Sacred Books of the Buddhists, Vol. XXXII

THE TEACHING

OF

VIMALAKĪRTI

THE TEACHING OF VIMALAKĪRTI

(VIMALAKĪRTINIRDEŚA)

from the French translation
with Introduction and Notes
(L'Enseignement de Vimalakīrti)

BY

ÉTIENNE LAMOTTE

rendered into English

BY

SARA BOIN

Published by
The Pali Text Society
Oxford
1994

First published 1976
Reprinted 1994

The original French version appeared as Volume 51 in the collection Bibliothèque du *Muséon*, Louvain 1962.

ISBN 0 86013 077 0

UNESCO COLLECTION OF REPRESENTATIVE WORKS

This Buddhist text has been accepted in the series of translations from the literature of Burma, Cambodia, India, Laos, Sri Lanka, and Thailand, jointly sponsored by the United Nations Educational, Scientific, and Cultural Organisation (UNESCO), and the National Commissions for Unesco in these countries.

Distributed by Lavis Marketing
73 Lime Walk
Oxford OX3 7AD

Printed in Great Britain by Antony Rowe Ltd

FOREWORD

The Vimalakīrtinirdeśa, or "Teaching of the Bodhisattva Unstained-Glory" is perhaps the crowning jewel of the Buddhist literature of the Great Vehicle. Vibrating with life and full of humour, it has neither the prolixity of other Mahāyānasūtras nor the technicality of the Buddhist Śāstras with which, however, it shares knowledge and wisdom alike.

Far from losing himself in a maze of abstract and impersonal doctrines, Vimalakīrti, simulating an ailing man, summons to his sick-bed the most illustrious of Śrāvakas and Bodhisattvas, and convicts them of ignorance and delusion in the very field of their speciality (Ch. III and VIII). He offends their sense of morals by inviting them to plunge into the sea of the passions (VII, § 3); he belittles their highest ideal, the conquest of enlightenment, by identifying Bodhi with the sixty-two kinds of false views (IV, § 8; VII, § 2).

Not satisfied with ridiculing the holy ones, he turns on the Tathāgatas themselves, for no sooner has he allowed them a transcendental body, a diamond body (II, § 12; III, § 43), than he denies their very existence (XI, § 1). The Bodhisattva, as he sees it, is not a being on the way to enlightenment, but an equivocal person, of ambiguous behaviour, "who follows the way of all the passions, but remains undefiled by them" (VII, § 1).

Vimalakīrti not only rejects all the Buddhist systems current at the time, he also attacks the physical and moral premises on which human society is based, and thus his censure takes on a universal value. Yielding to the taste of his time, he devises quantities of miracles of the most improbable kind with the sole aim of disconcerting his listeners. Hence the single parasol which shelters an entire cosmic system (I, § 8), the tiny house which easily makes room for thirty-two hundreds of thousands of immense thrones (V, § 7) testify to the relativity of space; the same length of time which for some lasts for a whole Kalpa, while for others is reduced to seven days (V, § 13), serves to illustrate the relativity of time; the young goddess who changes into a man at the same time that the elderly Śāriputra is transformed into a woman (VI, § 15) demonstrates the ambivalence of the sexes. "Absurd miracles", some might say. But do the contingencies on which humanity regulates its activities demand a more serious refutation?

For Vimalakīrti mind objects, from the most concrete to the most abstract, arise from false imagination (*abhūtaparikalpa*); false imaginations rest on a total baselessness (*apratiṣṭhāna*), and this itself, in turn, has no root (VI, § 6). From this it results that things, with no exception whatever, are, in the etymological sense of the word, *acintya* 'not to be thought of', and it is within this radical inconceivability that they lead to sameness (*samatā*) or, to be more exact, non-duality (*advaya*).

By adopting this position which is nothing but the absence of any position, Vimalakīrti cannot be taxed with either idealism or nihilism. He who does not think anything is not an idealist; he who does not deny anything is not a nihilist. But is he still a Buddhist?

At the risk of venturing a paradox myself, I dare to affirm that Vimalakīrti has fully grasped the spirit of the Tathāgatas by committing himself, without deviation or compromise, to the Middle Way discovered by Śākyamuni and taught by him in his first sermon: "That Middle Path which opens the eyes, achieves knowledge, and leads to stillness, to higher consciousness, to perfect awakening, to Nirvāṇa"[1].

For the Buddhas, liberating knowledge is not to be sought in the solution to the great philosophical problems which, for all time, have preoccupied the human mind: Is the world of beings eternal or transitory? limited or unlimited? Does the holy one emancipated from desire exist or not after death? Is the life principle the same as or different from the body[2]? The Buddhas have placed these difficult questions among the "undetermined points" (*avyākṛtavastu*) on which they refused to commit themselves. These lofty speculations surpass the capacity of human reason, distract the mind and provoke endless discussions. They are of purely theoretical interest and do not culminate in any practical result: "They make no contribution to disgust for the world, renunciation, stopping, stillness, higher consciousness, perfect awakening, Nirvāṇa"[3]. The only really efficacious knowledge consists in the liberating vision of the four Noble Truths: the universality of suffering, its origin, its extinction and the path which leads to this extinction.

Following their reasoning, the Buddhas have established that the world of existences is a purely subjective phenomenon, taking place in the mind[4]. The mind, or to be more

[1] Vinaya, I, p. 10; Majjhima, I, p. 15; III, p. 230, 236; Saṃyutta, V, p. 421: *Majjhimā paṭipadā tathāgatena abhisambuddhā cakkhukaraṇī ñāṇakaraṇī upasamāya abhiññāya sambodhāya nibbānāya saṃvattati.*

[2] Dīgha, I, p. 187 188; Majjhima, I, p. 157, 426, 484; Saṃyutta, III, p. 213-216, 258; IV, p. 286, 391-392; V, p. 418: *Sassato loko, asassato loko*, etc. In this passage, *loka* not only designates the receptacle-world (*bhājanaloka*), but also the world of beings (*sattaloka*). Moreover, besides the traditional formula *sassato loko, asassato loko*, a longer reading is often found: *sassato attā ca loko ca, asassato attā ca loko ca* (Dīgha, I, p. 16; III, p. 137; Majjhima, II, p. 233).

[3] Majjhima, I, p. 431; Saṃyutta, II, p. 222-223: *Etaṃ mayā abyākataṃ... Na h'etaṃ nibbidāya na virāgāya na nirodhāya na upasamāya na abhiññāya na sambodhāya na nibbānāya saṃvattati.*

[4] As far as I know, the idealist formula *Cittamātram idam yad idam traidhātukam* (Daśabhūmika, ed. Rahder, p. 49) does not yet appear in the canonical writings,

exact, the series (*saṃtāna*) of successsive thought moments is the seat of the passions (*kleśa*) and the false views (*mithyādṛṣṭi*). Intoxicated by the three-fold poison of craving (*rāga*), hatred (*dveṣa*) and delusion (*moha*), the mind lives and experiences the nightmare of Saṃsāra which, subjective though it may be, is painful nonetheless. "Everything that arises is nothing but suffering; suffering is that which persists and that which goes away; no other thing than suffering arises; no other thing than suffering dissipates" [5]. But there is no suffering without thought, and this led Śākyamuni to say: "The world (of beings) is led by the mind, manoeuvred by the mind. Everything obeys an one and only dharma: the mind" [6]. Vitiated by the passions and false views, the mind starts to function, and as a consequence of its actions, experiences suffering [7]. Freed from the passions of the false views, the mind calms,

but the latter never-endingly repeat that all the formations (dharmas arising from a cause) are impermanent and painful: *Sabbe saṅkhārā aniccā, sabbe saṅkhārā dukkhā* (Aṅguttara, I, p. 286, l. 8, 14 and 20). There is indeed no suffering without a mind to register it.

[5] Saṃyutta, I, p. 135; Kathāvatthu, I, p. 66: *Dukkhaṃ eva hi sambhoti, dukkhaṃ tiṭṭhati veti ca; nāññatra dukkhā sambhoti, nāññaṃ dukkhā nirujjhati.* Cf. Catuṣpariṣatsūtra, ed. Waldschmidt, p. 354: *Duḥkham idam utpadyamānam utpadyate, duḥkaṃ nirudhyamānaṃ nirudhyate.*

[6] Saṃyutta, I, p. 39, l. 10-11: *Cittena nīyati loko, cittena parikissati; cittassa ekadhammassa sabbeva vasaṃ anvagu.* Also see Aṅguttara, II, p. 177, l. 33; Kośavyākhyā, ed. Wogihara, p. 95, l. 22-23; Mahāyānasūtrālaṃkāra, ed. Lévi, p. 151, l. 7.

[7] It is true that a good action automatically leads to an agreeable feeling, but on experience, this reveals itself to be painful. The Buddha is formal in this respect: cf. Saṃyutta, IV, p. 216-217: *Tisso imā bhikkhu vedanā vuttā mayā sukhā vedanā dukkhā vedanā adukkhamasukhā vedanā: imā tisso vedanā vuttā mayā. Vuttaṃ kho panetaṃ bhikkhu mayā: Yaṃ kiñci vedayitaṃ taṃ dukkhasmin ti. Taṃ kho panetaṃ bhikkhu mayā saṅkhārānaṃ yeva aniccataṃ sandhāya bhāsitaṃ: Yaṃ kiñci vedayitaṃ taṃ dukkhasmin ti.* I have spoken, O monk, of three sensations: agreeable sensation, disagreeable sensation, neither disagreeable nor agreeable sensation. Yes, I have spoken of these three sensations. But I have also said, O monk: "All that is felt is felt in suffering". It is in alluding to the impermanence of the formations that I have said: "All that is felt is felt in suffering".

This canonical passage is commented on at length in the Kośabhāṣya, ed. Pradhan, p. 330, and the Kośavyākhyā, p. 519.

suffering disappears, Nirvāṇa is achieved. In other words and according to a canonical formula: "Through defilement of the mind are beings defiled; through the purification of the mind are they purified"[8].

It is at this point, in the direct prolongation of the teaching of the Buddhas, that the Mādhyamikas, for whom Vimalakīrti is one of their most remarkable spokesmen, come in. To be effective and suppress suffering, the calming (*upaśama*) of the mind is nothing but the stopping of its functioning (*cittapravṛttisamuccheda*).

Chapter VIII of the Vimalakīrtinirdeśa is significant in this respect. Asked to explain themselves over that Non-duality (*advaya*) which transcends extremes and keeps an equal distance between existence (*bhava*) and non-existence (*abhava*), thirty-two Bodhisattvas gathered in Vimalakīrti's home attempt in turn a definition which, valuable though it may be, still does not touch the heart of the matter. The best answer comes from Mañjuśrī, the Bodhisattva of Wisdom. "Penetrating Non-duality", he says, "is excluding all words, not saying anything, not thinking anything, not expressing anything, not teaching anything, not designating anything" (VIII, § 32). Would he not have done better to keep quiet? Anyway, Vimalakīrti puts a final end to this talk by enfolding himself in the silence of the wise (*āryāṇāṃ tūṣṇīṃbhāva*). This silence of which the Buddhas so often gave an example by not answering the questions posed to them (*sthāpanīya vyākaraṇa*)[9] has nothing in common with the disdainful reticence of western rationalism: it is a silence that has matured with time, that takes the middle way between affirmation

[8] Saṃyutta, III, p. 151, l. 22-23; 152, l. 8-9: *Cittasaṃkilesā bhikkhave sattā saṃkilissanti, cittavodānā satta visujjhanti.* Ratnagotravibhāga, ed. Johnston, p. 67, l. 1-2; Abhidharmadīpa, ed. Jaini, p. 45, l. 19; 78, l. 15; 363, l. 5-6: *Cittasaṃkleśāt sattvā saṃkliśyante, cittavyavadānād viśudhyante.*

[9] Dīgha, III, p. 229; Aṅguttara, I, p. 197; II, p. 46.

and negation and results from the previous cutting off of discussion and all practice (XI, § 1 : *sarvavādacaryoccheda*). This serene quietness, free of pride and aggression, is the mark of the Buddha's disciples.

*

In 1962, I published in French a work entitled *L'Enseignement de Vimalakīrti* (Vimalakīrtinirdeśa) *traduit et annoté* (Bibliothèque du Muséon, volume 51), Louvain. A desire to see my study available in the English language came to the attention of Miss I.B. Horner, President of the Pali Text Society. She made the suggestion to me of publishing an English version in the Society's Sacred Books of the Buddhist Series, with which I was only too happy to concur. I would like to express here my appreciation and gratitude for her great kindness and encouragement in seeing this proposal brought to fruition.

In accordance with its aims and as witness of its openmindedness, the Pali Text Society, in publishing another fundamental Mahāyānasūtra, continues its policy of making the teachings of Śākyamuni available in its various phases. The Great Vehicle, while marking a turning point in the evolution of the doctrines, is the natural development of the earlier Buddhist tradition. By taking up and explaining certain points of view which appeared in embryonic form in the old canonical texts, the Mahāyānasūtras lead us to a better understanding of the Buddhadharma,

The undertaking by the Pali Text Society has been greatly assisted by Mrs Sara Boin who made this English translation of my work on Vimalakīrti. This was a delicate task because, as applied to Buddhist texts, the English methods of translating are not quite the same as the French, and the English and French technical vocabulary used here and there does not necessarily coincide. Mrs Boin has triumphed brilliantly over these difficulties. Even if I am not able to appreciate her style fully, I am convinced that throughout the text she has faithfully rendered Vimalakīrti's thought, while making it accessible to the English-speaking public. May she find here the expression of my profound gratitude.

There remained the matter of providing the calligraphy of the Chinese characters and of indicating their pronunciation according to the English system of transliteration. Mrs M. Rowlands has carried out this awkward and thankless task with a care which is beyond all praise.

The present English translation is not, properly speaking, a revised and corrected edition of the French version. Nevertheless we have made use of the opportunity to rectify certain mistakes, make good some omissions and improve the notes. In undertaking this, Mrs Boin and myself benefitted from the valuable assistance of Dr Arnold Kunst, for which we would like to thank him most warmly.

Étienne LAMOTTE

The English translator would like to take this opportunity personally to thank Professor Lamotte for his unfailing assistance and encouragement, as well as Miss I.B. Horner and Dr A. Kunst for their generous advice and help throughout the undertaking, but especially at the proof-reading stage. However, the responsibility for any errors that may remain lies entirely with this translator.

ERRATA

Page, column & line	For	Read
p. xi, l. 18	benefitted	benefited
p. xxvi, l. 10	Li tai son pao chi	Li tai san pao chi
p. lxxxi, l. 1	absence	presence
p. 73b, l. 2	bings	beings
p. 139a, l. 29	thirty-two hundreds of thrones	thirty-two hundreds of thousands of thrones
p. 202, l. 21	implies	involves
p. 317b, l. 28	liberated 2	liberated 201
p. 318b, l. 40	wisdom eye 26 58 67n. 138	eye of the Law 26 58 67n. 138
p. 318b, l. 41	eye of the Law 49 67n. 202	wisdom eye 49 67n. 202

TABLE OF CONTENTS

FOREWORD v

TABLE OF CONTENTS XIII

ABBREVIATIONS AND EDITIONS XVII

INTRODUCTION XXV

I. The Translations of the Vkn XXVI
i. The Chinese Translations XXVI
ii. The Tibetan Translations XXXVII
iii. The Sogdian and Khotanese Translations . . . XLIII
iv. Concordance of the Translations of the Vkn . XLIV
II. The Titles of the Vkn LIV
III. The Philosophy of the Vkn LX
i. The Absolute in the Early Buddhism LX
ii. The Absolute in the Mahāyāna LXI
iii. The "Pure Mind" of the Vkn LXXII
1. The "Mind" in canonical Buddhism . . . LXXIII
2. The "Luminous Mind" in the Sects of the Small Vehicle LXXIV
3. The "Embryo of the Tathāgata" in the Yogācāra LXXVI
4. The "Non-Mind Mind" of the Prajñās and the Vkn LXXVIII
IV. The Sources of the Vkn LXXXI
i. Canonical Sūtras of the Tripiṭaka LXXII
ii. Vinaya LXXXIII
iii. Paracanonical Sūtras LXXXIII
iv. Mahāyāna Sūtras LXXXIV
V. The Date of the Vkn LXXXVII
i. The Buddhist Tradition LXXXVIII
ii. The *Terminus ad quem* of the Vkn LXXXIX
VI. The Divisions of the Vkn XCVIII
VII. The Localisation of the Vkn C
VIII. Vimalakīrti in Indian Tradition CIV
IX. References to the Vkn in Indian Śāstras CXI

NOTICE CONCERNING THE TRANSLATION CXVI

THE TEACHING OF VIMALAKĪRTI

TEXT

Chapter One — THE PURIFICATION OF THE BUDDHA-FIELDS 1
Introduction (1). — Arrival of Ratnākara and the 500 Licchavis (6). — Stanzas of Ratnākara (9). — The Purification of the Buddhafields (14). — Śāriputra and the Impurity of the Sahāloka (22). — Brahmā Śikhin and the Purity of the Sahāloka (22). — The Transformation of the Sahāloka (23).

Chapter Two — THE INCONCEIVABLE SKILL IN MEANS OF DELIVERANCE 28
Portrait of Vimalakīrti (28). — Simulated Illness of Vimalakīrti (32). — Vimalakirti's Homily on the Human Body (33). — Vimalakīrti's Homily on the Body of the Tathāgata (38).

Chapter Three — THE REFUSAL TO ENQUIRE BY THE ŚRĀVAKAS AND THE BODHISATTVAS 42
1. Śāriptura and the Pratisaṃlayana (42).
2. Maudgalyāyana and the Instruction to Laymen (45).
3. Kāśyapa and the Alms-seeking Round (49).
4. Subhūti and the Food (54).
5. Pūrṇamaitrāyaṇiputra and the Instruction to Monks (59).
6. Mahākātyāyana and the Summaries of the Law (62). — Vimalakīrti's Homily on the Summaries of the Law (64).
7. Aniruddha and the Heavenly Eye (65). — Question of the Mahābrahmā regarding the Heavenly Eye (66). — Intervention of Vimalakīrti and Stupefaction of the Brahmās (67).
8. Upāli and Morality (68). — The Confession of the Two Monks (70). — Vimalakīrti's Homily on Morality and Pure Mind (71). — Stupefaction of the Monks (74).
9. Rāhula and Leaving the World (74). Meeting with the Young Licchavis (75). — Vimalakīrti's Homily on Leaving the World (77). — Vimalakīrti's Exhortation to the Young Licchavis (78).
10. Ānanda and the Care of the Buddha (79). — Ānanda in Search of Milk (89). — Vimalakīrti's Homily on the Illness of the Buddha (81). — The Celestial Voice (84).
11. Maitreya and the Prediction (85). — Vimalakīrti's Address on Prediction (86). — Vimalakīrti's Homily on Enlightenment (90).
12. Prabhāvyūha and the Bodhimaṇḍa (94). — Vimalakīrti's Homily on the Seat of Enlightenment (95).
13. Jagatīṃdhara and the Assault of Māra (99). — Visit of Māra and his Daughters (99). — Vimalakīrti's Intervention (102). — Vimalakīrti's Homily on the Garden of the Law (102). — Stratagems Concerning the Daughters of the Gods (104). — Vimalakīrti's Advice to the Daughters of the Gods (105).
14. Sudatta and the Offering of the Law (106). — Sudatta's Great Offering (107). — Vimalakīrti's Homily on the Offering of the Law (107). — The Miracle of the Necklace (111).

Chapter Four — CONSOLATIONS TO THE SICK MAN . 113
Mañjuśrī's Acceptance (113). — Mañjuśrī at Vimalakīrti's House (115). — The Empty House (116). — Reciprocal Greetings (116). — Vimalakīrti's Sickness (117). — Universal Emptiness (118). — The Nature of Sickness (119). — How to Console a Sick Bodhisattva (120). — Considerations Proposed to the Sick (121). — Bondage and Deliverance (126). — Wisdom and Skillful Means (126). — The Domain of the Bodhisattva (128).

Chapter Five — THE INCONCEIVABLE LIBERATION . 134
The Search for the Law (134). — The Miracle of the Thrones (138). — The Inconceivable Liberation (141). — Kāśyapa's Wonder (149). — The Tempter-Bodhisattvas (150).

Chapter Six. — THE GODDESS 153
The Inexistence of a Living Being (153). — Goodwill (155). — Compassion, Joy and Equanimity (158). — Baselessness (158). — The Devī and the Miracle of the Flowers (160). — Deliverance (162). — Wisdom and Eloquence (163). — The Triple Vehicle (163). — The Eight Wonders of Vimalakīrti's House (168). — Equivalence and Miracle of the Sexes (169). — Inaccessible Enlightenment and Impossible Rebirth (171).

Chapter Seven — THE FAMILY OF THE TATHĀGATA . 173
The Roundabout Ways of a Bodhisattva (173). — The Family of the Tathāgata (176). — Mahākāśyapa's Lamentations (179). — Vimalakīrti's Stanzas (180).

Chapter Eight — INTRODUCTION TO THE DOCTRINE OF NON-DUALITY 188

Chapter Nine — THE OBTAINING OF FOOD BY THE IMAGINARY BODHISATTVA 204
Śāriputra's Anxiety (204). — The Revealing of the Sarvagandhasugandhā Universe (204). — An Imaginary Bodhisattva's Mission to the Sarvagandhasugandhā (206). — Return to the Sahāloka (210). — The Sacred Meal (211). — Sugandhakūṭa's Instruction in his Universe (213). — Śākyamuni's Instruction in the Sahā Universe (213). — The Virtues Particular to the Bodhisattvas of the Sahā Universe (216). — Conditions of Access to the Pure Lands (217).

Chapter Ten — INSTRUCTION REGARDING THE EXHAUSTIBLE AND THE INEXHAUSTIBLE 219
Visit to the Āmrapālīvana (219). — Duration and Effects of the Sacred Food (220). — Skillful Action of the Buddhakṣetras (223). — Variety and Similarity of Buddhakṣetras (226). — The Sameness and Inconceivability of the Buddhas (227). — Superiority of Bodhisattvas over Śrāvakas (228). — Request of the Bodhisattvas from the Sarvagandhasugandhā Universe (228). — Śākyamuni's Homily on the Exhaustible and the Inexhaustible (229). — The Return of the Sarvagandhasugandhā Bodhisattvas (236).

Chapter Eleven — THE APPROPRIATION OF THE ABHIRATI UNIVERSE and VISION OF THE TATHĀGATA AKṢOBHYA 238
The Inexistence of the Tathāgatas (238). — Antecedence of Vimalakīrti (242). — Vimalākīrti comes from the Abhirati Universe (243). — The Appearance of the Abhirati Universe (245). — Homages Paid to Akṣobhya (248). — Śāriputra's Wonder (249).

Chapter Twelve — ANTECEDENTS AND TRANSMISSION OF THE GOOD LAW 252
Śākra's Promises (252). — In Praise of the Vimalakīrtinirdeśa (253). — Jātaka of Ratnacchattra and his Sons (255). — Ratnacchattra's Pūjā (258). — Candracchattra's Pūjā (258). — Bhaiṣajyarāja's Homily on the Dharmapūjā (259). — Candracchattra, Guardian of the Law (263). — Identification of the Personalities in the Jātaka (265). — The Transmission to Maitreya (268). — Beginner Bodhisattvas and Veteran Bodhisattvas (268). — Maitreya's Promise (270). — The Bodhisattvas' Promise (271). — The Lokapālas' Promise (272). — Transmission to Ānanda and Title of the Sūtra (272).

APPENDIX 275
Note I: The Buddhakṣetras 275
Note II: Cittotpāda, Adhyāśaya and Āśaya 284
Note III: Nairātmya, Anutpāda and Kṣānti 286
Note IV: Morality in the Two Vehicles 292
Note V: The Illnesses of the Buddha 293
Note VI: Prajñā and Bodhi in the perspective of the Two Vehicles 298
Note VII: Gotra and Tathāgatagotra 303
Note VIII: Perfumed Amṛta and the Sacred Meal . . 307
INDEX 315
SYNOPSIS OF FORMULAE AND STOCK PHRASES 333

ABBREVIATIONS AND EDITIONS USED IN THIS WORK

Not listed here are the Pāli texts or their translations which are always quoted according to the editions of the Pali Text Society.

Abhidharmadīpa, ed. P.S. JAINI (Tibetan Sanskrit Works Series, IV), Patna, 1959.

Abhidharmasamuccaya, ed. V.V. GOKHALE, Journ. of the Bombay Branch R.A.S., XXIII, 1947, p. 13-38; rec. P. PRADHAN (Visvabharati Studies, 12), Santiniketan, 1950.

Abhisamayālaṃkāra, ed. TH. STCHERBATSKY and E. OBERMILLER (Bibl. Buddh., 23), Leningrad, 1929.

Ajitasenavyākaraṇa, ed. N. DUTT (Gilgit Man., I), Srinagar, 1939.

AKANUMA, *Noms propres* = C. AKANUMA, *Dictionnaire des noms propres du bouddhisme indien*, Nagoya, 1931.

Āloka = Abhisamayālaṃkārāloka, ed. U. WOGIHARA, Tōkyō, 1932-35.

Arthapada Sūtra, ed. and tr. P.V. BAPAT (Visvabharati Studies, 13), Santiniketan, 1951.

Arthaviniścaya, ed. and tr. A. FERRARI (Atti d. Reale Acc. d'Italia, Serie VII, Vol. IV, fasc. 13), Rome, 1944.

Aṣṭādaśasāhasrikā [Prajñāpāramitā], ed. and tr. E. CONZE (Lit. and hist. Doc. from Pakistan, 1), Rome, 1962.

Aṣṭasāhasrikā [Prajñāpāramitā], ed. U. WOGIHARA, incorporated in Āloka (see above).

Avadānaśataka, ed. J.S. SPEYER (Bibl. Buddh., 3), St Petersburg, 1902-09.

BAILEY, H.W., *Khotanese Buddhist Texts*, London, 1951.

BANERJEE, A.C., *Prātimokṣasūtra of the Mūlasarvāstivādins*, Calcutta, 1954.

BAREAU, *Sectes bouddhiques* = A. BAREAU, *Les Sectes bouddhiques du Petit Véhicule*, Saigon, 1955.

BEAL, *Life* = S. BEAL, tr., *The Life of Hiuen-Tsiang by the Shamans Hwui Li and Yen-Tsung* (Trübner's Oriental Series), London, 1888.

Bhadracarīpraṇidhāna, ed. K. WATANABE, Leipzig, 1912.

Bhaiṣajyaguru Sūtra, ed. N. DUTT (Gilgit Man., I), Srinagar, 1939.

BHATTACHARYYA, B., *Indian Buddhist Iconography*, 2nd. ed., Calcutta, 1958.

Bhāvanākrama I, ed. G. TUCCI, *Minor Buddhist Texts*, II (Serie Orientale Roma, IX, 2), Rome, 1958.

Bhāvanākrama III, ed. G. TUCCI, *Minor Buddhist Texts*, III (Serie Orientale Roma, XLIII), Rome, 1971.

BLOCH, J., *Les Inscriptions d'Aśoka* (Les Belles Lettres, Collection Émile Senart), Paris, 1950.

Bodhicaryāvatāra, ed. P. MINAYEFF, St Petersburg, 1890.

Bodhisattvaprātimokṣasūtra, ed. N. DUTT, IHQ, VII, Calcutta, 1931, p. 259-286.

Bodh. Bhūmi = Bodhisattvabhūmi, ed. U. WOGIHARA, Tōkyō, 1930.

Buddhacarita, ed. E.H. JOHNSTON (Panjab Univ. Publications, 31), Calcutta, 1936.

Bu-ston = E. OBERMILLER, tr., Bu-ston, *History of Buddhism*, 2 vol. (Mat. z. Kunde d. Buddh., 18, 19), Heidelberg, 1931-33.

Catalogue of the Tibetan Manuscripts from Tun-Huang in the India Office Library, compiled by L. DE LA VALLÉE POUSSIN, Oxford, 1962.

Catuḥśataka, ed. and tr. P.L. VAIDYA, *Étude sur Āryadeva*, Paris, 1923; ed. and rec. V. BHATTACHARYA (Visvabharati Series, 2), Calcutta, 1931.

Catuṣpariṣat Sūtra, ed. E. WALDSCHMIDT (Abh. d. Deutschen Akad. zu Berlin), Berlin, 1952-62.

CHAVANNES, *Contes* = É. CHAVANNES, *Cinq cents Contes et Apologues extraits du Tripiṭaka chinois*, 4 vol., Paris, 1910-34.

CH'EN, K.K.S., *The Chinese Transformation of Buddhism*, Princeton, 1973.

Cn = Chinese translation of the Vkn by Chih Ch'ien (T 474).

CONZE, E., *The Prajñāpāramitā Literature*, The Hague, 1960.

COOMARASWAMY, A.K., *History of Indian and Indonesian Art*, London, 1927.

COOMARASWAMY, A.K., *La Sculpture de Bhārhut*, Paris, 1956.

COOMARASWAMY, A.K., *La Sculpture de Bodh Gayā*, Paris, 1935.

CORDIER, P., *Catalogue du Fonds Tibétain de la Bibliothèque Nationale*, III, Paris, 1915.

Daśabhūmika Sūtra, ed. J. RAHDER, Louvain, 1926.

DEMIÉVILLE, P., *Le Concile de Lhasa* (Bibl. de l'Inst. des Hautes Études Chinoises, 7), Paris, 1952.

DEMIÉVILLE, P., *Les versions chinoises du Milindapañha*, BEFEO, XXIV, 1924.

Dharmasaṃgraha, ed. M. MÜLLER and H. WENZEL (Anec. Oxon. Aryan Series, vol. I. part V), Oxford, 1885.

Divyāvadāna, ed E.B. COWELL and R.A. NEIL, Cambridge, 1886.

DUMÉZIL, G., *Le Festin d'Immortalité*, Paris, 1924.

Dvādaśamukha Śāstra, rec. N.A. SASTRI, Visvabharati Annals, VI, Santiniketan, 1954, p. 165-231

ECKE, G. and DEMIÉVILLE, P., *The Twin Pagodas of Zayton*, Harvard, 1935.

EDGERTON, *Dictionary* = F. EDGERTON, *Buddhist Hybrid Sanskrit Dictionary*, New Haven, 1953.

FOUCHER, A., *Art Gréco-bouddhique du Gandhāra*, 2 vol., Paris, 1905-22.

FP = Fonds Pelliot tibétain de la Bibliothèque Nationale, Paris.

FRAUWALLNER, E., *Die Philosophie des Buddhismus*, Berlin, 1956.

Gaṇḍavyūha Sūtra, ed. D.T. SUZUKI and H. IDZUMI, Kyōto, 1934-36.

Gauḍapāda = Gauḍapādīya- kārikās, Ānandāśrama Sanskrit Series, 10, Poona, 1911.

GEIGER, M. and W., *Pāli Dhamma vornehmlich in der Kanonischen Litteratur*, Munich, 1920.

GERNET, J., *Les aspects économiques du bouddhisme* (Publ. de l'École Française d'Extrême Orient, XXXIX), Saigon, 1956.

H = Chinese translation of the Vkn by Hsüan-tsang (T 476).

HASHIMOTO, H., *A Study of the True Character of the Vimalakīrtinirdeśa, especially on the Idea of Acintyavimokṣa* (Indogaku Bukkyōgaku Kenkyū, VII), Tōkyō, 1958.

Hōbōgirin, Dictionnaire encyclopédique du bouddhisme d'après les sources chinoises et japonaises (Editor in chief, P. DEMIÉVILLE), Paris, 1929 and sq.

Hœrnle, A.F.R., *Manuscript Remains of Buddhist Literature found in Eastern Turkestan*, I, Oxford, 1916.

Hofinger, M., *Le Congrès du Lac Anavatapta* (Bibliothèque du Muséon, 34), Louvain, 1954.

Inde Classique, by L. Renou and J. Filliozat, Tome I (Bibliothèque Scientifique), Paris, 1947; Tome II (Bibl. Éc. Franç. Extrême Orient), Paris, 1953.

I-tsing, tr. Takakusu = J. Takakusu, tr., *A Record of the Buddhist Religion as Practised in India and the Malay Archipelago (A.D. 671-695), by I-tsing*, Oxford, 1896.

Jātakamālā, ed. H. Kern (Harvard Oriental Series, I), Boston, 1891.

K = Chinese translation of the Vkn by Kumārajīva (T 475).

Kāraṇḍavyūha, ed S.V. Samasrami, Calcutta, 1873.

Karatalaratna, rec. N.A. Sastri (Visvabharati Studies, 9), Santiniketan, 1949.

Karmasiddhiprakaraṇa, Tib. ed. and tr. É. Lamotte (off-print of MCB, IV), Bruges, 1935-36.

Karmavibhaṅga = Mahākarmavibhaṅga and Karmavibhaṅgopadeśa, ed. and tr. S. Lévi, Paris, 1932.

Karuṇāpuṇḍarīka, ed. S.C. Das and S.C. Sastri, Calcutta, 1898.

Kāśyapaparivarta, ed. A. v. Staël-Holstein, Commercial Press, 1926.

Kāvyamīmāṃsā, tr. L. Renou, *Kāvyamīmāṃsā de Rājasekhara*, Paris, 1946.

Kirfel, W., *Die Kosmographie der Inder*, Bonn, 1920.

Kośa = Abhidharmakośa, tr. L. de La Vallée Poussin, 6 vol., Paris, 1923-31; repr. (Mélanges chinois et bouddhiques, XVI), Brussels, 1971.

Kośabhāṣya = Abhidharmakośabhāṣya of Vasubandhu, ed. P. Pradhan (Tibetan Sanskrit Works Series, VIII), Patna, 1967.

Kośavyākhyā = Sphūṭārtha Abhidharmakośavyākhyā, ed. U. Wogihara, Tōkyō, 1932-36.

Lalitavistara, ed. S. Lefmann, Halle a.S., 1902.

Lalou, *Inventaire* = M. Lalou, *Inventaire des Manuscrits tibétains de Touen-houang*, 3 vol., Paris, 1939-61.

Lamotte, *Histoire* = É. Lamotte, *Histoire du bouddhisme indien, des origines à l'ère Śaka* (Bibliothèque du Muséon, 43), Louvain, 1958; repr. 1967.

Laṅkāvatāra, ed. B. Nanjio, Kyōto, 1923.

La Vallée Poussin, L. de, *Introduction à la pratique des futurs Bouddhas* (extrait de la Revue d'histoire et de littérature religieuse, vol. X, XI and XII, 1905, 1906, 1907), Paris, 1907.

La Valleé Poussin, L. de, *Nirvāṇa*, Paris, 1925.

La Valleé Poussin, L. de, *Théorie des douze causes*, Ghent, 1913.

Le Coq, A. von, *Bilderatlas zur Kunst und Kulturgeschichte Mittel-Asiens*, Berlin, 1925.

Legge, J., *A Record of Buddhistic Kingdoms*, Oxford, 1886.

Le Roy Davidson, J., *The Lotus Sūtra in Chinese Art*, Yale, 1954.

Leumann, E., *Buddhistische Litteratur nordarisch und deutsch*, Leipzig, 1920.

Longhurst, A.H., *The Buddhist Antiquities of Nāgārjunakoṇḍa* (Memoirs of the Arch. Surv. of India, No. 54), Delhi, 1938.

Madh. Avatāra = Madhyamakāvatāra, Tib. ed. L. de La Vallée Poussin (Bibl. Buddh. 9), St Petersburg, 1912.

Madh. vṛtti = Mūlamadhyamakakārikās of Nāgārjuna with the Prasannapadā, comm. by Candrakīrti, ed. L. DE LA VALLÉE POUSSIN (Bibl. Buddh., 4), St Petersburg, 1913; tr. J.W. DE JONG, *Cinq chapitres de la Prasannapadā*, Leiden, 1949; tr. J. MAY, *Candrakīrti Prasannapadā Mūlamadhyamakavṛtti, douze chapitres traduit du sanscrit* (Collection Jean Przyluski, II), Paris, 1959.

Madhyāntavibhāga, ed. S. YAMAGUCHI, 2 vol., Nagoya, 1934.

Mahāparinirvāṇa sanskrit = Mahāparinirvāṇasūtra, ed. E. WALDSCHMIDT (Abh. d. Deutschen Akad. zu Berlin), Berlin, 1950-51.

Mahāsaṃnipāta [Ratnaketudhāraṇī], ed. N. DUTT (Gilgit Man., IV), Calcutta, 1959.

Mahāvadāna sanskrit = Mahāvadānasūtra, ed. E. WALDSCHMIDT (Abh. d. Deutschen Akad. zu Berlin), Berlin, 1953-56.

Mahāvastu, ed. É. SENART. 3 vol., Paris, 1882-97.

Mahāvyutpatti, ed. R. SAKAKI, 2 vol., Kyōto, 1916-25.

Mahāyānaviṃśikā, ed. G. TUCCI, *Minor Buddhist Texts*, I (Serie Orientale Roma, IX, 1), Rome, 1956.

Mahāyānottaratantraśāstra (see Ratnagotravibhāga), tr. from the Tib. by E. OBERMILLER, *The Sublime Science of the Great Vehicle to Salvation*, Acta Orientalia, IX, 1931.

Maitreyavyākaraṇa, ed. N. DUTT (Gilgit Man., IV), Calcutta, 1959.

MALALASEKERA, *Proper Names* = G.P. MALALASEKERA, *Dictionary of Pāli Proper Names*, 2 vol. (Indian Texts Series), London, 1937-38.

Mañjuśrīmūlakalpa, ed. T. GANAPATI SASTRI (Trivandrum Sanskrit Series, No. 70, 76, 84), 3 vol., Trivandrum, 1920-22.

MARSHALL, Sir John H., *Taxila*, Cambridge, 1951.

MARSHALL, Sir John H. and FOUCHER, A., *The Monuments of Sāñchī*, Delhi, 1940.

Masterpieces of Chinese ju-i scepters in the National Palace Museum, Taipei, 1974.

MOCHIZUKI, *Encyclopaedia* = MOCHIZUKI, S., *Bukkyō Daijiten*, 2nd ed., 8 vol., Tōkyō, 1960.

N = Tibetan translation of the Vkn in the Narthang Kanjur (Fonds tibétain de la Bibliothèque Nationale, No. 419).

NAGAO, G.M., *Index to the Mahāyāna Sūtrālaṃkāra*, 2 parts, Tōkyō, 1958-61.

NĀGĀRJUNA, *Traité* = É. LAMOTTE, tr., *Traité de la Grande Vertu de Sagesse de Nāgārjuna*, vol. I and II (Bibliothèque du Muséon, 18), Louvain, 1944-49, repr. 1966-67; vol. III (Publ. de l'Institut Orientaliste de Louvain, 2), Louvain, 1970.

Niraupamyastava, ed. G. TUCCI, JRAS, 1932, p. 312-321.

NOBEL, J., *Wörterbuch zum Suvarṇaprabhāsa*, Leiden, 1950.

OBERMILLER, E., *Analysis of the Abhisamayālaṃkāra*, London, 1943.

OKC = A comparative analytical Catalogue of the Kanjur Division of the Tibetan Tripiṭaka, Kyōto, 1930-32.

OSHIKA, J., *Tibetan Text of the Vimalakīrtinirdeśa*, Acta Indologica of the Naritasan Shinshoji, I, 1970, p. 187-240. *Index to the Tibetan Translation*, id. ibid., III, 1974, p. 197-352.

P = Tibetan translation of the Vkn in the Peking Kanjur (OKC, 843).

PACHOW, W., *A Comparative Study of the Prātimokṣa*, Santiniketan, 1955.

Pañcakrama, ed. L. DE LA VALLÉE POUSSIN, Ghent, 1896.

Pañcaviṃśatisāhasrikā [Prajñāpāramitā], ed. N. DUTT (Calcutta Oriental Series, 28), London, 1934.

Pañjikā = Bodhicaryāvatārapañjikā, ed. L. DE LA VALLÉE POUSSIN (Bibl. Indica), Calcutta, 1901-14.

Paramārthastava, ed. G. TUCCI, JRAS, 1932, p. 322-325.

PELLIOT, P., *Les Grottes de Touen-Houang*, peintures et sculptures bouddhiques des époques des Wei, des T'ang et des Song, Mission Pelliot en Asie Centrale, Paris, 1920 (vol. 1-3), 1921 (vol. 4-5), 1926 (vol. 6).

PETECH, L., *North India according to the Shui-ching-shen*, Rome, 1950.

Prajñāpāramitāpiṇḍārtha, ed. and tr. G. TUCCI, JRAS, 1947, p. 53-75.

RĀHULA, W., *History of Buddhism in Ceylon*, Colombo, 1956.

Rāṣṭrapāla [paripṛcchā], ed. L. FINOT (Bibl. Buddh., 2), St Petersburg, 1901; Tib. ed. and tr. J. ENSINK, *The Question of Rāṣṭrapāla*, Zwolle, 1952.

Ratnagotra [vibhāga], ed. E.H. JOHNSTON (Bihar Research Society), Patna, 1950.

Ratnāvalī, ed. G. TUCCI, JRAS, 1934, p. 307-325.

REICHELT, H., *Die Sogdischen Handschriftenreste des Britischen Museums*, I. Teil: *Die Buddhistischen Texte*, Heidelberg, 1928.

RHYS DAVIDS, *Dictionary* = T.W. RHYS DAVIDS and W. STEDE, ed., *Pāli-English Dictionary*, Chipstead, 1925 and sq.

RUEGG, D.S., *La théorie du Tathāgatagarbha et du Gotra* (Publ. de l'École Franç. d'Extrême Orient), Paris, 1969.

Sad. puṇḍarīka = Saddharmapuṇḍarīka, ed. H. KERN and B. NANJIO (Bibl. Buddh., 10), St. Petersburg, 1908-12; tr. E. BURNOUF, *Le Lotus de la Bonne Loi*, 2 vol., Paris, 1852.

Sādhanamālā, ed. B. BHATTACHARYYA, 2 vol. (Gaekwad's Oriental Series, 26 and 41), Baroda, 1925-28.

SAEKI, J., *The Prince Shōtoku's Commentary on the Wei-mo-ching*, 2 vol., Tōkyō, 1937.

Śālistamba Sūtra, ed. N.A. SASTRI, Adyar Library, 1950.

Samādhirāja Sūtra, ed. N. DUTT, 3 parts (Gilgit Man., II), Srinagar, 1941-54.

Saṃdhinirmocana Sūtra, Tib. ed. and tr. É. LAMOTTE (Recueil de l'Univ. de Louvain, 34), Louvain, 1935.

Saṃgraha = Mahāyānasaṃgraha, tr. É. LAMOTTE, *La Somme du Grand Véhicule d'Asaṅga*, II (Bibliothèque du Muséon, 7), Louvain, 1938-39; repr. (Publ. de l'Institut Orientaliste de Louvain, 8), Louvain, 1973.

Saptaśatikā [Prajñāpāramitā], ed. G. TUCCI, Memorie d. R. Accademia dei Lincei, XVII, 1923, p. 115-139.

Sarvatathāgatādhiṣṭhāna, ed. N. DUTT (Gilgit Man., I), Srinagar, 1939.

Śatapañcāśatka, ed. and tr. D.R. SHACKLETON BAILEY, *The Śatapañcāśatka of Mātṛceṭa*, Cambridge, 1951.

Śatasāhasrikā [Prajñāpāramitā], ed. P. GHOSA (Bibl. Indica), Calcutta, 1914.

SCHIEFNER, A., tr. *Tibetische Lebensbeschreibung Śākyamuni's*, St Petersburg, 1848.

SHIH, R., *Biographies des Moines Éminents*, de Houei-kiao (Bibliothèque du Muséon, 54), Louvain, 1968.

Siddhi = Vijñaptimātratāsiddhi, tr. L. DE LA VALLÉE POUSSIN, 2 vol., Paris, 1928, and Index, 1948.

Śikṣāsamuccaya, ed. C. BENDALL (Bibl. Buddh., 1), St Petersburg, 1902.

Śrāvakabhūmi, Analysis by A. WAYMAN (Univ. of Calif. Publications, 17), Berkeley, 1961.

Śrīmālādevīsiṃhanādasūtra, tr. A. and H. WAYMAN, *The Lion's Roar of Queen Śrīmālā* (Translations from the Oriental Classics, Columbia Univ.), New York and London, 1974.

STCHERBATSKY, TH., *Buddhist Logic*, 2 vol. (Indo-Iranian Reprints, IV), The Hague, 1958.

STCHERBATSKY, TH., *The Conception of Buddhist Nirvāṇa*, Leningrad, 1927.

Subhāṣitasaṃgraha, *An anthology of extracts from Buddhist works compiled by an unknown author, to illustrate the doctrines of scholastic and of mystic (tāntrik) Buddhism*, ed. C. BENDALL, Le Muséon, IV, 1903, p. 375-402.

Sukhāvatīvyūha, ed. U. WOGIHARA, Tōkyō, 1931 [Reproduces, with corrections and a new pagination, the edition by M. MÜLLER which appeared in the Anec. Oxon. Aryan Series, vol. 1, part 2, Oxford, 1883].

Śūraṃgamasamādhisūtra, tr. É. LAMOTTE, *La Concentration de la Marche Héroïque* (Mélanges chinois et bouddhiques, XIII), Brussels, 1965.

Sūtrālaṃkāra = Mahāyānasūtrālaṃkāra, ed. S. LÉVI (Bibl. Éc. Hautes Études, 159), Paris, 1907.

Sūtrālaṃkāra, tr. HUBER = E. HUBER, *Aśvaghoṣa. Sūtrālaṃkāra*, Paris, 1908.

Suvarṇabhāsa [Uttamasūtra], ed. J. NOBEL, Leipzig, 1937.

Suvikrāntavikrāmi [Paripṛcchā Prajñāpāramitāsūtra], ed. R. HIKATA, Fukuoka, 1958.

SUZUKI, D.T., *Index to the Laṅkāvatāra*, Kyōto, 1934.

T = Taishō Issaikyō, ed. J. TAKAKUSU and K. WATANABE, 55 vol., Tōkyō, 1924-29.

TAKASAKI, J., *A Study on the Ratnagotravibhāga* (Serie Orientale Roma, XXXIII), Rome, 1966.

Tāranātha = A. SCHIEFNER, tr., Tāranātha, *Geschichte des Buddhismus*, St. Petersburg, 1869.

Tib. Trip. = Tibetan Tripiṭaka, ed. D.T. SUZUKI, 150 vol., Ōtani Univ., Kyōto, 1957.

Triṃśikā, ed. S. LÉVI, *Vijñaptimātratāsiddhi* (Bibl. Éc. Hautes Études, 245), Paris, 1925.

TUCCI, G., *Tombs of the Tibetan Kings*, Rome, 1950.

Udānavarga, ed. F. BERNHARD (Sanskrittexte aus den Turfanfunden X), Göttingen, 1965.

Udrāyaṇa, Tib. ed. and tr. J. NOBEL, *Udrāyaṇa, König von Roruka*, 2 vol., Wiesbaden, 1955.

Vajracchedikā, ed. E. CONZE (Serie Orientale Roma, XIII), Rome, 1957.

Vasumitra, tr. MASUDA = J. MASUDA, tr., *Origins and Doctrines of Early Indian Buddhist Schools... of Vasumitra's Treatise*, Asia Major, II, 1925.

Vimalakīrtinirdeśa, tr. É. LAMOTTE, *L'Enseignement de Vimalakīrti* (Bibliothèque du Muséon, 51), Louvain, 1962; tr. J. FISCHER and T. YOKOTA, *Das Sūtra Vimalakīrti*, Tōkyō, 1944; tr. and ed. C. LUK (LU K'UAN YU), *The Vimalakīrti Nirdeśa Sūtra* (Shamb(h)ala), Berkeley and London, 1972.

Viṃśikā, ed. S. Lévi, *Vijñaptimātratāsiddhi* (Bibl. Éc. Hautes Études, 245), Paris, 1925.

Vin. of the Mūlasarv. = Mūlasarvāstivāda-Vinayavastu, ed. N. Dutt, 4 parts, (Gilgit Man., III), Srinagar, 1942-50.

Vin. of the Sarvāstivādins = *Der Vinayavibhaṅga zum Bhikṣuprātimokṣa der Sarvāstivādins*, ed. V. Rosen (Sanskrittexte aus den Turfanfunden, 2), Berlin, 1959.

Visuddhimagga, ed. H.C. Warren and Dh. Kosambi (Harvard Oriental Series, 41), Cambridge, Mass., 1950.

Vkn = Vimalakīrtinirdeśa.

Waldschmidt, E., *Lebensende des Buddha*, Göttingen, 1944-48.

Waley, A., *Catalogue of Paintings recovered from Tun-Huang by Sir Aurel Stein*, London, 1931.

Watters, *Travels* = T. Watters, *On Yuan Chwang's Travels*, 2 vol., London, 1904-05.

Weller, F., *Tausend Buddhanamen des Bhadrakalpa*, Leipzig, 1928.

Windisch, E., *Māra und Buddha*, Leipzig, 1895.

Winternitz, M., *Geschichte der indischen Litteratur*, 2nd. ed., 3 vol., Leipzig, 1909-20.

Woodward, *Concordance* = F.L. Woodward and E.M. Hare, ed., *Pāli Tipiṭakaṃ Concordance*, London, 1952 and sq.

Yetts, W.P., *The George Eumorfolopoulos Collection: Buddhist Sculpture*, London, 1932.

Yogācārabhūmi, ed. V. Bhattacharya, I, Calcutta, 1957.

Yogācārabhūmi of Saṃgharakṣa, tr. P. Demiéville, BEFEO, XLIV, 1954, p. 339-436.

Zürcher, E., *The Buddhist Conquest of China*, 2 vol., Leiden, 1959.

INTRODUCTION

The Vimalakīrtinirdeśa (henceforth Vkn) "Teaching of the [bodhisattva named] Unstained Glory" is ranked as one of the developed Sūtras (*vaipulyasūtra*) of the Great Vehicle in Buddhism.

The work which consists of twelve chapters was in Sanskrit prose, except for two groups of stanzas (*gāthā*) in mixed or hybrid Sanskrit (I, § 10; VII, § 6). In the course of time it underwent some alterations and enlargements which concern only secondary points. The oldest state of the text is represented by the Chinese translation of Chih Ch'ien (third century); the intermediate state by the translation of Kumārajīva (fifth century), quite close to the Tibetan translations undertaken very much later (particularly in the ninth century); the most developed, if not the most recent, state appears in the Chinese translation by Hsüan-tsang (seventh century)[1].

Of the original Sanskrit, there only remain, to my knowledge, a few brief quotations in the *Prasannapadā* or *Madhyamakavṛtti* of Candrakīrti (seventh century), the *Śikṣāsamuccaya* of Śāntideva (seventh century) and the *Bhāvanākrama* of Kamalaśīla (eighth century). See the concordance below.

On the other hand the Vkn is known through a great many translations in Chinese, Tibetan, Sogdian and Khotanese which have come down to us in whole or in part.

[1] It is certain that the Vkn underwent modifications and enlargements in the course of time. The Śikṣāsamuccaya, p. 153,*20-22*, quotes an extract from it which is not found in any of the versions now known:

Tathāryavimalakīrtinirdeśe, pariśuddhabuddhakṣetropapattaye sarvasattveṣu śāstṛpremoktam, lokaprasādānurakṣārthaṃ tv āsanapādaprakṣālanakarma kurvatāpi cetasā strīṣu vākṣaṇaprāpteṣu vā vinipatiteṣu bodhisattvena premagauravābhyāsaḥ kāryaḥ.

"Thus in the noble Vkn, for the production of very pure Buddha fields, there is prescribed affection for all beings as if they were the Master himself; however, in order to protect the serenity of the world, the Bodhisattva, even when he rinses out his mouth or washes his feet, should mentally practise affection and respect towards women and towards those who live in unfavourable conditions and bad destinies".

I

THE TRANSLATIONS OF THE VKN

I. — THE CHINESE TRANSLATIONS

The information that we have at our disposal is taken from the Chinese Catalogues:

Ch'u = Ch'u san-tsang chi chi (T 2145), compiled by Sêng-yu in Chien-yeh (Nankin), in the first quarter of the sixth century, and published in 515.

Chung A = Chung ching mu lu (T 2146), compiled in Ch'ang-an, in 594, by the śramaṇas Fa-ching and others, of the Ta Hsing-shan ssŭ.

Li = Li tai son pao chi (T 2034), composed in Ch'ang-an, in 597, by the lay scholar Fei Chang-fang.

Chung B = Chung ching mu lu (T 2147), Ch'ang-an version, compiled in 602 by the bhadanta Yen-ts'ung.

Chung C = Chung ching mu lu (T 2148), Lo-yang version, compiled in 666 by Shih Ching-t'ai.

Nei = Ta T'ang nei tien lu (T 2149), compiled in 664 by Tao-hsüan, then Superior of the Hsi-ming ssŭ at Ch'ang-an.

T'u = Ku chin i ching t'u chi (T 2151), compiled in 664 in Ch'ang-an by the śramaṇa Ching-mai.

Wu = Ta Chou k'an ting chung ching mu lu (T 2153), compiled in Ch'ang-an in 695 on the orders of the Empress Wu, by Ming-ch'üan and others.

K'ai = K'ai yüan shih chiao mu lu (T 2154), compiled in 730 by the śramaṇa Chih-shêng of the Hsi Ch'ung-fu ssŭ in Ch'ang-an.

Chêng = Chêng-yüan hsin ting shih chiao mu lu (T 2157), published in 799-800 by Yüan-chao of the Hsi-ming ssŭ in Ch'ang-an.

For further details on these Chinese catalogues, see P. DEMIÉVILLE, *Les versions chinoises du Milindapañha*, BEFEO, XXIV, 1924, p. 4-20.

1. Ku Wei-mo-chieh ching 古維摩詰經, Old Vimalakīrtisūtra, translated in Lo-yang, in 188, by Yen Fo-t'iao 嚴佛調 of the Late Han.—Translation lost.

a. *Ch'u*, T 2145, p. 6 *c*, does not mention the translation of the Vkn among the works by Yen Fo-t'iao.

b. *Li*, T 2034, p. 54 *a* 14: *Ku Wei-mo-chieh ching*, 2 chüan. This is the first translation. See the Ku lu and the Chu Shih-hsing Han lu [2].

[2] This concerns two Chinese catalogues, already lost by the time of Fei Chang-fang, compiler of the Li tai san pao chi. According to an apocryphal and unreliable tradition, the Ku lu or Ku ching lu "Catalogue of old Sūtras", in one chüan, was brought to China by the Indian monk Shih Li-fang and his colleagues during the reign of the Emperor Shih Huang-ti, between 221 and 208 B.C. (*Nei*, T 2149, p. 336 *b* 11-13; *K'ai*, T 2154, p. 572 *c* 5-7). — The Chu Shih-hsing Han lu "Catalogue of the Han era compiled by Chu Shih-hsing", in one chüan, dating from the Wei period,

c. *Nei*, T 2149, p. 224 *c* 5: copies the aforementioned.

d. *T'u*, T 2151, p. 350 *b* 1: *Ku Wei-mo-chieh ching*, 2 chüan.

e. *K'ai*, T 2154, p. 483 *a* 12: *Ku Wei-mo-chieh ching*, 2 chüan. This is the first translation. See the Ku lu and the Chu Shih-hsing Han lu. An example similar to the Vimalakīrtisūtra of the T'ang (T 467).—Ibid., p. 483 *a* 19-20: A translation carried out in the fifth year of the *chung-p'ing* period (188) of the reign of Ling Ti.

2. Wei-mo-chieh ching 維摩詰經 Vimalakīrtisūtra.—**Wei-mo-chieh so-shuo pu-ssŭ-i fa-mên ching** 維摩詰所說不思議法門經, Vimalakīrtinirdeśa Acintyadharmaparyāyasūtra "Teaching of Vimalakīrti, Sūtra (containing) a treatise of the Law of the Inconceivable".—**Fo-fa p'u-ju tao-mên ching** 佛法普入道門經, Buddhadharmamukhasaṃpraveśasūtra "Sūtra of introduction to the doctrine of the Buddha attributes".—**Fo-fa p'u-ju tao-mên san-mei ching** 佛法普入道門三昧經[3], Buddhadharmamukhasaṃpraveśasamādhisūtra "Sūtra and Concentration on the Introduction to the doctrine of the Buddha attributes". Translated in Chien-yeh (Nankin), between 222 and 229, by Chih Ch'ien 支謙 of the Eastern Wu.—Translation preserved: T 474, 2 chüan.

a. *Ch'u*, T 2145, p. 6 *c* 14: *Wei-mo-chieh ching*, Vimalakīrtisūtra, 2 chüan, lost (!)

b. *Chung A*, T 2146, p. 119 *a* 9: *Wei mo chieh ching*, Vimalakīrtisūtra, 3 chüan. Translation by Chih Ch'ien, during the *huang-wu* period (222-229) of the Wu.

c. *Li*, T 2034, p. 57 *a* 21: *Wei-mo chieh so-shuo pu-ssŭ-i fa-mên ching*, Vimalakīrtinirdeśa Acintyadharmaparyāyasūtra, 3 chüan. Also called *Fo-fa p'u-ju tao-mên ching*, Buddhadharmamukhasaṃpraveśasūtra. Sometimes, in two chüan. This is the second translation. It differs slightly from the translation made by Yen Fo-t'iao of the Late Han. See the Wei Wu lu of Chu Tao-tsu[4] and the Ch'u san tsang chi chi (T 2145).

between A.D. 220 and 265 (*Li*, T 2034, p. 127 *b* 26; *Nei*, T 2149, p. 336 *b* 21-23; *K'ai*, T 2154, p. 572 *c* 15-18).

[3] In this title, as in the following one, the Chinese wording is not clear, but the catalogues certainly refer to one of the titles of the Vkn mentioned in Ch. X, § 11 (beginning): *Sarvabuddhadharmamukhasaṃpraveśa*, rendered in Tibetan by *Saṅs rgyas kyi chos thams cad kyi sgor ḥjug pa*, and in Chinese (Kumārajīva) by 入一切諸佛法門.

[4] Wei Wu lu, in four chüan, compiled by Chu Tao-tsu (d. A.D. 419), a disciple of Hui-yüan. The first two chüan deal with translations executed respectively under the Wei (220-265) and the Wu (220-280). See *Li*, T 2034, p. 127 *c* 4; *Nei*, T 2149, p. 336 *c* 16-22; *K'ai*, T 2154, p. 573 *a* 11-13.

d. *Nei*, T 2149, p. 227 *c* 22: repeats the aforementioned.

e. *T'u*, T 2151, p. 351 *b* 25: *Wei-mo-chieh so-shuo pu-ssŭ-i fa-mên ching*, Vimalakīrtinirdeśa Acintyadharmaparyāyasūtra, 3 chüan.

f. *K'ai*, T 2154, p. 488 *a* 3-4: *Wei-mo-chieh ching*, Vimalakīrtisūtra, 2 chüan. Called *Wei-mo-chieh shuo pu-ssŭ-i fa-mên*, Vimalakīrtinirdeśa Acintyadharmaparyāya. Another name is *Fo-fa p'u-ju tao-mên san-mei ching*, Buddhadharmamukhasaṃpraveśasamādhisūtra. This is the second translation. It is sometimes in 3 chüan. See the two catalogues of Chu Tao-tsu and Sêng-yu (T 2145). It differs slightly from the translation made by Yen Fo-[t'iao] of the Han.

This translation represents the oldest state of the Vkn. Certain paragraphs which appear in later translations are not yet to be found in it. There are missing the stanzas concerning the Buddha's instructing in a single sound (I, § 10, st. 11-18), the comparisons of the old well, the five killers, the four poisonous snakes (II, § 11), Dāntamati's opinion on the identity of Saṃsāra and Nirvāṇa (VIII, § 13), that of Padmavyūha on the absence of ideas (VIII, § 26), the famous passage concerning Vimalakīrti's silence (VIII, § 33), etc.

Sections that later will be greatly developed appear in embryonic form (III, § 1; IV, § 20; VI, § 1; VII, § 1; IX, § 15; X, § 6).

The stock phrases and courtesies with which the Sanskrit text is sprinkled are rendered briefly and clumsily (IV, § 5) or simply passed over (IX, § 4).

The technical vocabulary is hesitant and imprecise: *anātman* is rendered by *fei shên* 非身 (III, § 25); *ānantarya* by *chi-tsui* 極罪 (III, § 16) or *wu chien ch'u* 無間處 (VII, § 1); *parivāra* with the meaning of retinue by *yang* 養 (IV, § 8); *vedanā* with the meaning of feeling by *t'ung* 痛 (V, § 2); *ārya* by *hsien fu* 賢夫 (IV, § 20); *kleśa* by *wu* 污 (IV, § 20) or *lao ch'ên* 勞塵 (VI, § 5); *abhūtaparikalpa* by *pu ch'êng chih tsa* 不誠之雜 (VI, § 6); *upekṣā* with the meaning of equanimity by *hu* 護 (VI, § 3); *upāya* with the meaning of skillful means by *ch'üan* 權 (IV, § 16); *saṃskṛta* and *asaṃskṛta* by *shu* 數 and *wu shu* 無數 (X, § 16); *skandha-dhātu-āyatana* by *yin-chung-ju* 陰種入 (V, § 2); *duḥkha-samudaya-nirodha-pratipad* by *k'u-wu-tuan-hsi* 苦無斷習 (V, § 2).

The translation of the philosophical passages is often incoherent: in a phrase like this 意欲爲勞人執勞惡意已解 (III, § 34), no-one would be able to find the canonical saying: *Cittasaṃkleśāt sattvāḥ saṃkliśyante, cittavyavadānād viśudhyante*: "By the defilement of the mind are beings defiled, by the purification of the mind are they purified".

Showing all the faults—as well as all the merits—of archaic translations (*ku-i*), Chih Ch'ien's version was highly successful in South-East China, especially in Chih Tun's school (cf. III, § 35, note 69). It was to be completely supplanted by Kumārajīva's translation.

3. I Wei-mo-chieh ching 異維摩詰經 or **I P'i-mo-lo-chieh ching** 異毘摩羅詰經, Other Vimalakīrtisūtra. Translated in 291 or 296 by Chu Shu-lan 竺叔蘭 of the Western Chin.—Translation lost.

a. *Ch'u*, T 2145, p. 9 *c* 12-15; 98 *c*: *I Wei-mo-chieh ching*, Other Vimalakīrtisūtra, 3 chüan. Chu Shu-lan's translations appeared at the time of Hui Ti, the first year of the *yüan-k'ang* period (291).

b. *Li*, T 2034, p. 65 *b* 27: *I P'i-mo-lo-chieh ching*, Other Vimalakīrtisūtra, 3 chüan. Published in the sixth year of the *yüan-k'ang* period (296). This is the fifth translation. It greatly resembles and slightly differs from the translations made by Yen Fo-t'iao of the Han, Chih Ch'ien of the Wu, Chu Fa-hu (Dharmarakṣa) and Lo-shih (Kumārajīva). It is sometimes in two chüan. See the [Wei Wu] lu of Chu Tao-tsu.

c. *Nei*, T 2149, p. 236 *b* 26: repeats the aforementioned, but corrects the date: first year of the *yüan-k'ang* period (291).

d. *T'u*, T 2151, p. 354 *b* 15: *I P'i-mo-lo-chieh ching*, Other Vimalakīrtisūtra, 3 chüan.

e. *K'ai*, T 2154, p. 498 *a* 9: *I P'i-mo-lo-chieh ching*, Other Vimalakīrtisūtra, 3 chüan. [Sêng]-yu (T 2145) says: *I Wei-mo-chieh ching*. Sometimes the character *ssŭ* is written [instead of *i*]. It is sometimes in 2 chüan. It was translated during the sixth year of the *yüan-k'ang* period (296). It is the third translation. (Chinese) version of the same (Indian) original already translated by [Yen] Fo-t'iao and Chih Ch'ien. See the two catalogues of [Chu] Tao-tsu and Sêng-yu (T 2145).

4. Wei-mo-chieh ching 維摩詰經, Vimalakīrtisūtra.—**Wei-mo-chieh-ming-chieh** 維摩詰名解.—**Wei-mo-chieh so-shuo fa-mên ching** 維摩詰所說法門經, Vimalakīrtinirdeśadharmaparyāyasūtra "Teaching of Vimalakīrti; Sūtra of a Treatise of the Law". Translated in Ch'ang an, in 303, by Chu T'an-mo-lo-ch'a 竺曇摩羅察 alias Chu Fa-hu 竺法護 (Dharmarakṣa of India), of the Late Chin.—Translation lost.

a. *Ch'u*, T 2145, p. 7 *c* 1: *Wei-mo-chieh ching*, Vimalakīrtisūtra, 1 chüan. One sample says *Wei-mo-chieh ming-chieh*.

b. *Chung A*, T 2146, p. 119 *a* 10: *Wei mo-chieh ching*, Vimalakīrtisūtra, 1 chüan. Translated by Chu Fa-hu (Dharmarakṣa) of the Chin.

c. *Li*, T 2034, p. 63*c* 9: *Wei-mo-chieh so-shuo fa-mên ching*, Vimalakīrtinirdeśadharmaparyāyasūtra, 1 chüan. Translated the first day of the fourth moon of the second year of the *t'ai-an* period (3 May 303). This is the third translation. It greatly resembles and slightly differs from the translations by Yen Fo-t'iao of the Han and Chih Ch'ien of the Wu. See the [Chung ching] lu of Nieh Tao-chên [5].

d. *Nei*, T 2149, p. 234*b* 11-12: repeats the aforementioned.

e. *T'u*, T 2151, p. 353*c* 3-4: *Wei-mo-chieh so-shuo fa-mên ching*, Vimalakīrtinirdeśadharmaparyāyasūtra, 1 chüan.

f. *K'ai*, T 2154, p. 495*b* 16-17: *Wei-mo-chieh so-shuo fa-mên ching*, Vimalakīrtinirdeśadharmaparyāyasūtra, 1 chüan. Translated the first day of the fourth moon of the second year of the *t'ai-an* period (3 May 303). This is the fourth translation. The [Chung ching] lu by Nieh Tao-chên and the catalogue by [Sêng]-yu (T 2145) merely say *Wei-mo-chieh ching*, Vimalakīrtisūtra.

4ª. Shan Wei-mo-chieh ching 刪維摩詰經, Condensed Vimalakīrtisūtra, by the same Dharmarakṣa.—Text lost.

a. *Ch'u*, T 2145, p. 8*c* 16: *Shan Wei-mo-chieh ching*, Condensed Vimalakīrtisūtra, 1 chüan. I, [Sêng]-yu, think that the earlier Vimalas were boring and repetitive, and that [Fa]-hu (Dharmarakṣa) translated the sparse *gāthā* in a condensed form.

b. *K'ai*, T 2154, p. 495*b* 17: repeats the aforementioned.

5. Ho Wei-mo-chieh ching 合維摩詰經, The Combined (into one) Vimalakīrtisūtras. Compilation carried out, in the time of Hui Ti (290-307), by Chih Min-tu 支敏度 of the Western Chin.—Text lost.

a. *Ch'u*, T 2145, p. 10*a* 11: *Ho Wei-mo-chieh ching*, Combined Vimalakīrtisūtras, 5 chüan. It combines three copies (*pên* 本) of the Vimalas translated by Chih Ch'ien, Chu Fa-hu (Dharmarakṣa) and Chu Shu-lan, and unites them into a single work (*pu* 部).

Ibid., p. 58*b* 20-*c* 10: Preface by Chih Min-tu to his own book.—After having mentioned the many divergencies between the three translations, he continues: If, partially, one takes only one translation, one loses sight of the whole; if one consults, in great detail, the three translations, their reading becomes boring and difficult. This is why I have combined two [of the translations] so that they correspond

[5] Chung ching lu "Catalogue of all the Sūtras", in one chüan, compiled in the *yung-chia* period (307-312) by Nieh Tao-chên, disciple of Dharmarakṣa (*Li*, T 2034, p. 127*c* 2; *Nei*, T 2149, p. 336*b* 27-29; *K'ai*, T 2154, p. 572*c* 22-24).

[to the "basic" one]. I have taken as the basic text (*pên* 本) the translation made by [Kung]-ming (another name for Chih Ch'ien: cf. T 2059, ch. 1, p. 325 *a* 19) and as the secondary text (*tzŭ* 子) the translation made by [Chu Shu]-lan.

Ibid., p. 49 *b* 10-11: Equally, regarding his combined edition of the three translations of the Śūraṃgamasamādhi, Chih Min-tu remarks: Here, the translation drawn up by Yuëh (viz. Chih Ch'ien) is taken as the basic text (*mu* 母), that by [Chu Fa]-hu as the secondary text (*tzŭ* 子) and that by [Chu Shu]-lan as a supplementary text (*hsi* 繫)[6].

b. *Li*, T 2034, p. 66 *c* 7: *Ho Wei-mo-chieh ching*, The Combined Vimalakīrtisūtras. The three translations [in one], five chüan. This is the fourth version. It combines in a single work (*pu*) the three translations made respectively by Chih [Ch'ien] and the two Chu's [Chu Fa-hu and Chu Shu-lan]. See the [Ching lun tu] by Chih Min-tu[7].

c. *Nei*, T 2149, p. 237 *c* 18: repeats the aforementioned.

d. *K'ai*, T 2154, p. 501 *b* 16: The Vimala which combines the three translations by Chih Ch'ien and the two Chu's [Chu Fa-hu and Chu Shu-lan] and which consists of five chüan is not a new translation (*pie fan* 別翻) of the Sanskrit original (*fan pên* 梵本).

6. Wei-mo-chieh ching 維摩詰經, Vimalakīrtisūtra, 4 chüan, translated by Ch'i-to-mi 祇多蜜, Gītamitra of the Eastern Chin.— Text lost.

The *Ch'u*, T 2145, p. 12 *a* 18-19, does not mention it among the other works by Gītamitra. This would be the third translation. (*Li*, T 2034, p. 71 *c* 1; *Nei*, T 2149, p. 247 *b* 18; *Wu*, T 2153, p. 386 *a* 29-*b* 1), or the fifth (*K'ai*, T 2154, p. 508 *c* 6).

7. Hsin Wei-mo-chieh ching 新維摩詰經, New Vimalakīrtisūtra (or simply Wei-mo-chieh ching).—**Wei-mo-chieh so-shuo ching** 維摩詰所說經, Vimalakīrtinirdeśasūtra "Sūtra of the Teaching of Vimalakīrti".—**Wei-mo-chieh pu-ssŭ-i ching** 維摩詰不思議經 Vimalakīrtyacintyasūtra "Inconceivable Sūtra of Vimalakīrti".—

[6] It therefore is not a matter of a synoptic edition, but a composition consisting of: 1, a basic text; 2, followed by other texts, passage by passage (as notes). However it seems that at the time, notes were not yet in small characters. — Cf. T'oung Pao, XLVIII, p. 489.

[7] Ching lun tu lu "Complete Catalogue of Sūtras and Śāstras", in one chüan, compiled by Chih Min-tu, at the Yü chang shan monastery (Nan-ch'ang in Chiang-hsi), in the reign of Ch'êng-ti (A.D. 326-342). See *Li*, T 2034, p. 81 *c* 3; 127 *c* 5; *Nei*, T 2149, p. 336 *c* 23-25; *K'ai*, T 2154, p. 573 *a* 14-17.

Pu-k'o-ssŭ-i chieh-t'o 不可思議解脫, Acintyavimokṣa "Inconceivable Liberation". Translated in Ch'ang-an, in 406, by Kumārajīva of the Late Ch'in.—Translation preserved: T 475, 3 chüan.

a. *Ch'u*, T 2145, p. 10 *c* 22: *Hsin Wei-mo-chieh ching*, New Vimalakīrtisūtra, 3 chüan. Translated the eighth year of the *hung-shih* period (406), at the Ta ssŭ of Ch'ang-an.

Ibid., p. 58 *a-b*: Preface by Shih Sêng-chao 釋僧肇 who entitles this translation *Wei-mo-chieh pu-ssŭ-i ching*, Vimalakīrtyacintyasūtra. After having explained this title, he goes on: The sovereign of the Great Ch'in (Yao Hsing at that time), the eighth year of the *hung-shih* period (406), summoned the marshal, Duke of Ch'ang-shan, general of the guard of the Left, Marquis of An-ch'êng, and 1,200 exegetist śramaṇas. In the Ta ssŭ of Ch'ang-an, he invited Kumārajīva the master of the Law to make a new translation of the Vimalakīrtisūtra. Kumārajīva had superhuman capacities; he mysteriously penetrated the domain of truth and exactly reached the "circle's centre"; furthermore he knew foreign languages. Holding the Western text in his hands, he himself translated it orally. Devotees and laymen, filled with respect, repeated each of his words up to three times. He spared no effort in order to maintain absolutely the holy meaning. His style was concise and direct; his mind, elegant and clear; it perfectly reflected the subtle and strange Word. I (Sêng-chao), took part in the sessions for some time, and though my mind was lacking in depth, in the main I grasped the meaning of the text. According to what I had heard, I made a commentary, where I noted the words (of Kumārajīva): "I record them without inventing anything" (saying of Confucius).

b. *Li*, T 2034, p. 77 *c* 16: *Wei-mo-chieh ching*, 3 chüan, translated the eighth year of the *hung-shih* period (406), at the Ta ssŭ. This is the fourth translation. It greatly resembles and slightly differs from the translations by [Yen] Fo-t'iao, Chih Ch'ien and Dharmarakṣa. Sêng-chao took it down with his brush. See the Êrh Ch'in lu [8]. Kumārajīva himself made a commentary; [Shih Sêng]-jui 釋僧叡 composed the preface (cf. T 2145, ch. 8, p. 58 *c*-59 *a*).

c. *Nei*, T 2149, p. 252 *c* 8: repeats the aforementioned.

[8] Êrh Ch'in lu "Catalogue of the two Ch'in (dynasties)", in one chüan, compiled during the *hung-shih* period (399-415) by Sêng-jui, disciple and collaborator of Kumārajīva (*Li*, T 2034, p. 127 *c* 3; *Nei*, T 2149, p. 336 *c* 12-15; *K'ai*, T 2154, p. 573 *a* 7-10).

d. *T'u*, T 2151, p. 359 *a* 21: *Wei-mo-chieh so-shuo ching*, Vimalakīrtinirdeśasūtra, 3 chüan.

e. *K'ai*, T 2154, p. 512*b* 25: *Wei-mo-chieh so-shuo ching*, Vimalakīrtinirdeśasūtra, 3 chüan. Another name is *Pu-k'o-ssŭ-i chieh-t'o*, Acintyavimokṣa. Sometimes simply *Wei-mo-chieh ching*, Vimalakīrtisūtra, is used. The catalogue by Sêng-yu (T 2145) says *Hsin Wei-mo-chieh ching*, New Vimalakīrtisūtra. It was translated the eighth year of the *hung-shih* period (406), in the Ta ssŭ. Sêng-chao took it down with his brush; [Sêng]-jui composed the preface. This is the sixth translation. See the Êrh Ch'in lu and the catalogue by Sêng-yu (T 2145).

The Sanskrit original translated by Kumārajīva was more developed than the one used by Chih Ch'ien. We find in it the stanzas concerning the instruction in a single sound (I, § 10, stanzas 12-14), the comparisons of the old well, the five killers and the four poisonous snakes (II, § 11), the many comparisons serving to illustrate the inexistence of a being (VI, § 1), the long paragraph concerning the roundabout ways of the Bodhisattva (VII, § 1), the thirty-two definitions of *advaya* (VIII, § 1-32), the famous paragraph concerning Vimalakīrti's silence (VIII, § 33), the detailed account of Śākyamuni's instructions in the Sahā universe (IX, § 15), a lengthy elaboration on the effects of the sacred food (X, § 6).

Kumārajīva's style is concise and does not aim at literality: the stock phrases, commonplaces and courtesies are translated in brief or simply omitted (I, § 10 at the beginning; III, § 1; IV, § 5; IX, § 4-5). All the famous translator's attention is turned to the philosophical passages: here, his interpretation sticks as closely to the text as a Tibetan translation. The technical vocabulary has been completely revised, and the Chinese equivalent, once finalised, is regularly reproduced throughout the whole version.

The "New Vimalakīrtisūtra" of Kumārajīva, as it is called in the Chinese catalogues, cast all the earlier works into the shadow: of the six previous translations, only Chih Ch'ien's translation has come down to us, but it stopped being used.

For centuries, as much in Japan as China, the New Vimalakīrtisūtra was the subject of voluminous commentaries and in turn taxed the sagacity of Sêng-chao (T 1775), Hui-yüan (T 1776), Chih-i (T 1777), Chi-tsang (T 1780 and T 1781), Chan-jan (T 1778), Chih-yüan (T 1779) and the Japanese Prince Shōtoku[9].

[9] *The Prince Shotoku's Commentary on the Wei-mo-ching*, ed. by J. SAEKI, 2 vol., Tōkyō, 1937.

Among all the versions of the Vimalakīrti, Kumārajīva's was the only one to be translated into Western languages [10].

The Mahāprajñāpāramitopadeśa (T 1509), also translated by Kumārajīva, seems to have used an enlarged version of the Vkn. See below, III, § 44, note 82.

8. Wu-kou-ch'êng ching or **Shuo Wu-kou-ch'êng ching** 說無垢稱經, Vimalakīrtisūtra, translated in 650, in the Ta-tz'ŭ-ên ssŭ of Ch'ang-an, by Hsüan-tsang 玄奘 of the T'ang.—Translation preserved: T 476, 6 chüan.

a. *Chung C*, T 2148, p. 190 *c* 14: *Shuo Wu-kou-ch'êng ching*, Vimalakīrtisūtra, 6 chüan, 91 leaves. Translated by Hsüan-tsang, the [last] year of the *chêng-kuan* period (649-650) of the T'ang.

b. *Nei*, T 2149, p. 282 *b* 13: *Wu-kou-ch'êng ching*, Vimalakīrtisūtra, 1 book, 6 chüan.

c. *T'u*, T 2151, p. 367 *b* 11: *Wu-kou-ch'êng ching*, Vimalakīrtisūtra, 1 book, 6 chüan.

d. *Wu*, T 2153, p. 386 *b* 5-6: *Shuo Wu-kou-ch'êng ching*, Vimalakīrtisūtra, 1 book, 6 chüan, 110 leaves. Translated, the [last] year of the *chêng-kuan* period (649-650) of the Great T'ang, by the śramaṇa Hsüan-tsang, at the Ta-tz'ŭ-ên ssŭ.

e. *K'ai*, T 2154, p. 555 *c* 11: *Shuo Wu-kou-ch'êng ching*, Vimalakīrti-

[10] English translations, by K. Ōhara, in Hansei Zasshei, XIII, 1898; XIV, 1899; by H. Idzumi, in The Eastern Buddhist, III, 1924; IV, 1925-28; by C. Luk, *The Vimalakīrti Nirdeśa Sūtra*, translated and edited, Shamb(h)ala, Berkeley and London, 1972. — German translation by J. Fischer and T. Yokota, *Das Sūtra Vimalakīrti*, Hokuseidō Druckerei, Tōkyō, 1944. — French translation of Ch. VII, by R.H. Robinson, *Pensée bouddhique*, Bulletin des Amis du bouddhisme, VI, 2, April, 1957, p. 11-13.

With regard to the first Ch. of the Vkn, we would point out the masterly study by S. Yamaguchi, *Textual Explanation of the Buddhakṣetraparivarta of the Vkn*, Otani Gahuko, XXX, No. 2, 1950, p. 1-17; No. 3, 1951, p. 46-58.

Here are some Japanese articles concerning the Vkn, published in the Indogaku Bukkyōgaku Kenkyū of the University of Tōkyō:

H. Hashimoto, *On the transmission of Vkn*, I, No. 1, 1952, p. 196-201; *On the Middle Thought of Vkn*, II, No. 1, 1953, p. 334-337; *Yuima* (Vkn) *as a Zen Text*, II, No. 2, 1954, p. 661-663; *On Eon's Yuima-kyō-giki* (*Commentary on the Vkn*), V, No. 1, 1957, p. 204-207; *The Thought Construction of the Commentary on the Vkn*, VI, No. 2, 1957, p. 509-513; *A Study of the True Character of the Vkn, especially on the Idea of Acintyavimokṣa*, VII, No. 1, 1958, p. 215-219; *On the Position of the Vkn among Tz'u-ên's Teachings*, VIII, No. 1, 1960, p. 99-104. — K. Mochizuki, *A Study on the Chapter Buddha Countries of the Vkn*, IX, No. 2, 1961, p. 542-543.

Also see H. Hashimoto, *The Vkn as a Mādhyamika work*, in Kanazawa-daigaku-hōbunga-kubu-ronshū (Philosophy, History), V, Jan. 1958, p. 135-156.

sūtra, 6 chüan. See the Nei tien lu (T 2149). This is the seventh translation. Text similar to the Vimalasūtra translated by Kumārajīva. It was begun the eighth day of the second moon of the first year of the *yung-hui* period (15 March 650) at the Ta-tz'ŭ-ên ssŭ in the Sūtra Translation Hall, and completed the first day of the eighth moon (1st September 650). The śramaṇa Ta-ch'êng Kuang 大乘光 took it down with his brush.

There are near coincidences between Kumārajīva's translation and that by Hsüan-tsang, such as, for example, the order of the intervention of the first seven Bodhisattvas in Chapter VIII; however, Hsüan-tsang had the use of an Indian original which was far more developed than those of his predecessors. The synoptic arrangement of my translation enables the reader to ascertain this.

The courtesies and dogmatic stock phrases are quoted at length, and Hsüan-tsang was always careful to translate them literally (cf. III, § 25, 34, 58; IV, § 5; IX, § 4-5). In Chapter III, the Śrāvakas who encounter Vimalakīrti never fail to bow before him "saluting his feet with their heads" (*pādau śirasābhivandya*), a detail which is ignored or passed over by all the other versions.

The philosophical passages appear in a greatly enlarged form, as can be seen in the explanations concerning *bodhi* (III, § 52), *acintyavimokṣa* (V, § 11-18), *advaya* (VIII), the purity of the *buddhakṣetra* (IX, § 8), the Bodhisattvas of the Sahāloka (IX, § 16), etc. These explanations are enriched by the addition of several new paragraphs such as those, for example, concerning the gift of languages (V, § 17), *mahāmaitrī* (VI, § 2), the "roundabout ways" of the Bodhisattva (VII, § 2, note 12), etc. In certain sections, e.g. the passage referring to *dharmaparyeṣṭi* (V, § 2), each paragraph is introduced by a brief summary. These additions give Hsüan-tsang's version a remarkable clarity and precision, and that is why it has been chosen here in preference to all the others.

Hsüan-tsang, who spent the last nineteen years of his life translating some 75 Sūtras and Śāstras, was the greatest expert in Buddhist literature of all time. However, he was personally a convinced Vijñānavādin, and we might wonder if he did not interpret the Vkn in an idealistic sense. To answer in the affirmative would be to doubt his rigorous objectivity.

In the Vkn, the question of *ālaya* comes up several times, but it is in order to deny it (V, § 4, note 4; X, § 18, note 26). As with the other Chinese and Tibetan translators, Hsüan-tsang renders the original text faithfully, and avoids any trace of a parallel between this Mādhyamika *ālaya*—or rather, this absence of *ālaya*— and the famous *ālayavijñāna* "store-consciousness" of Vijñānavādin psychology. Moreover, so as to distinguish them clearly, he translates the *ālaya* of the Vkn with the characters *shê-tsang* 攝藏, while in his translations of Vijñānavādin treatises, he regularly transcribes *ālayavijñāna* by *a-lai-yeh shih* 阿賴耶識 (cf. Mahāyānasaṃgraha, T 1594, ch. 1, p. 133 *a* 6).

Very rare indeed are the passages in Hsüan-tsang's version where we can discern any trace of Vijñānavādin vocabulary or theories:

1. III, § 3. — The Tibetan, closely followed by Kumārajīva, says: "Not destroying the passions which come from the realm of rebirth, but entering Nirvāṇa, this is how to meditate". — Hsüan-tsang: "Not abandoning rebirth, but rejecting the passions; even while upholding Nirvāṇa, not abiding in it, this is how to meditate". The particulars given by Hsüan-tsang seem to be influenced by the theories relating to *apratiṣṭhitanirvāṇa*.

2. III, § 59. — According to the Tibetan and Kumārajīva: "The *bodhimaṇḍa* is the seat of the triple knowledge (*tisro vidyāḥ*)". — Hsüan-tsang translates: "The *bodhimaṇḍa* is the seat of the brightness of the mirror of the triple knowledge". We naturally think of the *ādarśajñāna* of Vijñānavādin Buddhology (see *ibidem* note No. 116).

3. IV, § 18. — According to the Tibetan: "Understanding that the body, mind and sicknesses are mutually and each in regular succession to the others without being new or old: this is wisdom". — Hsüan-tsang states: "Understanding that the body, mind and sickness rest on one another, form a series without beginning or end (*anādikālikasaṃtāna*) and that between their appearance and disappearance there is neither interval, nor posteriority nor anteriority: this is wisdom". These particulars recall the speculations on the Subtle Mind of certain Sautrāntikas (cf. Karmasiddhiprakaraṇa, p. 100 sq.), and the *anādikāliko dhātuḥ* of the Vijñānavādins (cf. Saṃgraha, p. 12).

4. V, § 5. — According to the Tibetan: "The Law (*dharma*) is neither conditioned (*saṃskṛta*) nor unconditioned (*asaṃskṛta*)". — For Hsüan-tsang, it is unconditioned. This, however, is also Kumārajīva's opinion and he cannot be suspected of idealism.

5. VI, § 9. — According to the Tibetan and Kumārajīva, deliverance (*vimukti*) is neither inward (*adhyātmam*) nor outward (*bahirdhā*) nor apart from either (*nobhayam antareṇa*): which is Madhyamaka. — But Hsüan-tsang adds that it is to be found in the middle: which is Vijñānavāda.

6. XI, § 1. — For the Tibetan, the Tathāgata is not the *bhūtakoṭi*; for Hsüan-tsang, he is *bhūtakoṭi* without being *koṭi*.

However, these are only very faint nuances, perhaps due to interpolations. In general Hsüan-tsang, like his predecessor Kumārajīva, faithfully reflects the philosophical thought of the Vkn which is pure Madhyamaka.

Despite its great value, Hsüan-tsang's version never got beyond the restricted and closed circle of Chinese śramaṇas, and, to my knowledge at least, was only commented on once, by his disciple K'uei-chi (T 1782) and, this one time, in a strictly idealistic sense. Kumārajīva's translation alone continued to be of interest to the general public.

II. — THE TIBETAN TRANSLATIONS

1. **Hphags pa Dri ma med par grags pas bstan pa** (Ārya-Vimalakīrtinirdeśa), translated by Chos ñid tshul khrims (Dharmatāśīla), representing the vulgate Tibetan of the Kanjur.

For the present work, I used:

a. The Narthang Kanjur (N) preserved in Paris (Fonds tibétain de la Bibliothèque Nationale, No. 419, from folio 274 *recto*, line 4, to folio 382 *recto*, line 2).

b. The Peking Kanjur (P) preserved at Ōtani University in Kyōto and published under the editorship of D.T. Suzuki (*The Tibetan Tripiṭaka*, Tōkyō-Kyōto, 1957: Volume 34, No. 843, from page 74, folio 180 *recto*, line 3, to page 102, folio 250 *verso*, line 3).

I have not been able to consult the Lhasa edition where the Vkn occupies the Mdo section, vol. Pha, folio 270v.1- 376v.3.

This Tibetan translation probably dates from the first quarter of the ninth century, for it is due to Dharmatāśīla who was one of the compilers of the Mahāvyutpatti. The compilation of this Sanskrit-Tibetan lexicon was begun in the reign of Khri-lde-sroṅ-bstan, in 802 or 814 [11]. Dharmatāśīla's translation adopts the Tibetan equivalents proposed by the Mahāvyutpatti.

The *Catalogue of the Tibetan Manuscripts from Tun-Huang in the India Office Library*, published in 1962 by Oxford University Press, lists under numbers 180 to 183 four Tibetan manuscripts of the Vimalakīrtinirdeśa, all in a fragmentary state. They reproduce, with a few variations, the Kanjur version. Number 180 includes the whole of Chapter VIII; No. 181, in 26 folios, goes from the beginning of the Vkn up to Ch. IV, § 10, of my translation; Nos. 182 and 183 only consist of one leaf.

[11] According to G. Tucci, *The Tombs of the Tibetan Kings*, Rome 1950, p. 15 and 18. — For T. Kagawa, *On the Compilation Date of the Mahāvyutpatti*, Indogaku Bukkyōgaku Kenkyū, VII, 1958, p. 160-161, the work, begun in 814, was completed in 824 or shortly after.

A transcription in Roman characters of the Kanjur version has been edited by JISSHU OSHIKA, with the title *Tibetan Text of the Vimalakīrtinirdeśa*, in Acta Indologica of the Naritasan Shinshoji, I, 1970, p. 137-240.

2. The four fragmentary manuscripts from Tun-huang from the Fonds Pelliot tibétain No. 610, 611, 613, 2203. They have been identified and described by M. LALOU, *Inventaire des Manuscrits tibétains de Touen-houang conservés à la Bibliothèque Nationale*, 3 vol., Paris, 1939-1961, I, p. 138-139; III, p. 217. — The first two (FP 610 and 611) have been reproduced in facsimile, edited and studied by J. W. DE JONG, *Fonds Pelliot tibétain Nos. 610 et 611*, Studies in Indology and Buddhology in honour of Prof. S. Yamaguchi, Kyōto, 1955, p. 58-67.

a. FP 610 — "2 f. (8 × 41) not pag., 6 l., mauve ruling and margins, uncircled hole on the left. The intersyllabic punctuation is made with two dots or placed in the middle of the letters. Cursive leaning to the left" (*Inventaire*, I. p. 139).

Folio 1, *recto* and *verso*, goes from Ch. XI, § 8 (end) to Ch. XII, § 2 (beginning) of my translation. — Folio 2, *recto* and *verso*, contains Ch. XII, § 5-7.

There is a considerable difference between FP 610 and the Kanjur. There is no doubt, says Professor de Jong, that the scribe of No. 610 knew nothing of either Dharmatāśīla's translation or the Mahāvyutpatti.

b. FP 611 — "1 f. (7,4 × 27,5) pag. 203 (*ñis-brgya-su*); 5 l., neither ruling nor margins, central hole with traces of a small yellowish circle. Badly written. Mutilated" (*Inventaire*, I, p. 139).

The single folio, *recto* and *verso*, goes from Ch. XI, § 9 (end) to Ch. XII, § 1 (beginning), of my translation.

Unlike the preceding one, FP 611 differs only slightly from the Kanjur text. According to Professor de Jong, it could not have been independent of Dharmatāśīla's translation.

c. FP 613 — "10 f. (7,2 × 48) not pag., plus 9 f. mutilated on the right; 4 l., black ruling and margins, two holes circled in violet. The intersyllabic dot is placed in the middle of the letters" (*Inventaire*, I, p. 139).

Taking into account the mutilated sections noted, FP 613 is related to the following passages of my translation:

Folios (complete) from 1 *recto* to 5 *verso* = Ch. I, § 4-12.
Folio 6 *recto* and *verso* (mutilated) = Ch. I, § 14-15 (beginning).
Folios (mutilated) from 7 *recto* to 8 *verso* = Ch. I, § 17-20, Ch. II, § 1 (beginning).
Folios (complete) from 9 *recto* to 12 *verso* = Ch. II, § 2-12 (beginning).
Folios (mutilated) from 13 *recto* to 14 *verso* = Ch. III, § 1-6 (beginning).
Folio 15 *recto* and *verso* (mutilated) = Ch. III, § 20-22 (beginning).
Folio 16 *recto* and *verso* (mutilated) = Ch. III, § 29 (end)-33 (beginning).
Folio 17 *recto* and *verso* (mutilated) = Ch. III, § 46-50 (beginning).
Folio 18 *recto* and *verso* (mutilated) = Ch. III, § 56 (end)-59 (beginning).
Folio 19 *recto* and *verso* (complete) = Ch. IV, § 16 (end)-17 (beginning).

d. FP 2203 — "30 strips (20 wide × 29,5 high). The first strip is half mutilated; the writing stops in the middle of the last strip. Red guide marks. Carefully written; leaving a space between double cuts" (*Inventaire*, III, p. 217).
Strip 1 (eleven lines preserved) = Ch. I, § 10, stanzas 1 to 6.
Strip 2, lines 1-12 = Ch. I, § 10, stanzas 13 to 18.
Strip 2,l.12-9,l.7 = Ch. I, § 11-20.
Strips 9,l.7-30,l.12 = Ch. II, § 1-13 (complete) and Ch. III, § 1-48.
For details see the Concordance of the version drawn up further on.
FP 613 and FP 2203 represent one and the same Tibetan translation of the Vkn, and this translation differs somewhat from the Kanjur version prepared by Dharmatāśīla.
In order to simplify their comparison, I reproduce here in a photograph (pl. I) and in a synoptic transcription the translation of Ch. II, § 8-9, given in the two versions. The left hand column consists of the text of FP 2203 and, in the critical apparatus, the variations in FP 613; the right hand column reproduces the Peking Kanjur text and, in the critical apparatus, the variations in the Narthang Kanjur.

FP 2203, strip 12, l. 1-14; FP 613, p. 11 *v.* 1 - 12 *r.* 3.	FP f. 188 *v.* 4 - 189 *r.* 2; N f. 287 *r.* 5 - *v.* 6.
II, § 8. der lhags pa de dag la |	II, § 8. der lhags pa de dag la

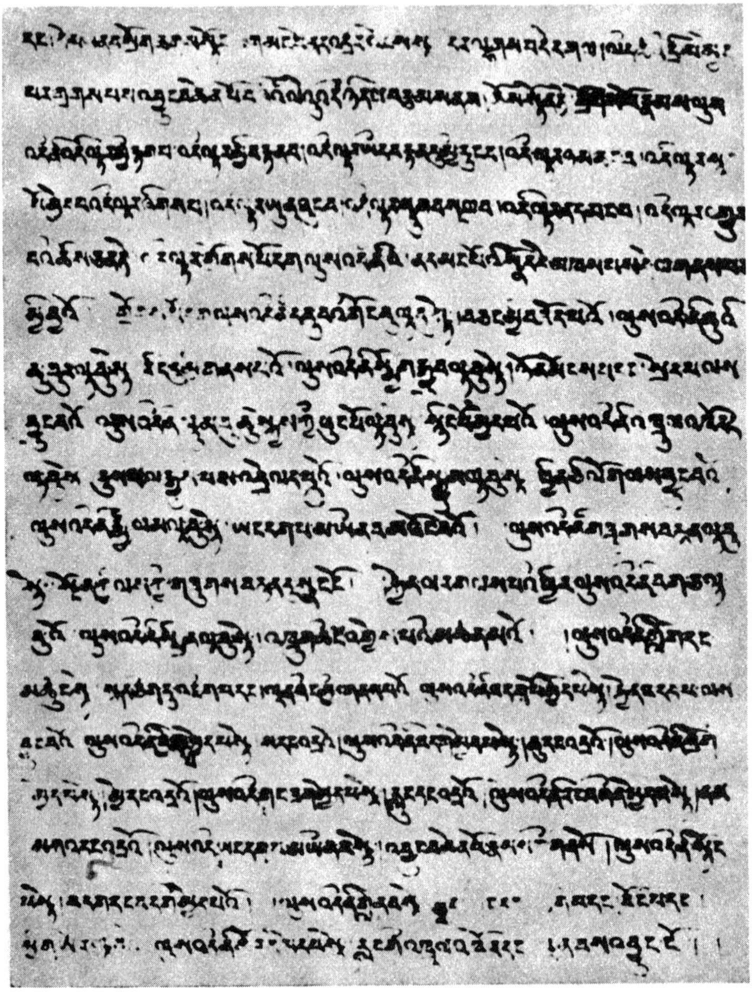

Fonds Pelliot Tibétain, No. 2203, strip 12.

translation from Tun-huang (II, §8-9),

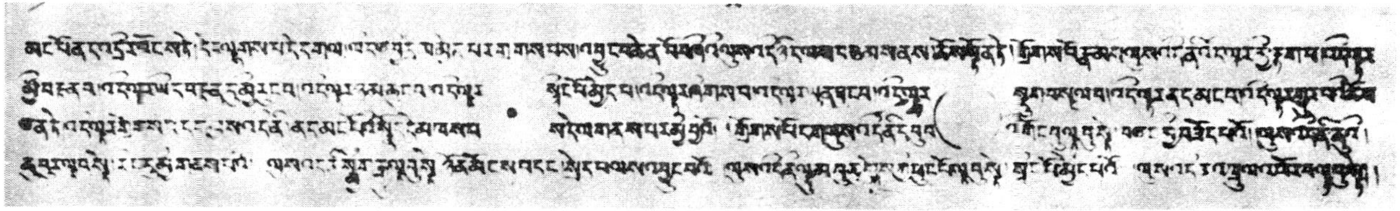

Fonds Pelliot tibétain, No. 613, folio 11 *verso*.

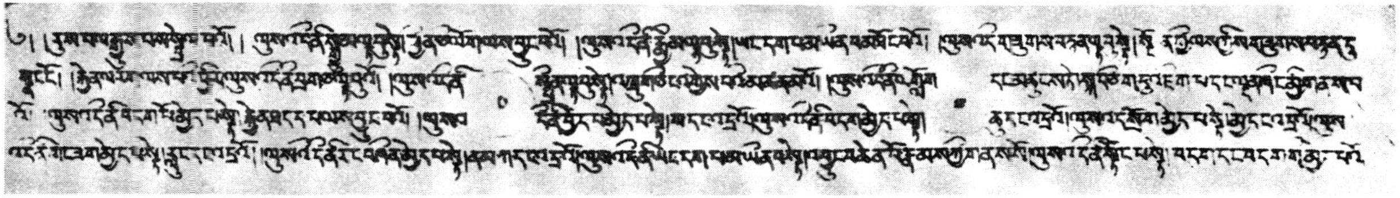

Fonds Pelliot tibétain, No. 613, tolio 12 *recto*.

lid tsha byi[1] dri ma myed par grags pas ḥbyuṅ ba chen po bźiḥi leḥu ḥdi ñid la[2] brtsams nas | chos ston te |

grogs po rnams lus ḥdi ni ḥdi ltar myi rtag pa | ḥdi ltar myi brtan ba | ḥdi ltar yid brtan du myi ruṅ ba | ḥdi ltar ñam chuṅ ba |

ḥdi ltar sñiṅ po myed pa ḥdi ltar źigs pa | ḥdi ltar yun thuṅ ba | ḥdi ltar sdug bsṅal ba | ḥdi ltar nad maṅ ba | ḥdi ltar ḥgyur baḥi[3] chos can te |

ḥdi ltar grogs po dag lus ḥdi ni ḥ[4] | nad maṅ poḥi snod de mkhas pas de la gnas par myi byaḥo ||

[1] *lid tsha byi* FP 2203: *lid tsa byi* FP 613 || [2] *leḥu ḥdi ñid la* FP 2203: *lus ḥdi ñid las* FP 613 || [3] *ḥgyur baḥi* FP 2203: *ḥgyur paḥi* FP 613 || [4] *ḥ* FP 2203: om. FP 613.

lid tsa byi[1] dri ma med par grags pas ḥbyuṅ ba chen po bźiḥi ḥdi ñid las brtsams nas chos ston te

grogs po dag lus ḥdi ni ḥdi ltar mi rtag pa | ḥdi ltar mi brtan pa | ḥdi ltar yid brtan du mi ruṅ ba | ḥdi ltar ñam chuṅ ba |

ḥdi ltar sñiṅ po med pa | ḥdi ltar źig... pa[2] | ḥdi ltar yun thuṅ ba | ḥdi ltar sdug bsṅal ba | ḥdi ltar nad maṅ ba | ḥdi ltar ḥgyur baḥi chos can no ||

grogs po dag ḥdi ltar lus ḥdi ni nad maṅ poḥi snod de mkhas pas de la gnas par mi byaḥo ||

[1] *lid tsa byi* P: *li tsa bhi* N || [2] *źig... pa* P: *źig pa* N ||

II, § 9. grogs po dag lus ḥdi ni dbu baḥi goṅ bu lta bu ste | bcad myi bzod paḥo |

lus ḥdi ni chuḥi chu bur lta bu ste | riṅ du myi gnas paḥo |

lus ḥdi ni smyig rgyu ba lta bu ste | ñon moṅs pa daṅ sred pa las byuṅ[1] baḥo |

lus ḥdi ni ldum bu chu skyes kyi phuṅ po lta bu ste | sñiṅ po myed paḥo |

lus ḥdi ni ḥkhrul ḥkhord[2] lta bu

[1] *byuṅ* FP 2203: *ḥbyuṅ* FP 613 || [2] *ḥkhord* FP 2203: *ḥkhor ba* FP 613 ||

II, § 9. grogs po dag lus ḥdi ni bcad[1] mi bzod pa ste | dbu ba rdos pa lta buḥo ||

lus ḥdi ni riṅ du mi gnas pa ste | chuḥi chu bur lta buḥo ||

lus ḥdi ni ñon moṅs paḥi srid pa las byuṅ ba ste | smig rgyu lta buḥo ||

lus ḥdi ni sñiṅ po med pa ste | chu śiṅ gi sdoṅ po lta buḥo ||

kye ma lus ḥdi ni rus pa la rgyus pas sbrel ba[2] ste | ḥkhrul

[1] *bcad* P: *cad* N || [2] *sbrel ba* P: *sprel ba* N. ||

ste | rus pa la rgyus pas ḥbreld[3] paḥo |

lus ḥdi ni sgyu ma lta bu ste | phyin ci log las byuṅ baḥo |

lus ḥdi ni rmyi lam[4] lta bu ste | yaṅ dag pa ma yin ba mthoṅ baḥo |

lus ḥdi ni[5] gzugs brñan lta bu ste | sṅon kyi[6] las kyi[7] gzugs brñan du snaṅ ṅo ||

rkyen la rag las[8] paḥi phyir lus ḥdi ni brag ca lta buḥo |

lus ḥdi ni sprin lta bu ste | ḥkhrug chiṅ[9] ḥgyes paḥi mtshan maḥo ||

lus ḥdi ni glog[10] daṅ mtshuṅse[11] | skad cig tu ḥjig pa daṅ | ldan źiṅ myi gnas paḥo |

lud ḥdi ni bdag po myed pa ste | rkyen tha dad pa las byuṅ baḥo |

[3] *ḥbreld* FP 2203: *sbrel* FP 613 || [4] *rmyi lam* FP 2203: *rmyim* FP 613 || [5] *ni* FP 2203: om. FP 613 || [6] *kyi* FP 2203: *gyi* FP 613 || [7] *kyi* FP 2203: *kyis* FP 613 || [8] *rag las* FP 2203 and FP 613, to be corrected to *rag lus* || [9] *chiṅ* FP 2203: *ciṅ* FP 613 || [10] *glog* FP 2203: *ḥglog* FP 613 || [11] *mtshuṅse* FP 2203: *mtshuṅs te* FP 613 ||

ḥkhor lta buḥo ||

lus ḥdi ni phyin ci log las byuṅ ba ste sgyu ma lta buḥo ||

lus ḥdi ni yaṅ dag pa ma yin par[3] mthoṅ ba ste | rmi lam lta buḥo ||

lus ḥdi ni sṅon gyi las kyis[4] gzugs brñan snaṅ ba ste | gzugs brñan lta buḥo ||

lus ḥdi ni rkyen la rag lus paḥi phyir brag cha[5] lta buḥo ||

lus ḥdi ni sems ḥkhrug ciṅ ḥgyes paḥi mtshan ñid de sbrin[6] lta buḥo ||

lus ḥdi ni skad cig tu ḥjig pa daṅ ldan źiṅ mi gnas pa ste glog daṅ mtshuṅs so ||

lus ḥdi ni rkyen sna tshogs las byuṅ ba ste bdag po med paḥo ||

[3] *ma yin par* P: *ma yin pa* N || [4] *kyis* P: *gyis* N || [5] *brag cha* P: *brag ca* N || [6] *sbrin* P: *sprin* N ||

It can be seen that the Tun-huang translation (FP 2203 and FP 613) differs from that of the Kanjur (*Dharmatāśīla*) by the intensive use of the da-drag and its phrase construction. However both translations are based on the same Indian original.

They palpably used the same technical vocabulary, recorded in the Mahāvyutpatti, of which Dharmatāśīla was one of the compilers. Here are a few places where the Tun-huang differs from the Kanjur:

I, § 10, stanza 16 — *Pha rol phyin te thaṅ la bźugs* (pāraṃgataḥ sthale tiṣṭhasi): *pha rol phyin nas skam la bźugs.*

I, § 17. — *Źabs kyi mthe bos brdabs* (pādāṅguṣṭhenotkṣipati sma): *źabs kyi mthe bos bsnun*.

I, § 18. — *Sems can tha ṁa* (hīnasattva): *sems can dman pa*.

II, § 1. — *Dbaṅ po mchog daṅ tha ma śes pa* (indriyavarāvarajñāna): *dbaṅ po mchog daṅ mchog ma yin pa śes pa*.

II, § 2. — *Sems can ṅan paḥi ṅaṅ tshul can* (duḥśīlasattva): *sems can tshul khrims ḥchal ba*.

III, § 3. — *Naṅ du yaṅ dag par ḥjog pa* (pratisaṃlayana): *naṅ du yaṅ dag par bźag pa*.

III, § 6. — *Thog maḥi mthaḥ daṅ tha maḥi mthaḥ* (pūrvāparānta): *sṅon gyi mthaḥ daṅ phyi maḥi mthaḥ*.

III, § 6. — *Gnas myed pa* (anālaya): *kun gźi med pa*.

III, § 22. — *Phyugs kyi rmyig* (gokhura): *ba laṅ gi rmig*.

Some differences can be noted in the manner of giving proper names: *Śa ri bu* (Śāriputra) instead of *Śā riḥi bu* (I, § 15, etc.); *Śag kyi thub pa* (Śākyamuni) instead of *Śā kya thub pa* (I, § 15, etc); *Meḥu dgal gyi bu* (Maudgalyāyana) instead of *Mo dgal gyi bu* (III, § 5); *Phyugs lhas kyi bu Ma ska ri* (Maskarin Gośālīputra) instead of *Kun tu rgyu Gnag lhas kyi bu* (III, § 17); *Beḥi ra taḥi bu Kun rgyal* (Saṃjayin Vairaṭīputra) instead of *Smra ḥdod kyi bu moḥi bu Yaṅ dag rgyal ba can* (III, § 17); *Gaṅ po byams paḥi bu* (Pūrṇa Maitrāyaṇīputra) instead of *Byams maḥi bu gaṅ po* (III, § 21); *U pa li* (Upāli) instead of *Ñe bar ḥkhor* (III, § 33); *Nor sbyin ḥdzin* (Rāhula) instead of *Sgra gcan ḥdzin* (III, § 38); *Dgaḥ bo* (Ānanda) instead of *Kun dgaḥ bo* (III, § 42).

However, these are only minor divergencies. If the Tibetan translation as represented by FP 613 and FP 2203 does differ in its phrase construction from the Kanjur version carried out by Dharmatāśīla, like the latter it makes great use of the technical vocabulary of the Mahāvyutpatti. Chronologically, no objection can be raised to such a use since the Mahāvyutpatti was compiled at the beginning of the ninth century and the grottoes of Tun-huang were not "closed" until 1035. Besides several of the Tun-huang manuscripts are translations for which compilers of the Mahāvyutpatti are responsible (*Inventaire*, I, Nos. 24, 51, 78, 99, 417, 551, 552, 797).

Briefly and provisionally then, the textual tradition regarding the Tibetan Vkn seems to be established in the following way:

1. The two folios of FP 610 represent the oldest Tibetan translation. It knows of the da-drag, and its method of rendering Indian words is still very far from the technical vocabulary later laid down by the Mahāvyutpatti (cf. DE JONG, *o.c.*, p. 66).

2. The long fragments of FP 613 and FP 2203 represent a second translation of the Vkn, perhaps the Tun-huang edition. It is characterized by the intensive use of the da-drag, but its technical vocabulary is very close to that of the Mahāvyutpatti.

3. Dharmatāśīla's translation, executed at the beginning of the ninth century and later incorporated into the Kanjur, is quite distinct from the preceding one, as much for the exclusion of the da-drag as for the arrangement of the words and members of the sentence. However, its technical vocabulary is also derived from the Mahāvyutpatti of which Dharmatāśīla was one of the compilers.

4. FP 611, consisting of a single folio, affords little material in comparison. However, in the light of the view expressed by Professor de Jong, it cannot be independent of Dharmatāśīla's translation: "Even though differences between these two texts exist, they are not great enough to allow for two distinct translations".

We should remember, in conclusion, that a Tibetan translation of the Vkn, entitled *Ḥphags pa dri ma med par grags pa bstan pa*, in 1,800 *śloka* and 6 *bam-po*, appears in the Catalogue of *āgama* and *śāstra* preserved in the palace of Ldan-kar, in Stod-thaṅ, under King Khri-sroṅ-lde-btsan, ca 755-797 (cf. M. Lalou, *Les textes bouddhiques au temps du roi Khri-sroṅ-lde-btsan*, JA, 1953, p. 322, line 1). With the information at present to hand, it is impossible to decide whether this concerns the Tun-huang edition represented by FP 613 and 2203, or Dharmatāśīla's translation.

III. — THE SOGDIAN AND KHOTANESE TRANSLATIONS

The sands of Central Asia have given up some Sogdian and Khotanese fragments of the Vkn.

1. The Sogdian fragment in the A. Stein Collection in the British Museum, Ch. 00352, at present Or. 8212 (159), is a scroll measuring 9,7 × 10,5 consisting of 207 lines. It has been edited and translated by H. Reichelt, *Die soghdischen Handschriftenreste des Britischen Museums*, I. Teil: *Die buddhistischen Texte*, Heidelberg, 1928, p. 1-13. Further studies have been published by E. Benveniste and F. Weller [12].

The fragment is a Sogdian translation of the Chinese version by Kumārajīva and not of a Sanskrit original. It corresponds to Ch. VII,

[12] E. Benveniste, *Notes sur les textes sogdiens bouddhiques du British Museum*, JRAS, Jan. 1933, p. 29-33; *Le nom de la ville de Ghazna*, JA, Jan.-Mar. 1935, p. 141-143. — F. Weller, *Bemerkungen zum soghdischen Vimalakīrtinirdeśasūtra*, Asia Major, X, 1935, p. 314-367; *Zum soghdischen Vimalakīrtinirdeśasūtra*, Abhandlungen für die Kunde des Morgenlandes, XXII, 6, Leipzig, 1937.

§ 1-6; VIII, § 1, 2 and 6 of my translation. See the Concordance further on.

2. For the Khotanese fragments, it is sufficient to refer to E. LEUMANN, *Buddhistische Litteratur nordarisch und deutsch*, Leipzig, 1920, p. 692 sq. — There is also a mention of Vimalakīrti in a Khotanese fragment (Ch. 00266) in the A. Stein Collection published by H.W. BAILEY, *Khotanese Buddhist Texts*, London, 1951, p. 104-113.

IV. — CONCORDANCE OF THE TRANSLATIONS OF THE VKN

In the notes that accompany my translation, I am frequently led to compare the various versions of the Vkn. In order to simplify the reference system and facilitate the reader's recourse to sources, I have found it useful to draw up a concordance of the translations known to us at present. There follows here a list of abbreviations and symbols used in this concordance:

§ refers to the paragraphs of my translation.
Cn = Chinese translation by Chih Ch'ien (T 474).
K = Chinese translation by Kumārajīva (T 475).
H = Chinese translation by Hsüan-tsang (T 476).
FP = Fonds Pelliot tibétain de la Bibliothèque Nationale (abbreviation always followed by the No. of the manuscript).
P = Peking Tibetan Kanjur, D.T. SUZUKI edition, Volume 34, No. 843.
N = Narthang Tibetan Kanjur, Fonds tibétain de la Bibliothèque Nationale, No. 419.
S = Original Sanskrit text quoted in extracts in Ś (Śikṣāsamuccaya, ed. C. BENDALL, St. Petersburg, 1897-1902), Bh K (Bhāvanākrama No. 1, ed. G. TUCCI, *Minor Buddhist Texts*, II, Rome, 1958; Bhāvanākrama, No 111, ed. G. TUCCI, *Minor Buddhist Texts*, III, Rome, 1971; MV (Madhyamakakavṛtti or Prasannapadā, ed. L. DE LA VALLÉE POUSSIN, S. Petersburg, 1903.
Sog = Sogdian fragment of the Vkn, ed. H. REICHELT, *Die soghdischen Handschriftenreste des Britischen Museums*, I, Heidelberg, 1928, p. 1-13.
a, *b*, *c*, in the Chinese translations, denote respectively the first, second and third horizontal column of the Taishō edition.
a, *b*, in the Tibetan translations, denote respectively the *recto* and *verso* of the leaf.
*, before a reference, indicates that the beginning of the paragraph is missing.
*, after the reference, indicates that the end of the paragraph is missing.
× indicates that the leaf is mutilated.
— indicates that the paragraph is missing.

CHAPTER I

§	Cn	K	H	FP 613	FP 2203	P	N
1	519 *a* 6	537 *a* 5	557 *c* 5			180 *a* 4	274 *a* 6
2	—	—	—			180 *a* 5	274 *a* 7
3	519 *a* 7	537 *a* 6	557 *c* 6			180 *a* 7	274 *b* 3
4	519 *b* 5	537 *b* 2	558 *a* 7	* 1 *a* 1		181 *a* 6	276 *a* 3
5	519 *b* 20	537 *b* 17	558 *a* 24	1 *b* 1		181 *b* 5	276 *b* 6
6	519 *b* 25	537 *b* 22	558 *b* 3	1 *b* 4		182 *a* 1	277 *a* 4
7	519 *b* 28	537 *b* 25	558 *b* 6	2 *a* 1		182 *a* 2	277 *a* 6
8	519 *c* 2	537 *b* 27	558 *b* 10	2 *a* 3		182 *a* 5	277 *b* 2
9	519 *c* 9	537 *c* 5	558 *b* 19	3 *a* 1		182 *b* 4	278 *a* 4
10	519 *c* 11	537 *c* 7	558 *b* 21	3 *a* 2	* 1,*1*	182 *b* 5	278 *a* 6
11	520 *a* 3	538 *a* 15	559 *a* 4	5 *a* 1	2,*13*	183 *b* 5	279 *b* 6
12	520 *a* 8	538 *a* 21	559 *a* 13	5 *b* 3 *	3,*6*	184 *a* 2	280 *a* 6
13	520 *a* 16	538 *a* 29	559 *a* 29		4,*1*	184 *a* 8	280 *b* 6
14	520 *b* 16	538 *b* 26	559 *c* 11	*× 6 *a* 1	6,*4*	185 *b* 2	282 *b* 2
15	520 *b* 24	538 *c* 6	559 *c* 26	* 6 *b* 1 *	6,*15*	185 *b* 8	283 *a* 2
16	520 *c* 1	538 *c* 12	560 *a* 4		7,*7*	186 *a* 5	283 *b* 2
17	520 *c* 7	538 *c* 20	560 *a* 15	*× 7 *a* 1	7,*18*	186 *b* 2	284 *a* 1
18	520 *c* 11	538 *c* 25	560 *a* 20	× 7 *a* 3	8,*6*	186 *b* 4	284 *a* 5
19	520 *c* 17	538 *c* 29	560 *a* 28	× 7 *b* 3	8,*14*	186 *b* 8	284 *b* 3
20	520 *c* 19	539 *a* 3	560 *b* 1	× 8 *a* 1	8,*18*	187 *a* 2	284 *b* 5

CHAPTER II

§	Cn	K	H	FP 613	FP 2203	P	N	S
1	520 *c* 24	539 *a* 8	560 *b* 6	× 8 *b* 1	9,*7*	187 *a* 5	285 *a* 2	
2	521 *a* 2	539 *a* 16	560 *b* 15	9 *a* 2	9,*18*	187 *b* 2	285 *b* 2	
3	521 *a* 5	539 *a* 19	560 *b* 20	9 *b* 1	10,*6*	187 *b* 5	285 *b* 6	
4	521 *a* 10	539 *a* 25	560 *b* 28	10 *a* 2	10,*14*	188 *a* 1	286 *a* 4	
5	521 *a* 15	539 *a* 29	560 *c* 5	10 *b* 1	11,*3*	188 *a* 5	286 *b* 2	
6	521 *a* 20	539 *b* 6	560 *c* 10	10 *b* 4	11,*10*	188 *a* 8	286 *b* 7	
7	521 *a* 25	539 *b* 9	560 *c* 15	11 *a* 3	11,*16*	188 *b* 3	287 *a* 3	
8	521 *a* 28	539 *b* 12	560 *c* 18	11 *b* 1	12,*1*	188 *b* 4	287 *a* 5	
9	521 *b* 2	539 *b* 15	560 *c* 22	11 *b* 3	12,*6*	188 *b* 7	287 *b* 1	
10	521 *b* 7	539 *b* 21	560 *c* 28	12 *a* 3	12,*14*	189 *a* 2	287 *b* 6	
11	521 *b* 9	539 *b* 22	561 *a* 2	12 *a* 4	12,*16*	189 a 3	287 *b* 7	
12	521 *b* 15	539 *c* 1	561 *a* 10	12 *b* 4 *	13,*6*	189 *a* 7	288 *a* 5	Bh K. III
13	521 *b* 26	539 *c* 11	561 *a* 23		14,*4*	189 *b* 5	289 *a* 1	13,7-9

CHAPTER III

§	Cn	K	H	FP 613	FP 2203	P	N
1	521 *b* 29	539 *c* 15	561 *b* 4	*× 13 *a* 1	14,*6*	189 *b* 7	289 *a* 3
2	521 *c* 1	539 *c* 16	561 *b* 6	× 13 *a* 1	14,*9*	189 *b* 8	289 *a* 4
3	521 *c* 4	539 *c* 19	561 *b* 11	× 13 *a* 4	14,*15*	190 *a* 3	289 *b* 1
4	521 *c* 10	539 *c* 26	561 *b* 18	× 14 *a* 1	15,*8*	190 *a* 8	290 *a* 1
5	521 *c* 13	539 *c* 28	561 *b* 21	× 14 *a* 2	15,*10*	190 *a* 8	290 *a* 3
6	521 *c* 16	540 *a* 2	561 *b* 26	× 14 *a* 4 *	15,*17*	190 *b* 3	290 *a* 6
7	521 *c* 28	540 *a* 17	561 *c* 17		16,*14*	191 *a* 2	291 *a* 2
8	522 *a* 2	540 *a* 19	561 *c* 21		16,*18*	191 *a* 4	291 *a* 4
9	522 *a* 5	540 *a* 22	561 *c* 25		17,*4*	191 *a* 6	291 *a* 7
10	522 *a* 8	540 *a* 24	561 *c* 29		17,*7*	191 *a* 7	291 *b* 2
11	522 *a* 10	540 *a* 11	562 *a* 4		17,*12*	191 *b* 1	291 *b* 4
12	522 *a* 14	540 *b* 3	562 *a* 10		18,*1*	191 *b* 4	292 *a* 1
13	522 *a* 17	540 *b* 6	562 *a* 14		18,*5*	191 *b* 6	292 *a* 4
14	522 *a* 23	540 *b* 13	562 *a* 22		18,*15*	192 *a* 2	292 *b* 2
15	522 *a* 28	540 *b* 18	562 *a* 29		19,*2*	192 *a* 5	292 *b* 5
16	522 *b* 2	540 *b* 21	562 *b* 5		19,*8*	192 *a* 7	293 *a* 1
17	522 *b* 8	540 *b* 29	562 *b* 14		19,*17*	192 *b* 4	293 *a* 7
18	522 *b* 12	540 *c* 5	562 *b* 18		20,*3*	192 *b* 6	293 *b* 3
19	522 *b* 18	540 *c* 12	562 *b* 26		20,*12*	193 *a* 2	294 *a* 1
20	522 *b* 24	540 *c* 20	562 *c* 6	× 15 *a* 1	21,*4*	193 *a* 6	294 *a* 7
21	522 *b* 27	540 *c* 22	562 *c* 11	× 15 *a* 2	21,*7*	193 *a* 8	294 *b* 2
22	522 *c* 1	540 *c* 26	562 *c* 15	× 15 *a* 4 *	21,*12*	193 *b* 2	294 *b* 5
23	522 *c* 7	541 *a* 5	562 *c* 28		22,*4*	193 *b* 6	295 *a* 5
24	522 *c* 11	541 *a* 10	563 *a* 5		22,*9*	194 *a* 1	295 *b* 2
25	522 *c* 14	541 *a* 12	563 *a* 10		22,*14*	194 *a* 3	295 *b* 5
26	522 *c* 18	541 *a* 16	563 *a* 16		23,*4*	194 *a* 6	296 *a* 2
27	522 *c* 23	541 *a* 21	563 *a* 23		23,*10*	194 *b* 1	296 *a* 5
28	522 *c* 25	541 *a* 23	563 *a* 26		23,*12*	194 *b* 2	296 *a* 7
29	522 *c* 27	541 *a* 25	563 *a* 28	* × 16 *a* 1	23,*15*	194 *b* 3	296 *b* 1
30	523 *a* 1	541 *a* 29	563 *b* 4	× 16 *a* 1	24,*5*	194 *b* 6	296 *b* 6
31	523 *a* 4	541 *b* 3	563 *b* 9	× 16 *a* 4	24,*11*	195 *a* 1	297 *a* 3
32	523 *a* 7	541 *b* 7	563 *b* 13	× 16 *b* 1	24,*16*	195 *a* 3	297 *a* 5
33	523 *a* 10	541 *b* 10	563 *b* 16	× 16 *b* 3 *	25,*4*	195 *a* 4	297 *a* 7
34	523 *a* 15	541 *b* 15	563 *b* 25		25,*12*	195 *a* 8	297 *b* 6
35	523 *a* 21	541 *b* 23	563 *c* 4		26,*6*	195 *b* 5	298 *a* 5
36	523 *a* 26	541 *b* 29	563 *c* 14		26,*14*	195 *b* 8	298 *b* 3
37	523 *a* 29	541 *c* 3	563 *c* 19		27,*2*	196 *a* 2	298 *b* 6

§	Cn	K	H	FP 613	FP 2203	P	N
38	523 *b* 3	541 *c* 7	563 *c* 23		27,*5*	196 *a* 4	299 *a* 1
39	523 *b* 8	541 *c* 13	564 *a* 1		27,*14*	196 *a* 8	299 *a* 7
40	523 *b* 14	541 *c* 22	564 *a* 14		28,*8*	196 *b* 6	299 *b* 7
41	523 *b* 17	541 *c* 27	564 *a* 20		28,*13*	197 *a* 1	300 *a* 4
42	523 *b* 20	542 *a* 1	564 *a* 24		28,*15*	197 *a* 2	300 *a* 5
43	523 *b* 24	542 *a* 5	564 *b* 1		29,*4*	197 *a* 5	300 *b* 2
44	523 *b* 27	542 *a* 9	564 *b* 7		29,*9*	197 *a* 7	300 *b* 5
45	523 *c* 6	542 *a* 16	564 *b* 16		29,*18*	197 *b* 3	301 *a* 3
46	523 *c* 8	542 *a* 19	564 *b* 19	× 17 *a* 1	30,*4*	197 *b* 6	301 *a* 7
47	523 *c* 11	542 *a* 22	564 *b* 24	× 17 *a* 2	30,*8*	197 *b* 8	301 *b* 3
48	523 *c* 12	542 *a* 23	564 *b* 27	× 17 *a* 3	30,*10*	198 *a* 1	301 *b* 4
49	523 *c* 15	542 *a* 27	564 *c* 3	× 17 *a* 4		198 *a* 2	301 *b* 5
50	523 *c* 19	542 *b* 1	564 *c* 8	× 17 *b* 4 *		198 *a* 5	302 *a* 2
51	523 *c* 23	542 *b* 8	564 *c* 16			198 *a* 8	302 *a* 6
52	524 *a* 4	542 *b* 20	565 *a* 3			198 *b* 5	302 *b* 6
53	524 *a* 19	542 *c* 8	565 *b* 3			199 *a* 5	303 *b* 6
54	524 *a* 21	542 *c* 10	565 *b* 6			199 *b* 1	303 *b* 7
55	524 *a* 25	542 *c* 15	565 *b* 12			199 *b* 5	304 *a* 5
56	524 *a* 28	542 *c* 17	565 *b* 16	*× 18 *a* 1		199 *b* 6	304 *a* 6
57	524 *b* 2	542 *c* 20	565 *b* 22	× 18 *a* 1		199 *b* 8	304 *b* 2
58	524 *b* 4	542 *c* 22	565 *b* 25	× 18 *a* 2		200 *a* 1	304 *b* 3
59	524 *b* 10	542 *c* 29	565 *c* 5	× 18 *b* 2 *		200 *a* 5	305 *a* 1
60	524 *b* 15	543 *a* 5	565 *c* 14			200 *a* 8	305 *a* 5
61	524 *b* 18	543 *a* 7	565 *c* 19			200 *b* 2	305 *b* 1
62	524 *b* 20	543 *a* 9	565 *c* 22			200 *b* 3	305 *b* 2
63	524 *b* 28	543 *a* 19	566 *a* 5			201 a 1	306 *a* 3
64	524 *c* 6	543 *a* 25	566 *a* 14			201 *a* 5	306 *b* 1
65	524 *c* 21	543 *b* 12	566 *b* 13			202 *a* 1	307 *b* 3
66	524 *c* 27	543 *b* 18	566 *b* 23			202 *a* 5	308 *a* 1
67	525 *a* 6	543 *b* 26	566 *c* 5			202 *b* 1	308 *a* 7
68	525 *a* 8	543 *c* 1	566 *c* 10			202 *b* 2	308 *b* 2
69	525 *a* 13	543 *c* 8	566 *c* 19			202 *b* 7	309 *a* 1
70	525 *a* 16	543 *c* 12	566 *c* 23			203 *a* 1	309 *a* 3
71	525 *a* 18	543 *c* 16	566 *c* 29			203 *a* 4	309 *a* 7
72	525 *a* 19	543 *c* 17	567 *a* 2			203 *a* 5	309 *b* 1
73	525 *a* 26	543 *c* 25	567 *a* 15			203 *b* 3	310 *a* 2
74	525 *a* 29	543 *c* 28	567 *a* 20			203 *b* 6	310 *a* 5
75	525 *b* 3	544 *a* 4	567 *a* 26			203 *b* 8	310 *b* 2

§	Cn	K	H	FP 613	FP 2203	P	N
76	525 *b* 11	544 *a* 11	567 *b* 6			204 *a* 5	310 *b* 7
77	525 *b* 13	544 *a* 14	567 *b* 10			204 *a* 6	311 *a* 2
78	525 *b* 15	544 *a* 16	567 *b* 14			204 *a* 8	311 *a* 4

CHAPTER IV

§	Cn	K	H	FP 613	P	N	S
1	525 *b* 18	544 *a* 23	567 *b* 22		204 *b* 1	311 *a* 5	
2	525 *b* 23	544 *b* 2	567 *c* 7		204 *b* 7	311 *b* 6	
3	525 *b* 28	544 *b* 9	567 *c* 16		205 *a* 3	312 *a* 5	
4	525 *c* 1	544 *b* 11	567 *c* 23		205 *a* 5	312 *a* 7	
5	525 *c* 3	544 *b* 18	568 *a* 1		205 *b* 1	312 *b* 5	
6	525 *c* 5	544 *b* 19	568 *a* 4		205 *b* 2	312 *b* 7	
7	525 *c* 10	544 *b* 24	568 *a* 11		205 *b* 5	313 *a* 4	
8	525 *c* 14	544 *b* 28	568 *a* 16		205 *b* 8	313 *a* 7	
9	525 *c* 25	544 *c* 10	568 *a* 28		206 *a* 6	314 *a* 1	
10	526 *a* 2	544 *c* 17	568 *b* 8		206 *b* 1	314 *a* 5	
11	526 *a* 8	544 *c* 26	568 *b* 19		206 *b* 4	314 *b* 3	
12	526 *a* 17	545 *a* 6	568 *b* 29		207 *a* 2	315 *a* 3	
13	526 *a* 24	545 *a* 13	568 *c* 11		207 *a* 7	315 *b* 2	
14	526 *a* 26	545 *a* 16	568 *c* 15		207 *b* 1	315 *b* 5	
15	526 *b* 6	545 *a* 25	569 *a* 2		207 *b* 6	316 *a* 5	
16	526 *b* 15	545 *b* 5	569 *a* 18	* 19 *a* 1	208 *a* 4	316 *b* 5	* Bh K.
17	526 *b* 18	545 *b* 8	569 *a* 23	19 *a* 1 *	208 *a* 7	317 *a* 2	194,*8-1*
18	526 *b* 26	545 *b* 18	569 *b* 11		208 *b* 5	317 *b* 3	and Bh K
19	526 *c* 2	545 *b* 23	569 *b* 17		208 *b* 8	317 *b* 7	22,*10-14*
20	526 *c* 5	545 *b* 27	569 *b* 21		209 *a* 2	318 *a* 2	* Ś 273,

CHAPTER V

§	Cn	K	H	P	N
1	526 *c* 20	546 *a* 4	570 *a* 28	210 *b* 5	320 *b* 2
2	526 *c* 24	546 *a* 8	570 *b* 4	210 *b* 7	320 *b* 5
3	526 *c* 28	546 *a* 12	570 *b* 9	211 *a* 2	321 *a* 1
4	527 *a* 7	546 *a* 19	570 *b* 22	211 *a* 7	321 *b* 1
5	527 *a* 13	546 *a* 24	570 *c* 1	211 *b* 2	321 *b* 6

§	Cn	K	H	P	N
6	527 *a* 16	547 *a* 29	570 *c* 7	211 *b* 4	322 *a* 1
7	527 *a* 24	546 *b* 5	570 *c* 17	212 *a* 2	322 *b* 1
8	527 *b* 2	546 *b* 11	570 *c* 26	212 *a* 6	322 *b* 7
9	527 *b* 10	546 *b* 20	571 *a* 10	212 *b* 5	323 *b* 2
10	527 *b* 13	546 *b* 24	571 *a* 15	212 *b* 7	323 *b* 6
11	527 *b* 18	546 *b* 29	571 *a* 24	213 *a* 3	324 *a* 4
12	527 *b* 21	546 *c* 3	571 *b* 5	213 *a* 6	324 *a* 7
13	527 *b* 24	546 *c* 8	571 *b* 16	213 *a* 7	324 *b* 2
14	527 *b* 26	546 *c* 12	571 *b* 26	213 *b* 2	324 *b* 6
15	527 *c* 2	546 *c* 20	571 *c* 9	213 *b* 6	325 *a* 3
16	527 *c* 5	546 *c* 24	571 *c* 19	213 *b* 8	325 *a* 6
17	527 *c* 8	546 *c* 27	571 *c* 26	214 *a* 3	325 *b* 2
18	—	547 *a* 1	572 *a* 6	214 *a* 5	325 *b* 5
19	527 *c* 11	547 *a* 3	572 *a* 13	214 *a* 7	325 *b* 7
20	527 *c* 21	547 *a* 15	572 *b* 2	214 *b* 6	326 *b* 2

CHAPTER VI

§	Cn	K	H	P	N	S
1	528 *a* 8	547 *a* 29	572 *a* 4	215 *b* 1	327 *b* 3	
2	528 *a* 19	547 *b* 13	572 *a* 24	217 *a* 1	329 *b* 5	
3	528 *b* 8	547 *c* 4	573 *a* 26	217 *b* 5	330 *b* 7	
4	528 *b* 11	547 *c* 7	573 *b* 4	217 *b* 6	331 *a* 2	Ś 145,*11-15*
5	528 *b* 14	547 *c* 12	573 *b* 8	218 *a* 1	331 *a* 5	
6	528 *b* 21	547 *c* 18	573 *b* 17	218 *a* 5	331 *b* 4	Ś 264,*6-9*
7	528 *b* 23	547 *c* 23	573 *b* 22	218 *a* 7	331 *b* 7	
8	528 *b* 26	547 *c* 26	573 *b* 27	218 *b* 2	332 *a* 3	
9	528 *c* 4	548 *a* 7	573 *c* 13	219 *a* 1	332 *b* 5	
10	528 *c* 14	548 *a* 18	573 *c* 27	219 *a* 8	333 *b* 1	
11	528 *c* 17	548 *a* 22	574 *a* 1	219 *b* 3	333 *b* 3	
12	528 *c* 19	548 *a* 25	574 *a* 9	219 *b* 4	333 *b* 5	
13	528 *c* 26	548 *b* 3	574 *a* 21	220 *a* 1	334 *a* 4	*Ś 269,*11-12**
14	529 *a* 14	548 *b* 22	574 *b* 19	220 *b* 4	335 *a* 6	
15	529 *a* 19	548 *b* 27	574 *b* 25	220 *b* 6	335 *b* 3	
16	529 *a* 29	548 *c* 9	574 *c* 9	221 *a* 5	336 *a* 4	
17	529 *b* 10	548 *c* 21	574 *c* 27	221 *b* 5	337 *a* 1	

CHAPTER VII

§	Cn	K	H	P	N	S	Sog
1	529 *b* 16	548 *c* 29	575 *a* 5	221 *b* 7	337 *a* 4		* ligne 1
2	529 *c* 1	549 *a* 28	575 *b* 23	223 *a* 3	339 *a* 2		l. *10*
3	529 *c* 6	549 *b* 4	575 *c* 2	223 *a* 6	339 *a* 7	* Ś 6,*10-11* *	l. *20*
4	529 *c* 16	549 *b* 16	575 *c* 21	223 *b* 5	340 *a* 2		l. *41*
5	529 *c* 20	549 *b* 20	575 *c* 29	223 *b* 8	340 *a* 5		l. *48*
6	529 *c* 25	549 *b* 27	576 *a* 9	224 *a* 4	340 *b* 3	* Ś 324,*11* > 327,*4*	l. *59*

CHAPTER VIII

§	Cn	K	H	P	N	Sog
1	530 *c* 24	550 *b* 29	577 *a* 12	226 *a* 1	343 *b* 2	l. *187*
2	530 *c* 28	550 *c* 5	577 a 19	226 *a* 3	343 *b* 5	l. *196*
3	531 *a* 3	550 *c* 11	577 *a* 26	226 *a* 4	343 *b* 6	—
4	531 *a* 6	550 *c* 13	577 *b* 1	226 *a* 6	344 *a* 1	—
5	531 *a* 8	550 *c* 19	577 *b* 9	226 *a* 7	344 *a* 2	—
6	531 *a* 1	550 *c* 8	577 *a* 22	226 *a* 8	344 *a* 4	l. *201*
7	531 *a* 11	550 *c* 16	577 *b* 5	226 *b* 2	344 *a* 6	—
8	531 *a* 14	550 *c* 22	577 *b* 13	226 *b* 3	344 *b* 1	
9	531 *a* 17	550 *c* 24	577 *b* 17	226 *b* 4	344 *b* 2	
10	531 *a* 19	550 *c* 27	577 *b* 21	226 *b* 5	344 *b* 3	
11	531 *a* 22	551 *a* 1	577 *b* 25	226 *b* 7	344 *b* 6	
12	531 *a* 25	551 *a* 4	577 *b* 29	226 *b* 8	344 *b* 7	
13	—	551 *a* 7	577 *c* 4	227 *a* 2	345 *a* 3	
14	531 *a* 28	551 *a* 10	577 *c* 7	227 *a* 3	345 *a* 4	
15	531 *b* 2	551 *a* 13	577 *c* 13	227 *a* 5	345 *a* 7	
16	531 *b* 4	551 *a* 16	577 *c* 17	227 *a* 6	345 *b* 1	
17	531 *b* 7	551 *a* 19	577 *c* 22	227 *a* 8	345 *b* 3	
18	531 *b* 10	551 *a* 23	577 *c* 26	227 *b* 2	345 *b* 6	
19	531 *b* 13	551 *a* 26	578 *a* 1	227 *b* 4	346 *a* 2	
20	531 *b* 17	551 *b* 2	578 *a* 7	227 *b* 6	346 *a* 4	
21	531 *b* 22	551 *b* 7	578 *a* 14	228 *a* 1	346 *b* 1	
22	531 *b* 25	551 *b* 11	578 *a* 20	228 *a* 3	346 *b* 4	

Cn	K	H	P	N
531 *b* 28	551 *b* 14	578 *a* 24	228 *a* 5	346 *b* 6
531 *c* 3	551 *b* 18	578 *b* 1	228 *a* 7	347 *a* 2
531 *c* 7	551 *b* 22	578 *b* 8	228 *b* 1	347 *a* 5
—	551 *b* 25	578 *b* 14	228 *b* 4	347 *b* 1
531 *c* 11	551 *b* 28	578 *b* 18	228 *b* 5	347 *b* 3
531 *c* 14	551 *c* 1	578 *b* 21	228 *b* 6	347 *b* 4
531 *c* 17	551 *c* 5	578 *b* 26	228 *b* 8	347 *b* 7
531 *c* 21	551 *c* 9	578 *c* 3	229 *a* 2	348 *a* 3
531 *c* 24	551 *c* 12	578 *c* 8	229 *a* 4	348 *a* 5
531 *c* 28	551 *c* 16	578 *c* 13	229 *a* 6	348 *a* 7
—	551 *c* 20	578 *c* 20	229 *a* 8	348 *b* 4

CHAPTER IX

Cn	K	H	P	N	S
532 *a* 4	552 *a* 4	579 *a* 4	229 *b* 4	349 *a* 2	
532 *a* 7	552 *a* 7	579 *a* 10	229 *b* 7	349 *a* 7	* MV 333, 6-9 *
532 *a* 17	552 *a* 17	579 *a* 26	230 *a* 7	350 *a* 2	
532 *a* 20	552 *a* 21	579 *b* 5	230 *b* 1	350 *a* 5	
532 *a* 26	552 *b* 2	579 *b* 17	230 *b* 8	351 *a* 1	
532 *b* 2	552 *b* 8	579 *b* 25	231 *a* 6	351 *b* 2	
532 *b* 8	552 *b* 16	579 *c* 8	231 *b* 4	352 *a* 3	
532 *b* 11	552 *b* 18	579 *c* 14	231 *b* 7	352 *a* 6	
532 *b* 17	552 *b* 27	579 *c* 29	232 *a* 4	352 *b* 6	
532 *b* 19	552 *b* 29	580 *a* 2	232 *a* 6	353 *a* 2	
532 *b* 27	552 *c* 9	580 *a* 16	232 *b* 3	353 *b* 2	
532 *b* 29	552 *c* 11	580 *a* 20	232 *b* 5	353 *b* 4	
532 *c* 4	552 *c* 17	580 *a* 29	232 *b* 8	354 *a* 2	Ś 209,*13*
532 *c* 9	552 *c* 21	580 *b* 7	233 *a* 3	354 *a* 5	> 270,*3*
532 *c* 13	552 *c* 25	580 *b* 14	233 *a* 6	354 *b* 3	
532 *c* 21	553 *a* 16	580 *c* 16	234 *a* 1	355 *b* 5	
532 *c* 25	553 *a* 22	581 *a* 2	234 *a* 5	356 *a* 2	
533 *a* 2	553 *a* 28	581 *a* 12	234 *b* 1	356 *b* 1	

CHAPTER X

§	Cn	K	H	P	N	
1	533 *a* 13	553 *b* 12	581 *b* 6	235 *a* 1	357 *a* 1	
2	533 *a* 17	553 *b* 17	581 *b* 12	235 *a* 4	357 *b* 2	
3	533 *a* 25	553 *b* 26	581 *b* 26	235 *b* 4	358 *a* 5	
4	533 *a* 28	553 *b* 29	581 *c* 2	235 *b* 6	358 *b* 2	
5	533 *b* 4	553 *c* 5	581 *c* 9	236 *a* 2	358 *b* 6	
6	533 *b* 7	553 *c* 8	581 *c* 14	236 *a* 3	359 *a* 2	* § 270,*4-7* *
7	533 *b* 10	553 *c* 13	581 *c* 24	236 *a* 6	359 *a* 5	
8	533 *b* 14	553 *c* 17	582 *a* 7	236 *a* 8	359 *b* 2	
9	533 *b* 19	553 *c* 24	582 *a* 16	236 *b* 5	360 *a* 1	
10	533 *b* 21	553 *c* 27	582 *a* 23	236 *b* 8	360 *a* 5	
11	533 *b* 24	554 *a* 1	582 *a* 29	237 *a* 2	360 *a* 7	
12	533 *b* 28	554 *a* 7	582 *b* 7	237 *a* 5	360 *b* 4	
13	533 *c* 1	554 *a* 9	582 *b* 12	237 *a* 6	360 *b* 6	
14	533 *c* 9	554 *a* 19	582 *b* 26	237 *b* 5	361 *b* 1	
15	533 *c* 15	554 *a* 28	582 *c* 8	238 *a* 2	361 *b* 7	
16	533 *c* 20	554 *b* 3	582 *c* 14	238 *a* 6	362 *a* 6	
17	533 *c* 23	554 *b* 7	582 *c* 20	238 *a* 7	362 *b* 1	
18	534 *a* 15	554 *c* 3	583 *b* 9	239 *a* 7	364 *a* 2	
19	534 *a* 26	554 *c* 15	583 *c* 2	239 *b* 7	364 *b* 5	
20	534 *b* 12	554 *c* 21	584 *a* 1	240 *b* 4	366 *a* 2	

CHAPTER XI

§	Cn	K	H	FP 610	FP 611	P	N
1	534 *b* 18	554 *c* 28	584 *a* 15			240 *b* 7	366 *a* [illegible]
2	534 *c* 9	555 *a* 25	584 *c* 1			242 *a* 4	368 *b*
3	534 *c* 20	555 *b* 5	584 *c* 17			242 *b* 4	369 *a*
4	534 *c* 30	555 *b* 14	584 *c* 28			243 *a* 1	369 *b*
5	535 *a* 14	555 *b* 29	585 *a* 21			243 *b* 4	370 *b*
6	535 *a* 16	555 *c* 1	585 *a* 23			243 *b* 5	371 *a*
7	535 *a* 23	555 *c* 8	585 *b* 5			244 *a* 1	371 *a*
8	535 *b* 1	555 *c* 16	585 *b* 20	* 1 *a* 1		244 *a* 7	371 *b*
9	535 *b* 5	555 *c* 22	585 *b* 28	1 *a* 1	* 1 *a* 1	244 *b* 3	372 *a*

CHAPTER XII

§	Cn	K	H	FP 610	FP 611	P	N
1	535 *b* 12	556 *a* 2	585 *c* 13	1 *b* 1	1 *b* 1 *	244 *b* 8	372 *b* 6
2	535 *b* 14	556 *a* 4	585 *c* 15	1 *b* 3 *		245 *a* 2	373 *a* 2
3	535 *b* 18	556 *a* 9	585 *c* 22			245 *a* 5	373 *a* 6
4	535 *b* 21	556 *a* 13	585 *c* 29			245 *a* 7	373 *b* 3
5	535 *b* 24	556 *a* 18	586 *a* 6	* 2 *a* 1		245 *b* 2	373 *b* 7
6	535 *c* 4	556 *a* 26	586 *a* 21	2 *a* 4		246 *a* 1	374 *b* 2
7	535 *c* 9	556 *b* 2	586 *a* 28	2 *b* 1 *		246 *a* 3	374 *b* 5
8	535 *c* 15	556 *b* 8	586 *b* 6			246 *a* 8	375 *a* 5
9	535 *c* 20	556 *b* 13	586 *b* 16			246 *b* 3	375 *b* 2
10	535 *c* 26	556 *b* 19	586 *b* 27			246 *b* 8	376 *a* 2
11	536 *a* 2	556 *b* 25	586 *c* 6			247 *a* 3	376 *a* 7
12	536 *a* 9	556 *c* 6	586 *c* 24			247 *b* 1	377 *a* 1
13	536 *a* 20	556 *c* 15	587 *a* 7			247 *b* 6	377 *b* 2
14	536 *a* 25	556 *c* 20	587 *a* 14			248 *a* 2	377 *b* 8
15	536 *b* 2	556 *c* 28	587 *a* 26			248 *a* 6	378 *a* 6
16	536 *b* 11	557 *a* 7	587 *b* 8			248 *b* 5	379 *a* 2
17	536 *b* 18	557 *a* 16	587 *b* 21			249 *a* 1	379 *b* 1
18	536 *b* 22	557 *a* 22	587 *b* 29			249 *a* 4	379 *b* 6
19	536 *b* 27	557 *a* 29	587 *c* 9			249 *a* 7	380 *a* 3
20	536 *c* 4	557 *b* 4	587 *c* 17			249 *b* 2	380 *a* 7
21	536 *c* 11	557 *b* 12	588 *a* 1			249 *b* 8	381 *a* 2
22	536 *c* 13	557 *b* 15	588 *a* 8			250 *a* 2	381 *a* 4
23	536 *c* 16	557 *b* 19	588 *a* 15			250 *a* 5	381 *b* 1

II

THE TITLES OF THE VKN

The Chinese catalogues examined earlier on attribute various titles to the Vkn. Not all are of Indian origin. Hence the distinctions that they make between the "old" (*ku*), "other" (*pie*) and "new" (*hsin*) Vkn are merely concerned with the chronology of the Chinese versions and have nothing to do with any Indian reference.

The Chinese versions and catalogues are the only ones to attribute the title of Sūtra (*ching*) to the Vkn. The Indian authors like Candrakīrti (Madh. vṛtti, p. 333, *6*), Śāntideva (Śikṣāsamuccaya, p. 6, *10*; 145, *11*; 153, *20*; 264, *6*; 269, *11*; 273, *6*; 324, *10*), Kamalaśīla (Bhāvanākrama I, p. 194, *8*), as well as the Tibetan translator, invariably cite the Vkn by the title of *Āryavimalakīrtinirdeśa* (*Ḥphags pa Dri ma med par grags pas bstan pa*). It is possible that they hesitated to call Sūtra a text in which the action and dialogue revolve round the bodhisattva Vimalakīrti and where the Buddha Śākyamuni plays only a secondary role.

As with all Mahāyāna texts, the Vkn itself indicates the titles which should be used in mentioning it. These are quite numerous and this diversity can be explained by the muliplicity of "religious subjects" (*dharmaparyāya* or *dharmamukha*) successively dealt with in the text.

In Ch. XII, § 23, the Chinese versions each mention two titles, while the Tibetan translation gives three. Further titles are mentioned in the body of the work.

1. The main title is *Vimalakīrtinirdeśa* "The Teaching of V.", in Chinese *Wei-mo-chieh so-shuo*, or *Shuo wu kou ch'êng*, in Tibetan *Dri ma med par grags pas bstan pa* (cf. XII, § 23).

2. A secondary title, possibly a sub-title, is *Acintyavimokṣadharmaparyāya* "Treatise of the law concerning the inconceivable liberation". The wording of it varies considerably:

a. Acintyadharmaparyāya (Pu-k'o-ssŭ-i fa-mên), according to Chih Ch'ien (XII, § 23).

b. Acintyavimokṣadharmaparyāya (Pu-k'o-ssŭ-i chieh-t'o fa-mên), according to Kumārajīva (XII, § 23).

c. Acintyavimokṣanirdeśo dharmaparyāyaḥ (Rnam par thar pa bsam gyis mi khyab pa bstan paḥi chos kyi rnam grańs), according to the Tibetan (XII, § 6).

d. Acintyavimokṣaparivarta (Bsams gyis mi khyab paḥi rnam par thar paḥi leḥu), according to the Tibetan (XII, § 23).

*e. *Acintyavikurvaṇa[niyata]bhūtanayasūtra* (Pu-k'o-ssŭ-i tzŭ-tsai-shên-t'ung chüeh-ting shih-hsiang ching-tien) "Sūtra of the true method (or true principle) of inconceivable wonder", according to Kumārajīva (XII, § 1, note 1).

*f. *Acintyavikurvaṇanayapraveśanirdeśa* (Rnam par sprul ba bsam gyis mi khyab paḥi tshul la ḥjug pa rab tu bstan pa) "Teaching [constituting] the entry into the method (or principle) of inconceivable wonder", according to the Tibetan (XII, § 1, note 1).

*g. *Acintyavikurvaṇavimokṣadharmaparyāya* (Pu-k'o-ssŭ-i tzŭ-tsai-shên-pien chieh-t'o fa-mên) "Treatise of the law [concerning] the liberation of inconceivable wonder", according to Hsüan-tsang (XII, § 1, note 1; § 6, note 9; § 23, note 42).

The Vkn owes this secondary title or sub-title, *Acintyavimokṣa* (with the variations as shown above in *a*, *b*, *c*, *d*), to its Chapter V entitled *Acintyavimokṣanirdeśa* and which in fact, from § 10 to § 18, deals with the inconceivable liberations of the Bodhisattva.

This section is presented in Ch. V, § 18, as the summary of an enormous *dharmaparyāya*. One naturally thinks of the *Avataṃsaka*, which also has the sub-title of *Acintyasūtra* or *Acintyavimokṣasūtra* (cf. V, § 10, note 11).

However, this section does not deal properly speaking with the three or eight *vimokṣa* of Buddhist scholasticism [1], but more with the super-knowledges (*abhijñā*), psychic power (*ṛddhi*), etc., which are the wondrous effects of them [2]. This explains the important variations noted in *e*, *f* and *g*, and which are aimed at further clarifying the vague title of *Acintyavimokṣa*. According to the variation *g*, *Acintyavikurvaṇavimokṣa* adopted by Hsüan-tsang, this concerns the Vimokṣa of inconceivable wonder(s).

3. A third title, known and pointed out by the Chinese catalogues [3], is formulated in Ch. X, § 11: *Sarvabuddhadharmamukhasampraveśa*, in Tibetan *Saṅs rgyas kyi chos thams cad kyi sgor ḥjug pa*, in Chinese

[1] See the references in RHYS DAVIDS and STEDE, *Pali-English Dictionary*, s.v. *vimokkha*; F. EDGERTON, *Buddhist Hybrid Sanskrit Dictionary*, p. 497 *a*, s.v. *vimokṣa*; *Kośa*, VIII, p. 206-211.

[2] Cf. Majjhima, III, p. 97-99, where it is clearly stated that the *abhijñā* are the fruit of the *vimokṣa*.

[3] See above, p. XXVII, note 3.

(tr. Kumārajīva) *Ju i ch'ieh chu fo fa mên* "Introduction to the doctrine of all the Buddha attributes".

This refers to another treatise of the law (*dharmaparyāya*) by the terms of which the Bodhisattva feels neither joy nor pride in the pure *buddhakṣetra*, neither sadness nor repugnance in the impure *buddhakṣetra*, but reveres all the Buddhadharmas indiscriminately.

4. Another title, completely unknown to the Chinese translations and catalogues, is mentioned in the Tibetan version in Ch. XII, § 23: *Phrugs su sbyar ba snrel źi(ṅ) mṅon par bsgrub pa*.

Phrugs-su-sbyar-ba "forming a pair, paired", in Sanskrit *yamaka*; snrel źi "inverted", in Sanskrit *vyatyasta*; mṅon par bsgrub pa "production", in Sanskrit *abhinirhāra*. The whole gives *yamaka-vyatyastābhinirhāra* which literally means: "Production of paireds and inverteds".

These expressions are recorded in the Mahāvyutpatti:

No. 3069: *vyatyasta[lokadhātuḥ]* = snrel źi [ḥi ḥjig rten gyi khams]. This concerns the *vyatyastalokadhātu* "inverted universe" mentioned in the Mahāvastu, I, p. 135, *6*; the Gaṇḍavyūha, p. 126, *2*; the Daśabhūmika, p. 15, *14*.

No. 534: *vyatyasto nāma samādhiḥ* = snrel źi źes bya baḥi tiṅ ṅe ḥdzin. This concerns the "Concentration called inverted" mentioned in the Śatasāhasrikā, p. 828, *2*; 1412, *21* (where *vyabhyasto* and *vyastato* are misreadings for *vyatyasto*).

No. 1497: *vyatyastasamāpattiḥ* = snrel ziḥi sñoms par ḥjug pa. This concerns the "Inverted Recollection" mentioned in the Pañcaviṃśati, p. 142, *17*.

No. 798: *yamakavyatyastāhārakuśalāḥ* = zuṅ snrel źiḥi rgyud la mkhas pa rnams, an obscure epithet which constitutes, according to the Mahāvyutpatti, the 12th exclusive attribute (*āveṇikadharma*) of a Bodhisattva.

The expression claimed the attention of F. EDGERTON, *Buddhist Hybrid Sanskrit Dictionary*, p. 112*b* and 444*b*. Here are his explanations:

āhāra in Mvy 798 = Tib. rgyud, usually = tantra; perhaps a *mystic technique* in general, or possibly *bringing in* in a more specific sense.

yamaka, designation of a kind of yoga practice, = Tib. zuṅ gzug (Das) or zuṅ ḥjug (Jäschke), 'a technical term of practical mysticism, the forcing the mind into the principal artery, in order to prevent distraction of mind' (Jäschke). Mvy yamaka-vyatyastāhārakuśalāḥ = zuṅ daṅ snrel zhi ḥi rgyud la mkhas pa rnams, *clever in the technique* (rgyud, see s.v. *āhāra*; or, *the bringing in*) *of the pair and the inverted* (yoga practices). How the word *pair* applies to the above definition, given by Jäschke and Das, is not clear to me.

In fact, the expression at issue in no way refers to yoga practices, but to linguistic or rhetorical processes and figures of style.

The Chinese equivalent, proposed by Ogiwara Unrai in his edition of the Mahāvyutpatti, Tōkyō 1915, is 於對偶及反轉文句善巧 "Skilled in paired and inverted word-sentences".

Among the various meanings of the word *yamaka*, Sanskrit dictionaries (Monier-Williams, p. 846 *c*; Apte, p. 455 *b*) always give: "In rhet., the repetition in the same stanza of words or syllables similar in sound but different in meaning, paranomasia". It concerns a figure of style whose invention is attributed to the master Yama[4].

Vyatyasta, in Tib. snrel źi, can designate another figure of style, probably the chiasmus. In the Vkn, IV, § 1, Mañjuśrī praises Vimalakīrti as "skilled in proffering inverted words (tshig snrel źi = *vyatyastapada*) and full words (rdzogs paḥi tshig = *pūrṇapada*)".

As for *āhāra*, it is not a synonym of *tantra*, as F. Edgerton would have it: it simply means the act of obtaining, producing.

That it is indeed a matter of sounds and not yoga practices is evident again from the Chinese versions of the Ratnameghasūtra detailing the list of the eighteen *āveṇikadharma* of the Bodhisattvas:

a. In T 660, ch. 4, p. 301 *c* 4, executed in A.D. 693, by Dharmaruci, *yamakavyatyastāhārakuśalāḥ* is rendered by 言音善巧能隨世俗文同義異 "Skilled in syllables: able to adapt to the homonyms of conventional (*saṃvṛti*) speech".

b. In T 489, ch. 7, p. 722*b* 26, executed, about A.D. 1000-1010, by Fa-hu and others, the expression is rendered by 於諸典章不滅文句 "From all the canonical texts, they do not abstract a word-sentence".

From this collection of agreeing evidence, it results that the title of *Yamakavyatyastābhinirhāra* attributed to the Vkn means: "Production of paired and inverted sounds".

*

I think, however, that the Indian authors and their translators did not always interpret the expression *yamakavyatyastāhāra* in this way, but that they sometimes saw in it an allusion to the contradictory qualities and attitudes of the Bodhisattvas.

A Bodhisattva practises conjointly and in turn skill in means (*upāyakauśalya*) and wisdom (*prajñā*). Through the former, he involves himself closely with the world and redoubles stratagems in order to

[4] Regarding *yamaka*, see the explanations and bibliography collated by L. Renou in his translation of the *Kāvyamimāṃsā de Rājaśekhara*, Paris, 1946, p. 24, note 27.

convert beings; through the latter, he transcends the world and aims for supreme and perfect enlightenment. This apparently contradictory attitude which consists of being involved with the world while turning the back to it is clearly defined in the Bodhisattvabhūmi (p. 261 ff) and amply detailed by the Vkn (II, § 3-6; III, § 3, 16-18; IV, § 20; VII, § 1; X, § 19).

Some Buddhist texts see a connection between this paired and inverted behaviour of the Bodhisattva and the *āveṇikabodhisattvadharma* formulated by the expression *yamakavyatyastāhārakuśalāḥ*. This is done in particular by the Avataṃsaka and its various translations:

a. Tib. Trip., vol. 26, p. 85, folio 208*b* 7-8:

"Besides, O Jinaputra, the Bodhisattva is skilled in pairing and inversion (*yamakavyatyastakuśala*) for, in that he plays with the knowledges (*jñānavikrīḍita*) and has obtained the excellence of the perfection of knowledge (*jñānapāramitāvaraprāpta*), he can, even while basing himself on Nirvāṇa (*nirvāṇāśrita*), manifest the ways of the round of rebirth (*saṃsāramukhasaṃdarśana*); although he possesses a domain absolutely devoid of a living being (*niḥsattva*), he does not cease ripening (*paripac-*) all beings" [5].

b. Chinese translation by Buddhabhadra, executed between 418 and 420: cf. T 278, ch. 40, p. 651 *a* 10-13:

"The Bodhisattva Mahāsattva well knows the concentration of conjunction (*chü-pien san-mei* 俱變三昧 = *yamakasamādhi*?) and the concentration of inversion (*fan-fu san-mei* 翻覆三昧 = *vyatyastasamādhi*: cf. Mahāvyut., No. 534). [On one hand], he plays (*vikrīḍati*) with the knowledges (*jñāna*) and the super-knowledges (*abhijñā*); [on the other], he has reached the other shore (*pāra*) of knowledge. Even while always dwelling in Nirvāṇa, he manifests (*saṃdarśayati*) the ways of the round of rebirth (*saṃsāramukha*). He knows a domain devoid of living beings (*niḥsattvagocara*), but he converts and ripens (*paripācayati*) all beings".

c. Chinese translations by Śikṣānanda, executed between 695 and 699: cf. T 279, ch. 56, p. 296 *c* 22-297 *a* 3:

"The Bodhisattva well knows the *ch'üan shih shuang hsing tao* 權實雙行道 "Path of the two-fold practice of Expediency and Truth". [On one hand], he possesses mastery over the knowledges (*jñānavaśitā*); [on the other], he has reached the summit of knowledge (*jñānaniṣṭhāgata*). Thus, even while remaining in Nirvāṇa, he manifests Saṃsāra. He knows that there are no

[5] *Kye rgyal baḥi sras gźan yaṅ byaṅ chub sems dpaḥ zuṅ daṅ snrel (b)źi la mkhas śiṅ ye śes kyis rnam par rtse ba daṅ | ye śes kyi pha rol tu phyin paḥi mchog thob pas | ḥdi ltar mya ṅan las ḥdas pa la gnas kyaṅ | ḥkhor baḥi sgo yoṅs su ston pa | sems can med paḥi mthaḥi spyod yul daṅ ldan yaṅ sems can thams cad yoṅs su smin par bya ba ma btaṅ ba* ...

beings, but he strives to convert them. He is definitively stilled (*śānta*), but he seems to experience the passions (*kleśa*). He inhabits the Body of the Law (*dharmakāya*), all mystery and knowledge, but he manifests himself everywhere, in the innumerable bodies of living beings. He is always immersed in deep trances (*dhyāna*), but he delights in the objects of desire (*kāmaguṇa*). He always keeps himself apart from the triple world (*traidhātuka*), but he does not abandon beings. He always delights in the pleasure of the Law (*dharmarati*), but he openly surrounds himself with women, songs and games. His body is adorned with the marks (*lakṣaṇa*) and sub-marks (*anuvyañjana*) of the [Mahāpuruṣa], but he takes on ugly and wretched forms. He ceaselessly accumulates good actions (*kuśalakarman*), and he is blameless (*niravadya*), but he goes to be reborn among the hell-bound (*naraka*), animals (*tiryagyoni*) and Pretas. Although he has reached the other shore of the knowledge of the Buddhas (*buddhajñānapāramitā*), he does not abandon the body of the knowledges (*jñānakāya*) of the Bodhisattva. The Bodhisattva Mahāsattva is gifted with such an unlimited (*aparyanta*) knowledge that neither the Śrāvakas nor the Pratyekabuddhas can understand it, and even less so, foolish beings (*bālasattva*). Such is the fifth exclusive attribute (*āveṇikadharma*) of the Bodhisattva, an attribute that does not rely on the teaching of others, and which consists in the two-fold practice of Expediency and Truth".

The relation between these three translations is significant. The Tibetan version, literal down to the smallest detail, reaffirms the presence in the Indian original of the expression *yamakavyatyasta*. Buddhabhadra somewhow or other rendered it in Chinese as "*samādhi* of conjunction" and "*samādhi* of inversion". In contrast, Śikṣānanda interprets the meaning and sees in this expression an allusion to the contradictory actions of the Bodhisattva, to that two-fold and inverted conduct through which the Bodhisattva, while being a holy one, behaves as an offender for the benefit of beings. To render this complex notion, Śiksānanda resorts to a specifically Chinese formula which opposes 權 to 實.

Śikṣānanda translated the Avataṃsaka at the end of the seventh century, between 695 and 699. At that time, the binomial 權實 had been current for nearly two centuries in the Chinese Buddhist schools of T'ien-t'ai and Hua-yen who claimed the Saddharmapuṇḍarīka and the Avatamsaka respectively as their authority. It had already been used by the brush of Chih-i (538-597), the great master of the T'ien-t'ai school[6]. Ever since, scholars of the two schools never stopped debating the Two Teachings (*êrh chiao* 二敎), the Two Knowledges

[6] Cf. Mo ho chih kuan, T 1911, ch. 3, p. 33-35.

(*êrh chih* 二智), and the Ten non-dual Gates (*shih pu êrh mên* 十不二門) of 權實[7].

In order to translate and interpret the Sanskrit originals, the missionaries whether Indian, or Khotanese like Śikṣānanda, did not hesitate to draw on Chinese philosophical vocabulary. But the liberties they took with it were sometimes to the detriment of the correct meaning. In the matter which occupies us here, it does seem that the title of *Yamakavyatyastābhinirhāra* applied to the Vkn had as its original and authentic meaning: "Production of paired and inverted sounds".

III

THE PHILOSOPHY OF THE VKN

It is not our intention here to go into all the philosophical ideas of the Vkn: this would only duplicate what follows in the annotated translation. However, it is indispensable to determine the position of the Vkn with regard to the Absolute and to show how it represents a pure Madhyamaka.

I. — THE ABSOLUTE IN EARLY BUDDHISM

All early Buddhism is contained in the four noble truths expounded by Śākyamuni in the sermon of Vārāṇasī:

1. All dharmas are impermanent (*anitya*), painful (*duḥkha*) and impersonal (*anātman*): they are not a Self and do not belong to a Self. This does not prevent them from having a self-nature (*svabhāva*) and specific marks (*lakṣaṇa*).

2. These dharmas are conditioned (*saṃskṛta*), causes and caused at the same time. Their arising (*utpāda*) and extinction (*nirodha*), during the course of the painful round of rebirth, are not left to chance, but ruled by the strict laws of the twelve-limbed dependent co-production (*pratītyasamutpāda*).

This dependent co-production constitutes the Suchness (*tathatā*) of dharmas. This is affirmed in a canonical passage often repeated, with some variations, in Pāli and Sanskrit texts:

[7] Regarding these subjects, see MOCHIZUKI SHINKŌ, *Bukkyō daijiten*, p. 1362-64; 2372-73.

Whether or not the Tathāgatas appear in the world, that Nature of things, that causal Status, that causal Certainty, the Relation of this with regard to that prevails [1].

3. "There is an unborn (*ajāta*), unbecome (*abhūta*), unmade (*akata*), unformed (*asaṃkhata*)" [2]: this is Nirvāṇa. It is unconditioned (*asaṃskṛta*), does not depend on causes and evades the mechanism of the dependent co-production.

4. The Buddha showed the Way (*mārga*), the Middle Path (*madhyamā pratipad*) which leads to Nirvāṇa.

It is easy to place Tathatā (here, dependent co-production) in the four noble truths. Suffering (the dharmas of Saṃsāra) should be known; its origin (the process of dependent co-production) should be extinguished; its extinction (Nirvāṇa) should be achieved; the Path of Nirvāṇa should be practised [3].

II. — THE ABSOLUTE IN THE MAHĀYĀNA

As has just been seen, early Buddhism, while categorically denying the existence of a Self or an Individual as a substantial entity, believes in the objective reality of the phenomena of existence or dharmas. The Abhidharma treatises, particularly those of the Sarvāstivādins, draw up a list of 75 dharmas which they see as having a real nature; and they add that the 72 conditioned dharmas are endowed with marks (*lakṣaṇa*) by virtue of which they arise, endure and disappear according to the immutable mechanism of dependent co-production.

Certain Hīnayānist sects had already risen up against this realism, which they considered to be exaggerated. The Sautrāntikas, for the sake of brevity and reason, carried out severe cuts in the lists of the dharmas, reduced their appearance to an infinitesimal duration and asserted that they perished without cause. Nevertheless, they still

[1] *Uppādā vā tathāgatānaṃ anuppādā vā tathāgatānaṃ ṭhitā va sā dhātu dhammaṭṭhitatā dhammaniyamata idappaccayatā*: Saṃyutta, II, p. 25,*18*; Aṅguttara, I, p. 286,*6*; Kathāvatthu, p. 321,*6*; Saṃyukta, T 99, ch. 12, p. 84 *b* 19; Śālistamba, p. 4,*4*; Kośavyākhyā, p. 293,*26*; Aṣṭasah., p. 562,*17*; Sad. puṇḍarīka, p. 53,*9*, Laṅkāvatāra, p. 143,*11*; Madh. vṛtti, p. 40,*1*; Śikṣāsamuccaya, p. 14,*18*; Pañjikā, p. 588,*5*.

[2] Udāna, p. 80,*23*.

[3] *Idaṃ dukkhaṃ ariyasaccaṃ pariññeyyaṃ, idam dukkhasamudayaṃ ariyasaccaṃ pahātabbaṃ, idaṃ dukkhanirodhaṃ ariyasaccaṃ sacchikātabbaṃ, idaṃ dukkhanirodhagāminī paṭipadā ariyasaccaṃ bhāvetabbaṃ*: Vinaya, I, p. 11; Saṃyutta, V, p. 422; Kośa, VI, p. 248; Madh. vṛtti, p. 516,*17-18*; Āloka, p. 381,*24* - 382,*5*; Mahāvyutpatti, No. 1316-19.

accepted as real the existence of some dharmas which their judgement considered it worthwhile retaining.

A new step was made by the thinkers and scholars of the Mahāyāna who delightedly undermined the grandiose, but fragile, edifice of the Abhidharmas. Not satisfied in denying, as their predecessors had been, the substantiality of the soul, they further proclaimed the inexistence of things of experience, which were caused or relative. They claimed both the inexistence of the individual (*pudgalanairātmya*) and the inexistence of things (*dharmanairātmya*); they sought to implant in their followers the "conviction of the non-arising of dharmas" (*anutpattikadharmakṣānti*).

The emptiness of things is the basic doctrine of the greatly developed Sūtras (*mahāvaipulyasūtra*) which proliferated from the beginning of our era: Prajñāpāramitā, Saddharmapuṇḍarīka, Avataṃsaka, Ratnakūṭa, Mahāparinirvāṇasūtra, Mahāsaṃnipāta and quantities of others of lesser size. These texts or collections of texts each have their own particular viewpoint, but all are agreed on the basic emptiness of things: it is a real obsession with them.

The theories expounded in the Vaipulyasūtras were systematized, probably in the third century, by Nāgārjuna, author of the famous Madhyamakakārikā which demonstrate the absurdity of all intellectual notions, the logical impossibility of any sensorial or mental experience. His school of the Madhyamaka or "Middle" won renown for centuries through reputed scholars: Āryadeva, Piṅgalākṣa (Ch'ing-mu), Buddhapālita, Bhāvaviveka, Siṃharaśmi and Jñānaprabha, Candrakīrti, Śāntideva, Śāntarakṣita and Kamalaśīla, Prajñākaramati, Advayavajra.

Because of its relatively early date, because of its sources of inspiration as much as the theories it develops, the Vkn ranks among the oldest Mahāyānasūtras. Like the Prajñāpāramitā, the Avataṃsaka, the Ratnakūṭa and the Mahāsaṃnipāta, it represents that Madhyamaka in the raw state which served as the foundation for Nāgārjuna's school. It is quite separate from the Sūtras with idealistic tendencies, Saṃdhinirmocana, Laṅkāvatāra, Śrīmālādevīsiṃhanāda, etc., which were only translated into Chinese in the mid-fifth century, and which were considered as authoritative by the epistemological school of the Vijñānavādins.

I shall outline here the most important theses of the Madhyamaka [4]

[4] There can be found in J. MAY, *Prasannapadā*, Paris, 1959, p. 22-45, a complete bibliography on the Madhyamaka.

and, by means of appropriate quotations, attempt to show how the Vkn has professed them all.

PROPOSITION A: All dharmas are without self-nature (*niḥsvabhāva*), empty of self-nature (*svabhāvaśūnya*).

The Bodhisattva does not apprehend (*nopalabhate*) the ātman, whatever the words used to designate it: *sattva, jīva, poṣa, puruṣa, pudgala, manuja, mānava, kāraka, vedaka, jānaka, paśyaka.* He does not apprehend things, *skandha, dhātu, āyatana,* nor their *pratītyasamutpāda.* He does not apprehend the noble truths, *duḥkha, samudaya, nirodha, mārga.* He does not apprehend the triple world, *kāma, rūpa, ārūpyadhātu.* He does not apprehend the mystical planes, *apramāṇa, dhyāna* and *ārūpyasamāpatti.* He does not apprehend the thirty-seven auxiliaries of enlightenment, *smṛtyupasthāna, samyakprahāṇa, ṛddhipāda, indriya, bala, bodhyaṅga, mārga.* He does not apprehend the Buddha attributes, *daśabala, caturvaiśāradya, aṣṭādaśāveṇika.* He does not apprehend the categories of the holy ones, *srotāapanna, sakṛdāgāmin, anāgāmin, arhat, pratyekabuddha, bodhisattva, buddha.* If he does not apprehend them, it is because of their absolute purity (*atyantaviśuddhitā*). And what is this purity? Non-arising (*anutpāda*), non-manifestation (*aprādurbhāva*), inexistence (*anupalambha*), inactivity (*anabhisaṃskāra*)[5].

*

The Vkn returns on every page to the inexistence of dharmas: The body is like a ball of foam, etc. (II, § 9-11). The Law is without essence (III, § 6). The six sense objects have no reality (III, § 12). The self-nature of dharmas is like an illusion, a transformation (III, § 19). The five *skandha* are absolutely empty of self-nature (III, § 26). The mind exists neither on the inside nor on the outside nor between the two (III, § 34). All dharmas are false visions, born of the imagination (III, § 35). The *bodhimaṇḍa* is the seat of all dharmas for it is perfectly enlightened regarding their emptiness (III, § 59). The *skandha* are like killers, the *dhātu* like poisonous snakes, the *āyatana* like an empty village (III, § 64). The notion of dharma is a perversion (IV, § 12). He who seeks the Law does not seek the *skandha, dhātu* and *āyatana* (V, § 2). All dharmas rest on a baseless root (VI, § 6). All dharmas are unreal and of a nature created by illusion (VI, § 14). The five *upādānaskandha* are naturally and originally empty (VIII, § 17). All dharmas are void, vain, worthless, dependent, abodeless (X, § 18).

[5] Pañcaviṃśati, p. 146.

PROPOSITION B: All dharmas are unarisen (*anutpanna*) and unextinguished (*aniruddha*).

Empty of self-nature, dharmas are without production and disappearance, for empty things arising from empty things in reality do not arise. Not arising, they are not extinguished. In consequence, the dependent co-production of phenomena is a non-production.

That which is born of causes is not born; its arising is not real; that which depends on causes is proclaimed empty; he who knows emptiness does not swerve[6].

That which arises because of this or that does not arise of itself; that which has not arisen of itself, how can it be said that it has arisen[7]?

Of dharmas purely and simply empty are only empty dharmas born[8].

The dependent co-production you consider to be emptiness; there is no existence dependent on itself; this is your incomparable roar[9].

Dependent co-production is what we call emptiness; it is the designation "by reason of"; it is the Middle Path[10].

*

[6] *Yaḥ pratyayair jāyati sa hy ajāto*
na tasya utpādu sabhāvato 'sti,
yaḥ pratyayādhīnu sa śūnya ukto
yaḥ śūnyatāṃ jānati so 'pramattaḥ.

Cf. Anavataptahrada quoted in Madh. vṛtti, p. 239,*10*; 491,*11*; 500,*7*; 504,*1*; Madh. avatāra, p. 229,*2*; Catuḥśataka Comm., ed. V. BHATTACHARYA, p. 294,*13*; Pañjikā, p. 355,*10*; Karatalaratna, p. 40,*1*.

[7] *Tat tat prāpya yad utpannaṃ*
notpannaṃ tat svabhāvataḥ,
svabhāve na yad utpannam
utpannaṃ nāma tat katham?

Cf. Madh. vṛtti, p. 9,*5*; Madh. avatāra, p. 228.

[8] *Śūnebhya eva śūnyā dharmāḥ prabhavanti dharmebhyaḥ*: Pratītyasamutpādahṛdaya, stanza 3 (cf. L. DE LA VALLÉE POUSSIN, *Théorie des douze causes*, Gand, 1913, p. 123); Pañjikā, p. 355,*14*; 532,*5*; Pañcakrama, p. 40,*35*.

[9] *Yaḥ pratītyasamutpādaḥ*
śūnyatā saiva te matā,
bhāvaḥ svatantro nāstīti
siṃhanādas tavātulaḥ.

Cf. Lokātītastava, stanza 20; Pañjikā, p. 417,*7*; 528,*11*; Āloka, 173,*12*; 297,*19*; 414,*12*; 557,*19*; 698,*5*; 916,*17*.

[10] *Yaḥ pratītyasamutpādaḥ*
śūnyatāṃ tāṃ pracakṣmahe,
sā prajñaptir upādāya
pratipat saiva madhyamā.

Cf. Madh. vṛtti, p. 503,*10*; Madh. avatāra, p. 228,*17*.

The Vkn in turn insists on the non-arising, non-production of dharmas, on the *pratītyasamutpāda* "in its deep meaning", which does not function.

The Bodhisattva penetrates the *pratītyasamutpāda* in its deep meaning...; he rejects the diamond weapon of the *pratītyasamutpāda* (I, §3). Vimalakīrti is convinced of the non-arising of dharmas (II, §1). The Law is without grasping and rejecting for it is free from arising and extinction (III, § 6). It is forbidden to speak of dharmas endowed with activity, endowed with production and endowed with destruction; in fact absolutely nothing has been produced, is produced, will be produced; absolutely nothing has been destroyed, is destroyed and will be destroyed (III, §26). All dharmas are without arising, disappearance and duration, like an illusion, a transformation, a cloud and a flash of lightning; all dharmas are false visions like a dream, a mirage and a town of the Gandharvas; all dharmas are born of imagination like the moon in the water and the reflection in a mirror (III, § 35). The past birth is already exhausted, the future birth has not yet come, the present birth is without foundation (III, § 50). The *bodhimaṇḍa* is the seat of the *pratītyasamutpāda* because it goes from the exhaustion of *avidyā* to the exhaustion of *jarāmaraṇa* (III, § 58). The Bodhisattva's domain is that where it is reflected that dharmas have non-arising and non-extinction as their mark (IV, § 20, No. 31). He who seeks the Law does not seek birth and does not seek extinction (V, § 3). The Bodhisattva rightly makes the effort concerning non-arising and non-extinction (VI, § 5). Dharmas, all just as they are, are neither made nor changed (VI, § 15). Dharmas are linked to *śūnyatā*, *ānimitta*, *apraṇihita*, *anabhisaṃskāra* and *anutpāda* (XII, § 11). It must be considered that the outcome of an invincible belief in being is the twelve-fold *pratītyasamutpāda*, according to which "through the extinction of ignorance, are extinguished old-age, death, lamentation, suffering, grief and despair" (XII, §12).

PROPOSITION C: All dharmas are originally calm (*ādiśānta*) and naturally Nirvāṇa-ised (*prakṛtiparinirvṛta*).

Being without arising, dharmas are, from the start and by nature, stilled and extinguished. He who says emptiness says Nirvāṇa. According to early Buddhism, that which is Saṃsāra is that which is subject to the *pratītyasamutpāda*, and that which is Nirvāṇa is that which eludes this process. But for the Madhyamaka, dharmas, which do not arise at all, are not produced by reason of causes and do not enter the round of rebirth (*na saṃsaranti*): thus they are Nirvāṇa-ised. For them, Saṃsāra is intermixed with Nirvāṇa. Emptiness, Saṃsāra and Nirvāṇa are intermixed.

Emptiness having as its mark the stopping of all development is called Nirvāṇa [11].

Briefly the Tathāgatas say that the Law is harmlessness (i.e. morality) and that Emptiness is Nirvāṇa. In Buddhism, these two things (morality and emptiness) are the only ones (to ensure heaven and deliverance) [12].

Between Saṃsāra and Nirvāṇa, there is no difference; between Nirvāṇa and Saṃsāra, there is no difference [13].

In conclusion, for the Small Vehicle, the Tathatā "suchness of things" was the *pratītyasamutpāda*; for the Madhyamaka, it is Śūnyatā.

*

The same propositions are formulated by the Vkn:

That which is without self-nature and without other-nature does not burn, and that which does not burn cannot be stilled; that which admits of no stilling is absolutely stilled: such is the meaning of the word *śānta* (III, § 26). There is not one single being who is not in Parinirvāṇa already. The Tathāgata has said that true Tathatā is Parinirvāṇa. Seeing that all beings are originally calmed and in Parinirvāṇa, the Buddha has said of true Tathatā that this is Parinirvāṇa (III, § 51). Saṃsāra and Nirvāṇa are both empty (*śūnya*). And why? As simple designations (*nāmadheya*) they are both empty and unreal (IV, § 12). He who seeks the Law does not seek birth and extinction (that is, Saṃsāra and Nirvāṇa). And why? The Law is calm and stilled (V, § 3). It is said, Saṃsāra and Nirvāṇa are two. But the Bodhisattvas who see the self-nature of Nirvāṇa as originally empty are not reborn and do not enter Nirvāṇa: this is penetrating non-duality (VIII, § 13). The absence of delight in Nirvāṇa and the absence of repugnance for Saṃsāra constitute non-duality (VIII, § 29).

[11] *Śūnyataiva sarvaprapañcanivṛttilakṣaṇatvān nirvāṇam ity ucyate*: Madh. vṛtti, p. 351,*11*.

[12] *Dharmaṃ samāsato 'hiṃsāṃ varṇayanti tathāgatāḥ,*
śūnyatām eva nirvāṇaṃ kevalaṃ tad ihobhayam.

Cf. Madh. vṛtti, p. 351,*13*.

[13] *Na saṃsārasya nirvāṇāt kiṃcid asti viśeṣaṇam,*
na nirvāṇasya saṃsārāt kiṃcid asti viśeṣaṇam.

Cf. Madh. vṛtti, p. 535,*2*.

PROPOSITION D: Dharmas are without marks (*alakṣaṇa*) and, in consequence, inexpressible (*anirvacanīya, anabhilāpya*) and unthinkable. Being inexistent, dharmas are devoid of marks. Nothing can be said of them or, if anyone does speak of them, it is only out of convention (*saṃvṛti*). To know them, is not to think of them.

All dharmas are neither conjoined nor disjoined; they are formless, invisible, unresisting, of a single mark, that is, without a mark [14].

Is there (among dharmas) a true self-nature? — It cannot be said that there is, nor that there is not in itself. However, to avoid frightening our listeners, we say, through convention and uncalled-for affirmation, that there is. For the Blessed One has said: "Of an unutterable dharma, what can be heard, what can be taught? And yet this unutterable dharma is heard and taught, but by virtue of an uncalled-for affirmation" And in the Madhyamakakārikā (XXII, 11), it will also be said: "It cannot be said that it is empty, or that it is non-empty, or that it is empty and non-empty at the same time, or that it is neither empty nor non-empty; but this is what is said in order to speak of it" [15].

It is in the detachment from all dharmas and their unreality that the Bodhisattva should train himself; it is by basing himself on the total absence of ideas that he should know all dharmas [16].

Thus yogins, dwelling in the vision of emptiness no longer perceive the *skandha, dhātu, āyatana* as being things. Not perceiving them as things, they avoid all idle chatter concerning them. Avoiding all idle chatter concerning them, they do not think of them... It is through the extinction of idle chatter that ideas are abolished... Thus emptiness, characterized by the extinction of all idle chatter, is called Nirvāṇa [17].

[14] *Sarva ete dharmā na saṃyuktā na visaṃyuktā arūpiṇo 'nidarśanā apratighā ekalakṣaṇā yadutālakṣaṇāḥ*: Pañcaviṃśati, p. 164,*8*; 225,*23*; 244,*7*; 258,*16*; 261,*19*; 262,*24*.

[15] Madh. vṛtti, p. 264,*2* sq.: *Kiṃ khalu taditthaṃ svarūpam asti? — Na tad asti na cāpi nāsti svarūpataḥ. yady apy evaṃ tathāpi śrotṝṇām uttrāsaparivarjanārthaṃ saṃvṛtyā samāropya tad astīti brūmaḥ. yathoktaṃ bhagavatā:*

anakṣarasya dharmasya śrutiḥ kā deśanā ca kā,
śrūyate deśyate cāpi samāropād anakṣaraḥ iti.

ihāpi ca vakṣyati:

sunyam iti na vaktavyam aśunyam iti vā bhavet,
ubhayaṃ nobhayaṃ ceti prajñaptyarthaṃ tu kathyate.

[16] *Sarvadharmāṇāṃ hi bodhisattvenāsaktatāyām asadbhūtatāyaṃ sikṣitavyam. akalpanatām akalpanatāṃ copādāya sarvadharmāś ca bodhisattvenāvaboddhavyāḥ:* Pañcaviṃśati, p. 164,*9*.

[17] Madh. vṛtti, p. 351,*4* sq.: *Evaṃ yogino 'pi śūnyatādarśanāvasthā niravaśeṣaskandhadhātvāyatanāni svarūpato nopalabhante. na cānupalabhamānā vastusvarūpaṃ tadviṣayaṃ prapañcam avatārayanti. na cānavatārya tadviṣayaṃ prapañcaṃ vikalpam avatārayanti... prapañcavigamāc ca vikalpanivṛttiḥ... tasmāc chūnyataiva sarvaprapañcanivṛttilakṣaṇatvān nirvāṇam ity ucyate.*

The Vkn expresses identical views:

The Law is signless; thus those who pursue the signs of dharmas do not seek the Law, but seek signs... The Law cannot be seen, or heard, or thought, or known (V, § 4). Not withdrawing from the recollection of extinction (of notions and feelings), this is how to meditate; acting so that the mind does not stop inwardly and does not spread outwardly, this is how to meditate (III, § 3). The Law is calm and appeasing for it destroys the marks of things... It has no syllables for it suppresses discourse. It is inexpressible for it avoids all thought "waves" (III, § 6). The Law escapes the sphere of all imaginations for it ends absolutely all idle chatter (III, § 6). The wise are not attached to words and do not fear them. And why? Because all words are without self-nature or mark. Words being without self-nature or mark, everything that is not a word is deliverance (III, § 19). Imagining, this is passion; the absence of imagining and mental construction, this is self-nature (III, § 35). Bodhi is the appeasing of all the signs; it is without uncalled-for affirmation concerning objects; it is the non-functioning of all attention ...; it is the abandoning of all imaginings (III, § 52). The (true) grasping of an object is a non-grasping avoiding the two false views of an internal subject and an external object (IV, § 14). The wisdom and eloquence of the Devī are due to the fact that she has not obtained anything, achieved anything (VI, § 10). The destruction of all ideas is the entry into non-duality (VIII, § 3). To that which does not exist there cannot be applied either uncalled-for affirmation or unjustified negation (VIII, § 6).

Proposition E: All dharmas are the same (*sama*) and without duality (*advaya*).

Empty and inexistent, all dharmas are the same. It is in this sense that there is non-duality (*advaya*). However, this non-duality consisting of a common inexistence does not imply any kind of monism whatsoever.

Being, from the absolute point of view, equally without production and equally without birth, all dharmas are the same from the absolute point of view [18].

*

[18] *Paramārthataḥ sarvadharmānutpādasamatayā paramārthataḥ sarvadharmātyantājātisamatayā paramārthataḥ samāḥ sarvadharmāḥ*: Satyadvayāvatārasūtra quoted in Madh. vṛtti, p. 374,*15*. — Going into details, the Sūtra gives as being absolutely the same the five acts of immediate fruition (*ānantarya*), the sixty-two kinds of false views

For its part the Vkn returns ceaselessly to the sameness and non-duality of all things:

The Buddha, equally beneficent towards all beings, penetrates the sameness of all dharmas (I, § 10, st. 8). In order to beg correctly, one should penetrate the sameness of all dharmas (III, § 11). One must, through the sameness of the depravities, penetrate the sameness of the Absolute Good (III, § 13). Subhūti is promised recompense if he can, through the sameness of material objects, penetrate the sameness of all dharmas, through the sameness of all dharmas penetrate the sameness of all Buddha attributes, through the sameness of the five acts of immediate fruition penetrate the sameness of deliverance (III, § 16). The mind exists neither on the inside, nor on the outside, nor between the two; so it is with a fault as it is with the mind, and with all dharmas as with a fault: they are not separated from Tathatā (III, § 34). Bodhi is undifferentiated because it penetrates the sameness of all dharmas (III, § 52). The *bodhimaṇḍa* is the seat of goodwill because of its sameness of mind regarding all beings (III, § 57). There is an integral sameness, going from the sameness of Self to the sameness of Nirvāṇa (IV, § 12). There is sameness of the sexes, and dharmas are neither male or female (VI, § 15).

The whole of Chapter VIII of the Vkn is devoted to non-duality. Thirty-two Bodhisattvas intervene in it in turn to bridge the gap separating the purely apparent antinomies, and proclaim *advaya.*

PROPOSITION F: Emptiness is not an entity.

The Prajñāpāramitā and Madhyamaka reject all forms of monism, whether overt or disguised. They assert that dharmas are inexistent, but refuse to hypostasize inexistence. The self-nature (*svabhāva*) of dharmas "which do not arise" (*anutpādātmaka*) is not something (*akiṃcid*), mere non-existence (*abhāvamātra*): it is not.

It is not through emptiness that form is empty; apart from form there is no emptiness; form is emptiness, emptiness is form. In fact, form is nothing but a word [19].

(*dṛṣṭigata*), the qualities of Pṛthagjana, Śaikṣa, Aśaikṣa and Samyaksaṃbuddha, Nirvāṇa and Saṃsāra, defilement (*saṃkleśa*) and purification (*vyavadāna*): in brief, all dharmas.

The Madh. vṛtti, p. 375,7, ends the quotation by remarking: *Tad evam anānārthatā tattvasya lakṣaṇaṃ veditavyaṃ śūnyatayaikarasatvāt*: "It should be known that this indifferentiation is a mark of reality because of the sole flavour of Emptiness".

[19] *Na śūnyatayā rūpaṃ śūnyaṃ, nānyatra rūpāc chūnyatā, rūpam eva śūnyatā śūnyataiva rūpam... tathā hi nāmamātram idaṃ yad idaṃ rūpam*: cf. Pañcaviṃśati, p. 38,*2-8*; Śatasāhasrikā, p. 118,*18*; 812,*3-5*; 930,*11-16*; T 220, ch. 402, p. 11 *c* 1;

The Prajñāpāramitā, which repeats this topic tirelessly, adds that this reasoning is not only valid regarding form, but for the other *skandha* and for all dharmas without distinction.

The Madhyamaka in turn sees Śūnyatā as not being something:

Perpetual non-production, because it does not depend on others and is not artificial, is called the self-nature (of dharmas), fire, etc. This is what is meant: This kind of self-nature perceived by the power of that visual trouble which is ignorance but which, among the holy ones cured of that visual trouble, is known in that it is not seen, this nature, say I, is given as the self-form, the self-nature of dharmas. And its mark should be understood as the masters have defined it: "Non-artificial self-nature, independent of others". This self-nature of essences consisting in their non-production not being something, being simply non-existence, is only non-self-nature: thus the self-nature of things is not. Thus it is that the Blessed One said: "He who knows natures as non-natures, he is not attached to any nature. He who is not attached to any nature, he is in touch with concentration without a sign" [20].

The Madhyamaka compares Emptiness to a raft (*kaula*) which is abandoned after crossing, to a drug (*bhaiṣajya*) which is thrown out after the cure, to a serpent (*alagarda*) bearing treasure but which must be well handled, to a magical formula (*vidyā*) to be pronounced exactly [21]. It then concludes:

T 221, ch. 1, p. 4 *c* 18; T 222, ch. 1, p. 152 *a* 16; T 223, ch. 1, p. 221 *b* 25-221 *c* 10; T 1509, ch. 35, p. 318 *a* 8-22. — The Logicians and Vijñānavādins see in this text the refutation of the ten *vikalpa-vikṣepa*: cf. Diṅnāga, Prajñāpāramitāpiṇḍārtha (ed. G. Tucci, JRAS, 1947), stanzas 19-58; Mahāyānasūtrālaṃkāra, p. 76; Saṃgraha, p. 115-118; Siddhi, p. 521.

[20] Madh. vṛtti, p. 265,*1-8*: *Sarvadānutpāda eva hy agnyādīnāṃ paranirapekṣatvād akṛtrimatvāt svabhāva ity ucyate. etad uktaṃ bhavati. avidyātimiraprabhāvopalabdhaṃ bhāvajātaṃ yenātmanā vigatāvidyātimirāṇām āryāṇām adarśanayogena viṣayatvam upayāti tad eva svarūpam eṣāṃ svabhāva iti vyavasthāpyate. tasya cedaṃ lakṣaṇam:*

akṛtrimaḥ svabhāvo hi nirapekṣaḥ paratra ca

iti vyavasthāpayāmbabhūvur ācārya iti vijñeyam. sa caiṣa bhāvānām anutpādātmakaḥ svabhāvo 'kiṃcittvenābhāvamātratvād asvabhāva eveti kṛtvā nāsti bhāvasvabhāva iti vijñeyam. yathoktaṃ Bhagavatā:

bhāvān abhāvān iti yaḥ prajānati
sa sarvabhāveṣu na jātu sajjate,
yaḥ sarvabhāveṣu na jātu sajjate
sa ānimittaṃ spṛśate samādhiṃ.

[21] See the references in L. de La Vallée Poussin, *Madhyamaka*, MCB, II, 1932-33, p. 31-32.

The Victorious Ones have proclaimed Emptiness to be the outlet of all the false views, but they have pronounced as incurable those who believe in Emptiness[22].

By adopting this agnostic position, the Madhyamaka knowingly and voluntarily avoids Sarvāstivādin realism and Yogācāra idealism.

Here, some invent three unconditioned things: space, extinction not due to knowledge and Nirvāṇa[23]; others imagine as unconditioned Emptiness which is defined as the suchness of things[24], but it is clear and evident that none of this exists, since the conditioned things are lacking[25].

All the same, Madhyamaka agnosticism should not be confused with common nihilism[26].

*

The Vkn also refuses to hypostasize emptiness and allows no other basis for experience than ignorance.

[22] *Śūnyatā sarvadṛṣṭīnāṃ proktā niḥsaraṇaṃ jinaiḥ,*
yeṣāṃ tu śūnyatādṛṣṭis tān asādhyān babhāṣire.

Cf. Madh. vṛtti, p. 247,*1-2*; Madh. avatāra, p. 119,*6-9*; [illegible] Ratnakūṭa quoted in Madh. vṛtti, p. 248,*4*-249,*2*; Laṅkāvatāra, p. 146,*11-13*; Ratnagotra, p. 28,*11-12*; Kāśyapaparivarta, p. 95.

[23] These are the Sārvāstivādin-Vaibhāṣikas: cf. Kośa, I, p. 8.

[24] These are the Vijñānavādin-Yogācāras: cf. Siddhi, p. 75: "The three *asaṃskṛta* exist as designations of the true nature of dharmas (*dharmatā*), another name being *bhūtatathatā*. Bhūtatathatā is revealed by Emptiness (*śūnyatā*), by the Not-Self (*nairātmya*), it is above the progression of the mind and the path of the words which course in existence, non-existence, both existence and non-existence, neither existence nor non-existence; it is neither the same as dharmas, nor different from dharmas, neither both, nor neither. Since it is the 'true principle' (*tattva*) of dharmas, it is called Dharmatā".

For the Yogācāras, there exists a true Suchness — the "Mind only" (*cittamātra*) — subjacent to appearance, to the false aspect from which the intellect sees reality. The Mādhyamika, on the contrary, believes that experience or appearance is *anadhiṣṭhāna* (Śikṣāsamuccaya, p. 264,*3-5*) "without a basis in true reality", *ajñānamātrasamutthāpita* (Madh. vṛtti, p. 495,*3*) "arisen from non-knowledge only".

[25] Madh. vṛtti, p. 176,*9-11*: *Atraike ākāśapratisaṃkhyānirodhanirvāṇāny asaṃskṛtāniti kalpayanti. apare śūnyatāṃ tathatālakṣaṇām asaṃskṛtāṃ parikalpayanti. tad etat sarvaṃ saṃskṛtasyāprasiddhau satyāṃ nāsty eveti spaṣṭam ādarśitam.*

[26] The Nihilist (*nāstika*) denies the reality he sees, and thus demolishes the basis of morality (cf. Madh. vṛtti, p. 159,*10*). The Mādhyamika says nothing of the reality which he does not see: he conforms to the relative truth (*saṃvṛtisatya*) and the absolute truth (*paramārthasatya*) by saying: Everything that is by reason of causes (relative truth) is inexistent with regard to its self-nature (absolute truth). Concerning this see Madh. vṛtti, p. 153, 159, 188, 222-224, 231, 273-274, 368-369, 490-491, 495; Madh. avatāra, p. 292; NĀGĀRJUNA, *Traité*, p. 1090-1094.

Suchness (*tathatā*) which is unarisen and unextinguished does not arise and is not extinguished. The suchness of all beings, of all dharmas, of all holy ones, this is also your own suchness, O Maitreya... It is not constituted of duality or multiplicity (III, § 51). The Tathāgata has said that true suchness, this is Parinirvāṇa (III, § 51). Imaginings are empty of emptiness, imagination is empty, and emptiness does not imagine emptiness. Emptiness is found in the 62 kinds of false views, the said false views are found in the deliverance of the Tathāgatas, the said deliverance is found in the first thought activity of all beings (IV, § 8). Dharmas, good or bad, do not arise and are not extinguished; they have aggregation (*kāya*) as their root; the root of aggregation is craving; the root of craving is false imagination; the root of false imagination is distorted perception, the root of distorted perception is the absence of a basis (*apratiṣṭhāna*); the absence of a basis has no root: that is why all dharmas rest on a baseless root (VI, § 5-6). Supreme enlightenment rests on a non-base. In the absence of any base, who could reach supreme enlightenment? I have obtained the state of holiness because there was nothing to obtain; it is the same with Bodhi: it is achieved because there is nothing to achieve (VI, § 16). Form and the other *skandha* are empty; it is not through the destruction of form that there is emptiness; the self-nature of form is emptiness (VIII, § 17).

Whether it is conceived of as inexistence pure and simple (*abhāvamātra*) or as true suchness (*bhūtatathatā*), the Absolute is designated in Buddhist texts by a whole stock of synonyms [27]. The most commonly used terms in the Vkn are: Tathatā "suchness", Dharmadhātu "element or plan of the Law", Śūnyatā "emptiness", Bhūtakoṭi "limit of reality", Samatā "sameness", Advaya "non-duality", Parinirvāṇa, Apratiṣṭhāna "baselessness" [28].

From the Vkn's viewpoint, this Absolute is not something.

III. — THE "PURE MIND" OF THE VKN

I think I have shown that the Vkn represents a pure Madhyamaka.

[27] Lists of synonyms can be found in Pañcaviṃśati, p. 168,*14-17*; Śatasāh., p. 1262,*13-17*; T 220, vol. VI, ch. 360, p. 853 *c* 11; Madh. vṛtti, p. 264,*11*; Upadeśa, T 1509, ch. 44, p. 382 *a*; Daśabhūmika, p. 63,*26*; Laṅkāvatāra, p. 192-193; Madhyāntavibhāga, p. 49-50; Abhidharmasamuccayavyākhyā, T 1606, ch. 2, p. 702 *b*; Buddhabhūmiśāstra, T 1530, ch. 7, p. 323 *a*; Siddhi, Appendice, p. 743-761.

[28] See particularly Ch. III, § 6, 16, 52; IV, § 1, 8, 12; VI, § 2, 4, 6, 16; VIII (devoted entirely to Advaya); X, § 16.

However, in Ch. III, § 34, it accepts as its own a saying of the Buddha asserting that beings are defiled by the defilement of the mind and purified by the purification of the mind, and from this it concludes that the nature of the mind is originally pure and undefiled. The Yogācāras based themselves on this passage from the Vkn to demonstrate the existence of the *ālayavijñāna* (Siddhi, p. 214) and of the *vijñaptimātratā* (Siddhi, p. 421). Should we then place the Vkn among the Mahāyāna-sūtras of idealistic tendency like the Saṃdhinirmocana, the Laṅkāvatāra, the Śrīmālādevī, etc? I do not think so, since the Pure mind of which the Vkn speaks should be interpreted in its context as a Non-mind.

It is appropriate here to outline the evolution of the concept of "Mind" in Buddhist philosophy.

1. — The "Mind" in canonical Buddhism.

1. The general tendency of the Canon is clear. Thought (*citta*), mind (*manas*) and consciousness (*vijñāna*) are synonymous. *Vijñāna* constitutes the fifth aggregate (*skandha*) and, like all the aggregates, is transitory, painful and impersonal.

> That which is called thought, mind or consciousness arises and disappears in a continual changing of day and night. Just as a monkey, gamboling in a forest or wood, seizes a branch, then lets it go and seizes another one, so that which is called thought, mind or consciousness arises and disappears in a continual changing of day and night [29].

In the process of dependent co-production, *vijñāna* is conditioned by actions (*saṃskāra*), and is itself the conditioning of names and forms (*nāmarūpa*), i.e. the psychophysical phenomena of existence.

It is understood that if the *vijñāna* does not descend into the mother's womb, the *nāmarūpa* would not be organised in the mother's womb; if the *vijñāna*, after having descended into the mother's womb, went away, the *nāmarūpa* would not be born; if the *vijñāna* were to be cut off in the child, young man, young girl, the *nāmarūpa* would not get bigger, grow or develop [30].

[29] Saṃyutta, II, p. 95,*1-9*: *yaṃ ca kho etaṃ bhikkhave vuccati cittaṃ iti pi mano iti pi viññāṇaṃ iti pi taṃ rattiyā ca divasassa ca aññad eva uppajjati aññaṃ nirujjhati. seyyathapi bhikkhave makkaṭo araññe pavane caramāno sākhaṃ gaṇhati taṃ muñcitvā aññaṃ gaṇhati evaṃ eva kho bhikkhave yad idaṃ vuccati cittaṃ iti pi mano iti pi viññāṇaṃ iti pi taṃ rattiyā ca divasassa ca aññad eva uppajjati aññaṃ nirujjhati.*

[30] Cf. Dīgha, II, p. 63,*2-14*; Kośavyākhyā, p. 669,*1-8*.

2. However, we find in the Canon certain passages which seem to attribute a more stable value to the mind:

a. Saṃyutta, I, p. 39, *10-11*; Saṃyukta, T 99, No. 1009, ch. 36, p. 264 *a* 26-27; T 100, No. 236, ch. 12, p. 459 *b* 14-15:

Cittena nīyati loko cittena parikissati,
cittassa ekadhammassa sabbeva vasaṃ anvagu.

"By the mind is the world led, by the mind manoeuvred: this one dharma, the mind, does everything obey".

The same stanza is given in Sanskrit in the Kośavyākhyā, p. 95, *22-23*:

Cittena nīyate lokaś cittena parikṛṣyate,
ekadharmasya cittasya sarve dharmā vaśānugāḥ.

The same *logion*, in prose, can be found elsewhere:

Aṅguttara, II, p. 177, *33* (Madhyama, T 26, No. 172, ch. 45, p. 709 *a* 20): *cittena kho bhikkhu loko niyyati cittena parikissati cittassa uppannassa vasaṃ gacchati.*

Sūtrālaṃkāra, p. 151, *7*: *cittenāyaṃ loko nīyate cittena parikṛṣyate cittasyotpannasya vaśe vartate.*

b. Aṅguttara, I, p. 10, *5-8*; Atthasālinī, p. 140, *25*: *pabhassaram idaṃ bhikkhave cittaṃ tañ ca kho āgantukehi upakkilesehi upakkiliṭṭhaṃ ... tañ ca kho āgantukehi upakkilesehi vippamuttaṃ.*

"Luminous is this mind, but sometimes it is defiled by chance passions; sometimes it is free of chance passions".

c. Saṃyutta, III, p. 151, *31-32*, 152, *8-9*; Saṃyukta, T 99, No. 267, ch. 10, p. 69 *c* 17: *Cittasaṃkilesā bhikkhave sattā saṃkilissanti, cittavodānā sattā visujjhanti.*

"By defilement of the mind, O monks, are beings defiled; by purification of the mind are they purified".

This *logion*, put into Sanskrit, is quoted by the Ratnagotravibhāga, p. 67, *1-2*, and the Abhidharmadīpa, p. 45, *19*; 78, *15*; 363, *5-6*: *Cittasaṃkleśāt sattvāḥ saṃkliṣyante, cittavyavadānād viśudhyante.*

The Sūtras and Śāstras of both Vehicles frequently refer to it: Vimalakīrtinirdeśa, III, § 34; Vibhāṣā, T 1545, ch. 142, p. 731 *b* 11-12; Pên shêng hsin ti kuan ching, T 159, ch. 4, p. 306 *b* 25-26; Śāsanaśāstra, T 1563, ch. 5, p. 795 *b* 27; Siddhi, p. 214, 421.

2. — The "Luminous Mind" in the Sects of the Small Vehicle.

1. Basing themselves on the passage from the Aṅguttara quoted

above, certain sects of the Small Vehicle — Mahāsāṃghikas [31] and Vibhajyavādins [32], — as well as the Śāriputrābhidharma [33], say that the mind is originally and naturally luminous (*cittaṃ prabhāsvaram*), but that it can be defiled (*kliṣṭa*) by the passions (*kleśa*), or liberated (*vipramukta*) from the passions. These latter, not being the original nature of the mind, are termed chance (*āgantuka*).

These sects conclude from this, as do the Andhakas [34], that it is the mind equipped with craving (*rāga*), etc., which obtains deliverance. Just as the filth is removed from a dirty vessel, as a crystal takes on various colours because of the diversity of colour of the body it covers, so the pure mind, defiled by craving, etc., receives the name of "equipped with craving" (*sarāga*) and later becomes delivered (*vimukta*). Hence the formula: *sarāgaṃ cittaṃ vimuccati* "it is the mind equipped with craving that is delivered [of craving]".

2. The great schools of the Small Vehicle reject both the thesis and its corollary. No, the mind is not naturally and originally pure: on the contrary, it is defiled by passion and action. In consequence, the final link with the passions must first be broken and, this break having been made, the mind of a Holy One (*arhat*, *aśaikṣa*) will be born freed of the passions.

a. The Theravādins see in the luminous mind of the Aṅguttara a reference to the *bhavaṅga* "subconscious vital influx".

> [In the Aṅguttara], the mind is called "clear", in the sense of extremely pure with reference to the *bhavaṅga*. It is because it comes from the *bhavaṅga* that, even when bad, it is called clear, exactly as a tributary of the Ganges is like the Ganges, and a tributary of the Godhāvarī is like the Godhāvarī [35].

That a mind still possessed of craving can be delivered is a contradiction in terms. This would presuppose that craving and mind would both be delivered.

b. Polemizing with the Vibhajyavādins, the Sarvāstivādin-Vaibhāṣikas

[31] See A. Bareau, *Les Sectes bouddhiques du Petit Véhicule*, Saigon, 1955, p. 67 68, No. 44.

[32] Idem, *ibidem*, p. 175, No. 23; Vibhāṣā, T 1545, ch. 27, p. 140 *b* 25-26.

[33] Idem, *ibidem*, p. 194, No. 6; Śāriputrābhidharma, T 1548, ch. 27, p. 697 *b* 18.

[34] Cf. Kathāvatthu, p. 238-241.

[35] Atthasālinī, p. 140,*24-29*; *taṃ (cittaṃ) eva parisuddhaṭṭhena paṇḍaraṃ. bhavaṅgaṃ sandhāy' etaṃ vuttaṃ. yathāha: pabhassaram idam bhikkhave cittaṃ tañ ca kho āgantukehi upakkilesehi upakkiliṭṭhan ti. tato nikkhantattā pana akusalaṃ pi Gaṅgāya nikkhantā nadī Gaṅgā viya, Godhāvarīto nikkhantā Godhāvarī viya ca paṇḍaran tveva vuttaṃ.*

remark that an originally luminous mind cannot be defiled by the filth of chance passions. On this hypothesis, the chance passions, naturally defiled, once associated with the originally and naturally luminous mind, would become pure. Or, if they remained impure, the luminous mind would not be defiled by their actions [36].

It therefore results that it is not a luminous mind accidentally possessed of craving that is liberated. Dharmas, whether of the mind or passions, perish from instant to instant. Filth cannot be removed from a vessel, for filth and vessel arise from instant to instant. The mind, ceaselessly renewed, is in possession of the passions. The final link with the passions must first be broken. Once this is broken, there will be born, finally delivered, the mind of a Holy One (*arhat* or *aśaikṣa*). Hence the formula in the Kośa: *vimucyate jāyamānam aśaikṣaṃ cittam āvṛteḥ* "Delivered of obstacle is the Aśaikṣa mind, nascent". By "nascent", "future" should be understood [37].

3. — The "Embryo of the Tathāgata" in the Yogācāra.

There is a close relationship between the "Luminous Mind" of the Hīnayānist sects and the Tathāgatagarbha "Embryo of the Tathāgata", as it is described in certain Sūtras and Śāstras of the idealist school of the Yogācāras.

1. In these Sūtras, which are not among the earliest products of the Mahāyāna, the Tathāgatagarbha is in principle luminous, pure, eternal, immanent in all beings, but accidentally defiled by chance passions.

Tathāgatagarbhasūtra as quoted in the following way by the Laṅkāvatāra, p. 77, *14*-78, *1*:

> As it is described by yourself, O Blessed One, in the text of a Sūtra, the Tathāgatagarbha is described as being naturally luminous, pure, pure in origin, endowed with the thirty-two marks, hidden in the body of all beings, girt by the aggregates, elements and bases of consciousness like a jewel of great value enveloped in dirty garments, soiled by the defilements of craving, hatred and delusion and other false imaginings, but permanent, stable, auspicious and eternal [38].

[36] Cf. Vibhāṣā, T 1545, ch. 27, p. 140 *b-c*.

[37] Regarding this problem, cf. Vibhāṣā, *l.c.*; Kośa, VI, p. 299; Nyāyānusāraśāstra, T 1562, ch. 72, p. 731 *c*.

[38] *Tathāgatagarbhaḥ punar Bhagavatā sūtrāntapāṭhe 'nuvarṇitaḥ, sa ca kila tvayā prakṛtiprabhāsvaraviśuddhādiviśuddha eva varṇyate dvātriṃśallakṣaṇadharaḥ sarvasattvadehāntargato mahārgharatna(ṃ) malinavastraparivesṭitam iva skandhadhātvāyatanavastu-*

Śrīmālādevī, section of the Ratnakūṭa, T 310, ch. 119, p. 677 *c*:

In this way, the Dharmakāya not yet free of the *kleśa* is called Tathāgatagarbha... Birth-death by reason of the Tathāgatagarbha. It is because of the Tathāgatagarbha that it is said that the starting point [of Saṃsāra] is not known (*pūrvā koṭir na prajñāyate*)... These two Dharmas, birth and death, make up the Tathāgatagarbha... Death is the extinction of the organs of feeling (*vedanendriyanirodha*); birth is their arising (*utpāda*). The Tathāgatagarbha is not born, does not die, does not ascend, does not descend; it is free of any saṃskṛta mark: never does it deteriorate... Were the Tathāgatagarbha lacking, there would be no aversion to suffering, no aspiration for Nirvāṇa. And why? Because the six vijñānas and their object, seven dharmas, do not last for an instant; therefore no feeling of suffering; no aversion; no aspiration for Nirvāṇa. The Tathāgatagarbha has no origin, is not born, does not die, feels suffering, is averse to suffering, aspires to Nirvāṇa... The Tathāgatagarbha is the Dharmadhātugarbha, the Dharmakāyagarbha, the Lokottaragarbha, the Prakṛtiprabhāsvaragarbha. It is originally and naturally pure. The Tathāgatagarbha, as I explained, can indeed be defiled by chance defilements, nevertheless it is incomprehensible (*acintya*), of the domain (*gocara*) of the Tathāgatas [39].

The Great Parinirvāṇa, T 374, ch. 7, p. 407 *b*; T 375, ch. 8, p. 648 *b*, discussing the fourth perversion — taking that which is not a "self" (*anātman*) for a self (*ātman*) — remarks:

The ātman is the Tathāgatagarbha. All beings possess a Buddha Nature: this is what the ātman is. This ātman, from the start, is always covered by innumerable passions (*kleśa*): this is why beings are unable to see it. It is as if, in a poor woman's hut, there was a treasure of pure gold without absolutely anyone in her family knowing anything about it... The Tathāgata, today, reveals to beings this precious treasure, that is, Buddha Nature. When all beings have seen it, they experience great joy and take refuge in the Tathāgata. The Tathāgata is he who excels in skillful means (*upāya*); the poor woman

veṣṭito rāgadveṣamohābhūtaparikalpamalamalino nityo dhruvaḥ śivaḥ śāśvataś ca Bhagavatā varṇitaḥ.

The Chinese versions of the Tathāgatagarbha (T 666, p. 457 *c*; T 667, p. 461 *c*) differ slightly from this quotation: cf. P. DEMIÉVILLE, *Le Concile de Lhasa*, Paris, 1952, p. 116-117 in the notes. In the Laṅkāvatāra, the Tathāgatagarbha is identified with the *ālayavijñāna*.

Regarding the Embryo of the Tathāgata, we now have two very valuable works available: J. TAKASAKI, *A Study on the Ratnagotravibhāga* (Serie Orientale Roma, XXXIII), Rome, 1966; D.S. RUEGG, *La théorie du Tathāgatagarbha et du Gotra* (Publications de l'École Française d'Extrême Orient, LXX), Paris, 1969.

The Śrīmālādevīsiṃhanādasūtra has been translated and annotated in English by A. and H. WAYMAN, *The Lion's Roar of Queen Śrīmālā* (Columbia University), New York and London, 1974.

[39] Translation based on that by DE LA VALLÉE POUSSIN, Siddhi, p. 756.

represents the innumerable beings; the treasure of pure gold is the Buddha Nature.

2. The naturally luminous Mind (*cittaṃ prakṛtiprabhāsvaram*), the Tathāgatagarbha, with which these Sūtras are concerned, inspired the great scholars of the Yogācāra School. Some, such as Sāramati, use it as an authority to contrive an absolute monism, more Brahmanical than Buddhist; others, like Asaṅga, interpret it within the framework of their psychological system and identify it with the Bhūtatathatā or the "reversed" or "revolutionized" Ālaya. To go into details would be to leave the subject which occupies us; moreover it suffices to draw the reader's attention to the masterly account by Professor E. Frauwallner[40].

4. — The "Non-Mind Mind" of the Prajñās and the Vkn.

To return to the Vkn, it will be noted that in Ch. III, § 34, it posits an originally and naturally pure mind which has never been defiled and which — this is most important — is not separated from Tathatā.

Chronologically speaking, the Vkn lies between the Hīnayānist Sects which talk of the Luminous Mind and the relatively recent Mahāyānasūtras, which liken this Luminous Mind to the Tathāgatagarbha, the Buddha Nature present in all beings.

However, in the reasoning of the Vkn, this Tathatā, from which the pure mind is not separated, is a plain non-existence (*abhāvamātra*). In fact we have seen that, after the fashion of the Prajñāpāramitās and the Madhyamaka, the Vkn refuses to hypostasize emptiness and does not allow of any basis to experience: "All dharmas", it says, "rest on a baseless root".

It is therefore through purely gratuitous means that the Siddhi uses the authority of the Vkn to set up its *ālayavijñāna* and *vijñaptimātratā*.

But, one might say, if the Tathatā of the Vkn is plain non-existence of what can this pure Mind "which is not separated from Tathatā" consist? This pure mind can only be a "Non-Mind Mind" or "Non-Thought Thought" (*cittam acittam*).

Now the theory of the "Non-thought Thought" has been formulated by the Prajñāpāramitās in a passage that has passed unnoticed, but which is strictly authentic since it already appears in the Aṣṭasāhasrikā

[40] E. FRAUWALLNER, *Die Philosophie des Buddhismus*, Berlin, 1956, p. 255-407.

(considered to be the oldest composition [41]) and which is faithfully reproduced in the Śatasāhasrikā and the Pañcaviṃśatisāhasrikā [42].

Subhūti said: The Bodhisattva Mahāsattva who courses in the Perfection of Wisdom should know [all dharmas, form, etc.], should know the thought — thought of Enlightenment, the thought the same as that which has no equal, noble thought — but should not make anything of it [43]. And why? This thought is Non-Thought, for the original nature of thought is luminous [44].

Śāriputra said to Subhūti: What, then, O Honourable Subhūti, is this luminosity of thought?

Subhūti replied: The fact that this thought is not associated with or dissociated

[41] See E. CONZE, *The Composition of the Aṣṭasāhasrikā Prajñāpāramitā*, BSOAS, XIV, 1952, p. 251-262; *The Oldest Prajñāpāramitā*, The Middle Way, XXXII, 1958, p. 136-141; *The Prajñāpāramitā Literature*, The Hague, 1960, p. 9-17; R. HIKATA, *Introd. to Suvikrāntavikrāmin*, Fukuoka, 1958, p. XIV, XLVII, L.

[42] Aṣṭasāh., p. 37,*16*-40,*12*; T 224, ch. 1, p. 425 *c*; T 225, ch. 1, p. 478 *c*; T 226, ch. 1, p. 508 *c* 15-22; T 227, ch. 1, p. 537 *b* 13-19; T 220, vol. VII, ch. 538, p. 763 *c* 16-25; ch. 556, p. 866 *a* 8-17.

Śatasāh., p. 495,*3-21*; T 220, vol. V, ch. 36, p. 202 *a* 8-25.

Pañcaviṃśati, p. 121,*12*-122,*11*; T 221, ch. 2, p. 13 *b* 24-*c* 7; T 222, ch. 3, p. 166 *b* 21-*c* 10; T 223, ch. 3, p. 233 *c* 20-234 *a* 5; T 220, vol. VII, ch. 408, p. 44 *c* 20-45 *a* 7.

Aṣṭādaśasāh., T 220, vol. VII, ch. 484, p. 456 *b* 24-*c* 10.

Bodhisattvena mahāsattvena prajñāpāramitāyāṃ caratā bodhicittaṃ nāma jñātavyam asamasamacittaṃ nāmodāracittaṃ nāma jñātavyaṃ na ca tena mantavyam. tat kasya hetoḥ. tathā tac cittam acittaṃ prakṛtiś cittasya prabhāsvarā.

Śāriputra āha. kā punar āyuṣman Subhūte cittasya prabhāsvaratā.

Subhūtir āha. yad āyuṣman Śāriputra cittaṃ na rāgeṇa saṃyuktaṃ na visaṃyuktaṃ na dveṣeṇa … na mohena … na paryutthānair … nāvaraṇair … nānuśayair … na saṃyojanair … na dṛṣṭikṛtaiḥ saṃyuktaṃ na visaṃyuktam iyaṃ Śāriputra cittasya prabhāsvaratā.

Śāriputra āha. kiṃ punar āyuṣman Subhūte asti tac cittaṃ yac cittam acittam.

Subhūtir āha. kiṃ punar āyuṣman Śāriputra yā acittatā tatrāstitā vā nāstitā vā vidyate vā upalabhyate vā.

Śāriputra āha. na khalv āyuṣman Subhūte.

Subhūtir āha. sa ced āyuṣman Śāriputra tatrācittatāyām astitā vā nāstitā vā na vidyate nopalabhyate vā api nu te yukta eṣa paryanuyogaḥ. yad āyuṣman Śāriputra evam āha asti tac cittaṃ yac cittam acittam iti.

Śāriputra āha. kā punar eṣā āyuṣman Subhūte acittatā.

Subhūtir āha. avikārā āyuṣman Śāriputra avikalpā acittatā yā sarvadharmāṇāṃ dharmatā. iyam ucyate acittatā.

[43] *Na ca tena mantavyam*, in Aṣṭasāh. *tenāpi bodhicittena na manyeta*. The Āloka, p. 38,*6*, glosses *abhiniveśaṃ na kuryāt* "let him not give it his allegiance". This is also Hsüan-tsang's interpretation. Kumārajīva understands: "let him not take pride in it".

[44] The Āloka, p. 38,*24-26*, explains: This thought (*citta*) is in reality non-thought (*acitta*) because, devoid of a single or multiple self-nature (*ekānekasvabhāvavaidhuryāt*), the nature of this thought (*cittasya prakṛtiḥ*) which is not to arise of itself (*svabhāvonutpādatā*) is luminous (*prabhāsvarā*), that is, exempt from the shadows resulting from false conceptions (*vidhamitasarvāsatkalpanāndhakāra*).

from craving, hatred, delusion, invasions, obstacles, residues, shackles and the various categories of false views, this, O Śāriputra, is what this luminosity of thought is.

Śāriputra said: Well then, O Honourable Subhūti, this thought that is "Non-thought Thought", does it exist?

Subhūti replied: Well, then, Honourable Śāriputra, wherever the thought is lacking, the existence or inexistence [of the thought] does it exist or is it perceived?

Śāriputra replied: No, indeed, O Honourable Subhūti.

Subhūti went on: If wherever the thought is lacking, the existence or inexistence [of the thought] cannot be found and is not perceived, can the Honourable Śāriputra reasonably ask if the thought which is "Non-Thought Thought" exists?

Śāriputra went on: So what then, Honourable Subhūti, is the absence of thought?

Subhūti replied: The absence of thought without modification or concept, the Dharma Nature of all dharmas, such is, Honourable Śāriputra, the absence of thought [45].

We can compare with this passage ascertained in the oldest Prajñāpāramitās this extract from the Suvikrāntavikrāmin, p. 85, *15*-86, *5*:

The Bodhisattva well knows the prejudices of beings, prejudices born of perverse thought, but never does he rouse a thought concerning these perversities. And why? Because the Perfection of wisdom is exempt from thought, and the natural luminosity of thought, the natural purity of thought does not

[45] Whoever says *acittam* says *cittābhāvamātram* "pure and simple inexistence of thought" (Āloka, p. 40,*6*).

See the commentary of this passage in the Upadeśa, T 1509, ch. 41, p. 363 *a* 20 sq.: The Bodhisattva who has obtained the thought of great knowledge takes no pride in it, because that thought is always pure. Just as space (*ākāśa*), always pure, is not defiled by smoke, clouds, dust, mist and other chance (*āgantuka*) things which cover it, so thought, eternally pure in itself, is not defiled by ignorance (*avidyā*) and other chance passions (*āgantukakleśa*) which cover it. Once the passions have been avoided, it is as pure as at the start. The yogin's ability means little: this purity of thought is not his work. He should not take pride in it or dwell on it. And why? Because [the thought] is absolutely empty (*atyantaśūnya*)...

Śāriputra asks if this thought without the characteristics of thought (*yac cittam acittam*) exists or does not exist. In fact, if it exists, why call it non-thought (*acittam*)? And if it does not exist, why make much of that incomparable thought (*asamasamacitta*) which is destined to produce Bodhi?

Subhūti replies: In the absolute purity (*atyantaviśuddhi*) of the absence of thought (*acittatā*) neither existence (*astitā*) nor non-existence (*nāstitā*) can be found.

Śāriputra then asks of what the absence of thought (*acittatā*) consists, and Subhūti replies that it is pure emptiness (*atyantaśūnya*), the inconceivability (*avikalpanatā*) of all dharmas.

consist in any thought production. It is in the absence of an object that foolish worldlings produce a thought. The Bodhisattva who knows the object also knows [the mechanism] from which thought arises. Where does thought arise from? The Bodhisattva knows that thought is naturally luminous, and he says to himself: "It is because of the object that the thought arises". Having understood the object [to be wrong], he does not produce or destroy any thought. His own thought is luminous, undefiled, loving, perfectly pure. Based on the non-arising of thought, the Bodhisattva neither produces nor destroys any dharma [46].

Thus then, for the Prajñāpāramitā and the Madhyamaka, the luminous thought or mind (*cittaṃ prabhāsvaram*) is, purely and simply, the inexistence of thought (*cittābhāvamātra*). And for the Vkn which denies any basis (*pratiṣṭhāna*) to the phenomenal world (VI, § 5-6). the Luminous Mind, to which it refers in Ch. III, § 34, comes down to the absence of all thought (*acittatā*): "The mind", it says, "is immaterial (*arūpin*), invisible (*anidarśana*), without support (*aniśraya*) and without intellect (*avijñaptika*)" (Ch. III, § 52, at the end).

The Vkn is purest Madhyamaka, and the Yogācāras cannot use it as an authority on which to build their systems.

IV

THE SOURCES OF THE VKN

Written in the grammar and style particular to Buddhist Sanskrit, the Vkn abounds in turns of phrases, formulae, stock phrases, comparisons and repetitions which are the rule in the Sūtras of both Vehicles. We have been obliged here, in the notes, to point out all these conventionalisms and supply each of them with a certain number of parallels drawn from other Pāli and Sanskrit texts. With the lexicons and concordances we have now to hand, this was mere

[46] *Tatra bodhisattva imān evaṃrūpān abhiniveśān sattvānāṃ viparyāsacittajān samanupaśyan na kvacid viparyāse cittam utpādayati. tat kasmād dhetoḥ. cittāpagatā hi prajñāpāramitā, yā ca cittasya prakṛtiprabhāsvaratā prakṛtipariśuddhitā, tatra na kācic cittasyotpattiḥ. ārambaṇe sati bālapṛthagjanāś cittam utpādayanti. tatra bodhisattvo 'py ārambaṇaṃ prajānann api cittasyotpattiṃ prajānāti. kutaś cittam utpadyate. sa evam pratyavekṣate: prakṛtiprabhāsvaram idaṃ cittam. tasyaivaṃ bhavaty ārambaṇaṃ pratītya cittam utpadyata iti. sa ārambaṇaṃ parijñāya na cittam utpādayati nāpi nirodhayati. tasya tac cittaṃ prabhāsvaraṃ bhavati, asaṃkliṣṭaṃ kamanīyaṃ pariśuddham. sa cittānutpādasthito na kaṃcid dharmam utpādayati, na nirodhayati.*

child's play. But as the same formula or stock phrase appears in many texts, it is practically impossible to know from which of these the Vkn borrowed them. Experienced in the reading of Sūtras, the author of the Vkn may well have taken them from his memory, without referring, even mentally, to any particular text.

This state of affairs makes the problem of sources particularly delicate, Buddhist Sūtras not being in the habit of acknowledging their references. Omitting therefore what are simply stylistic formulae, I have limited myself to pointing out a certain number of texts from which the Vkn has borrowed an idea or a theory.

I. — CANONICAL SŪTRAS OF THE TRIPIṬAKA

Dīgha, I, p. 76, *18*, etc.: The body which has as its law to be always anointed and massaged... (II, § 11, n. 25).

Dīgha II, p. 30, *26*, etc.: The world is fallen into wretchedness: it is born, grows old, dies... (III, § 50, n. 91).

Dīgha II, p. 36, *3*, etc.: Beings, most certainly, love the Ālaya... (V, § 4, n. 4).

Dīgha, II, p. 157, *8*, etc.: *Aniccā vata saṃkhārā*... (I, § 20, n. 86).

Sanskrit Mahāparinirvāṇa, p. 356, etc.: Rarity of the Buddhas (III, § 40, n. 73).

Saṃyutta, II, p. 95, *5*: The mind is like a monkey (IX, § 15, n. 17).

Saṃyutta, II, p. 178, *18*, etc.: Saṃsāra has no beginning or end (III, § 39, n. 72).

Saṃyutta, II, p. 198, *3*: The body is like an old well (II, § 11, n. 27).

Saṃyutta, III, p. 26, *28*, etc.: The exhaustion of craving, hatred... (VI, § 9, n. 31).

Saṃyutta, III, p. 140, *16*, etc.; As the lotus, born in water... (I, § 10, st. 17, n. 55).

Saṃyutta, III, p. 132, *26*, etc.: The three (or four) Summaries of the Law, *sabbe saṅkhārā aniccā*... (III, §25, n. 51; IV, §10, n. 15; X, § 18, n. 24; XII, § 11, n. 21).

Saṃyutta, III, p. 142: Form is like a ball of foam... (II, § 9, n. 23).

Saṃyutta, III, p. 151 and 152: *Cittasaṃkilesā, bhikkhave*... (III, § 34).

Saṃyutta, IV, p. 172-174, etc.: *Āsīvisa Sutta* (II, §11, n.28; III, §11; III, § 64, n. 130).

Saṃyutta, IV, p. 174, *19*: *Tiṇṇo pārāṅgato*... (I, § 10, st. 16, n. 54).

Saṃyutta, V, p. 422, etc.: Suffering should be known... (V, § 3, n. 2).

Aṅguttara, I, p. 23-26: On the pre-eminences of the Śrāvakas. — Like all Mahāyānasūtras, the Vkn is fully conversant with the special qualities which characterise a particular disciple of the Buddha. It is precisely over their specialities that, in Ch. III, Vimalakīrti takes ten great Śrāvakas to task.

Aṅguttara, I, p. 63, *6-8*: Respect for Śaikṣa and Aśaikṣa (IX, § 3, n. 5).

Aṅguttara, I, p. 287: *Assakhaluṅka* (IX, § 15, n. 16).

Dhammapada, v. 11-12: *Asāre sāramatino*... (III, § 62, n. 124; III, § 72, n. 142).

Dhammapada, v. 92-93: *Ākāse va sakuntānaṃ padam* (VI, § 1, n. 11).

II. — VINAYA

Vinaya, I, p. 83, *37* (seventh *śikṣāpada*): Prohibition of the use of garlands (VI, § 8, n. 27).

Vinaya, I, p. 83, *12*, etc.: Prohibition of ordaining a child without the authorisation of his parents (III, § 40, n. 74).

Vinaya, II, p. 214, *12*, etc. (33rd *sekhiya*): Obligation of alms-seeking from door to door (III, § 10, n. 19).

III. — PARACANONICAL SŪTRAS

This is a question of Sayings of the Buddha (*vacana*) not mentioned in the Nikāyas-Āgamas and which the Small Vehicle does not generally recognize as being authoritative.

1. Rātridvayasūtra (modification of a canonical logion, Dīgha, III, p. 135, etc., made by the Mahāsāṃghikas and other Hīnayānist sects): The Buddha teaches the Law with a single sound (I, § 10, st. 12-13, n. 52).

2. Catuṣpratisaraṇasūtra: The Law is the refuge and not the man... (XII, § 12, n. 23). Set up as a formula of canonical teaching, the Sūtra of the Four Refuges is recognized and adopted by the treatises of both Vehicles, mainly the Kośa, the Upadésa and the Yogācārabhūmi. Among all the Mahāyānasūtras, the Vkn was possibly the first to formulate it.

3. Vatsasūtra (T 808, tr. by Chih Ch'ien): Ānanda begs for milk at the home of a Śrāvastin brahman. But, for the Vkn, it is a question of a brahman from Vaiśālī and it is while going to see him that Ānanda meets up with Vimalakīrti (III, § 42, n. 77). The Vatsasūtra was in consequence modified in order to insert these new facts and was the object of a long recension entitled *Kṣiraprabuddhasūtra "Sūtra

of the Buddha Brilliance of Milk". This new recension was translated by Dharmarakṣa (T 809).

4. Maitreyavyākaraṇa: Śākyamuni predicts to Maitreya that he will succeed him (Śākyamuni) as Buddha. This prediction had already been mentioned in the canonical Nikāyas (Dīgha, III, p. 75-76, etc.), but it was only later that it instigated a whole surge of Maitreyan literature, recognized, apparently, by both Vehicles (Cf. É. LAMOTTE, *Histoire du bouddhisme indien*, p. 777-783). It seems that on the coming of Maitreya, four inexhaustible treasures (*akṣayanidhāna*) will appear in the world. They are mentioned in the Sanskrit Āgamas and other later sources, particularly the numerous Maitreyavyākaraṇas. The Vkn alludes to these four treasures, but only to locate them in Vimalakīrti's house (VI, § 13, n. 34).

Finally the Vkn quotes freely from stanzas which are tirelessly repeated in the collections of Buddhist stories and fables, for example: *na praṇaśyanti karmāṇi*... (I, § 10, st. 4, n. 48).

IV. — MAHĀYĀNA SŪTRAS

The question of the relationship of the Vkn to other Mahāyānasūtras is particularly delicate because the uncertainties of relative chronology do not enable us to decide which is the borrower and which the borrowed. The present summary is of only provisional value.

1. The Histories of Indian literature place the Prajñāpāramitās at the head of the Mahāyānasūtras. The fact is that Lokakṣema and his collaborator Chu Fo-so published, from 24th November 179 on, a translation of the Aṣṭasāhasrikā with the title of Tao hsing pan jê ching (T 224) and that some Chinese masters of the third and fourth centuries, Chu Shih-hsing (203-282), Tao An (313-385) and Shih Tao-lin (314-366) considered this Aṣṭasāhasrikā to be the abbreviation of a much longer Prajñāpāramitā — in 90 scrolls — compiled "after the Buddha's Nirvāṇa" by a foreign priest, i.e. an Indian. Unless this is a matter of the old Chinese prejudice regarding the antecedence of long recensions in relation to short ones, these ancient opinions confirm the great antiquity of the Prajñāpāramitās.

If, as we believe, the Chinese version by Chih Ch'ien (T 474), carried out between 222 and 229, represents the oldest translation of the Vkn, the latter is later than what E. CONZE calls the *Basic Prajñāpāramitā* and may well have been inspired by it.

We have seen above how the Vkn conceived the Pure Mind:

exactly in the sense of the "Non-Thought Thought" of the Prajñās. Even more, in Ch. VIII, § 17, it seems to have quoted freely the famous stock phrase of the Prajñās concerning the inexistence of Emptiness (cf. above, p. LXIX).

2. The Mahāratnakūṭa, as it appears in translations in Chinese (T 310) and Tibetan (OKC, No. 760), is a compendium of 49 sūtras. Bodhiruci alias Dharmaruci, who edited the Chinese compilation at the beginning of the eighth century (706-713), reproduced, just as they were, earlier translations of 23 sūtras, slightly modified the translations of 15 other sūtras and personally translated 11 sūtras. Among the 23 sūtras reproduced unchanged, appears the *Tathāgataguhyanirdeśa*, or *Tathāgataguhyaka*, translated by Dharmarakṣa of the Western Chin, on 16th November 280.

The Vkn refers twice to this Sūtra: 1. It speaks of the "Secrets of the Buddha", and Kumārajīva himself sees in this passage an allusion to the Mi chi ching = *Guhyakasūtra* (cf. IV, § 1, n. 3). 2. Moreover, and this settles the question, it claims that innumerable Buddhas come to expound the *Tathāgataguhyaka* in Vimalakīrti's house (VI, § 13, n. 36).

In the Ratnakūṭa compendium there appears in the sixth place (T 310, ch. 19-20, p. 101-112) an *Akṣobhyatathāgatasya vyūhaḥ* translated by Bodhiruci himself. There does, however, exist an earlier translation, in archaic style, entitled A ch'u fo kuo ching (T 313). The old catalogue by Chu Shih-hsing compiled under the Wei (220-265) and quoted in the Li tai san pao chi (T 2034, ch. 4, p. 52 *c* 23), as well as the K'ai yüan shih chiao mu lu (T 2154, ch. 1, p. 478 *c* 5) assign this translation the date of A.D. 147 (first year of the *chien-ho* period) and ascribe it to Lokakṣema. This information is probably wrong, since it was only in the second half of the second century that Lokakṣema made his first appearance as a translator. This does not lessen the fact that the Sūtra concerning the Tathāgata Akṣobhya was among the first to be translated into Chinese.

In all probability, it was due to the inspiration of this text that the Vkn (XI, § 3-7) attaches so much importance to the Buddha Akṣobhya and his Abhirati universe, where it locates Vimalakīrti before his appearance in Sahāloka.

3. "A certain number of [Mahāyāna] texts, without forming special classes, have some denominations in common that bring them together, their titles ending in *-nirdeśa* "display, index, explanation", *-vyūha* "development", *-parivarta*, "survey, roundabout words", *-paripṛcchā*

"enquiry, questioning, interrogation" [1]. The most common denomination is *-dharmaparyāya* "treatise, explanation of the Law", or *-dharmamukha* "introduction to the Law".

The Vkn refers to itself equally as *sūtra*, *nirdeśa*, *dharmaparyāya* or *parivarta* (cf. XII, § 1, n. 1; § 6, n. 9; § 23, n. 42).

However the same terms can also designate part of the work, a chapter. Thus Ch. V of the Vkn is entitled *Acintyavimokṣanirdeśa* "Teaching of the inconceivable liberation"; and Ch. X includes a *dharmamukha* called Introduction to all the Buddha attributes (cf. X, § 11, at the beginning).

Finally, it occurs that the Vkn refers to explanations dealt with elsewhere. Thus Vimalakīrti advises the daughters of Māra to study a *dharmamukha* entitled *Akṣayapradīpa* "Inexhaustible Lamp" (cf. III, § 66, n. 134), but I have not been able to identify it. Conversely, in its chapter on Inconceivable Liberation, Vimalakīrti remarks (in Ch. V, § 18) that he has only expounded a small part of the subject and refers his questioner Śāriputra to a full teaching (*nirdeśa*) which it would take more than a kalpa to recite. Rightly or wrongly, I think I see in this reference an allusion to the Avataṃsaka, which bears the sub-title of *Acintyavimokṣasūtra* "Sūtra of inconceivable liberation", and which, according to well implanted tradition, *originally* consisted of a countless number of *gāthā* (cf. V, § 10, n. 11).

From the chronological point of view, nothing prevents the Vkn from having been inspired by the Avataṃsaka, since portions of this enormous collection were clearly translated into Chinese at the same time as the Vkn. According to the Ch'u san-tsang chi chi (T 2145, ch. 2, p. 6*b* 20, and 6*c* 19), Lokakṣema, who was active from A.D. 167 to 186, translated the *Tou-sha ching* (T 280); and Chih Ch'ien, who worked from 223 to 253, translated the **Bodhisattvapūrvacaryasūtra* (T 281). The Li tai san pao chi (T 2034, ch. 6, p. 63*b* 5; 62*a* 2; 62*c* 10; 62*a* 23 and 62*a* 18) attributes to Dharmarakṣa the translation of five Sūtras from the Avataṃsaka: *Bodhisattvadaśavyavasthāna* (T 283), *Daśabhūmika* (T 285), *Samantanetrabodhisattvaparipṛcchāsamādhi* (T 288), *Tathāgatotpattisaṃbhavanirdeśa* (T 291) and *Lokottarasūtra* (T 292). Let us not forget that translations of the Vkn were made by these same Chih Ch'ien and Dharmarakṣa.

4. Finally, there is a close connection between the Vkn and the Mahāsaṃnipāta, without it being possible to decide which is the

[1] J. FILLIOZAT, in *Inde classique*, II, Paris, 1953, p. 367.

borrower and which the borrowed. The Chinese *Mahāsaṃnipāta* (T 397) is a compendium of seventeen texts which was compiled by Sêng-chiu in 594. But several of these texts had already been translated earlier, in the second and third centuries A.D.: Even disregarding the translations ascribed to An Shih-kao (148-170), we can turn to the authority of the Li tai san pao chi (T 2034, ch. 6, p. 62 *b* 3, 62 *a* 11, 62 *a* 25 and 63 *c* 21) according to which Dharmarakṣa translated the *Mahāyānopadeśa* (T 399) on the 26th May 287, the *Tathāgatamahākaruṇānirdeśa* (T 398) in 291, the *Akṣayamatinirdeśa* (T 403) on the 10th January 308, and the *Sūtra of the young Mute* (T 401) at an unknown date.

However it may be, apart from the seven texts devoted *ex professo* to Vimalakīrti and his family (T 474 to 480), the Mahāsaṃnipāta is one of the few Mahāyānasūtras to give a role to Vimalakīrti (T 397, ch. 31, p. 217 *a* 25-26; ch. 35, p. 240 *c* 17-21; ch. 48, p. 312 *b* 17 and 312 *c* 25).

There are close analogies between the conversion of the Apsarases related by the Vkn (III, § 62-67) and the account of the defeat of Māra which appears at the beginning of the ninth section of the Mahāsaṃnipāta, the *Ratnaketudhāraṇīsūtra*, preserved in Sanskrit (N. Dutt, *Gilgit Manuscripts*, IV, p. 1-82) and Chinese (T 397, ch. 19, p. 129-137).

In conclusion, the Vkn is closely linked to the earliest known recensions of the Prajñāpāramitās, the Ratnakūṭa, the Avataṃsaka and the Mahāsaṃnipāta, and belongs to the same philosophico-mystical movement. We know how this developed later and culminated in the vast collections known by the generic name of Vaipulyasūtras.

V

THE DATE OF THE VKN

All the events related in the Vkn would have taken place at the time of the Buddha Śākyamuni, in the sixth and fifth centuries before our era. But this is only a question of a literary fiction, derived from an old Buddhist tradition.

I. — THE BUDDHIST TRADITION

Having dealt with this subject elsewhere [1], I shall do no more here than recall the main points.

Immediately after his enlightenment, the Buddha Śākyamuni went to the Deer Park in Vārāṇasī and, for the first time, caused "the turning of the Wheel of the Law": he taught the Śrāvakas, his immediate disciples, the four noble truths and the *tripiṭaka.* A few years later, in the course of a second, even third turning of the Wheel of the Law, Śākyamuni gathered, in Śrāvastī or Vaiśālī, chosen assemblies of Śrāvakas and Bodhisattvas, taught them the Mahāyāna and expounded to them the voluminous Vaipulyasūtras. In general, the Śrāvakas, who would have been incapable of understanding it, got no wind of this teaching, but it was noted by the gods.

After the death of the Buddha, the Śrāvakas, under the leadership of Mahākāśyapa, gathered in Rājagṛha and there compiled the Hīnayānist scriptures: the *tripiṭaka.* Concurrently, the great Bodhisattvas, assisted by Ānanda, reached Mount Vimalasvabhāva and there they compiled the Mahāyānasūtras.

Only the Hīnayānist *tripiṭaka* was immediately expounded to men. The Mahāyānasūtras, entrusted to the safe-keeping of the great Bodhisattvas, were stored in hiding places, among the Devas, Nāgas or Gandharvas. The majority of these Mahāyānasūtras, such as the Prajñāpāramitā and the Avataṃsaka, existed in three versions: a long version consisting of an infinite quantity of *gāthā*, a medium-length version numbering about fifty myriad *gāthā*, a short version in 100,000 *gāthā*.

Five hundred years after the Buddha's Nirvāṇa, when the Good Law was gradually declining and the Buddha's work threatened, the Mahāyānasūtras began to spread in the world. The Bodhisattva Nāgārjuna discovered, in the Nāgas' palace, seven precious coffers filled with Mahāyānasūtras. In 90 days he recited them and learnt by heart the short versions of 100,000 *gāthā.* At a later date, the Bodhisattva Vasubandhu was to repeat this feat.

Nāgārjuna and his emulators propagated the Mahāyānasūtras, but, in order to adapt themselves to listeners with weak faculties, they limited themselves to summarizing or condensing the 100,000 *gāthā* version. Thus it is that the Prajñāpāramitā was first known in China

[1] *Sur la formation du Mahāyāna*, Asiatica (Festschrift F. Weller), Leipzig, 1954, p. 381-386; *Mañjuśrī*, T'oung Pao, XLVIII, 1960, p. 40-46, 61-73.

through a *Tao-hsing-p'in* in 8,000 *gāthā* (*Aṣṭasāhasrikā*) translated in A.D. 179 by Lokakṣema (T 224), then through a *Kuang-tsan-ching* in 25,000 *gāthā* (*Pañcaviṃśatisāhasrikā*) translated in 286 by Dharmarakṣa (T 222). The Avataṃsaka the Chinese only ever had in a version in 36,000 *gāthā* translated by Buddhabhadra in 418-420 (T 278) and a version in 40,000 *gāthā* put into Chinese by Śikṣānanda in 695-699 (T 279). However, according to the information supplied by the Indian Jinagupta, about 560, there was in existence in Khotan, to be more precise Karghalik, a collection of twelve Mahāyānasūtras, each one consisting of 100,000 *gāthā*.

The Indian tradition's sole aim is to attribute the Mahāyānasūtras, which developed in the course of time, with an antiquity equal to that of the Hīnayāna *tripiṭaka* going back directly to Śākyamuni's time Historically speaking, this tradition is valueless and supplies no exact information on the date of Mahāyānasūtras in general or the Vkn in particular. All the same we must remember that, according to the traditional reckoning, it was only five centuries after Śākyamuni's Nirvāṇa that the Mahāyānasūtras began to be spread in the world.

II. — THE *TERMINUS AD QUEM* OF THE VKN

In the absence of more precise indications, the *terminus ad quem* of the Vkn is supplied by the date of publication of the oldest Chinese translation. The Chinese catalogues consulted at the beginning of this Introduction give Yen Fo-t'iao (A.D. 188) and Chih Ch'ien (between 222 and 229) as the first translators of the Vkn, but their allegations should not be accepted blindly.

We have, regarding Fo-t'iao[2]—also called Fou-t'iao or Fu-t'iao—documents from the third century reproduced in the Ch'u san-tsang chi chi (T 2145) by Sêng-yu:

1. Ch. 10, p. 69 *c*: A preface by Yen a-chih-li (ācārya) Fou-t'iao to his own work entitled *Sha-mi shih hui chang-chü* "Commentary on the ten (kinds) of Intelligences (for the use) of śrāmaṇeras". Although the title is not very precise, it is seemingly a matter of explanations on the ten *śikṣāpada* of the novice (Vinaya, I, p. 83-84; Aṅguttara,

[2] On this author, see H. MASPERO, *Communautés et moines bouddhistes chinois aux IIe et IIIe siècles*, BEFEO, X, 1910, p. 228 229; P. PELLIOT, in T'oung Pao, XIX, 1920, p. 344-345, note 64; E. ZÜRCHER, *The Buddhist Conquest of China*, Leiden, 1959, p. 34; R. SHIH, *Biographies des Moines éminents* de Houei-kiao (Bibliothèque du Muséon, 54), Louvain, 1968, p. 17.

I, p. 211). In this preface, Yen Fo-t'iao praises the Bodhisattva An Shih-kao of Parthian origin "who spread the Buddha's Law in the land of the Han".

2. Ch. 7, p. 50 *a*: An old preface, dating back to the beginning of the third century and written by an unknown hand, concerning a translation of the Fa-chü ching (Dharmapada). It says there (l. 6-8): "Formerly, Lan-t'iao, the Parthian marquis Shih-kao, the commander [An Hsüan] and Yen Fu-t'iao, translating *hu* (Sanskrit) into the language of the Han (Chinese), found the (true) method: they are considered as the Inimitable (*nan-chi*) (translators)". Consequently Yen Fo-t'iao belonged to the team of translators which brought fame to the Church of Lo-yang in the second half of the second century.

3. Ch. 6, p. 46 *c*: A preface by K'ang Sêng-hui, a Sogdian who reached Chien-yeh (Nankin) in 247, to the translation of the Fa-ching ching = Ugradattaparipṛcchā (T 322; OKC 760, No. 19), a section of the Ratnakūṭa. In it we read (l. 2-6) that the *ch'i-tu-yü* (cavalry commander) An Hsüan and Yen Fou-t'iao, the latter from Lin-huai (in the locality of An-hui), translated the Fa-ching ching: the commander interpreted it out loud and Yen t'iao took it down with his brush.

4. Ch. 13, p. 96 *a*: A biographical note on An Hsüan, in an unknown hand. There it is said that [An] Hsüan and the śramaṇa Yen Fo-t'iao translated the Fa-ching ching in collaboration (l. 14), that the latter also composed the Shih-hui (l. 19) and that, together with An Shih-kao, they were called the three Inimitable Translators (l. 18).

On the basis of these documents, the Ch'u san-tsang chi chi (ch. 2, p. 6 *c* 3-4) only recognizes two works to be by Yen Fo-t'iao: the translation of the Fa-ching ching and the composition of the Shih-hui.

In his Kao sêng chuan (T 2059, ch. 1, p. 324 *c*), written between 519 and 544, Hui-chiao repeats, almost without change, the information supplied by the Ch'u san-tsang chi chi.

The Chung ching mu lu (T 2146, ch. 1, p. 119 *a*), compiled in 594 by Fa-ching and his team, mentions the translation of the Fa-ching ching by An Hsüan and Fo-t'iao. It details four translations of the Vkn, but the one by Yen Fo-t'iao is not among them.

It follows that, until the end of the sixth century, the Chinese knew nothing of a translation of the Vkn by Yen Fo-t'iao. The first to mention it was the Li tai san pao chi (T 2034, p. 54 *a* 14), reproduced in subsequent catalogues[3]. The K'ai yüan shih chiao mu lu (T 2154, p. 483 *a* 19-20) dates this translation from the fifth year of the *chung-p'ing* period (188).

In attributing the first translation of the Vkn to Yen Fo-t'iao, these seventh and eighth century catalogues refer to two ancient catalogues, already lost by the sixth century: the Ku lu and the Chu Shih-hsing Han lu. However, according to tradition[4], the Ku lu dates from the reign of the Emperor Shih Huang-ti who ruled from 221 to 208 B.C. It is difficult to see how a catalogue from the third century before our era could mention the work of an author (Yen Fo-t'iao) who lived in the second century of our time.

Moreover, Chih Min-tu who, between 290 and 307, published a combined edition of the existing versions of the Vkn[5], would not have failed to make use of the translation by Yen Fo-t'iao if it had existed, or he would at least have mentioned it in his preface which has come down to us. However, this is not the case.

We must conclude from this that the "old" (*ku*) translation of the Vkn by Yen Fo-t'iao never existed, but that the seventh century Chinese did not consider the translation of the Vkn by Chih Ch'ien between 222 and 229 to be the oldest and thought that there had been a considerable time lapse between the original edition of the Vkn and the version by Chih Ch'ien.

The latter is known to us: it is the T 474. Its authenticity cannot be doubted: it was used as the basic text by Chih Min-tu in his combined edition of the Vimalakīrtisūtras (ca 290-307) and is mentioned by all the Chinese catalogues which assign it the date of the *huang-wu* period (222-229) of the Wu. Through an error which I find incomprehensible, the Ch'u san-tsang chi chi (T 2145, p. 6 *c* 14) gives this translation as having been lost.

The *terminus ad quem* of the original edition of the Vkn is established by this first Chinese translation made between A.D. 222 and 229.

*

By this date, however, the Vkn was already considered as authoritative in India, where the Mahāyānist school of the Mādhyamikas or Śūnyavādins was in the course of being formed. The time was near when Nāgārjuna, the great master of that school, would publish his

[3] See above, p. XXVI-XXVII.

[4] See above, p. XXVI, note 2.

[5] See above, p. XXX.

Mūlamadhyamakakārikā or Madhyamakaśāstra in 445 stanzas, his Dvādaśamukhaśāstra in 26 stanzas, his Daśabhūmikavibhāṣā and perhaps other works as well. Āryadeva, his immediate disciple, would in turn, publish his famous Centuries (Śatakaśāstra and Catuḥśataka)[6].

Doubtless the Vkn is not quoted by name in these stanzas, the extreme conciseness of which did not allow for any references. Conversely, it is copiously invoked[7] in the Mahāprajñāpāramitopadeśa (abbreviated to Upadeśa), a voluminous encyclopaedia of Mādhyamika Buddhism. Kumārajīva, who translated this work from 402 to 404, attributes it to Nāgārjuna himself, but R. Hikata[8] has pointed out several passages in it which could only have come from the translator Kumārajīva or non-Indian authors and, according to P. Demiéville the attribution of the Upadeśa to Nāgārjuna is based on a legend that was current in Kaśmīr in the fourth century: "In reality it is a matter of a work composed in Kaśmīr or North-West India by an author or, which is more likely, by a team of anonymous authors who alleged that they were still steeped in the tradition of the Small Vehicle"[9].

All these Mādhyamika works were only translated into Chinese at the beginning of the fifth century, by Kumārajīva[10]. By that time, Nāgārjuna and his emulators had already become legendary, as can be seen by the fantastic *Biography* of *Nāgārjuna* (Lung-shu p'u-sa chuan, T 2047), wrongly attributed to Kumārajīva. It involves Nāgārjuna in incredible adventures and makes him live for more than 300 years, a figure which later biographies were to go so far as to double[11].

[6] There is in J. MAY, *Candrakīrti Prasannapadā*, Paris 1959, p. 22-45, a complete bibliography of the Madhyamaka. Additionally, the Dvādaśamukhaśāstra by Nāgārjuna has been reconstructed into Sanskrit by N.A. SASTRI, Visva-Bharati Annals, VI, 1954, p. 165-231.

[7] See below, p. CXI.

[8] R. HIKATA, in his Introduction to the Suvikrāntavikrāmin, Fukuoka, 1958, p. LII ff.

[9] P. DEMIÉVILLE in *Inde Classique*, II, Paris, 1953, p. 443.

[10] According to the Chinese catalogues, in 404 Kumārajīva translated the Śatakaśāstra of Āryadeva with the comm. by the bodhisattva (*k'ai-shih*) Vasu (T 1569); in 404-405, the Upadeśa "of Nāgārjuna" (T 1509); in 409, the Dvādaśamukhaśāstra of Nāgārjuna (T 1568); in 409, the Madhyamakaśāstra of Nāgārjuna with the commentary by Piṅgala (T 1564); later still the Daśabhūmikavibhāṣa of Nāgārjuna (T 1521).

[11] Cf. the bibliography on the life of Nāgārjuna in É. LAMOTTE, Introduction to the *Traité*, Louvain, 1944, p. XI-XIV. Also see the reservations expressed in the Introduction to Volume III of this same *Traité*, Louvain, 1970, p. LI-LV.

This does not lessen the fact that the Madhyamaka sprang into life and defined its basic philosophical positions during the third century of our era; the name of Nāgārjuna is indissolubly linked with it, if not as its founder, at least as its most illustrious representative.

In the chronological study that concerns us here, it is important to know his date, if only approximately. Summarizing many earlier works, M. WINTERNITZ [12] concludes: "An dieser Legende dürfte wohl so viel richtig sein, dass Nāgārjuna ebenso wie der etwas ältere Aśvaghoṣa — Nāgārjuna lebte wahrscheinlich gegen Ende des 2. Jahrhunderts n. Chr. — ursprünglich Brahmane war": this is the generally accepted date. However, taking note of the legends associating Nāgārjuna with Kaniṣka, Śātavāhana and Nahapāna, S. LÉVI [13] and D.R. SHACKLETON BAILEY [14] place Nāgārjuna's birth in the first century. The latter proposes the following dates:

A.D. 70: Birth of Nāgārjuna.
A.D. 90: Birth of Āryadeva.
A.D. 105: Birth of Mātṛceṭa.
A.D. 128: Accession of Kaniṣka I. — *Suhṛllekha* of Nāgārjuna.
A.D. 145: Conversion of Mātṛceṭa.
A.D. 170: Mātṛceṭa's Epistle to Kaniṣka II.

But this connecting of philosophers and sovereigns is practically worthless, since Buddhists have always endeavoured to attach their great men to illustrious sovereigns: Moggaliputtatissa and Upagupta to Aśoka, Aśvaghoṣa, Nāgārjuna, Pārśva, Saṃgharakṣa, etc., to Kaniṣka. In the same spirit they attribute Kaniṣka with a Buddhist council which is only a pastiche of the Aśokan one.

The Chinese sources analysed in the *Chronology* of Mochizuki's Encyclopaedia (p. 78) place Nāgārjuna's birth in the year 200, 300, 500, 530, 600, 700 or 800 after the Buddha's Nirvāṇa. These contradictions are partly explained by the divergencies concerning the date of the Nirvāṇa, which was never established by the Chinese and their Indian or Serindian informants [15].

Having no desire to deal with such a complicated subject in a few lines, I will merely point out the earliest information supplied by

[12] *Geschichte der Indischen Litteratur*, II, Leipzig, 1920, p. 253.
[13] *Kaniṣka et Śātavāhana*, JA, 1936, p. 61-121.
[14] *The Śatapañcāśatka of Mātṛceṭa*, Cambridge, 1951, p. 9.
[15] Cf. A. BAREAU, *La date du Nirvāṇa*, JA, 1953, p. 46-47.

Kumārajīva, his disciples and contemporaries regarding the date of Nāgārjuna.

In a note, dating from A.D. 568, in the Êrh chiao lun by Tao-an [16], reproduced by Tao-hsüan (596-667) in his Kuang hung ming chi (T 2103, ch. 8, p. 142 *a* 18-20), we read:

> According to the chronology of the dharmācārya Shih (Kumārajīva) and the *Shih chu ming* (inscribed pillar in the region of Wu-hsing), in agreement with the *Springs and Autumns* (Chronicle of the principality of Lu), the Tathāgata was born in the fifth (correction: fourth) year of the king Huan of the Chous, *i-ch'ou* cycle (716 B.C.). He left home, the 23rd (correction: 22nd) year of King Huan, *kuei-wei* cycle (698 B.C.). He reached enlightenment the tenth year of King Chuang, *chia-wu* cycle (687 B.C.). He entered Nirvāṇa the 15th year of King Hsiang, *chia-shên* cycle (637 B.C.): which makes up to to-day (A.D. 568) 1205 years.

If the note is authentic — but that cannot be guaranteed — this would be a matter of a correction made by Kumārajīva to a pseudo-historical chronology which was current in China until the beginning of the sixth century, and which placed the birth (not enlightenment) of Śākyamuni on the eighth day of the fourth month of the tenth year of King Chuang (687 B.C.) [17].

According to the note which we have just quoted, Kumārajīva fixed the Nirvāṇa in 637 B.C. This supplies us with information on the chronology of the Madhyamaka as Kumārajīva, his disciples and contemporaries conceived it in the fourth and fifth centuries of our era, since it is in years after the Nirvāṇa that they dated the great scholars Aśvaghoṣa, Nāgārjuna, Āryadeva and Harivarman.

The eighth year of the *hung-shih* period (A.D. 408) [18], Kumārajīva translated the Ch'êng shih lun (Satyasiddhiśāstra, T 1646) of Harivarman, and ordered his disciple Sêng-jui to make a commentary of it. After Kumārajīva's death in 413 or, more likely, 409, Sêng-jui put his master's last teachings into writing and composed a preface to the Satyasiddhiśāstra. This last is quoted in extracts by Chi-tsang (549-623) in his commentaries on the Śatakaśāstra of Āryadeva (Po

[16] No connection with the famous Tao-an of the fourth century.

[17] Cf. E. ZÜRCHER, *Conquest* ..., p. 271-272.

[18] According to the *Li* (T 2034, ch. 8, p. 78 *c* 22). — By the terms of the *K'ai* (T 2154, ch. 4, p. 513 *a* 18) translation started on the 8th day of the 9th month of the 13th *hung-shih* year (11 October 411) and ended the 15th day of the 9th month of the 14th *hung-shih* year (4 November 412). The date put forward by the *Li* is to be preferred, Kumārajīva probably having died in 409.

lun shu, T 1827), the Madhyamakaśāstra of Nāgārjuna (Chung kuan lun shu, T 1824) and the Three Treatises (San lun hsüan i, T 1852).

T 1827, ch. 1, p. 233 *a* 8-14: The master [Sêng]-jui, in the preface to the Satyasiddhiśāstra which he composed after the death of his master Shih (Kumārajīva), quotes the latter's words: "After the Buddha's Nirvāṇa, in the year 350, Ma-ming (Aśvaghoṣa) was born; in 530, Lung-shu (Nāgārjuna) was born". He also said: "Aśvaghoṣa made the end of the Good Law (*saddharma*) illustrious; Nāgārjuna appeared at the beginning of the counterfeit Law (*pratirūpaka*)" ... [19] [Sêng]-chao and [Sêng]-jui together say that T'i-p'o (Āryadeva) was born in the year 800 or so".

T 1824, ch. 1, p. 18 *b* 23-25: At what moment of the counterfeit Law (*pratirūpakadharma*) was Nāgārjuna born? The master [Sêng]-jui, in his preface to the Satyasiddhiśāstra, quotes the words of his master Lo-shih (Kumārajīva) and says: "Aśvaghoṣa was born in the year 350, and Nāgārjuna in the year 530".

T 1852, p. 3 *c* 10-14: In bygone days, the dharmācārya Lo-shih (Kumārajīva), after having translated the Satyasiddhiśāstra, ordered Sêng-jui to make a commentary of it. After the death of the master Kumārajīva, Sêng-jui put his last teachings down in writing and composed the preface to the śāstra; he says: "The Satyasiddhiśāstra was composed by a sage of the Hīnayāna, from the land of Chi-pin (Kaśmīr), in the 890 years after the Buddha's Nirvāṇa, Harivarman, the most illustrious of the disciples of Kumarāta".

These accounts which proffer several variations could lead to confusion: two interpretations are possible:

a. Aśvaghoṣa and Nāgārjuna were born respectively in 350 and 530 after the Nirvāṇa. According to the chronological system of Kumārajīva, described above, the Nirvāṇa occured in 637 B.C. It follows that Aśvaghoṣa was born in 637 — 350 = 287 B.C., and Nāgārjuna in 637 — 530 = 107 B.C.

b. Aśvaghoṣa was born in 350 after the Nirvāṇa (287 B.C.), and Nāgārjuna 530 years after Aśvaghoṣa [20], or 350 + 530 = 880 years after the Nirvāṇa, which gives us A.D. 243.

It is evidently this last date which was adopted by Kumārajīva, his disciples Sêng-chao and Sêng-jui and his contemporary Hui-yüan.

In his *Biography of Āryadeva* (T'i-p'o p'u-sa chuan, T 2048, p. 186 *c* 8; 187 *a* 18), Kumārajīva makes Nāgārjuna the master and predecessor of Āryadeva. This is a matter of a well-established tradition and which was to be reproduced for centuries [21].

[19] On the respective duration of the *saddharma* and the *pratirūpaka*, see LAMOTTE, *Histoire*, p. 211-217.

[20] A difference of 530 years between Aśvaghoṣa and Nāgārjuna is more than unlikely, but the many forgeries which circulated in China in the name of Aśvaghoṣa made his dating impossible.

[21] Cf. Fu fa tsang, T 2058, ch. 6, p. 318 *c*; Hsüan-tsang, in T. WATTERS, *Travels*,

The disciples and contemporaries of Kumārajīva invariably place Āryadeva in the "800 years or so" after the Nirvāṇa:

a. Sêng-chao, disciple of Kumārajīva, reached Ch'ang-an with him in 401 and worked there until his death in 414. With the aid of Kumārajīva's notes, he composed his famous commentary on the Vkn (Chu Wei-mo-chieh ching, T 1775) and edited, among other things, a preface to the Śatakaśāstra (T 1569) by Kumārajīva. In this preface, which has come down to us (T 1569, p. 167 *c* 12; *Ch'u*, T 2145, ch. 11, p. 77 *b* 12), it is said: "After the Buddha's Nirvāṇa, 800 years or so, there was a great *pravrajita* scholar, named T'i-p'o (Āryadeva)".

b. We have seen above that Sêng-jui, another of Kumārajīva's disciples, was of the same opinion.

Finally, Hui-yüan (334-417), the master of the Lu shan, who was closely connected with Kumārajīva, wrote in his preface to the Ta chih lun ch'ao (T 2145, ch. 10, p. 75 *b* 27-29): "There was an eminent scholar of the Mahāyāna, named Lung-shu (Nāgārjuna); he was born in India and came from a brahman family... He shared his lot with the 900 years after the Nirvāṇa (接九百之運)".

Therefore, when Kumārajīva and his followers placed Nāgārjuna's birth in 530, we should understand 530 after Aśvaghoṣa who was himself born in 350 after the Nirvāṇa. Thus Nāgārjuna, born in 880 after the Nirvāṇa (= A.D. 243), lived during the ninth century after the Nirvāṇa and could have been the master of Āryadeva whom all the sources place in "800 or so" after the Nirvāṇa. In short, the chronological facts supplied by Kumārajīva and which represent the Kaśmīrian tradition of the fourth century can be interpreted in the following way:

637 B.C. The Buddha's Nirvāṇa.

287 B.C. Birth of Aśvaghoṣa.

A.D. 243 Birth of Nāgārjuna succeeded by Āryadeva.

A.D. 253 Composition of the Satyasiddhiśāstra by Harivarman.

Two indications, pointed out by R. Hikata[22], enable us to check the correctness of the date A.D. 243 proposed for the birth of Nāgārjuna.

a. Kumārajīva, in fact, was not the first to translate Nāgārjuna's works. The Upadeśa (T 1509) quotes at least once (ch. 49, p. 411 *a* 29)

II, p. 100, 200, and S. BEAL, *Life*, p. 135; I-tsing, tr. J. TAKAKUSU, p. 181; Bu-ston, II, p. 130; Tāranātha, p. 83.

[22] Introduction to the Suvikrāntavikrāmin, p. LII-LIII, in the notes.

from the Daśabhūmikasūtra destined to form the 22nd section of the Avataṃsaka. Nāgārjuna composed a commentary on this sūtra entitled Daśabhūmikavibhāṣā which Kumārajīva translated at the end of the *hung-shih* period, probably in 408, under the title of Shih chu p'i-p'o-sha lun (T 1521). In fact the Chinese catalogues list among the works translated by Dharmarakṣa at Ch'ang-an, between A.D. 265 and 313, a P'u-sa hui-kuo ching 菩薩悔過經. This translation is noted in the *Ch'u* (T 2145, ch. 2, p. 8 *b* 17), and the *Li* (T 2034, ch. 6, p. 63 *a* 23) which remark: "The colophon says that this is an extract from the Daśabhūmikaśāstra of Nāgārjuna". It therefore results that a work by Nāgārjuna had already reached China about A.D. 265.

b. Kumārajīva, supposed author of the Lung-shu p'u-sa chuan (T 2047), ends his observations by remarking (p. 185 *b* 2-3; 186 *b* 28-29): "From the time that Nāgārjuna left this world until today, more than a hundred years have passed". If this biography, mentioned for the first time in the Li tai san pao chi (T 2034, ch. 8, p. 79 *a* 7), was really drawn up at the beginning of the fifth century of our era, Nāgārjuna's death would have occurred towards the end of the third century.

It therefore really does seem that, for Kumārajīva and his school, Nāgārjuna was placed between A.D. 243 and 300[23].

However, Nāgārjuna was a pupil of the brahman Rāhulabhadra, author of a Prajñāpāramitāstotra which usually appears at the head of the Sanskrit manuscripts of the Prajñās and which is reproduced in full in the Upadeśa[24]. The main theses of the Madhyamaka are formulated in it. This would lead us to believe that the "Nāgārjunian" phase of the Madhyamaka covered the whole of the third century A.D. and overlapped into the fourth.

*

This long digression throws some light on the date of the Vkn which, among other Mahāyānasūtras, was one of the sources of the

[23] According to the *Tibetische Lebensbeschreibung Śākyamuni's*, tr. A. SCHIEFNER, St. Petersburg, 1848, p. 310, Nāgārjuna lived for 60 years. Other sources make him live for 100, more than 200, more than 300, 529 or 571, 600 years. Account must also be taken of Nāgārjuna's previous births, reincarnation of Ānanda (cf. P. DEMIÉVILLE, BEFEO, XXIV, 1924, p. 218, 227-228).

[24] Cf. NĀGĀRJUNA, *Traité*, p. 1060, note 2.

Madhyamaka. It is best to place it at the latest in the second century of our era.

It has been seen above (p. LXXXVI) how it was closely connected with the oldest known portions or recensions of the Prajñāpāramitās, the Ratnakūṭa, the Avataṃsaka and the Mahāsaṃnipāta.

Internal evidence supports this great antiquity. Only the enlarged Prajñāpāramitās (Pañcaviṃśatisāh., p. 214-225; Śatasāh., p. 1454-1473; Aṣṭādaśasāh., T 220, ch. 490-491, p. 490*b* - 497*b*) mention the ten Stages (*bhūmi*) of the Bodhisattvas. The Aṣṭasāhasrikā, the earliest known text of the Prajñās, does not breathe a word about them. The Vkn, which also remains silent on this subject, ranks as one of the oldest Mahāyānasūtras.

So when did these really begin to appear? The Indian Mahāyānist tradition would have it to be 500 years after the Nirvāṇa, but without supplying us with any valid synchronism. Some modern authors, "roughly speaking", place the elaboration of the "basic text" of the Prajñās between 100, or even 200 B.C., and A.D. 100. In fact, the present state of information does not allow any hypothesis on the *terminus a quo* of the Mahāyānasūtras.

VI

THE DIVISIONS OF THE VKN

In the three Chinese versions that have come down to us, the Vkn consists of 14 chapters bearing more or less the same titles. I reproduce here a synoptic table drawn up by H. HASHIMOTO, *A Study of the True Character of the Vimalakīrtinirdeśa*, Indogaku Bukkyōgaku Kenkyū, VII, 1958, p. 216. (See page XCIX).

The Tibetan version of the Kanjur only consists of 12 chapters of which these are the titles:

1. *Saṅs rgyas kyi źiṅ yoṅs su dag pa gleṅ gźi*: Introduction (with reference) to the purification of the Buddha fields.
2. *Thabs la mkhas pa bsam gyis mi khyab pa*: The inconceivable skill in means.
3. *Ñan thos daṅ byaṅ chub sems dpaḥ gtaṅ bar rmas pa*: The refusal to enquire by the Śrāvakas and Bodhisattvas.
4. *Na ba yaṅ dag par dgaḥ bar bya ba*: Consolations to the sick man.

譯 品	支謙			羅什		玄奘	
I	Ⓐ 卷上	佛國	Ⓑ 卷上	佛國	卷上	序	卷一
II		善權		方便		顯不思議方便善巧	
III		弟子		弟子		聲聞	卷二
IV		菩薩		菩薩		菩薩	
V		諸法言	Ⓑ 卷中	文殊師利問疾	卷中	問疾	卷三
VI		不思議		不思議		不思議	
VII	Ⓐ 卷下	觀人物		觀衆生		觀有情	卷四
VIII		如來種		佛道		菩提分	
IX		不二入		入不二法門		不二法門	
X		香積佛	Ⓑ 卷下	香積佛	卷下	香台佛	卷五
XI		菩薩行		菩薩行		菩薩行	
XII		見阿閦佛		見阿閦佛		觀如來	
XIII		法供養		法供養		法供養	卷六
XIV		囑累彌勒		囑累		囑累	
大藏正本	pp. 519 a—536 c			pp. 537 a—557 b		pp. 557 c—588 a	

5. *Rnam par thar pa bsam gyis mi khyab pa bstan pa*: Teaching on the inconceivable liberation.

6. *Lha mo*: The goddess.

7. *De bźin gśegs paḥi rigs*: The family of the Tathāgata.

8. *Gñis su med paḥi chos kyi sgor ḥjug pa*: Introduction to the doctrine of Non-duality.

9. *Sprul pas źal zas blaṅs pa*: Obtaining of food by the imaginary (bodhisattva).

10. *Zad pa daṅ mi zad pa źes bya baḥi chos kyi rdzoṅs*: Instruction on the Exhaustible and the Inexhaustible.

11. *Ḥjig rten gyi khams mṅon par dgaḥ ba blaṅs pa daṅ de bźin gśegs pa mi ḥkhrugs pa bstan pa*: Appropriation of the Abhirati universe and vision of the Tathāgata Akṣobhya.

12. *Sṅon gyi sbyor ba daṅ dam paḥi chos gtaṅ ba*: Antecedents and Transmission of the Good Law.

The reader can easily find the beginning of these chapters by consulting the concordance of the versions of the Vkn which appears at the beginning of this introduction.

Here now is a synoptic table of the contents of the Vkn according to the Tibetan and Chinese versions, with the titles reconstructed in Sanskrit:

Kanjur	Chih Ch'ien	Kumārajīva	Hsüan-tsang
I. *Buddhakṣetrapariśodhananidānam.*	I. *Buddhakṣetram.*	I. *Buddhakṣetram.*	I. *Nidānam.*
II. *Acintyam upāyakauśalyam.*	II. *Upāyakauśalyam.*	II. *Upāyāḥ.*	II. *Acintyam upāyakauśalyam.*
III. *Śrāvakabodhisattvānaṃ praśnatyāgaḥ.*	III. *Śrāvakāḥ.*	III. *Śrāvakāḥ.*	III. *Śrāvakāḥ.*
	IV. *Bodhisattvāḥ.*	IV. *Bodhisattvāḥ.*	IV. *Bodhisattvāḥ.*
IV. *Glānasaṃmodanam.*	V. *Dharmavacanam.*	V. *Mañjuśriyo glānapṛcchā.*	V. *Glānapṛcchā.*
V. *Acintyavimokṣanirdeśaḥ.*	VI. *Acintyam.*	VI. *Acintyam.*	VI. *Acintyam.*
VI. *Devī.*	VII. *Sattvasaṃdarśanam.*	VII. *Sattvasaṃdarśanam.*	VII. *Sattvasaṃdarśanam*
VII. *Tathāgatagotram.*	VIII. *Tathāgatagotram.*	VIII. *Tathāgatagotram.*	VIII. *Bodhyaṅgāni.*
VIII. *Advayadharmamukhapraveśaḥ.*	IX. *Advayapraveśaḥ.*	IX. *Advayadharmamukhapraveśaḥ.*	IX. *Advayadharmamukh*
IX. *Nirmitena bhojanādānam.*	X. *Sugandhakūṭas tathāgataḥ.*	X. *Sugandhakūṭas tathāgataḥ.*	X. *Sugandhakūṭas tathāgataḥ.*
X. *Kṣayākṣayam iti dharmavisarjanam.*	XI. *Bodhisattvacaryā.*	XI. *Bodhisattvacaryā.*	XI. *Bodhisattvacaryā.*
XI. *Abhiratilokadhātor grahaṇam, Akṣobhyasya tathāgatasya darśanam.*	XII. *Akṣobhyas tathāgataḥ.*	XII. *Akṣobhyas tathāgataḥ.*	XII. *Tathāgatasya darś*
XII. *Pūrvayogaḥ, saddharmasya parīndanā.*	XIII. *Dharmapūjā.*	XIII. *Dharmapūjā.*	XIII. *Dharmapūjā.*
	XIV. *Maitreye parīndanā.*	XIV. *Parīndanā.*	XIV. *Parīndanā.*

VII

THE LOCALISATION OF THE VKN

Early exegetists attached considerable importance to the localities and assemblies in which the Sūtras were expounded. The action of the Vkn is a coming and going between the Āmrapālīvana and Vimalakīrti's house in Vaiśālī (Basarh, district of Muzaffarpur, in Tirhut), with a quick trip to the Sarvagandhasugandhā universe (zenith region).

I. In the Āmrapālīvana in Vaiśālī (Ch. I). — The Buddha Śākyamuni expounds the Law there, surrounded by an immense assembly of Śrāvakas, Bodhisattvas and Devas.

Ratnākara, accompanied by 500 young Licchavis, comes to find him there (I, § 7).

II. In Vimalakīrti's dwelling (Ch. II). — Vimalakīrti, remaining at home, simulates a sick man (II, § 1); the notables of the town come in a crowd to enquire after his health (II, § 7).

III. In the Āmrapālīvana in Vaiśālī (III-IV, § 1). — One by one, Śākyamuni invites ten Śrāvakas, three Bodhisattvas and an Upāsaka to go for news of Vimalakīrti's health. All refuse. Mañjuśrī alone accepts the mission.

IV. In Vimalakīrti's dwelling (IV, §2 - IX, §4). — Mañjuśrī, accompanied by an enormous crowd of Śrāvakas, Bodhisattvas and Devas, leaves the Āmrapālīvana and goes to Vimalakīrti's home (IV, § 2). The assembly sits on gigantic thrones purposefully sent by the Tathāgata Merupradīparāja of the Merudhvajā universe (V, § 7).

V. In the Sarvagandhasugandhā universe (IX, § 5-8). — On Vimalakīrti's orders, an imaginary bodhisattva goes to the universe in question, asks the Tathāgata Sugandhakūṭa for some remains from his meal and is given satisfaction.

VI. In Vimalakīrti's dwelling (IX, §9-18). — The imaginary bodhisattva, accompanied by countless Bodhisattvas from the Sarvagandhasugandhā universe, returns to Vimalakīrti's dwelling (IX, § 9).

VII. In the Āmrapālīvana in Vaiśālī (X-XII). — The whole assembly gathered in Vimalakīrti's home is transported to the Āmrapālīvana, into the presence of Śākyamuni (X, § 2). At a particular moment, the Bodhisattvas of the Sarvagandhasugandhā universe leave the Āmrapālīvana to return to their own universe (X, § 20). The Abhirati universe of the Tathāgata Akṣobhya is miraculously brought into the Āmrapālīvana, and then put back in place (XI, § 4-7).

*

In the mind of the Indian author, all these movements are purely fictitious: mere changes of decor to give more emphasis to the action and dialogue. The positive and meticulous Chinese, however, took them literally and whenever their pilgrims went to Vaiśālī, they did not fail to enquire about the various places mentioned in the Vkn. The cicerones naturally had an answer for everything and, when the need arose, invented things they knew nothing about whatsoever. Their survey data were piously collected by the Chinese pilgrims, committed to memory and reproduced through the centuries.

1. Fa-hsien stayed in India from 402 to 411 and, between 414 and 416, wrote out an account of his journey. In this Fa-hsien chuan, the record devoted to Vaiśālī is very short (T 2085, p. 861 *c* 13-15):

Inside the town of Vaiśālī, the Lady Āmrapālī built a stūpa in honour of the Buddha: it is still exactly as it was originally. Three li to the south of the town, west of the road, there is the garden which this same Āmrapālī presented to the Buddha so that he could take up residence there [1].

2. The *Shui ching* "Classic of the Waters" is a small text which is traditionally attributed to the Han dynasty, but which was probably written during the period of the Three Kingdoms (220-265). In 527, Li Tao-yüan published a *Shui ching chu*, "Commentary on the Classic of the Waters" in which he made use of various sources. One of them, the *Wai kuo shih*, "Matters concerning foreign kingdoms" by Chih Sêng-tsai, is the first to mention Vimalakīrti's house:

The town of Vaiśālī has a perimeter of three *yojana*. The house of Wei-chieh (Vimalakīrti) is to the south of the palace in the great enclosure, seven li distant from the palace. The building is destroyed and only the spot where it was can be seen [2].

3. Hsüan-tsang, who visited Vaiśālī around 635, was particularly interested in the holy places mentioned in the Vkn. The information that he collected is recorded in the Hsi-yü-chi by Pien-chi (T 2087, ch. 7, p. 908 *b*) published in 646, and the Ta-T'ang ta tz'ŭ ên ssŭ san tsang fa shih chuan (T 2053, ch. 3, p. 235 *c*) published by Hui-li and Yen-ts'ung in 664 and revised in 688. Here are some extracts from them:

The foundations of the old town of Vaiśālī have a perimeter of 60 or 70 li; the palace has a perimeter of four or five li and contains few inhabitants. Five or six li to the north-west of the palace, a saṃghārāma is reached where some monks, not many in number, teach the doctrines of the Saṃmitīya sect of the Hīnayāna. Nearby, there is a stūpa, on the spot where, in olden days, the Tathāgata expounded the Vimalakīrtisūtra and where the śreṣṭhiputra Pao-chi (Ratnākara) and others presented him with precious parasols (*ratnacchattra*)...

Three li to the north-east of the saṃghārāma [situated on the banks of the Markaṭahrada "Monkey Pool"], there is a stūpa on the spot of the foundations of Vimalakīrti's ruined house: this house has many wonders. Not far from there, there is a sacred dwelling (*shên shê*): one would say a pile of bricks, but tradition has it that it is a pile of stones; this is the place where the śreṣṭhin Vimalakīrti appeared sick and expounded the Law. Not far from there, there is a stūpa: it is the ruined house of the śreṣṭhiputra Ratnākara. Not far from there, there is a stūpa: it is the ruined house of the lady Āmrapālī...

[1] Cf. J. LEGGE, *A Record of Buddhistic Kingdoms*, Oxford, 1886, p. 72.

[2] Cf. L. PETECH, *Northern India according to the Shui-ching-chu*, Rome, 1950, p. 28-30.

A little to the south [of the stūpa called "The Last Look"], there is a vihāra and, in front of it, a stūpa: this is the Āmrapālīvana which that lady presented to the Buddha [3].

Here, Hsüan-tsang differs considerably from the written tradition. According to the Vkn (I, § 1 and 7), it was in the Āmrapālīvana that Śākyamuni expounded the Sūtra and received the offering of parasols from Ratnākara and his companions; for Hsüan-tsang, these two scenes were set in a spot further north, not far from the palace. Furthermore, the Vkn (II, § 7; IV, § 3) has it that Vimalakīrti simulated sickness in his own home, whereas for Hsüan-tsang it is a question of two different places.

4. A score or so years after Hsüan-tsang, the Chinese envoy Wang Hsüan-ts'ê visited Vaiśālī, measured the ruins of Vimalakīrti's house with his tablet and found it one *chang* (ten feet) square. The event is noted in the Fa yüan chu lin (T 2122, ch. 29, p. 501 *c* 10-13) compiled by Tao-shih in 668:

During the *hsien-ching* period (656-660) of the Great T'angs, an imperial order entrusted the *wei-ch'ang-shih* (chief of the guard and archivist) Wang Hsüan-ts'ê with a mission. That is why he set out for India. He went to the dwelling of Ching-ming (Vimalakīrti). He measured it with his official tablet (*hu*); it was exactly ten times its dimension (ten *hu*), that is why he named it Fang-chang 方丈 "The squared chang".

P. Pelliot [4] accepts the date of 656-660 proposed by the Fa yüan chu lin; but for S. Lévi [5], Wang Hsüan-ts'ê carried out this measuring several years earlier. In fact, the Shih chia fang chih by Tao-hsüan (T 2088, ch. 1, p. 960 *c* 17-21), published in the first *yung-hui* year (650), has it that this measuring took place "recently", and the Fo tsu t'ung chi (T 2035, ch. 39, p. 365 *c* 10-12) by Chih-p'an (1269-1271) places this event in the 17th year of the *chêng-kuan* period (643).

5. Whatever the details are, the expression *fang-chang* became traditionally used in China to describe Vimalakīrti's house. It flows from the brush of I-ching (635-713) in his Ch'iu fa kao sêng chuan (T 2066, ch. 2, p. 8 *b* 8), of Chan-jan (711-782) in his Wei-mo ching lüeh shu (T 1778, ch. 7, p. 669 *c* 13-14), of Hui-lin (737-820) in his

[3] T. Watters, *On Yuan Chwang's Travels*, II, London, 1905, p. 63, 66-67.

[4] P. Pelliot, *Autour d'une traduction sanscrite du Tao-tö king*, T'oung Pao, XII, 1912, p. 380, note 2.

[5] S. Lévi, *Les Missions de Wang Hiuan-ts'e dans l'Inde*, JA, 1900, p. 19-20 of the off-print.

I ch'ieh ching yin i (T 2128, ch. 6, p. 342 *b* 11), of Tao-yüan (ca 1004) in his Ching tê ch'uan têng lu (T 2076, ch. 6, p. 251 *a* 8-9), etc.

It does not seem as though the expression *fang-chang* had its equivalent in Sanskrit. In modern Chinese it is still used to describe the abbot of a monastery.

VIII

VIMALAKĪRTI IN INDIAN TRADITION

The Bodhisattva is, by definition, an enlightenment-being (*bodhisattva*). His career includes two crucial moments: 1. The production of the thought of enlightenment (*bodhicittotpāda*) or high resolve (*adhyāśaya*) to become a fully and perfectly enlightened Buddha in order to ensure the welfare and happiness of all beings; 2. The attainment of the supreme and perfect enlightenment (*anuttarā samyaksaṃbodhiḥ*) which characterises the Buddhas.

In consequence, the role of the Vaipulyasūtras devoted to the great Bodhisattvas is to tell us where, when and before which Buddha the Bodhisattva produces his *bodhicitta* and determines through his vows (*praṇidhāna*) the qualities with which he intends adorning his future Buddha field (*buddhakṣetra*), and where and when this same Bodhisattva reaches supreme and perfect enlightenment. Thus the Sukhāvatīvyūha informs us about these two essential moments in the life of the Buddha Amitābha and, with regard to Mañjuśrī, similar details are supplied by the Mañjuśrībuddhakṣetraguṇavyūha [1].

In contrast, Indian tradition is silent on the *cittotpāda* and *abhisaṃbodhi* of Vimalakīrti (abridged form, Vim.). This silence can be explained by the relatively modest place held by this Bodhisattva in Mahāyānist hagiography; it is also justified by the philosophical radicalism of Vim. for whom "enlightenment is already acquired by all beings" (III, § 51). If enlightenment is an innate and universal property, the question of reaching enlightenment does not arise.

The Vkn itself only gives rather vague details about its hero. In the Buddha Śākyamuni's time, Vim. was a lay bodhisattva, living in Vaiśālī. He was married, father of a family, and enjoyed a great fortune (II, § 2; VII, § 6). However his presence on earth was only

[1] See article *Mañjuśrī*, T'oung Pao, XLVIII, 1960, p. 17-23.

skillful means (*upāya*) in order to convert beings to the Buddha's Law and the doctrines of the Great Vehicle. Theoretically, he did not believe in beings or things; in practice, he worked for the benefit and happiness of all creatures. Hence his contradictory actions, arising both from wisdom (*prajñā*) and great compassion (*mahākaruṇā*), which made him appear sometimes as a sceptic and sometimes as a believer (II, § 3-6; III, § 3, 16-18; IV, § 20; VII, § 1; IX, § 19).

Endowed with invincible eloquence (*apratihatapratibhāna*), he also had inconceivable psychic powers (*ṛddhyabhijñā*) at his command which enabled him to reduce or enlarge his home at will (IV, § 3; V, § 7), curb Māra (III, § 63), transform a necklace into a belvedere (III, § 75), create imaginary bodhisattvas and instantaneously send them off to the furthermost universes (IX, § 4, 7), shrink these universes and pack one inside the other (XI, § 5-6), etc.

Vim., who denies the birth and death of beings, refuses to make his provenance known to Śāriputra. However, the Buddha Śākyamuni explains that, before making his appearance in Sahāloka, Vim. dwelt in the Abhirati universe, ruled over by Akṣobhya (XI, § 2-3). We know no more than this, and it is strange that Vim. does not come into the long jātaka related by Śākyamuni at the end of the Vkn (XII, § 7-15)*.

*

Outside the Vkn, Vimalakīrti is also mentioned in some Sūtras and Śāstras of the Great Vehicle. Here are some references which have no pretentions to being complete.

1. Mahāsaṃnipāta (T 397). — We have seen above (p. LXXXVI) that certain texts which went into the compilation of this voluminous compendium had already been translated by the beginning of the third, even second century of our era, but the passages where Vim. is mentioned do not belong to these oldest parts.

T 397, ch. 31, p. 216 *b*-217 *c*: In the Eastern region, there is an universe called *Wu-liang* (Apramāṇa): there, a Buddha named *Wu-kung-tê* (Pañcaguṇa) always expounds the Good Law and converts beings; also there, a bodhisattva named *Jih-mi* (Sūryaguhya) listens attentively to the Law and contemplates space. He perceives innumerable Bodhisattvas going from East to West and asks the Buddha where they are going. Pañcaguṇa explains to him that those

* However, see Professor Lamotte's remarks on this in his translation of the Śūraṃgamasamādhisūtra, *La Concentration de la Marche Héroïque*, Brussels, 1965, p. 191-192, § 78, note 181 (translator's note).

Bodhisattvas, responding to a previous vow by Śākyamuni, are gathering in the Sahā universe in the Western region in order to spread the Law there. He asks Sūryaguhya also to set out for the Sahā universe with a miraculous *dhāraṇī*. Faced with the bodhisattva's fears and hesitations, he insists, saying: "Sūryaguhya, are you not the Vimalakīrti of the Sahā universe, why should you be afraid?" The bodhisattva admits this identification: "Yes, that Vimalakīrti there is myself. In that universe, I am present in the form of a layman (*avadātavasana*) and I expound the principles of the Law to beings. I sometimes appear as a brāhmaṇa, kṣatriya, vaiśya, śūdra, Īśvaradeva, Śakra devendra, Brahmā deva, Nāgarāja, Asurarāja, Garuḍarāja, Kiṃnararāja, pratyekabuddha, śrāvaka, śreṣṭhin, strī, kumāraka, kumārikā, tiryagyoni, preta or nāraka, in order to convert beings". Finally, Sūryaguhya, alias Vimalakīrti, equipped with the *dhāraṇī*, goes to Śākyamuni.

T 397, ch. 35, p. 239 (Tib. trip., vol. 36, p. 181, folio 114 *a* 5 *sq.*): In the Eastern region, beyond buddhakṣetras as numerous as the sands of an infinite number of Ganges, there is a Buddha universe called *Wu-chin-tê* (Yoṅs su gduṅ ba med pa = Niṣparidāha); there, a Buddha named *Chan-po-chia-hua-sê* (Tsam pa kaḥi mdog = Campakavarṇa) always expounds the Good Law and converts beings; there also, a bodhisattva named *Jih-hsing-tsang* (Ñi maḥi śugs kyi sñiṅ po = Sūryakośagarbha) listens to the Law attentively and contemplates space. He perceives innumerable Bodhisattvas going from East to West... [Rest as above].

T 397, ch. 48, p. 311 *c* 312 *b*: The Buddha said to Maitreya: In times gone by, during the 31st kalpa, the Buddha Viśvabhū appeared in the world and expounded the Law to the four assemblies. At that time, there was a great brahman named Puṣyayajña who took his refuge in the Three Jewels and observed the five precepts. He had eight pupils: 1. Puṣyavajra, 2. Puṣyanābhika, 3. Puṣyajālika, 4. Puṣyavarman, 5. Puṣyakṣatriya, 6. Puṣyavṛkṣa, 7. Puṣyavīrya, 8. Puṣyanandika. The brahman invited them to take their refuge in the Three Jewels, observe the five precepts, drive out all negligence and produce the *cittotpāda*. His pupils refused, but faced with their teacher's insistence, they said to him: If, for a thousand years, you make use of only two bodily attitudes (*īryāpatha*), walking and standing, without ever sitting or lying down, if you eat only one ball of food a week and you practise these austerities for a thousand years, then we will take refuge in the Three Jewels". The brahman took them at their word and swore to observe these austerities; a voice from the sky predicted to him that one day he would be the Buddha Śākyamuni of the Bhadrakalpa.

Then follows the application of the jātaka to persons of the present: the brahman Puṣyayajña of that time is the present Buddha Śākyamuni; Puṣyavajra is Rāhula Asurarāja; Puṣyanābhika is Vemacitra Asurarāja; Puṣyajālika is Prahārāda Asurarāja; Puṣyavarman is Bali Vairocana; Puṣyakṣatriya is Mārarāja Pāpīyān; Puṣyavṛkṣa is Maitreya; Puṣyavīrya is Vimalakīrti; Puṣyanandika is Devadatta.

2. A sequel to the Vkn consists of an early Sūtra which styles itself *Ting-wang ching* 頂王經 (T 477, p. 595 *c* 14; T 478, p. 604 *a* 2,

6) or *Kuan-ting-wang ching* 灌頂王經 (T 479, ch. 2, p. 613 *c* 6), in Sanskrit Mūrdhābhiṣiktarājasūtra "Sūtra of the King with capital Consecration". The *Tables du Taishō Issaikyō*, Nos 477-479, mistakenly give it the title of Vimalakīrtinirdeśa.

To judge by the Chinese translations that have come down to us, this Sūtra existed in three very different versions:

a. Ting wang ching (T 477), in one chüan, translated in Ch'ang-an, between 265 and 313, by Dharmarakṣa of the Western Chin. This translation is mentioned in the catalogues by Chih Min-tu (compiled between 326 and 342) and Tao-an (374). It had other names as well: *Ta fang têng ting wang ching*, Mahāvaipulya Mūrdhābhiṣiktarājasūtra; *Wei-mo-chieh tzŭ wên ching*, Vimalakīrtiputraparipṛcchāsūtra; *Shan-ssŭ t'ung-tzŭ ching*, Sucintakumārasūtra. This is the first translation. See *Ch'u*, T 2145, p. 8 *a* 15; *Chung A*, T 2146, p. 118 *a* 3; *Li*, T 2034, p. 63 *a* 2; *Nei*, T 2149, p. 241 *a* 12; *T'u*, T 2151, p. 353 *b* 23; *K'ai*, T 2154, p. 494 *a* 17.

The Buddha, staying in the Āmrapālīvana in Vaiśālī, goes alms-seeking at the home of Vimalakīrti who had a son named *Shan-ssŭ* (Bhadracinta or Sucinta). The latter is with his wife, in the middle of watching women's games from the top of a storied house, when he sees the Buddha arrive. He addresses his wife with verses in praise of the Buddha's merits. The Buddha stops before the Kumāra's house. Exchange of *gāthā* referring in particular to the *bhūtakoṭi*. The Kumāra offers the Buddha a lotus. Śāriputra requests the Kumāra to expound his ideas on the *bhūtakoṭi*, etc. Pūrṇamaitrāyaṇīputra in turn addresses him with *gāthā*, to which he replies with further *gāthā*. These arouse the admiration of Pūrṇa. The Buddha approves of them by treating the Kumāra as a Bodhisattva and questions him in turn. The Kumāra replies by again returning to the *bhūtakoṭi*. Ānanda in turn expresses his admiration, in prose and in verse. The Kumāra replies with *gāthā*. The Buddha asks him if he is "fearless", etc. Long instruction by the Buddha in prose and verse: *śūnyatā* style, archaistic Chinese... The Kumāra obtains the *anutpattikadharmakṣānti*, leaps in the air for joy. The Buddha smiles and predicts to Ānanda that the Kumāra will become a Buddha with the name of *Wu-kou-kuang* (Vimalaprabha). Śāriputra asks the title of the Sūtra: it is *Ting-wang ching*. Explanation of this title and transmission (*parīndanā*) of the Sūtra.[2]

b. Ta ch'êng ting wang ching, Mahāyāna Mūrdhābhiṣiktarājasūtra (T 478), in one chüan, translated in Chin-ling, about 546, by Upaśūnya (or Ūrdhvaśūnya) of the Eastern Wei. This translation, also called *Wei-mo êrh ching*, Vimalakīrtiputrasūtra, would be the

[2] I reproduce here the summaries of the Mūrdhābhiṣiktarājasūtra and the Candrottaradārikāparipṛcchā which Professor P. Demiéville was kind enough to send me and for which I am extremely grateful.

second or third; the catalogues consider it quite close to Dharmarakṣa's version. See *Chung A*, T 2146, p. 118 *a* 4; *Li*, T 2034, p. 98 *c* 17; *Nei*, T 2149, p. 266 *a* 18; *T'u*, T 2151, p. 365 *b* 27; *Hsü kao sêng chuan*, T 2060, ch. 1, p. 430 *c* 21-23; *K'ai*, T 2154, p. 538 *a* 18.

In this translation, the Kumāra is named *Shan-ssŭ-wei* (Bhadracinta or Sucinta). It is not expressly said that he is Vimalakīrti's son; he is a Kumāra "from Vimalakīrti's neighbourhood". On the Buddha's chance arrival, he is not with his wife on top of the storied building, but with his nurse who is carrying him in her arms.

The Kumāra is playing with a lotus flower which he is holding. He addresses his nurse with *gāthā* requesting her to let him go down to the Buddha. Stupefaction of the nurse. Exchange of *gāthā* between the Buddha and the Kumāra (on *bhūtakoṭi*, etc.). He offers his lotus flower to the Buddha and invites him to expound on his Law, (free of pṛthagjana or śrāvaka). Śāriputra questions him on his Law, and the Kumāra replies with *gāthā*. Intervention by Pūrṇamaitrāyaṇīputra, etc. Admiration of Ānanda. The Buddha asks the Kumāra if he is fearless. What follows is similar to the T 477, but in a clearer style and more classical terminology. The Kumāra will become a Buddha with the name of *Ching-yüeh* (Vimalacandra). Title of Sūtra and *parīndanā*.

c. *Shan ssŭ t'ung tzŭ ching*, Sucintakumārasūtra (T 479), in two chüan, translated in Ta-hsing (near Ch'ang-an) by Jinagupta of the Sui. Begun the seventh month of the 11th year of the *k'ai-huang* period (July-August 591), the translation was finished two months later; the upāsaka Fei Chang-fang took it down with his brush, and the śramaṇa Yen-ts'ung wrote the preface. According to one catalogue, this would be the fourth translation. See *Li*, T 2034, p. 103 *c* 9; *Nei*, T 2149, p. 276 *a* 17; *T'u*, T 2151, p. 366 *a* 9-10; *K'ai*, T 2154, p. 548 *b* 24.

Here, the Kumāra is a member of the household or family of Vimalakīrti the Licchavi. Same setting as in T 478, with the nurse... The text follows closely that of T 478, but the style is even more classical.

3. Expanded version of the Vatsasūtra, the Kṣīraprabhabuddhasūtra (T 809, p. 754 *c* 23 - 755 *a* 20), translated by Dharmarakṣa, tells of a meeting between Vimalakīrti and Ānanda, probably borrowed from the Vkn (cf. III, § 42, note 77).

4. Candrottaradārikāparipṛcchā, quoted with this title by Śāntideva in his Śikṣāsamuccaya, p. 78, *19*. Jinagupta of the Sui translated it into Chinese with the title of Yüeh shang nü ching (T 480). According to the Li tai san pao chi (T 2034, ch. 12, p. 103 *c* 8), reproduced by the other catalogues, the translation was begun the fourth month of the 11th year of the *k'ai-huang* period (April-May 591) and completed

two months later; the upāsaka Liu-p'ing took it down with his brush and the śramaṇa Yen-ts'ung wrote the preface. According to the Tibetan version (OKC No. 858) executed at the beginning of the ninth century by Jinamitra and his team, the Sūtra had the title of Candrottaradārikāvyākaraṇa.

Candrottaradārikā is the daughter of Vimalakīrti and his wife Vimalā. Only just born, she is as tall as a child of eight. She is sought in marriage on every side. Her father announces that in seven days time she herself will choose her husband by ringing a bell at a crossroad. On the sixth day a lotus flower grows on her hand in which appears a *nirmāṇa* Buddha who exhorts her to promise herself to the Buddha. On the seventh day she goes to the Buddha by flying through the air so as to avoid the crowd of her suitors. On the way, she converses with Śāriputra. Having reached the Buddha, she debates with Kāśyapa, Ānanda, Mañjuśrī, etc. She transforms herself into a man so as to become a monk. At first sight, this text seems to have no doctrinal resemblance to the Vkn.

5. The Ta ch'êng pên shêng hsin ti kuan ching (T 159) is a late Sūtra which was translated in Ch'ang-an in the Li-ch'üan ssŭ by the Kaśmīrian Prājña, in the sixth year of the *chêng-yüan* period (790); the Emperor Tai-tsung wrote the preface (cf. Chêng yüan mu lu, T 2157, ch. 17, p. 891 *c* 2).

T 159, ch. 1, p. 291 *b* 18: The Bodhisattva Vimalakīrti is a member of the assembly of the Sūtra expounded in Rājagṛha on the Gṛdhrakūṭaparvata.

In the Gupta and Post-Gupta period Stotras circulated in praise of the eight Great Caityas. Of these we possess in Tibetan translation two *Aṣṭamahāsthānacaityastotra* (Bstod, I, Nos 24, 25) attributed to one Nāgārjuna, fictitious or late; we also have a *Pa ta ling t'a ming hao ching* (T 1685) translated by Fa-t'ien at the end of the tenth century; and finally we have an *Aṣṭamahāsthānacaityavandanastava* in a Tibetan translation (Bstod, I, No. 57) and a Chinese transliteration (T 1684) by Fa-t'ien [3]. According to the Chinese transliteration, this last work was by King Harṣa Śīlāditya; according to the Tibetan version, the author was King Harṣadeva of Kaśmir: these attributions are worthless.

The eight great caityas in question commemorate eight great miracles of the Buddha: 1. his birth in Kapilavastu, in the Lumbinī

[3] On the caityastotras, see S. LÉVI, *Une poésie inconnue du roi Harṣa Śīlāditya*, Actes du Xe Congrès international des Orientalistes, II, 1, 1897, p. 189-203 (article reprinted in the *Mémorial Sylvain Lévi*, Paris, 1937, p. 244-256); P.C. BAGCHI, *The Eight Great Caityas and their Cult*, IHQ, XVII, 1941, p. 223-235.

gardens, 2. his enlightenment at Gayā, 3. his first sermon in Vārāṇasī, 4. his victory over the heretics in Śrāvastī, 5. his descent from the Trāyastriṃśa heaven in Sāṃkāśya (near Kanyākubja), 6. his sermon on the schism in Rājagṛha, 7. his announcement of his death in Vaiśālī, 8. his entry into Nirvāṇa in Kuśinagara.

According to the T 159 with which we are concerned here, there was a great light in which there appeared "the eight inconceivable great precious stūpas of the Tathāgata". However, in enumerating them, the T 159 differs from the traditional list:

T 159, ch. 1, p. 294 *b* 1-4: 6. In Magadha, near Rājagṛha, on the Gṛdhrakūṭaparvata, there is the ratnastūpa where the Buddha expounded the Mahāyāna, namely the Mahāprajñā, the Saddharmapuṇḍarīka, the Ekayānacittabhūmisūtra (T 159), etc. — 7. In Vaiśālī, in the Āmrapālīvana, there is the ratnastūpa where the śreṣṭhin Vimala the Inconceivable feigned sickness.

The introduction of Vimalakīrti into the Buddha's feats shows how much prestige he enjoyed at the time.

T 159, ch. 4, p. 306 *b* 23 - *c* 12: The Buddha is very benevolent and very compassionate. One day in Vaiśālī, he expounded the most deep Law to Vimalakīrti: Vimalakīrti, he said, the pure mind is the root of good actions; the impure mind is the root of bad actions: *Cittasaṃkleśāt saṃkliśyante, cittavyavadānād viśudhyante* (cf. above, p. LXXIV). In my Law the mind is sovereign: all dharmas depend on the mind. You are now a *gṛhastha*, but you possess great qualities. You abound in jewels and necklaces; the men and women who surround you are at peace and joyful. You possess the *samyagdṛṣṭi*; you do not decry the *triratna*; animated by filial piety, you honour your parents. You have produced great *maitrī* and *karuṇā*, you give to orphans and you spare even the ants. *Kṣānti* is your clothing, *maitrī* and *karuṇā* are your abode. You revere virtuous people; your mind is free of pride; you have pity for all beings as if they were little children. You do not covet wealth; you always practise *muditā* and *upekṣā*; you revere the *triratna* without ever tiring. You sacrifice yourself for the Law, and that without regret. You are an *avadātavasana*, but, without leaving the world, you possess countless and infinite qualities. In times to come, after having fulfilled the ten thousand practices, you will go beyond the triple world and experience great *bodhi*. Skilled in the mind as you are, you are a true *śramaṇa*, a true *brāhmaṇa*, a true *bhikṣu*, a true *pravrajita*. A man such as you is what is called a "householder-monk" (*gṛhasthapravrajita*).

6. The Tathāgatācintyaviṣayasūtra, translated by Devaprajña in 691, by Śikṣānanda about 700, includes Vimalakīrti in its assembly of Bodhisattvas (cf. T 300, p. 905 *b* 18; T 301, p. 909 *a* 20).

7. Vimalakīrti also participates in the assembly of the Mañjuśrīmūlakalpa (T 1191, ch. 1, p. 838 *a* 13; ch. 5, p. 855 *a* 7), translated under the Sung, between 980 and 1000, by T'ien-hsi-tsai.

Indian records of Vimalakīrti are somewhat scanty. However, in the sixth century, quite a few legends circulated in China regarding his family, father, mother, wife, son. Chi-tsang (549-623) reports them in his commentaries of the Vkn (T 1780, 1781). To go into them here would be to go beyond our self-assigned compass.

IX

REFERENCES TO THE VKN IN INDIAN ŚĀSTRAS

Once again, we only draw attention to quotations of the Vkn in Indian Buddhist treatises, whether they have been preserved for us in the original or in Chinese translations.

1. Tsa p'i yü ching (T 205), translated by an unknown hand under the Late Han (A.D. 25-220).

Ch. 2, p. 509 *b* 8: Vimalakīrti has said: "This body is like a heap of foam. Purify it by washing it, and do violence to it so as to become patient" [1]. A free reference: cf. II, § 9; III, § 34; VI, § 1; X, § 9.

2. Mahāprajñāpāramitopadeśa (T 1509), translated by Kumārajīva between 402 and 404.

Ch. 9, p. 122 *a* 22 - *b* 14 = III, § 42-43.
Ch. 15, p. 168 *b* 14-15 = summary of Ch. VIII.
Ch. 17, p. 188 *a* 1-3 = III, § 3.
Ch. 28, p. 267 *c* 7-10 = summary of Ch. III.
Ch. 30, p. 278 *b* 14-16 = I, § 17-18.
Ch. 30, p. 284 *a* 1-3 – V, § 13.
Ch. 85, p. 657 *b* 7-8 = I, § 16.
Ch. 88, p. 682 *b* 4-9 = X, § 5; IX, § 11.
Ch. 92, p. 709 *a* 4-5 = I, § 13, *sub-fine*.
Ch. 95, p. 727 *a* 19-21 = general reference to Ch. VIII.
Ch. 98, p. 744 *b* 15 = VII, § 3, *sub fine*.

3. Maitreyaparipṛcchopadeśa (T 1525), commentary on the Maitreyaparipṛcchā of the Ratnakūṭa, translated between 508 and 534 by Bodhiruci of the Northern Wei:

Ch. 3, p. 245 *a* 10 = 1, § 14.

[1] This quotation, which appears at the end of the narration, is possibly an interpolation.

4. Ratnakūṭacaturdharmopadeśa (T 1526). Commentary by Vasubandhu on section 47 of the Ratnakūṭa. It was translated by Vimokṣasena of the Eastern Wei, in Yeh, in the monastery of Chin-hua, on the first day of the ninth month of the third year of the *hsing-ho* period (6 October 541). Cf. *K'ai*, T 2154, ch. 6, p. 543 *a* 24.

P. 277 *a* 8 - 277 *b* 15 = 1, § 14 *in fine* up to and including § 18.

5. Mahāyānāvatāraśāstra (T 1634) by Sāramati (in Chinese, Chien-i 堅意 or Chien-hui 堅慧[2]), translated into Chinese, between 437 and

[2] Chien-i, author of the Mahāyānāvatāraśāstra, composed, at the beginning of the 600 years after the Nirvāṇa, a commentary of the Saddharmapuṇḍarīkaśāstra by Nāgārjuna (cf. T 2068, ch. 1, p. 52 *c* 27-28); he is also attributed with an abridged commentary on the Daśabhūmikaśāstra by Vasubandhu (cf. T 2073, ch. 1, p. 156 *c* 12).

According to Chinese tradition (T 1838, ch. 1, p. 63 *c* 5-21), the bodhisattva Chien-hui 堅慧 whose name in Sanskrit is spelt *So-lo-mi-ti* 娑囉末底 (Sāramati) was a bodhisattva of superior standing. In the 700 years after the Buddha's Nirvāṇa, he was born in Central India into the kṣatriya caste ... He composed the Mahāyānottara Ratnagotraśāstra = Ratnagotravibhāga Mahāyānottaratantraśāstra (T 1611) and the [Mahāyāna] dharmadhātunirviśeṣaśāstra (T 1626 and 1627).

The Sanskrit original of the Ratnagotravibhāga Mahāyānottaratantraśāstra, discovered in Tibet by R. Sāṃkṛtyāyana, has been edited by E.H. JOHNSTON, Patna, 1950, and translated by J. TAKASAKI, *A Study on the Ratnagotravibhāga* (Serie Orientale Roma, XXXIII), Rome, 1966. The Tibetan version, which attributes the work to Maitreya-Asaṅga, and has the title of *Theg pa chen poḥi rgyud bla maḥi bstan bcos* (Mahāyānottaratantraśāstra) has been translated into English by E. OBERMILLER, *The Sublime Science ...*, Acta Orientalia, IX, 1931, p. 81-306. — This work has been the subject of many studies in Japanese: K. TSUKINOWA, *Kukyō-ichijō-hōshō-ron ni tsuite* (On the Uttaratantraśāstra), The Journal of the Nippon Research Association, Vol. 7, 1934; M. HATTORI, *Busshō-ron no ichikōsatsu* (A Study on the Fo sing louen), Bukkyō Shigaku, Vol. 4, No. 3/4, 1950; H. UI, *Hōshō-ron Kenkyū* (A Study on RGV), Tōkyō, 1959; J. TAKASAKI, *Structure of the Anuttarāśrayasūtra* (Wu-shang-i-ching), Journal of Indian and Buddhist Studies, Vol. VIII, No. 2, 1960.

In this work, Sāramati professes a Buddhism heavily tinged with monism where the immaculate and luminous mind (*amalaṃ prabhāsvaraṃ cittam*) is raised to the level of a supreme entity. There can be found in E. FRAUWALLNER, *Die Philosophie des Buddhismus*, 1956, p. 255-264, an excellent account of this system.

As for the Dharmadhātunirviśeṣaśāstra, this is a short treatise in 24 verses which was commented upon and translated by Devaprajña in 691. In the version of the Ch'i-tan (T 1626) the commentary is inserted between groups of verses; in that of the Sung (T 1627), the commentary follows the verses. Its attribution to Chien-hui (Sāramati) is firmly established. Fa-tsang (643-712) compiled a sub-commentary of this work (T 1838).

The majority of modern exegetists distinguish two Sāramatis: the first being the author of the Ratnagotravibhāga and the Dharmadhātunirviśeṣa; the second being the author of the Mahāyānāvatāra. This was already the opinion of N. PÉRI in his

439, by Shih Tao-t'ai of the Liang (cf. *Li*, T 2034, ch. 9, p. 85 *a* 23; *K'ai*, T 2154, ch. 4, p. 522 *a* 11):

Ch. 2, p. 45 *b* 5-10 = abbreviated quotation of Ch. V, § 20.

6. The Vkn appears in the long list of the Sūtras of the two Vehicles drawn up by the Nandimitrāvadāna (T 2030, p. 14 *a* 26), a work translated by Hsüan-tsang in 654.

7. The Vijñaptimātratāsiddhi (T 1585), established and translated by Hsüan-tsang in 659-660, contains several implicit references to the Vkn. Cf. the tr. by L. DE LA VALLÉE POUSSIN, p. 110, 214, 421, 425, 427, 531, 697.

8. In his Madhyamakavṛtti (p. 333, *6-8*), a commentary on the Kārikās by Nāgārjuna, Candrakīrti (seventh century) has a vague reference to Ch. IX of the Vkn. This reference is missing in the Tibetan version.

9. Śikṣāsamuccaya of Śāntideva (seventh century). The Sanskrit original has been edited by C. BENDALL (abridged form: B). A Chinese translation (abridged form: C), T 1636, was carried out in Pien-liang, in the first half of the eleventh century, by Dharmarakṣa of the Sung.

B. p. 6,*10-11* = C. p. 76 *b* 14-16 = VII, § 3.

B. p. 145,*11-15* = C. p. 103 *b* 19-24 = VI, § 4.

B. p. 153,*20-22* = C. p. 105 *b* 23-24: Missing in our versions of the Vkn.

B. p. 264,*6-9* = C. p. 126 *b* 15-19 = VI, § 6.

article: *A propos de la date de Vasubandhu*, BEFEO, 1911, p. 10-17 of the off-print; it is also the opinion of Dr H. UI, *Indo-tetsugaku Kenkyū* (Studies in Indian Philosophy), Vol. 5, Tokyo 1929, p. 138; *Hōshō-ron Kenkyū* (A Study on RGV), Tokyo, 1959.

However, Professor M. Hattori, to whom I owe this information, considers Sāramati I and Sāramati II to be one and the same person and who would have lived between Nāgārjuna and Asaṅga-Vasubandhu. The arguments he put forward to me in his letter of 27 March 1962 are most impressive and I sincerely hope that he will make them public one day.

Anyway, Sāramati antedates Sthiramati, in Chinese An-hui 安慧 or Hsi-ch'ih-lo-mo-ti 悉恥羅末底 A native of Lāṭa in Southern India (Central or Southern Gujarat), a pupil of Guṇamati, bestowed with a monastery by the Maitraka Guhasena (556-567), Sthiramati was, in the sixth century, one of the ten great Indian commentators of the Triṃśikā (cf. K'uei-chi, in T 1830, ch. 1, p. 231 *c* 19-23). He was director of the Vijñānavādin school of Valabhī whose rival was that of Nālandā represented by Dharmapāla. It seems that Sthiramati's ideas were spread in China by Paramārtha (500-569).

B. p. 269,*11-12* (C. missing) = VI, § 13.
B. p. 269,*13*-270,*3* (C. missing) = IX, § 13.
B. p. 270,*4-7* (C. missing) = X, § 6.
B. p. 273,*6-7* (C. missing) = IV, § 20.
B. p. 324,*11*-327,*4* = C. p. 136 *c* 21-137 *b* 10[3] = VII, § 6, st. 16, 18-41.

10. Sūtrasamuccaya (T 1635) of Dharmakīrti (alias Śāntideva) translated in the first half of the eleventh century by Dharmarakṣa of the Sung, assisted by Wei-ching. According to the Tibetan translation (CORDIER, III, p. 323), this is a work by Nāgārjuna[4].
Ch. 8, p. 69 *c* 10-14 = IV, § 14.
Ch. 8, p. 69 *c* 14-17 = VIII, § 17.
Ch. 9, p. 72 *c* 16-25 = V, § 20.

11. During the Council of Lhasa (792-794), the Vkn was frequently invoked as a scriptural authority.
a. In the Chinese records (tr. P. DEMIÉVILLE, *Le Concile de Lhasa*, Paris, 1952), defended by Mahāyāna (Hva-śaṅ; Ho-shang), we find the following quotations: p. 80 = III, § 52; p. 113-114 = VIII, § 33; p. 126 = VIII, § 6; p. 152 = I, § 10, stanza 12.
b. In the Bhāvanākramas of Kamalaśīla, protagonist of the Indian side:
Bhāvanākrama I, ed. G. TUCCI, *Minor Buddhist Texts*, II, Rome, 1958, p. 194,*8-11* = IV, § 16.
Bhāvanākrama III, ed. G. TUCCI, *Minor Buddhist Texts*, III, Rome, 1971, p. 13,*7-9* = II, § 12 *in fine*; p. 22,*10-14* = IV, § 16.

[3] In his translation of the stanzas, Dharmarakṣa of the Sung reproduces textually the version by Kumārajīva (T 475).

[4] In his Bodhicaryāvatāra, V, verses 105-106, Śāntideva recommends the reading of the Śikṣāsamuccaya and the Sūtrasamuccaya, but we are none too sure if he attributes the latter work to himself or if he considers it to be a work by Nāgārjuna. Hence the hesitation of modern critics: C. BENDALL, *Śikṣāsamuccaya*, Introduction, p. IV; L. DE LA VALLÉE POUSSIN, *Introduction à la pratique des futurs Bouddhas*, Paris, 1907, p. 48, note 1; A BANERJEE, *Sūtrasamuccaya*, IHQ, XVII, 1941, p. 121-126. However the problem has now been clarified by Professor J. FILLIOZAT who, in his article *Śikṣāsamuccaya et Sūtrasamuccaya* (JA, 1964, p. 473-478), reaches the following conclusion: "Śāntideva did not compose a *Sūtrasamuccaya* independently of his *Śikṣāsamuccaya* where, furthermore, he illustrates his exposition with many quotations of extracts from *Sūtras*. This is why no trace can be found of such a work. On the contrary, he attributes to Nāgārjuna a *Sūtrasamuccaya* and which indeed exists in a Tibetan version as a work by Nāgārjuna".

The quotations given here range over six centuries and have been taken from nearly all the chapters of the Vkn, which only proves the remarkable stability of the text. Moreover, the writers who quote it are Mādhyamikas for the most part. As we said earlier, the Vkn is pure Madhyamaka and was considered as such by Indian scholars.

NOTICE CONCERNING THE TRANSLATION

The present translation is based on the Tibetan version of the Kanjur (Ōtani Kanjur Catalogue, No. 843). It is printed in *large format*.

Printed in *small format* are the variations and additions found in the Chinese version by Hsüan-tsang (Taishō, No. 476): the greatest variations appear in the *right-hand column*; additions of lesser importance are inserted in the text, but always in *small format*.

Interesting points brought out by the Chinese translations by Chih Ch'ien (Taishō, No. 474) and especially by Kumārajīva (Taishō, No. 475) are indicated in the notes.

The passages in *underlined italics* are fragments of the original Sanskrit quoted in the Śikṣāsamuccaya of Śāntideva. Other passages in *italics* are reconstructions.

I am responsible for the division into paragraphs and the sub-titles in brackets.

THE TEACHING OF VIMALAKĪRTI

CHAPTER ONE

THE PURIFICATION OF THE BUDDHA-FIELDS

Homage to all the Buddhas, Bodhisattvas, Āryaśrāvakas and Pratyekabuddhas, past, present and to come!

[*Introduction*]

1. Thus have I heard. At one time the Blessed One was in the town of Vaiśālī, in the Āmrapālī grove[1], with a large troop of monks, eight thousand monks (*Evaṃ mayā śrutam ekasmin samaye Bhagavān Vaiśālīnagare viharati smāmrapālīvane mahatā bhikṣusaṃghena sārdham aṣṭābhir bhikṣusahasraiḥ*).

2. All these monks were holy men (*arhat*), free from impurities (*kṣīṇāsrava*), without passions (*niḥkleśa*), come to great strength (*vaśībhūta*), their minds delivered (*suvimuktacitta*) and their wisdom equally delivered (*suvimuktaprajñā*); of noble birth (*ājāneya*) and resembling great elephants (*mahānāga*); they had fulfilled their duty (*kṛtakṛtya*), done what they had to do (*kṛtakaraṇīya*), laid down their burden (*apahṛtabhāra*), achieved their aim (*anuprāptasva-*

[1] Vaiśālī, capital of the Licchavis, now Basarh in the district of Muzaffarpur, in Tirhut. It was an opulent and prosperous town at the time of the Buddha (Vinaya, I, p. 268; Lalitavistara, p. 21). A mango grove, situated three leagues to the south of the town (Fa hsien chuan, T 2085, p. 861 *c* 14; Hsi yü chi, T 2087, ch. 7, p. 908 *c* 4) frequently served as a residence for the Buddha. There he expounded important sermons (e.g. Saṃyutta, V, p. 141 sq.). During the Buddha's final visit to Vaiśālī, this grove was given to him by the courtesan Āmrapālī (Vinaya, I, p. 231-233; Vin. of the Mahīśāsakas, T 1421, ch. 20, p. 135 *c*; Vin. of the Dharmaguptakas, T 1428, ch. 40, p. 856 *a*): it took on the name of Āmrapālīvana, Ambapālivana in Pāli.

kārtha), completely destroyed the shackles of existence (*parikṣīṇa-bhavasaṃyojana*); their minds were delivered by perfect knowledge (*samyagājñāsuvimuktacitta*); they had obtained the supreme perfection of being complete masters of their thoughts (*sarvacetovaśitāpa-ramapāramitāprāpta*)[2].

3. Also to be found there were thirty-two thousand Bodhisattvas, Bodhisattvas who are great beings (*mahāsattva*); universally known (*abhijñānābhijñāta*)[3]; devoted to the exercise of the great super-knowledges (*mahābhijñāparikarmaniryāta*); upheld by the supernatural action of the Buddhas (*buddhādhiṣṭhānādhiṣṭhita*); guardians of the town of the Law (*dharmanagarapālaka*); roaring the lion's roar (*mahāsiṃhanā-danādin*) in response to the cry echoing in the ten regions (*daśadikṣu prakīrtitanādaḥ*)[4]; having become, without being asked (*anadhyeṣita*) the good friends (*kalyāṇamitra*) of all beings; refraining from interrupting the lineage of the triple jewel (*triratnagotra*); vanquishers of Māra and adversaries (*nihatamārapratyarthika*); victoriously resisting all opponents (*sarvaparapravādyanabhibhūta*); free from any obstacle and the invasion of the passions (*vigatasarvāvaraṇaparyutthāna*); gifted with awareness, intelligence, knowledge, concentration, magical formulae and eloquence (*smṛtimatyadhigamasamādhidhāraṇīpratibhānasaṃpanna*); based on the liberations without obstacle (*anāvaraṇavimokṣa*); gifted with indestructible eloquence (*anācchedyapratibhāna*)[5], complying with the perfections of giving, morality, patience, vigour, concentration, wisdom, skillful means, vows, power and knowledge (*dānaśīlakṣāntivīryadhyānaprajño-pāyakauśalyapraṇidhānabalajñānapāramitāniryāta*)[6]; convinced of the

[2] List of the Śrāvakaguṇas appearing at the start of the majority of Mahāyānasūtras: Sukhāvatīvyūha, p. 4,*14*; Pañcaviṃśati, p. 4,*2*; Aṣṭasāh., p. 8,*18*; Śatasāh., p. 3,*1*; Sad. puṇḍarīka, p. 1,*6*; Mahāvyutpatti, No. 1075 sq. It is commented on at length in the Upadeśa (NĀGĀRJUNA, *Traité*, p. 203-219) and the Āloka, p. 9-11.

[3] The epithet *abhijñānābhijñāta* is usually applied to Śrāvakas and not to Bodhisattvas: cf. Sad. puṇḍarīka, p. 1,*9*.

[4] The instructing by the Buddha is often described as *sīhanāda* "lion's roar": Aṅguttara, III, p. 122,*6*; V, p. 33,*6*; *bhagavā ... bhikkhūnaṃ dhammaṃ deseti sīho va nadatī vane* (Suttanipāta, v. 1015).

[5] *Anācchedyapratibhāna*: cf. Mahāvyutpatti, No. 851.

[6] List of the ten *pāramitā*: Saṃgraha, p. 207-209. It is not quoted in full in all the versions.

ungraspability of all dharmas (*anupalabdhadharmakṣāntipratilabdha*); turning the irreversible wheel of the Law (*avaivartikadharmacakrapravartaka*); marked with the seal of signlessness (*ānimittamudrāmudrita*); skilled in knowing the faculties of all beings (*sarvasattvendriyajñānakuśala*); braving all the assemblies (*sarvaparṣadanabhibhūta*) and appearing there without fear (*nirbhayavikrāmin*); accumulating great stores of merit and knowledge (*mahāpuṇyajñānasaṃbhāra*); their bodies adorned with all the primary and secondary marks (*sarvalakṣaṇānuvyañjanālaṃkṛtakāya*)[7]; beautiful (*abhirūpa*) but without adornments (*ābharaṇa*); raised on high in glory and renown (*yaśaḥkīrtyabhyudgata*) like the highest peak of Sumeru; filled with high resolve, as firm as a diamond (*vajravad dṛḍhādhyāśaya*); having in the Buddha, the Law and the Community the faith of understanding (*buddhe dharme saṃghe 'vetyaprasādena samanvāgataḥ*)[8]; emitting the ray of the jewel of the Law (*dharmaratnaraśmipramokṣaka*) and causing to rain down a shower of ambrosia (*amṛtavarṣābhivarṣaka*); gifted with excellent and pure clarity of speech (*varaviśuddhasvaranirghoṣopeta*); penetrating the dependent co-production in its deep meaning (*gambhīrārthapratītyasamutpāda*)[9]; having interrupted the course of the pervasion left by false views concerning the finite and the infinite (*antānantadṛṣṭivāsanābhisaṃdhisamucchedaka*); fearlessly giving the lion's roar (*viśāradaḥ siṃhanādanādin*); causing the thunder of the great Law to reverberate (*mahādharmameghasvaranādin*); absolutely unequalled (*asamasama*) and immeasurable (*pramāṇaviṣayasamatikrānta*); great leaders of caravans (*sārthavāha*) obtaining the jewels of the Law (*dharmaratna*), that is, stores of merit and knowledge (*puṇyajñānasaṃbhāra*); versed in the principle of the Law which is correct, calm, subtle, sweet, difficult to see and difficult to know (*ṛjukaśantasukṣmamṛdudurdṛśadurvigāhyadharmanayakuśala*); penetrating the comings and goings (*āgamanirgama*) of beings and their intentions (*āśaya*); anointed with the unction of the knowledge of the unequalled Buddhas (*asamasamabuddhajñānābhiṣekābhiṣikta*); approaching through their high resolve

[7] The 32 *lakṣaṇa* and the 80 *anuvyañjana* are explained in the Upadeśa (NĀGĀRJUNA, *Traité*, p. 271-281) and the Sanskrit Mahāvadāna, p. 101-113, where other references are to be found.

[8] *Avetyaprasāda, aveccappasāda* in Pāli: Dīgha, II, p. 93; Majjhima, I, p. 37; Saṃyutta, II, p. 69; Aṅguttara, II, p. 56; Aṣṭasah., p. 213,*13*; Bodh. bhūmi, p. 161,*2*; 327,*2*; Mahāvyutpatti, No. 6823.

[9] All dharmas being non-arisen (*anutpanna*) and non-extinguished (*aniruddha*), the Pratītyasamutpāda in its deepest meaning is a non-production: see Ch. XII, §12.

(*adhyāśaya*), the ten powers (*bala*), the convictions (*vaiśāradya*) and the exclusive attributes of the Buddhas (*āveṇikabuddhadharma*); crossing the fearful ditch (*bhairavaparikhā*) of bad destinies (*apāyadurgativinipāta*)[10]; rejecting the diamond weapon of the dependent co-production (*pratītyasamutpāda*) and voluntarily (*saṃcintya*) assuming rebirth (*janman*) in the paths of existence (*bhavagati*); great healing kings (*mahābhaiṣajyarāja*), skilled in the treatment of beings to be disciplined (*vaineyasattva*), knowledgeable of all the diseases of the passions (*kleśavyādhi*) which affect beings, and correctly (*yathāyogam*) administering the medicine of the Law (*dharmabhaiṣajya*); having at their disposal an immense mine of virtues (*apramāṇaguṇākara*) and adorning, with the unfolding of these virtues (*guṇavyūha*), innumerable Buddha-fields (*buddhakṣetra*); propitious to see and hear and unstoppable in their tasks (*amoghaparākrama*). Even if one were to devote innumerable hundreds of thousands of *koṭinayuta* of kalpas in praising their virtues (*guṇa*), one could not exhaust the flood of their virtues (*guṇaugha*)[11].

4. There were particularly (*tad yathā*) the Bodhisattvas:

[Tibetan list]: 1. Samadarśana, 2. Asamadarśana, 3. Samādhivikurvitarāja, 4. Dharmeśvara, 5. Dharmaketu[12], 6. Prabhāketu[13], 7. Prabhāvyūha, 8. Ratnavyūha[14], 9. Mahāvyūha[15], 10. Pratibhānakūṭa[16], 11. Ratnakūṭa[17], 12. Ratnapāṇi[18], 13. Ratnamudrāhasta[19], 14. Nityapralambahasta, 15. Nityotkṣiptahasta[20], 16. Nityatapta, 17. Nityamuditendriya, 18. Prāmodyarāja, 19. Devarāja, 20. Praṇidhānapraveśaprāpta, 21. Prasiddhapratisaṃvitprāpta, 22. Gaganagañja[21], 23. Ratnolkāpa-

[10] Canonical expression: *apāyaṃ duggatiṃ vinipātaṃ nirayaṃ upapannā*; cf. WOODWARD, *Concordance*, p. 187, s.v. *apāya*.

[11] Cf. Sad. puṇḍarīka, p. 121,*3*: *ete ca guṇā ataś cānye 'prameyā asaṃkhyeyā yeṣāṃ na sukaraḥ paryanto 'dhigantum aparimitān api kalpān bhāṣamāṇaiḥ*.

[12] Dharmaketu: Sukhāvatīvyūha, p. 14,*14*; Gaṇḍavyūha, p. 3,*18*.

[13] Prabhāketu: Gaṇḍavyūha, p. 3,*19*.

[14] Ratnavyūha: Lalitavistara, p. 60,*18*; 61,*12*; 63,*2*; 73,*3*; also I, §17 below.

[15] Mahāvyūha: Śatasāh., p. 7,*7*.

[16] Pratibhānakūṭa: Mahāvyutpatti, No. 703.

[17] Ratnakūṭa: Mahāvyutpatti, No. 659.

[18] Ratnapāṇi: Sad. puṇḍarīka, p. 3,*5*; Kāraṇḍavyūha, p. 1,*12*; 17,*1*; Mañjuśrīmūlakalpa, p. 425,*19*; Mahāvyutpatti, No. 655.

[19] Ratnamudrāhasta: Śatasāh., p. 7,*5*; Mahāvyutpatti, No. 656; ZÜRCHER, *Conquest of China*, p. 392, n. 89.

[20] Nityotkṣiptahasta: Śatasāh., p. 7,*6*.

[21] Gaganagañja: Lalitavistara, p. 295,*10*; Kāraṇḍavyūha, p. 38,*13*; 39,*8*; 49,*17*; Śikṣāsamuccaya, p. 127,*1*; Mañjuśrīmūlakalpa, p. 40,*13*; 68,*21*; Sādhanamālā, p. 49,*16*; Dharmasaṃgraha, §12; Mahāvyutpatti, No. 700.

rigṛhīta, 24. Ratnaśūra[22], 25. Ratnapriya, 26. Ratnaśrī[23], 27. Indrajāla[24], 28. Jālinīprabha[25], 29. Nirālambanadhyāna, 30. Prajñākūṭa[26], 31. Ratnadatta, 32. Mārapramardaka, 33. Vidyuddeva, 34. Vikurvaṇarāja[27], 35. Kūṭanimittasamatikrānta, 36. Siṃhanādanādin, 37. Giryagrapramardirāja, 38. Gandhahastin[28], 39. Gandhakuñjaranāga, 40. Nityodyukta[29], 41. Anīkṣiptadhura[30], 42. Pramati, 43. Sujāta, 44. Padmaśrīgarbha[31], 45. Padmavyūha[32], 46. Avalokiteśvara, 47. Mahāsthāmaprāpta[33], 48. Brahmajāla, 49. Ratnadaṇḍin(?), 50. Mārakarmavijetā, 51. Kṣetrasamalaṃkāra, 52. Maṇiratnacchattra, 53. Suvarṇacūḍa, 54. Maṇicūḍa, 55. Maitreya, 56. Mañjuśrī kumārabhūta.

[H's Chinese list]: 1. Samadarśana, 2. Asamadarśana, 3. Asamasamadarśana, 4. Samādhivikurvitarāja, 5. Dharmeśvara, 6. Dharmaketu, 7. Prabhāketu, 8. Prabhāvyūha, 9. Mahāvyūha, 10. Ratnakūṭa, 11. Pratibhānakūṭa, 12. Ratnapāṇi, 13. Ratnamudrāhasta, 14. Nityotkṣiptahasta, 15. Nityapralambahasta, 16. Nityodgrīva, 17. Nityapramuditendriya, 18. Nityapramuditarāja, 19. Akuṭilapratisaṃvid, 20. Gaganagañja, 21. Ratnolkāparigṛhīta, 22. Ratnaśrī, 23. Ratnadatta, 24. Indrajāla, 25. Jālinīprabha, 26. Anāvaraṇadhyāna, 27. Prajñākūṭa, 28. Devarāja, 29. Mārapramardaka, 30. Vidyuddeva, 31. Vikurvaṇarāja, 32. Kūṭanimittasamalaṃkāra, 33. Siṃhanādanādin, 34. Meghasvara, 35. Giryagrapramardirāja, 36. Gandhahastin, 37. Mahāgandhahastin, 38. Nityodyukta, 39. Anikṣiptadhura, 40. Pramati, 41. Sujāta, 42. Padmaśrīgarbha, 43. Samādhirāja, 44. Padmavyūha, 45. Avalokiteśvara, 46. Mahāsthāmaprāpta, 47. Brahmajāla, 48. Ratnadaṇḍin, 49. Ajita[34], 50. Māravijetā, 51. Kṣetrasamalaṃkāra, 52. Suvarṇacūḍa, 53. Maṇicūḍa, 54. Maitreya, 55. Mañjuśrī, 56. Maṇiratnacchattra.

[22] Ratnaśūra: Rin chen dpaḥ in N and FP 613; Rin chen dpal in P.

[23] Ratnaśrī: Sukhāvatīvyūha, p. 14,*15*; Gaṇḍavyūha, p. 4,*4*.

[24] Indrajāla: Lalitavistara, p. 291,*18*.

[25] Jālinīprabha: Mahāvyutpatti, No. 705.

[26] Prajñākūṭa: Sad. puṇḍarīka, p. 260,*14*.

[27] Vikurvaṇarāja: Mahāvyutpatti, No. 1409; Vikurvaṇarājabodhisattvasūtra, T 421; OKC 834.

[28] Gandhahastin: Aṣṭasāh., p. 890,*24*; Sukhāvatīvyūha, p. 194,*11*; Samādhirāja, I, p. 194,*1*; Mahāvyutpatti, No. 704.

[29] Nityodyukta: Sad. puṇḍarīka, p. 3,*4*.

[30] Anikṣiptadhura: Sad. puṇḍarīka, p. 3,*5*; Kāraṇḍavyūha, p. 1,*11*; Mahāvyutpatti, No. 719.

[31] Padmaśrīgarbha: Gaṇḍavyūha, p. 2,*26*; Daśabhūmika, p. 2,*6*.

[32] Padmavyūha: Gaṇḍavyūha, p. 66,*17*, Mahāvyutpatti, No. 753.

[33] Mahāsthāmaprāpta: Sukhāvatīvyūha, p. 114,*8*; Kāraṇḍavyūha, p. 1,*13*; Sad. puṇḍarīka, p. 3,*4*; 375.*1*; Samādhirāja, p. 194,*6*; Sādhanamālā, p. 71,*4*.

[34] Ajita, epithet of Maitreya (cf. LAMOTTE, *Histoire*, p. 782).

5. Ten thousand Brahmās, Brahmā Śikhin[35] at their head, come from the Aśoka universe of four continents (*Aśoko nāma caturdvīpako lokadhātuḥ*) to see, revere, serve the Blessed One and hear the Law from his lips (*bhagavato darśanāya vandanāya paryupāsanāya dharmaśravaṇāya ca*)[36], were present in this assembly (*tasyāṃ parṣadi saṃnipatitā abhūvan saṃniṣaṇṇāḥ*) — Twelve thousand Śakras from various universes of four continents (*caturmahādvīpaka*) were also present in this assembly. — Equally, other very powerful divine beings (*maheśākhyamaheśākhya*), Brahmās, Śakras, Lokapālas, Devas, Nāgas, Yakṣas, Gandharvas, Asuras, Garuḍas, Kiṃnaras, and Mahoragas were present in this assembly. — Finally, the fourfold community (*catuṣpariṣad*), monks, nuns, laymen and laywomen (*bhikṣubhikṣuṇyupāsakopāsikā*), were there also.

6. Then the Blessed One, seated on a majestic throne, surrounded and revered by several hundreds of thousands of those present, expounded the Law (*atha khalu bhagavāñ śrīgarbhe siṃhāsane niṣaṇṇo 'nekaśatasahasrayā parṣadā parivṛtaḥ puraskṛto dharmaṃ deśayati sma*). Dominating all the assemblies, like Sumeru the king of the mountains rising from the oceans, the Blessed One was shining, gleaming and resplendent, seated as he was on his majestic throne (*sumerur iva parvatarājaḥ samudrābhyudgato bhagavān sarvāḥ parṣado 'bhibhūya bhāsate tapati virocate sma śrīgarbhe siṃhāsane niṣaṇṇaḥ*)[37].

[*Arrival of Ratnākara and the 500 Licchavis*]

7. Then the Licchavi Bodhisattva Ratnākara[38] and five hundred

[35] Mahābrahmā, king of the *rūpadhātu*, more usually known by the name of Brahmā Sahāpati (Sahampati in Pāli). The epithet of *śikhin* (Lalitavistara, p. 393,*20*; 397,*12*; Sad. puṇḍarīka, p. 4,*9*; 175,*1*), translated in Chinese sometimes by "topknot" and sometimes by "fire", is due to the fact that Brahmā is at the summit (topknot) of the cosmic fire which stops after having consumed his palace (T 1723, ch. 2, p. 675 *c* 16) and because he breaks up the passion of the *kāmadhātu* by means of the trance of the fire's brilliance (T 1718, ch. 1, p. 11 *b*).

[36] *Bhagavato darśanāya*, etc., is a stock phrase: Sad. puṇḍarīka, p. 367,*5*; 425,*2*; 427,*7*; 458,*10*; 463,*3*.

[37] Cf. Sukhāvatīvyūha, p. 128,*9*: *adrākṣus tathāgatam arhantaṃ samyaksaṃbuddhaṃ sumerum iva parvatarājaṃ sarvakṣetrābhyudgataṃ sarvā diśo 'bhibhūya bhāsamānaṃ tapantaṃ virocamānaṃ vibhrājamānam.*

The formula *bhāsate tapati virocate* (*bhāsati tapati virocati* in Pāli) is common: Majjhima, II, p. 33,*27*; III, p. 102,*4*; Pañcaviṃśati, p. 10,*10*; Mahāvyutpatti, No. 6289-91.

[38] The Bodhisattva Ratnākara "Mine of virtues" appears in the *nidāna* of several Mahāyānasūtras: Pañcaviṃśati, p. 5,*6*; Śatasāh., p. 6,*5*; Sad. puṇḍarīka, p. 3,*11*. A great Bodhisattva of the tenth stage, he was a Licchavi, a guildsman's son

young Licchavis (*licchavikumāra*), each holding a parasol (*chattra*) formed of seven jewels (*saptaratnamaya*), left the town of Vaiśālī and went to the Āmrapālī grove, approaching the Blessed One (*yenāmrapālīvanaṃ yena ca bhagavāṃs tenopasaṃkrāntāḥ*); having reached him (*upasaṃkramya*), after having saluted the feet of the Blessed One with their heads (*bhagavataḥ pādau śirobhir vanditvā*) and after having circled round him seven times (*saptakṛtvaḥ pradakṣiṇīkṛtya*), they each offered him their parasols and, having made this offering, stood to one side (*niryātyakānte sthitā abhūvan*).

8. As soon as these precious parasols had been set down suddenly by the power of the Buddha, they joined together into one single precious parasol (*samanantarasamarpitāni tāni ratnacchattrāṇi sahasā buddhānubhāvenaikaṃ ratnacchattram abhūvan*)[39], and that one single precious parasol covered (*ācchādayati sma*) all that trichiliomegachiliocosm (*trisāhasramahāsāhasralokadhātu*)[40]. The surface (*parimaṇḍala*) of the trichiliomegachiliocosm appeared on the inside itself of that great precious parasol. Thus there could be seen on the inside of that great precious parasol all that the trichiliomegachiliocosm contained: Sumeru the king of mountains (*parvatarāja*), Himadri, Mucilinda, Mahāmucilinda, Gandhamādana, Ratnaparvata, Kālaparvata, Cakravāḍa and Mahācakravāḍa[41]; the great oceans (*mahāsamudra*), water-

(*śreṣṭhiputra*) and native of Vaiśālī (Bhadrapālasūtra, T 418, ch. 1, p. 903 *a* 7-8; Upadeśa, T 1509, ch. 7, p. 111 *a* 6; Hsi yü chi, T 2087, ch. 7, p. 908 *b* 7).

He is part of the group of eight Bodhisattvas mentioned in the Aṣṭabuddhaka, T 427, p. 73 *a* 17, and the sixteen Satpuruṣas "Worthy men", beginning with Bhadrapāla, and recorded, with certain variations, in several Mahāyānasūtras: Sad. puṇḍarīka, p. 3,*10*-4,*2*; Sukhāvatīvyūha, T 360, ch. 1, p. 265 *c* 17-21; Viśeṣacintābrahmaparipṛcchā, T 585, ch. 1, p. 1 *a* 13-16; T 586, ch. 1, p. 33 *b* 9-13; T 587, ch. 1, p. 62 *b* 12-17; Ratnakūṭa, T 310, ch. 17, p. 91 *c* 14-15; ch. 111, p. 623 *b* 13-14; Mañjuśrīparinirvāṇa, T 463, p. 480 *b* 6; Upadeśa, T 1509, ch. 7, p. 111 *a* 4, etc.

[39] By virtue of his *pariṇāmikī ṛddhi* (cf. Bodh. bhūmi, p. 58-64; Saṃgraha, p. 221-222), the Buddha, with a single touch of his thumb or by means of his *adhimuktibala*, can concentrate into one objects of the same type which are offered to him, bowls, flowers, parasols, etc. One of his first miracles was to unite into one the four bowls which the king of the gods offered to him:

Mahāvastu, III, p. 304,*16*: *bhagavatā sarveṣāṃ caturṇāṃ lokapālānāṃ catvāri pātrāṇi pratigṛhṇitvā aṃguṣṭhena ākrāntā ekapātro ca adhiṣṭhito.*

Catuṣpariṣad, p. 88: *atha bhagavāṃś caturṇāṃ mahārājñāṃ pātrāṇi pratigṛhyaikaṃ pātram adhimuktavān*

Lalitavistara, p. 385,*4*: *pratigṛhya caikaṃ pātram adhitiṣṭhati sma, adhimuktibalena.*

[40] Regarding this cosmology, see Appendix, Note I: The *Buddhakṣetra*.

[41] Series of mountains which can be found, with some variations, in other Sūtras:

courses (*saras*), lakes (*taḍāga*), ponds (*puṣkariṇī*), rivers (*nadī*), streams (*kunadī*) and springs (*utsa*)[42]; then, in infinite quantities, the suns (*sūrya*), moons (*candra*) and stars (*tārakā*), the dwellings (*bhavana*) of the Devas, Nāgas, Yakṣas, Gandharvas, Asuras, Garuḍas, Kiṃnaras, Mahoragas, as well as the dwellings of the Caturmahārājas; finally, the villages (*grāma*), towns (*nagara*), boroughs (*nigama*), provinces (*janapada*), kingdoms (*rāṣṭra*), capitals (*rājadhānī*) and all the surrounding territories (*maṇḍala*)[43]. And the instruction in the Law expounded in the world of ten regions by the Blessed Lord Buddhas could be heard in its entirety (*yaṃ ca daśadigloke te buddhā bhagavanto dharmaṃ deśayanti sa ca sarvo nikhilena śrūyate sma*)[44], as if their voices came from that one single great precious parasol.

9. Then the whole assembly, having seen this great wonder accomplished by the Blessed One, was astonished; satisfied, delighted, transported, joyful, filled with happiness and pleasure, all paid homage to the Tathāgata, and stood to one side, watching him fixedly (*atha khalu sarvāvatī sā parṣad bhagavato 'ntikād idaṃ evaṃrūpaṃ mahāprātihāryaṃ dṛṣṭvāścaryaprāptābhūt*[45]. *tuṣṭodagrāttamanāḥ pramuditā prīti-*

Sukhāvatīvyūha, p. 128,*2*: Kālaparvata, Ratnaparvata, Meru, Mahāmeru, Mucilinda, Mahāmucilinda, Cakravāḍa, Mahācakravāḍa.

Sad. puṇḍarīka, p. 244,*10*; 246,*3*: Kālaparvata, Mucilinda, Mahāmucilinda, Cakravāḍa, Mahācakravāḍa, Sumeru.

Kāraṇḍavyūha, p. 91,*12*: Cakravāḍa, Mahācakravāḍa, Mucilinda, Mahāmucilinda, Kāla, Mahākāla.

Samādhirāja, II, p. 276,*13*: Cakravāḍa, Meru, Sumeru, Mucilinda, Mahāmucilinda, Vindhya, Gṛdhrakūṭa, Himavat.

These disordered lists do not conform with the traditional data of Buddhist cosmology (Kośa, III, p. 141; Atthasālinī, p. 297; Jātaka, VI, p. 125) which places nine great mountains on the golden land: in the centre, Meru; concentrically, seven mountains; outside the Nimindhara, the four great continents; enveloping the whole, the Cakravāḍa. — Some sūtras conform to these data:

Mahāvastu, II, p. 300,*16*: *pṛthivīcālena iyaṃ trisāhasramahāsāhasrā lokadhātu samā abhūṣi pāṇitalajātā sumeruś ca parvatarājā cakravāḍamahācakravāḍā ca parvatā nimindharo yugandharo iṣāṃdharo ca parvatā khadirakāśvakarṇo vinatako sudarśano ca sapta parvatā dvīpāntarikā tathānye kālaparvatā pṛthivyāṃ osannā abhūṣi bodhisattvasyānubhāvena.*

Also see Divyāvadāna, p. 217.

[42] Cf. Mahāvyutpatti, No. 4170 sq.

[43] The sequence *grāma-nagara-nigama*, etc., is a stock phrase in Sanskrit texts: Aṣṭasāh., p. 685,*17*; Sad. puṇḍarīka, p. 72,*1*; 102,*5*; 244,*10*; 246,*3*; 247,*3*; Mahāsaṃnipāta, p. 129,*1*; 133,*10-11*; below, V, § 7 and 9; XII, § 3 and 22. The Pāli is less prolix: Dīgha, II, p. 249,*30*; Mahāniddesa, p. 268,*27*.

[44] Cf. Sad. paṇḍarīka, p. 6,*10*.

[45] To show astonishment, the Sad. puṇḍarīka uses the two expressions *āścaryaprāpta*

saumanasyajātā[46] *tathāgatam abhivandyaikānte sthitābhūd animiṣābhyāṃ netrābhyāṃ*[47] *saṃprekṣamāṇā*).

[*Stanzas of Ratnākara.*]

10. Then the young Licchavi Ratnākara, having seen the great wonder accomplished by the Blessed One, placed his right knee on the ground, raised his joined hands to the Blessed One and, having paid homage to him, praised him with the following stanzas (*atha khalu Ratnākaro licchavikumāro bhagavato 'ntikād idam evaṃrūpaṃ mahāprātihāryaṃ dṛṣṭvā dakṣiṇaṃ jānumaṇḍalaṃ pṛthivyāṃ pratiṣṭhāpya yena bhagavāṃs tenāñjaliṃ praṇamya taṃ bhagavantaṃ namaskṛtvābhir gāthābhir abhiṣṭauti sma*):

1. Pure (*śuci*) and beautiful (*sundara*), your eyes (*netra*) are as large (*viśāla*) as a lotus leaf (*padmapattra*); pure are your intentions (*āśaya*); you have reached the other shore (*pāra*) of tranquillity (*śamatha*); you have accumulated good actions (*kuśalakarman*) and conquered a great sea of virtues (*guṇasamudra*). Holy One (*śramaṇa*), you lead to the path of peace (*śāntimārga*), all homage to you!

2. Bull-like man (*puruṣarṣabha*), Leader (*nāyaka*), we see your wonder (*prātihārya*). The fields (*kṣetra*) of the Sugatas are illumined (*prabhāsita*) with a brilliant light (*pravarāloka*), and their instructions in the Law (*dhārmyā kathā*), greatly developed (*vipula*) and leading to immortality (*amṛtaga*), can be heard throughout the reaches of space (*ākāśatala*).

3. King of the Law (*dharmarāja*), you reign through the Law over all beings, you lavish on them the riches of the Law (*dharmavasu*). Skillful analyst of dharmas (*dharmapravicayakuśala*), Instructor in the Good Law (*saddharmadeśaka*), Sovereign of the Law (*dharmeśvara*), King of the Law (*dharmarāja*), all homage to you!

4. "Neither being (*sat*) nor not-being (*asat*), all dharmas are born dependent on causes (*hetūn pratītya samutpannāḥ*); there is in them

adbhutaprapta, p. 125,*1*; 183,*4*; 199,*3*; 206,*5*; 249,*11*. We also find after them, *audbilyaprāpta*, p. 6,*5*; 20,*13*; 389,*5*; *vismayaprāpta*. p. 310,*14*; *kautūhalaprāpta*, p. 8,*1*. — In Pāli, the traditional expression is *acchariyabbhutacittajāta*: Majjhima, I, p. 254,*2*; 330,*16*; II, p. 144,*27*; Saṃyutta, I, p. 156,*20*.

[46] Joy is shown by a series of five adjectives: *tuṣṭa udagra āttamanas pramudita prītisaumanasyajāta*: Sad. puṇḍarīka, p. 60,*1*; 69,*7*; 103,*13*; 209,*9*; 222,*10*; 257,*7*; 288,*13*; 367,*2*; 404,*7*; 406,*2*; Suvarṇabhāsottama, p. 9,*7*; Gaṇḍavyūha, p. 99,*15*; Rāṣṭrapāla, p. 47,*18*; Divyāvadāna, p. 297,*15*; Mahāvyutpatti, No. 2929-33; below, VI, §7; XII, §20.

[47] *Animiṣābhyāṃ netrābhyām*: cf. Sad. puṇḍarīka, p. 199,*10*.

no self (*ātman*), no sensing subject (*vedaka*), no activator (*kāraka*); but good (*kuśala*) or bad (*akuśala*), no action (*karma*) withers"[48]: such is your teaching.

5. Great Ascetic (*munīndra*), you have overcome Māra and his hordes; you have conquered supreme enlightenment (*pravarabodhi*), peace (*śānta*), immortality (*amṛta*), happiness (*sukha*). But unaware, deprived of thought (*citta*) and attention (*manasikāra*), the hordes of the sectaries (*tīrthika*) do not understand it.

6. Wondrous King of the Law (*adbhuta dharmarāja*), in the presence of gods and men (*devamanuṣya*), you turn the wheel of the Law which has a threefold revolution and twelve aspects (*dharmacakraṃ pravartayasi triparivartaṃ dvādaśākāram*)[49]; it is calmed (*praśānta*)

[48] This is a resumé of the ancient Buddhist doctrine teaching the Pratītyasamutpāda, Anātman and the fruition of actions. The last point recalls this stanza:

na praṇaśyanti karmāṇi kalpakoṭiśatair api,
sāmagrīṃ prāpya kālaṃ ca phalanti khalu dehinām.

Cf. Divyāvadāna, p. 54,*9*; 131,*13*; 141,*14*; 191,*19*; 282,*17*; 311,*22*; 504,*23*; 582,*4*; 584,*20*; Avadānaśataka, I, p. 74,*7*; 80,*13*; 86,*6*; 91,*11*; 100,*10*; 105,*1*.

[49] We have, in Sanskrit, *triparivartaṃ dvādaśākāraṃ dharmacakram* (Mahāvastu, III, p. 333,*11*; Divyāvadāna, p. 205,*21*; 393,*23*; Lalitavistara, p. 422,*2*; Aṣṭasāh., p. 380,*13*; Sad. puṇḍarīka, p. 179,*1*). We have in Pāli, *tiparivaṭṭaṃ dvādasākāraṃ yathābhūtaṃ ñānadassanaṃ* (Vinaya, I, p. 11,*20*; 11,*25*; Saṃyutta, V, p. 422,*32*).

The expression is explained in Vinaya, I, p. 11; Saṃyutta, V, p. 420-424; Saṃyukta, T 99, ch. 15, p. 104 *c*-105 *a*; Mahāvastu, III, p. 332-333; Lalitavistara, p. 417-418; Mahāvyutpatti, No. 1309-1324; Āloka, p. 381-382.

The first turning (*parivarta*) of the noble truths is the path of vision (*darśanamārga*) and consists of four aspects (*ākāra*): 1. This is suffering (*idaṃ duḥkham*); 2. This is its origin (*ayaṃ samudayaḥ*); 3. This is its extinction (*ayaṃ nirodhaḥ*); 4. This is the path of the extinction of suffering (*iyaṃ duḥkhanirodhagāminī pratipat*).

The second turning is the path of meditation (*bhāvanāmārga*) and consists of four aspects: 1. The noble truth of suffering should be known (*duḥkham āryasatyaṃ parijñeyam*); 2. The origin of suffering should be ended (*duḥkhasamudayaḥ prahātavyaḥ*); 3. The extinction of suffering should be achieved (*duḥkhanirodhaḥ sākṣātkartavyaḥ*); 4. The path of the extinction of suffering should be practised (*duḥkhanirodhagāminī pratipad bhāvitavyā*).

The third turning is the path of the Arhat (*aśaikṣamārga*) and also consists of four aspects: 1. Suffering is known (*duḥkhaṃ parijñātam*); 2. Its origin is destroyed (*samudayaḥ prahīṇaḥ*); 3. Extinction is achieved (*nirodhaḥ sākṣātkṛtaḥ*); 4. The path of the extinction of suffering has been practised (*duḥkhanirodhagāminī pratipad bhāvitā*).

It is in the light of this traditional meaning that we should interpret the expression "wheel of the Law which has a three-fold revolution and twelve aspects" used here by the Vimalakīrtinirdeśa. Neither did Kumārajīva have any doubts about it (T 1775, ch. 1, p. 333 *b* 4-5). Without ignoring the ancient exegesis, K'uei-chi (T 1782, ch. 2, p. 1021 *b-c*) also sees in the triple turning the successive teachings of the Vehicles of

and naturally pure (*svabhāvaviśuddha*). From then on, the three jewels (*triratna*) are revealed to the world.

7. Those who are well-disciplined (*suvinīta*) by your precious Law (*ratnadharma*) are unruffled (*avitarka*) and always calm (*nityapraśānta*). You are the great Healer (*mahāvaidya*) who puts an end to birth (*jāti*), old age (*jarā*) and death (*maraṇa*). You have conquered a great sea of virtues (*guṇasamudra*), all homage to you!

8. Before homages (*satkāra*) and good deeds (*sukṛta*) [50], you remain as immovable (*acala*) as Sumeru; towards beings moral (*śīlavat*) or immoral (*duḥśīla*), you are equally beneficent; penetrating the sameness (*samatā*) of all things, your mind (*manas*) is like space (*ākāśasama*). Jewel among beings (*sattvaratna*), who would not honour you?

9. Under this little parasol offered to the Blessed One, there appear the trichiliocosm and the dwelling of the Devas and Nāgas; thus it is that we salute his knowledge and vision (*jñānadarśana*) and the assemblage of his virtues (*guṇakāya*).

10. With this wonder (*prātihārya*) the being with ten powers (*daśabala*) reveals the worlds (*loka*) to us, and all are like plays of light. Beings cry out in wonder (*adbhuta*). This is why we salute the being with ten powers, gifted with knowledge and vision [51].

11. Great Ascetic (*mahāmuni*), the assemblies united here (*parṣatsaṃnipāta*) in your presence contemplate you full of faith (*prasannena manasā*). Each one sees the Victorious One (*jina*) facing him; this is an exclusive attribute (*āveṇikalakṣaṇa*) of the Victorious One.

12. The Blessed One expresses himself in a single sound (*ekasva-*

the Śrāvakas, Pratyekabuddhas and Bodhisattvas. Regarding this new interpretation of the turning of the wheel, see Aṣṭasāh., p. 442,*8-9*; Pañcaviṃśati, T 223, ch. 12, p. 311 *b* 16; Upadeśa, T 1509, ch. 65, p. 517 *a*; Sad. puṇḍarīka, p. 69,*12-13*; 291,*1-3*; Saṃdhinirmocana, VII, § 30; Bu-ston, *History of Buddhism*, II, p. 41-56; E. OBERMILLER, *The Doctrine of Prajñāpāramitā*, Acta Orientalia, XI, 1932, p. 90-100.

[50] According to H: "before the eight worldly states". These eight *lokadharma* are gain (*lābha*), loss (*alābha*), glory (*yaśas*), ignominy (*ayaśas*), praise (*praśaṃsā*), blame (*nindā*), happiness (*sukha*) and suffering (*duḥkha*): cf. Dīgha, III, p. 260; Aṅguttara, IV, p. 156; Mahāvyutpatti, No. 2342-48.

[51] Stanzas 9 and 10 are missing in the Tibetan versions. Conversely, stanzas 11 to 18 are missing in Cn, the oldest Chinese translation. They were perhaps not part of the original composition.

reṇodāharati)[52] and beings, each according to his category, grasp its meaning; each one says to himself that the Blessed One speaks his own language; this is an exclusive attribute (*āveṇikalakṣaṇa*) of the Victorious One (*jina*).

[52] Conceptions concerning the instruction of the Buddha have varied considerably during the course of time:

1. According to ancient Buddhism, Śākyamuni taught throughout the forty-five years of his public life, and all that he said is true. This is confirmed by a common theme, entitled the Sūtra of the Two Nights (*dharmarātridvayasūtra*), frequently invoked in the texts: Dīgha, III, p. 135; Aṅguttara, II, p. 24; Itivuttaka, p. 121; Madhyamāgama, T 26, ch. 34, p. 645 *b* 18; Sumaṅgala, I, p. 66; Upadeśa, T 1509, ch. 1, p. 59 *c* 5-7: *yañ ca rattiṃ tathāgato anuttaraṃ sammāsambodhiṃ abhisambujjhati yañ ca rattiṃ anupādisesāya nibbānadhātuyā parinibbāyati, yaṃ etasmiṃ antare bhāsati lapati niddisati, sabbaṃ taṃ tath'eva hoti no aññathā.*

2. Possessing the gift of languages, the Buddha did not only teach in the Āryan tongue (*āryā vāc*) or in the tongue of the middle Country (*madhyadeśavāc*), but also in barbarian languages (*dasyuvāc*) and in the common language of the frontier-lands of Southern India. This is brought out in the tale of the conversion of the four kings of the gods (Vin. of the Sarvāstivādins, T 1435, ch. 26, p. 193 *a*; Vin. of the Mūlasarvāstivādins, *Gilgit Manuscripts*, III, 1, p. 256-259; Ch'u yao ching, T 212, ch. 23, p. 734 *b*; Vibhāṣā, T 1545, ch. 79, p. 410 *a*; T 1546, ch. 41, p. 306 *c*; T 1547, ch. 9, p. 482 *c*).

Commenting on this episode, the Vibhāṣā (T 1545, ch. 79, p. 410 *b*) remarks: "It is in order to show that the Buddha can express himself clearly in all languages that he expresses himself in various ways so as to cut off the doubts of those who suspect him of only being able to teach in the holy tongue... The Tathāgata can express all that he wishes in any language. If he expresses himself in Chinese, it is because this language is the best for the inhabitants of China; equally he expresses himself in the Balkh language... Furthermore the word of the Buddha is light and sharp, the flow is rapid, and even though he speaks all sorts of languages, it can be said that he speaks them all at once: thus, if he expresses himself in turn in Chinese, in Balkh language, in Śaka (Scythian) language, he pronounces all these languages uninterruptedly and, as it were, at the same time".

3. There was but a single step to take to suggest that the Buddha taught all the Law with a single sound (*ekasvareṇa*) or with an instant's utterance (*ekakṣaṇavāgudāhāreṇa*): Thesis No. 4 of the Mahāsāṃghikas (BAREAU, *Sectes*, p. 58); Vibhāṣā, T 1545, ch. 79, p. 410 *a* 16; Avataṃsaka, T 278, ch. 60, p. 787 *a* 27; T 279, ch. 80, p. 443 *c* 28; Bhadracarīpraṇidhāna, v. 30 (= T 293, ch. 39, p. 843 *b* 11): Great Parinirvāṇa, T 374, ch. 10, p. 423 *c* 10-14; T 375, ch. 9, p. 665 *a* 2; Daśabhūmika, p. 79,*27-29*.

This is the view formulated here by the Vimalakīrtinirdeśa which, further on (X, § 9), explains that it is enough for the Buddha to have a sound, a word, a syllable to teach the self-nature and the character of all dharmas.

4. According to an even more radical formula, certain scholars of the Small, as of the Great Vehicle, affirm that the Buddha does not speak.

Thesis 12 of the Mahāsāṃghikas (BAREAU, *Sectes*, p. 60): "The Buddhas never

13. The Blessed One expresses himself in a single sound (*ekasvarenodāharati*) and beings, each according to his understanding, are affected by it and profit from it (*svakārtha*): this is an exclusive attribute of the Tathāgata.

14. The Buddha expounds the Law in a single sound (*ekasvareṇa dharmaṃ deśayati*), and to some this brings fear (*bhaya*), to some joy (*muditā*); to others, repulsion (*saṃvega*); and to yet others, the suppression of their doubts (*saṃśayaccheda*): this is an exclusive attribute of the Tathāgata [53].

15. All homage to you, Being with ten powers (*daśabala*), Leader (*nāyaka*), Hero (*vikrāmin*)! All homage to you, who are fearless (*nirbhaya*) and free from dread (*vigatabhaya*)! All homage to you who fulfil the exclusive attributes (*āveṇikadharma*)! All homage to you, Leader of all creatures (*sarvajagannāyaka*).

pronounce a word, for they stay eternally in *samādhi*, but beings, thinking they have pronounced words, jump for joy".

Thesis of the Vetullakas, in Kathāvatthu, p. 560,*14*: *na vattabbaṃ Buddhena Bhagavatā dhammo desito*. — Cf. Avataṃsaka, T 279, ch. 52, p. 275 *c* 19.

Niraupamyastava, v. 7, of Nāgārjuna (JRAS, 1932, p. 314): *nodāhṛtaṃ tvayā kiṃcid ekam apy akṣaraṃ vibho, kṛtsnaś ca vaineyajano dharmavarṣeṇa tarpitaḥ*.

The "Sūtra of the Two Nights" was modified in consequence:

Madh. vṛtti, p. 366, 539: *yāṃ ca, Śāntamate, rātriṃ tathāgato 'nuttarāṃ samyaksaṃbodhim abhisaṃbuddho yāṃ ca rātrim anupādāya parinirvāsyati, asminn antare tathāgatenaikākṣaram api nodāhṛtaṃ na pravyāhṛtaṃ nāpi pravyāhariṣyati*.

Pañjikā, p. 419: *yasyāṃ rātrau tathāgato 'bhisaṃbuddho yasyāṃ ca parinirvṛto 'trāntare tathāgatenaikam apy akṣaraṃ nodāhṛtam. tat kasya hetoḥ. nityaṃ samāhito bhagavān. ye cākṣarasvararutavaineyāḥ sattvās te tathāgatamukhād ūrṇākośād uṣṇīṣād dhvaniṃ niścarantaṃ śṛṇvanti*.

Laṅkāvatāra, p. 142-143: *yāṃ ca rātriṃ tathāgato 'bhisaṃbuddho yāṃ ca rātriṃ parinirvāsyati, atrāntara ekam apy akṣaraṃ tathāgatena nodāhṛtaṃ na pravyāhariṣyati avacanaṃ buddhavacanam*.

The Vimalakīrti says further on (X, § 9): "There are pure and calm Buddhakṣetras, which actuate Buddha-deeds through silence (*avacana*), through muteness (*anabhilāpa*), by saying nothing and speaking nothing. And beings to be disciplined, because of this calm, spontaneously penetrate the self-nature and the marks of dharmas".

5. Finally, the work of the Buddhas, the instruction of the Law, is not only carried out with words or the absence of words, but with a quantity of other means on which the Vimalakīrti (X, § 8) expatiates at length. With regards to Śākyamuni, it seems to allow (IX, § 15-16) that, in the Sahāloka, he occupies himself with many oral expositions of the Law (*dharmaparyāya*).

In conclusion, I do not think that the theses referred to above are mutually exclusive. The Buddhas expound the Law by sermons, by a single sound, by silence or quantities of other means according to the needs or exigencies of beings to be disciplined. It is solely through expediency that they adopt such or such a means.

[53] Stanza translated from H.

16. All homage to you, who have broken the fetters and links (*samucchinnasaṃyojanabandhana*)! All homage to you who "having reached the other shore, are standing on firm ground" (*tīrṇaḥ pāraṃgataḥ sthale tiṣṭhasi*)[54]! All homage to you, saviour of creatures who are lost! All homage to you who have escaped the course of rebirth (*saṃsāragati*)!

17. You associate yourself with beings by going into their course of existence (*gati*), but your mind is delivered (*vimukta*) from all courses of existence "As the lotus, born in water, is not defiled by water" (*padmam ivodake jātam udakena na lipyate*)[55], so the Ascetic One (*muni*), like the lotus, dwells in emptiness (*śūnyatāṃ prabhāvayati*).

18. You have eliminated signs (*nimitta*) in all their aspects (*ākāra*); you have no wishes (*praṇidhāna*) regarding anything. The great power (*mahānubhāva*) of the Buddhas is inconceivable (*acintya*). All homage to you, who are as unsupported (*asthita*) as space (*ākāśa*)!

[*The Purification of the Buddha-fields*[56].]

11. Then the young Licchavi Ratnākara, having praised the Blessed One with these stanzas, also said to him: Blessed One, the five hundred young Licchavis who are on the path to supreme and perfect enlightenment (*anuttarāyāṃ samyaksaṃbodhau saṃprasthitāḥ*) question me regarding the purification of the Buddha-fields (*buddhakṣetrapariśodhana*) and ask me what this purification of the Buddha-fields is. May the Blessed Tathāgata through pity for them (*anukampām upādāya*) then explain to these Bodhisattvas the purification of the Buddha-fields.

[54] Canonical reminiscence probably taken from the Āsīviṣopamasutta to which the Vimalakīrti often refers; cf. Saṃyutta, IV, p. 174,*19*; 175,*23*: *tiṇṇo pāraṅgato thale tiṭṭhati brāhmaṇo*.

It goes without saying that the "brahman" in question here is really an Arhat possessed of Nirvāṇa on earth; cf. Aṅguttara, II. p. 6,*1*: *idha ekacco puggalo āsavānaṃ khayā anāsavaṃ cetovimuttiṃ paññāvimuttiṃ diṭṭh' eva dhamme sayaṃ abhiññā sacchikatvā upasampajja viharati ayaṃ vuccati puggalo tiṇṇo pāraṅgato ṭhale tiṭṭhati brāhmaṇo*.

[55] Another canonical reminiscence; cf. Aṅguttara, II, p. 38-39; Saṃyutta, III, p. 140: *seyyathāpi uppalaṃ vā padumaṃ vā puṇḍarīkaṃ vā udake jātaṃ udake saṃvaddhaṃ udakā accuggamma ṭhāti anupalittaṃ udakena*. The Mahāsāṃghikas and Vetullakas derived their *lokottaravāda* from this text (cf. Vibhāṣā, T 1545, ch. 44, p. 229 *a* 17-18; Kathāvatthu, p. 560,*7*).

[56] Regarding the Buddhakṣetras, see Appendix, Note I.

This having been said, the Blessed One expressed his approval to the young Licchavi Ratnākara: Excellent, excellent, young man, you are right to question the Tathāgata regarding the purity of the Buddha-fields. Now listen and engrave it on your mind: I shall begin by speaking to you of the purification of the Buddha-fields by the Bodhisattvas. — Excellent, O Blessed One, answered the young Licchavi Ratnākara and the five hundred young Licchavis, and they began to listen (*evam ukte bhagavāṃs tasya licchavikumārasya ratnākarasya sādhukāram adāt. sādhu sādhu kumāra. sādhu yas tvaṃ buddhakṣetraviśuddhim ārabhya tathāgataṃ paripṛcchasi. tac chṛṇu sādhu ca suṣṭhu ca manasikuru. bhāṣiṣye 'haṃ te bodhisattvair buddhakṣetraviśodhanam ārabhya. — sādhu bhagavann iti licchavikumāro ratnākarāḥ pañcamātrāṇi ca licchavikumāraśatāni bhagavataḥ pratyaśrauṣuḥ*)[57].

12. The Blessed One then said to them: Sons of good family (*kulaputra*), the field of beings (*sattvakṣetra*) is the Buddhakṣetra of the Bodhisattvas. And why is it so (*tat kasya hetoḥ*)? To the extent (*yāvatā*) that Bodhisattvas favour (*upabṛṃhayanti*) beings do they acquire (*parigṛhṇanti*) Buddhakṣetras. To the extent that beings produce all sorts of pure qualities (*nānāvidhān viśuddhaguṇān utpādayanti*) do Bodhisattvas acquire Buddhakṣetras. To the extent that beings are disciplined (*vinīta*) by these pure Buddhakṣetras do Bodhisattvas acquire Buddhakṣetras. To the extent that beings, entering these Buddhakṣetras, penetrate the knowledge of the Buddhas (*buddhajñānaṃ praviśanti*) do Bodhisattvas acquire Buddhakṣetras. To the extent that beings, entering these Buddhakṣetras, produce noble dominant faculties (*āryendriyāṇy utpādayanti*) do Bodhisattvas acquire Buddhakṣetras. And why is it so? Sons of good family, the Buddhakṣetras of the Bodhisattvas draw their origin from the benefits (*arthakriyā*) rendered by them to beings.

For example, O Ratnākara, if one desires to build (*māpayitum*) on something which resembles space (*ākāśasama*), it can be done; but, in space (*ākāśa*) itself, nothing

For example, O son of good family, if somebody wanted to build a palace on some piece of land and adorn it, he could do so easily and without obstacle; but, if he wanted to build in space (*ākāśa*)

[57] Series of formulae:
Sādhukāram adāt: *sādhu*...: Sad. puṇḍarīka, p. 302,*9*; 397,*5*; 407,*11*; 419,*10*.
Tena hi śṛṇu...: Sad. puṇḍarīka, p. 38,*10*; 332,*8*; 346,*5*.
Sādhu bhagavann iti... pratyaśrauṣīt: Sad. puṇḍarīka, p. 39,*6*.

can be built (*māpayitum*), nothing can be adorned (*alaṃkartum*)[58]. Similarly, O Ratnākara, knowing that all dharmas are like space (*ākāśasama*) and to help beings ripen (*sattvaparipācanārtham*), the Bodhisattva who wishes to build something resembling a Buddhakṣetra can build a simulated Buddhakṣetra, but it is impossible to build a Buddhakṣetra in the void and it is impossible to adorn it.

itself, he would never succeed. Similarly, the Bodhisattva who knows that all dharmas are like space (*ākāśasama*) produces for the progress (*vṛddhi*) and welfare (*hita*) of beings pure qualities (*viśuddhaguṇa*). This is the Buddhakṣetra he acquires. To acquire a Buddhakṣetra of this type is not to build in the void (*śūnya*).

13.

Also, O Ratnākara, you must know that the field where the thought of supreme enlightenment (*anuttarabodhicitta*)[59] is produced is the pure Buddhakṣetra of the Bodhisattva: the instant he obtains great enlightenment, all beings who have started towards the Great Vehicle (*mahāyānasaṃprasthita*)[60] come to be born in his field.

Also, O Ratnākara, the field of good intentions (*āśayakṣetra*) is the Buddhakṣetra of the Bodhisattva: the instant he obtains enlightenment (*bodhi*), beings free from hypocrisy (*śāṭhya*) and deceit (*māyā*)[61] are born in his Buddhakṣetra.

Son of good family, the field of high resolve (*adhyāśaya*)[62] is the Buddhakṣetra of the Bodhi-

[58] Close comparison in Majjhima, I, p. 127,*30*: *seyyathā pi bhikkhave puriso āgaccheyya lākhaṃ vā haliddiṃ vā nīlaṃ vā mañjiṭṭhaṃ vā ādāya, so evaṃ vadeyya: ahaṃ imasmiṃ ākāse rūpāni likhissāmi rūpapātubhāvaṃ karissāmīti. taṃ kiṃ maññatha bhikkhave: api nu so puriso imasmiṃ ākāse rūpaṃ likheyya rūpapātubhāvaṃ kareyyāti. — no h' etaṃ bhante. taṃ kissa hetu: ayaṃ hi bhante ākāso arūpī anidassano, tattha na sukaraṃ rūpaṃ likhituṃ rūpapātubhāvaṃ kātuṃ.*

[59] Regarding *bodhicittotpāda*, *adhyāśaya* and *āśaya*, see Appendix, Note II.

[60] At the instant that a Bodhisattva enters into the great stages, he is called *bodhisattvayānasaṃprasthita* or *mahāyānasaṃprasthita*: Vajracchedikā, p. 28,*17*; Pañcaviṃśati, p. 214,*6*; Śatasāh., p. 1454,*3*.

[61] *Śāṭhya* and *māyā* are two *upakleśa*: Kośa, V, p. 93; Triṃśikā, p. 30,*29*; Siddhi, p. 367.

[62] Regarding *adhyāśaya*, see Appendix, Note II.

sattva: the instant he obtains enlightenment, beings who have accumulated all the stores of good roots (*kuśalamūlasaṃbhāra*) are born in his Buddhakṣetra.

The field of effort (*prayoga*)[63] is the Buddhakṣetra of the Bodhisattva: the instant he obtains enlightenment, beings who are established in all good dharmas (*kuśaladharmapratiṣṭhita*) are born in his Buddhakṣetra.

The field of right effort (*kuśalaprayoga*) is the pure Buddhakṣetra of the Bodhisattva: the instant he obtains great enlightenment, all beings who have produced and maintained right effort come to be born in his field.

The production of the great thought (*uttaracittotpāda*) of the Bodhisattva is the Buddhakṣetra of the Bodhisattva: the instant he obtains enlightenment, beings who have started towards the Great Vehicle (*mahāyānasaṃprasthita*) are born in his Buddhakṣetra.

The field of high resolve (*adhyāśaya*) is the pure Buddhakṣetra of the Bodhisattva: the instant he obtains great enlightenment, beings gifted with good dharmas (*kuśaladharmasamanvāgata*) come to be born in his field.

The field of giving (*dāna*)[64] is the Buddhakṣetra of the Bodhisattva: the instant he obtains enlightenment, beings who have abandoned their worldly goods (*parityaktasarvasva*) are born in his Buddhakṣetra.

The field of morality (*śīla*) is the Buddhakṣetra of the Bodhisattva: the instant he obtains enlightenment, beings gifted with all the good intentions (*āśayasamanvāgata*) and who observe the ten paths of good conduct (*kuśalakarmapatha*) are born in his Buddhakṣetra.

The field of patience (*kṣānti*) is the Buddhakṣetra of the Bodhisattva: the instant he obtains enlightenment, beings who are adorned with the thirty-two primary marks (*lakṣaṇālaṃkṛta*), and who are gifted with the lovely perfections (*pāramitā*) of patience (*kṣānti*), discipline (*vinaya*) and calm (*śamatha*) are born in his Buddhakṣetra.

The field of vigour (*vīrya*) is the Buddhakṣetra of the Bodhisattva: the instant he obtains enlightenment, beings who apply their vigour

[63] *Prayoga* is the efficacious effort extended by a Bodhisattva in the two-fold interest of himself and others. It consists of several types: Sūtrālaṃkāra, p. 164,*18*; Bodh. bhūmi, p. 288.

[64] This paragraph and the following five concern the six *pāramitā*.

to all good dharmas (*sarveṣu kuśaleṣu dharmeṣv ārabdhavīryaḥ*) are born in his field.

The field of meditation (*dhyāna*) is the Buddhakṣetra of the Bodhisattva: the instant he obtains enlightenment, beings gifted with memory (*smṛti*), presence of mind (*saṃprajñāna*) and concentration (*samāpatti*) are born in his Buddhakṣetra.

The field of wisdom (*prajñā*) is the Buddhakṣetra of the Bodhisattva: the instant he obtains enlightenment, beings certain to acquire the Absolute Good (*samyaktvaniyata*)[65] are born in his Buddhakṣetra.

The field of the four infinite states (*apramāṇa*)[66] is the Buddhakṣetra of the Bodhisattva: the instant he obtains enlightenment, beings

[65] *Niyāma* (variations, *niyama, nyāma*) or, more completely, *samyaktvaniyāmāvakrānti* is the entry into the absolute certainty of acquiring the supreme Good. It concerns a *kṣānti* through which one enters into possession of a state of predestination relative to the future acquisition of *samyaktva*, that is to say, Nirvāṇa.

The question of *niyāma* appears in the two Vehicles; cf. Saṃyutta, I, p. 196,*17*; III, p. 225,*10*; Aṅguttara, I, p. 121,*26* and *31*; Suttanipāta, v. 55, 371; Kathāvatthu, p. 307-309, 317, 480; Lalitavistara, p. 31,*20*; 34,*10*; Aṣṭasāh., p. 131,*10*; 662,*20*; 679,*6*; Śatasāh., p. 272,*8*; Gaṇḍavyūha, p. 320,*22*; Daśabhūmika, p. 11,*27*; Kośa, VI, p. 180-182; Sūtrālaṃkāra, p. 171,*22*; Bodh. bhūmi, p. 358,*2*; Madhyāntavibhāga, p. 256,*2*; Āloka, p. 131,*18*; 662,*25*; 663,*22*; 679,*16*; below, I, § 13; III, § 50; IV, § 20; VII, § 3; X, § 6.

In the Small Vehicle, a Śrāvaka obtains the *niyāma* the instant he enters the *darśanamārga*, the path of the vision of the truths, and where he produces the *duḥkhe dharmajñānakṣāntiḥ*. This is explained in the Madhyāntavibhāga, p. 256: *āryamārgotpādo niyāmāvakrāntisamudāgama iti... tathā hy utpannadarśanamārgo niyato bhavati sugatau nirvāṇe ca*, and the Āloka, p. 131,*18*: *samyaktvaniyāmaḥ svaśrāvakadarśanādimārgaḥ*; p. 679,*16*: *bodhisattvaniyāmaṃ duḥkhe dharmajñānakṣāntim adhigato 'vakrāntaḥ san*. — At the moment of the *niyāma*, the Śrāvaka abandons the quality of a worldly one (*pṛthagjana*) to become an ārya, abandons the wrong (*mithyātva*) to obtain the great Good (*samyaktva*).

In the Great Vehicle, a Bodhisattva obtains the *niyāma* when he produces the *cittotpāda* and enters the first stage (Daśabhūmika, p. 11,*26-27*). This stage, called *śuddhādhyāśayabhūmi* or *pramuditāvihāra* (cf. Bodh. bhūmi, p. 367,*8*), constitutes the third of the twelve *vihāra* of the Bodhisattva and coincides with the *niyāmāvakrāntivihāra* of the Śrāvaka (ibidem, p. 358,*2-3*).

However, the predestination of a Bodhisattva takes clearer shape in the course of his career. It is in the eighth stage that he becomes "absolutely predestined" (*atyantaniyata*) when he acquires the *anutpattikadharmakṣānti* and becomes an *avaivartika* Bodhisattva (cf. Upadeśa, T 1509, ch. 93, p. 713 *b*).

[66] The four *apramāṇa*, infinite states, also called *brahmavihāra*, Brahmā dwellings, are goodwill (*maitrī*), compassion (*karuṇā*), joy (*muditā*) and equanimity (*upekṣā*). Being of pre-Buddhist origin, these practices play a large part in both Vehicles: Dīgha, I, p. 251; Majjhima, I, p. 38; Saṃyutta, IV, p. 296; Aṅguttara, I, p. 183; other references in Woodward, *Concordance*, p. 201 *a*; Kośa, VIII, p. 196; Sūtrālaṃkāra, p. 121-123; 184; Bodh. bhūmi, p. 241-249; below, II, § 12; III, § 57, 69; VI, § 2-3.

established in goodwill (*maitrī*), compassion (*karuṇā*), joy (*muditā*) and equanimity (*upekṣā*) are born in his Buddhakṣetra.

The four means of conversion (*saṃgrahavastu*)[67] are the Buddhakṣetra of the Bodhisattva: the instant he obtains enlightenment, beings possessing all the liberations (*sarvavimokṣaparigṛhīta*) are born in his Buddhakṣetra.

Skill in means (*upāyakauśalya*)[68] is the Buddhakṣetra of the

[67] The four *saṃgrahavastu* are giving (*dāna*), kind words (*priyavāditā*), service rendered (*arthacaryā*) and the pursuit of a common aim (*samānārthatā*): Dīgha, III, p. 152, 232; Aṅguttara, II, p. 32, 248; IV, p. 219, 364; Lalitavistara, p. 38,*16*; 160,*6*; 182,*6*; 429,*13*; Mahāvastu, I, p. 3,*11*; II, p. 395,*8*; Dharmasaṃgraha, § 19; Sūtrālaṃkāra, p. 116,*1*; Bodh. bhūmi, p. 112,*11*; 217,*2*.

[68] Unlike the Śrāvaka for whom *prajñā* is the ultimate element of the path, the Bodhisattva seeks a *prajñā* completed by *upāyakauśalya*, skill in means of salvation (IV, § 17, below).

Upāyakauśalya fulfils a double role: it brings about the welfare of the Bodhisattva himself and the welfare of others (*svaparārthasādhana*). We need to distinguish, with the Bodh. bhūmi, p. 261-272, a two-fold *upāyakauśalya*:

1. *Upāyakauśalya* for oneself, aiming at the acquisition of the Buddha attributes (*buddhadharmasamudāgama*): 1. compassionate solicitude for all beings (*sarvasattveṣu karuṇāsahagatāpekṣā*), 2. exact knowledge of all conditioned things (*sarvasaṃskāreṣu yathābhūtaparijñānam*), 3. desire for that most excellent knowledge which is supreme and perfect enlightenment (*anuttarasamyaksaṃbodhijñāne spṛhā*), 4. an undefiled passage through the round of rebirth (*asaṃkliṣṭā saṃsārasaṃsṛtiḥ*), 5. fervent vigour (*uttaptavīryatā*).

2. *Upāyakauśalya* for others, so as to ripen beings (*sattvaparipāka*), consisting of the four means of conversion listed in the previous note. Through their use, a Bodhisattva: 1. assures immense fruit to the small good roots of beings (*sattvānāṃ parīttāni kuśalamūlāny apramāṇaphalatāyām upanayati*), 2. causes to be acquired with little effort immense good roots (*alpakṛcchreṇāpramāṇāni kuśalamūlāni samāvartyati*), 3. averts obstacles preventing beings from accepting the Buddhist doctrine (*buddhaśāsanapratihatānām sattvānāṃ pratighātam apanayati*), 4. causes the crossing of those who are still in mid-path (*madhyasthān avatārayati*), 5. ripens those who have already crossed (*avatīrṇān paripācayati*), 6. delivers those who are already ripened (*paripakvān vimocayati*).

The Sūtrālaṃkāra, p. 147,*3*, distinguishes five categories of means:

1. Knowledge free of concepts (*nirvikalpaṃ jñānam*) which brings about the acquisition of the Buddha attributes.

2. The means of conversion (*saṃgrahavastu*) which cause beings to ripen.

3. The confession of faults (*pratideśanā*), delight (*anumodanā*) in the Buddhas, the invitation (*adhyeṣaṇā*) to the Buddhas and the transference (*pariṇāmanā*) which speed enlightenment (*kṣiprābhisaṃbodhi*).

4. The concentrations (*samādhi*) and formulae (*dhāraṇī*) which purify action.

5. The "baseless" (*apratiṣṭhita*) Nirvāṇa which does not interrupt the course through *saṃsāra*.

It should further be noted that the wisdom of means (*upāyaprajñā*) is particularly intense in the seventh stage (Daśabhūmika, p. 60,*6*; Bodh. bhūmi, p. 349,*24*).

Bodhisattva: the instant he obtains enlightenment, beings skilled in all the means and practices of deliverance (*sarvopāyacaryākuśala*) are born in his Buddhakṣetra.

The thirty-seven auxiliaries of enlightenment (*saptatriṃśad bodhipākṣikā dharmāḥ*) [69] are the Buddhakṣetra of the Bodhisattva: the instant he obtains enlightenment, there come to be reborn in his Buddhakṣetra beings who understand the four applications of mindfulness (*smṛtyupasthāna*), the four right efforts (*samyakpradhāna*), the four bases of psychic power (*ṛddhipāda*), the five dominant faculties (*indriya*), the five powers (*bala*), the seven limbs of enlightenment (*bodhyaṅga*) and the eight limbs of the Path (*mārgāṅga*).

The transference of merit (*pariṇāmanācitta*) [70] is the Buddhakṣetra of the Bodhisattva: the instant he obtains enlightenment, the adornments of all the virtues (*sarvaguṇālaṃkāra*) appear in his Buddhakṣetra.

The teaching intended to suppress the eight unfavourable conditions for birth (*akṣaṇapraśamananirdeśa*) [71] is the Buddhakṣetra of the Bodhisattva: the instant he obtains enlightenment, all the wrong paths (*apāya*) are eliminated; and there are not, in his Buddhakṣetra, any unfavourable conditions for birth (*akṣaṇa*).

Observing the rules of training (*śikṣāpadarakṣaṇa*) [72] oneself and not blaming the faults of others (*aparāpattipaṃsana*) is the Buddhakṣetra of the Bodhisattva: the instant he obtains enlightenment, the word for fault is not even suggested in his Buddhakṣetra.

The purity of the ten paths of good action (*daśakuśalakarmapathapariśuddhi*) [73] is the Buddhakṣetra of the Bodhisattva: the instant he

[69] See the detailed definition of these thirty-seven *bodhipākṣikadharma* in Visuddhimagga, ed. Warren, p. 582 sq.; Arthaviniścaya, Ch. XII-XVIII; Kośa, VI, p. 283 sq; Pañcaviṃśati, p. 203-208.

[70] *Pariṇāmanā* is the transference of all merits to supreme and perfect enlightenment: Āloka, p. 246,*25*; 247,*10*; Sutrālaṃkāra, p. 130,*16*; Bodh. bhūmi, p. 309-310.

[71] The eight or nine *akṣaṇa* are conditions for birth unfavourable to the religious life (*asamayā brahmacaryavāsāya*): 1-5. rebirths among the hellbound (*narakāḥ*), animals (*tiryañcaḥ*), Pretas, the gods of long life (*dīrghāyuṣo devāḥ*); 6. crippling (*indriyavaikalya*); 7. false view (*mithyādarśana*); 8. periods when Buddhas do not appear (*tathāgatānām anutpādaḥ*): cf. Dīgha, III, p. 263-264, 287; Aṅguttara, IV, p. 225, 227; Mahāvastu, II, p. 363,*3*; Lalitavistara, p. 412,*14*; Śikṣāsamuccaya, p. 2,*4*; 114,*14*; Gaṇḍavyūha, p. 116,*16*; Suvarṇabhāsa, p. 41,*13*; Mahāvyutpatti, No. 2299-2306; Dharmasaṃgraha, § 134.

[72] The five or ten *śikṣāpada* apply, depending on their level, to monks and lay people: Vinaya, I, p. 83-84; Aṅguttara, I, p. 211. For details, see Nāgārjuna, *Traité*, p. 819-852.

[73] The ten good *karmapatha* consist in avoiding: 1. taking life (*prāṇātipāta*), 2. taking

obtains enlightenment, there are born in his Buddhakṣetra beings who are gifted with long life (*dīrghāyuḥ*), are very wealthy (*mahābhoga*), continent (*brahmacārin*), whose speech conforms with the truth (*satyānulomikaśabda*), gentle (*ślakṣṇa*), who do not break up the assembly (*na pariṣadbhedaka*), are skilled in reconciling adversaries (*bhinnānāṃ saṃdhānakuśalaḥ*), free from hypocrisy (*amrakṣa*), free from malicions thought (*avyāpādacitta*) and holding right views (*samyagdṛṣtisamanvāgata*).

14. In fact, son of good family (*kulaputra*), as is the production of the thought of enlightenment, so is the intention (*yādṛśo bodhicittotpādas tādṛśa āśayaḥ*). — As is the intention, so is the effort (*prayoga*). — As is the effort, so is the high resolve (*adhyāśaya*). — As is the high resolve, so is deep meditation (*nidhyapti*). — As is deep meditation, so is conduct (*pratipatti*). — As is conduct, so is the transference of merit (*pariṇāmanā*).

As is the transference of merit, so are skillful means (*upāya*). — As are skillful means, so is the pure field (*pariśuddhakṣetra*). — As is the pure field, so are pure beings (*pariśuddhasattva*). — As are pure beings, so is pure knowledge (*pariśuddhajñāna*). — As is pure knowledge, so is pure teaching (*pariśuddhadeśanā*). — As is pure teaching, so is pure action of knowledge (*pariśuddhajñānasādhana*). — As is pure action of knowledge, so is pure personal mind (*pariśuddhasvacitta*).

As is the transference of merit, so is appeasement (*vyupaśama*). — As is appeasement, so is a pure being (*pariśuddhasattva*). — As is a pure being, so is a pure field (*pariśuddhakṣetra*). — As is a pure field, so is pure teaching (*pariśuddhadeśanā*). — As is pure teaching, so is pure merit (*pariśuddhapuṇya*). — As is pure merit, so is pure wisdom (*pariśuddhaprajñā*). — As is pure wisdom, so is pure knowledge (*pariśuddhajñāna*). — As is pure knowledge, so is pure action (*pariśuddhasādhana*). — As is pure action, so is pure personal mind (*pariśuddhasvacitta*). — As is pure mind, so are pure virtues (*pariśuddhaguṇa*).

That is why, son of good family, the Bodhisattva who wishes to purify his Buddhakṣetra should, first of all, skillfully adorn (*alaṃkartum*)

what is not given (*adattādāna*), 3. sexual misconduct (*kāmamithyācāra*), 4. false speech (*mṛṣāvāda*), 5. slanderous speech (*paiśunyavāda*), 6. harsh speech (*pāruṣyavāda*), 7. useless speech (*saṃbhinnapralāpa*), 8. covetousness (*abhidhyā*), 9. animosity (*vyāpāda*), 10. false views (*mithyādṛṣṭi*). Cf. Vinaya, V, p. 138; Majjhima, I, p. 42, 360; III, p. 23; Saṃyutta, IV, p. 313; V, p. 469; Aṅguttara, I, p. 226; Mahāvastu, I, p. 107,*13*; Divyāvadāna, p. 301,*22*; Daśabhūmika, p. 23,*6*, Śikṣāsamuccaya, p. 69,*13*; Dharmasaṃgraha, § 56; Mahāvyutpatti, No. 1687-1698; below, IX, § 15.

Regarding the rewards for these good actions and the penalties for the faults that are opposed to them, see Karmavibhaṅga, p. 78-80; NĀGĀRJUNA, *Traité*, p. 782-819.

his own mind (*svacitta*). And why? Because to the extent that the mind of a Bodhisattva is pure is his Buddhakṣetra purified.

[*Śāriputra and the Impurity of the Sahāloka*]

15. At that moment, through the power of the Buddha, the Venerable Śāriputra had this thought (*atha khalu buddhasyānubhāvenāyuṣmataḥ śāriputrasyaitad abhavat*): If the mind of a Bodhisattva must be pure in order for his Buddhakṣetra to be purified, then, when the Blessed Lord Śākyamuni exercised the practices (*caryā*) as a Bodhisattva, his mind must have been impure, since today his Buddhakṣetra appears to be so impure.

Then the Blessed One, knowing the Venerable Śāriputra's thought in his mind, said to him (*atha khalu bhagavāṃs tasyāyuṣmataḥ śāriputrasya cetasaiva cetaḥparivitarkam*[74] *ājñāyāyuṣmantam śāriputram etad avocat*): What do you think of this (*tat kiṃ manyase*)[75] Śāriputra? Is it because the sun (*sūrya*) and the moon (*candra*) are impure (*apariśuddha*) that those born blind (*jātyandha*)[76] cannot see them? — Śāriputra replied: Not so, Blessed One (*no hīdaṃ bhagavan*); it is the fault of those born blind, it is not the fault of the sun and moon. — The Buddha continued: Similarly, Śāriputra, if beings cannot see the splendour of the virtues (*guṇavyūha*) of the Buddhakṣetra of the Tathāgata, the fault (*doṣa*) is in their ignorance (*ajñāna*); the fault is not the Tathāgata's. Śāriputra, my Buddhakṣetra is pure, but you yourself cannot see it.

[*Brahmā Śikhin and the Purity of the Sahāloka*]

16. Then Brahmā Śikhin said to Śāriputra the Elder (*sthavira*): Honourable (*bhadanta*) Śāriputra, do not say that the Buddhakṣetra of the Tathāgata is impure (*apariśuddha*); the Buddhakṣetra of the Blessed One is pure.

[74] Traditional formula. — In Pāli, *cetasā cetoparivitakkaṃ aññāya*: Dīgha, II, p. 36,*23*; Majjhima, I, p. 458,*12*; Saṃyutta, I, p. 137,*3*. — In Sanskrit, *cetasaiva cetaḥparivitarkam ājñāya*: Sad. puṇḍarīka, p. 8,*4*; 33,*13*; 148,*3*; 206,*7*; 218,*8*; 250,*8*; 303,*1*; below, V, § 1; IX, § 1; XI, § 4.

[75] Traditional interrogation: Sad. puṇḍarīka, p. 76,*5*; 322,*13*; 347,*12*; below, XI, § 2, 3; XII, § 5.

[76] The comparison of the *jātyandha* is often exploited in Buddhist texts: Dīgha, II, p. 328,*3*; Majjhima, I, p. 509,*14*; Udāna, p. 68,*6*; Sad. puṇḍarīka, p. 133,*3*; below, III, § 22; V, § 19.

Śāriputra asked: Great Brahmā, king of the gods, how can you say that, at this moment, this Buddhakṣetra is pure?

Brahmā Śikhin replied: On my part, Honourable Śāriputra, I can see that the splendour (*vyūha*) of the Buddhakṣetra of the Blessed Lord Śākyamuni equals the splendours of the dwellings (*bhavana*) of the Paranirmitavaśavartin gods [77].

Then Śāriputra the Elder said to Brahmā Śikhin: On my part, O Brahmā, I can see this great land with rises (*utkūla*) and dips (*nikūla*), with thorns (*kaṇṭaka*), precipices (*prapāta*), peaks (*śikhara*) and chasms (*śvabhra*), and all filled with filth (*gūthoḍigallaparipūrṇa*) [78].

Brahmā Śikhin replied:

If you see the Buddhakṣetra as being so impure, it is because there are rises and dips in your mind, O Honourable Śāriputra, and because you have certainly not purified your intentions (*āśaya*) in the knowledge (*jñāna*) of the Buddha. On the contrary, those who possess sameness of mind (*cittasamatā*) regarding all beings and who have purified their intentions in the knowledge of the Buddha can see the Buddhakṣetra as being perfectly pure (*pariśuddha*) [79].

Honourable Sir, your mind has rises and dips, and it is impure. This is why you suggest that the knowledge (*jñāna*) and intentions (*āśaya*) of the Buddha are the same, and this is why you see the Buddhakṣetra as being impure. On the contrary, the Bodhisattvas who possess perfect sameness of mind (*cittasamatā*) regarding all beings say that the knowledge and intentions of the Buddha are the same; and so they can see the Buddhakṣetra as being very pure.

[*The Transformation of the Sahāloka*]

17. Then the Blessed One touched, with his toe (*pādāṅ-*

Then the Blessed One, aware of the perplexity (*vimati*) of the great assembly

[77] The Paranirmitavaśavartins "divinities who control desirable objects created by others" from the sixth class of the gods of the *kāmadhātu* (cf. MALALASEKERA, *Proper Names*, II, p. 153). The pure lands are often compared to their paradise; cf. Sukhāvatīvyūha, p. 86,*17*. *yathā devāḥ paranirmitavaśavartina evaṃ Sukhāvatyaṃ lokadhatau manuṣyā draṣṭavyāḥ*.

[78] Cf. Sad. puṇḍarīka, p. 144,*10*; 425,*10*.

[79] K is, as often, close to the Tibetan: "Men whose minds have rises and dips and who do not lean on the Buddha-knowledge see this kṣetra as being impure. But Bodhisattvas are the same (*sama*) towards all beings; their high resolve (*adhyāśaya*) is pure and they lean on the knowledge (*jñāna*) and wisdom (*prajñā*) of the Buddha: then they can see that this Buddhakṣetra is pure".

guṣṭhenotkṣipati sma)[80], the trichiliomegachiliocosm (*trisāhasramahāsāhasralokadhātu*), and, as soon as he had touched it, that universe (*lokadhātu*) became like a heap of many jewels (*anekaratnakūṭa*), a collection of several hundreds of thousands of jewels (*anekaratnaśatasahasrasaṃcaya*), a pile of several hundreds of thousands of jewels. And the Sahā universe appeared like the Anantaguṇaratnavyūhā universe belonging to the Tathagāta Ratnavyūha[81].

(*mahāsaṃgha*), touched with his toe that great land, and the trichiliocosm, adorned with countless hundreds of thousands of precious jewels, appeared like the Anantaguṇaratnavyūhā universe belonging to the Buddha Guṇaratnavyūha.

The whole assembly (*sarvāvatī parṣad*) was astonished (*āścaryaprāpta*) when it found itself sitting on a splendid seat of precious lotuses (*ratnapadmavyūhāsana*).

18. Then the Blessed One said to the venerable Śāriputra: Can you see, Śāriputra, the splendour of the virtues of my Buddha-field (*paśyasi tvaṃ, Śāriputra, etaṃ buddhakṣetrasya guṇavyūham*)? — Śāriputra replied: Yes, I can see, O Blessed One, that splendour that has never been seen or heard before (*paśyāmi, bhagavan, etam adṛṣṭāśrūtapūrvaṃ vyūham*); now the splendour of the Sahā universe is entirely manifested. — The Buddha continued: Śāriputra, my Buddhakṣetra is always as pure as this, but, to help inferior beings ripen, the Tathāgata makes it appear (*saṃdarśayati*) like a field vitiated with many flaws (*bahudoṣaduṣṭa*).

For example, O Śāriputra, the sons of the Trāyastriṃśa[82] gods (*devaputra*) take their food (*bhojana*) from one single precious receptacle (*ekasmin ratnabhājane*), but the ambrosia (*amṛta*) which is the food of the gods varies according to the diverse merits accumulated by those gods (*puṇyasaṃcayaviśeṣāt*).

Equally, Śāriputra, beings born in the same Buddhakṣetra see,

Equally, Śāriputra, countless beings born in the same Buddhakṣetra have

[80] Same action by the Buddha in Majjhima, I, p. 337,*31*; Aṣṭasāh., p. 876,*17*.

[81] Cf. above, I, § 4, note 14.

[82] The Trāyastriṃśas "Gods of the Thirty-three" form the second class of the gods of the *kāmadhātu*; they inhabit the summit of Meru. Cf. MALALASEKERA, *Proper Names*, I, p. 1002-1004; AKANUMA, *Noms Propres*, p. 681-683; Kośa, III, p. 160-163.

in proportion to their purity (*pariśuddhi*), the splendour of the virtues (*guṇavyūha*) of the Buddhakṣetra of the Buddhas.

different views of it, depending on whether their minds are pure (*śuddha*) or sullied (*kliṣta*). If the mind of a man is pure, he can see this universe adorned with innumerable virtues and precious jewels (*anantaguṇaratnālaṃkṛta*).

19. When the splendour of the virtues (*guṇavyūha*) of the Buddhakṣetra appeared to them, the minds of eighty-four thousand living beings (*prāṇin*) turned towards supreme and perfect enlightenment (*anuttarāyāṃ samyaksaṃbodhau cittāny utpāditāni*)[83], and the five hundred young Licchavis who accompanied the Licchavikumāra Ratnākara obtained the preparatory certainty (*anulomikī kṣāntiḥ*)[84].

When the Buddha had shown them this splendid Buddhakṣetra, the five hundred young men (*kumāra*) brought by Ratnākara obtained the certainty concerning the non-arising of dharmas (*anutpattikadharmakṣāntipratilābho 'bhūt*), and the minds of eighty-four thousand living beings (*prāṇin*) turned towards supreme and perfect enlightenment (*anuttarāyāṃ samyaksaṃbodhau cittāny utpāditāni*).

20. Then the Blessed One withdrew his psychic power (*ṛddhi*)[85], and the Buddha-field reappeared as it had been before (*pūrveṇa svabhāvena saṃdṛśyate sma*).

Then the Bhagavat Buddha withdrew the bases of his psychic power (*ṛddhipāda*), and immediately the Buddha-field became as before.

Then the gods and men (*devamanuṣya*) who belonged to the Listeners' Vehicle (*śrāvakayānika*) thought: Alas! conditioned things are transitory (*anityā bata saṃskārāḥ*)[86], and knowing this, thirty-two

[83] These 84,000 living beings produced the thought of Bodhi (*bodhicittotpāda*), the starting point of the Bodhisattva career.

[84] There are divergencies here between the versions:

1. According to the Tibetan translation and Cn, the five hundred Licchavis — who are already Bodhisattvas — obtained the preparatory certainty (*anulomikī kṣāntiḥ*).

2. According to K and H, they obtained the certainty concerning the non-arising of dharmas (*anutpattikadharmakṣānti*).

In both cases, it concerns a certainty (*kṣānti*) relating to the same object: the non-arising of dharmas, but taken from a different level: *anulomikī* is from the sixth stage; *anutpattikā*, from the eighth. See Appendix, Note III: *Nairātmya, anutpāda* and *kṣānti*.

[85] Cf. Aṣṭasāh., p. 875,1: *atha khalu Bhagavāṃs tam ṛddhyabhisaṃskāraṃ punar eva pratisaṃharati sma.*

[86] Beginning of a famous stanza (cf. NĀGĀRJUNA, *Traité*, p. 688, n. 4):

1. Sanskrit Mahāparinirvāṇa, p. 398; Avadānaśataka, II, p. 198,9:

thousand living beings (*prāṇin*) obtained the pure eye of the Law regarding dharmas, without dust or stain (*virajo vigatamalaṃ dharmeṣu dharmacakṣur viśuddham*)[87].

The minds of eight thousand monks (*bhikṣu*) were, through detachment, delivered from their impurities (*anupādāyāsravebhyaś cittāni vimuktāni*)[88].

Finally, in eighty-four thousand living beings (*prāṇin*) who nobly aspired to the Buddha-fields (*buddhakṣetreṣūdārādhimuktikaḥ*) and who had understood the mark of all dharmas to be created by mental illusion (*sarvadharmān viṭhapanapratyupasthānalakṣaṇān viditvā*)[89], their minds turned to

anityā vata saṃskārā utpādavyayadharminaḥ,
utpadya hi nirudhyante teṣāṃ vyupaśamaḥ sukham.

2. Dīgha, II, p. 157; Saṃyutta, I, p. 6, 158, 200; II, p. 193; Theragāthā, No. 1159; Jātaka, I, p. 392; Visuddhimagga, ed. WARREN, p. 448:

aniccā vata saṃkhārā uppādavayadhammino,
uppajjitvā nirujjhanti tesaṃ vūpasamo sukho.

[87] It should be noted that the teaching of Mahāyānasūtras not only profits the followers of the Great Vehicle (*mahāyānika*), but also those of the Small (*śrāvakayānika*). See NĀGĀRJUNA, *Traité*, p. 196. Here, among the Śrāvakas, 32,000 are converted, and 8,000 bhikṣus achieve Arhatship.

A stereotyped formula serves to define conversion:

1. In Pāli: Vinaya, I, p. 11,*34*; 16,*6*; 40,*31*; Dīgha, I, p. 110,*11*; II, p. 288,*21*; Saṃyutta, IV, p. 47,*28*; Aṅguttara, IV, p. 186,*22*: *tassa virajaṃ vītamalaṃ dhammacakkhuṃ udapādi yaṃ kiñci samudayadhammaṃ sabbaṃ taṃ nirodhadhammaṃ ti*: In him, there arose the eye of the Law that is without dust or stain, and he recognised that all that has arising as its law also has extinction as its law".

2. In Sanskrit: Catuṣpariṣad, p. 152, 162; Sanskrit Mahāparinirvāṇa, p. 378; Mahāvastu, III, p. 61,5; 339,*2*; Sukhāvatīvyūha, p. 154,*1*; Kāśyapaparivarta, § 138, 149; Sad. puṇḍarīka, p. 471,*3*: *tasya virajo vigatamalaṃ dharmeṣu dharmacakṣur viśuddham* (*viśuddham* is sometimes replaced by *utpannam*).

[88] This deliverance of mind (*cetovimukti*) in fact constitutes Arhathood, holiness:

1. In Pāli: Vinaya, I, p. 14,*35*; Dīgha, II, p. 35,*23*; Majjhima, I, p. 219,*32*. WOODWARD, *Concordance*, I, p. 148 *b*: *anupādāya āsavehi cittāni vimucciṃsu*.

2. In Sanskrit: Mahāvastu, I, p. 329,*19*; III, p. 67,*1*; 337,*4*; 338,*20*; Kāśyapaparivarta, § 138, 145; Rāṣṭrapāla, p. 59,*19*; Sad. puṇḍarīka, p. 179,*17*: *anupādāyāsravebhyaś cittāni vimuktāni*.

[89] *Viṭhapanapratyupasthānalakṣaṇa* is a traditional expression (cf. Mahāvyutpatti, No. 185). Viṭhapana is Middle-Indian for *viṣṭhāpana*, literally, stabilisation. For the

supreme and perfect enlightenment (*anuttarāyāṃ samyaksaṃbodhau cittāny utpāditāni*)[90].

meaning, cf. Madh. vṛtti, p. 52,*14*: *vitathā ime sarvadharmāḥ, asanta ime sarvadharmāḥ, viṭhapitā imc sarvadharmāḥ, māyopamā imc sarvadharmāḥ*.

Also see Daśabhūmika, p. 39,*14*; 45,*6*; 55,*17*; 74,*4*; Gaṇḍavyūha, p. 524,*1*; Śikṣāsamuccaya, p. 180,*4*; 236,*1-4*; Madh. vṛtti, p. 51,*1*; 363,*5*; 565,7.

[90] This paragraph, which is a repetition of § 19, is missing in the Chinese versions.

CHAPTER TWO

THE INCONCEIVABLE SKILL IN MEANS OF DELIVERANCE

[*Portrait of Vimalakīrti*[1]]

1. At that time, there lived in the great town of Vaiśālī a certain Licchavi Bodhisattva named Vimalakīrti.

In the presence of the Victorious Ones of the past (*pūrvajina*), he had planted good roots (*avaropitakuśalamūla*). He had served numerous Buddhas. He was convinced of the non-arising of dharmas (*anutpādakṣāntipratilabdha*)[2]. He was gifted with eloquence (*pratibhāna*). He exercised the great super-knowledges with ease (*mahābhijñāvikrīḍita*). He knew the formulae (*dhāraṇī*). He was possessed of the convictions (*vaiśāradya*)[3]. He had overcome Māra and his adversaries (*nighātamārapratyarthika*). He had penetrated the deep principle of the Law (*gambhīradharmanaya*). He had achieved the perfection of wisdom (*prajñāpāramitāniryāta*). He was skilled in the means of deliverance (*upāyakauśalyagatiṃgata*). He had fulfilled the great vows (*paripūrṇamahāpraṇidhāna*)[4]. He knew the intentions (*āśaya*) and conduct (*carita*) of beings. He understood perfectly the strength or weakness of the faculties of beings (*sattvendriyavarāvara*)[5]. He expounded the Law as it should be (*yathāpratyarhadharmadeśaka*). He applied himself energetically to the Great Vehicle (*mahāyānābhiyukta*). He accomplished his deeds with resolution (*suniścitaḥ karmakārakaḥ*). He adopted the bodily attitudes (*īryāpatha*) of the Buddhas. He had great intelligence (*paramamati*), as vast as the sea (*samudra*)[6]. He was praised (*stuta*), complimented (*stomita*) and congratulated (*praśaṃsita*) by all the Buddhas. He was venerated (*namaskṛta*) by all the Śakras, Brahmās

[1] The moral portrait of Vimalakīrti will be resumed further on (IV, § 1) by Mañjuśrī.

[2] *Anutpādakṣānti* (cf. Lalitavistara, p. 33,*10*; Laṅkāvatāra, p. 203,*11*) is synonymous with *anutpattikadharmakṣānti*.

[3] This concerns the four *vaiśāradya* of the Bodhisattva (Mahāvyutpatti, No. 782-785), not to be confused with the four *vaiśāradya* of the Buddha (ibidem, No. 131-134).

[4] The ten *mahāpraṇidhāna* of the Bodhisattva: cf. Daśabhūmika, p. 14,*15*.

[5] This concerns the five moral faculties of beings, faith (*śraddhā*), etc: cf. Mahāvyutpatti, No. 976-981; Kośa, I, p. 111.

[6] On the intelligence of the great sea which slopes gradually, throws up bodies, etc., cf. Aṅguttara, IV, p. 198; Daśabhūmika, p. 97.

and Lokapālas. It was in order to help beings ripen (*sattvaparipācanārtham*) that, through skillful means (*upāyakauśalya*), he lived in the great town of Vaiśālī.

2. In order to convert (*saṃgrahāya*) orphans (*anāthasattva*) and poor people (*daridra*), he had inexhaustible riches (*akṣayabhoga*)[7] available. In order to convert immoral beings (*duḥśīla*), he practised pure morality (*pariśuddhaśīla*). In order to convert beings who were cruel (*caṇḍa*), very cruel (*pracaṇḍa*), violent (*raudra*), angry (*krodhana*), he observed patience (*kṣānti*) and self-discipline (*vinaya*). In order to convert lazy beings (*kusīdasattva*), he was full of the utmost vigour (*uttaptavīrya*). In order to convert distracted beings (*vikṣiptacittasattva*), he based himself on the meditations (*dhyāna*), right mindfulness (*samyaksmṛti*), the liberations (*vimokṣa*), concentrations (*samādhi*) and recollections (*samāpatti*). In order to convert stupid beings (*duṣprajñāsattva*), he possessed firm wisdom (*niyataprajñā*)[8].

3. He wore the white clothing of a layman (*avadātavasana*), but observed the conduct of a monk (*śramaṇacaritasaṃpanna*)[9]. He lived in a house (*gṛha*), but kept himself away (*asaṃsṛṣṭa*) from the world of desire (*kāmadhātu*), the world of form (*rūpadhātu*) and the world of no-form (*ārūpyadhātu*). He said he had a son (*putra*), a wife (*bhāryā*), an harem (*antaḥpura*), but practised continence (*brahmacarya*). He appeared surrounded by servants (*parijanaparivṛta*), but always sought solitude (*praviveka*). He appeared adorned with ornaments (*bhūṣaṇālaṃkṛta*), but he always possessed the primary and secondary marks (*lakṣaṇānuvyañjanasamanvāgata*). He seemed to take food (*anna*) and drink (*pāna*), but he always sustained himself with the flavour of the trances (*dhyānarasa*)[10]. He showed himself in amusement parks and gaming houses (*krīḍādyūtasthāna*), but it was always only in order to help ripen (*paripācana*) beings who were attached (*sakta*) to entertainments (*krīḍā*) and games of chance (*dyūta*). He followed

[7] In Vimalakīrti's house there were four inexhaustible treasures (*akṣayanidhāna*); cf. below, VI, § 13, No. 6. Regarding the concept of the inexhaustible treasure, see VII, § 6, v. 34.

[8] This paragraph concerns the six *pāramitā*.

[9] There are frequent references in the Vimalakīrti to the "roundabout ways" or contradictory actions of the Bodhisattvas in general and Vimalakīrti in particular (II, §3-6; III, §3, 16-18; IV, §20; VII, §1; X, §19). See the Introduction, above, p. LVII-LX.

[10] The *dhyānarasāsvādana* consisting in tasting the flavour, the delights of transic meditation is generally condemned by the texts: Laṅkāvatāra, p. 212,*14*; Sūtrālaṃkāra, p. 160,*14*; NĀGĀRJUNA, *Traité*, p. 1027, 1045; Kośa, VIII, p. 144. See P. DEMIÉVILLE, *Le Concile de Lhasa*, p. 62-70.

in the wake of wandering sectaries (*carakapāṣaṇḍikagaveṣin*)[11], but retained for the Buddha and the Law (*dharma*) a flawless attachment (*abhedyāśaya*). He understood the invocations (*mantra*) and commentaries (*śāstra*), whether worldly or transcendental (*laukikalokottara*), but always delighted in the pleasures of the Law (*dharmarati*). He mixed with the crowds (*saṃsarga*), but among all he was revered (*pūjita*) as the foremost (*pramukha*).

4. In order to conform with the world (*lokānuvartanārtham*), he frequented (*sahāyībhūta*) the old (*jyeṣṭha*), the middle-aged (*antara*) and the young (*kumāra*), but spoke to them in conformity with the Law. He undertook all sorts of business deals (*vyavahāra*), but was uninterested (*niḥspṛha*) in gain (*lābha*) or profit (*bhoga*). In order to discipline (*damana*) beings, he showed himself in squares (*catvara*) and at crossroads (*śṛṅgāṭaka*), and in order to protect (*pālana*) beings, he exercised the royal functions (*rājakriyā*). In order to draw away (*samudghāta*) followers of the Small Vehicle (*hīnayānādhimukta*) and attract (*samādāna*) beings to the Great Vehicle (*mahāyāna*), he showed himself among the Listeners (*dharmaśrāvaka*) and reciters of the Law (*dharmabhāṇaka*). In order to help children ripen (*bālaparipācana*), he entered the writing rooms (*lekhanāśālā*). In order to expose the defects of sexual misconduct (*kāmādīnavasamprakāśana*), he went into all the houses of prostitution (*veśyāgṛha*)[12]. In order to bring (drunkards) to right mindfulness (*samyaksmṛti*) and right knowledge (*samyagjñāna*), he entered all the drinking houses (*śauṇḍikagṛha*).

[11] Regarding this expression, see below, III, § 44, note 81.

[12] Regarding this, Kumārajīva (T 1775, ch. 2, p. 340 *a* 9-21) narrates the following tale: Once upon a time, in a foreign land, there was a woman whose body was the colour of gold. A śreṣṭhiputra named Dharmottara, for a consideration of a thousand ounces of gold, was just about to enter a bamboo grove taking the woman with him. Mañjuśrī, on their path, transformed himself into a layman dressed in valuable clothes and richly adorned. On seeing him, the woman conceived a thought of desire. Mañjuśrī said to her: "If you want this clothing, produce the thought of *bodhi*." The woman asked: "What is the thought of *bodhi*?" Mañjuśrī replied: "It is yourself". The woman went on: "How can this be?" Mañjuśrī replied: "*Bodhi* is empty of self-nature and you yourself are also empty". Previously this woman, in the presence of the Buddha Kāśyapa, had planted good roots and cultivated wisdom. Thus, on hearing these words, she obtained the *anutpattikadharmakṣānti*. Having obtained this *kṣānti*, she confessed her sexual misdeeds. She returned to the śreṣṭhiputra and went with him into the bamboo grove. However, once in there, she transformed herself into a swollen and fetid corpse. At the sight of which the śreṣṭhiputra, quite terrified, went to the Buddha. And when the Buddha had expounded the Law to him, he also obtained the *dharmakṣānti* and confessed his sexual misconduct.

5. Because he made the fairest regulations (*dharmaśreṣṭha*), he was recognised (*saṃmata*) as the guildsman (*śreṣṭhin*) among guildsmen [13]. Because he overcame (through his generosity) the avidity (*upādāna*) of beggars (*pratigrāhaka*), he was recognised as the householder (*gṛhapati*) among householders. Because he taught endurance (*kṣānti*), resolution (*niścaya*) and strength (*bala*), he was recognised as the warrior (*kṣatriya*) among warriors. Because he had destroyed pride (*māna*), vanity (*mada*) and arrogance (*darpa*), he was recognised as the brahman among brahmans. Because he taught the method of exercising the royal functions (*rājakriyā*) in conformity with the laws, he was recognised as the minister (*amātya*) among ministers.

Because he attacked attachment (*saṅga*) to royal pleasures (*rājabhoga*) and the exercise of power (*aiśvarya*), he was recognised as the prince (*kumāra*) among princes.

Because he taught faithfulness and filial piety, he was recognised as the prince among princes [14].

Because he educated young women (*kumārī*), he was recognised as an eunuch (*klība*) in the midst of the harem (*antaḥpura*).

6. Because he caused ordinary merits to be highly appreciated, he was in harmony with the common people (*prākṛtapuṇyā-*

Among the common people he was the foremost, because he encouraged a singular estimation (*viśiṣṭāśaya*) for similar merits (to theirs) [15].

[13] Turn of phrase to be interpreted according to the Chinese versions: "Among all the guildsmen, he was the best guildsman", and so on for the rest of the paragraph.

[14] Here H textually reproduces K who diverges considerably from the Tibetan version.

[15] K merely says: "Among the common people he was the foremost, in causing them to extol the power of merits". This evidently concerns the merits of the common people. Regarding this, Kumārajīva (T 1775, ch. 2, p. 340 *c* 1-8) narrates the following anecdote: In days gone by, on entering a town, a poor wretch saw a splendidly dressed man, astride a great horse and holding a valuable parasol. The wretch sighed and said. "It is not good" and this up to three times. The man was astonished and asked him: "Before myself, who am so elegant, why do you say that it is not good?" The wretch answered: "Lord, it is because you planted good roots in the past that you have obtained this reward: you are majestically clothed and looked upon by everyone. As to myself who have not planted any merits, I am as wretched as this. Compared to you, my Lord, I am like an animal. That is why I was saying to myself that it is not good. I did not mean to offend you in the least". After this, the wretch reformed himself and took up many acts of merit; the elegance of forms had been a lesson to him; the advantages that he gained from it were considerable. What then can be said of those who convert beings through teaching?

dhyālambanatayā janakāyasamīcī-pratipannaḥ).

Because he proclaimed the precariousness of power (*ādhipatyānityatā*), he was recognised as the Śakra among Śakras [16].

Because he taught them superior knowledge (*jñānaviśeṣa*), he was recognised as the Brahmā among Brahmās [17].

Among Brahmās, he was the foremost, because he taught the Brahmakāyikas superior meditation (*dhyānaviśeṣa*).

Because he caused all beings to ripen (*sarvasattvaparipācanāt*), he was recognised as the Lokapāla among Lokapālas [18].

Thus it was that the Licchavi Vimalakīrti, gifted with an immense knowledge of skill in means (*apramāṇopāyakauśalyajñānasamanvāgata*), was to be found in the great town of Vaiśālī.

[*Simulated Illness of Vimalakīrti*]

7. Through skill in means (*upāyakauśalyena*), Vimalakīrti made it known that he was ill (*glāna*) [19]. In order to ask him about his illness,

[16] I have adopted here the reading of FP 2203 and FP 613: *bdag po mi rtag par bstan paḥi phyir brgya byin gyi naṅ du yaṅ brgya byin du kun gyis rig*. This reading is confirmed by the Chinese versions.

In the delights of his paradise, Śakra would be tempted to forget the precariousness of his condition; this is why Vimalakīrti reminds him of the great truth of *anityatā*. King of the Trāyastriṃśa gods, Śakra is not freed of old age, sickness and death (cf. Aṅguttara, I, p. 144,*24*). He is regularly warned of his imminent end by the overheating of his throne (Jātaka, IV, p. 8,*29*).

[17] Mahābrahmā is the king of the *rūpadhātu* and the chief of the Brahmakāyika gods spread among the seventeen levels of the four *dhyāna* (Kośa, III, p. 2-4). These *dhyāna* constitute mystical heavens of great value, but they still belong to the triple world. This is why Vimalakīrti teaches the Brahmā gods the most excellent *jñāna* or *dhyāna*: that of the Buddha who transcends the triple world (*lokottara*).

[18] In Buddhism, the four Lokapālas, also called Caturmahārājikadevas, have as their task to report on the conduct of beings to the Trāyastriṃśa gods (Dīgha, II, p. 225; Aṅguttara, I, p. 142), and they are the recognized protectors of the Good Law (Vin. of the Mūlasarv., *Gilgit Manuscripts*, III, part 1, p. 259-260; Aśokāvadāna, T 2042, ch. 3, p. 112 *a*; Aśokasūtra, T 2043, ch. 6, p. 150 *b*).

[19] This concerns a simulated sickness forming part of the arsenal of skillful means used by the Bodhisattva. It will be said later, VII, § 1 and § 6, stanza 18, that the Bodhisattvas make themselves old, sick and even simulate death, but only in order to ripen beings. In Ch. IV, § 7, it is said that the Bodhisattva, who cherishes beings like his only son, is sick when beings are sick and well when beings are well.

It is in basing himself on these passages that, in the sixth century, the Chinese Chih-i, founder of the T'ien-t'ai school, built up his theory of the sicknesses of expediency (*ch'üan ping*). Cf. Mo ho chih kuan, T 1911, ch. 8, p. 110 *c*-111 *a*: "Through the

the king (*rājan*), the ministers (*amātya*), the governors (*adhipati*), the young people (*kumāramaṇḍala*), the brahmans, the householders (*gṛhapati*), the guildsmen (*śreṣṭhin*), the citizens (*naigama*), the country folk (*jānapada*) and several thousands of other people left the great town of Vaiśālī and went to ask him about his illness (*glānapṛcchaka*) [20].

[*Vimalakīrti's Homily on the Human Body* [21]]

8. When they had all gathered, the Licchavi Vimalakīrti addressed them with a discourse on the four great elements (*catvāri mahābhūtāny adhikṛtya dharmaṃ deśayati sma*).

Then Vimalakīrti addressed them at length with a discourse on bodily diseases (*kāyavyādhi*).

Friends (*sakhi*), he said to them, the body consisting of four great elements (*mahābhūta*), is transitory (*anitya*), fragile (*adṛḍha*), unworthy of trust (*aviśvāsya*) and weak (*durbala*); it is unsubstantial (*asāra*), perishable (*vināśin*), lasts for a short while (*acira*), full of suffering (*duḥkha*), full of sickness (*vyādhiparigata*) and subject to changes (*vipariṇāmadharma*). And so, my friends, the body being the receptacle

examination of emptiness (or the middle way), the sick Bodhisattva controls his mind; the mind being controlled, the real sickness is cured. Then, through compassion, there is born in him the "sickness of expediency": The Bodhisattva produces particular lands and men (*fên tuan*); he considers these men like his only son, whom he consoles through his own sickness, just as the parents of a sick only son fall sick themselves".

[20] Visiting the sick is a Buddhist tradition. The visitors are commonly known as *gilānapucchaka* (Vinaya, IV, p. 88,*12-13*; 115,*26-27*; 118,*4*; Majjhima, III, p. 263,*23*; Saṃyutta, IV, p. 56,*4*).

These visits take place according to a traditional ceremony. The sick man sends a nurse to inform the Buddha or a great disciple, and asks for someone to come and visit him. The Master or a disciple accepts the invitation by remaining silent. Then, alone or accompanied by an assistant, he goes to the sick man and sits beside his bed. He asks for news of his health according to an established form of address: *Kacci te khamanīyaṃ*, etc. The sick man admits how much his state leaves to be desired. Thereupon the Master or the great disciple exhorts him to patience, to observe the rules, the faith which delivers from all fear, detachment from the world of feeling, the impermanence of the conditioned, etc. Visits of this kind are frequently mentioned in the canonical texts: cf. Majjhima, II, p. 192; III, p. 258-259, 263-264; Saṃyutta, III, p. 119-120; 124-125; 126-127; IV, p. 55-56; V, p. 79-80; Aṅguttara, III, p. 379.

[21] This homily takes its inspiration from the traditional *kāyasmṛtyupasthāna* (Majjhima, I, p. 56-59, etc.), but seen from the angle of the negativist concepts of the Great Vehicle. See also below, IV, § 9-11.

of so much sickness (*bahuvyādhibhājana*), knowledgeable people (*kuśala*) place no reliance on it[22].

9. The body, which cannot be grasped (*avimardanakṣama*), is like a ball of foam (*phenapiṇḍa*)[23]. The body, which does not last for long (*acirasthitika*), is like a bubble of water (*budbuda*). The body, arisen from the thirst of the passions (*kleśatṛṣṇotpanna*), is like a mirage (*marīci*). The body, deprived of substance (*asāra*), is like the trunk of a banana tree (*kadalīgarbha*). Alas! the body, a collection of bones and tendons (*asthisnāyubandha*), is like a mechanical thing (*yantra*). The body, arisen from perverted views (*viparyāsasamutthita*), is like a magical illusion (*māyā*). The body, a false vision (*abhūtadarśana*), is like a dream (*svapna*). The body, a replica of previous action (*pūrvakarmapratibimba*), is like a reflection (*pratibimba*). The body, dependent on conditions (*pratyayādhīna*), is like an echo (*pratiśrutkā*). The body, which dissipates and dissolves itself (*vikṣepavidhvaṃsalakṣaṇa*), is like a cloud (*megha*). The body, which perishes instantaneously (*kṣaṇabhaṅga*) and is unstable (*avyavasthita*), is like a flash of lightning (*vidyut*). The body, born of multiple conditions (*vividhapratyayotpanna*), has no master (*asvāmika*).

10. The body, like earth (*pṛthivī*), is immobile (*niśceṣṭa*). The body, like water (*ap*), is impersonal (*nairātmya*). The body, like fire (*tejas*),

[22] It is a typically Buddhist concept that sickness is the normal state of the body: cf. NĀGĀRJUNA, *Traité*, p. 584; Hōbōgirin, p. 232 *b*.

[23] This and the following paragraph multiply comparisons taken for the most part from the stock of the ten *Upamāna*, frequently exploited in Mahāyānasūtras. These Upamāna are commented on at length in NĀGĀRJUNA, *Traité*, p. 357-387; where there are several references to be found which it would be easy to complete (e.g. Suvikrānta, p. 92; Mahāvyutpatti, No. 2812-2828). The Vimalakīrti resorts to them again in other places: III, § 35; X, § 9, and particularly VI, § 1, where the comparisons reach the number of thirty-five.

The accuracy of these comparisons deeply impressed the Chinese, and the poet and calligrapher Hsieh Ling-yün (385-433), who took an active part in the Buddhist controversies of his time, composed a "Eulogy to the ten Upamānas of the Vimalakīrtisūtra" (cf. Kuang hung ming chi, T 2103, ch. 15, p. 220 *a* 29 - *c* 1). However, these comparisons are not an invention of either the Vimalakīrti or other Mahāyānasūtras: they go back, for the most, to the old canonical Sūtras, in particular the Saṃyutta, III, p. 142:

phenapiṇḍūpamaṃ rūpaṃ vedanā bubbulupamā,
marīcikūpamā saññā saṅkhārā kadalūpamā,
māyūpamañca viññānaṃ dīpitādiccabandhunā.

Also see Saṃyukta, T 99, ch. 10, p. 69 *a* 18-20; Wu yin p'i yü ching, T 105, p. 501 *b* 18-20; Shui mo so p'iao ching, T 106, p. 502 *a* 26; Visuddhimagga, ed. WARREN, p. 406,7; Cullaniddesa, p. 279; Madh. vṛtti, p. 41; Madh. avatāra, p. 22; Śrāvakabhūmi, p. 170.

is without life (*nirjīva*). The body, like wind (*vāyu*), has no individuality (*niṣpudgala*). The body, like air (*ākāśa*), has no self-nature (*niḥsvabhāva*)[24].

11. The body, receptacle of the four great elements (*mahābhūtasthāna*), is unreal (*abhūta*). The body, which has no self (*anātman*) and belongs to no self (*anātmīya*), is empty (*śūnya*). The body, like a blade of grass (*tṛṇa*), a piece of wood (*kāṣṭha*), a wall (*bhitti*), a clod of earth (*loṣṭa*), an image (*pratibhāsa*), is unintelligent (*mūrkha*). The body, moved by the wind like a mechanical thing (*yantra*), is unfeeling (*nirvedaka*). The body, an accumulation of pus (*pūya*) and excrement (*mīḍha*), is dirty (*tuccha*). The body, which is always subject (not only) to being washed and rubbed (but also) to breaking and being destroyed (*nityasnāpanaparimardanabhedanavidhvaṃsanadharma*)[25], is false (*rikta*). The body is tormented (*upadruta*, *pratāpita*)

[24] Cf. Dīgha, I, p. 55,*21*.

[25] This long compound is an extract from a canonical topic, confirmed in Pāli and Sanskrit:

Dīgha, I, p. 76,*18*; 173,*27*; 209,*4*; Majjhima, I, p. 144,*3*; 500,*2-3*; II, p. 17,*19*; Saṃyutta, IV, p. 83,*26*; 194,*30*; 292,*9*; V, p. 370,*1* and *16*; Aṅguttara, IV, p. 386,*23*: *ayaṃ kāyo rūpī cātummahābhūtiko mātapettikasaṃbhavo odanakummāsupacayo anicc' ucchādanaparimaddanabhedanaviddhaṃsanadhammo*: "The material body, made of the four great elements, born of mother and father, fattened with boiled rice and gruel, which has as its law to be always anointed and massaged, but nevertheless to breaking and being destroyed".

Mahāvastu, II, p. 269,*15*: *mātāpitṛsaṃbhavaḥ kāyo odanakulmāṣopacaya ucchādanaparimardanasvapnabhedanavikiraṇavidhvaṃsanadharmaḥ*: "Body born of mother and father, fattened with boiled rice and gruel, which has as its law to be anointed, massaged, committed to sleep, but which all the same breaks, transforms itself and perishes".

Mahāvastu, II, p. 278,*1*, offers the variation *ācchādana* instead of *ucchādana*: "which has as its law to be dressed ..."

Kāśyapaparivarta, § 152, presents the variation *ucchāda(na)snāpana*: "which has as its law to be anointed, bathed ..."

Here, the Tibetan version of the Vimalakīrti has: *lus ḥdi ni rtag tu bsku ba* (to correct *ḥkhru ba*) *daṅ mñe ba daṅ ḥjig pa daṅ ḥgyes paḥi chos can te*, which presupposes in Sanskrit *ayaṃ kāyo nityasnāpanaparimardanabhedanavidhvaṃsanadharmaḥ*: "This body has as its law to be always bathed and massaged, but nevertheless it breaks and is destroyed".

The translation proposed here, which contrasts *snāpanaparimardana* with *bhedanavidhvaṃsana*, diverges from current interpretation. All modern translators follow T.W. Rhys Davids, *Dialogues of the Buddha*, I, p. 87: "This body is subject to erasion, abrasion, dissolution and disintegration". Cf. I.B. Horner, *Middle Length Sayings*, I, p. 185,*11-12*; F.L. Woodward, *Kindred Sayings*, IV, p. 50,*20-21*; E.M. Hare,

by the four hundred and four diseases (*vyādhi*)[26]. The body, always overcome by old age (*jarābhibhūta*), is like an old well (*jarodapāna*)[27].

Gradual Sayings, IV, p. 258,*3-4*; J.J. JONES, *Mahāvastu translated*, II, p. 253,*3-4*; F. EDGERTON, *Buddhist Hybrid Sanskrit Dictionary*, p. 119 *a*.

However, it is necessary to diverge from these authorities so as to follow the formal advice of Sinhalese commentators and Chinese translators:

1. Buddhaghosa in his Commentaries of the Dīgha, I, p. 220,*21*, and the Majjhima, II, p. 129,*32*, explains: "The body is *ucchādanadhamma* because it is gently coated (*tanuvilepanena*); it is *parimaddanadhamma* because it is lightly massaged (*khuddakasambāhanena*); but even if it is thus cared for (*evaṃ pariharato pi*), it has as its law to break and be destroyed".

2. Translation by Saṃgharakṣa and Saṃghadeva, in Madhyamāgama, T 26, ch. 28, p. 603 *a* 25: This body is material (*rūpin*), gross (*audārika*), made of the four great elements (*cāturmahābhūtika*), born of mother and father (*matāpitṛsaṃbhava*). With extreme patience, it is provided with nourishment and drink (*annapānopacaya*), dressed in clothes (*ācchādana*), massaged (*parimardana*) and bathed (*snāpana*). But it is subject to impermanence (*anityadharma*), and it has as its law to break (*bhedanadharma*) and be destroyed (*vidhvaṃsanadharma*).

3. Translation of Kumārajīva in Vimalakīrtinirdeśa, T 475, ch. 1, p. 539 *b* 25: This body is false (*rikta*): although it is bathed (*snāpana*), it is dressed (*ācchādana*), it is nourished with food and drink (*annapānopacaya*), it necessarily ends by breaking and being destroyed.

[26] There are 404 diseases, 101 for each of the four great elements: Hsiu hsing pên ch'i ching, T 184, ch. 2, p. 466 *c* 20-21; Prajñāpāramitā, T 220, ch. 502, p. 556 *c* 8; ch. 540, p. 778 *a* 17; T 223, ch. 9, p. 287 *a* 1; T 1509, ch. 58, p. 469 *c* 23; Fo i ching, T 793, p. 737 *a*; Great Parinirvāṇa, T 374, ch. 5, p. 392 *b* 5; Vin. of the Mahāsāṃghikas, T 1425, ch. 10, p. 316 *c* 20; Vin. of the Mūlasarv., T 1451, ch. 12, p. 257 *b* 26; Catuḥsatyaśāstra, T 1647, ch. 1, p. 382 *c* 22-23; Bodhicaryāvatāra, II, v. 55. — For details, see Hōbōgirin, p. 255-257.

[27] The reading *khron paḥi rñiṅ pa*, confirmed in N, FP 2203 and FP 603, is preferable to *khron paḥi sñiṅ po* of P. *Khron paḥi rñiṅ pa*, *ch'iu ching* 丘井 in K, *ch'iu sui chi* 水隧級 in H, corresponds to the Pāli *jarūdapāna* or *jarudapāna* and to the Sanskrit *jarodapāna* "old well" or "dried up well". The expression is found in canonical texts, especially in the Candropamasūtra (Saṃyutta, II, p. 198,*3*; HOERNLE, *Manuscript Remains*, p. 43,*3*; Saṃyukta, T 99, ch. 41, p. 299 *c* 8; T 100, ch. 6, p. 414 *a* 22; T 121, p. 544 *b* 18).

However Kumārajīva, in his Commentary of the Vimalakīrti, T 1775, ch. 2, p. 342 *b* 2 sq., sees in this an allusion to the familiar parable of the "Man in the well":

1. Mahābhārata, Strīparvan, adhyāya V-VI.

2. Chung ching hsüan tsa p'i yü ching, T 208, ch. 1, p. 533 *a* 27 - 533 *b* 13, translated into French in É. CHAVANNES, *Cinq cents contes et apologues extraits du Tripiṭaka chinois*, Paris, 1910-34, vol. II, p. 83. According to this version, the old well symbolises the dwelling place of all living beings.

3. P'in t'ou lu t'u lo shê wei yu t'o yen wang shuo fa ching, T 1690, p. 787 *a* 19. According to this version, the well symbolises the human body, an interpretation identical to that of the Vimalakīrti.

4. Fo shuo p'i yü ching, T 217, p. 801 *b*, translated into French by P. DEMIÉVILLE

The body, which comes to an end in death (*maraṇānta*), cannot fix its own end (*aniyatānta*). The body, which comprises [five] aggregates (*skandha*), [eighteen] elements (*dhātu*) and [twelve] bases of consciousness (*āyatana*), is like five killers (*vadhaka*), four poisonous snakes (*āśīvisa*) and an empty village (*śūnyagrāma*)[28]. Thus it is that,

in CHAVANNES, *Contes*, IV, p. 236-238. According to this version, the well symbolises Saṃsāra.

5. Ching lü i hsiang, T 2121, ch. 44, p. 233 *c* 28-234 *a* 10, translated into French in CHAVANNES, *Contes*, III, p. 257.

6. Various figurative representations:

a. A bas-relief in the Musée Guimet: cf. J.Ph. VOGEL, *The Man in the Well*, Revue des Arts Asiatiques, XI, 1937, p. 109-115, pl. XXXIII b.

b. A sculpture from Nāgārjunakoṇḍa: cf. A.H. LONGHURST, *The Buddhist Antiquities of Nāgārjunakoṇḍa*, Delhi, 1938, pl. 49 b and 31 b.

c. A bas-relief on the base of the Eastern pagoda in Zayton: cf. G. ECKE and P. DEMIÉVILLE, *The Twin Pagodas of Zayton*, Harvard, 1935, p. 53 and pl. 36 b. The sculpture bears the four Chinese characters *ch'iu ching k'uang hsiang* "the empty well and the enraged elephant", taken directly from Kumārajīva's translations (T 208 and 475, *l.c.*).

d. Representations on the Southern door of the baptistry of Parma and the pulpit in Ferrara cathedral: cf. ECKE-DEMIÉVILLE, *l.c.*, p. 54.

This is how Kumārajīva, T 1775, ch. 2, p. 342 *b*, summarises this parable: A man, having committed an offence against the king and fearful of this offence, took flight. The king sent a drunken elephant in his pursuit, and the man, in his fear and haste, threw himself into a dried up well. In the middle of the well, he found some rotten grass and clung to it with his hands. At the bottom of the well, there was an evil dragon who spat venom in his direction. On the walls, five poisonous snakes also tried to reach him. Two rats gnawed at the blade of grass, and the grass was on the point of giving way. The great elephant, leaning over the well, tried to grasp him. Faced with all these dangers, the man felt very much afraid. But, above the well, there was a tree and, on the tree, honey. Drops of honey fell into his mouth and when he had tasted its flavour, he forgot his fears. The empty well is *saṃsāra*. The drunken elephant is impermanence (*anityatā*). The venomous dragon represents the bad destinies (*durgati*). The five poisonous snakes are the five aggregates (*skandha*). The rotten grass is the vital organ (*jīvitendriya*). The two rats, one white and the other black, are respectively the white fortnight (*śuklapakṣa*) and the black fortnight (*kṛṣṇapakṣa*). The drops of honey are the five objects of desire (*kāmaguṇa*). The man who, in tasting them, forgets his fears, is the being (*sattva*) who, obtaining the five objects of desire, no longer fears suffering.

[28] The Vimalakīrti will return further on (III, § 11 and 64) to these closely linked comparisons. Cf. Dharmasaṃgītisūtra (T 761, ch. 5, p. 639 *c*), quoted in Bhavanākrama No. I, ed. G. TUCCI, *Minor Buddhist Texts*, II, p. 222, *12-16*: *skandheṣu māyāvat pratyavekṣaṇā ..., dhātuṣv āśīviṣavat pratyavekṣaṇā ..., āyataneṣu śūnyagrāmavat pratyavekṣaṇā*. Regarding the *āśīviṣa*, see also the Upadeśa, T 1509, ch. 2, p. 67 *a* 27;

full of disgust (*nirvid*) and repugnance (*udvega*) for a body such as this, you should turn your aspirations (*adhimukti*) to the body of the Tathāgata.

[*Vimalakīrti's Homily on the Body of the Tathāgata*]

12. Friends (*sakhi*), the body of the Tathāgata (*tathāgatakāya*) is

Sūtrālaṃkāra of Aśvaghoṣa, trans. É. Huber, p. 153, 387; Tsa p'i yü ching, T 205, ch. 1, p. 503 *a*.

These three comparisons are taken from a parable of canonical origin:

1. Āśīviṣopamasūtra, in Saṃyutta, IV, p. 172-175; Saṃyukta, T 99, ch. 43, p. 313*b*-314*a*; Ekottara, T 125, ch. 23, p. 669*c*-670*a*. — According to tradition, this sūtra would have been expounded to Aravāla, the Nāga king, and the people of Kaśmīra-Gandhāra by the sthavira Madhyāntika; eighty thousand listeners were converted and an hundred thousand took up the religious life (Samantapāsādikā, I, p. 66; Shan chien lü, T 1462, ch. 2, p. 685 *b*; Mahāvaṃsa, XII, v. 26).

2. Great Parinirvāṇa, T 374, ch. 23, p. 499 *a-b*; T 375, ch. 21, p. 742 *c*-743 *a* (French trans. in Nāgārjuna, *Traité*, p. 705).

3. Upadeśa, T 1509, ch. 12, p. 145 *b* (French trans. in Nāgārjuna, *Traité*, p. 702-707).

4. Chu wei mo chieh ching, T 1775, ch. 2, p. 342 *b* 22 - *c* 6.

Here is a short summary of this parable:

A man, being guilty of some offence, the *king* (rājan) gives him a *coffer* (karaṇḍaka) containing *four poisonous snakes* (āśīviṣa), and orders him to rear these snakes. Terrified, the man takes flight, but the king sends *five killers* (vadhaka) in his pursuit. A *sixth killer*, guessing his intentions, advises him to comply with the king's orders. Suspecting a trap, the man continues on his way and comes to an *empty village* (śūnyagrāma). A *good person* (satpuruṣa) warns him of the imminent arrival of *six big thieves* (mahācaura) and persuades him to leave the village as soon as possible. The man continues on his way and comes across a *stretch of water* (udakārṇava): the *near bank* (oratīra) was highly dangerous, while the *far bank* (pāratīra) was entirely safe. The man builds himself a *raft* (kaula), gets on it and *manoevering his hands and feet* (hastaiś ca pādaiś ca vyāyāmaḥ), manages to *cross* (tīrṇa) the stretch of water.

The *king* is Māra; the *coffer* is the human body (*kāya*); the *four poisonous snakes* are the four great elements (*mahābhūta*) entering into the composition of the body. The *five killers* are the five psychophysical aggregates (*skandha*) constituting the false personality; the *sixth killer* is joy and pleasure (*nandirāga*). The *empty village* represents the six internal bases of consciousness (*ādhyātmikāyatana*), eye, etc. The *good person* who advises flight is the good Master (*śāstṛ*): he puts the man on guard against the *six thieves*, that is, the six external bases of consciousness (*bāhyāyatana*), colour, etc. The *stretch of water* is the sea of yearning (*tṛṣṇā*), fed by the rivers of craving (*kāma*), becoming (*bhava*), false view (*dṛṣṭi*) and ignorance (*avidyā*). The *near bank*, full of dangers, is the world (*loka*), the aggregation of perishable things (*satkāya*); the *far bank* is Nirvāṇa. The *raft* which the man uses is the noble eight-fold path (*āryāṣṭāṅgamārga*). The *manoeuvering of hands and feet* is vigour (*vīrya*). And finally, the man who has *crossed* is the Arhat.

the body of the Law (*dharmakāya*)[29], born of knowledge (*jñāna*). The body of the Tathāgata is born of merit (*puṇya*), born of giving (*dāna*); — born of morality (*śīla*), born of concentration (*samādhi*), born of wisdom (*prajñā*), born of deliverance (*vimukti*), born of the knowledge and vision of deliverance (*vimuktijñānadarśana*)[30]; — born

[29] All the versions, with the exception of H, begin with this statement: "The body of the Tathāgata is the body of the Law"; H merely says: "The body of the Tathāgata consists of innumerable good dharmas (*apramāṇakuśaladharmasaṃbhava*)". This practically comes to the same thing, the *dharmakāya* being the series of pure dharmas (*anāsravadharmasaṃtāna*).

The Buddhology of the Vimalakīrti is very simple and is practically unaware of speculations concerning the Triple Body of the Buddha.

1. The true body of the Tathāgata is not the material body (*rūpakāya*), body of fruition (*vipākakāya*), or birth (*janmakāya*), born in the Lumbinī garden, but the body of the Law born of all the good dharmas (II, § 12; III, § 43); it is a transcendental body, pure and unconditioned (III, § 45). All the Tathāgatas are the same among themselves, in that they possess the fullness of all the Buddha attributes and, even if one wanted to, one could not enumerate all the qualities of those who are fully and perfectly enlightened (X, § 13).

All this is Sarvāstivādin Buddhology, as can be seen in the Kośa, III, p. 198; IV, p. 76, 220-221; VI, p. 267; VII, p. 66-85; VIII, p. 195.

2. However, if the true body of the Buddha is the synthesis of all qualities, this in no way prevents Vimalakīrti from "seeing the Tathāgata as if there was nothing to see" (XI, § 1). Because of his transcendency, or, better, his inexistence (*niḥsvabhāvatā*), the Tathāgata eludes time, place, causality, movement, experience and activity. He is unknowable and undefinable.

This is the position of the Prajñāpāramitā (Pañcaviṃśati, p. 146,*9-17*) according to which the Bodhisattva does not perceive (*nopalabhate*) either being, or dharma, or conditioned co-production, or arhat, or pratyekabuddha, or bodhisattva, or Buddha "because of their absolute purity" (*atyantaviśuddhitā*).

Even more, this absolute purity is originally and universally acquired. And the Vimalakīrti will explain further on (VII, § 2-3) that the family of the Tathāgata is the accumulation of all the passions and all the false views. The Śrāvaka who sees the noble truths and aspires to the unconditioned (*asaṃskṛta*), to Nirvāṇa, will never reach the supreme and perfect enlightenment of the Buddhas. The production of the thought of Bodhi is reserved for those who, leaning on conditioned things (*saṃskṛta*), still course in all the passions and all errors. These latter form the true family (*gotra*) of the Tathāgatas.

Hence this supreme paradox (III, § 51) that enlightenment is already acquired by all beings, and that there is not a single being who is not already in parinirvāṇa.

[30] *Śīla, samādhi, prajñā, vimukti* and *vimuktijñānadarśana* are the five *dhammakkhandha* of the canon (Dīgha, III, p. 279,*14*; Saṃyutta, I, p. 99,*30*; Aṅguttara, I, p. 162,*4*; Itivuttaka, p. 106,*21*), the *lokottaraskandha* of the Dharmasaṃgraha, § 23; the *asamasamāḥ skandhāḥ* of the Mahāvyutpatti, No. 104-108; the *anāsravaskandha* of the Kośa, I, p. 48; VI, p. 297, and of the Kośavyākhā, p. 607,*10*.

According to the Ratnakūṭa, quoted in Madh. vṛtti, p. 48,*5*, these skandhas define

of goodwill (*maitrī*), compassion (*karuṇā*), joy (*muditā*) and equanimity (*upekṣā*)[31]; born of giving (*dāna*), discipline (*vinaya*) and self-mastery (*saṃyama*); — born of the ten paths of good action (*daśa kuśalakarmapatha*); — born of patience and kindness (*kṣāntisauratya*)[32]; — born of the good roots resulting from unflinching vigour (*dṛḍhavīryaḳuśalamūla*); — born of the four ecstatic states (*dhyāna*), the (eight) liberations (*vimokṣa*), the (three) concentrations (*samādhi*) and the (four) recollections (*samāpatti*); — born of learning (*śruta*), wisdom (*prajña*) and skillful means (*upāya*); — born of the thirty-seven auxiliaries of enlightenment (*bodhipākṣikadharma*)[33]; — born of calm (*śamatha*) and insight (*vipaśyanā*)[34]; — born of the ten powers (*bala*)[35], the four convictions (*vaiśāradya*)[36], and eighteen exclusive attributes of the Buddhas (*āveṇikabuddhadharma*)[37]; — born of all the perfections (*pāramitā*); — born of the (six) super-knowledges (*abhijñā*) and the (triple) knowledge (*tisro vidyāḥ*)[38]; — born of the destruction of all bad dharmas (*sarvākuśaladharmaprahāṇa*) and born of the assemblage of all good dharmas (*sarvakuśaladharmasaṃgraha*); — born of truth (*satya*), righteousness (*samyaktva*) and heedfulness (*apramāda*).

Friends, the body of the Tathāgata is born of countless good actions (*apramāṇakuśalakarman*). It is towards a body such as this

Nirvāṇa: *śīlaṃ na saṃsarati na parinirvāti*; *samādhiḥ prajñā vimuktir vimuktijñānadarśanaṃ na saṃsarati na parinirvāti*: *ebhir dharmair nirvāṇaṃ sūcyate*.

One also speaks of the five-limbed Body of the Law (*pañcāṅgadharmakāya*), in honour of which Aśoka built five stūpas in addition to the 84,000: cf. Hsi yü chi, T 2087, ch. 8, p. 912 *b* 7.

31 See above, I, § 13, n. 66.

32 *Kṣāntisauratya*, in Pāli *khantisoracca*, Saṃyutta, I, p. 100,*10*; 222,*15*; Aṅguttara, II, p. 68,*15*; Daśabhūmika, p. 13,*19*; 37,*11*; Sad. puṇḍarīka, p. 234,*8*; 236,*9*; Bodh. bhūmi, p. 20,*12*; 143,*27*; Śikṣāsamuccaya, p. 183,*14*; 326,*12*.

33 See above, I, § 13, n. 69.

34 Cf. Bodh. bhūmi, p. 260,*11-14*: *tatra vā bodhisattvasyaiṣā dharmāṇām evam avikalpanā, so 'sya śamatho draṣṭavyaḥ. yac ca tad yathābhūtajñānaṃ pāramārthikaṃ, yac ca tad apramāṇavyavasthānanayajñānaṃ dharmeṣu, iyam asya vipaśyanā draṣṭavyā.*

Also see Sūtrālaṃkāra, p. 146,*4-9*; Bhāvanākrama II, in P. DEMIÉVILLE, *Le Concile de Lhasa*, p. 336-348.

35 Regarding the ten *bala*, cf. Pañcaviṃśati, p. 210,*11*; EDGERTON, *Dictionary*, p. 397 *b*.

36 Regarding the four *vaiśāradya*, cf. Pañcaviṃśati, p. 211,*1*; EDGERTON, *Dictionary*, p. 512 *b*.

37 Regarding the eighteen *āveṇikabuddhadharma*, cf. Pañcaviṃsati, p. 211,*17*; Arthaviniścaya, p. 579; Kośa, VII, p. 66; EDGERTON, *Dictionary*, p. 108 *b*.

38 Of the six *abhijñā*, three are *vidyā* "knowledges" and make upt the *tisro vidyāḥ* cf. Kośa, VII, p. 108.

that you should turn your aspirations (*adhimukti*) and, so as to destroy the diseases of the passions (*kleśavyādhi*)[39] of all beings, you should produce the thought of supreme and perfect enlightenment.

13. While the Licchavi Vimalakīrti was thus expounding the Law to those who came to ask about his illness (*glānapṛcchaka*), several hundreds of thousands of beings produced the thought of supreme and perfect enlightenment (*bahuśatānāṃ sattvasahasrāṇām anuttarāyāṃ samyaksaṃbodhau cittāny utpāditāni*).

[39] This concerns the mental diseases (*mānasa*), numbering 84,000: 21,000 of *rāga*, 21,000 of *dveṣa*, 21,000 of *moha* and 21,000 combined; cf. Upadeśa, T 1509, ch. 59, p. 478 *b* 15; Hōbōgirin, p. 255. They are distinct from the 404 bodily diseases mentioned above, II, § 11.

CHAPTER THREE

THE REFUSAL TO ENQUIRE BY THE ŚRĀVAKAS AND THE BODHISATTVAS

1. Then the Licchavi Vimalakīrti had this thought (*atha khalu licchaver vimalakīrter etad abhavat*): I am ailing (*ābādhika*), suffering (*duḥkhita*), lying on a couch (*mañcakopaviṣṭa*), and the Tathāgata, holy one (*arhat*), perfectly and fully enlightened (*samyaksaṃbuddha*), is not concerned about me (*mām anabhipretya*), has no pity whatever (*anukampām anupādāya*), and sends no-one to enquire about my illness (*na kaṃcid eva glānapṛcchakaṃ preṣayati*).

[1. *Śāriputra and the Pratisaṃlayana*]

2. Then the Blessed One, knowing in his mind the thought that had arisen in the mind of Vimalakīrti (*atha khalu bhagavāṃs tasya vimalakīrteś cetasaiva cetaḥparivitarkam ājñāya*), took pity on him (*anukampām upādāya*) and said to the Venerable (*āyuṣmant*) Śāriputra: Śāriputra, do go and ask the Licchavi Vimalakīrti about his illness[1].

[1] In the course of this chapter, the Buddha will successively invite ten bhikṣus, three bodhisattvas and one upāsaka to go and seek news of Vimalakīrti. They all decline the invitation, and justify their refusal by narrating a misadventure that befell them when meeting Vimalakīrti on a previous occasion.

Śāriputra was the chief disciple (*agraśrāvaka*) of Śākyamuni and the foremost of the great wise men (*mahāprajñāvatām agryaḥ*).

He was born in Nālandā of the brahman Vaṅgānta and Rūpaśārī. He left the world and with his friend Maudgalyāyana joined the school of the sectarian master Sañjaya. The latter conferred on the two young men the leadership of five hundred disciples. Śāriputra and Maudgalyāyana soon left their teacher in order to seek the Immortal, each in his own way. The first to find it would immediately tell his friend.

One day in Rājagṛha, Śāriputra met the bhikṣu Aśvajit, one of the first five disciples of Śākyamuni. He questioned him about the doctrine of the Buddha, and Aśvajit condensed for him, in a stanza which is still famous, the four noble truths: *ye dharmā hetuprabhāvāḥ*, etc. Śāriputra immediately told Maudgalyāyana of the Buddha's appearance. The two friends, followed by their five hundred pupils, went to Rājagṛha, to the Veṇuvana. The Buddha ordained them forthwith. The five hundred pupils obtained Arhatship on the spot, Maudgalyāyana after seven days, and Śāriputra after fifteen, when the Master had expounded the Dīghanakhasutta to him.

Enjoying the Buddha's complete confidence, Śāriputra seconded him in his teaching, gave counsel to his colleagues and undertook the most delicate of missions on behalf

This having been said (*evam ukte*), Venerable Śāriputra answered the Blessed One: Blessed One, I am not capable (*utsāha*) of going to ask the Licchavi Vimalakīrti about his illness. And why (*tat kasya hetoḥ*)? Blessed One, I remember (*anusmarāmi*) that one day in the Mahāvana [2], where I was absorbed in meditation (*pratisaṃlīna*) at the foot of a tree (*vṛkṣamūla*), the Licchavi Vimalakīrti came to the foot of that tree (*yena vṛkṣamūlaṃ tenopasaṃkrāntaḥ*) and having saluted my feet by touching them with his head (*pādau śirasābhivandya*), addressed these words to me:

3. Honourable (*bhadanta*) Śāriputra, you should not absorb yourself in meditation as you are doing (*yathā tvaṃ pratisaṃlīyase naivaṃ pratisaṃlayane pratisaṃlayitavyam*) [3].

of the Saṃgha. He died in his native village a few months before Śakyamuni's Nirvaṇa. His great reputation for wisdom led him later to be considered as an Abhidharma master and to figure in Mahāyānasūtras as the main interrogator of the Buddha.

Regarding Śāriputra, see MALALASEKERA, *Proper Names*, II p. 1108-1118; AKANUMA, *Noms propres*, p. 593-602; NĀGĀRJUNA, *Traité*, p. 623-640; A. MIGOT, *Un grand disciple du Buddha*: *Śāriputra*, BEFEO XLVI, 1954, p. 405-554.

[2] A great forest which stretched from Vaiśālī to the Himālayas: Comm. of the Dīgha, I, p. 309; Comm. of the Majjhima, II, p. 73, 267; NĀGĀRJUNA, *Traité*, p. 183, footnote; Hsi yü chi, T 2087, ch. 7, p. 908 *b*. It was here that the Belvedere Hall (*kūṭāgāraśālā*) beside the Monkey Pool (*markaṭahrada*) was to be found.

[3] Śāriputra was a past master in *pratisaṃlayana* "siesta, rest, retreat, solitude, away from all worldly sounds". Cf. Comm. of the Majjhima, I, p. 181: *tehi tehi sattasaṅkhārehi paṭinivattitvā sallānaṃ*; *nilīyanaṃ ekībhāvo paviveko ti vuttaṃ hoti.*

The *pratisaṃlayana* was practised in the jungle, at the foot of a tree, after the alms round and the midday meal. It was carried out during the hot afternoon hours, and the monk only came out of it towards evening (*sāyāhnasamaye*).

Saṃyutta, III, p. 235; Majjhima, I, p. 447, etc.: *atha kho āyasmā Sāriputto pubbaṇhasamayaṃ nivāsetvā pattacīvaraṃ ādāya Sāvatthiṃ piṇḍāya pāvisi. Sāvatthiyaṃ piṇḍāya caritvā pacchābhattaṃ piṇḍapātapaṭikkanto yena andhavanaṃ ten' upasaṅkami divāvihārāya, andhavanaṃ ajjhogāhitvā aññatarasmiṃ rukkhamūle divāvihāraṃ nisīdi. atha kho āyasmā Sāriputto sāyaṇhasamayaṃ paṭisallāṇā vuṭṭhito yena ...*

From the viewpoint of the Small Vehicle, the *pratisaṃlayana* cannot degenerate into somnolence pure and simple, and Śākyamuni recommended his monks to apply all their efforts to the *pratisaṃlayana* in order to understand exactly the origin and disappearance of the *skandha*, the impermanence of the *dhātu*, the four noble truths, etc.: cf. Saṃyutta, III, p. 15,*21*; IV, p. 80,*30*; V, p. 414,*18*.

In contrast, for Vimalakīrti the true *pratisaṃlayana* is a meditation without content, the recollection of the extinction of consciousness and feeling (*saṃjñāvedayitanirodha-samāpatti*). This recollection constitutes Nirvāṇa on earth (*dṛṣṭadharmanirvāṇa*), but should not be followed by the entry into complete Nirvāṇa (*nirupadhiśeṣanirvāṇa*) after death, for the Bodhisattva renounces this so as to devote further himself to the

Not displaying either one's body (*kāya*) or one's mind (*citta*) in the triple world (*traidhātuka*), this is how to meditate. Not withdrawing (*vyutthātum*) from the recollection of extinction (*nirodhasamāpatti*), but displaying ordinary attitudes (*īryāpathasaṃdarśana*), this is how to meditate[4]. Not renouncing the spiritual marks already acquired (*prāptalakṣaṇaparityāga*), but displaying all the marks of the worldly (*pṛthagjanalakṣaṇasaṃdarśana*), this is how to meditate[5]. Acting so that the mind does not stop inwardly (*adhyātmam*) and does not spread outwardly (*bahirdhā*), this is how to meditate. Not avoiding false views (*dṛṣṭigata*), but basing oneself on the thirty-seven auxiliaries of enlightenment (*bodhipākṣikadharma*), this is how to meditate[6].

Not destroying the passions which come from the realm of rebirth (*saṃsārāvacarakleśa*), but

Not abandoning rebirth (*saṃsārāparityāga*), but rejecting the passions (*kleśa*); even while upholding Nirvāṇa (*nirvāṇa*-

welfare and happiness of all creatures. The Bodhisattva establishes himself in *apratiṣṭhitanirvāṇa*.

To tell the truth, the Small Vehicle too already recommended the meditation without content, as it appears from the Sandhakaccānasutta where it is said:

Namo te purisājañña namo te purisuttama,
yassa te nābhijānāma yaṃ pi nissāya jhāyasi.

"Homage to you, peerless man; homage to you, excellent man, for we know not on what you meditate".

Cf. Aṅguttara, V, p. 323-326; Saṃyukta, T 99, ch. 33, p. 235 *c* - 236 *b*; T 100, ch. 8, p. 430 *c*-431 *b*.

This concerns an old canonical Sūtra in which the doctors of the Great Vehicle later sought confirmation of their metaphysical theses: Upadeśa of Nāgārjuna, T 1509, ch. 2, p. 66 *c*; Karatalaratna of Bhāvaviveka, ed. N.A. SASTRI, p. 88, and T 1578, ch. 2, p. 276 *c*; Yogācārabhūmi of Asaṅga in Bodh. bhūmi, p. 49-50, or T 1579, ch. 36, p. 489 *b*.

[4] By virtue of this contradictory behaviour which has been mentioned earlier (II, § 3, note 9), the Bodhisattva, even while remaining in the recollection of extinction, participates in everyday life and adopts normal attitudes: he walks, stands, sits and lies down.

[5] The Bodhisattva does not make anything of his state of *ārya* (cf. Kośa, V, p. 25), but behaves outwardly as a worldling (*pṛthagjana*). Besides, as will be said further on (III, § 51), all beings participate in the same suchness (*tathatā*). Hence the formulae *fan shêng i ju* 凡聖一如 or *fan shêng pu êrh* 凡聖不二 invented by Sêng-chao to identify the worldly and the holy (T 1775, ch. 4, p. 362 *a*).

[6] This concerns the 62 kinds of false or heretical views recounted in Dīgha, I. p. 39,*10-19*, and commented on in the Sumaṅgalavilāsinī, I, p. 99-123. Even while pursuing his own perfecting, the Bodhisattva should take them into account in order to be able to benefit beings. It will be said further on (IV, § 8) that the false views are found in the deliverance of the Tathāgatas and that Bodhisattvas never avoid them.

entering Nirvāṇa (*nirvāṇasamavasaraṇa*), this is how to meditate [7].

sākṣātkāra) not abiding (*apratiṣṭhāna*) in it, this is how to meditate [8].

Honourable Śāriputra, those who absorb themselves in meditation in this way are declared by the Blessed One to be the truly "absorbed ones" (*pratisaṃlīna*) and marked with the seal of the Buddhas (*buddhamudrāmudrita*).

4. As for myself, O Blessed One, having heard these words, I was incapable of replying (*prativacana*) and I remained silent (*tūṣṇībhūto 'bhūvam*). That is why I am not capable of going to ask that worthy man (*satpuruṣa*) about his illness.

[2. *Maudgalyāyana and the Instruction to Laymen*]

5. Then the Blessed One said to the Venerable (*āyuṣmant*) Maudgalyāyana [9]: Maudgalyāyana, go and ask the Licchavi Vimalakīrti about his illness.

[7] H diverges somewhat from the Tibetan which is however confirmed by K: "Not cutting off the passions, but entering Nirvāṇa". For this concept, see Upadeśa, T 1509, ch. 15, p. 169 *a-b*: The Bodhisattva should practise patience with regard to his own passions, and not cut off their bonds (*bandhana*). And why? Because, if he cut off those bonds, the disadvantage would be too grave: he would fall to the Arhat level and would not differ at all from a man deprived of his senses. This is why he stops his passions, but does not cut them off at all... The Bodhisattva, through the power of knowledge, would know how to cut off his bonds; however, in the interest of beings, he prefers to remain in the world for a long time. Nevertheless, he knows that these bonds are his enemies, and that is why, even while bearing them, he does not follow them".

[8] H's translation betrays the influence of the scholastic theories relating to the *apratiṣṭhitanirvāṇa*, the Nirvāṇa "where one does not abide definitively" (*nirvāṇaṃ yatra na pratiṣṭhīyate*), or better, the Nirvāṇa of him "who does not abide in either the conditioned element or the unconditioned element, but does not avoid them either" (*sa naiva saṃskṛte dhātau sthito nāpy asaṃskṛte dhātau sthito na ca tato vyutthitaḥ*: Aṣṭasāh., p. 151,*23-24*). These ideas will be developed at length below, X, § 16-19.

On the *apratiṣṭhitanirvāṇa*, or again *apratiṣṭhitasaṃsāranirvāṇatva*, see Sūtrālaṃkāra, p. 41,*21*; 47,*6*; 147,*7*; 171,*26*; G.M. NAGAO, *Index to the Mahāyāna Sūtrālaṃkāra*, Tokyo, 1958, p. 24; Madhyāntavibhāga, p. 4,*1*; 108,*14*; 160,*17*; 187,*13*; 200,*15* and *19*; 266,*24*; 267,*18*; Saṃgraha, p. 259 and *47; Siddhi, p. 668-680; Th. STCHERBATSKY, *The Conception of Buddhist Nirvāṇa*, Leningrad, 1927, p. 235; L. DE LA VALLÉE POUSSIN, *Nirvāṇa*, Paris, 1925.

[9] Maudgalyāyana formed, with Śāriputra, the *agrayuga*, the *bhadrayuga*, that is the foremost pair of the good disciples of Śākyamuni (Dīgha, II, p. 5,*4*; Mahāvadānasūtra in Sanskrit, p. 76). He was, besides, the foremost of those in possession of magical powers (*agrya ṛddhimatām*).

He was born in Kolita, near Rājagṛha, into a rich brahman family and with his friend Śāriputra, was converted to Buddhism in the circumstances related above (III,

Maudgalyāyana replied: Blessed One, I am not capable of going to ask that worthy man (*satpuruṣa*) about his illness. And why? Blessed One, I remember that one day, at a road intersection (*vīthimukha*) in the great town of Vaiśālī, I was expounding the Law to householders (*gṛhapati*) when the Licchavi Vimalakīrti approached and after having saluted my feet by touching them with his head, addressed these words to me:

6. Honourable (*bhadanta*) Maudgalyāyana, expounding the Law in that way is not expounding the Law to white-robed (*avadātavasana*)[10]

§ 2, note 1). His magical powers enabled him to battle with Māra, vanquish the Nāgas and reach at will the celestial spheres of the triple world. When Śākyamuni went to the Trāyastriṃśa heaven to expound the Law to his mother, Maudgalyāyana served as intermediary between the Buddha and the Community on earth. He died a few days after Śāriputra, for whom he was still able to give the funeral oration.

Regarding Maudgalyāyana, see MALALASEKERA, *Proper Names*, II, p. 541-547; AKANUMA, *Noms propres*, p. 375-380.

[10] Since he was addressing laymen, Maudgalyāyana was certainly expounding the "gradual teaching" (*anupūrvī kathā*) consisting of three discourses on giving, morality and heaven and a succinct treatise on the noble truths. Canonical texts have given us the wording of these in Pāli and Sanskrit:

Vinaya, I, p. 15-16, 18, 20, 23, 37, 180, 225, 237, 242-243, 248; II, p. 156, 192; Dīgha, I, p. 110, 148; II, p. 41, 44; Majjhima, I, p. 379; II, p. 145; Aṅguttara, IV, p. 186, 209, 213; Udāna, p. 49; Milinda, p. 228; Sumaṅgala, I, p. 277, 308; Mahāvastu, III, p. 408-409; Vin. of the Mūlasarv. in *Gilgit Manuscripts*, III, part 3, p. 142,*11*; Catuṣpariṣatsūtra, p. 178-180; Divyāvadāna, p. 616-617.

Ekamantaṃ nisinnassa kho Yasassa kulaputtassa Bhagavā anupubbikathaṃ kathesi seyyath' idaṃ dānakathaṃ sīlakathaṃ saggakathaṃ kāmānaṃ ādīnavaṃ okāraṃ saṃkilesaṃ nekkhamme ānisaṃsaṃ pakāsesi. yadā Bhagavā aññāsi Yasaṃ kulaputtaṃ kallacittaṃ muducittaṃ vinīvaraṇacittaṃ udaggacittaṃ pasannacittaṃ atha yā buddhānaṃ sāmukkaṃsikā dhammadesanā taṃ pakāsesi dukkhaṃ samudayaṃ nirodhaṃ maggaṃ.

We know the leading role played by the teaching and hearing of the Law in ancient Buddhism (cf. M. and W. GEIGER, *Pāli Dhamma vornehmlich in der kanonischen Literatur*, Munich, 1920, p. 39-52), and Maudgalyāyana, in faithfully repeating the teaching of his Master, gained the latter's praise (cf. Saṃyutta, IV, p. 187,*27*).

Such is not Vimalakīrti's opinion for he reproaches the disciple for his manner of expounding to layman "like an illusionary being expounding to other illusionary beings". Theoretically, the Buddhist Law which is based on the *pudgala-* and *dharma-nairātmya* as well as absolute quietism does not lend itself to instruction: there is neither instructor, nor listener, nor object to be instructed. However, in practice, the instruction should respond to the spiritual needs of beings by favouring them in all ways: it is a work of compassion rather than of teaching.

These ideas are not absolutely new: for the Prajñāpāramitā, the Bodhisattva expounds the Law with the sole aim of eradicating all views from the mind and not of inculcating a doctrine of positive content.

Aṣṭasāh., p. 80-81: *kenārthena bodhisattvo mahāsattva ity ucyate? — mahatyā*

householders. The Law should be expounded according to the Law (*yathādharmam*).

I asked him: What does expounding according to the Law mean? — He answered me:

The Law (*dharma*) is without being (*niḥsattva*), for it is free of the stains of being (*sattvarajas*)[11]. It is without self (*nirātman*) for it is free of the stains of craving (*rāgarajas*). It is without a life principle (*nirjīva*), for it is free from birth (*jāti*) and death (*maraṇa*). It is without personality (*niṣpudgala*) for it is free from an initial point (*pūrvānta*) and a final point (*aparānta*)[12].

The Law is calm (*śama*) and appeasing (*upaśama*), for it destroys the marks of things (*lakṣaṇa*). It is without craving (*rāga*) for it has no object (*ālambana*). It has no syllables (*akṣara*) for it suppresses discourse (*vākya*). It is inexpressible (*anabhilāpya*) for it avoids all thought-waves (*taraṅga*)[13]. It is omnipresent (*sarvatraga*) for it is the same as space (*ākāśasama*). It is without colour (*varṇa*), without trait (*liṅga*) and without shape (*saṃsthāna*) for it avoids all motion (*caraṇa*). It is without 'Mine' (*ātmīya*) for it has no belief in a 'Mine' (*ātmīya-grāha*). It has no ideas (*vijñapti*) for it is deprived of thought (*citta*), mind (*manas*) and consciousness (*vijñāna*). It is incomparable (*asama*) for it has no rival (*pratipakṣa*). It has no dependence on causes (*hetvanapekṣa*) for it does not rely on conditions (*pratyaya*)[14].

It is linked to the element of the Law (*dharmadhātum samavasarati*) for it penetrates all dharmas equally (*sarvadharmān sampraviśati*). It follows suchness (*tathatām anugacchati*) but by the method that consists in not following (*ananvayanayena*). It rests on the limit of reality (*sthito bhūtakoṭyām*) for it is absolutely immovable (*atyantā-*

ātmadṛṣṭyāḥ sattvadṛṣṭyā jīvadṛṣṭyāḥ pudgaladṛṣṭyā bhavadṛṣṭyā vibhavadṛṣṭyā uccheda-dṛṣṭyāḥ śāśvatadṛṣṭyāḥ svakāyadṛṣṭyā etāsām evamādyānāṃ dṛṣṭīnāṃ prahāṇya dharmaṃ deśayiṣyatīti tenārthena bodhisattvo mahāsattva ity ucyate.

Āloka, p. 81,*11*: *dṛṣṭīnām ātmadharmasaṃtīraṇākārābhiniveśasvabhāvānāṃ prahāṇāya savāsanāparityāgāya dharmaṃ deśayati.* "The Bodhisattva expounds the Law to destroy, together with all their pervasion, the views consisting of any attachment whatsoever to all consideration regarding the self and things".

[11] The twenty kinds of *satkāyadṛṣṭi*, false view concerning the aggregation of all perishable things: cf. Kośa, V, p. 15-16; Mahāvyutpatti, No. 4685-4704.

[12] This passage concerns the *pudgalanairātmya*. Cf. Vajracchedikā, p. 49,*17*: *nir-ātmānaḥ sarvadharmā niḥsattvāḥ nirjīvā niṣpudgalāḥ sarvadharmāḥ*; below, XII, §11.

[13] Waves symbolise mental agitation: cf. Laṅkāvatāra, p. 43-47; 314-315; below, III, § 52, n. 102.

[14] This passage concerns the *dharmanairātmya*.

cala)[15]. It is immovable (*acala*) for it does not rely on the six sense objects (*ṣaḍviṣaya*). It is without coming or going (*gamana-āgamana*) for it does not stop. It is linked to emptiness (*śūnyatā*), signlessness (*ānimitta*) and wishlessness (*apraṇihita*)[16] (for) it avoids all affirmation (*samāropa*) and negation (*apavāda*)[17]. It is without grasping (*utkṣepa*) or rejecting (*prakṣepa*) for it is free from arising (*utpāda*) and extinction (*nirodha*). It is without a resting place (*ālaya*) for it is beyond the path (*mārgasamatikrānta*) of the eye (*cakṣus*), the ear (*śrotra*), the nose (*ghrāṇa*), the tongue (*jihvā*), the body (*kāya*) and the mind (*manas*). It has no high (*ucca*) and no low (*nīca*) for it is always fixed (*sthita*) and immovable (*acala*). It escapes the sphere of all imaginations (*sarvavikalpagocarātikrānta*) for it ends absolutely (*atyantam*) all idle chatter (*prapañca*).

7. Honourable Maudgalyāyana, what instruction (*deśanā*) could there be regarding such a Law? The word instructor (*deśaka*) is an uncalled-for affirmation (*ā-*

Maudgalyāyana, the characteristics of the Law being such, how can it be expounded? When one speaks of an instructor of the Law (*dharmadeśaka*), there is room for affirmation (*samāropa*) or negation (*apavāda*). When one also

[15] To indicate the unconditioned, the absolute, without positive content and immobile, the Vimalakīrti turns to traditional phraseology:

Pañcaviṃśati, p. 168,*14-17*; Śatasāh., p. 1262,*13-17*: *katame 'saṃskṛtā dharmāḥ. yeṣāṃ dharmāṇāṃ notpādo na nirodho nānyathātvaṃ prajñāyate rāgakṣayo dveṣakṣayo mohakṣayaḥ. tathatā avitathatā ananyatathatā dharmatā dharmadhātur dharmasthititā dharmaniyāmatā acintyadhātur bhūtakoṭir ayam ucyate 'saṃskṛto dharmaḥ.* — Cf. T 220, ch. 360, p. 853 *c* 11, where twelve names are listed: Tathatā, Dharmatā, Avitathatā, Avikāratathata, Samatā, Niyāmatā, Dharmaniyama, Dharmasthiti, Ākāśadhātu, Bhūtakoṭi, Acintyadhātu, Yathāvattathatā.

For the definition of these terms, see Upadeśa, T 1509, ch. 44, p. 382 *a*; Madhyāntavibhāga, p. 49-50; Abhidharmasamuccayavyākhyā, T 1606, ch. 2, p. 702 *b*; Buddhabhūmiśāstra, T 1530, ch. 7, p. 323 *a*; Siddhi, Appendice, p. 743-761.

[16] This concerns the *samādhi* practised in both Vehicles and considered as the three doors to deliverance (*vimokṣamukha*). *Śūnyatā* looks at things from the aspects of emptiness (*śūnya*) and not-self (*anātman*) and counteracts the belief in a self (*satkāyadṛṣṭi*); *ānimitta* which relates to Nirvāṇa has an objective free of all characteristic sign (*nimitta*); *apraṇihita* is the *samādhi* where there is no intention (*āśaya*), no wish (*praṇidhāna*) regarding any dharma of the triple world.

For the Small Vehicle, see Dīgha, III, p. 219; Dhammasaṅgaṇi, p. 70-73; Paṭisambhidāmagga, II, p. 36-57; Visuddhimagga, ed. WARREN, p. 563-565; Vibhāṣā, T 1545, ch. 104, p. 538 *a*; Kośa, VIII, p. 184.

For the Great Vehicle, see e. g., Sūtrālaṃkāra, p. 148,*6-23*; Bodh. bhūmi, p. 276,*2-13*.

The three *samādhi* present both Vehicles with the best grounds for a comparative approach.

[17] On the expressions *samāropa*, *samāropita*, see Th. STCHERBATSKY, ***Buddhist Logic***, II, p. 74, 133, 364; below, III, § 52; VIII, § 2 and 6.

ropitavākya); the word listener (*śrāvaka*) is also an uncalled-for affirmation. Where there exists no uncalled-for affirmation, there is no-one to instruct (*deśaka*), to hear (*śrāvaka*) or to understand.

speaks of a listener to the Law (*dharmaśrāvaka*), there is room for affirmation and negation. But with a subject (like the Law), where there is neither affirmation nor negation, there is no-one who can expound, no-one who can listen, no-one who can understand.

It is as if an illusionary being (*māyāpuruṣa*) expounded the Law to other illusionary beings.

8. This is the attitude with which the Law should be expounded. You should evaluate the degree of spiritual faculties (*indriyaviśeṣa*) of all beings. Then, through correct vision with the eye of wisdom (*prajñācakṣuḥsaṃdarśana*) which knows no obstacles (*pratigha*), by opening yourself to great compassion (*mahākaruṇāsammukhībhāva*), by extolling the Great Vehicle (*mahāyānavarṇana*), by recognising the beneficence of the Buddha (*buddhe kṛtajñatā*), by purifying your intentions (*āśayaviśodhana*) and by penetrating the language of the Law (*dharmaniruktikauśalya*), you should expound the Law so that the lineage of the triple jewel (*triratnavaṃśa*) is never interrupted (*samucchinna*).

9. Blessed One, when Vimalakīrti had expounded in this manner, eight hundred householders among the crowd (*maṇḍala*) of householders produced the thought of supreme and perfect enlightenment (*aṣṭānāṃ gṛhapatiśatānām anuttarāyāṃ samyakṣambodhau cittāny utpāditāni*). As for myself, I was reduced to silence (*niṣpratibhāna*). That is why, Blessed One, I am not capable of going to ask that worthy man (*satpuruṣa*) about his illness.

[3. *Kāśyapa and the Alms-seeking Round*]

10. Then the Blessed One said to the Venerable (*āyuṣmant*) Mahākāśyapa[18]: Kāśyapa, go and ask the Licchavi Vimalakīrti about his illness.

[18] Mahākāśyapa, originally named Pippali, was born in Mahātīrtha, in Magadha. His father was a rich brahman named Kapila and his mother, Sumanādevī. On the insistence of his parents, he married Bhadrā Kāpilānī, a young girl who was a native of Śākala (Sialkot), but the marriage was not consummated. By mutual agreement, the couple both took up the robe and set off on their own way. Kāśyapa met the Buddha under the Bahuputraka Nyagrodha, a famous tree situated between Rājagṛha and Nālandā. The Master gave him three injunctions and ordained him. While on their way together to Rājagṛha, the Buddha and Kāśyapa proceeded to exchange clothes (Saṃyutta, II, p. 221); eight days later, Kāśyapa became an Arhat, and the Buddha proclaimed him to be "the foremost of those who observe the

Mahākāśyapa replied: Blessed One, I am not capable of going to ask that worthy man (*satpuruṣa*) about his illness. And why? I remember that one day, I had gone into the town of Vaiśālī and I was going along the street of the poor (*daridravīthi*) begging for my food (*piṇḍāya caran*)[19], when the Licchavi Vimalakīrti approached and

ascetic rules" (cf. Aṅguttara, I, p. 23,*19*: *aggo dhutavādānaṃ*; Mahāvastu, I, p. 66,*16*; 72,*19*: *dhutadharmadhārin*; Divyāvadāna, p. 61,*28*: *dhūtaguṇavādinām agraḥ*).

[Regarding these ascetic rules which number thirteen in Pāli sources and twelve in Sanskrit sources, cf. Vinaya, V, p. 131, 193; Milinda, p. 359; Visuddhimagga, ed. WARREN, p. 48-67; Aṣṭasāh., p. 773-774; Dharmasaṃgraha, § 63; Mahāvyutpatti, No. 1127-1139].

Kāśyapa was not present at the Buddha's death, but took part in his funeral ceremony. Shortly afterwards, he summoned, in Rājagṛha, the first Buddhist council and presided over the compilation of the scriptures.

Kāśyapa lived to great old age. Feeling his life drawing to a close, he went to the summit of Mount Gṛdhrakūṭa near Rājagṛha and entered Nirvāṇa, still wearing the monk's outer robe that he had received from Śākyamuni. The mountain parted and closed over him. It will retain his body until the end of time. When Maitreya the future Buddha comes, he will go to the Gṛdhrakūṭa and touch the mountain with his toe. The rock will open up, Kāśyapa will rise and solemnly hand over Śākyamuni's robe to Maitreya.

Regarding Kāśyapa, see MALALASEKERA, *Proper Names*, II, p. 476-483; AKANUMA, *Noms propres*, p. 369-372; NĀGĀRJUNA, *Traité*, p. 191-196.

[19] The fourth dhutaṅga of the Pāli list is *sapadānacārika* (Vinaya, V, p. 131,*16*; 193,*10*; Visuddhimagga, p. 49,*12*). It is taken up again in the 33rd *sekhiya* of the Pāṭimokkha: *sapadānaṃ piṇḍapātaṃ bhuñjissāmi* (Vinaya, IV, p. 191,*28*). — Also see Vinaya, II, p. 214,*12*; Majjhima, I, p. 30,*20*; II, p. 7,*30*; Saṃyutta, III, p. 238,*24*.

To the *sapadānam* of the Pāli correspond:

a. In Sanskrit, *sāvadānam* (Mahāvastu, I, p. 301,*9*; 327,*8*; Karmavibhaṅga, p. 21,*14*; Śikṣāsamuccaya, p. 128,*8*; Mahāvyutpatti, No. 8567).

b. In Tibetan, *ḥthar chags* or *mthar chags*.

c. In Chinese, *i tz'ŭ* 以次 or *tz'ŭ hsing* 次行.

If the etymology remains obscure, the meaning is clear: *sapadānam* means "without a break, going from house to house" (*avakhaṇḍanarahitaṃ anugharaṃ*: Visuddhimagga, p. 49,*9-10*) "proceeding from family to family" (*kulā kulaṃ abhikkamanto*: Cullaniddesa, p. 267,*29*), "without making any distinction and systematically" (*tattha tattha odhiṃ akatvā anupaṭipātiyā*: Kaṅkhāvitaraṇī, p. 150,*3*).

In brief, according to the fourth dhutaṅga, the monk who begs for his food should go regularly from house to house, to the poor as well as to the rich, without neglecting anyone.

Kāśyapa conforms to this rule by going from house to house, but bends it somewhat by seeking alms in the street of the poor. The Vimalakīrti is here recalling a well-known habit of the great disciple:

Udāna, p. 29-30; Comm. of the Dhammapada, I, p. 423-429: After seven days of meditation, Kāśyapa decides to go to Rājagṛha: "I am going", he says, "on an alms seeking round in Rājagṛha, in a systematic order" (*Rājagahe sapadānaṃ piṇḍāya*

after having saluted my feet by touching them with his head, addressed these words to me:

11. Honourable (*bhadanta*) Kāśyapa, avoiding thus the houses of the aristocracy (*mahāsattva*) and going only to the houses of the poor (*daridra*), that is only partial goodwill (*ekadeśamaitrī*) [20].

Honourable Mahākāśyapa, you should base yourself (*sthātavyam*) on the sameness of dharmas (*dharmasamatā*) and go begging (*piṇḍā-*

Mahākāśyapa, even if it is through goodwill (*maitrī*), you should not avoid the rich and beg (only) from the poor.

Honourable Kāśyapa, basing yourself on the sameness of dharmas, you should beg for your food in systematic order (*sāvadānam*).

carissāmi). Five hundred nymphs, wives of Śakra, prepare some food for him and present themselves on his path. They ask the disciple to accept their offerings. Kāśyapa drives them away, saying "Go away! It is to the poor that I grant my favours" (*gacchatha tumhe, ahaṃ duggatānaṃ saṃgahaṃ karissāmi*).

Mo ho chia shê tu pin mu ching, T 497, p. 761 *c* 6-9: At that time, Mahākāśyapa, making an alms seeking round, reached Rājagṛha. He always practised great compassion (*mahākaruṇā*) regarding beings and, neglecting the rich, went to beg from the poor. When he was about to go begging (*piṇḍapāta*), Mahākāśyapa did not set out before entering concentration in order to know: Where are there some poor whom I can favour?

[20] In his homily, Vimalakīrti not only counters this acceptance of people which Kāśyapa displays, he launches a formal attack on the disciplinary prescriptions ruling the alms seeking round and the Hīnayānist conception of the morality of giving.

The old Buddhist discipline carefully regulated the begging and meal of the monks; cf. Vinaya, IV, p. 185-199 (tr. I.B. HORNER, *Book of the Discipline*, III, p. 120-141); L. FINOT, *Le Prātimokṣasūtra des Sarvāstivādin*, JA, 1913, p. 527-533; A.C. BANERJEE, *Prātimokṣasūtra of the Mūlasarv.*, Calcutta, 1954, p. 31-32; W. PACHOW, *Comparative Study of the Prātimokṣa*, Santiniketan, 1955, p. 179-203. Furthermore, early Buddhism built up, especially with regards to laymen, a whole morality of giving. It distinguishes material giving (*āmiṣadāna*) from the giving of the Law (*dharmadāna*) and states that the value of giving does not derive only from the nature and importance of the thing given, but also, in fact even more so, from the qualities of the giver and the excellence of the beneficiary (cf. Kośa, IV, p. 233-240; NĀGĀRJUNA, *Traité*, p. 658-723).

Vimalakīrti sweeps away all these scholastic distinctions and extols, in the spirit of purest Mahāyāna, the giving which is triply pure (*trimaṇḍalapariśuddha*) and leads to the unity of the giver, the beneficiary and the thing given, according to the formula: *bodhisattvo mahāsattvo dānaṃ dadat nātmānam upalabhate pratigrāhakaṃ nopalabhate dānaṃ ca nopalabhate* (cf. Pañcaviṃśati, p. 18,*9*; 264,*17*; Śatasāh., p. 92,*14*; NĀGĀRJUNA, *Traité*, p. 676, 724; Bodhicaryāvatāra, IX, st. 168; Pañjikā, p. 604,*5*; Sūtrālaṃkāra, p. 90,*2*; 103,*32*; 112,*3*; Saṃgraha, p. 185, 225; Ratnagotra, p. 6,*5*; 117,*1*; Siddhi, p. 629).

This refined conception of giving is based on the Mahāyānist doctrine of universal sameness (*sarvadharmasamatā*) to which the Vimalakīrti refers frequently (III, § 11, 16; IV, § 12). Regarding *samatā*, see P. DEMIÉVILLE, *Byōdō*, Hōbōgirin, p. 270-276.

ya caritavyam) always keeping all beings in mind (*sarvakāle sarvasattvān saṃcintya*).

It is in order not to eat (*apiṇḍāya*)[21] that you should beg for your food (*piṇḍāya caritavyam*).

It is in order to destroy in others belief in a material object (*anyeṣāṃ piṇḍagrāhaprahāṇāya*)[22] that you should beg for your food.

It is in order to take the food given to you by others that you should beg for your food.

It is in representing the village to yourself as empty (*grāmaṃ śūnyam adhiṣṭhāya*) that you should enter the village (*grāma*). It is in order to ripen (*vipācanārtham*) men and women (*naranarī*), the great and the small, that you should enter the town (*nagara*). It is in thinking of penetrating the family of the Buddha (*buddhagotra*) that you should enter the houses (*gṛha*)[23].

12. It is in not taking anything that the food should be taken: 1. to see forms (*rūpa*) as those blind from birth (*jātyandha*) see them; 2. to hear sounds (*śabda*) as one hears an echo (*pratiśrutkā*); 3. to smell odours (*gandha*) as one smells the wind (*vāyu*); 4. to taste flavours (*rasa*) without distinguishing them; 5. to touch tangibles (*spraṣṭavya*), but in spirit, without touching them; 6. to know the dharmas, but as one knows illusionary beings (*māyāpuruṣa*)[24]; that which is without self-nature (*svabhāva*) and without other-nature

[21] "Not to eat, this is a property of Nirvāṇa, for Nirvāṇa is sheltered from the sufferings of birth and death, heat and cold, hunger and thirst" (Sêng-chao, in T 1775, ch. 2, p. 348 *a* 22).

[22] Cf. Vajracchedikā, p. 60,*5-8*: *saced lokadhātur abhaviṣyat sa eva piṇḍagrāho 'bhaviṣyat. yaś caiva piṇḍagrāhas tathāgatena bhāṣitaḥ, agrāhaḥ sa tathāgatena bhāṣitaḥ.*

[23] Better than the Śrāvakas and Pratyekabuddhas, already set on the absolute, do the worldly, prey to false views and passions, represent the family of the Tathāgata, for it is in them that there arises the thought of enlightenment and that the Buddhadharmas develop: see below, VII, § 2-3.

[24] Even while consuming the food, the Bodhisattva does not "take" it, for he does not perceive any real character in it. Early Buddhism, without denying the reality of a material object, advised the bhikṣu to disregard it. Cf. Majjhima, III, p. 294: *Sace bhikkhu paccavekkhamāno evaṃ jānāti: yena cāhaṃ maggena gāmaṃ piṇḍāya pāvisiṃ, yasmiñ ca padese piṇḍāya acariṃ, yena ca maggena gāmato piṇḍāya paṭikkamiṃ, na 'tthi me tattha… rūpesu saddesu gandhesu rasesu phoṭṭhabbesu dhammesu chando vā rāgo vā doso vā moho vā paṭighaṃ vā pi cetaso ti, — tena bhikkhunā ten' eva pītipāmujjena vihātabbaṃ ahorattānusikkhinā kusalesu dhammesu.*

(*parabhāva*) does not burn (*na prajvalati*), and that which does not burn cannot be extinguished (*na śāmyate*).

13. Honourable Mahākāśyapa, if you can, without exceeding (*atikrāntum*) the eight depravities (*mithyātva*), concentrate yourself in the eight liberations (*vimokṣa*)[25]; if, through the sameness of the depravities (*mithyātvasamatā*), you penetrate the sameness of the Absolute Good (*samyaktvasamatā*); if, with this single morsel of food (*ekenaiva piṇḍapātena*), you can satiate all beings and make an offering to all the Buddhas and all the Holy Ones (*ārya*), only then can you yourself eat.

He who eats thus is neither defiled (*saṃkliṣṭa*) nor undefiled (*asaṃkliṣṭa*), neither concentrated (*samāhita*) nor withdrawn from concentration (*samādher vyutthitaḥ*), neither abiding in rebirth (*saṃsārasthita*) nor abiding in Nirvāṇa (*nirvāṇasthita*)[26].

Honourable Sir, those who give this noble food will obtain from it neither much fruit (*mahāphala*) nor little fruit (*alpaphala*), neither loss (*apacaya*) nor gain (*upacaya*): they follow (*samavasaranti*) the way of the Buddhas (*buddhagati*), but do not follow the way of the Listeners (*śrāvakagati*).

Honourable Mahākāśyapa, this is what is called eating the food of the village (*grāmapiṇḍapāta*) befittingly (*amogham*).

14. As for myself, Blessed One, on hearing this expounding of the Law (*dharmadeśanā*), I marvelled (*āścaryaprāpta*) and I paid homage (*namas*) to all the Bodhisattvas. If lay (*gṛhastha*) Bodhisattvas are gifted with such eloquence (*pratibhāna*) and such wisdom (*prajñā*), then what wise man, after having heard this discourse would not produce the thought of supreme and perfect enlightenment (*anuttarā samyaksaṃbodhiḥ*)? From then on, I no longer exhorted beings to seek the Vehicles (*yāna*) of the Listeners (*śrāvaka*) or of the Solitary Buddhas (*pratyekabuddha*), but I only taught them to produce the thought of enlightenment (*cittotpāda*) and to seek supreme and perfect enlightenment. That is why, Blessed One, I am not capable of going to ask that worthy man (*satpuruṣa*) about his illness.

[25] The eight *mithyātva* are the exact antithesis of the eight limbs of the noble path (*āryamārga*). As to the eight *vimokṣa*, see Dīgha, III, p. 261; Aṅguttara, I, p. 40; IV, p. 306; Paṭisambhidā, II, p. 38-40; Pañcaviṃśati, p. 166-167; Dharmasaṃgraha, § 59; Mahāvyutpatti, No. 1510-1518.

[26] See above, III, § 3, note 8.

[4. *Subhūti and the Food*]

15. Then the Blessed One said to the Venerable (*āyuṣmant*) Subhūti[27]: Subhūti, go and ask the Licchavi Vimalakīrti about his illness.

[27] Son of the merchant Sumana and younger brother of Anāthapiṇḍada, Subhūti took up the religious life the very day of the dedication of the Jetavana. He studied the summaries of the Discipline, was given some points for meditation (*kammaṭṭhāna*) and retired to the forest to devote himself to the ascetic life. Having developed insight (*vipassanā*) and taking as his base the meditation on good-will (*mettajjhānaṃ pādakaṃ katvā*), he attained Arhatship (Manorathapūraṇī, I, p. 223).

In the early canonical sūtras, he only played a minor role (cf. Aṅguttara, V, p. 337-341); In contrast, in the Mahāyānasūtras he is, along with Śāriputra, one of the main interrogators of the Buddha. The texts credit him with a threefold excellence:

1. He was the foremost of those who practise the *araṇā* (Majjhima, III, p. 237,*16*; Aṅguttara, I, p. 24,*8*; Avadānaśataka, II, p. 131,*5-6*; Aṣṭasāh., p. 40,*19*; 83,*17*; Śatasāh., p. 502,*21*; Vajracchedikā, p. 35,*8*).

Araṇā means absence of passions (*kleśa*), or dispute (*raṇa*). However, there are certain divergencies on the interpretation:

Buddhaghosa, in Manorathapūraṇī, I, p. 221: *therena pana dhammadesanāya etaṃ nāmaṃ laddhaṃ. aññe bhikkhū dhammaṃ desentā odissakaṃ katvā vaṇṇaṃ avaṇṇaṃ vā kathenti, thero pana dhammaṃ desento satthārā desitaniyāmato anokkamitvā deseti. tasmā araṇavihārīnaṃ aggo nāma jāto*: "The Thera Subhūti owes this epithet to his method of expounding the Law. The other monks, when expounding the Law, make distinctions and distribute praise and blame, but the Thera, when he expounds the Law, never swerves from the method fixed by the Master. That is why he is called the foremost of those who dwell in the absence of passion".

Completely different is the explanation supplied by Sanskrit sources: the *araṇā* is the power through which the ascetic prevents others from producing some passion (*rāga*, *dveṣa* or *moha*) regarding him; he puts an end, among beings, to that *raṇa* — dispute, battle, cause of defilement and torment — which is passion. Cf. Kośa, VII, p. 86; Āloka, p. 917,*2*; Sūtrālaṃkāra, p. 184,*15*; Saṃgraha, p. *53; Abhidharmasamuccaya, p. 18,*11-17*; 96,*15-16*; Bodh. bhūmi, p. 89,*1*.

2. Subhūti was also the foremost of those who practised the concentration on emptiness (*śūnyatāsamādhi*). Thus, when the Buddha descended from the Trāyastriṃśa heaven where he had been expounding the Law to his mother, the fourfold community set off for Sāṃkāśya to go and greet him. However, Subhūti remained quietly in his retreat at Rājagṛha. Convinced that the best way of seeing the Buddha was to contemplate the body of the Law, he imperturbably continued his meditation on the emptiness of dharmas. And the Buddha declared that Subhūti, who had not stirred, had been the first to greet him. Cf. Ekottara, T 125, ch. 28, p. 707 *c* 15-708 *a* 20; I tsu ching, T 198, ch. 2, p. 185 *c*; Ta ch'êng tsao hsiang kung tê ching, T 694, ch. 1, p. 792 *c*-793 *a*; Fên pie kung tê lun, T 1507, ch. 3, p. 37 *c*-38 *a*; Upadeśa, T 1509, ch. 11, p. 137 *a*; Hsi yü chi, T 2087, ch. 4, p. 893 *b*.

3. Finally, Subhūti was the foremost of those who are worthy of offerings (*dakkhiṇeyyānaṃ aggo*: Aṅguttara, p. 24,*9*).

Manorathapūraṇī, I, p. 221,*9*: *thero piṇḍāya caranto ghare ghare mettajjhānaṃ samāpajjitvā samāpattito vuṭṭhāya bhikkhaṃ gaṇhati 'evaṃ bhikkhādāyakānaṃ mahappha-*

Subhūti replied: Blessed One, I am not capable of going to ask that worthy man (*satpuruṣa*) about his illness. And why? Blessed One, I remember that one day, in the great town of Vaiśālī, I went according to the systematic order (*sāvadānam*)[28], begging for my food (*piṇḍāyācaram*) to the house of the Licchavi Vimalakīrti, when the latter after having saluted me, seized my bowl (*pātra*), filled it with excellent food (*praṇītabhojana*)[29], and said to me:

16. Honourable (*bhadanta*) Subhūti, take, then, this food (*piṇḍapāta*) if you can, through the sameness of material objects (*āmiṣasamatā*), penetrate the sameness of all dharmas (*sarvadharmasamatā*) and, through the sameness of all dharmas, penetrate the sameness of all the attributes of the Buddha (*sarvabuddhadharmasamatā*).

Take this food if, without destroying craving (*rāga*), hate (*dveṣa*) or delusion (*moha*), you do not remain in their company[30]; if, without destroying the false view of self (*satkāyadṛṣṭi*), you penetrate the one-way path (*ekayāno mārgaḥ*)[31]; if, without destroying ignorance (*avidyā*), or the thirst for existence (*bhavatṛṣṇā*), you produce[32] knowledge (*vidyā*) and deliverance (*vimukti*); if through the sameness of the five acts of immediate fruition (*ānantaryasamatā*), you penetrate the sameness of deliverance (*vimuktisamatā*)[33], without being

laṃ bhavissatī' ti. tasmā dakkhiṇeyyānaṃ aggo ti vutto: "When the Thera begged for his food by going from house to house, he first entered the trance on good-will; then, having come out of this trance, he accepted the offering, thinking that in this way the donor would derive much fruit from it. That is why he is called the foremost of those who are worthy of offerings".

It is on this last point that Vimalakīrti will take him to task.

[28] Regarding *sāvadānam*, see above, III, § 10, note 19.

[29] This excellent food, to be of profit, should be eaten in a certain state of mind, namely a deep-seated conviction of the perfect sameness of all dharmas. Vimalakīrti will successively explain: 1. The sameness between bad dharmas and the Buddha attributes, between enslavement (*bandhana*) and deliverance (*vimukti*): cf. § 16; 2. The sameness between good and bad systems: cf. § 17; 3. The sameness between fault and merit: cf. § 18.

[30] A Śrāvaka, who aspires to Nirvāṇa, seeks to destroy *rāga*, *dveṣa* and *moha*, while a worldling (*pṛthagjana*) accepts them. A Bodhisattva avoids both Nirvāṇa and Saṃsara.

[31] According to K'uei-chi (T 1782, p. 1046 *b* 2-3), the *ekayānamārga* is the inexistence of the self (*anātman*).

[32] P and N add a negative which does not appear in the Chinese versions.

[33] There are five *ānantarya* misdeeds, so called because he who has committed them immediately goes to hell (*samanantaraṃ narakeṣūpapadyate*). They are: 1-3. the murder of mother, father or an Arhat (*mātṛghāta*, *pitṛghāta*, *arhadghāta*), 4. schism (*saṃghabheda*), 5. the intentional infliction of a wound on the Buddha (*tathāgatasyāntike*

either delivered (*vimukta*) or bound (*baddha*); if, without having seen the four Truths (*satya*), you are not "he who has not seen them" (*na dṛṣṭasatya*); if, without having obtained the fruits (*phala*) of the religious life, you are not "he who has not obtained them" (*aprāptaphala*); if, without being a worldly man (*pṛthagjana*), you are not lacking in the characteristics of the worldly (*pṛthagjanadharma*); if, without being an *ārya*, you are also not an *anārya*[34]; if you are equipped with all the dharmas (*sarvadharmasamanvāgata*), but exempt from all notion (*saṃjñā*) concerning dharmas.

duṣṭacittarudhirotpādanam). The sources often quote them jumbled up with other misdeeds: Vinaya, I, p. 168,*8*; 321,*17*; II, p. 193,*38*; Aṅguttara, I, p. 27; III, p. 436; Vibhaṅga, p. 378; Kośa, IV, p. 201; Dharmasaṃgraha, § 60; Mahāvyutpatti, No. 2324-2328.

However, from the point of view of the absolute and integral sameness, misdeed equals merit. Cf. Madh. vṛtti, p. 374,*6*: *yat samāḥ paramārthatas tathatā dharmadhātur atyantājātiś ca tat samāni paramārthataḥ pañcānantaryāṇi.*

Śikṣāsamuccaya, p. 257,*10*: *sarvadharmā bodhiḥ, svabhāvavirahitā boddhavyāḥ, antaśa ānantaryāṇy api bodhiḥ.*

[34] Below, VII, § 4. Vimalakīrti does not accept the various stages of the Buddhist path established by the theoreticians of the Small Vehicle:

1. State of *pṛthagjana*, worldling, in whom the five spiritual faculties are completely lacking, and who, as a consequence, has not pledged himself to the path (cf. Saṃyutta, V, p. 204).

2. State of *ārya*, predestined to the acquisition of the absolute Good or Nirvāṇa (*samyaktvaniyāmāvakrānta*): stage which coincides with the first thought of the path of the vision of the noble truths (*satyadarśanamārga*).

3. State of *dṛṣṭasatya*, or of him who has seen the four noble truths concerning the triple world: stage coinciding with the 15th thought of the *darśanamārga*.

4. State of *srotaāpanna*, or ascetic who has entered the stream, and is in possession of the first fruit of the religious life (*śrāmaṇyaphala*): stage coinciding with the 16th thought of the *darśanamārga* and the first moment of the path of meditation (*bhāvanāmārga*).

5. State of *sakṛdāgāmin*, or of him who will be reborn only once again in the *kāmadhātu* and who is in possession of the second fruit: stage coinciding with the 12th moment of the *bhāvanāmārga*.

6. State of *anāgāmin*, or of him who will no longer be reborn in the *kāmadhātu* and who is in possession of the third fruit: stage coinciding with the 18th moment of the *bhāvanāmārga*.

7. State of *vajropamasamādhi* "diamond-like concentration", where the ascetic abandons the last category of the passions of the triple world: stage coinciding with the 161st moment of the *bhāvanāmārga*,

8. State of *arhat*, holy one, or *aśaikṣa*, of him who has no more to practise with regard to the destruction of the vices: this is the fourth and last fruit of the religious life and ensures possession of Nirvāṇa.

For details see Kośa, V, p. I-XI; LAMOTTE, *Histoire*, p. 678-685.

17. Honourable Subhūti, take this food if, without seeing the Buddha, nor hearing the Law (*dharma*), nor serving the community (*saṃgha*), you go forth as a religious mendicant (*pravrajasi*) under the six sectarian masters (*tīrthikaśāstṛ*) and you follow the way followed by the six sectarian masters, namely, Pūraṇa Kāśyapa, Maskarin Gośālīputra, Saṃjayin Vairaṭīputra, Kakuda Kātyāyana, Ajita Keśakambala and Nirgrantha Jñātiputra [35].

18. Honourable Subhūti, take this food if, falling into all the false views (*dṛṣṭigata*), you reach neither the middle (*madhya*) nor the extremes (*anta*) [36]; if, entering the eight unfavourable conditions for birth (*akṣaṇa*), you do not attain the favourable conditions (*kṣaṇa*); if, relating yourself to defilement (*saṃkleśa*), you do not achieve purification (*vyavadāna*); if the *araṇā* won by all beings is your own *araṇā* [37], O Honourable Sir; if, for all those who give to you, you do not constitute a purifying field of merit (*puṇyakṣetra*) [38], and if those who offer you food, O Honourable Sir, still fall into bad destinies (*vinipāta*) [39]; if you link yourself with all the Māras and if you consort with all the passions

[35] This concerns the heterodox systems represented by the six heretical masters whom the Buddha had put to confusion in Śrāvastī (Vinaya, II, p. 111; Mahāvastu, I. p. 253; Divyāvadāna, p. 143). Their doctrines are set forth in the Dīgha, 1, p. 52-59; see J. FILLIOZAT, *Inde Classique*, II, Paris, 1953, p. 514-515.

[36] K translates: "If entering into all the false views, you do not reach the other shore". — The 62 kinds of false views (*dṛṣṭigata*) are based on the two beliefs in extremes (*antagrāhadṛṣṭi*) which consist of the views of existence and non-existence (*bhavābhavadṛṣṭi*), the views of eternity and annihilation (*śāśvatocchedadṛṣṭi*). The belief in extremes is condemned by both Vehicles:

Saṃyutta, II, p. 17,*21*; III, p. 135,*12*: *sabbaṃ atthīti ayaṃ eko anto, sabbaṃ natthīti ayaṃ dutiyo anto. ete te ubho ante anupagamma majjhena tathāgato dhammaṃ deseti.*

Ratnakūṭa quoted in Madh. vṛtti, p. 270,*7*: *astīty ayam eko 'nto nāstīty ayam eko 'nto. yad enayor dvayor antayor madhyaṃ tad arūpyam anidarśanam apratiṣṭham anābhāsam aniketam avijñaptikam iyam ucyate madhyamā pratipad dharmāṇāṃ bhūtapratyavekṣā.*

Also see Mahāvastu, III, p. 448,*10*; Aṣṭasāh., p. 66,*9*; Madh. vṛtti, p. 272,*14*; 445,*3*; Pañjikā, p. 346,*5*.

According to the Small Vehicle, the middle path between the extremes is the *pratītyasamutpāda*; for the Great Vehicle it is emptiness (*śūnyatā*) but this emptiness itself should not be hypostasized (see Introduction, p. LXIX). This is why Vimalakīrti advises Subhūti not to reach either the middle or the extremes.

[37] See above, I, § 13, note 71.

[38] Paradox directed against the old speculations concerning the field of merit; cf. Majjhima, III, p. 254-255; Kośa, IV, p. 236-238.

[39] According to the old writings, a generous donor, after his death, is reborn in a happy heavenly world; cf. Aṅguttara, III, p. 41,*4*: *kāyassa bhedā parammaraṇā sugatiṃ saggaṃ lokaṃ upapajjati.*

(*kleśa*); if the self-nature of the passions (*kleśasvabhāva*) is your own self-nature, O Honourable Sir; if, against all beings you nurture hostile thoughts (*pratighacitta*); if you slander (*apavadasi*) all the Buddhas, if you criticize (*avarṇaṃ bhāṣase*) the whole of the Law (*dharma*), if you do not take part in the community (*saṃgha*)[40]; if, finally, you never enter Parinirvāṇa. In such conditions, you can take this food.

19. Blessed One, having heard Vimalakīrti's words, I wondered what I should say (*kiṃ vaktavyam*), what I should do (*kiṃ karaṇīyam*): on ten sides (*daśadikṣu*), I was in the dark (*andhakāra*). Abandoning my bowl (*pātraṃ chorayitvā*), I was about to leave the house when the Licchavi Vimalakīrti said to me:

Honourable Subhūti, do not fear these words and take up your bowl. What do you think of this (*tat kiṃ manyase*), O Honourable Subhūti? If it was a transformation-body (*nirmāṇa*) of the Tathāgata who addressed these words to you, would you be afraid? — I answered him: No, certainly not, son of good family (*no hīdaṃ kulaputra*). — Vimalakīrti continued: Honourable Subhūti, the self-nature (*svabhāva*) of all dharmas is like an illusion (*māyā*), a transformation (*nirmāṇa*); all beings (*sattva*) and all words (*vākya*) have such a self-nature. That is why the wise (*paṇḍita*) are not attached (*nābhiniviśante*) to words and do not fear them. And why? Because all words are without self-nature (*svabhāva*) or mark (*lakṣaṇa*). Why is it so? These words being without self-nature or mark, everything that is not a word is deliverance (*vimukti*), and all dharmas have this deliverance as their mark (*vimuktilakṣaṇa*).

20. When Vimalakīrti had spoken these words, two hundred [H's variant: twenty thousand] sons of the gods obtained, regarding dharmas, the pure eye of the Law, without dust or stain (*dviśatānāṃ devaputrāṇāṃ virajo vigatamalaṃ dharmeṣu dharmacakṣur viśuddham*), and five hundred sons of the gods obtained the preparatory certainty (*pañcānāṃ ca devaputraśatānām anulomikīkṣāntipratilābho 'bhūt*). As for myself, I was reduced to silence (*niṣpratibhāna*) and could not answer him at all. That is why, Blessed One, I am not capable of going to ask that worthy man (*satpuruṣa*) about his illness.

[40] Another paradox, the first duty of a Buddhist being to nurture utter faith (*aveccappasāda*) in the Buddha, the Dharma and the Saṃgha; cf. Saṃyutta, IV, p. 304; LAMOTTE, *Histoire*, p. 74.

[5. *Pūrṇamaitrāyaṇīputra and the Instruction to Monks*]

21. Then the Blessed One said to the Venerable (*āyuṣmant*) Pūrṇamaitrāyaṇīputra[41]: Pūrṇa, go and ask the Licchavi Vimalakīrti about his illness.

Pūrṇa replied: Blessed One, I am not capable of going to ask that worthy man (*satpuruṣa*) about his illness. And why? Blessed One, I remember that one day, somewhere in the Mahāvana, I was expounding the Law to some new monks (*navakabhikṣu*)[42], when

[41] Pūrṇa, son of Maitrāyaṇī, was a brahman who was a native of Droṇavastu, a place near Kapilavastu, in Śākyan country. He was a nephew of Ājñāta Kauṇḍinya, one of the first five of Śākyamuni's disciples.

His life story is not well known: cf. MALALASEKERA, *Proper Names*, II, p. 222-223; AKANUMA, *Noms propres*, p. 519.

According to the Pāli tradition (Manorathapūraṇī, I, p. 202-204; Majjhima, I, p. 145 sq.), he received ordination in Kapilavastu at his uncle's hands, and quickly attained Arhatship. Five hundred young men took up the religious life under his guidance. He sent them to the Buddha in Rājagṛha. He himself did not meet the Master until later, in Śrāvastī. The Buddha welcomed him in his own cell (*gandhakuṭī*). Pūrṇa then withdrew to the Andhavana and was visited there by Śāriputra, who wanted to make his acquaintance.

According to the Sanskrit tradition (Mahāvastu, III, p. 377-382; Pên hsing chi ching, T 190, ch. 37, p. 824 *a*-825 *a*), Pūrṇa and his twenty-nine disciples were ordained by the Buddha himself, in the Ṛṣipatana at Vārāṇasī.

The Wei ts'êng yu yin yüan ching, T 754, ch. 2, p. 586 *b* 25-*c* 8, making use of a well-known theme, has it that Pūrṇa, bearing a light on his head and with his torso armoured with copper plates, went to Rājagṛha in order to challenge the Buddha. A simple thought was enough to overcome him: "Wise or ignorant, a proud man is like a blind man who produces light without seeing anything".

However, all the texts are in agreement in making Pūrṇa "the foremost of those who expound the Law" (*dharmakathikānām agryaḥ*): cf. Aṅguttara, I, p. 23,*24*; Saṃyutta, II, p. 156,*7-10*; Ekottara, T 125, ch. 3, 557 *c* 18; A lo han chü tê ching, T 126, p. 831 *a* 24; Pên hsing chi ching, T 190, ch. 37, p. 825 *a* 6; Hsien yü ching, T 202, ch. 6, p. 396 *a* 13; Sad. puṇḍarīka, p. 200,*3*.

[42] Pūrṇa, as testified to by Ānanda himself, was highly useful (*bahūpakāra*) to the new monks (Saṃyutta, III, p. 105,*10-11*). He taught the five hundred young men who entered the religious life under his guidance the "ten good subjects of conversation" (*dasa kathāvatthu*): 1. reduced desire (*appiccha*), 2. internal contentment (*santuṭṭhi*), 3. solitude (*paviveka*), 4. withdrawal from the world (*asaṃsagga*), 5. vigorous effort (*viriyārambha*), 6. morality (*sīla*), 7. concentration (*samādhi*), 8. wisdom (*paññā*), 9. deliverance (*vimutti*), 10. knowledge and vision of deliverance (*vimuttiñāṇadassana*): cf. Majjhima, I, p. 145,*19-30*; Aṅguttara, V, p. 67,*20-23*; 129,*12-14*; Mahāniddesa, p. 472,*28-31*.

Thanks to these good subjects of conversation, the five hundred young men attained Arhatship. And the Buddha solemnly gave his approval of Pūrṇa's instructions to the young monks (Majjhima, I, p. 145-146).

In the present passage, the Vimalakīrti is obviously referring to this incident.

the Licchavi Vimalakīrti approached and after having saluted my feet by touching them with his head, addressed me with these words:

22. Honourable (*bhadanta*) Pūrṇa, collect yourself and examine the minds (*citta*) of these monks, and then you can expound the Law to them[43]. Do not pour rotten food (*pūtikabhojana*) into a precious bowl (*ratnapātra*). Understand first of all what the intentions (*āśaya*) of these monks are. Do not confuse a beryl (*vaiḍūrya*) which is a priceless stone (*anarghamaṇiratna*)[44] with a brittle and cheap glass gem (*kācakamaṇi*).

Honourable Pūrṇa, do not, without knowing the degree of the spiritual faculties of beings (*indriyaviśeṣa*), implant in them teachings conceived by limited faculties (*prādeśikendriya*). Do not inflict a wound (*vraṇa*) on those who have none. Do not direct to a little pathway those who seek a great path (*mahāmārga*). Do not pour the great sea (*mahāsamudra*) into the footprints of an ox (*gokhura*). Do not insert Sumeru, king of the mountains (*parvartarāja*), into a mustard seed (*sarṣapa*)[45]. Do not confuse the brightness of the sun (*sūryaprabhā*) with the glimmer of a glow-worm (*khadyotaka*)[46]. Do not compare the roaring of a lion (*siṃhanāda*) with the yelping of a jackal (*sṛgāla*)[47].

Honourable Pūrṇa, all these monks who, formerly, were pledged to the Great Vehicle (*mahāyānasaṃprasthita*) have recently lost the thought of enlightenment (*bodhicitta*).

Do not, therefore, O Honourable Pūrṇa, teach them the List- | Why teach them the Law of the Listeners' Vehicle? I consider the knowledge

[43] Vimalakīrti's criticism is not aimed at the foundation of the teaching, but at its opportuneness. Pūrṇa was teaching his monks the doctrine of the Śrāvakas without realising that he was addressing fallen Bodhisattvas. It is only in the eighth stage, the Acalā, that Bodhisattvas are irreversible (*avaivartika*). In the preceding stages, they are subject to slipping back. This was particularly the case for Śāriputra who, after having followed the Bodhisattva path for sixty Kalpas, had returned to the Small Vehicle (cf. NĀGĀRJUNA, *Traité*, p. 701).

[44] The *vaiḍūrya* is considered to be a stone of great value; cf. Dīgha, I, p. 76,*21*; Majjhima, II, p. 17,*8*; 33,*26*; 41,*8*; III, p. 102,*3*; 121,*20*: *seyyathā pi maṇiveḷuriyo subho jātimā aṭṭhaṃso suparikammakato accho vippasanno anāvilo sabbākārasampanno* ... The Vimalakīrti will return to this comparison below (VII, § 3).

[45] Regarding the *sarṣapa*, the smallest of masses, cf. Saṃyutta, II, p. 137,*26*; V, p. 464,*2*; Jātaka, VI, p. 174,*18*; Divyāvadāna, p. 359,*19*; below, V, § 10.

[46] Regarding the *khadyotaka* (in Pāli, *khajjopanaka*), the smallest of lights, cf. Majjhima, II, p. 34,*2*; 41,*17*; Lalitavistara, p. 120,*11*; 304,*20*; 334,*4*; Divyāvadāna, p. 359,*19*; Śatapañcaśatka, v. 37; Pañcaviṃśati, p. 41,*5*; below, V, § 20.

[47] Cf. Aṅguttara, I, p. 187,*35*: *seyyathā pi brahārañie jarasigālo sīhanādaṃ nadissāmī ti segālakaṃ yeva nadati bheraṇḍakaṃ yeva nadati*.

eners' Vehicle (*śrāvakayāna*). The Vehicle of the Listeners is shallow (*abhūta*). With regard to knowing the degree of the faculties of beings (*sattvendriyakramajñāna*), I consider the Listeners (*śrāvaka*) comparable to those blind from birth (*jātyandha*)[48].

(*jñāna*) of the Listeners to be a minimal and base knowledge, even more than that of those blind from birth (*jātyandha*). They do not have the wondrous knowledge of the Mahāyānists, which evaluates the faculties of beings (*sattvendriya*); they cannot distinguish if the faculties of beings are keen (*tīkṣṇa*) or dull (*mṛdu*).

23. At that moment, the Licchavi Vimalakīrti went into such a deep concentration (*tathārūpaṃ samādhiṃ samāpadyate sma*) that those monks recalled their various previous existences (*nānākarapūrvanivāsa*), existences during which they had, in the presence of five hundred Buddhas of the past, planted good roots (*kuśalamūla*) and accumulated innumerable superior virtues (*guṇa*) with a view to the thought of supreme and perfect enlightenment (*anuttarasamyaksaṃbodhicitta*). When this thought of enlightenment (*bodhicitta*) took shape (*āmukhībhūta*) in their memory, the monks saluted the feet of the worthy man Vimalakīrti with their heads and joined their hands (*pragṛhītāñjali*). And Vimalakīrti expounded the Law to them in such a way that they became incapable of turning from supreme and perfect enlightenment (*avaivartikāḥ kṛtā anuttarāyāṃ samyaksaṃbodhau*).

24. As for myself, I had this thought: The Listeners (*śrāvaka*) who do not know either the minds (*citta*) or the intentions (*āśaya*) of others cannot expound the Law to anyone. And why? These Listeners have no skill in discerning the degrees of the faculties of beings (*sarvasattvendriyaparāparakauśalya*) and they are not, like the Tathāgata, holy (*arhat*) and perfectly enlightened (*samyaksaṃbuddha*), perpetually collected (*nityaṃ samāhitāḥ*).

As for myself, Blessed One, I had this thought: The Listeners who do not know the various faculties (*indriyaviśeṣa*) of beings and do not understand the Tathāgata, are not entirely capable of expounding the Law to others. And why? Because the Listeners do not know the degrees of the faculties (*indriyaparāpara*) in beings and they are not always collected like the Blessed Lord Buddha.

[48] Regarding the superiority of Bodhisattvas over Śrāvakas, see below, V, § 19; X, § 14. However, this in only a provisional point of view: in fact the Great Vehicle is the One Vehicle (VI, § 11-12), and the Śrāvaka mind like the Bodhisattva mind is empty of self-nature and like an illusion (VIII, § 5).

That is why, O Blessed One, I am not capable of going to ask that worthy man (*satpuruṣa*) about his illness.

[6. *Mahākātyāyana and the Summaries of the Law*]

25. Then the Blessed One said to the Venerable (*āyuṣmant*) Mahākātyāyana[49]: Kātyāyana, go and ask the Licchavi Vimalakīrti about his illness.

[49] Kātyāyana's biography can be found in MALALASEKERA, *Proper Names*, II, p. 468-470; AKANUMA, *Noms propres*, p. 364-366.

Son of the brahman Tirīṭivaccha and Candapadumā, Kātyāyana was born in Ujjayinī, capital of the kingdom of the Avanti. He studied the Vedas and succeeded his father in the post of chaplain to the king Caṇḍapradyota. Sent by the king to the Buddha, Kātyāyana heard the Master's sermons, attained Arhatship and entered the Buddhist order. The Buddha entrusted him with the mission of expounding the Good Law in Avanti. However, the activities of the good disciple widely exceeded the kingdom's frontiers. In the North-West, he carried out a great teaching tour (cf. Divyāvadāna, p. 580 sq.; J. NOBEL, *Udrāyaṇa, König von Roruka*, I, Wiesbaden, 1955, p. XVI-XVII). In Avanti, Kātyāyana had as his disciple and collaborator Śroṇa Koṭikarṇa and it is through his intervention that he obtained from the Buddha, to the profit of the Avanti, certain relaxations in the matter of monastic discipline (Vinaya, I, p. 194-198).

Some Sanskrit and Chinese sources identify Kātyāyana with Naradatta (variations, Nārada, Nālada, Nālaka), nephew of the recluse Asita who examined the physical signs of the child Śākyamuni and predicted his future enlightenment (Mahāvastu, III, p. 386,*8*; Chung hsü mo ho ti ching, T 191, ch. 3, p. 941 *c* 10; Vin. of the Mūlasarv., T 1450, ch. 3, p. 110 *b* 3-4; T 1451, ch. 20, p. 299 *c* 6-7; ch. 21, p. 304 *c* 20; p. 305 *a* 16; Fo pên hsing chi ching, T 190, ch. 38, p. 830 *c* 18-20). But this identification came late (cf. J.W. DE JONG, *L'épisode d'Asita dans le Lalitavistara*, Asiatica, Festschrift F. Weller, Leipzig, 1954, p. 314). It had, however, the effect of modifying Kātyāyana's biography quite considerably:

According to the Mahāvastu, III, p. 382-389, and the Fo pên hsing chi ching, T 190, ch. 37-38, p. 825 *a* 18-831 *b* 9, Nālaka Kātyāyana was the younger son of a brahman from the Avanti, chaplain to the king Ujjhebhaka Toṇehāraka; he was the nephew of the ṛṣi Asita in the Vindhya. Most wonderfully gifted, he devoted himself to the religious life under the guidance of his uncle. Apprised by the latter of the appearance of a Buddha, and on his advice, he came to Vārāṇasī to be ordained and experienced the inadequacy of the six heretical masters, Kāśyapa Pūraṇa and the others. Impressed by the ease with which the Buddha solved the enigmas put by the Nāga Elapatra, Kātyāyana asked him for ordination, and the Master explained to him the essential laws of the religious life.

Scholastic tradition places Mahākātyāyana among the Abhidharma masters. During the Buddha's lifetime, he had composed a Peṭaka in order to explain the Master's words (Upadeśa, T 1509, ch. 2, p. 70 *a* 20-23; Fên pie kung tê lun, T 1507, ch. 1, p. 32 *a* 19). In the two hundred years after the Nirvāṇa, he is said to have emerged from Lake Anavatapta and founded, in Magadha, the Mahāsāṃghika sub-sect of the Prajñaptivādins (P. DEMIÉVILLE, *L'origine des sectes bouddhiques*, MCB, I, 1932,

Kātyāyana replied: Blessed One, I am not capable of going to ask that worthy man (*satpuruṣa*) about his illness. And why? Blessed One, I remember that one day the Blessed One, after having briefly expounded his instructions to the monks, returned to his cell (*bhagavān bhikṣubhyaḥ saṃkṣiptenoddeśam uddeśya vihāraṃ praviṣṭaḥ*) and that, subsequently (*pṛṣṭhataḥ*), I myself explained at length the meaning of the instructions given by the Blessed One (*asya bhagavata uddeśasya vistareṇārthaṃ vyabhākṣam*)[50], namely: "Impermanent are all formations, painful are all formations, empty are all dharmas, impersonal are all dharmas; calm is Nirvāṇa" (*anityāḥ sarvasaṃskārāḥ, duḥkhāḥ sarvasaṃskarāḥ, śūnyāḥ sarvadharmāḥ, anātmānaḥ sarvadharmāḥ, śāntaṃ nirvāṇam*)[51]. At that moment, the Licchavi Vimalakīrti approached

p. 49-50). In any case, in the fifth century, in Southern India, exegetical works (Peṭakopadesa, Nettippakaraṇa) and grammatical ones (Kaccānavyākaraṇa) were circulated in his name. On these points, see LAMOTTE, *Histoire*, p. 206-208, 356-357.

On several occasions (Aṅguttara, I, p. 23,*26*, etc.), the Buddha proclaimed Kātyāyana to be "the foremost of those who explain at length the meaning of the concise sayings of the Buddha" (*aggo saṅkhittena bhāsitassa vitthārena atthaṃ vibhajantānaṃ*). It is over this very quality that Vimalakīrti will take him to task.

[50] It happened that the Buddha, after having briefly expounded the Law, would retire to his cell. Then, doubting if they had understood properly, the monks would go to Kātyāyana to make him explain at length the meaning of the concise words of the Buddha. The scene is described, in stereotype terms, by the old sūtras:

Majjhima, I, p. 110; III, p. 193-194; 223-224; Aṅguttara, V, p. 255; 259-260: *Idam avoca Bhagavā, idaṃ vatvā Sugato uṭṭhāy' āsanā vihāraṃ pāvisi. Atha kho tesaṃ bhikkhūnaṃ acirapakkantassa Bhagavato etad ahosi: Idaṃ kho no āvuso Bhagavā saṅkhittena uddesaṃ uddisitvā vitthārena atthaṃ avibhajitvā uṭṭhāy' āsanā vihāraṃ paviṭṭho: Yatonidānam bhikkhu purisaṃ – pe – aparisesā nirujjhantīti. Ko nu kho imassa Bhagavatā saṅkhittena uddesassa uddiṭṭhassa vitthārena atthaṃ avibhattassa vitthārena atthaṃ vibhajeyyāti. Atha kho tesaṃ bhikkhūnaṃ etad ahosi: Ayaṃ kho āyasmā Mahākaccāno Satthu c'eva saṃvaṇṇito sambhāvito ca viññūnaṃ sabrahmacārīnaṃ, pahoti c' āyasmā Mahākaccāno imassa Bhagavatā saṅkhittena uddesassa uddiṭṭhassa vitthārena atthaṃ avibhattassa vitthārena atthaṃ vibhajituṃ. Yan nūna mayaṃ yen' āyasmā Mahākaccāno ten' upasaṅkameyyāma, upasaṅkamitvā āyasmantaṃ Mahākaccānaṃ etaṃ atthaṃ paṭipuccheyyāmāti...*

Atha kho te bhikkhū yen' āyasmā Mahākaccāno ten' upasaṅkamiṃsu, upasaṅkamitvā āyasmatā Mahākaccānena saddhiṃ sammodiṃsu, sammodanīyaṃ kathaṃ sārāṇīyaṃ vītisāretvā ekamantaṃ nisīdiṃsu. Ekamantaṃ nisinnā kho te bhikkhū āyasmantaṃ Mahākaccānaṃ etad avocuṃ: Idaṃ kho no... (as the preceding paragraph up to *paṭipuccheyyāmāti*). *Vibhajat' āyasmā Mahākaccāno ti.*

For a more concise rendering, see also Saṃyutta, III, p. 9,*18-25*; p. 13,*5-10*; Aṅguttara, V, p. 46,*19*-47,*2*; L. DE LA VALLÉE POUSSIN, *Documents sanskrits de la seconde collection A. Stein*, JRAS, 1913, p. 571.

[51] Depending on whether it is reproduced more or less completely, this summary

me and after having saluted my feet by touching them with his head, addressed me with these words:

[*Vimalakīrti's Homily on the Summaries of the Law*]

26. Honourable (*bhadanta*) Mahākātyāyana, do not speak of dharmas endowed with activity (*ācārasaṃyukta*), endowed with production (*utpādasaṃyukta*), and endowed with destruction (*bhaṅgasaṃyukta*). And why?

Honourable Mahākātyāyana, do not speak of dharmas having a real mark (*bhūtalakṣaṇadharma*), with production (*utpāda*), destruction (*bhaṅga*), discrimination (*vikalpa*) and activities of mind (*cittācāra*). And why?

a. Honourable Mahākātyāyana, absolutely nothing has been produced, is produced, or will be produced; absolutely nothing has been destroyed, is destroyed or will be destroyed: such is the meaning of the word "impermanent" (*anitya*)[52].

b. Understanding that the five aggregates (*skandha*) are absolutely

concerning the characteristics of dharmas, and eventually, Nirvāṇa, is mentioned under different names:

1. Three-fold mark (*lakṣaṇa*): Jātaka, I, p. 48,*28*; 275,*23*; III, p. 377,*5*.

2. Three-fold Seal of the Law (*dharmamudrā*): Lien hua mien ching, T 386, ch. 2, p. 1077 *a* 23-24 and 26-27; Vin. of the Mūlasarv., T 1442, ch. 9, p. 670 *c* 2-3; Upadeśa, T 1509, ch. 22, p. 222 *b*; ch. 26, p. 253 *c* 13-14; ch. 32, p. 297 *c* 23-24; Satyasiddhiśāstra, T 1646, ch. 1, p. 243 *c* 17-18.

3. Four-fold Summary of the Law (*dharmoddāna*): Sūtrālaṃkāra, p. 17,*3*; 55,*6*; 73,*22*; Bodh. bhūmi, p. 277,*5*; below, XII, § 11.

4. Four-fold 'Alpha and Omega' of the Law (*dharmapūrvāparānta*): Ekottarāgama, T 125, ch. 18, p. 640 *b* 13-17.

Here are some references:

Saṃyutta, III, p. 132,*26*; 133,*1* and *31*; 134,*3*: *sabbe saṅkhārā aniccā, sabbe dhammā anattā.*

Aṅguttara, I, p. 286, line *8*, *14* and *20*: *sabbe saṅkhārā aniccā, sabbe saṅkhārā dukkhā, sabbe dhammā anattā.*

Saṃyukta, T 99, ch. 10, p. 66 *b* 14; 66 *c* 7 and 21; Great Parinirvāṇa, T 374, ch. 13, p. 443 *a* 2-3; Vibhāṣā, T 1545, ch. 9, p. 45 *a* 21: *sarve saṃskārā anityāḥ, sarve dharmā anātmānaḥ, nirvāṇaṃ śāntam.*

Sūtrālaṃkāra, p. 149,*1-3*: *sarvasaṃskārā anityāḥ, sarvasaṃskārā duḥkhāḥ, sarvadharmā anātmānaḥ, śāntaṃ nirvāṇam.*

Bodh. bhūmi, p. 277,*5-10*: *anityāḥ sarvasaṃskārāḥ, duḥkhāḥ sarvasaṃskārāḥ, anātmānaḥ sarvadharmāḥ, śāntaṃ nirvāṇam.*

See also below, IV, § 10, note 15; X, § 18, note 24; XII, § 11, note 21.

[52] Cf. Bodh. bhūmi, p. 277,*17-19*: *iha bodhisattvaḥ sarvasaṃskārāṇām abhilāpyasvabhāvaṃ nityakālam eva nāstīty upalabhyānityataḥ sarvasaṃskārān paśyati.*

empty of self-nature (*atyantasvabhāvaśūnya*) and consequently, not born (*anutpanna*): such is the meaning of the word "painful" (*duḥkha*)[53].

c. All dharmas are absolutely indiscernible (*atyantānupalabdha*): such is the meaning of the word "empty" (*śūnya*).

d. Knowing that self (*ātman*) and not-self (*anātman*) do not constitute a duality (*advaya*): such is the meaning of the word "impersonal" (*anātman*)[54].

e. That which is without self-nature (*svabhāva*) and without other-nature (*parabhāva*) does not burn (*na prajvalati*), and that which does not burn cannot be stilled (*na praśāmyati*); that which admits of no stilling is absolutely stilled (*atyantapraśānta*): such is the meaning of the word "calm" (*śānta*)[55].

27. When Vimalakīrti had pronounced these words, the minds of the monks were, through detachment, delivered from their impurities (*teṣāṃ bhikṣūṇām anupādāyāsravebhyaś cittāni vimuktāni*). As for myself, O Blessed One, I was reduced to silence (*niṣpratibhāna*). That is why I am not capable of going to ask that worthy man (*satpuruṣa*) about his illness.

[7. *Aniruddha and the Heavenly Eye*]

28. Then the Blessed One said to the Venerable (*āyuṣmant*) Aniruddha[56]: Aniruddha, go and ask the Licchavi Vimalakīrti about his illness.

[53] Cf. Bodh. bhūmi, p. 280,*12-17*: *tān punar evam anityān saṃskārān ... bodhisattvaḥ triprakārāyā duḥkhatāyāḥ paśyati: saṃskāraduḥkhatāyā vipariṇāmaduḥkhatāyā duḥkha-duḥkhatāyāś ca. evaṃ hi bodhisattvaḥ sarvasaṃskārā duḥkhā iti yathābhūtaṃ prajānāti.*

[54] Cf. Bodh. bhūmi, p. 280,*18* sq.: *punaḥ sarvadharmāṇāṃ bodhisattvaḥ saṃskṛtā-saṃskṛtānāṃ dvividhaṃ nairātmyaṃ yathābhūtaṃ prajānāti, pudgalanairātmyaṃ dharma-nairātmyaṃ ca... yat sarveṣv abhilāpyeṣu vastuṣu sarvābhilāpasvabhāvo dharmo na saṃvidyate. evaṃ hi bodhisattvaḥ sarvadharmā anātmāna iti yathābhūtaṃ prajānāti.*

[55] K, more briefly: "The dharmas which did not burn originally, cannot be stilled now". Cf. Tathāgataguhyasūtra in Madh. vṛtti, p. 363,*9*: *tad yathāpi nāma, Śāntamate, agnir upādānato jvalaty anupādānataḥ śāmyati, evam evālambanataś cittaṃ jvalati, anālambanataḥ śāmyati*: "Just as fire burns due to fuel and becomes stilled through lack of fuel, so the mind burns due to an object and calms down through lack of an object".

For this line of reasoning, cf. Bodh. bhūmi, p. 281,*2-5*: *yaḥ punar eṣām eva saṃskārāṇāṃ pūrvaṃ hetusamucchinnānāṃ paścād aśeṣoparamas tadanyeṣāṃ cātyantam anabhinirvṛttir aprādurbhāvaḥ, idam ucyate nirvāṇam. tac ca śāntaṃ kleśopaśamād duḥkhopaśamāc ca veditavyam.*

[56] Regarding Aniruddha, see MALALASEKERA, *Proper Names*, I, p. 85-90; AKANUMA, *Noms propres*, p. 47-51.

Son of Amṛtodana, the Śākyan Aniruddha was the true cousin of the Buddha. During the Buddha's first visit to Kapilavastu, five hundred Śākyas entered the order. Frail in health, Aniruddha did not join them. However, on being told by his older

Aniruddha replied: Blessed One, I am not capable of going to ask that worthy man (*satpuruṣa*) about his illness. And why?

[*Question of the Mahābrahmā regarding the Heavenly Eye*]

29. Blessed One, I remember that one day when I was taking a walk in the Mahāvana, the Mahābrahmā named Śubhavyūha, accompanied by ten thousand Brahmās, illuminating the spot, came to where I was and, after having saluted my feet by touching them with his head, he stood to one side (*mayi mahāvane caṅkramaṃ caṅkramyamāṇe Śubhavyūho nāma Mahābrahmā daśabrahmasahasraparivṛtas taṃ pradeśam avabhāsya yenāhaṃ tenopasaṃkrama. upasaṃkramya matpādau śirasābhivandyaikānte 'sthāt*). He then addressed these words to me: Honourable (*bhadanta*) Aniruddha, you have been proclaimed by the Blessed One as the foremost among those who possess the

brother Mahānāman about the difficulties that would await him in the world, he changed his mind and even persuaded his friend Bhadrika, the "king" of the Śākyas, to take up the religious life with him. Aniruddha and Bhadrika, joined by the princes Ānanda, Bhṛgu, Kimbila, Devadatta and the barber Upāli, caught up with the Buddha in Anupiya, in Malla country, and were ordained by him (Vinaya, II, p. 180-183; Manorathapūraṇī, I, p. 191-192; Dhammapada Commentary, I, p. 136-138; *Psalms of the Brethren*, p. 325-326; Mahāvastu, III, p. 176-178; Vin. of the Mahīśāsakas, T 1421, ch. 3, p. 16 *c* 21-17 *c* 14; Vin. of the Dharmaguptas, T 1428, ch. 4, p. 590 *b* 13-591 *c* 16; Vin. of the Mūlasarv., T 1450, ch. 9, p. 144 *b* 9-147 *b* 22).

Aniruddha withdrew to Ceḍi country in order to meditate on the eight reflections fit for a Great Man (*mahāpuruṣavitarka*) the formula for which he had received from Śāriputra. The eighth *vitarka* concerned the cessation of mental development (*niṣprapañca*). As Aniruddha was vainly seeking to understand it, the Buddha came to give him the necessary explanations and taught him the qualities which engender the birth of the holy ones (*āryavaṃśa*). Aniruddha understood and attained Arhatship (Aṅguttara, IV, p. 228-235; Madhyama, T 26, ch. 18, p. 540 *c*-542 *a*; Ekottara, T 125, ch. 37, p. 754 *a*).

Of meditative temperament, forever plunged into the practices of *smṛtyupasthāna*, Aniruddha played only a minor role in the Community. He was present at the death of the Buddha and, on that occasion, uttered a famous stanza which bore witness to his perfect detachment (Dīgha, II, p. 157,*11*; E. WALDSCHMIDT, *Lebensende des Buddha*, Göttingen, 1944-48, p. 256-259). According to some sources, he took part in the Council of Rājagṛha and received the guardianship of the Aṅguttaranikāya (Sumaṅgalavilāsinī, I, p. 15,*12*). He died in Beluva, near Vaiśālī (Theragāthā, v. 919).

Aniruddha was in possession of the six *abhijñā*. His psychic power (*ṛddhi*) enabled him to go at will to the spheres of the Brahmās (cf. Saṃyutta, I, p. 145,*14-20*), and the Buddha had proclaimed him to be "the foremost of those who possess the heavenly eye" (*aggo dibbacakkhukānaṃ*: cf. Aṅguttara, I, p. 23,*20*; Hsien yü ching, T 202, ch. 6, p. 395 *c* 26).

heavenly eye (*divyacakṣukānām agryaḥ*)[57]. To what distance does the heavenly vision of the Venerable Aniruddha extend?

I replied to the Brahmās: Friends (*mitra*), I see the trichiliomegachiliocosm (*trisāhasramahāsāhasralokadhātu*) of the Blessed Lord Śākyamuni in the same way that a man endowed with an ordinary eye can see a myrobalan fruit (*āmalakaphala*) on the palm of his hand (*hastatala*)[58].

[*Intervention by Vimalakīrti and Stupefaction of the Brahmās*]

30. This having been said (*evam ukte*), the Licchavi Vimalakīrti approached and, having saluted my feet by touching them with his head, said to me: Honourable Aniruddha, this heavenly eye that you possess, is it of constituted mark (*abhisaṃskṛtalakṣaṇa*) or of unconstituted mark (*anabhisaṃskṛtalakṣaṇa*)? If it is constituted, it is the same (*sama*) as the five super-knowledges (*abhijñā*) of outsiders (*bāhya*)[59]. If it is unconstituted, it is unconditioned (*asaṃskṛta*), and,

[57] There are five eyes: 1. fleshly eye (*māṃsacakṣus*), 2. heavenly eye (*divyacakṣus*), 3. wisdom eye (*prajñācakṣus*), 4. eye of the Law (*dharmacakṣus*), 5. Buddha eye (*buddhacakṣus*): cf. Atthasālinī, p. 306; Suttanipāta Comm., p. 351; Mahāvastu, I, p. 158-160; Pañcaviṃśati, p. 77-82; Sūtrālaṃkāra, p. 143,*8*; Dharmasaṃgraha, § 66.

The heavenly eye perceives exactly the deaths and births of all the beings in the universes of the ten regions; cf. Pañcaviṃśati, p. 78,*5*: *tenaiva pariśuddhena divyena cakṣuṣā daśāsu dikṣu gaṅgānadīvālukopameṣu lokadhātuṣu sarvasattvānāṃ cyutopapādaṃ yathābhūtaṃ prajānāti*.

The heavenly eye coincides with the knowledge of the death and birth of beings (*cyutyupapādajñāna*) which is the fifth of the six *abhijñā* of the Sūtra (Dīgha, I, p. 77-84; Majjhima, I, p. 35-36; Aṅguttara, III, p. 280-281; Paṭisambhidā, II, p. 207 sq.; Visuddhimagga, ed. WARREN, p. 314-368; Pañcaviṃśati, p. 83-88; Kośavyākhyā, p. 654; Mahāvyutpatti, No. 211-230).

Cf. Pañcaviṃśati, p. 87,*3-15*: *sa divyena cakṣuṣā viśuddhenātikrāntamānuṣyakeṇa sattvān paśyati cyavamānān utpadyamānān suvarṇān durvarṇān hīnān praṇītān sugatau durgatau yathākarmopagān sattvān prajānāti ... iti hi divyena cakṣuṣā viśuddhenātikrāntamānuṣyakeṇa daśadiśi loke sarvalokadhātuṣu dharmadhātūparame ākāśadhātuparyavasāne ṣaḍgatikānāṃ sattvānāṃ cyutopapādaṃ yathābhūtaṃ prajānāti*.

It goes without saying that the range of the heavenly eye is not the same for all: cf. Kośa, VII, p. 124; NĀGĀRJUNA, *Traité*, p. 331.

[58] Compare Majjhima, I, p. 213,*25-31*, where Aniruddha explains to Śāriputra: *Idha bhikkhu dibbena cakkhunā visuddhena atikkantamānusakena sahassaṃ lokānaṃ voloketi. seyyathā pi cakkhumā puriso uparipāsādavaragato sahassaṃ nemimaṇḍalānaṃ volokeyya, evam eva kho bhikkhu dibbena cakkhunā visuddhena atikkantamānusakena sahassaṃ lokānaṃ voloketi*.

[59] The *abhijñā*, of which the heavenly eye is one, are qualities common to both the worldly (*pṛthagjana*) and the holy (*ārya*); only the sixth *abhijñā*, the knowledge

as such, incapable of seeing[60]. This being so, how do you see, O Elder (*sthavira*)? — At these words, I kept silent (*tūṣṇībhūto 'bhūvam*).

31. The Brahmās, having heard the discourse of the worthy man, were overcome with astonishment (*āścaryaprāpta*), and after having paid homage to him (*namaskṛtya*), asked him: In the world (*loka*), who then possesses the heavenly eye (*divyacakṣus*)? — Vimalakīrti replied: In the world, it is the Blessed Lord Buddhas who possess the heavenly eye; these, without even abandoning the state of concentration (*samāhitasthāna*), see all the Buddha-fields (*buddhakṣetra*) without being affected (*prabhāvita*) by either duality (*dvaya*) or multiplicity (*nānātva*)[61].

32. Then the ten thousand Brahmās [K and H var.: the Brahmarāja and five hundred of his companions (*parijana*)], having heard these words, inspired by high resolve (*adhyāśaya*), produced the thought of supreme and perfect enlightenment (*anuttarāyāṃ samyaksaṃbodhau cittāny utpāditāni*). Having addressed their homages (*vandana*) and their respects (*satkāra*) to myself and to the worthy man (*satpuruṣa*), they disappeared (*antarhita*). As for myself, I was reduced to silence (*niṣpratibhāna*). That is why I am not capable of going to ask that worthy man about his illness.

[8. *Upāli and Morality*]

33. Then the Blessed One said to the Venerable (*āyuṣmant*) Upāli[62]: Upāli, go and ask the Licchavi Vimalakīrti about his illness.

of the destruction of impurites (*āsravakṣayajñāna*), is reserved for the holy ones (Kośa, VII, p. 97 and 100). However, this is a disputed point among the sects and only admitted by the Haimavatas, Sarvāstivādins and Vātsīputrīyas; according to the Mahīśāsakas and Dharmaguptas, outsiders (*bāhya*) do not possess the *abhijñā* (cf. A. BAREAU, *Les Sectes bouddhiques*, p. 263,*13*).

[60] Vimalakīrti enfolds Aniruddha in a dilemma: if the heavenly eye is *saṃskṛta*, it is a mundane property; if it is *asaṃskṛta*, it cannot see for the *asaṃskṛta* is devoid of activity; in fact "if the *saṃskṛta* is not proven, how can an *asaṃskṛta* be postulated?" (Madh, vṛtti, p. 176,*8*).

Here Vimalakīrti shares the Nāgārjunian theory, the terms of which are that vision, transcendental or not, does not exist, for it cannot see itself *svātmani kriyāvirodhāt*, much less others. Besides, with or without vision, he who sees does not exist: Madh. vṛtti, p. 113-122; tr. J. MAY, p. 78-87.

[61] Only Buddhas possess the real heavenly eye, in that they see nothing. Their Buddha-fields are empty of self-nature (below, IV, § 8) and the Tathāgatas see them as if there were nothing to see (VII, §6, st. 15).

[62] A native of Kapilavastu, Upāli was a barber in the service of the Śākya family. He took up the religious life with his masters, but was ordained before them so that

Upāli replied: Blessed One, I am not capable of going to ask that worthy man (*satpuruṣa*) about his illness. And why?

they owed him precedence. However, the sources differ over the circumstances of the ordination:

a. Vinaya, II, p. 182-183; Vin. of the Mahīśāsakas, T 1421, ch. 3, p. 17 *a-b*; Vin. of the Dharmaguptas, T 1428, ch. 4, p. 591 *b*; Dhammapada Comm., I, p. 137-138: We have seen above (note 56) that it was after the 500 Śākyas that the Buddha's cousins, Aniruddha, Ānanda, Devadatta, etc., decided to take up the religious life. At the time, the Buddha had already left Kapilavastu and was in Anupiyā. The princes went to catch him up in the company of Upāli, their barber. On the way, they took off their jewels and gave them to Upāli, telling him to return to Kapilavastu. "If I return to the town with these jewels", thought Upāli, "I shall be taken for a thief and killed. If those princes can leave home to become monks, it is even easier for me to do the same thing". Upon which, he hung the package containing the jewels on a tree and followed the princes to Anupiyā. In order to destroy their own pride, the princes asked the Buddha to ordain Upāli before them so that they would owe him precedence, and the Master agreed to their request.

b. Vin. of the Mūlasarv., T 1450, ch. 9, p. 145 *c* - 146 *b*: Upāli, under the guidance of Śāriputra, is supposed to have joined the Buddha before the arrival of the princes, and the Buddha to have ordained him immediately so as to force the proud Śākyas to prostrate themselves before him.

c. Mahāvastu, III, p. 179-192; Fo pên hsing chi ching. T 190, ch. 53, p. 899 *c*; Chung hsü mo ho ti ching, T 191, ch. 13, p. 974 *c*; Hsien yü ching, T 202, ch. 4, p. 377 *a*: Upāli had been taken by his mother to the Buddha to carry out his service as a barber and, while shaving the Buddha, he attained the four *dhyāna*. When the 500 Śākyas decided to leave the world, they made a gift to Upāli of their clothes and ornaments. This example inspired in Upāli the desire to take up the religious life. He went and asked admittance of the Buddha who ordained him immediately while the others were still taking leave of their families. Afterwards, when the 500 Śākyas received their ordination in turn, the Master called upon them to prostrate themselves before Upāli, their senior in the religious life. This they did and, together with them, King Śuddhodana and the entire court.

Upāli wanted to devote himself to meditation, but the Buddha urged him to remain among his brothers so as to progress in both holiness and knowledge. The Thera developed his insight (*vipaśyanā*) and attained Arhatship. The Master taught him the Basket of the Vinaya (Manorathapūraṇī, I, p. 312; *Psalms of the Brethren*, p. 168-169), and Upāli thus became "the foremost of the guardians of the Vinaya" (*aggo vinayadharānaṃ*: cf. Aṅguttara, I, p. 25,9), an enviable title which presupposes many qualities (Aṅguttara, V, p. 11).

Tradition has it that Upāli compiled the Vinayapiṭaka at the Council of Rājagṛha and, later, the Buddhist sects fought over the honour of keeping Upāli's old Vinaya (cf. LAMOTTE, *Histoire*, p. 137, 188). After the Buddha's death, Upāli became the chief Vinaya master (*vinayapāmokkha*) and retained this function for 30 years (Dīpavaṃsa, IV, v. 27-35). He died 30 years after the Nirvāṇa and had spent 74 years in the religious life.

[*The Confession of the Two Monks*]

Blessed One, I remember that one day, two monks (*bhikṣu*) committed an infraction (*atyayo 'tyagamat*); filled with shame (*lajjā*), they did not dare go near the Blessed One, but they came to me and after having saluted my feet by touching them with their heads, said to me: Honourable (*bhadanta*) Upāli, we have both committed an infraction, but, since we are ashamed, we have not gone near the Blessed One. May the Honourable Upāli relieve our remorse and recognise this infraction as an infraction so that in future we will avoid it (*teṣāṃ no bhadanta Upāliḥ saṃśayam apaharatu, atyayam atyayataḥ pratigṛhṇātv āyatyāṃ saṃvarāya*)[63].

[63] Every fortnight, during the *uposatha*, Buddhist monks had to admit their failings with regard to the articles of the *prātimokṣa*. As well as this public admittance, Buddhists practised a sort of private confession. An offender conscious of a misdeed would present himself before the Buddha or a great disciple and, prostrating himself at his feet, would say to him: "I have committed an infraction (*atyaya*), O Master, when in my foolishness, my straying and my wrong-doing; I did such and such a thing. May the Master accept this infraction as an infraction (*atyayam atyayataḥ pratigṛhṇātu*) so that in future I may abstain from it". The "confessor" accepted the infraction by saying: "Since you have acknowledged the infraction as an infraction and since you make amends for it according to the Law (*yathādharmaṃ pratikaroṣi*), we accept it. It is progress in the Noble One's discipline when one acknowledges an infraction as an infraction and when one makes amends according to the Law and when in future one can abstain from it".

Such private confessions are frequently mentioned as much in the Pāli texts as the Sanskrit: Vinaya, II, p. 126, 192; IV, p. 18; Dīgha, I, p. 85; III, p. 55; Majjhima, I, p. 438; III, p. 246-247; Saṃyutta, I, p. 24; II, p. 127, 205; Aṅguttara, I, p. 238; II, p. 146; IV, p. 377; Vin. of the Mūlasarv. in *Gilgit Manuscripts*, III, part 4, p. 222-223; Divyāvadāna, p. 617; Lalitavistara, p. 379; Suvarṇabhāsa, p. 30; Gaṇḍavyūha, p. 122; Sad. puṇḍarīka, p. 210.

The phrasing is not exactly the same in Pāli and Sanskrit. Here are two examples which can be compared:

Vinaya, II, p. 126: *atha kho Vaḍḍho licchavi... yena Bhagavā ten' upasaṃkami, upasaṃkamitvā Bhagavato pādesu sirasā nipatitvā Bhagavantaṃ etad avoca: accayo maṃ bhante accagamā yathā bālaṃ yathā mūḷhaṃ yathā akusalaṃ yo 'haṃ ayyaṃ Dabbaṃ Mallaputtaṃ amūlikāya sīlavipattiyā anuddhaṃsesiṃ, tassa me bhante Bhagavā accayaṃ accayato paṭigaṇhātu āyatiṃ saṃvarāyā ti. taggha tvaṃ āvuso Vaḍḍha accayo accagamā... yato ca kho tvaṃ āvuso Vaḍḍha accayaṃ accayato disvā yathādhammaṃ paṭikarosi tan te mayaṃ paṭigaṇhāma, vuḍḍhi h' esā āvuso Vaḍḍha ariyassa vinaye yo accayaṃ accayato disvā yathādhammaṃ paṭikaroti āyatiṃ saṃvaraṃ āpajjatīti.*

Gilgit Manuscripts, III, part 4, p. 222-223: *atha rājā māgadho 'jātaśatrur Vaidehīputraś cīvarakarṇikenāśrūṇy utsṛjya Bhagavataḥ pādayor nipatya Bhagavantam idam avocat: atyayo Bhagavann atyayaḥ Sugata yathā bālo yathā mūḍho yathā avyakto yathā akuśalo*

[*Vimalakīrti's Homily on Morality*[64] *and Pure Mind*]

34. Blessed One, while I was instructing these two monks with a righteous discourse (*dhārmyā kathayā saṃdarśayāmi*), the Licchavi Vimalakīrti approached and addressed these words to me:

I myself instructed them in conformity with the Law, so that they could rid themselves of their remorse (*vipratisāra*) and cleanse themselves of their infraction (*atyaya*): I edified them, I incited them, I inflamed them and I heartened them (*saṃdarśayāmi samādāpayāmi samuttejayāmi saṃpraharṣayāmi*)[65]. At that moment, Vimalakīrti approached me and, having saluted my feet by touching them with his head, addressed these words to me:

Honourable Upāli, without further aggravating the fault (*āpatti*) of these two monks or doing wrong (*āvila*) by them, just destroy the remorse (*vipratisāra*) they feel for their fault.

Upāli, without further aggravating the fault (*āpatti*) of these two monks, just destroy their remorse (*vipratisāra*) directly. The fault that they have committed should not torture their minds. And why?

Honourable Upāli, a fault exists neither on the inside, nor on the

yena mayā pāpamitrasahāyena pāpamitravaśaṃ gatena pāpamitropagūḍhakena pitā dhārmiko dharmarājo jīvitād vyaparopitaḥ. tasya mama bhadanta atyayaṃ jānato 'tyayaṃ paśyato 'tyayam atyayataḥ pratigṛhṇiṣvānukampām upādāya. tathyaṃ tvaṃ mahārāja atyayam atyayatas tadyathā bālo ... yena ... pitā ... jīvitād vyaparopitaḥ. yataś ca tvaṃ mahārāja atyayaṃ jānāsi atyayaṃ paśyasi ca dṛṣṭvādeśayasi, āyatyāṃ ca saṃvaram āpadyase vṛddhir eva te pratikāṅkṣitavyā kuśalānāṃ dharmāṇāṃ na hāniḥ.

According to popular belief, private confession could lessen, maybe even suppress the misdeed. Hence the very frequent suggestion made to the offender: *atyayam atyayato deśaya, apy evaitat karma tanutvaṃ parikṣayaṃ paryādānaṃ gaccheta*: "Confess your infraction as an infraction and thus your action will undergo diminution, disappearance and suppression" (cf. Divyāvadāna, p. 5,*5*; 55,*1*; 567,*29*). This is a twisting of the orthodox theory in the terms of which action only disappears when the fruit of its fruition is exhausted. We can quote the Dhammapada, st. 127: "Neither in the realm of the air, nor in the midst of the sea, nor if you were to bury yourself in a mountain cleft, nowhere can you find on earth a place where you can escape the fruit of your bad actions".

[64] Regarding morality in both Vehicles, see Appendix, Note IV.

[65] H is the only one to reproduce in full a well-known canonical stock phrase:

Dīgha, II, p. 42,*8*; 95,*23*: *Bhagavā dhammiyā kathāya sandassesi samādapesi samuttejesi sampahaṃsesi.*

Sanskrit Mahāvadāna, p. 162: *ahaṃ dhārmyā kathayā saṃdarśayāmi samādāpayāmi samuttejayāmi saṃpraharṣayāmi.*

Further references in Woodward, *Concordance*, II, p. 11 *b*, s.v. *dhammiyā kathāya sandassetvā*; Edgerton, *Hybrid Dictionary*, p. 568 *a*, s.v. *samādāpayati*, No. 4.

outside, nor between the two (*nāpattir adhyātmaṃ na bahirdhā nobhayam antareṇopalabhyate*)[66]. And why?

Because the Blessed One has said: "By the defilement of the mind are beings defiled; by the purification of the mind are they purified" (*cittasaṃkleśāt sattvāḥ saṃkliśyante, cittavyavadānād viśudhyante*)[67].

Honourable Upāli, the mind (*citta*) exists neither on the inside, nor on the outside, nor between the two. So it is with a fault (*āpatti*) as it is with the mind, and with all dharmas as with a fault: they are not separated from suchness (*na tathatāyā atikrāmanti*)[68].

Honourable Upāli, this nature of mind (*cittasvabhāva*) by virtue of which your own mind, O Honourable Sir, is a delivered mind (*vimuktacitta*), could it ever

Upāli, your mind is originally pure (*ādiśuddha*). When it obtains deliverance (*vimukti*), was this originally pure mind initially defiled (*saṃkliṣṭa*)? I replied that it was not.

[66] A passage in the Ratnakūṭa, quoted in Madh. vṛtti, p. 47-48, may throw light on this reasoning: Two imaginary monks are questioning five hundred devotees: Honourable Sirs, what are you trying to destroy?

The devotees replied: We are trying to destroy craving (*rāga*), hatred (*dveṣa*) and delusion (*moha*).

The imaginary monks went on: But, Honourable Sirs, do craving, hatred and delusion exist in you?

The devotees answered: They cannot be found either on the inside (*adhyātmam*), or on the outside (*bahirdhā*) or between the two (*ubhayam antareṇa*), but they are not born without being imagined (*parikalpita*).

The imaginary monks went on: Then, O Honourable Sirs, do not imagine them (*mā kalpayata*), do not conceive them (*mā vikalpayata*). If you do not imagine them, if you do not conceive them, you will not experience either craving or hatred. And he who is free of craving (*na rakta*) and repulsion (*na virakta*) is called "calmed" (*śānta*). Morality (*śīla*), Honourable Sirs, is not dependent on either Saṃsāra or Nirvāṇa (*na saṃsarati na parinirvāti*). Concentration (*samādhi*), wisdom (*prajñā*), deliverance (*vimukti*), the knowledge and vision of deliverance (*vimuktijñānadarśana*) are not dependent on either Saṃsāra or Nirvāṇa: they are dharmas through which Nirvāṇa is suggested (*sūcyate*). These dharmas are empty (*śūnya*), devoid of a nature (*prakṛtivivikta*). Therefore reject, Honourable Sirs, the concept of Parinirvāṇa. Do not formulate a concept regarding a concept (*na saṃjñāyāṃ saṃjñāṃ kārṣṭa*), do not conceive a concept regarding a concept. For he who formulates a concept on a concept incurs the bondage of the concept (*saṃjñābandhana*). Enter, Honourable Sirs, the recollection of the extinction of consciousness and sensation (*saṃjñāvedayitanirodhasamāpatti*). We affirm that the monk who has entered this recollection has no further progress to make.

[67] Regarding this Saying of the Buddha and the problem of Pure Mind, see Introduction, p. LXXII-LXXXI.

[68] Cf. Madhyāntavibhāga, p. 221,*24*; Āloka, p. 297,*20*: *dharmadhātuvinirmukto yasmād dharmo na vidyate.*

have been defiled (*saṃkliṣṭa*)? — I replied: No, certainly not (*no hīdam*).

Vimalakīrti continued: Honourable Upāli, the minds of all beings (*sarvasattvacitta*) are of such a nature (*tatsvabhāva*).

Vimalakīrti continued: Equally, among all bings, the nature of the mind (*cittasvabhāva*) is originally pure (*ādiśuddha*) and undefiled (*asaṃkliṣṭa*).

35. Honourable Upāli, imagining (*saṃkalpa*), this is passion (*kleśa*); the absence of imagining (*akalpanā*) and of mental construction (*avikalpanā*), this is self-nature (*svabhāva*).

Upāli, if there is imagining (*kalpanā*) and mental construction (*vikalpanā*), there is passion (*kleśa*). If there is neither imagining nor mental construction, there is pure nature (*svabhāvaviśuddhi*).

Perversion (*viparyāsa*), this is defilement (*saṃkleśa*); the absence of perversion, this is self-nature.

If there is perversion (*viparyāsa*), this is passion (*kleśa*); if there is no perversion, there is pure nature.

Uncalled-for affirmation of self (*ātmasamāropa*), this is defilement (*saṃkleśa*); the inexistence of self (*nairātmya*), this is self-nature.

If one believes in self (*ātmagrāha*), one is defiled (*saṃkliṣṭa*): if one does not believe in self, the nature is pure.

Honourable Upāli, all dharmas are without arising (*utpāda*), disappearance (*vyaya*) and duration (*sthiti*), like an illusion (*māyā*), a transformation (*nirmāṇa*), a cloud (*megha*) and a flash of lightning (*vidyut*). — All dharmas are without interdependence (*ananyo'nyāpekṣa*) and do not last even an instant (*kṣaṇamātra*). — All dharmas are false visions (*abhūtadarśana*), like a dream (*svapna*), a mirage (*marīci*) and a town of the Gandharvas (*gandharvanagara*). — All dharmas are born of imagination (*parikalpotpanna*), like the moon in the water (*udakacandra*)[69] and a reflection in a mirror (*ādarśapratibimba*). Those who know this are called the true guardians of the discipline (*vinayadhara*); those who know this are well-disciplined (*suvinīta*).

[69] K, H and the Tibetan version agree; but Cn (T 474, ch. 1, p. 523 *a* 25) understands: "All dharmas are knowable like the moon in the water; all dharmas arise from and are formed by the mind". It is this translation that is used, in his Fêng-fa Yao "Vade-mecum of the Convert", by the Chinese Hsi Ch'ao (336-377), a lay disciple of the master Chih Tun (cf. Hung ming chi, T 2102, ch. 13, p. 88 *b* 12). On Hsi Ch'ao, his family and work, see E. ZÜRCHER, *The Buddhist Conquest of China*, Leiden, 1959, I, p. 134-135; 164-176.

[*Stupefaction of the Two Monks*]

36. Then the two monks having heard these words, were filled with astonishment (*adbhutaprāpta*) and said: It is extraordinary (*adbhutam etat*) that a householder (*gṛhapati*) should be gifted with such wisdom (*prajñā*) and such eloquence (*pratibhāna*); Upāli himself, whom the Buddha has proclaimed as "the foremost of the guardians of the Vinaya" (*vinayadharāṇām agryaḥ*), cannot equal them.

I said to the two monks: Do not consider him at all as a householder (*na tasmin gṛhapatisaṃjñotpādayitavyā*). And why? Except for the Tathāgata (*tathāgataṃ sthāpayitvā*), there is no-one, neither Listener (*śrāvaka*) nor Bodhisattva, who is capable of interrupting the flow of his eloquence (*pratibhānaprabandha*) nor who equals him in brilliance of wisdom (*prajñāprabhāsa*).

37. Then the two monks, freed from their remorse (*chinnasaṃśaya*) and filled with high resolve (*adhyāśaya*), produced the thought of supreme and perfect enlightenment (*anuttarāyāṃ samyaksaṃbodhau cittāny utpāditāni*), and, saluting the worthy man (*satpuruṣam abhivandya*), they said to him: May all beings obtain such wisdom (*prajñā*) and such eloquence (*pratibhāna*). As for myself, I kept silent (*tūṣṇīm*) and could not answer at all: that is why I am not capable of going to ask that worthy man about his illness.

[9. *Rāhula and Leaving the World*]

38. Then the Blessed One said to the Venerable (*āyuṣmant*) Rāhula [70]: Rāhula, go and ask the Licchavi Vimalakīrti about his illness.

[70] Regarding Rāhula, the son of Śākyamuni and Yaśodharā, see MALALASEKERA, *Proper Names*, II, p. 737-740; AKANUMA, *Noms propres*, p. 526-528; NĀGĀRJUNA, *Traité*, p. 1001-1008.

The sources disagree over the date of his birth and of his leaving the world. During the Buddha's first visit to Kapilavastu, Rāhula, on Yaśodharā's instigation, claimed his inheritance from him. The Master feigned not to hear and left the town, still followed by his son. When he reached the monastery, he called Śāriputra and ordered him to confer the leaving of the world (*pravrajyā*), on Rāhula. This episode is recounted in Vinaya, I, p. 82-83; Jātaka, I, p. 91-92; Dhammapada Comm., I, p. 116-117; Mahāvastu, III, p. 142; Vin. of the Mahīśāsakas, T 1421, ch. 17, p. 116 *c* 6-14; Vin. of the Mahāsāṃghikas, T 1425, ch. 29, p. 460 *b* 22-25; Vin. of the Dharmaguptas, T 1428, ch. 34, p. 809 *c* 3-22; Vin. of the Mūlasarv., T 1450, ch. 12, p. 159 *a* 8-*b* 10.

The Buddha gave several religious instructions to his son, and it is after one of them, the Cūḷarāhulovāda (Majjhima, III, p. 277-280; Saṃyutta, IV, p. 105-107), that Rāhula attained Arhatship. He distinguished himself by the gentleness of his character and

Rāhula replied: Blessed One, I am not capable of going to ask that worthy man (*satpuruṣa*) about his illness. And why?

[*Meeting with the Young Licchavis*]

Blessed One, I remember that one day, many young Licchavis (*licchavikumāra*) came to where I was and, after having saluted my feet by touching them with their heads, addressed me with these words:

Honourable (*bhadanta*) Rāhula, you are the son of the Blessed One and, having renounced the royalty of a wheel-turning king (*cakravartirājya*), you have left the world (*pravrajita*). Which are, in your opinion, the virtues (*guṇa*) and advantages (*anuśaṃsa*) of leaving the world (*pravrajyā*)?

Then I was explaining suitably (*yathāyogam*) to them the virtues and advantages of leaving the world (*pravrajyā*)[71], when the Licchavi

his scrupulous faithfulness to his religious duties. He was considered to be the foremost of those "who love to train" (*aggo sikkhākāmānaṃ*: cf. Aṅguttara, I, p. 24,*17*).

Rāhula died in Tāvatiṃsa, before the death of his father Śākyamuni and his master Śāriputra. Cf. Dīgha Comm., II, p. 549,*21*; Saṃyutta Comm., III, p. 213,*22*.

[71] The Buddhist religion relies above all on the community (*saṃgha*) of monks and nuns. This is why the Buddha was so eager to recruit those of religious vocation for his order, and the Vinayas have carefully regulated the ceremonies of *pravrajyā*, the leaving of the world (e.g., Vinaya, I, p. 22; 82) and of *upasampadā*, ordination (e.g., Vinaya, I, p. 56, 95).

The Majjhima, II, p. 66-68, explains in its own way the genesis of religious vocations. They are usually provoked by personal or family disappointments: old age (*jarā*), disease (*vyādhi*), loss of wealth (*bhogapārijuñña*) or the death of parents (*ñatipārijuñña*). They are encouraged by exhortations (*dhammuddesa*) from the Buddha who points out the degree to which the world is frail (*addhuva*), without protection (*attāṇa*) and without protector (*anabhissara*); he does not belong to it and should leave, forsaking everything (*assuko loko sabbaṃ pahāya gamaniyaṃ*); he is deficient (*ūna*), always unsatisfied (*atitta*) and the slave of desire (*taṇhādāsa*).

Weighing up all the vanity of things human, the householder introspects and takes a decision: "Life in the home is hampering, it is the way of the passions; life outside is freedom. For him who remains in the house, it is not easy to observe the brahma life (namely, chastity) to the absolute full, in its absolute purity, polished like a conch shell. So, I want to have my hair and beard cut off, to wear the yellow robe and leave my family, exchanging my home for the homeless state".

This is a stock phrase found widespread in the Pāli texts as much as the Sanskrit:

a. Pāli formula in Dīgha, I, p. 63; 250; Majjhima, I, p. 179, 267, 344; II, p. 211; III, p. 33; Saṃyutta, II, p. 219; V, p. 350; Aṅguttara, II, p. 208; V, p. 204: *sambādho gharāvāso rajāpatho abbhokāso pabbajjā; nayidaṃ sukaraṃ agāraṃ ajjhāvasatā ekantaparipuṇṇaṃ ekantaparisuddhaṃ saṃkhalikhitaṃ brahmacariyaṃ carituṃ; yan nūnāhaṃ kesamassuṃ ohāretvā kāsāyāni vatthāni acchādetvā agārasmā anagāriyaṃ pabbajeyyaṃ*

b. Sanskrit formula in Mahāvastu, II, p. 117,*16*; III, p. 50,*9*: *saṃbādho punar ayaṃ*

Vimalakīrti approached me and, after having saluted my feet by touching them with his head, addressed me with these words:

gṛhavāso abhyavakāśaṃ pravrajyā tu; na śakyaṃ agāram adhyāvasatā ekāntasaṃlikhitam ekāntānavadyaṃ pariśuddhaṃ paryavadātaṃ brahmacaryaṃ carituṃ; yaṃ nūnāham agārasyānagāriyaṃ pravrajeyam.

The canonical texts enumerate the virtues and advantages of the religious life and proclaim the superiority of the religious life over that of the lay life (Dīgha, I, p. 47-86; Majjhima, I, p. 91; Madhyama, T 26, ch. 36, p. 659 *b-c*; Suttanipāta, v. 60 sq.; Hsien yü ching, T 202, ch. 4, p. 376 *b* 4-16; Ch'u chia kung tê ching, T 707, p. 813 *c*-815 *a*). If it is admitted that an upāsaka, living at home, can attain the first three fruits of the religious life (Majjhima, I, p. 467; 490-491), it is doubtful whether he can reach Nirvāṇa without having first put on the religious robe (Majjhima, I, p. 483; Saṃyutta, V, p. 410; Kathāvatthu, I, p. 267; Milindapañha, p. 264-265). One thing is certain, that a monk attains holiness more surely and quickly than a layman (Tsa pao tsang ching, T 203, No. 111, ch. 9, p. 492 *c* sq.).

One might think that the Great Vehicle which substitutes the ideal of Saṃbodhi for that of holiness (*arhattva*) would have a tendency to minimise the importance of the religious life. But India is the land of the yellow robe and the prestige of a monk remained practically intact.

The Prajñāpāramitā (Pañcaviṃśati, p. 218,*6*; Śatasāh., p. 1459,*17*) avers that, from the moment he enters the bhūmis, the Bodhisattva perpetually practises the leaving of the world (*abhīkṣṇaṃ naiṣkramyaparikarma*) and that, invariably throughout all his lives, he leaves home and takes up the Tathāgata's religion without anyone being able to obstruct him (*sarvajātiṣv avyavakīrṇo 'bhiniṣkrāmati tathāgataśāsane pravrajati na cāsya kaścid antarāyaṃ karoti*). — The Daśabhūmika, p. 22,*13*; 41,*1*; 46,*10*, emphasizes the role played by the *pravrajyā* in the Bodhisattva's career. — The Ratnakūṭa, T 310, ch. 82, p. 476 *a* 24-*c* 21, lists the innumerable advantages of the *pravrajita* over the *gṛhastha*. — The Upadeśa, T 1509, ch. 13, p. 161 *a-b* (cf. NĀGĀRJUNA, *Traité*, p. 839-846) demonstrates, with the support of proofs and examples, that the layman, even if he is dedicated to the five-fold morality (*pañcaśīla*), is far inferior to the monk. — Finally, the Bodh. bhūmi, p. 310-311, stresses the very great difference which divides the monk Bodhisattva from the lay Bodhisattva: the former is free of family and professional worries; he practises continence, quickly reaches the peak of the *bodhipakṣyadharma*, and he speaks with authority.

However, all this is on the level of conventionality (*saṃvṛti*) and not of reality (*paramārtha*). If it is true, as the Great Vehicle asserts, that the world does not exist, the leaving of the world makes no sense. This is the viewpoint adopted here by Vimalakīrti (III, § 40) according to whom the true leaving of the world is the *cittotpāda*. Taken literally, this theory would lead straight to the closing of the monasteries.

The Upadeśa, T 1509, ch. 18, p. 197 *a-b* (cf. NĀGĀRJUNA, *Traité*, p. 1111-1112) also teaches that all practices (*caryā*) are false and in vain and that the noble practice (*āryacaryā*) is the absence of all practice, for nothing can be acquired that is not already possessed.

In the same spirit, the Mañjuśrīvikrīḍita, T 818, ch. 2, p. 830 *b* 17-*c* 7, remarks: "The leaving of the world is not shaving the head, but producing great vigour (*vīrya*) in order to destroy the passions (*kleśa*) of all beings; it is not putting on the yellow

[*Vimalakīrti's Homily on Leaving the World*]

39. Honourable Rāhula, it is not thus that one should expound the virtues and advantages of leaving the world. And why? Leaving the world is precisely the absence of virtues and the absence of advantages. Honourable Rāhula, when it concerns conditioned (*saṃskṛta*) dharmas, one can speak of virtues and advantages, but leaving the world is unconditioned (*asaṃskṛta*) and, with the unconditioned, there can be no question of either virtues or advantages.

Honourable Rāhula, leaving the world is not material (*rūpin*), but freed of matter (*rūpavigata*). It is freed from extreme views of beginning and end (*avarāgrānta-dṛṣṭivigata*)[72]. It is the path (*mārga*) of Nirvāṇa.

Rāhula, leaving the world is without beginning or end or middle (*anavarāgrama-dhya*) and frees from all false views (*dṛṣṭi*). Being neither material (*rūpin*) nor immaterial (*arūpin*), it is the path of Nirvāṇa.

robe (*kāṣāya*), but diligently destroying in beings the mind defiled by the three-fold poison (*triviṣakliṣṭacitta*); it is not observing a moral conduct (*śīlacaryā*) oneself but helping the immoral (*duḥśīla*) to abide happily (*sukhavihārāya*) by pure morality (*viśuddhaśīla*); it is not meditating in the solitude of the jungle (*araṇya*), but remaining in [the whirlpool of] Saṃsāra and using wisdom (*prajñā*) and skillful means (*upāya*) in order to discipline beings and lead them to deliverance (*vimukti*); it is not keeping to the restraint (*saṃvara*) oneself, but widely producing the four infinite states (*apramāṇacitta*) and sustaining (*pratiṣṭhāpana*) beings; it is not cultivating good dharmas (*kuśaladharma*) oneself, but causing beings to develop their good roots (*kuśalamūla*); it is not entering Nirvāṇa oneself, but making beings disposed to enter great Nirvāṇa; it is not eliminating the passions (*kleśa*) for oneself, but diligently destroying the passions of all beings; it is not controlling one's own body and mind, but controlling all beings; it is not unravelling the bonds (*bandhana*) of one's own body and mind, but unravelling the bonds imprisoning the bodies and minds of all beings; it is not freeing oneself from the fears of Saṃsāra, but destroying in all beings the fear of Saṃsāra and leading them to deliverance (*vimukti*); it is not delighting in Nirvāṇa, but extending one's vigour so that all beings fulfil all the Buddhadharmas".

[72] In the canonical texts, the Buddha affirms that the round of rebirth, having no beginning or end, is eternal:

Saṃyutta, II, p. 178,*18*; III, p. 151,*3*; Kathāvatthu, p. 29,*19*: *anamataggāyaṃ bhikkhave saṃsāro pubbākoṭi na paññāyati avijjānīvaraṇānaṃ sattānaṃ taṇhāsaṃyojanā-naṃ sandhāvataṃ saṃsarataṃ*: "The round of rebirth of beings, O monks, has no conceivable starting point. It is impossible to discover any beginning from which beings, involved in ignorance, impeded by desire, wander at random from rebirth to rebirth".

Divyāvadāna, p. 197,*15*: *anavarāgro bhikṣavaḥ saṃsāro 'vidyānivaraṇānāṃ sattvānāṃ tṛṣṇāsaṃyojanānāṃ tṛṣṇārgalabaddhānāṃ dīrgham adhvānaṃ saṃdhāvatāṃ saṃsaratāṃ pūrvā koṭir na prajñāyate duḥkhasya*: "The round of rebirth, O monks, is without beginning or end. It is impossible to discover the starting point of suffering for beings

Leaving the world is praised by the wise (*paṇḍitavarṇita*) and adopted by the holy (*āryaparigṛhīta*). It is victory over all Māras (*māranirjaya*), release from the five destinies (*pañcagatimokṣa*), purification of the five eyes (*pañcacakṣurvyavadāna*), acquisition of the five powers (*pañcabala-lābha*), establishment of the five spiritual faculties (*pañcendriyaniśraya*). It does not disturb others (*na paraghātaka*) and does not tangle with bad dharmas (*na pāpadharmasaṃsṛṣṭa*). It disciplines alien sectaries (*paratīrthikavināyaka*). It transcends all designation (*prajñaptisamati-krānta*). It is the bridge (*setu*) erected over the quagmire of desire (*kāmapaṅka*). It is without a link (*grantha*), without grasping (*parigraha*) and exempt from belief in me and mine (*ātmātmīyagrāha*). Being without attachment (*upādāna*), it destroys all attachments; being without trouble (*upāyāsa*), it destroys trouble. It disciplines one's own mind (*svacitta*) and protects the minds of others (*paracitta*). It favours tranquillity (*śamathānukūla*), and stimulates insight (*vipaśyanāsaṃcodaka*). Being, in all ways, irreproachable (*sarvatrānavadya*), it cultivates everything good (*kuśala*). This is what is called leaving the world (*pravrajyā*), and those who leave the world in this way have "truly left the world" (*supravrajita*).

[*Vimalakīrti's Exhortation to the Young Licchavis*]

40. Then Vimalakīrti said to the young people (*kumāra*): Young people, together leave the world and enter the well-established religious order (*svākhyāte dharmavinaye*). The appearance of Buddhas (*buddhot-*

impeded by desire, bound by the tether of desire, following the long path and wandering from rebirth to rebirth".

Madh. vṛtti, p. 218,*4*: *anavarāgro hi bhikṣavo jātijarāmaraṇasaṃsāra iti. avidyāni-varaṇānāṃ sattvānāṃ tṛṣṇāsaṃyojanānāṃ tṛṣṇagardūrabaddhānāṃ saṃsaratāṃ saṃdhā-vatāṃ pūrvā koṭir na prajñāyata iti*: "Without beginning or end, O monks, is the round of rebirth, birth, old age and death. It is impossible to discover the starting point of beings involved in ignorance, impeded by desire, bound by the tether of desire, wandering and coursing from rebirth to rebirth".

Commenting on this passage (Madh. vṛtti, p. 220), Nāgārjuna establishes that the round of rebirth that has no beginning or end could not have a middle (*naivāgraṃ nāvaraṃ yasya tasya madhyaṃ kuto bhavet*), and he concludes from this that "in weighing up the real, the round of rebirth does not exist" (*vastukacintāyāṃ tu saṃsāra eva nāsti*).

It thus results that Saṃsāra not existing, Nirvāṇa is acquired originally and the religious life that leads to it is a path that has already been followed. This is why Vimalakīrti considers it as unconditioned (*asaṃskṛta*).

pāda) is difficult to come by (*durlabha*)[73]; to escape unfavourable conditions (*akṣaṇa*) is difficult (*durlabha*), to acquire a human destiny (*manuṣyagati*) is difficult; to acquire favourable conditions (*kṣaṇa*) is very difficult (*sudurlabha*).

The young people objected to Vimalakīrti: Householder (*gṛhapati*), we have heard the Buddha say that "without the consent of his father and mother, a son cannot leave the world" (*na bhikkhave ananuññāto mātāpitūhi putto pabbājetabbo*)[74].

Vimalakīrti replied to them: Young people, only produce the thought of supreme and perfect enlightenment (*anuttarā samyaksaṃbodhiḥ*) and vigorously cultivate right conduct (*samyakcarita*), for this is the leaving the world (*pravrajyā*) and the ordination (*upasampadā*) which make a monk (*bhikṣu*).

41. Then three thousand two hundred [K and H var.: thirty-two] young Licchavis produced the thought of supreme and perfect enlightenment (*anuttarāyāṃ samyaksaṃbodhau cittāny utpāditāni*) and applied themselves sincerely to right conduct. As for myself, I kept silent (*tūṣṇīm*) and could not answer at all. That is why, Blessed One, I am not capable of going to ask that worthy man (*satpuruṣa*) about his illness.

[10. *Ānanda and the Care of the Buddha*]

42. Then the Blessed One said to the Venerable (*āyuṣmant*) Ānanda[75]: Ānanda, go and ask the Licchavi Vimalakīrti about his illness.

[73] Cf. Sanskrit Mahāparinirvāṇa, p. 356; Divyāvadāna, p. 19,*13*; Lalitavistara, p. 105,*1*; Sad. puṇḍarīka, p. 39,*8*; Sukhāvatīvyūha, p. 10,*15*: *kadācit karhicit tathāgatā arhantaḥ samyaksaṃbuddhā loka utpadyante tadyathodumbare puṣpam*: "It is only at certain times and in certain places that the Tathāgatas appear in the world, like a flower on an Udumbara tree".

[74] Rāhula was ordained by Śāriputra without the consent of his grandfather Śuddhodana. The latter, extremely displeased, asked the Buddha to prescribe that in future the holy ones were not to admit a son into their order without the parents' permission. The Master agreed to this request. Cf. Vinaya, I, p. 83,*12*; Vin. of the Mahīśāsakas, T 1421, ch. 17, p. 117 *a* 15; Vin. of the Mahāsāṃghikas, T 1425, ch. 24, p. 421 *b* 10; Vin. of the Dharmaguptas, T 1428, ch. 34, p. 810 *a* 21; Vin. of the Mūlasarv., T 1444, ch. 3, p. 1035 *b* 4.

[75] It would take a whole book to tell the story of the life of Ānanda, the Buddha's cousin and favourite disciple: cf. MALALASEKERA, *Proper Names*, I, p. 249-268; AKANUMA, *Noms propres*, p. 24-32. In the Aṅguttara, I, p. 23,*32*-25,*3*, the Buddha credited him with no less than five pre-eminences: *aggo bahussutānaṃ, satimantānaṃ, gatimantānaṃ, dhitimantānaṃ, upaṭṭhākānaṃ*.

It is in this last aspect that he is presented here as assistant to the Buddha.

Upasthāyakasūtra, in Madhyama, T 26, No. 33, ch. 8, p. 471 *c*-475 *a*; Vin. of the

Ānanda replied: Blessed One, I am not capable of going to ask that worthy man (*satpuruṣa*) about his illness. And why?

[*Ānanda in Search of Milk*]

Blessed One, I remember that one day, when the body of the Blessed One evinced some illness (*glānya*)[76] and when he was in need of milk (*kṣīra*), I dressed myself in the morning (*pūrvāhṇe nivasya*) and, having taken bowl and robe (*pātracīvaram ādāya*), I went to Vaiśālī to the dwelling of a great brahman family (*brāhmaṇamahāśālakula*); and there, standing on the porch, I begged for some milk[77]. At that moment, the Licchavi Vimalakīrti

Mūlasarv., in W.W. ROCKHILL, *Life of the Buddha*, London, 1884, p. 88; Fo pao ên ching, T 156, ch. 6, p. 155 *c* 22-25; Hsien yü ching, T 202, ch. 8, p. 404 *b-c*; Ch'u ch'u ching, T 730, p. 526 *a-b*; Vinayavibhāṣā, T 1440, ch. 1, p. 504 *c* 12-15; Manorathapūraṇī, I, p. 292-296; Theragāthā Comm. in *Psalms of the Brethren*, p. 350-352. In the twentieth year of his public ministry, Śākyamuni, conscious of old age coming on, felt the need for a helper who would be attached to him and named Ānanda as his assistant (*upasthāyaka*). Before accepting this responsibility, the disciple made certain conditions, particularly not to share the food or clothing of the Buddha, not to accompany him when he went to see laymen and to have access to the Master at all times of the day.

Ānanda fulfilled this mission with the greatest devotion throughout the twenty-five years which preceded the Buddha's death (Dīrgha, T 1, ch. 3, p. 19 *c* 2-6; Upadeśa, T 1509, ch. 2, p. 68 *a* 10; Sumaṅgalavilāsinī, II, p. 570,*12*).

[76] According to K'uei-chi (T 1782, ch. 4, p. 1056 *a* 18), the Buddha suffered from back-ache, a common indisposition for him: cf. Majjhima, I, p. 354,*24-25*; other references in NĀGĀRJUNA, *Traité*, p. 509 in the notes.

[77] According to the old commentators, Hui-yüan (T 1776, ch. 2, p. 459 *c* 19 sq.), Chih-yüan (T 1779, ch. 7, p. 797 *b* 1 sq.) and Chi-tsang (T 1781, ch. 3, p. 947 *c*), the Vimalakīrti is referring to an episode narrated in a paracanonical Sūtra, the *Vatsasūtra*, of which there exist two versions: a short version translated into Chinese by Chih Ch'ien (ca 222-253) with the title of Tu tzŭ ching = *Vatsasūtra (T 808); a long version translated into Chinese by Dharmarakṣa (ca 265-313) with the title of Ju kuang fo ching = *Kṣīraprabhabuddhasūtra (T 809). Cf. Ch'u san tsang chi chi, T 2145, ch. 2, p. 8 *b* 19; Chung ching mu lu, T 2146, ch. 1, p. 118 *b 1-2*; T 2147, ch. 2, p. 157 *c* 27-28; T 2148, ch. 2, p. 192 *c 11-12*; Li tai san pao chi, T 2034, ch. 6, p. 63 *a* 24; Ta t'ang nei tien lu, T 2149, ch. 2, p. 234 *a* 2; T'u chi, T 2151, ch. 2, p. 353 *c* 13; K'ai yüan shih chiao mu lu, T 2154, ch. 2, p. 488 *a* 9; 494 *b* 18.

According to the short version (T 808), the Buddha was staying in Śrāvastī, in the Jetavana, at the Anāthapiṇḍadārāma. Suffering from a "wind ailment", he sent Ānanda to ask for some milk from a neighbouring brahman. The latter had, in his stable, a very vicious cow which no-one could approach. He invited Ānanda to go and milk her. Śakra, disguised as a brahman, offered to take his place. The cow was told that if she would consent to give her milk, she would gain immense merit. The cow offered a part of her milk but asked that the other part be kept for her calf. But the calf, who had heard this request, offered his part of the milk to the Buddha:

approached me and, after having saluted my feet by touching them with his head, he addressed me with these words:

[*Vimalakīrti's Homily on the Illness of the Buddha*[78]]

43. Honourable (*bhadanta*) Ānanda, why, since daybreak (*kalyam eva*), have you been with a bowl (*pātra*) on the porch of this house?

I replied to him: The body of the Blessed One is stricken with an illness (*glānya*) and, as he has need of milk (*kṣīra*), I have come to get some here.

Vimalakīrti went on:

Honourable Ānanda, say not so.	Stop, stop (*tiṣṭha tiṣṭha*), O Honourable Sir (*bhadanta*). Do not use such words. Do not slander the Blessed One; do not denigrate the Tathāgata with such deceitful remarks. And why?

he would be satisfied, he said, with eating grass and drinking water. Ānanda returned to the Buddha and gave him the milk. The Master then told him about the jātaka: In olden days, the cow and the calf who did not believe in the Buddha's Sūtras had fallen to the rank of animals for sixteen kalpas. Today they had understood and heard the name of the Buddha, they had conceived a thought of good-will and given their milk. In future times, they will be śramaṇa disciples of the Buddha Maitreya and will become great Arhats. The calf, after its death, will offer the Buddha silken banners, will scatter flowers, burn perfumes, observe the Sūtras and the discipline. At the end of twenty kalpas, he will be the Tathāgata Kṣīraprabha "Brilliance of Milk" and will save everyone.

The Vimalakīrtinirdeśa is obviously using this Sūtra to introduce its section about Ānanda. According to it, Ānanda, while going begging for his milk, would have met the Bodhisattva Vimalakīrti in the brahman's house and the former would have addressed him with a long homily on the illness of the Buddha, a purely fictitious illness and simply skillful means.

In later times, the Vatsasūtra (T 808) was altered in consequence, and was the object of a new, much longer version (T 809). We find in it (T 809, p. 754 *c* 23 - 755 *a* 12), almost word for word, Vimalakīrti's homily just as it appears in the Vimalakīrtinirdeśa, and since that great Bodhisattva lived in Vaiśālī, and not Śrāvastī, the setting of the Sūtra was modified: instead of saying, like T 808, p. 754 *a* 4: "One day, the Buddha was staying in Śrāvastī, in the Jetavana, at the Anāthapiṇḍadārāma", the T 809, p. 754 *b* 19, says: "One day, the Buddha was in Vaiśālī, at the home of the brahmacārin *Mo tiao* (Mahādeva?), under the music tree".

The Vimalakīrtinirdeśa seems to come chronologically between the short version and the long version of the Vatsasūtra.

[78] On the much discussed problem of the illnesses of the Buddha, see Appendix, Note V.

Honourable Ānanda, the body of the Tathāgata (*tathāgatakāya*) is as hard as a diamond (*vajravat kaṭhinaḥ*)[79]. It has destroyed the pervasion of all bad dharmas (*akuśaladharmavāsanā*); it is endowed with all good dharmas (*sarvakuśaladharmasamanvāgata*): where then (*kutra*) could illness (*glānya*) quicken? Where could suffering (*ātaṅka*) exist?

44. Honourable Ānanda, go, without replying and in silence (*anabhyākhyānena tūṣṇīṃbhāvena nivartaya*). May no-one else hear your coarse words. Neither the very powerful sons of the gods (*mahaujaskā devaputrāḥ*) nor the Bodhisattvas come from the various Buddha-fields (*buddhakṣetra*) can be allowed to hear these words.

Honourable Ānanda, a Cakravartin king, who possesses only little good roots (*parīttakuśalamūlasamanvāgata*), is free from sickness (*roga*)[80]. Then how can the Tathāgata, endowed with infinite good roots (*anantakuśalamūlasamanvāgata*), with merit (*puṇya*) and knowledge (*jñāna*), be ill? This is absolutely impossible (*asthānam etat*).

Honourable Ānanda, go quickly and in silence, so as not to fill us with shame (*hrepaṇa*). The Anyatīrthikas, Carakas, Parivrājakas, Nirgranthas and Jīvikas[81] must not hear your coarse words. They would say to themselves: O, beware (*aho bata*)! the master (*śāstṛ*) of these people: if he is incapable of curing his own sickness, how then could he cure the sickness of others? Steal away, so that no-one may hear you[82].

[79] See above, II, § 12, note 29.

[80] A minute amount of merit can ensure many years of good health. Kumārajīva (T 1775, ch. 3, p. 359 *b* 20) points out, regarding this, the case of the Arhat Vākula who, at the age of 90, still did not know what sickness was, and who, for 90 kalpas, continued to enjoy this privilege, merely because earlier he had offered a harītakī fruit to a sick bhikṣu. This is a well-known episode: cf. Vin. of the Mūlasarv. in *Gilgit Manuscripts*, III, part 1, p. 193, *7-8*; T 1448, ch. 17, p. 82 *c*; Fo wu po ti tzŭ, T 199, p. 194 *b*; Upadeśa, T 1509, ch. 22, p. 223 *c* 27-29; M. Hofinger, *Le Congrès du lac Anavatapta*, p. 228-229.

[81] We have met above (II, § 3) the expression *carakapāṣaṇḍika* describing wandering sectaries. Here the Tibetan translation *gźan mu stegs can spyod pa daṅ kun tu rgyu daṅ gcer bu pa daṅ ḥtsho ba* presupposes a Sanskrit original of *anyatīrthika-caraka-parivrājaka-nirgrantha-jīvika*, a traditional expression used to describe the whole of the heretical sects, and which we meet, with slight variations, in the Lalitavistara, p. 2,*21*; 380,*12*; Sad. puṇḍarīka, p. 276,*2*; Śikṣāsamuccaya, p. 331,*11*; Mahāvastu, III, p. 412,*7*. H simply renders the expression by *Wai-tao P'o-lo-mên*, i.e. *tīrthika-brāhmaṇa*.

With regard to the old heretical sects, see also the listing in the Aṅguttara, III, p. 276,*31*.

[82] Presented as they are here according to the Tibetan translation and the Chinese

45. Honourable Ānanda, the body of the Tathāgata, this is the body of the Law (*dharmakāya*) and not a body mixed with excrement: it is not a body that can be cured with food (*āhāra*). The body of the Tathāgata is a transcendental body (*lokottarakāya*) which goes beyond all worldly dharmas (*sarvalokadharmasamatikrānta*). The body of the Tathāgata is a pure body (*anāsravakāya*)[83], apart from all impurities (*āsrava*). The body of the Tathāgata is an unconditioned body (*asaṃskṛtakāya*),

version by H, paragraphs 43 and 44 are rendered in exactly the same way by Kumārajīva in his translation of the Vimalakīrtinirdeśa, T 475, ch. 1, p. 542 *a* 5-16. However, the same paragraphs appear in a much longer version in a quotation from the Upadeśa, T 1509, ch. 9, p. 122 *a* 27-*b* 13, also translated by Kumārajīva:

Vim. — Why, since this morning, have you been here with your bowl?

Ān. — The Buddha is somewhat ill; he has need of milk; that is why I have come here.

Vim. — Stop, stop, O Ānanda. Do not slander the Tathāgata. The Buddha who is blessed has gone beyond all bad dharmas (*sarvākuśaladharmasamatikrānta*). What illness could he have? Take care that the sectaries do not hear such coarse words: they would despise the Buddha and say: "Can the Buddha, incapable of curing his own illness, cure others?"

Ān. — It is not my idea. I personally received an order from the Buddha, and need milk.

Vim. — This order of the Buddha's is skillful means (*upāya*): in the period of the five corruptions (*pañcakaṣāyakāla*), he makes use of this fiction in order to save all beings. When, in generations to come, bhikṣus who are ill will go and ask laymen (*avadātavasana*) for broths and medicaments (*bhaiṣajya*) should the laymen say to them: "You cannot cure yourselves, how can you cure others?", the bhikṣus will be able to reply: "If our great Master himself was subject to illness, then how could we not be ill, we whose bodies are like black mustard-seeds (*sarṣapa*)?" Thus the laymen will offer the bhikṣus broths and medicaments, and the bhikṣus, enjoying peace (*kṣema*) and tranquillity, will practise the Way. If heretical ṛṣis, by means of medicinal plants (*oṣadhi*) and formulae (*mantra*), can chase away the illnesses of other men, then how could the Tathāgata who is omniscient (*sarvajña*) be incapable of chasing away his own illnesses? So be quiet and take this milk in your bowl. Take care that nonbelievers do not learn of it.

Faced with these quite considerable variations, we might ask if the author of the Upadeśa did not quote the Vimalakīrtinirdeśa from memory, not without adding his own inventions or, which is more likely, if during Kumārajīva's time, there were not some very different versions of the Vimalakīrtinirdeśa in circulation.

Furthermore it is quite strange that Kumārajīva always transcribes Vimalakīrti's name by *Wei mo chieh* in his translation of the Vimalakīrtinirdeśa, but by *P'i mo lo chieh* in his translation of the Upadeśa. However, we know that the bibliographers tended to attribute to Kumārajīva translations which were not by him (cf. P. Demiéville, in *L'Inde Classique*, II, p. 416).

[83] Reading by K and H; the Tibetan version has a variation: *de bźin gśegs paḥi sku la gnod pa med de*: "The body of the Tathāgata has no troubles".

apart from all conditioned things (*saṃskṛta*). It avoids all reckoning (*saṃkhyā*); within it, all reckonings are eternally stilled (*nityaśānta*). Honourable Ānanda, to have it that such a body is ill is foolish and improbable.

[*The Celestial Voice*]

46. When I had heard these words, I wondered if, even while being so close to the Blessed One [84], I had not misheard and misunderstood him, and I was thoroughly ashamed (*hrīta*).

At that moment, I heard a voice which came from the sky (*antarīkṣān nirghoṣam aśrauṣam*) [85] and which said: Ānanda, what the householder (*gṛhapati*) has told you is quite true: the true body of the Blessed One is truly free of illness. However, as the Blessed One has appeared at the era of the five corruptions (*pañcakaṣāyakāla*) [86], he manifests these things so as to discipline (*vinayanārtham*) beings who are poor (*daridra*), suffering (*duḥkhita*), and of bad conduct (*duścarita*). Therefore, do not be ashamed, O Ānanda, but take that milk and go back.

47. This is how, Blessed One, the Licchavi Vimalakīrti replies to questions (*praśnān vyākaroti*). And, as for myself, on hearing that worthy man speaking so eloquently, I did not know what to say, I kept silent and did not answer at all. That is why, Blessed One, I am not capable of going to ask that worthy man about his illness.

*

48. In the same way, the five hundred Śrāvakas, incapable (of going to ask Vimalakīrti), related to the Blessed One their own adventures (*svanidāna*) and reported to him all the conversations (*kathā*) that they had with the Licchavi Vimalakīrti.

In the same way, the Blessed One invited, one after the other, the five hundred great Śrāvaka disciples to go to Vimalakīrti to ask him about his illness. But, these Śrāvakas, each individually, related to the Buddha their own adventures (*svanidāna*), reported the words of the worthy man Vimalakīrti, and all declared themselves incapable of going to ask him about his illness.

[84] Ānanda was close to the Buddha in his capacity of *upasthāyaka*.

[85] The hearing of celestial voices — the voices of the *antarīkṣa deva* — is common in Mahāyāna texts: cf. Lalitavistara, p. 266,*1*; 401,*1*; Aṣṭasāh., p. 442,7; Sad. puṇḍarīka, p. 69,*12*; 379,*10*; 389,*5*; 390,*1*; below, III, § 63; XII, § 9.

[86] The five corruptions are concerned respectively with the life span (*āyus*), false view (*dṛṣṭi*), passion (*kleśa*), being (*sattva*) and the cosmic period (*kalpa*): cf. Lalitavistara, p. 248,*13*; 257,*21*; Sad. puṇḍarīka, p. 43,*4*; 56,*8*; 58,*11*; Bodh. bhūmi, p. 15,*3*; 252,*17*; Śikṣāsamuccaya, p. 60,*14*; Mahāvyutpatti, No. 2335-40.

[11. *Maitreya and the Prediction*]

49. Then the Blessed One said to the Bodhisattva Mahāsattva Maitreya[87]: Maitreya, go and ask the Licchavi Vimalakīrti about his illness.

The Bodhisattva Maitreya replied: Blessed One, I am not capable of going to ask that worthy man (*satpuruṣa*) about his illness. And why? Blessed One, I remember that, one day, with the son of the gods (*devaputra*), Saṃtuṣita[88], and other sons of the gods of the family of the Tuṣitas (*tuṣitakuladevaputra*), I was holding a righteous conversation (*dhārmī kathā*) concerning the irreversible stage (*avaivartikā bhūmiḥ*) of the Bodhisattva Mahāsattvas, when the Licchavi Vimalakīrti approached and, after having saluted my feet by touching them with his head, said these words to me:

[87] After having met with the refusal of the ten Śrāvakas, the Buddha now turns to three Bodhisattvas of whom the first and most famous is Maitreya. There can be found in LAMOTTE, *Histoire*, p. 775-788, an outline of the enormous amount of literature devoted to this Bodhisattva by both Vehicles.

Maitreya was a Bodhisattva of the eighth stage, the *acalā*, also called the irreversible stage (*avaivartikā bhūmiḥ*), when Śākyamuni made him his prediction (see below, Appendix, Note III, *in fine*): "When the life-span of men is 84,000 years in length, the Lord Maitreya will be born in the world, holy and perfectly enlightened".

The direct successor of Śākyamuni, Maitreya is at present dwelling in the Tuṣita heavens, separated by one birth only from accession to supreme and perfect enlightenment. Hence his title of *ekajātipratibaddha* Bodhisattva, "bound by a single rebirth", expression rendered in Tibetan by *skye ba gcig gis thogs pa*, and in Chinese by *i-shêng-pu ch'u* 一生補處 (translation by Chih Ch'ien and Kumārajīva) or *i-shêng so hsi* 一生所繫 (translation by Hsüan-tsang).

The Prajñāpāramitā (Pañcaviṃśati, p. 62,*14*-63,*5*; Satasāh., p. 270,*9*-271,*3*) defines this epithet clearly: *santi bodhisattvā mahāsattvā ekajātipratibaddhā ye prajñāpāramitāyāṃ caranta upāyakauśalyena catvāri dhyānāni samāpadyante yāvad apraṇihitasamādhiṃ samāpadyante. na ca teṣāṃ vaśena gacchanti saṃmukhībhūtāṃś ca buddhān bhagavata ārāgayitvā tatra brahmacaryaṃ caritvā punar eva tuṣitānāṃ devānāṃ sabhāgatāyai upapadyante. te tatra yāvad āyus tiṣṭhanti. te tatra yāvad āyuḥ sthitvā ahīnendriyāḥ smṛtimantaḥ saṃprajānanto anekair devakoṭīniyutaśatasahasraiḥ parivṛtāḥ puraskṛtā ihopapattiṃ darśayitvā nānābuddhakṣetreṣv anuttarāṃ samyaksaṃbodhiṃ abhisaṃbudhyante.*

[88] Like all the Buddhas before their last birth, Maitreya is dwelling in the Heavens of the Tuṣitas, the fourth class of gods of the *kāmadhātu*. The king of these gods is known by the name of Saṃtuṣita: cf. Dīgha, I, p. 218,*15*; Anguttara, IV, p. 243,*1*; Jātaka, I, p. 48,*16*; 81,*11*; Upadeśa, T 1509, ch. 54, p. 443 *b* 17. He surpasses his companions in ten superior ways, life-span, beauty etc. (Aṅguttara, IV, p. 243,*1-4*; Dīgha, III, p. 146,*3-7*).

[*Vimalakīrti's Address on Prediction*[89]]

50. Honourable Maitreya, the Blessed One predicted to you that after only one birth you would come to supreme and perfect enlightenment

[89] The prediction (*vyākaraṇa*) plays an important part in the later works of the Pāli Tipiṭaka and in postcanonical Sanskrit literature. The Buddha no longer expatiates in long dogmatic sūtras of greatly advanced technique, but frequently intervenes in order to reveal to his listeners their past actions or announce their future rebirths. These predictions, which take place according to an established ceremonial, are common in the Avadānaśataka, I, p. 4-7; 10-12; 19-22, etc; the Divyāvadāna, p. 67-69; 138-140; 265-267; 366-368; 568-570, and the Vin. of the Mūlasarvāstivādins, T 1442, ch. 46, p. 879 *a-c*; T 1448, ch. 8, p. 36 *a-b*:

The Buddha smiles. It is a rule that when the Buddhas come to smile, there issue from their lips rays of blue, yellow, red and white light; some descending, others rising. Those which descend go to the depths of the hells and, as the case may be, refresh or warm the hell-bound, who are metamorphosed into devas. The rays which rise infiltrate into the twenty-three celestial spheres, and the gods, seized with admiration, cry out to each other:

"Begin, come out of your houses; devote yourselves to the Buddha's Law; annihilate the army of death, as an elephant overturns a reed hut".

"He who will walk without distraction under the discipline of this Law, avoiding birth and the revolving of the world, will put an end to suffering".

Then the rays, after having enveloped the trichiliomegachiliocosm, return to the Blessed One from behind. If the Buddha wishes to explain an action accomplished in the past, the rays disappear into his back. If it is a future action that he wants to predict, they disappear into his chest. According to whether he predicts a birth in hell, among animals, among Pretas, among men, among the Bālacakravartin kings, among Cakravartin kings or among the Devas, the rays disappear respectively under the soles of his feet, into his heel, into his big toe, into his knee, into the palm of his left hand, into the palm of his right hand or, finally, into his navel. If he wants to predict to someone that he will have a Śrāvaka *bodhi*, they disappear into his mouth; if it is the *bodhi* of a Pratyekabuddha, they disappear into his ears; if it is the *anuttarā samyaksaṃbodhiḥ* they disappear into his cranial protuberance.

Ānanda then asks the Buddha the reason for his smile and the return of the rays: "No, it is not without motive that the Victorious Ones, who have triumphed over the enemy, who are exempt from lightheartedness, who have given up pride and discouragement, and who are the cause of the happiness of the world, permit the sight of a smile like the yellow fibres of the lotus ...".

The Buddha replies to him that in fact his smile is not without motive and that such and such a person, because of a thought he has conceived or an offering he has made, will go to such and such a birth or will even become, in the world, a perfectly accomplished Buddha with a set name.

The texts of the Great Vehicle like the Śūraṃgamasamādhisūtra, T 642, ch. 2, p. 638 *c*-639 *b* (tr. LAMOTTE, *La Concentration de la Marche Héroïque*, Brussels, 1965, p. 202, §100-213, §108; also cf. P. DEMIÉVILLE, *Le Concile de Lhasa*, p. 141-142), the Sūtrālaṃkāra, p. 166,9, and the Bodh. bhūmi, p. 290,6-7, distinguish four kinds of prediction: 1. the prediction conferred on the *gotrastha* who has not yet produced the thought of Bodhi (*anutpādacittavyākaraṇa*); 2. the prediction conferred on him who has just produced the thought of Bodhi (*utpāditacittavyākaraṇa*); 3. the prediction in secret, known to the assembly, but not to the one concerned (*asamakṣavyākaraṇa* or *viparokṣāvasthita*); 4. the public prediction, made in the presence of the one concerned (*saṃmukhapudgalavyākaraṇa*).

The supreme *vyākaraṇa* is conferred in the eighth stage, the *acalā* or *avaivartikā bhūmiḥ*, on a Bodhisattva who is in possession of the *anutpattikadharmakṣānti* (cf. below, Appendix, Note III, *in fine*).

However the *vyākaraṇa* is of only provisional value and is not directly compatible with the doctrine of *pudgalanairātmya*.

Upadeśa, T 1509, ch. 38, p. 336 *b* 24 - *c* 3: "Bodhisattva is only a name (*nāmamātra*)... But, within the Buddha's Law there are two kinds of truths: 1. the truth of experience (*saṃvṛtisatya*), 2. the real truth (*paramārthasatya*). It is a truth of experience when one says that a being (*sattva*) exists; in real truth, one says it does not exist. There are two kinds of people: those who understand the marks of a name (*nāmalakṣaṇa*) and those who do not understand them, Similarly when the army establishes a pass-word, some know it, others do not know it".

All the texts are of the opinion that, the being not existing, any prediction concerning it is meaningless:

Aṣṭasāh., p. 800,*12-17*: *nāhaṃ bhagavaṃs taṃ dharmaṃ samanupaśyāmi yo dharmo vyākṛto vyākariṣyate vyākariyate vānuttarāyāṃ samyaksaṃbodhau. tam apy ahaṃ bhagavan dharmaṃ na paśyāmi yo dharmo 'bhisaṃbudhyate yo dharmo 'bhisaṃboddhavyo yena vā dharmeṇābhisaṃbudhyate*: "I do not see any dharma which has been predicted, will be predicted or is predicted to supreme and perfect enlightenment; I do not see any dharma reaching enlightenment, due to reach enlightenment or by which to reach enlightenment".

Pañcaviṃśati, p. 58,*20* - 59,*14*: Among the efforts in which the Bodhisattva engages, the effort devoted to the truth of wisdom is defined as the best (*agra*)... And why? Because the supreme effort is the effort devoted to the perfection of wisdom, to emptiness (*śūnyatā*), signlessness (*ānimitta*), wishlessness (*apraṇihita*). The Bodhisattva who strives in this way should be taken as the object of the prediction (*vyākṛta*) and close to the prediction (*āsannībhūto vyākaraṇasya*). Striving in this way, he will benefit innumerable and incalculable beings, all the same he will never think: "The blessed Lord Buddhas will give me the prediction", or "I am close to prediction", or "I will purify a Buddha-field", or "I shall cause beings to ripen", or again "After having obtained supreme and perfect enlightenment, I shall cause the wheel of the Law to turn". And why? Because he does not isolate the element of the Law (*dharmadhātum na viviktīkaroti*) and because he does not see any dharma distinct from the element of the Law (*na dharmadhātor anyadharmaṃ samanupaśyati*) which could practise the perfection of wisdom or to which the blessed Lord Buddhas could predict supreme and perfect enlightenment. And why? When the Bodhisattva practises the perfection of wisdom, the notion of being (*sattvasaṃjñā*) does not occur to him. In fact the being absolutely does not arise (*atyantatayā sattvo notpadyate*), absolutely is not extinguished (*na nirudhyate*) because it has as its law non-arising and non-extinction (*anutpādānirodhadharmatvāt*). How can that which is without arising or extinction practise the perfection of wisdom?

(*tvam ekajātipratibaddho bhagavatā vyākṛto 'sy anuttarāyāṃ samyaksaṃbodhau*)[90]. With regard to which birth (*jāti*) did you receive this prediction (*vyākaraṇa*)? Is it the past (*atīta*) birth, the future (*anāgata*) or the present (*pratyutpanna*) one? If it is the past birth, it is already exhausted (*kṣīṇa*); if it is the future birth, it has yet to come (*ananuprāpta*); if it is the present birth, it is without foundation (*asthāna*), for the Blessed One has said: "Thus it is, O monk, that in a single moment, you are born, you grow old, you die, you pass on and you are reborn" (*kṣaṇe tvaṃ bhikṣu jāyase jīryase mriyase cyavase upapadyase*)[91]. It is therefore by not being born that you obtained the prediction.

But non-arising (*anutpāda*), this is the entry into the absolute certainty of acquiring the Supreme Good (*niyāmāvakrānti*)[92]. That which is not born (*ajāta*), that which has already entered into the said certainty (*avakrāntaniyāma*) is not the subject of a prediction (*na vyākṛtaḥ*) and does not reach supreme enlightenment (*nābhisaṃbudhyate*).

In the Ratnakūṭa, T 310, ch. 28, p. 154 *c* 8, the Buddha declares: "Son of good family, when I predict to the Śrāvakas that they will obtain supreme and perfect enlightenment, it is not accurate".

The same viewpoint is adopted here by Vimalakīrti. The Buddha, it is said, predicted to Maitreya that after one last birth he would attain bodhi. But the more the assertions, the more the nonsense.

1. The prediction concerns future existence. But the distinction between past, present and future does not hold. Regarding the refutation of the three phases of time, cf. Madh. vṛtti, p. 382-389; tr. J. DE JONG, *Cinq chapitres de la Prasannapadā*, Leiden, 1949, p. 37-43.

2. Maitreya, the object of the prediction, is not born and is identical with the universal Tathatā which is non-arising (*anutpāda*) and non-extinction (*anirodha*); in consequence, no prediction can be ascribed to him.

If Maitreya is, by virtue of this Tathatā, originally enlightened and in Parinirvāṇa, all beings are also at the same time as he. Maitreya enjoys no privilege.

3. The Bodhi predicted to Maitreya is a mere absence, an idea of purely negative content. It therefore can not be acquired by anyone.

[90] Cf. Sad. puṇḍarīka, p. 307,*11*: *eṣa Maitreyo nāma bodhisattvo mahāsattvo bhagavataḥ Śākyamuner anantaraṃ vyākṛto 'nuttarāyāṃ samyaksaṃbodhau.*

[91] A saying of the Buddha, quoted as such, in the Khuddakapātha Commentary, p. 78: *khandhesu jāyamānesu jīyamānesu mīyamānesu ca khaṇe khaṇe tvaṃ bhikkhu jāyase ca jīyase ca mīyase ca.*

Also see Dīgha, II, p. 30,*26*; Saṃyutta, II, p. 5,*10*; 10,*3*: *kicchaṃ vatāyaṃ loko āpanno, jāyati ca jīyati ca mīyati ca cavati ca uppajjati ca.*

Sanskrit Mahāvadāna, p. 134; Lalitavistara, p. 346,*1-2*: *kṛcchraṃ baṭāyaṃ loka āpanno yad uta jāyate pi jīryate mriyate cyavate upapadyate.*

[92] Regarding the *niyāma*, see above, I, § 13, note 65.

51. How then, O Maitreya, would you receive the prediction? Would it be by virtue of the arising of suchness (*tathatotpāda*) or by virtue of the extinction of suchness (*tathatānirodha*)?

But suchness which is unarisen (*anutpanna*) and unextinguished (*aniruddha*) does not arise (*notpadyate*) and is not extinguished (*na nirudhyate*)[93].

If it is by virtue of the arising of suchness that you receive the prediction, suchness has no arising. If it is by virtue of the extinction of suchness that you receive the prediction, suchness has no extinction. That which is without arising (*anutpāda*) and without extinction (*anirodha*) does not admit logically (*nyāya*) of any prediction.

The suchness of all beings (*sarvasattvatathatā*), the suchness of all dharmas (*sarvadharmatathatā*), the suchness of all the holy ones (*sarvāryatathatā*), this is also your own suchness, O Maitreya. If therefore, you receive the prediction, all beings also receive this same prediction. And why? Because suchness is not constituted of duality (*dvayaprabhāvita*), is not constituted of multiplicity (*nānātvaprabhāvita*). Honourable Maitreya, the instant that you reach supreme and perfect enlightenment (*anuttarāṃ samyaksaṃbodhim abhisaṃbhotsyase*), at that instant, all beings also will reach that same enlightenment (*evaṃrūpāṃ bodhim abhisaṃbhotsyante*). And why? Because that enlightenment (*bodhi*) is already acquired (*anubuddha*) by all beings. Honourable Maitreya, the instant that you achieve complete Nirvāṇa (*parinirvṛta*), at that instant, all beings also will be in complete Nirvāṇa. And why? Because there is not one single being who is not in complete Nirvāṇa already. The Tathāgata has said that true suchness (*tathatā*), this is Parinirvāṇa[94]. Seeing that all beings are originally calmed (*ādiśānta*) and in complete Nirvāṇa, the Buddha has said of true suchness, that this is Parinirvāṇa[95].

[93] Regarding Tathatā which is the absence of self-nature (*niḥsvabhāvatā*), without arising, or extinction, the same for all, see the Introduction, p. LXIX-LXXII.

[94] Regarding the synonyms of Tathatā, see Introduction, p. LXXII.

[95] Mādhyamika speculations on a famous formula tendered by Mahāyānasūtras (*yathoktaṃ Vaipulye*):

a. Ratnameghasūtra, in Madh. vṛtti, p. 225,*9*, and Subhāṣitaṃgraha, (Muséon, 1903, p. 394,*13*):

> *ādiśāntā hy anutpannāḥ prakṛtyaiva ca nirvṛtāḥ,*
> *dharmās te vivṛtā nātha dharmacakrapravartane.*

b. Saṃdhinirmocana, VII, § 1; Abhidharmasamuccaya (ed. V.V. Gokhale, Journ. Bombay Branch R.A.S., XXIII, 1947, p. 35,*15-20*; ed. P. Pradhan, p. 84,*11-19*):

Therefore, O Maitreya, do not try, do not mislead these sons of the gods (*devaputra*) with your addresses.

[*Vimalakīrti's Homily on Enlightenment*[96]]

52. Bodhi, no-one can draw near it or away from it. Therefore act O Honourable Maitreya, so that these sons of the gods (*devaputra*) reject these imaginary views (*saṃkalpadṛṣṭi*) concerning Bodhi.

Bodhi is not verified (*abhisaṃbuddha*) by the body (*kāya*) and it is not verified by the mind (*citta*).

Bodhi is the appeasing of all the signs (*sarvanimittopaśānti*).	Bodhi is extinction (*nirodha*), because in it the signs (*nimitta*) of all beings (*sattva*) and all dharmas are entirely extinguished (*niruddha*).
Bodhi is without uncalled-for affirmation (*samāropa*)[97] concerning all objects (*ālambana*).	Bodhi is without uncalled-for affirmation (*samāropa*) because it does not affirm anything about any object (*ālambana*).
Bodhi is the non-functioning of all mental attention (*manasikārapracāra*).	Bodhi is non-functioning (*apracāra*), for all idle chatter (*prapañca*) and all mental attention (*manasikāra*) do not function in it.
Bodhi is the cutting off of all kinds of false views (*sarvadṛṣṭigataparicchedа*).	Bodhi is eternal cutting off (*paricchedа*) because all the kinds of false views (*dṛṣṭigata*) are definitively cut off in it.
Bodhi is the abandoning of all imaginings (*sarvaparikalpatyāga*).	Bodhi is abandoning (*tyāga*), because all beliefs (*grāha*) are abandoned in it.
Bodhi is free from movement (*iñjita*), anxiety (*cintanā*) and disturbance (*utkṣepa*).	Bodhi is without fetters (*bandhana*) because it is free from movement (*iñjita*) and disturbance (*utkṣepa*).
	Bodhi is appeasement (*upaśānti*) because all discrimination (*vikalpa*) is appeased (*upaśānta*) in it.

niḥsvabhāvāḥ sarvadharmā anutpannāḥ sarvadharmā
aniruddhā ādiśāntāḥ prakṛtiparinirvṛtāḥ.

c. Sūtrālaṃkāra, XI, v. 51; Saṃgraha, p. 128-129:
niḥsvabhāvatayā siddhā uttarottaraniśrayāt,
anutpādānirodhādiśāntaprakṛtinirvṛtiḥ.

d. Gauḍapāda, IV, 93:
ādiśāntā hy anutpannāḥ prakṛtyaiva sunirvṛtāḥ.

[96] By means of a series of paradoxes, Vimalakīrti is explaining here the Mahāyānist viewpoint of *bodhi* without content. Regarding this matter, see the Appendix, Note VI. Prajñā and Bodhi in the perspective of the two Vehicles.

[97] Regarding *samāropa*, cf. above, III, § 6, n. 17; VIII, § 6.

Bodhi is the non-functioning of all vows (*praṇidhānāpravṛtti*).

Bodhi is freedom and detachment from all beliefs (*grāha*).

Bodhi has as its abode (*sthāna*, *vihāra*) the element of the Law (*dharmadhātu*).

Bodhi is in conformity with suchness (*tathatānvaya*).

Bodhi is non-duality (*advaya*) because there is neither discriminating mind (*manas*) nor object of thought (*dharma*).

Bodhi is founded on the limit of reality (*bhūtakoṭi*)[98].

Bodhi is the same (*sama*) for it is the same as space (*ākāśasama*).

Bodhi, being without origination (*utpāda*), disappearance (*vyaya*), duration (*sthiti*) or modification (*anyathātva*)[99] is unconditioned (*asaṃskṛta*).

Bodhi is complete knowledge (*parijñā*) of the minds (*citta*), conduct (*carita*) and intentions (*āśaya*) of all beings.

Bodhi does not have the bases of consciousness (*āyatana*) for doors.

Bodhi, exempt from the passions of rebirth (*pratisaṃdhikleśa*) and

Bodhi is immense (*vipula*) for all its great vows (*praṇidhāna*) are unfathomable (*duravagāha*).

Bodhi is pacifying (*akalaha*) because it rejects all attachment (*abhiniveśa*) and all argument (*vivāda*).

Bodhi is well-established (*supratiṣṭhita*) because it rests on the element of the Law (*dharmadhātu*).

Bodhi is conformity (*anvaya*) because it is in conformity with true suchness (*tathatā*).

Bodhi is non-duality (*advaya*) because all qualified dharmas (*viśiṣṭadharma*) are excluded from it.

Bodhi is founded because it is founded (*sthita*) on the limit of reality (*bhūtakoṭi*).

Bodhi is the same (*sama*) because all the elements (*dhātu*), from the eye (*cakṣus*) and form (*rūpa*) to the discriminating mind (*manas*) and dharmas, are all the same (*sama*) and the same as space (*ākāśasama*).

Bodhi is unconditioned (*asaṃskṛta*) because it is absolutely freed of origination (*utpāda*), duration (*sthiti*), modification (*anyathātva*) and disappearance (*vyaya*).

Bodhi is complete knowledge (*parijñā*) because it knows in depth the minds (*citta*) and conduct (*carita*) of all beings.

Bodhi is without doors (*dvāra*) because it is not connected with the six inward bases of consciousness (*ādhyātmika āyatana*).

Bodhi is without involvement (*asaṃsṛṣṭa*), because it is definitively exempt

---

[98] Regarding the synonyms of Tathatā, see Introduction, p. LXXI, above, III, §6, note 15.

[99] This concerns the three or four marks of the conditioned (*saṃskṛtalakṣaṇa*): cf. Kośa, II, p. 222.

all their pervasion (*vāsanā*), is without involvement (*asaṃsṛṣṭa*).

Bodhi, which is neither somewhere (*sthāna*) nor nowhere (*asthāna*), can be found neither here (*na deśastha*) nor there (*na pradeśastha*). Bodhi, which is without intrusion (*paryutthāna*), does not rely on suchness (*tathatā*)[100].

Bodhi is only a name (*nāmamātra*) and that name itself is immovable (*acala*).

Bodhi, beyond grasping or rejection (*āyūhaniryūhavigata*)[101], is without "waves" (*ataraṅga*)[102].

Bodhi which is non-functioning (*apravṛtti*) is pure in nature (*svabhāvapariśuddha*).

Bodhi is luminous (*ābhāsa*) and naturally pure (*prakṛtiviśuddha*).

Bodhi is without prehension (*grāha*) and has absolutely no object (*ālambana*).

Bodhi, which penetrates the

from all the passions (*kleśa*) and pervasions of rebirth (*pratisaṃdhivāsanā*).

Bodhi is without localisation (*asthāna*) because, in true suchness (*tathatā*), all localisation is avoided. Bodhi is without abode (*avihāra*) because it is not visible anywhere.

Bodhi is only a name (*nāmamātra*) for the name of Bodhi is unfunctional (*akāritra*).

Bodhi is without waves (*ataraṅga*) because all grasping (*āyūha*) and rejection (*niryūha*) are avoided.

Bodhi is non-disturbance (*anutkṣepa*) because it is eternally pure in itself (*svabhāvaparisūddha*).

Bodhi is really stilled (*praśānta*) because it is originally pure (*ādiśuddha*).

Bodhi is luminous (*abhāsa*) because it is naturally uninvolved (*prakṛtyasaṃsarga*).

Bodhi is without prehension (*grāha*) because it is exempt from all objects of perception (*adhyālambana*)[103].

Bodhi is undifferentiated (*abhinna*) be-

[100] Bodhi conforms with suchness, as has been said above, but it does not rely on suchness. See further on, VI, § 6, the passage relating to baselessness (*apratiṣṭhāna*). — K simply says: "Bodhi is without localisation (*asthāna*), for it has no shape (*saṃsthāna*) or form (*rūpa*)".

[101] The Tibetan *blaṅ ba daṅ dor ba med pa* renders the Sanskrit expression *āyūhaniryūhavigata* which will be found further on, III, § 73, and which is also to be found in the Laṅkāvatāra, p. 80,*7*; 115,*15*. Cf. D.T. Suzuki, *Index to the Laṅkāvatāra*, Kyōto, 1934, p. 41.

[102] Regarding *taraṅga*, see above, III, § 6, note 13. — Cf. Laṅkāvatāra, p. 127,*12*:

yathā kṣiṇe mahā-oghe taraṅgāṇām asaṃbhavaḥ,
tathā vijñānavaicitryaṃ niruddhaṃ na pravartate.

[103] *P'an-yüan* 攀緣 in the versions by K and H. In Ch. IV, § 14, note 21, these two characters have as their correspondent in Tibetan *lhag par dmigs pa*, in Sanskrit *adhyālambana* according to the Mahāvyutpatti, No. 6991.

sameness of all dharmas (*sarvadharmasamatā*), is undifferentiated (*abhinna*).

Bodhi, which is without example (*udāharaṇa*) is incomparable (*anupama*).

Bodhi, being very difficult to understand (*duranubodha*), is subtle (*aṇiman*).

Bodhi, having the nature of space (*ākāśasvabhāva*) is omnipresent (*sarvatraga*).

This Bodhi cannot be verified (*abhisaṃbuddha*) either by the body (*kāya*) or by the mind (*citta*). And why? The body is like grass (*tṛṇa*), a tree (*vṛkṣa*), a wall (*bhitti*), a path (*mārga*) and a reflection (*pratibhāsa*). As for the mind, it is immaterial (*arūpin*), invisible (*anidarśana*), without support (*aniśraya*) and without intellect (*avijñapti*).

cause it penetrates (*avabodha*) the sameness of all dharmas (*sarvadharmasamatā*).

Bodhi is incomparable (*anupama*) because it is without example (*udāharaṇa*).

Bodhi is subtle (*aṇiman*) because it is very difficult to understand (*duranubodha*).

Bodhi is omnipresent (*sarvatraga*) because, by nature, it encompasses everything, like space (*ākāśa*).

Bodhi attains the summit (*niṣṭhāgata*) because it reaches the supreme summit of all dharmas.

Bodhi is without defilement (*asaṃkleśa*) because no worldly dharma (*lokadharma*) can defile it.

This Bodhi cannot be verified (*abhisaṃbuddha*) either by the body (*kāya*) or by the mind (*citta*).

53. Blessed One, when Vimalakīrti had pronounced this address, within the gathering of the gods (*devamaṇḍala*), two hundred sons of the gods obtained the certainty concerning the non-arising of dharmas (*dviśatānāṃ devaputrāṇām anutpattikadharmakṣāntipratilābho 'bhūt*). As for myself, I was reduced to silence (*niṣpratibhāna*) and could not answer at all. That is why, O Blessed One, I am not capable of going to ask that worthy man (*satpuruṣa*) about his illness.

[12. *Prabhāvyūha and the Bodhimaṇḍa*]

54. Then the Blessed One said to the young Licchavi (*licchavikumāra*) Prabhāvyūha [104]: Prabhāvyūha, go and ask the Licchavi Vimalakīrti about his illness.

Prabhāvyūha replied: Blessed One, I am not capable of going to ask that worthy man (*satpuruṣa*) about his illness. And why? Blessed One, I remember that one day as I was leaving the great town of Vaiśālī, the Licchavi Vimalakīrti was entering it. I saluted him and asked him: Householder (*gṛhapati*), where have you come from? — He replied to me: I have come from the seat of enlightenment (*bodhimaṇḍa*) [105]. — I asked him: What then is the seat of enlightenment? — He then said these words to me:

[104] This kumāra Prabhāvyūha is perhaps the same as the Bodhisattva Prabhāvyūha listed in the *nidāna*, Ch. I, § 4, No. 7.

[105] The question of the *bodhimaṇḍa* often comes into the Sanskrit sources: Mahāvastu, III, p. 278,*1*; Divyāvadāna, p. 392,*17*; Lalitavistara, p. 36,*2*; 44,*17*, etc.; Aṣṭasāh., p. 205,*27*; 206,*1*; Pañcaviṃśati, p. 24,*6*; 42,*3*; Sad. puṇḍarīka, p. 16,*3*; 54,*13*; 159,*3*; 165,*8*; 340,*5*; Suvarṇabhāsa, p. 89,*15*; Madh. vṛtti, p. 594,*10*; Ratnagotra, p. 88,*2*; Abhisamayālaṃkāra, V, v. 28.

Bodhimaṇḍa is rendered in Tibetan by *byaṅ chub kyi sñiṅ po* "quintessence of enlightenment", in Chinese by *tao-ch'ang* 道場 "area of bodhi" (tr. by Cn and K), or *miao-p'u-t'i* 妙菩提 "marvellous bodhi" (tr. by H).

Āloka, p. 206,*7*: *bodher maṇḍaḥ sāro 'treti bhūpradeśaḥ paryaṅkākrānto bodhimaṇḍaḥ*: "The *bodhimaṇḍa*, used as a seat, is a spot so named because the *maṇḍa*, that is, the quintessence of bodhi, is present there".

Pañjikā, p. 58,*11*: In the compound *bodhimaṇḍa*, the word *maṇḍa* means quintessence (*maṇḍaśabdo 'yaṃ sāravacanam*), as one says quintessence of butter (*ghṛtamaṇḍa*) to describe cream.

The word *maṇḍa* is often strengthened by a synonym, as in the expressions *bodhimaṇḍavara* (Ratnagotra, p. 4,*1*) or *bodhimaṇḍavarāgra* (Sad. puṇḍarīka, p. 165,*8*; 316,*3*; Survarṇabhāsa, p. 90,*6*).

1. Literally, the bodhimaṇḍa is a seat on which one sits as appears from the expressions *bodhimaṇḍe niṣīdati* (Bodh. bhūmi, p. 405,*11*; Karuṇāpuṇḍarīka, T 157, ch. 3, p. 184 *b* 2); *bodhimaṇḍaniṣadanam* or *niṣadanatā* (Sūtrālaṃkāra, p. 102,*22*; 103,*13*; Bodh. bhūmi, p. 94,*5*); *bodhivṛkṣamūle siṃhāsanopaviṣṭaḥ* (Sad. puṇḍarīka, p. 165,*8*).

This concerns the seat situated in Gayā, at the foot of the tree of enlightenment under which the Buddhas reach supreme and perfect enlightenment (cf. Sad. puṇḍarīka, p. 316,*3-4*).

Śākyamuni sat there after having strewn on it the *kuśa* grass which had been given to him by the grass cutter Sotthiya or Svastika (cf. Jātaka, I, p. *70-71*; Mahāvastu, II, p. 131,*13-15*; Lalitavistara, p. 286-288; Sad. puṇḍarīka, p. 421,*6-7*; Hsiu hsing pên ch'i ching, T 184, ch. 2, p. 470 *a*; Yin kuo ching, T 189, ch. 3, p. 639 *c*; Abhiniṣkramaṇa, T 190, ch. 26, p. 773 *a*; Chung hsü mo ho ti ching, T 191, ch. 6,

[*Vimalakīrti's Homily on the Seat of Enlightenment*]

55. Son of good family (*kulaputra*), the seat of enlightenment (*bodhimaṇḍa*) is the seat of good intentions (*kalyāṇāśaya*), for they

p. 950 *a*; Vin. of the Dharmaguptas, T 1428, ch. 31, p. 781 *a*; Vin. of the Mūlasarv., T 1450, ch. 5, p. 122 *c*).

The cult of the tree and seat goes back to the far past and is corroborated in the Maurya period. During his visit to the Saṃbodhi in the year 10 after his consecration (cf. J. BLOCH, *Inscriptions d'Aśoka*, p. 112), the emperor Aśoka "attached a four-sided enclosure to the bodhi tree" (*bodhivṛkṣasya caturdiśaṃ vāraṃ baddhvā*), and getting on to it, he sprinkled it with 4,000 precious vases filled with a perfumed liquid (cf. Divyāvadāna, p. 404,*2*; Aśokāvadāna, T 99, ch. 23, p. 170 *b*; T 2042, ch. 2, p. 105 *c*; T 2043, ch. 3, p. 141 *a*). Later, in the year 34 of his reign, after Tiṣyarakṣitā's attack on the bodhi tree (cf. Mahāvaṃsa, XX, v. 4-5), Aśoka erected round the earlier sanctuary an enclosure made of stone and brick, the traces of which were still visible in the seventh century, in Hsüan-tsang's time (Hsi yü chi, T 2087, ch. 8, p. 915 *c*).

Representations of this unroofed temple appear, from the second and first centuries B.C. onwards, on the sculptures of Bhārhut and Sāñcī (cf. A.K. COOMARASWAMY, *La sculpture de Bhārhut*, Paris, 1956, pl. 8, fig. 23, or pl. 9, fig. 27; J. MARSHALL and A. FOUCHER, *The Monuments of Sāñchi*, Delhi, 1940, vol. II, pl. 51 *a*). The existence of a Bodhimaṇḍavihāra in the Śuṅga period is noted by the Mahāvaṃsa, XXIX, v. 41 (cf. LAMOTTE, *Histoire*, p. 440).

During his visit to Bodh-Gayā in approximately A.D. 636, Hsüan-tsang noticed, in the enclosure round the bodhi tree, the existence of the Diamond Seat (*vajrāsana*) which came into being at the same time as the world, at the beginning of the Bhadrakalpa. This seat is to be found at the centre of the trichiliomegachiliocosm (*trisāhasramahāsāhasralokadhātu*). Even while resting on the Golden Circle, or *kāñcana-vajramaṇḍala* (cf. Kośa, III, p. 140), it is level with the ground. It is made of diamond (*vajra*), and has a circumference of more than a hundred feet. It is called the Diamond Seat because it is on this spot that the thousand Buddhas of the Bhadrakalpa acquired or will acquire the Diamond-like Concentration (*vajropamasamādhi*) which immediately precedes the attainment of enlightenment. It is also called the Area of Enlightenment (*tao-ch'ang* = *bodhimaṇḍa*) because the Buddhas attained bodhi on that spot. The place is protected from cosmic upheavals; however, since the recent decline of Buddhism, the Diamond Seat is no longer visible, and is covered by sand (cf. Hsi yü chi, T 2087, ch. 8, p. 915 *b*).

The excavations carried out by A. Cunningham at Bodh-Gaya have brought to light a whole series of *vajrāsana*: see A.K. COOMARASWAMY, *History of Indian and Indonesian Art*, London, etc., 1927, p. 81-82; *La sculpture de Bodh-Gayā*, Paris, 1935, p. 12, and pl. 44 and 45.

2. Figuratively speaking, bodhimaṇḍa merely means the wholly spiritual presence of the Law, or of the *dharmakāya* of the Buddhas, and this is quite independent of any material localisation. According to the Saddharmapuṇḍarīka, p. 391,*6-13*, any spot where the Sūtra has just been recited, hermitage, monastery, house, etc., should be considered as the *bodhimaṇḍa*: "It must be realised that on that spot (where the Sūtra is recited) all the Tathāgatas, holy and perfectly enlightened ones, have attained

are unfeigned (*akṛtrima*)[106]. It is the seat of effort (*yoga*) for it accomplishes deeds of strength (*udyogakarman*). It is the seat of high resolve (*adhyāśaya*) for it penetrates in depth the excellent Law (*viśiṣṭadharmāvabodhāt*). It is the seat of the great thought of enlightenment (*mahābodhicitta*), for it does not forget any dharmas (*sarvadharmāsaṃpramoṣāt*)[107].

56. It is the seat of pure giving (*pariśuddhadāna*) for it does not seek the fruits of worldly fruition (*laukikavipākaphalaniḥspṛha*). It is the seat of firm morality (*dṛḍhaśīla*), for it fulfils the vows (*praṇidhānaparipūraṇāt*). It is the seat of patience and kindness (*kṣāntisauratya*)[108], for it does not have towards beings any thought of aversion (*pratighacitta*). It is the seat of heroic vigour (*śūravīrya*), for it does not retreat (*avinivartanīya*) before any strenuous endeavour (*ādīptaprayatna*). It is the seat of tranquillity (*śamatha*) and meditation (*dhyāna*), for it makes use of mental ability (*cittakarmaṇyatā*)[109]. It is the seat of excellent wisdom (*viśiṣṭaprajñā*) for it discerns (*sākṣātkaroti*) all dharmas[110].

57. It is the seat of goodwill (*maitrī*) because of its sameness of mind regarding all beings (*sarvasattveṣu samacittatā*). It is the seat of compassion (*karuṇā*) because it withstands all adversity (*upadruta*). It is the seat of joy (*muditā*) because it experiences (*anubhavati*) the

supreme and perfect enlightenment, turned the wheel of the Law and entered complete Nirvāṇa". From this point of view, Bodh-Gayā, Vārāṇasī and Kuśinagara are indistinguishable.

Vimalakīrti takes the same point of view when he affirms here, in § 60, that, wherever they may have set out from, the Bodhisattvas come from the bodhimaṇḍa and the Buddhadharmas.

Vimalakīrti's homily on the bodhimaṇḍa, or marvellous bodhi according to H's translation, serves as a sort of corrective to the preceding homily concerning bodhi (§ 52). If it is true that bodhi is only a name, it is no less true that all possible good can be said about it. Inept from the philosophical point of view, this panegyric is justified from the mystical angle.

[106] In the whole of this paragraph, the Chinese versions by K and H invert the order of the words adopted by the Tibetan translation: the subject becomes the predicate and vice versa: "Good intentions are the seat of enlightenment for they are unfeigned", and so on.

[107] Regarding *āśaya*, *adhyāśaya* and *bodhicitta*, see above, I, § 13, and Appendix, Note II.

[108] Regarding *kṣāntisauratya*, see above, II, § 12, note 32.

[109] *Cittakarmaṇyatā*, a synonym of *cittapraśrabdhi* "mental aptitude" (Kośa, II, p. 157).

[110] This paragraph is concerned with the six *pāramitā*.

pleasure of the garden of the Law (*dharmārāmarati*). It is the seat of equanimity (*upekṣā*) because it has destroyed affection (*anunaya*) and aversion (*pratigha*)[111].

58. It is the seat of super-knowledge (*abhijñā*) because it is in possession of the six super-knowledges (*ṣaḍabhijñā*). It is the seat of the liberations (*vimokṣa*) because it rejects the movement of mental constructions (*vikalpa*). It is the seat of skillful means (*upāya*) because it causes beings to ripen (*paripācayati*). It is the seat of the means of conversion (*saṃgrahavastu*) because it wins over (*saṃgṛhṇāti*) all beings. It is the seat of learning (*bahuśruta*) because it consolidates religious practice (*pratipatti*)[112]. It is the seat of self-control (*dama*)[113] because of its correct motive (*bhūtapratyavekṣā*). It is the seat of the thirty-seven auxiliary dharmas of enlightenment (*bodhipākṣikadharma*) because it destroys conditioned dharmas (*saṃskṛtadharma*). It is the seat of the truths (*satya*) because it does not mislead (*na vañcayati*) beings.

It is the seat of the dependent co-production (*pratītyasamutpāda*) because it goes from the exhaustion of ignorance (*avidyāsravakṣaya*) to the exhaustion of old age and death (*jarāmaraṇāsravakṣaya*).

It is the twelve-limbed dependent co-production (*dvādaśāṅgapratītyasamutpāda*) because ignorance (*avidyā*) is inexhaustible (*akṣaya*), etc., and because old age (*jarā*), death (*maraṇa*), sorrow (*śoka*), lamentation (*parideva*), pain (*duḥkha*), grief (*daurmanasya*) and despair (*upāyāsa*) are inexhaustible[114].

[111] This paragraph is concerned with the four *apramāṇacitta*: cf. above, I, § 13, note 66.

[112] Regarding the relative importance of learning (*bahuśruta, paryāpti*) and religious practice (*pratipatti*), see W. RĀHULA, *History of Buddhism in Ceylon*, Colombo, 1956, p. 158-159.

[113] Here and elsewhere, wherever the Tibetan has *ṅes par sems pa*, the Chinese versions have *tiao-hsin* 調心 (K) and *tiao-fu* 調伏 (H). The meanings do not tally at all. According to the Mahāvyutpatti, No. 7460, *ṅes par sems pa* corresponds to the Sanskrit *nidhyapti* (Pāli, *nijjhatti*) "deep meditation", while *tiao-hsin* or *tiao-fu* usually renders the Sanskrit *dama* "self-control" or *vinaya* "discipline". The Chinese reading seems preferable.

[114] Cf. K: "The *pratītyasamutpāda* is the *bodhimaṇḍa* because [its twelve aṅgas] from *avidya* to *jarāmaraṇa* are inexhaustible (*akṣaya*)". The *pratītyasamutpāda* in reverse order: "From the extinction of *avidyā*, extinction of the *saṃskāra*, and so on" is meaningless, because not having arisen (*anutpanna*), the limbs of the chain of causation can never be extinguished (*aniruddha*). We could say along with the Chinese versions that they are inexhaustible (*akṣaya*) or, with the Tibetan version, that they are already extinguished. In other words, all dharmas, being originally calmed (*ādiśānta*) and essentially in Nirvāṇa (*prakṛtiparinirvṛta*), elude the mechanism of the *pratītyasamutpāda*. Cf. Introduction, p. LXIV-LXVI.

It is the seat of the stilling of all the passions (*sarvakleśapraśamana*) because it is perfectly enlightened (*yathābhūtam abhisaṃbuddha*) on the true nature of things (*dharmatā*).

59. It is the seat of all beings (*sarvasattva*) because all these beings are without self-nature (*niḥsvabhāva*).

It is all beings, for all these beings have non-self (*anātman*) as their self-nature (*svabhāva*).

It is the seat of all dharmas (*sarvadharma*) for it is perfectly enlightened (*abhisaṃbuddha*) regarding their emptiness (*śūnyatā*). It is the seat of the crushing of all Māras (*sarvamārapramardana*) for it remains immovable (*acala*) before them. It is the seat of the triple world (*traidhātuka*) because it refrains from entering it (*praveśa*). It is the seat of the vigour characterising those who give the lion's roar (*siṃhanādanādivīrya*)[115], for it discerns (*pravicinoti*) without fear (*bhaya*) or trembling (*saṃtrāsa*). It is the seat of the [ten] powers [*bala*], the [four] convictions (*vaiśāradya*) and the [eighteen] exclusive attributes of the Buddhas (*āveṇikabuddhadharma*) because it is everywhere irreproachable (*sarvatrāninditа*). It is the seat of the brightness of the mirror[116] of the triple knowledge (*tisro vidyāḥ*) because it eliminates the passions (*kleśa*) and wins the knowledge which is definitive and without a trace of error (*atyantaṃ niravaśeṣajñāna*). It is the seat of the complete penetration of all dharmas in a single instant of thought (*cittaikakṣaṇikaḥ sarvadharmaniravaśeṣādhigamaḥ*) because it fully achieves omniscience (*sarvajñajñānasamudāgamāt*).

60. If Bodhisattvas, O son of good family (*kulaputra*), are thus endowed (*saṃpanna*) with the true course (*bhūtapraskanda*)[117], with the perfections (*pāramitā*), the power to ripen beings (*sattvaparipācana*), good roots (*kuśalamūla*), the winning of the good Law (*saddharmasaṃgraha*) and the devotion to the Tathāgatas (*tathāgataparyupāsana*), then and whatever they do — whether they go somewhere or return from it (*abhikrānte pratikrānte*), whether they advance or stop (*gate sthite*)[118], whether they lower their feet or raise

[115] Cf. above, I, § 3, note 4.

[116] H is the only one to speak of the brightness of the mirror: *Chien-chao* 鑒照. This is perhaps a Vijñānavādin interpolation, for the "mirror wisdom" (*ādarśajñāna*) of the Buddhas is not referred to in India before the fourth century of our era. On this matter, see Sūtrālaṃkāra, p. 46,*16*; Saṃgraha, p. 278-279; Buddhabhūmisūtra, T 680, p. 721 *b* 12-*c* 26; Buddhabhūmisūtraśāstra, T 1530, ch. 3, p. 302 *a* 12-19; Siddhi, p. 681-682. Regarding this philosophical form, cf. P. DEMIÉVILLE, *Le miroir spirituel*, in Sinologica, I, 1947, p. 112-137.

[117] This concerns the passage of the Bodhisattvas through the stages (*bhūmi*).

[118] These passive past participles used substantively are common in Buddhist texts:

their feet (*caraṇanikṣepaṇe caraṇotkṣepaṇe*)[119] — then, say I, all these Bodhisattvas come from the seat of enlightenment (*bodhimaṇḍa*), come from the Buddhadharmas, are established (*sthita*) in the Buddhadharmas.

61. Blessed One, when Vimalakīrti had given this address, five hundred gods and men produced the thought of supreme and perfect enlightenment (*pañcamātrāṇāṃ devamanuṣyaśatānām anuttarāyāṃ samyaksaṃbodhau cittāny utpāditāni*). As for myself, I was reduced to silence (*niṣpratibhāna*) and could not answer at all. That is why, O Blessed One, I am not capable of going to ask that worthy man (*satpuruṣa*) about his illness.

[13. *Jagatiṃdhara and the Assault of Māra*]

62. Then the Blessed One said to the Bodhisattva Jagatīṃdhara[120]: Jagatīṃdhara, go and ask the Licchavi Vimalakīrti about his illness.

Jagatīṃdhara replied: Blessed One, I am not capable of going to ask that worthy man (*satpuruṣa*) about his illness. And why?

[*Visit of Māra and his Daughters*]

Blessed One, I remember that one day when I was at home (*matsthāna*), Māra the Evil One (*Māraḥ pāpīyān*)[121], surrounded by

Sanskrit Mahāparinirvāṇa, p. 174: *iha bhikṣur abhikrānte pratikrānte saṃprajāno bhavaty ālokite vilokite saṃmiñjite prasārite saṃghāṭīcīvarapātradhāraṇe gate sthite niṣaṇṇe śayite jāgarite bhāṣite tūṣṇīṃbhāve supte śrame viśrame saṃprajāno bhavati.* — For the corresponding Pāli formula, see WOODWARD, *Concordance*, I, p. 211, s.v. *bhikkhu ... sampajānakārī.*

[119] In Tibetan, *gom pa ḥdor daṅ ḥdeg pa.* The stanzas in hybrid Sanskrit in the Lalitavistara, p. 114,*10*, have *caraṇotkṣipaṇe*. Also see Aṣṭasāh., p. 670,*21*: *so 'bhikrāman vā pratikrāman vā na bhrāntacitto 'bhikrāmati vā pratikrāmati vā, upasthitasmṛtir abhikrāmati, upasthitasmṛtiḥ pratikrāmati; na vilambitaṃ pādaṃ bhūmer utkṣipati na vilambitaṃ pādaṃ bhūmau nikṣipati, sukham evotkṣipati sukhaṃ nikṣipati; na ca sahasā pādaṃ bhūmer utkṣipati na ca sahasā pādaṃ bhūmau nikṣipati; paśyann eva bhūmipradeśam ākrāmati.*

[120] *Ḥgro ba ḥdzin pa* is clearly Jagatīṃdhara, a Bodhisattva mentioned in the Mahāvyutpatti, No. 728, and the Rāṣṭrapālaparipṛcchā, ed. L. FINOT, p. 2,*1*; ed. J. ENSINK, p. 2,*9*. Jagatīṃdhara is rendered by *Ch'ih-jên* 持人 in Cn, by *Ch'ih-shih* 持世 in K and H. *Ch'ih-shih* can also mean the Bodhisattva Vasudhara, in Tibetan *Nor gyi rgyun* (cf. MOCHIZUKI, *Encyclopaedia*, IV, p. 3590 *a*).

[121] Regarding Māra, the work by E. WINDISCH, *Māra und Buddha*, Leipzig, 1895, should be supplemented by the notes in MALALASEKERA, *Proper Names*, II, p. 611-620,

and AKANUMA, *Noms propres*, p. 412-415. Also see NĀGĀRJUNA, *Traité*, I, p. 339-346; II, p. 880-884; 906-908.

Māra is the ruler of the world of desire (*kāmadhātu*) and the direct head of the sixth and last class of the gods of the *kāmadhātu*. His palace is exactly like the Paranirmitavaśavartin heaven (Yin kuo ching, T 189, ch. 3, p. 639 *c* 17; Yogācārabhūmi, p. 75,*7-8*: *Mārabhuvanaṃ punaḥ parinirmitavaśavartiṣu deveṣu paryāpannaṃ na sthānāntaraviśiṣṭam*; T 1579, ch. 4, p. 294 *c* 25); however, certain sources place it immediately above (Dīrgha, T 1, ch. 20, p. 136 *a* 2).

Māra is the direct adversary of the Buddha, sworn enemy of desire. Whether alone or in the company of his armies and his daughters, he made countless assaults on Śākyamuni, his monks and his nuns. Always overcome, he returns regularly to the attack and, so as to deceive his adversaries, taking on the most varied of forms, including that of the Buddha himself.

He is the personification of the forces of evil, and this is why Buddhist texts distinguish between several kinds of Māras, particularly the "four-fold Māra": 1. Aggregates-Māra (*skandhamāra*), 2. Passion-Māra (*kleśamāra*), 3. Death-Māra (*mṛtyumāra*), 4. "Son of the gods" Māra (*devaputramāra*). Cf. Mahāvastu, III, p. 273,*2*; 281,*7*; Lalitavistara, p. 224,*18-19*; 354,*11-12*; Madh. vṛtti, p. 49,*10*; 442,*3*; Dharmasaṃgraha, § 80; Upadeśa, T 1509, ch. 5, p. 99 *b* 11; Yogācārabhūmi, T 1579, ch. 29, p. 447 *c* 17; Great Parinirvāṇa, T 374, ch. 2, p. 372 *b* 4; Ch'ao jih ming san mei ching, T 638, ch. 1, p. 536 *c* 2-4.

There is also a mention of a Formation-Māra (*abhisaṅkhāramāra*) in the Udāna Commentary, p. 216,*11*, and a Misdeed-Māra (*āpattimāra*) in the Ma i ching, T 732, p. 530 *c* 12.

In even the earliest of sources, such as the Padhānasutta, the "internal" armies of Māra are personified faults: desire, sadness, hunger, thirst, greed, etc. (Suttanipāta, v. 436-449; Lalitavistara, p. 262-263; NĀGĀRJUNA, *Traité*, p. 341). As for his daughters, they have names such as "Passion", "Sadness" and "Greed" (Taṇhā, Arati and Rāga in Saṃyutta, I, p. 124; Tantrī, Aratī and Ratī in Mahāvastu, III, p. 286; Rati, Arati and Tṛṣṇā in Lalitavistara, p. 378; Arati, Prīti and Tṛṣ in Buddhacarita, XIII, v. 3).

A supposed conversion of Māra is mentioned in the Legend of Aśoka and related sources: Aśokāvadāna, T 2042, ch. 5, p. 118 *c* 9-120 *b* 6; Aśokasūtra, T 2043, ch. 8, p. 159 *a* 12-161 *a* 25; Divyāvadāna, p. 356,*25*-364,*3*; Hsien yü ching, T 202, ch. 13, p. 442 *b*-443 *c*; Fu fa tsang yin yüan chuan, T 2058, ch. 3, p. 304 *c* sq. ; Vibhāṣā, T 1545, ch. 135, p. 697 *c*-698 *a*. Upagupta, the fifth Buddhist patriarch, was teaching in Mathurā when Māra interrupted and annoyed the audience with a shower of precious objects and the appearance of heavenly maidens. In order to punish the Evil One, Upagupta attached the corpses of a serpent, dog and man to his neck. Māra was unable to get rid of them and had to apologize publicly. He confessed his past misdeeds and committed himself not to bother the monks ever again. In return Upagupta freed him of his troublesome necklace.

However, the forces of good and evil are irreconcilable. In the Mahāyānasūtras, Māra takes on the role of tempter, as appears in the present section of the Vimalakīrtinirdeśasūtra. The episode recounted here is not dissimilar from a section in the Mahāsaṃnipāta, the Ratnaketudhāraṇīsūtra, the original Sanskrit of which, rediscovered in Gilgit, has been published by N. DUTT, *Gilgit Manuscripts*, IV, 1959, p. 1-82.

twelve thousand daughters of the gods (*devakanyā*) and disguised as Śakra (*śakraveṣeṇa*)[122], approached me with music (*tūrya*) and singing (*gītā*). With his retinue (*saparivāra*), he saluted my feet by touching them with his head (*pādau śirasābhivandya*); he played celestial music and paid homage to me; then joining his hands as a sign of respect (*añjaliṃ praṇamya*), he stood to one side (*ekānte 'sthāt*).

Then, taking him for Śakra, the king of the gods (*devendra*), I said to him: May you be welcome (*sugata*), O Kauśika[123]! But, in the midst of all these pleasures (*kāmanandeṣu*), remain attentive (*apramāda*). Ponder carefully on how these pleasures are transitory (*anitya*) and, whilst in the body (*kāya*), life (*jīvita*) and riches (*bhoga*), make an effort to hold on to whatever is substantial (*sāra*)[124].

Māra then said to me: Worthy man (*satpuruṣa*), do accept these twelve thousand daughters of the gods, and make them your servants (*bhṛtyā*).

In the first chapter "Mara's disappointment" (*Mārajiṃhikaraṇa*), the Evil One goes to see the Buddha in a disguised form, but is immediately recognised. He sends his daughters, but the seductions they attempt meet with no success, and a few words are enough to convert them. Then follows an attack by Māra's sons which also ends in defeat: their throwing-weapons are miraculously turned into flowers.

The second chapter is devoted to "Retrospectives" (*pūrvayoga*) and explains the conversion of Māra's daughters by certain meritorious actions in their previous lives.

Finally, in the third chapter entitled "Māra's Submission" (*Māradamana*), the Evil One, held prisoner by the Buddha's magic, only regains his freedom by taking his refuge in the Triple Jewel.

Just like the texts of the Small Vehicle, the Mahāyāna Sūtras recognize the forces of evil; they put the Bodhisattvas on guard against Māra's works: cf. Aṣṭasāh., p. 499-527; 771-784; Pañcaviṃśati, T 223, ch. 13, p. 318 *b*-320 *b*; Śikṣāsamuccaya, p. 151,*13*-152,*19*.

However, "discernment of minds" needs to be practised because, alongside the real Māras, there are false Māras, that is, compassionate Bodhisattvas who, in order to convert beings, make use of skillful means and occasionally transform themselves into tempters. This original point of view will be taken up further on by the Vimalakīrtinirdeśa, IV, § 8; V, § 20.

[122] Regarding the various disguises that Māras can make use of, cf. Mahāsaṃnipāta, p. 77,*7*-79,*2*.

[123] Kauśika, in Pāli Kosiya (cf. Dīgha, II, p. 270,*3*; Majjhima, I, p. 252,*32*), is an epithet of Śakra (Indra), a guardian deity of the brahman clan of the Kuśikas.

[124] A canonical reminiscence of a famous stanza in the Dhammapada, I, v. 11:

Asāre sāramatino sāre cāsāradassino,
te sāraṃ nādhigacchanti micchāsankappagocarā,

paradoxically modified in the Sūtrālaṃkāra, p. 82,*20*, the Saṃgraha, p. 132, 225, and the Abhidharmasamuccaya, ed. P. PRADHAN, p. 107,*5*. Also see below, III, § 72.

I answered him: Stop (*tiṣṭha*), O Kauśika! Do not offer to me, who am a recluse (*śramaṇa*) and son of the Śākya (*śākyaputrīya*), such unfitting things (*ayogyavastu*)[125]. It is unfitting for me.

[*Vimalakīrti's Intervention*]

63. I had not finished speaking, when the Licchavi Vimalakīrti arrived and, after having saluted my feet by touching them with his head, said to me: Son of good family (*kulaputra*), do not, in any way, take him for Śakra: it is Mārah pāpīyān, come [in disguise] to hold you up to ridicule (*viḍambanārtham*); it is not Śakra.

Then the Licchavi Vimalakīrti said to Māra the Evil One: Māra pāpīyān, since these daughters of the gods (*devakanyā*) are not fitting (*ayogya*) to a monk, son of the Śākya (*bhikṣu śākyaputrīya*), give them to me. They are fitting for me, who am a layman (*gṛhastha*), dressed in white clothing (*avadātavasana*).

Then Māra the Evil One, stricken with terror (*bhayabhīta*) and troubled (*parikhinna*), thought that the Licchavi Vimalakīrti had come to torment him. He wanted to disappear (*antardhātum*), but, held by the psychic power (*ṛddhibala*) of Vimalakīrti, he was incapable of doing so. Try as he might to deploy the various resources (*nānāvidhopāya*) of his psychic power (*ṛddhibala*), he could not disappear[126].

At that moment, a voice (*nirghoṣa*) came from the sky (*antarīkṣa*)[127], which said: Māra pāpīyān, hand over (*samarpaya*) these daughters of the gods to the worthy man (*satpuruṣa*) Vimalakīrti, then you can return to your celestial dwelling (*devabhavana*).

Then Māra the Evil One, terror-stricken (*bhayabhīta*), reluctantly[128] gave up the daughters of the gods.

[*Vimalakīrti's Homily on the Garden of the Law*]

64. The Licchavi Vimalakīrti, after having received the daughters of the gods, addressed them with these words: Since you have been given to me by Māra the Evil One, then produce the thought of supreme and perfect enlightenment (*anuttarā samyaksaṃbodhiḥ*).

[125] In his quality of monk Bodhisattva, Jagatīṃdhara is bound to continence.

[126] Cf. Mahāsaṃnipāta, p. 81,*1*: *tathāpi na śaknoti antardhātuṃ vā digvidikṣu palāyituṃ vā, tatraiva kaṇṭhe pañcabandhanabaddham ātmānaṃ dadarśa.*

[127] See above, III, § 46, note 85.

[128] In Tibetan, *mi ḥtshal bźin du*. K and H have *mien-yang* 俛仰 "eyes [successively] lowered and raised".

After Vimalakīrti had addressed to them discourses aimed at ripening them with a view to enlightenment (*saṃbodhivipācanānulomikā kathā*), the daughters of the gods produced the thought of enlightenment.

Vimalakīrti addressed them further: You have just produced the thought of supreme and perfect enlightenment; henceforth (*sāṃpratam*), it is in the great garden of the Law (*dharmārāma*)[129] that you will place your pleasure (*rati*) and your confidence (*adhimukti*), and not in the five objects of desire (*kāmaguṇa*).

The daughters of the gods asked: What is this pleasure (*rati*) that has as its object the garden of the Law (*dharmārāma*)?

Vimalakīrti replied: It is the pleasure which consists in believing firmly in the Buddha (*buddhe 'vetyaprasādaḥ*), in desiring to hear the Law (*dharmaśravaṇakāma*), attending to the community (*saṃghaparyupāsana*), driving away pride (*māna*) and respecting the teachers (*gurusatkāra*), extricating oneself from the triple world (*traidhātukavyutthāna*), not stopping over any object (*viṣaya*), considering the (five) aggregates (*skandha*) as transitory (*anitya*) and like killers (*ghātaka*), unerringly considering the (eighteen) elements (*dhātu*) like poisonous snakes (*āśīviṣa*), unerringly considering the (twelve) bases of consciousness (*āyatana*) like an empty village (*śūnyagrāma*)[130], protecting the thought of enlightenment (*bodhicittasaṃrakṣaṇa*), benefiting beings (*sattvahitakriyā*), respecting the teachers (*gurusatkāra*), excluding all avarice (*mātsarya*) in giving, avoiding all relaxation (*sraṃsanā*) in pure morality (*śīla*), exercising endurance (*kṣama*) and self-control (*dama*) in patience (*kṣānti*), cultivating good roots (*kuśalamūla*) in vigour (*vīrya*), possessing undisturbed (*anutkṣepa*) knowledge in meditation (*dhyāna*), excluding even a shadow of defilement (*kleśābhāsa*) in wisdom (*prajñā*), spreading enlightenment (*bodhivistaraṇa*), overcoming Māras (*māranigrahaṇa*), destroying passions (*kleśanirghātana*), purifying the Buddha-fields (*buddhakṣetraviśodhana*), accumulating all good roots (*sarvakuśalasaṃnicaya*) with a view to perfecting the primary and secondary marks (*lakṣaṇānuvyañjanapariniṣpattyartham*)[131], practising correctly (*samyagbhāvanā*) in the double store of merit and knowledge (*puṇyajñānasaṃbhāra*), adorning the

[129] Here Vimalakīrti is contrasting the Garden of the Law, the image of perfect renunciation, with the heavenly parks, Nandanavana, etc., where the daughters of the gods enjoy the five objects of desire: forms, sounds, scents, tastes and tangibles.

[130] Regarding the images of the killers, serpents and the empty village, see above, II, § 11, note 28.

[131] The *mahāpuruṣalakṣaṇa* are the fruit of meritorious actions undertaken by the Bodhisattva during the hundred complementary cosmic ages: cf. Kośa, IV, p. 223-224.

seat of enlightenment (*bodhimaṇḍālaṃkriyā*), not trembling on hearing the profound dharmas (*gambhīradharmaśravaṇe 'nuttrāsanam*)[132], penetrating in depth the three doors to deliverance (*vimokṣamukhapravicaya*), taking Nirvāṇa as an objective (*adhyālambana*) but without obtaining it inopportunely (*akālaprāpti*)[133], seeing the virtues (*guṇa*) of one's equals (*sabhāgajana*) and always serving them (*sevanā*), not seeing the flaws (*doṣa*) of strangers (*visabhāgajana*) and having for them neither hatred (*dveṣa*) nor aversion (*pratigha*), serving good friends (*kalyāṇamitrasevanā*) and improving bad friends (*pāpamitrottāpana*), according to the Law (*dharma*) confidence (*adhimukti*) and delight (*prāmodya*), assembling comptetent skillful means (*upāyasaṃgrahaṇa*), and finally, attentively (*apramādam*) cultivating the auxiliary dharmas of enlightenment (*bodhipākṣikadharma*).

Thus it is that the Bodhisattva places his pleasure (*rati*) and his confidence (*adhimukti*) in the garden of the Law (*dharmārāma*).

Such is, O my sisters (*bhaginī*), the pleasure (*rati*) having as its object the great garden of the Law (*dharmārāma*) of the Bodhisattvas; and it is in this garden of the Law that the great Bodhisattvas always reside. Place your pleasure there, and no longer in the object of desire (*kāmaguṇa*).

[*Stratagems concerning the Daughters of the Gods*]

65. Then Māra the Evil One said to the daughters of the gods: Come here, I wish to return with you to our celestial dwelling (*devabhavana*).

The daughters of the gods replied: Māra pāpīyān, go away; we will not return with you. And why? You have given us to this householder (*gṛhapati*); how, then, could we return with you? Henceforth we shall place our pleasure (*rati*) and our confidence (*adhimukti*) in the garden of the Law (*dharmārāma*), and no longer in the objects of desire (*kāmaguṇa*). So return alone.

Then Māra the Evil One said to the Licchavi Vimalakīrti: If it

[132] The Bodhisattva should accept the profound doctrine of the Great Vehicle without discouragement or fear. This is what is ceaselessly recommended by the Prajñā literature, particularly the Aṣṭasāh., p. 45,*19-24*: *saced bodhisattvasya mahāsattvasya gambhīrāyāṃ prajñāpāramitāyāṃ bhāṣyamāṇāyāṃ deśyamānāyām upadiśyamānāyāṃ cittaṃ nāvalīyate na saṃlīyate na viṣīdati na viṣādam āpadyate nāsya vipṛṣṭhī bhavati mānasaṃ na bhagnapṛṣṭhī bhavati nottrasyati na saṃtrasyati na saṃtrāsam āpadyate* ...

[133] The Tibetan simply says: *dus ma yin par thob par mi byed pa*. Regarding the expression *p'an-yüan* (*adhyālambana*) used by H, see above, III, § 52, note 103.

is true that a Bodhisattva Mahāsattva feels no regret in giving away all that he possesses (*sarvasvaparityāga*), then, O householder (*gṛhapati*), give me back these daughters of the gods.

Vimalakīrti replied: I give them to you, O Evil One (*pāpīyan*). Return with your retinue (*saparivāra*), but act so as to fulfil (*paripūraṇa*) the spiritual aspirations (*dharmāśaya*) of all beings.

Then the daughters of the gods, saluting Vimalakīrti, said these words to him: Householder (*gṛhapati*), how shall we conduct ourselves when we have returned to the dwelling of Māra?

[*Vimalakīrti's Advice to the Daughters of the Gods*]

66. Vimalakīrti replied: My sisters (*bhaginī*), there is a treatise of the Law (*dharmamukha*) called "The Inexhaustible Lamp" (*akṣayapradīpa*)[134]. Study it. What then is it? My sisters, a single and only lamp (*pradīpa*), were it used to light an hundred thousand lamps, suffers no diminution (*apacaya*) of brilliance at all: equally, O my sisters, if a single and only Bodhisattva established in full and perfect enlightenment several hundreds of thousands of *koṭinayuta* of beings, his own thought of Bodhi not only does not suffer either exhaustion (*kṣaya*) or diminution (*apacaya*), but, in the course of time, increases (*vardhate*).

Equally, to the extent that, making use of his skill in means (*upāyakauśalya*), he teaches others all the good dharmas (*sarveṣāṃ sarvakuśaladharmān uddeśayati*), to that same extent does he progress (*vardhate*) in all these good dharmas without suffering either exhaustion (*kṣaya*) or diminution (*apacaya*). Such is the treatise of the Law (*dharmamukha*) entitled "The Inexhaustible Lamp" (*akṣayapradīpa*) which you should study. Even while residing in the palace of Māra, you will exhort countless sons and daughters of the gods (*apramāṇadevaputradevakanyā*) to produce the thought of enlightenment (*bodhicitta*). Thus you will truly recognise the beneficence of the Tathāgata (*tathāgate kṛtajñaḥ*) and you will benefit all beings.

[134] Here Vimalakīrti is referring to a text (*chos kyi sgo* in Tib.; *fa-mên* in the Chinese versions) entitled *Akṣayapradīpa*. I can find no trace of it in the catalogues of the Tripiṭaka. However, the short quotation given from it here recalls Ovid's distich, *Ars amatoria*, III, 90-93:

Quis vetet adposito lumen de lumine sumi?
Mille licet sumant, deperit inde nihil.

On the allegory of the inexhaustible lamp. cf. H. DURT, in Hōbōgirin, IV, p. 363, *chōmyōtō* article.

67. Then the daughters of the gods, having saluted the feet of the Licchavi Vimalakīrti by touching them with their heads (*pādau śirasābhivandya*), returned with Māra.

Then the daughters of the gods saluted the feet of Vimalakīrti by touching them with their heads. Vimalakīrti removed his psychic power (*ṛddhibalaṃ pratisaṃharati sma*) which held Māra the Evil One prisoner so well that the latter disappeared suddenly with his retinue and returned to his dwelling.

Blessed One, having seen the extent of the magical strength (*vikurvaṇāspharaṇa*) of the Licchavi Vimalakīrti, I am not capable of going to ask that worthy man (*satpuruṣa*) about his illness.

Such are, O Blessed One, in Vimalakīrti, the control (*aiśvarya*), the psychic power (*ṛddhibala*), the knowledge (*jñāna*) and the wisdom (*prajñā*), the eloquence (*pratibhāna*), the magical strength (*vikurvaṇa*) and the instruction of the Law (*dharmadeśanā*). That is why I am not capable of going to ask him about his illness.

[14. *Sudatta and the Offering of the Law*]

68. Then the Blessed One said to the guildsman's son (*śreṣṭhiputra*), Sudatta[135]: Son of good family (*kulaputra*), go and ask the Licchavi Vimalakīrti about his illness.

Sudatta replied: Blessed One, I am not capable of going to ask that worthy man (*satpuruṣa*) about his illness. And why?

[135] Having brought onto the scene ten Śrāvaka monks and three Bodhisattvas, the text ends by introducing a lay (*upāsaka*) Śrāvaka, the śreṣṭhiputra Sudatta, better known by the name of Anāthapiṇḍada, Anathapiṇḍika in Pāli. He was a native of Śrāvastī in Kosala and considered to be the most generous of donors (*aggo dāyakānaṃ*: cf. Aṅguttara, I, p. 26,*3*).

His first encounter with the Buddha in the Śītavana at Rājagṛha, his conversion and donation of the Jetavana at Śrāvastī are told with a great profusion of detail in canonical and other texts: Saṃyutta, I, p. 210-212; Saṃyukta, T 99, ch. 22, p. 157 *b*; T 100, ch. 9, p. 440 *b*; Pāli Vinaya, II, p. 154-159, 163-165; Vin. of the Mahīśāsakas, T 1421, ch. 25. p. 166 *c* 10-167 *b* 19; Vin. of the Mahāsāṃghikas, T 1425, ch. 23, p. 415 *a* 29-*c* 8; Vin. of the Dharmaguptas, T 1428, ch. 50, p. 938 *b* 20-939 *c* 15; Vin. of the Sarvāstivādins, T 1435, ch. 34, p. 243 *c* 20-245 *a* 3; Vin. of the Mūlasarv., T 1450, ch. 8, p. 138 *b* 18-142 *b* 13; Hsien yü ching, T 202, ch. 10, p. 418 *b*-421 *b*; Ch'u yao ching, T 212, ch. 27, p. 756 *c* 17 sq.; Pāli Jātaka, I, p. 92-93; Fa hsien chuan, T 2085, p. 860 *b*; Hsi yü chi, T 2087, ch. 6, p. 899 *b*. — The donation of the Jetavana is depicted from the time of the earliest representational monuments: cf. A.K. Coomaraswamy, *La sculpture de Bhārhut*, Paris, 1956, pl. 26, fig. 67; Idem, *La sculpture de Bodh-Gayā*, Paris, 1935, pl. 51, fig. 2; J. Marshall and A. Foucher, *The Monuments of Sāñchī*, II, New Delhi, 1940, pl. 34 *a* 2; A. Foucher, *Art Gréco-bouddhique du Gandhāra*, I, Paris, 1905, p. 474, fig. 239.

[*Sudatta's Great Offering*]

Blessed One, I remember that one day, at my father's house (*matpitṛghara*), for seven days and seven nights, I performed a great offering (*mahāyajña*) and I distributed gifts to recluses (*śramaṇa*), brahmans, sectaries (*tīrthika*), the poor (*daridra*), the suffering (*duḥkhita*), the wretched (*kṛpaṇa*), supplicants (*vanīyaka*) and all those in need. This great offering had gone on for seven days when the Licchavi Vimalakīrti came to the site of the great offering (*mahāyajñabhūmi*) and said these words to me: Guildsman's son (*śreṣṭhiputra*), an offering is not performed in this way [136]; you should perform the offering of the giving of the Law (*dharmadānayajña*). Enough for you of this material offering of giving (*alaṃ tava tenāmiṣadānayajñena*).

I asked him then how to perform this offering of the giving of the Law, and he replied to me:

[*Vimalakīrti's Homily on the Offering of the Law*]

69. The offering of the Law (*dharmayajña*) is that thanks to which beings ripen without beginning or end (*yenāpūrvam acaramaṃ sattvāḥ paripacyante*) [137]. And what does this mean?

The great goodwill resulting from enlightenment (*bodhisamudānītā mahāmaitrī*), the great com-

The offering of the giving of the Law (*dharmadānayajña*) has neither beginning nor end (*apūrvo 'caramaḥ*); in a single moment it honours (*pūjayati*) all beings; this is the complete offering of the giving of the Law (*paripūrṇo dharmadānayajñaḥ*). And what does this mean?

The great goodwill (*mahāmaitrī*) resulting from the practice of supreme enlightenment (*anuttarā bodhiḥ*) [138], the great

[136] In canonical sources, the Buddha has already explained the mediocre value of material offerings: Dhammapada, v. 106-107; Suttanipāta, v. 462-485, 506-509; Saṃyutta, I, p. 76, 169; Aṅguttara, II, p. 42-43; IV, p. 42-45; Itivuttaka, p. 21. However, here we are less concerned with the ceremonial of a ritual than with the generosity occasioned by the offering of which Velāma gave the best example (Aṅguttara, IV, p. 392-396).

It has always been admitted that the gift of the Law (*dharmadāna*), i.e. religious instruction, is far more beneficial than a material gift (*āmiṣadāna*): cf. Aṅguttara, I, p. 91; Itivuttaka, p. 98; Bodh. bhūmi, p. 133. Concerning this cliché, Vimalakīrti utters some generalities which are the object of a lengthy elaboration in the Upadeśa (NĀGĀRJUNA, *Traité*, p. 650-769).

[137] A material gift, bound by circumstances of time and place, is occasional. In contrast, the gift of the Law, strictly spiritual, is unlimited.

[138] Here I have adopted the word sequence in Sanskrit as it appears from the Tibetan version. The requirements of Chinese syntax have forced H to invert it: "Through the practice of supreme enlightenment, producing great good will", and so on until §74.

passion resulting from the grasping of the Good Law (*saddharma-samundānītā mahākaruṇā*), the great joy resulting from what can be perceived of satisfaction in beings (*sattvaprāmodyālambanasamud-ānītā mahāmuditā*), the great equanimity resulting from the grasping of knowledge (*jñānasaṃ-grahasamudānītā mahopekṣā*)[139].

compassion (*mahākaruṇā*) resulting from the practice of the liberation of beings (*sattvavimokṣa*), the great joy (*mahāmuditā*) resulting from the practice of the delighting of beings (*sattvānumodanā*), the great equanimity (*mahopekṣā*) resulting from the grasping of the Good Law (*saddharmasaṃ-graha*) and the grasping of knowledge (*jñānasaṃgraha*).

70. The perfection of giving (*dānapāramitā*) resulting from calm (*śama*) and self-control (*dama*), the perfection of morality (*śīlapāramitā*) resulting from the ripening of immoral beings (*duḥśīlasattvaparipācana*), the perfection of patience (*kṣāntipāramitā*) resulting (from endurance) with regard to impersonal dharmas (*anātmyadharma*), the perfection of vigour (*vīryapāramitā*) resulting from the efforts made with a view to enlightenment (*bodhyārambha*), the perfection of meditation (*dhyāna-pāramitā*) resulting from the isolation of body and mind (*kāyacittavi-veka*), the perfection of wisdon (*prajñāpāramitā*) resulting from omni-science (*sarvajñajñāna*)[140].

71. The meditation of emptiness (*śūnyabhāvanā*) resulting from the ripening of all beings (*sarvasattvaparipācana*), the meditation of sign-lessness (*ānimittabhāvanā*) resulting from the purification of conditioned things (*saṃskṛtapariśodhana*), the meditation of wishlessness (*apraṇihitabhāvanā*) resulting from the births assumed according to the aspirations (*yathāśayotpatti*)[141].

72. The gathering of power (*balopasaṃhāra*) resulting from the grasping of the Good Law (*saddharmasaṃgraha*), the vitality (*jīviten-driya*) resulting from the skillful use of the means of conversion (*saṃ-grahavastu*); the absence of pride (*nirmānatā*) acquired by making oneself the slave and servant of all beings (*sarvasattvānāṃ dāsaśiṣya-parivartanam*), the gains of body, life and riches (*kāyajīvitabhogalābha*) resulting from the action of taking for substantial that which is not substantial (*asāre sāropādānam*)[142], the right mindfulness (*samyaksmṛti*) re-

[139] This paragraph concerns the four *apramāṇa* or *brahmavihāra*: cf. above, I, § 13, note 66.

[140] Paragraph concerning the six *pāramitā*.

[141] Paragraph concerning the three *vimokṣamukha*: cf. above, III, § 6, note 16.

[142] Canonical reminiscence: *asāre sāramatayaḥ* ...: cf. above, III, § 62, note 124.

sulting from the six recollections (*anusmṛti*)[143], the good intention (*āśaya*) resulting from the exercising of the pleasant dharmas (*saṃmodanīya*), the purity of livelihood (*ājīvapariśuddhi*) resulting from right effort (*samyagvyāyāma*), the respect for the holy ones (*āryāṇāṃ sevā*) resulting from faithful and joyful service (*śraddhāprāmodyasevanā*), the control of the mind (*cittadama*) due to the action of not feeling any hostility towards unbelievers (*anāryeṣv apratighacittam*), the high resolve (*adhyāśaya*) resulting from leaving the world (*pravrajyā*), the ability in skillful means and learning (*upāyabahuśrutakauśalya*) resulting from religious practice (*pratipatti*), the dwelling in the forest (*araṇyavāsa*) resulting from the knowledge of the peaceful dharmas (*araṇādharmāvabodhana*), the solitary absorption in meditation (*pratisaṃlayana*) resulting from the search for the knowledge of the Buddhas (*buddhajñānaparyeṣṭi*), the sphere of the practice of yoga (*yogācārabhūmi*) resulting from the efforts aimed at freeing all beings from their passions (*sarvasattvakleśapramocanaprayoga*).

73. The store of merit (*puṇyasaṃbhāra*) resulting from the primary and secondary marks (*lakṣaṇānuvyañjana*), from the adorning and purification of the Buddha-fields (*buddhakṣetrālaṃkāra*) and from the ripening of beings (*sattvaparipācana*); the store of knowledge (*jñānasaṃbhāra*) resulting from the knowledge of the minds and conduct of beings (*sarvasattvacittacaritajñāna*) and the instruction of the Law conforming to need (*yathāyogadharmadeśanā*); the store of wisdom (*prajñāsaṃbhāra*) resulting from the knowledge relating to the single principle without the grasping or rejection of any dharma (*sarvadharmāyūhaniryūhavigatam ekanayajñānam*)[144]; the store of good roots

[143] The six *anusmṛti* relate respectively to the Buddha, the Law (*dharma*), the Community (*saṃgha*), morality (*śīla*), generosity (*tyāga*) and the divinities (*deva*): cf. Dīgha, III, p. 250, 280; Aṅguttara, III, p. 284; 312 sq.; Visuddhimagga, ed. WARREN, p. 162-188; Lalitavistara, p. 31,*18-22*; Dharmasaṃgraha, §54; Mahāvyutpatti, No. 1148-1154.

[144] The expression *āyūhaniryūhavigata* has already been met with above, III, §52, note 101.

In the minds of Buddhists the ideas of *ekanaya* "single principle" and *ekayāna* "single or one vehicle" are frequently connected, possibly because of their homonymy.

The assertion of an *ekanaya* in no way involves a monistic view of things, the single principle being no other than the inexistence of all dharmas (*dharmāṇāṃ niḥsvabhāvatā*) and in no way consisting of a metaphysical entity. Since all the Vehicles lead, more or less directly, to the understanding of this single principle (*ekanaya*), the One Vehicle (*ekayāna*) is spoken of.

Here are some quotations concerning the *ekanaya*:

In the present passage of the Vimalakīrtinirdeśa, *ekanayajñāna* is rendered by *tshul*

(*sarvakuśalamūlasaṃbhāra*) resulting from the abandoning (*utsarga*) of all passions (*kleśa*), of all obstacles (*āvaraṇa*) and of all bad dharmas (*akuśaladharma*).

gcig paḥi śes in Tibetan; *ju i hsiang mên* 入一相門 "to pass through the door of the single characteristic" by K; *i chêng li mên wu ju* 一正理門悟入 "to pass through the door of the single right principle intellectually" by H.

For the Prajñāpāramitā, the *ekanaya* is simply non-duality (*advaya*), the non-existence (*abhāva*) of all things. Cf. Pañcaviṃśati, p. 223,*8*; Śatasāh., p. 1468,*21*: *tatra katamo bodhisattvasya mahāsattvasyaikanayanirdeśaḥ — yā advayasamudācaratā, ayaṃ bodhisattvasya mahāsattvasyaikanayanirdeśaḥ*: "For a Bodhisattva Mahāsattva the demonstration of the single principle is not to course in duality". Translating this passage, Kumārajīva (T 223, p. 259 *a* 21) renders *ekanayanirdeśa* by *shuo chu fa i hsiang* 說諸法一相 "to tell the single characteristic of dharmas"; and Hsüan-tsang (T 220, vol. VII, p. 87 *b* 5) by *shuo i ch'ieh fa i hsiang li ch'ü* 說一切法一相理趣 "to tell the principle with a single characteristic of all dharmas". Commenting on this passage, the Upadeśa (T 1509, ch. 50, p. 417 *c* 8-12) explains: "The Bodhisattva knows that the twelve bases of consciousness (*āyatana*), internal (*ādhyātmika*) and external (*bāhya*), are all nets of Māra (*mārajāla*), deceptive (*vañcaka*) and unreal (*abhūta*). From these bases of consciousness arise the six kinds of consciousnesses (*vijñāna*), also nets of Māra and deceptive. What therefore is real (*bhūta*)? Only non-duality (*advaya*). The inexistence (*abhāva*) of the eye (*cakṣus*) and the inexistence of colour (*rūpa*), and so on [for the other *āyatana*], up to the inexistence of the mind (*manas*) and the inexistence of dharmas, this is what is called reality. To make all beings reject the twelve *āyatana*, the Bodhisattvas, always and by all manner of teachings, expound non-duality (*advaya*) to them".

The Abhisamaya, I, v. 62, places the *ekanayajñatā* among the practices of the seventh stage. The Āloka, p. 102,*2*, explains: *mahāyānatvenaikayānāvabodhād dhetugrahatyāgaḥ*; in Tibetan, *theg pa chen po ñid du theg pa gcig par rtogs pas rgyur ḥdzin pa spaṅs pa*: "The knowledge of the One Vehicle in the form of the Great Vehicle provokes the abandoning of belief [in the various ways of salvation]". Cf. E. OBERMILLER, *Analysis of the Abhisamayālaṃkāra*, London, 1943, p. 166.

Saṃdhinirmocana, T 676, ch. 4, p. 708 *a* 13-21: The Bodhisattva Avalokiteśvara asked the Buddha: With what hidden intention (*kiṃ saṃdhāya*) did the Blessed One say that the Śrāvakayāna and the Mahāyāna are but a single Vehicle (*ekayāna*)? — The Buddha replied: Kulaputra, in the Śrāvakayāna I explained the various self-natures (*svabhāva*) of dharmas, that is, the five *skandha*, the six *ādhyātmikāyatana*, the six *bāhyāyatana* and other categories of this kind. In the Mahāyāna I said that all dharmas form but a one and only element of the Law (*t'ung-i fa-chieh* = *ekadharmadhātu*), but a one and only principle (*t'ung-i li-ch'ü* = *ekanaya*). That is why I deny any distinction (*bheda*) between Vehicles. But here certain people interpreting my words to the letter (*yathārutam*) moot false distinctions: some make uncalled-for affirmations (*āropayanti*), others object abusively (*apavadanti*). Regarding the various methods of the Vehicles, they affirm that they oppose one another, and all this leads to arguments. It is with that intention that I assert the oneness of the Vehicles.

In all these explanations one suspects a certain amount of confusion between

74. The acquisition of all the auxiliaries of enlightenment resulting from the penetration of omniscience and the store of good dharmas (*sarvajñajñānādhigamena ca kuśaladharmasaṃbhāreṇa ca samudānītaḥ sarvabodhipākṣikadharmasamudāgamaḥ*), such is, O son of good family (*kulaputra*), the offering of the giving of the Law (*dharmayajña*). Bodhisattvas faithful to this offering of the Law are the best offerers, the "great masters of giving" (*mahādānapati*), worthy of offerings among gods and men (*sadevaloke dakṣiṇīyāḥ*).

Blessed One, when the householder (*gṛhapati*) had pronounced this address, two hundred brahmans among the crowd of brahmans produced the thought of supreme and perfect enlightenment (*dviśatānāṃ brāhmaṇānām anuttarāyāṃ samyaksaṃbodhau cittāny utpāditāni*).

[*The Miracle of the Necklace*]

75. I, myself, filled with astonishment, after having saluted the feet of the worthy man by touching them with my head, removed from my neck a necklace of pearls worth an hundred thousand (gold pieces), and offered it to him. But he would not accept it. Then I said to him: Accept, O worthy man, this necklace of pearls to show evidence of your compassion and give it to whomsoever you wish. Then Vimalakīrti accepted the necklace of pearls and, having accepted it, divided it into two parts. He gave one half to the poor of the town, who had been disdained by those who were present at the offering. The other half he gave to the Tathāgata Duṣprasaha[145]. And he performed such a wondrous feat that all the assemblies could see the Marīci universe and the Tathāgata Duṣprasaha. And, on the head of the Tathāgata Duṣprasaha, the necklace of pearls took on the form of a belvedere, adorned with necklaces of pearls, resting on four supports, having four columns, uniform, well built and lovely to see (*atha khalv aham āścaryaprāptas tasya satpuruṣasya pādau śirasābhivandya matkaṇṭhād avatārya śatasahasramūlyaṃ muktāhāram anupra-*

ekanaya "single principle" and *ekayāna* "single Vehicle". Nevertheless *ekanaya* is a synonym of *ekadharmadhātu*. Hence the reasoning is clear: the non-substantiality of all dharmas (*dharmāṇāṃ niḥsvabhāvatā*) constituting a single truth, all the Vehicles that lead to it also revert to unity themselves.

[145] The Buddha Duṣprasaha "Hard to attain" is so named because his Marīci universe is located beyond sixty-one great chiliocosms. This Buddha stopped teaching when Śākyamuni turned the wheel of the Law at Vārāṇasī (Mahāvastu, III, p. 341,*18*-342,*4*). Also see Sukhāvātī, p. 142,*1*; Mañjuśrīmūlakalpa, p. 64,*1*; 130,*3*; below, VI, §13, No. 7).

yacchāmi sma. sa na pratīcchati sma. atha khalv aham etad avocam. pratigṛhāṇa tvaṃ satpuruṣemaṃ muktāhāram asmākam anukampām upādāya. yaṃ cādhimucyase tasmai dehi. atha khalu Vimalakīrtis taṃ muktāhāraṃ pratigṛhṇāti sma. pratigṛhya ca dvau pratyaṃśau kṛtavān kṛtvā caikaṃ pratyaṃśaṃ yajñasthānasthaninditānāṃ nagaradaridrāṇāṃ dadāti sma, dvitīyaṃ pratyaṃśaṃ Duṣprasahāya tathāgatāya niryātayām āsa. tathārūpaṃ ca prātihāryaṃ saṃdarśayati sma yathā sarvābhiḥ parṣadbhir Marīcir nāma lokadhātur Duṣprasaho nāma tathāgataś ca saṃdṛśyete sma. sa ca muktāhāras tasya Duṣprasahasya tathāgatasya mūrdhni muktāhāraḥ kūṭāgāraḥ saṃsthito 'bhūc caturasraś catuḥsthūṇaḥ samabhāgaḥ suvibhakto darśanīyaḥ)[146].

76. Having performed such a wondrous feat (*prātihārya*), Vimalakīrti said further: The giver (*dāyaka*) who bestows his gifts on the poor of the town (*nagaradaridra*) while thinking that they are as worthy of offerings (*dakṣiṇīya*) as the Tathāgata, the giver who gives to all without making distinctions (*asaṃbhinnam*), impartially (*samacittena*), with great goodwill (*mahāmaitrī*), great compassion (*mahākaruṇā*), and without expecting any reward (*vipākaniḥspṛha*), this giver, say I, fully performs the offering of the giving of the Law (*dharmayajñaṃ paripūrayati*).

77. Then the poor of the town, having seen this wondrous feat (*prātihārya*) and having heard this address, obtained the irreversible high resolve (*avaivartikādhyāśaya*) and produced the thought of supreme and perfect enlightenment.

O Blessed One, that great householder (*gṛhapati*) having at his disposal such powerful wonders and such irresistible eloquence (*pratibhāna*), I am not capable of going to ask him about his illness.

*

78. In the same way, all the Bodhisattva Mahāsattvas recounted in turn the conversations (*kathā*) that they had with that person and declared themselves incapable of going to find him.

In the same way, the Blessed One invited, one after the other, the great Bodhisattvas to go and ask that householder about his illness, but all those Bodhisattvas, having in turn recounted to the Buddha their own particular story (*nidāna*) and related the conversations (*kathā*) that they had had with the worthy man Vimalakīrti, declared themselves incapable of going to ask him about his illness.

[146] Original reconstructed with the help of two passages from the Saddharmapuṇḍarīka, p. 445,*13*-446,*11*; 468,*5-8*. Regarding the miracle of the necklace and the belvedere, also see Ajātaśatrukaukṛtyavinodana, T 628, ch. 3, p. 436 *b* 13-18; Pañcaviṃśati, p. 97,*5-7*.

CHAPTER FOUR

CONSOLATIONS TO THE SICK MAN

[*Mañjuśrī's Acceptance*]

1. Then the Blessed One said to Māñjuśrī the crown prince (*kumārabhūta*)[1]: Mañjuśrī, go and ask the Licchavi Vimalakīrti about his illness.

Mañjuśrī replied: Blessed One, the Licchavi Vimalakīrti is hard to approach (*durāsada*).

He has such consummate eloquence on the profound principle (*gambhīranaye praskannapratibhānaḥ*).	He penetrates in depth the treatises of the Law (*dharmamukha*).
He excels in proffering inverted word-sentences and full word-sentences (*vyatyastapadapūrṇapadāhārakuśala*)[2].	It is with skill that he can discourse.

[1] Regarding this great Bodhisattva, see É. LAMOTTE, *Mañjuśrī*, T'oung Pao, XLVIII, 1960, Fasc. 1-3, p. 1-96. The meeting between Mañjuśrī and Vimalakīrti which is the subject of this chapter is depicted on Chinese stelae of the sixth century: P. PELLIOT, *Les grottes de Touen-Houang*, Paris, 1921, VI, pl. 324; H. FERNALD, *An Early Chinese Sculptured Stele of 575 A.D.*, Eastern Art, III, p. 73-111; A. WALEY, *Catalogue of Paintings recovered from Tun-Huang by Sir Aurel Stein*, London, 1931, pl. 41 and 42, p. 91-95; W.P. YETTS, *The George Eumorfopoulos Collection: Buddhist Sculpture*, London, 1932, p. 26-28, 41-46; J. LE ROY DAVIDSON, *Traces of Buddhist Evangelism in Early Chinese Art*, with 7 ill., Artibus Asiae, XI, 1948, p. 251-265; *The Lotus Sūtra in Chinese Art*, Yale University, 1954, p. 32-36.

On these monuments, Mañjuśrī usually holds a curved sceptre, commonly known as *ju-i* 如意 "back-scratcher", in reality a *t'an-ping* 談柄 "conversation sceptre", symbol of triumphant eloquence. Regarding this *ju-i*, see *Masterpieces of Chinese ju-i scepters in the National Palace Museum*, Taipei, 1974; J. LE ROY DAVIDSON, *The Origin and Early Use of the Ju-i*, Artibus Asiae, XIII, 1950, p. 239-249; E. ZÜRCHER, *The Buddhist Conquest of China*, Leiden, 1959, p. 407. Mañjuśrī and Vimalakīrti had become the paragons of *ch'ing t'an* 清談, "pure conversation", then in fashion in China.

[2] This obviously concerns the linguistic technique (rhetoric, dialectic) which constitutes one of the twenty *āveṇikadharma* of the bodhisattva (see the Introduction, p. LVI-LVII).

K translates: "He penetrates the real mark (*bhūtalakṣaṇa*) in depth and skillfully expounds the principle of the Law (*dharmanaya*)". — Sêng-chao (T 1775, ch. 5, p. 371 *a* 1) explains: "He excels in bringing out a great deal of sense with concise words".

He has invincible eloquence (*anācchedyapratibhāna*). He possesses, among all beings, an irresistible intelligence (*sarvasattveṣv apratihatamatisamanvāgataḥ*). He complies with all the practices of the Bodhisattvas (*bodhisattvakāryaniryāta*).

He easily enters the secret reserves of all the Bodhisattvas and Pratyekabuddhas (*sarvabodhisattvapratyekabuddhaguhyasthānasupratipanna*)[3].

He easily enters the secret reserves (*guhyasthāna*) of all the great Bodhisattvas and all the Tathāgatas.

He is skilled in overturning the dwellings of all the Māras (*sarvamārabhavanasamudghātanakuśala*). He is at ease with the great super-knowledges (*mahābhijñāvikrīḍita*). He excels in skillful means and wisdom (*upāyaprajñāniryāta*). He has reached the other shore of the domain of the element of the Law without duality or confusion (*advayāsaṃbhinnadhar-*

He is skilled in converting Māras (*mārasaṃgraha*). His skillful means (*upāyakauśalya*) are unobstructed (*apratihata*). He has achieved supreme and unconfused non-duality. He has reached the other shore (*pāra*) of the domain of the element of the Law (*dharmadhātugocara*). Regarding the element of the Law which is of unique harmony (*ekākāravyūhadharmadhātu*), he is capable of giving discourses of infinite variety (*anantākāravyūhadharmamukha*). He penetrates the spiritual faculties (*indriya*) and practices (*carita*) of all beings.

[3] Kumārajīva translates: "There are no secrets of the Buddha which he does not penetrate", and he explains (T 1775, ch. 5, p. 371 *a* 7): "According to the Mi chi ching, this concerns the body, speech and mind [of the Buddhas]".

The Mi chi ching in question is the Tathāgataguhyaka or Tathāgatācintyaguhyanirdeśa of which there are three translations:

1. A Chinese translation carried out by Dharmarakṣa of the Western Chin. It was completed on the eighth day of the tenth month of the first year of the *t'ai-k'ang* period (16 November 280), a date supplied by the Li tai san pao chi (T 2034, ch. 6, p. 62 *a* 19). Later, at the beginning of the eighth century (706-713), it was incorporated by Bodhiruci, alias Dharmaruci, into his compilation of the Ratnakūṭa (T 310, ch. 8-14, p. 42-80).

2. A Tibetan translation, undertaken in the first quarter of the ninth century by Jinamitra and his team (OKC, No. 760, 3).

3. A Chinese translation carried out, in the eleventh century, by Dharmarakṣa of the Sung (T 312).

The passage regarding the secrets of the Buddha which is alluded to here appears in T 310, ch. 10, p. 53 *b* 11 and T 312, ch. 6, p. 716 *c* 10: "The secrets of the Tathāgata are three in number: secret of the body, secret of speech and secret of mind". Then follows a long and particularly interesting development which is quoted in full in the Upadeśa, T 1509, ch. 10, p. 127 *c* (cf. NĀGĀRJUNA, *Traité*, p. 560-561).

Further on (VI, §13, note 36), the Vimalakīrti will again refer to the Tathāgataguhyaka, this time quoting it by name. It asserts that countless Tathāgatas come to expound the Tathāgataguhyaka in Vimalakīrti's house.

madhātugocarapāramiṃgata). Upon the element of the Law which is of unique harmony (*ekavyūhadharmadhātu*), he excels in enlarging through instructions of infinite variety (*anantākāravyūhadharmadeśanā*). He understands the spiritual faculties (*indriya*) of all beings. He excels in skillful means and knowledge (*upāyakauśalyajñānagatiṃgata*). He possesses the answer to all questions (*praśnanirṇaya*).

He is at ease with the supreme super-knowledges (*mahābhijñāvikrīḍita*). He has attained great knowledge (*mahājñāna*) and skillful means (*upāyakauśalya*). He possesses the answer to all questions (*praśnanirṇaya*).

Even though he is in no way satisfied with little preparedness (*parīttasaṃnāha*), nevertheless, thanks to the supernatural intervention of the Buddha (*buddhādhiṣṭhāna*), I will go to him and I will debate with him as well as possible (*yathābhūtam*) and according to my ability (*yathānubhāvaṃ*)[4].

This fearless sovereign (*viśāradeśvara*) cannot be attacked by the edge of my feeble eloquence. Nevertheless, benefiting from the supernatural intervention (*adhiṣṭhāna*) of the Buddha, I will go to him to ask him about his illness and, in his presence, I will debate with him according to my capacity.

[*Mañjuśrī at Vimalakīrti's House*]

2. Then, in the assembly, the Bodhisattvas, the great Listeners (*śrāvaka*), the Śakras, the Brahmās, the Lokapālas, the sons of the gods (*devaputra*) and the daughters of the gods (*devakanyā*) had this thought: the two Bodhisattvas, both of them, possess profound and vast convictions (*gambhīraviśālādhimukti*); wherever Mañjuśrī the crown prince and the worthy man (*satpuruṣa*) converse, there will certainly (*niyatam*) be a great and virtuous dialogue (*dhārmī kathā*). We should all together accompany Mañjuśrī to Vimalakīrti's to hear the Law (*dharmaśravaṇāya*).

Immediately, eight thousand Bodhisattvas, five hundred Listeners (*śrāvaka*), and countless hundreds of thousands of Śakras, Brahmās, Lokapālas and sons of the gods (*devaputra*), with the aim of listening to the Law, followed in the wake of Mañjuśrī the crown prince.

Then Mañjuśrī the crown prince, surrounded (*parivṛta*) and followed

[4] This paragraph is missing in Cn and K.

(*puraskṛta*) by these Bodhisattvas, great Śrāvakas, Śakras, Brahmās, Lokapālas and Devaputras, after having bowed respectfully before the Blessed One, left the Āmrapālīvana, entered the great town of Vaiśālī and reached the house of Vimalakīrti.

[*The Empty House*]

3. At that moment the Licchavi Vimalakīrti had this thought: Since Mañjuśrī the crown prince is coming to my house with an immense following to inquire about my illness, I shall, with a supernatural action (*adhiṣṭhāna*), empty this house. I shall eject the couches (*mañcaka*), the furniture (*pariṣkāra*), the servants (*antevāsin*) and the door-keeper (*dauvārika*); I shall leave only a single couch where I shall lie as if sick.

Having had this thought, Vimalakīrti supernaturally made his house empty (*gṛhaṃ śūnyam adhiṣṭhāya*), and there was not even a door-keeper (*dauvārika*) left in it. Except for (*sthāpayitvā*) a single couch (*mañcaka*) where he lay as if sick, the couches (*mañcaka*), the seats (*pīṭha*), the chairs (*āsana*), all had disappeared.

[*Reciprocal Greetings*]

4. Then Mañjuśrī, with his following (*saparivāra*), reached the place where Vimalakīrti's house was (*yena Vimalakīrteḥ sthānaṃ tenopajagāma*) and, having reached it (*upetya*), went inside. He saw that the house was empty: there was not even a door-keeper (*dauvārika*) there. Except for the sickbed occupied by Vimalakīrti, he saw neither couch (*mañcaka*), nor seat (*pīṭha*) nor chair (*āsana*).

Then the Licchavi Vimalakīrti perceived Mañjuśrī the crown prince and, having perceived him, said to him: Mañjuśrī, you are welcome (*sugata*), Mañjuśrī, you are most welcome. You had not come and you come; you had not seen and you see; you had not heard and you hear.

Mañjuśrī replied: It is indeed so, O householder, it is indeed as you say (*evam etad gṛhapate, evam etad yathā vadasi*)[5]. He who has already come (*āgata*) comes no more; he who has already left (*gata*) leaves no more. And why? Because he who has come no longer comes, he who has left no longer leaves, he who has seen no longer sees and he who has heard no longer hears[6].

[5] Very common stock phrase: cf. Saddharmapuṇḍ., p. 77,*4-5*, etc.

[6] Experience does not consist of either arrival or departure. The Buddha demonstrated that the *pratītyasamutpāda* is *anāgama* and *anirgama* (Madh. vṛtti, p. 11,*14*). Nāgārjuna

5. O worthy man, is this tolerable? Is it viable? In you are not the physical elements troubled? Do painful sensations diminish and not increase? Can one establish in them diminution and not increase? (*kaccit te satpuruṣa kṣamaṇīyaṃ, kaccid yāpanīyaṃ, kaccit te dhātavo na kṣubhyante, kaccid duḥkhā vedanāḥ pratikrāmanti nābhikrāmanti, pratikrama āsāṃ prajñāyate nābhikramaḥ*)[7]. The Blessed One would have you ask yourself if you have little affliction and little suffering, if you are alert and well-disposed, if you are strong, physically well and morally without reproach, and if you rejoice in agreeable contacts (*bhagavāṃs tvām alpābādhatāṃ pṛcchaty alpātaṅkatāṃ yātrāṃ laghūtthānatāṃ balaṃ sukham anavadyatāṃ sukhasparśavihāratām*)[8].

[*Vimalakīrti's Sickness*]

6. *Mañj.* — Householder (*gṛhapati*), your sickness (*vyādhi*), from where has it come? For how long will it last? On what is it based? After how long will it abate?

Vim. — Mañjuśrī, my sickness will last while there lasts in beings ignorance (*avidyā*) and the thirst for existence (*bhavatṛṣṇā*). My sickness comes from afar, from the round of rebirth at its beginning (*pūrvakoṭisaṃsāra*).

demonstrates in the Madh. vṛtti, p. 92-97 (tr. MAY, p. 51-59) the inexistence of movement by basing himself on simple temporal analysis. Movement which has already been carried out (*gatam*) does not consist of movement (*na gamyate*) because its motive action has stopped (*uparatagamikriyam*). Movement which has not yet been carried out (*agatam*) does not consist of movement (*na gamyate*) either, because its motive action has not yet originated (*anupajātagamikriyam*). As for present movement (*gamyamānam*), there is no movement (*na gamyate*), being independent of the other two (*gatāgatavinirmuktam*).

[7] Very common stock phrase: cf. Saddharmapuṇḍ., p. 429,*4*; Divyāvadāna, p. 110,*2*; Mahāvastu, III, p. 347,*19*; Sanskrit Mahāparinirvāṇa, p. 194. — The Pāli formula is: *kacci te khamanīyaṃ, kacci yāpanīyaṃ, kacci dukkhā vedanā paṭikkamanti no abhikkamanti, paṭikkamo 'sānaṃ paññāyati no abhikkamo*: cf. Majjhima, II, p. 192,*29*; III, p. 259,*2*; 264,*3*; Saṃyutta, IV, p. 46,*21*; 56,*11*; V, p. 79,*28*; 177,*6*; 345,*2*; 381,*17*; 385,*25*.

[8] Same or similar formula in Sanskrit Mahāparinirvāṇa, p. 102; Mahāvastu, I, p. 254,*16*; 323,*20*; Avadānaśataka, I, p. 325,*13*; II, p. 90,*13*; 93,*15*; Divyāvadāna, p. 156,*22*; Kāraṇḍavyūha, p. 89,*12*; Pañcaviṃśati, p. 13,*17*; Saddharmapuṇḍ., p. 429,*3*; Mahāvyutpatti, No. 6284-88; J. BLOCH, *Inscriptions d'Aśoka*, p. 154; below, IX, § 4 and 5. — The Pāli wording is: *appābādhaṃ appātaṅkaṃ lahuṭṭhānaṃ balaṃ phāsuvihāraṃ pucchati* (references in WOODWARD, *Concordance*, I, p. 193, s.v. *appātaṃkaṃ*).

All these terms are commented on at length in NĀGĀRJUNA, *Traité*, p. 582-586. Also see, concerning *phāsuvihāra*, C. CAILLAT, *Deux études de moyen-indien*, JA, 1960, p. 41-55.

As long as beings are sick, I myself will also be sick; when beings recover, I also shall recover. And why? Mañjuśrī, for Bodhisattvas, the realm of the round of rebirth (*saṃsārasthāna*), this is beings (*sattva*), and sickness rests on this round of rebirth (*saṃsārastha*)[9]. When all beings have escaped the pains of this sickness, then Bodhisattvas also will be free of sickness.

7. For example, O Mañjuśrī, if the only son (*ekaputra*) of a guildsman (*śreṣṭhin*) falls sick, his father and mother (*mātāpitṛ*) would also both fall sick. As long as this only son does not recover, his father and mother will also both continue suffering (*duḥkhita*). Equally, O Mañjuśri, a Bodhisattva who cherishes beings as his only son is sick when beings are sick, and is free of sickness when they are free of sickness.

Let us suppose that somewhere in the world a wealthy guild member (*śreṣṭhipuruṣa*) has but an only son (*ekaputra*); he loves him tenderly, always delights in seeing him and never leaves him for a single instant. If that son falls sick, his father and mother would also both fall sick; but as soon as he recovers, they would also both recover. Equally, a Bodhisattva who cherishes beings as his only son, is sick when beings are sick and recovers when beings recover.

You asked me, O Mañjuśrī, where my sickness comes from: in a Bodhisattva sickness arises from great compassion (*mahākaruṇā*).

[*Universal Emptiness*]

8. *Mañj.* — Householder (*gṛhapati*), why is your house (*gṛha*) empty (*śūnya*) and why have you no retinue (*parivāra*)?

Vim. — Mañjuśrī, all the Buddha-fields (*buddhakṣetra*) themselves are also empty.

Mañj. — Of what are they empty?

Vim. — They are empty of emptiness (*śūnyatāśūnya*).

Mañj. — What is empty of emptiness?

Vim. — Imaginings (*saṃkalpa*) are empty of emptiness.

Mañj. — Can emptiness (*śūnyatā*) be imagined?

Vim. — Imagination (*parikalpa*) itself is also empty (*śūnya*), and emptiness (*śūnyatā*) does not imagine emptiness.

[9] In Tib: *byaṅ chub sems dpaḥi ḥkhor baḥi gnas ni sems can te; nad ni ḥkhor ba la gnas so.* — K: It is for beings that Bodhisattvas enter Saṃsāra; and if there is Saṃsāra, there is sickness. — H: All Bodhisattvas count on the long lasting Saṃsāra [incurred] by beings, and it is because they count on this Saṃsāra that they undergo sickness.

Mañj. — Householder (*gṛhapati*), where is this emptiness found?

Vim. — Mañjuśrī, emptiness is found in the sixty-two kinds of false views (*dṛṣṭigata*)[10].

Mañj. — Where are the sixty-two kinds of false views found?

Vim. — They are found in the deliverance (*vimukti*) of the Tathāgatas.

Mañj. — Where is the deliverance of the Tathāgatas found?

Vim. — It is found in the first thought activity (*cittapūrvacarita*)[11] of all beings.

You further asked me, O Mañjuśrī, why I am without a retinue (*parivāra*), but all Māras and all adversaries (*parapravādin*) are my retinue. And why?

Māras praise the round of rebirth (*saṃsārasya varṇaṃ vadanti*), and the round of rebirth (*saṃsāra*) constitutes the retinue (*parivāra*) of a Bodhisattva. Adversaries (*parapravādin*) praise all kinds of false views (*dṛṣṭigata*) and a Bodhisattva does not avoid (*na calati*) any kind of false view. That is why all Māras and adversaries are my retinue.

Māras praise the round of rebirth, and sectaries (*tīrthika*) praise false views. Now, a Bodhisattva has no repugnance for (the round of rebirth and false views). That is why Māras and sectaries are my retinue[12].

[*The Nature of Sickness*]

9. *Mañj.* — Householder (*gṛhapati*), of what kind is your sickness?

Vim. — It is formless (*arūpin*) and invisible (*anidarśana*).

Mañj. — This sickness, is it associated with the body (*kāyasaṃprayukta*) or associated with the mind (*cittasaṃprayukta*)?

[10] Supreme paradox which establishes, without any possible argument, the position, or rather, the absence of a metaphysical position in Vimalakīrti. After having destroyed, through the view of emptiness, the belief in permanence (*sasvatagraha*) and the belief in annihilation (*ucchedadarśana*), Vimalakīrti relegates emptiness itself among the sixty-two kinds of false views. He refuses to hypostasise emptiness, to make of it a *dharmadhātu*, a *dharmatā*, a *tathatā*. This is pure Madhyamaka. See above, Introduction, p. LXVIII-LXXII.

[11] Tib: *sems can thams cad kyi sems daṅ po spyod pa las btsal lo.* — K and H: In the activity of the mind of all beings.

[12] K: Māras delight in the round of rebirth, and Bodhisattvas do not abandon the round of rebirth; Tīrthikas delight in the false views, and Bodhisattvas do not avoid these false views.

Vim. — It is not associated with the body because it is distinct from the body (*kāyavivikta*) and, besides, that which is associated with the body is like a reflection (*pratibimba*). It is not associated with the mind because it is distinct from the mind (*cittavivikta*) and, besides, that which is associated with the mind is like an illusion (*māyā*).

Mañj. — Householder, among the four elements (*dhātu*), that is, the earth element (*pṛthivīdhātu*), the water element (*abdhātu*), the fire element (*tejodhātu*) and the wind element (*vāyudhātu*), which is the one that suffers (*bādhyate*)?

Vim. — Mañjuśrī, the sickness of beings, this is precisely the element (*dhātu*) which makes me sick myself[13].

Vim. — The bodies (*kāya*) of beings spring from the four great elements (*mahābhūta*), and it is because they are sick that I am sick. However, this sickness does not stem from the four elements (*dhātu*) for it avoids the nature of an element.

[*How to Console a Sick Bodhisattva*]

10. *Mañj.*[14] — How does a Bodhisattva console (*saṃmodana*) a sick Bodhisattva so as to gladden him?

Vim. — He tells him that the body is impermanent (*anitya*), but does not prompt him to feel for it any disgust (*nirveda*) or repugnance (*virāga*). He tells him that the body is painful (*duḥkha*), but does not exhort him to delight in Nirvāṇa. He tells him that the body is without self (*anātman*), but prompts him to ripen beings (*sattvaparipācana*). He tells him that the body is calm (*śānta*), but does not exhort him to seek the definitive calm (*atyantaśānti*)[15].

He exhorts him to repent of previous misdeeds (*pūrvaduścarita*), but does not say that these misdeeds are past (*saṃkrānta*)[16]. He exhorts him to use his own sickness to have pity on sick beings and drive away their sickness. He exhorts him to recall (*anusmaraṇa*) sufferings previously undergone

[13] K differs slightly: [My] sickness does not stem from the earth element but is not separate from it. And, related to the other great elements — water, fire and wind —, it is the same. But the sickness of beings comes from the four great elements, and it is because they are sick that I am sick.

[14] In Tib. and in K, Mañjuśrī questions and Vimalakīrti replies; in Cn and H (Taishō edition), it is the reverse.

[15] The definitive calm, i.e. Nirvāṇa. Regarding *anitya, duḥkha, anātman, śānta*, see above, III, § 25, note 51.

[16] Misdeeds are not eternal and irreparable; they exist only through their present effects, and can be expiated through repentance.

(*pūrvakoṭyanubhūtaduḥkha*) to promote the welfare of beings (*sattvārthakriyā*). He exhorts him to recall (*anusmaraṇa*) the countless good roots (*kuśalamūla*) already nurtured for practising a pure life (*viśuddhājīva*). He exhorts him not to fear, but to give himself over to vigour (*vīryārambha*). He exhorts him to pronounce the great vow (*mahāpraṇidhāna*) to become the great king-physician (*mahāvaidyarāja*) who heals all beings and definitively appeases the sicknesses of body and mind (*kāyacittavyādhi*). It is thus that a Bodhisattva should console (*saṃmodana*) a sick Bodhisattva, so as to gladden him[17].

[*Considerations Proposed to the Sick*]

11. Mañjuśrī asked: How does a sick Bodhisattva subdue his own mind (*svacittaṃ niyamati*)?

Vimalakīrti answered: Mañjuśrī, a sick Bodhisattva should subdue his own mind with the following considerations:

Sickness results from the conjunction of the radically perverted views (*pūrvāntābhūtaviparyāsakarmaparyutthāna*). Since it arises from imaginations (*abhūtaparikalpa*) and passions (*kleśa*), there is in truth (*paramārthataḥ*) no dharma there which can be said to be sick.

My sickness arises from the actions produced by the radically perverted views (*pūrvāntābhūtaviparyāsa*), imaginations (*parikalpa*) and passions (*kleśa*). In the body, there does not really (*paramārthataḥ*) exist any dharma that can undergo this sickness.

How is this so? The body derives from the four great elements (*mahābhūta*) and, among these elements (*dhātu*), there is neither a master (*adhipati*) nor a begetter (*janayitṛ*).

How is this so? The body (*kāya*) is called a complex of the four great elements (*cāturmahābhūtasāmagrī*) and, among these great elements, there is no master (*adhipati*).

In this body, there is no self (*atman*). If one avoids attachment to self (*ātmābhiniveśam sthāpayitvā*), there is not, here, in truth (*paramārthataḥ*), anything that can be called sickness (*vyādhi*). That

In a body, there is no self (*ātman*). If sickness arises, it is because of attachment to self (*ātmābhiniveśa*). Therefore, one must not mistakenly produce attachment to self, but understand that this attachment is the root of sickness (*vyādhimūla*). For this reason one should suppress all notion

[17] In this paragraph, I have followed the interpretation by H; the Tibetan is more concise.

is why, rejecting all attachment (*abhiniveśa*), I must rely (*sthātavyam*) on the true understanding (*ājñā*) of the roots of sickness (*vyādhimūla*) and, after having suppressed the notion of self (*ātmasaṃjñā*), produce the notion of dharma (*dharmasaṃjñā*)[18].

(*saṃjñā*) of being (*sattva*) or of Ātman and abide in the notion of dharma (*dharmasaṃjñā*).

This body is an assemblage of numerous dharmas (*saṃbahuladharmasaṃgraha*)[19]. When it arises (*utpadyate*), it is only dharmas that arise; when it is extinguished (*nirudhyate*), it is only dharmas that are extinguished. But these dharmas are not aware of each other, do not mutually (*parasparam*) know each other. When these dharmas arise, they do not think: "I am arising", when they are extinguished, they do not think: "I am being extinguished".

A Bodhisattva should make the following consideration: The body is constituted of an assemblage of numerous dharmas (*saṃbahuladharmasaṃgraha*), a process of births and extinctions (*utpādanirodhasaṃvṛtti*). When it arises, it is only dharmas that arise; when it is extinguished, it is only dharmas that are extinguished. But these dharmas, which form a continuous series (*paraṃparaprabandha*), do not know each mutually and are absolutely free from mental activity (*manasikāra*). When they arise, they do not say: "I am arising"; when they are extinguished, they do not say: "I am being extinguished".

12. A sick Bodhisattva should endeavour to understand (*ājñā*) clearly this notion of dharma (*dharmasaṃjñā*): "For me", he says to himself, "this notion of dharma is a perversion (*viparyāsa*), and this perversion is a grave sickness (*mahāvyādhi*). I must therefore free myself of this sickness and endeavour to drive it away (*prahāṇa*). I should also drive away this grave sickness in all beings".

And how drive away this grave sickness?—By driving away belief in "me" (*ātmagrāha*) and belief in "mine" (*ātmīyagrāha*).

And how drive away belief in me and mine?—By avoiding two things (*dvayaviyoga*).

And how avoid two things? — By abstaining from all internal and external activity (*adhyātmabahirdhāsamudācāra*).

And how abstain from all internal and external activity? — By

[18] However, as we shall see, the notion of dharma will be discarded in its own turn.

[19] The numerous dharmas which go into the composition of the body are the subject of the *kāyasmṛtyupasthāna* (Majjhima, I, p. 57,*15-20*).

considering integral sameness (*samatā*), unmoved (*acalita*), unshaken (*apracalita*) and altogether unperturbed (*asaṃpracalita*)[20].

What is integral sameness (*samatā*)? — That which goes from the sameness of Self (*ātmasamatā*) to the sameness of Nirvāṇa (*nirvāṇasamatā*).

And why so? — Because the round of rebirth (*saṃsāra*) and Nirvāṇa are both empty (*śūnya*).

And why are they both empty? — As simple designations (*nāmadheya*), they are both empty (*śūnya*) and unreal (*apariniṣpanna*).

Thus he who sees the integral sameness (*samatā*) makes no distinction between sickness on the one hand and emptiness on the other: sickness (*vyādhi*), this is emptiness (*śūnyatā*).

13. That this sensation (*vedanā*) is a non-sensation (*avedanā*) should be known, but the complete extinction of sensation (*vedanānirodha*) should not be effected (*sākṣātkṛ-*). Even though the two-fold sensation may be eliminated (*vijahita*) in him who fulfils to perfection the attributes of the Buddhas (*paripūrṇabuddhadharma*)[21], he is not without feeling great compassion (*mahākaruṇā*) towards beings fallen into bad destinies (*durgatija*) and acts so as to drive away through correct dis-

And why so? — Because they are both empty of self-nature (*svabhāvaśūnya*).

If both are imperceptible, what then is empty? — It is only verbally that they are qualified as empty: both are unreal (*apariniṣpanna*). From the point of view of sameness (*samatādarśana*), there is no separate sickness, there is only an empty sickness. Emptiness and sickness should be considered as equally empty. And why? Because this emptiness and this sickness are absolutely empty (*atyantaśūnya*).

A sick Bodhisattva should experience sensation (*vedanā*) without experiencing anything. Not yet fulfilling to perfection the attributes of the Buddhas (*aparipūrṇabuddhadharma*), he should not destroy all sensation thus achieving Nirvāṇa (*nirvāṇasākṣātkāra*); but he should eliminate notions of a "sensing subject" (*vedaka*) and "things to be sensed" (*vedanīyadharma*). When suffering touches his body, he should have pity on beings fallen into bad destinies (*durgati*) and, gripped by great compassion (*mahākaruṇā*), he should drive away the sufferings of beings.

[20] Vocabulary borrowed from the description of an earthquake: cf. Mahāvyutpatti, No. 3004-06.

[21] In Tib.: *saṅs rgyas kyi chos yoṅs su rdzogs pa la tshor ba gñis ka dor mod kyi, ṅan ḥgror skyes paḥi sems can thams cad la sñiṅ rje chen po mi skyed paḥaṅ ma yin no.* However, the Chinese versions by K and H which introduce a negative and read *yü fo fa wei tê yüan man* (aparipūrṇabuddhadharma) give a preferable reading.

cipline (*yoniśoniyama*) the sickness of beings.

14. Among these beings, there is not any dharma to be produced (*upasaṃhartavya*) or destroyed (*apahartavya*); the Law should be expounded to them only so that they clearly understand the foundation (*ādhāra*) from which sickness derives.

What is the foundation (*ādhāra*) of sickness? The foundation of sickness is the grasping of an object (*adhyālambana*)[22]. This grasping being the foundation, as long as there is grasping, there is sickness.

To what does grasping relate? It relates to the triple world (*traidhātuka*).

And how understand (*parijñā*) the grasping (*adhyālambana*) which is the foundation (*ādhāra*) of sickness? It is a non-grasping (*anupalambha*), a non-perception (*anupalabdhi*). This non-perception (*anupalabdhi*) is "non-grasping" (*anadhyālambana*).

And what is not perceived? It is the dual view (*dṛṣṭidvaya*), the view of an internal subject (*adhyātmadṛṣṭi*) and the view of an external object (*bahirdhādṛṣṭi*) which is not perceived. That is why one speaks of non-perception (*anupalabdhi*).

A sick Bodhisattva should make the consideration: To drive away my own sickness, the sickness of others must also be driven away. But in driving away my own sickness and that of others, there is not the least dharma to drive away. One should carefully examine the causes and conditions (*hetupratyaya*) from which sickness derives and, to drive it away rapidly, expound the Good Law (*saddharma*).

What are the causes and conditions (*hetupratyaya*) of sickness? It is the grasping of an object (*adhyālambana*). All grasping is the cause of sickness. As long as there is grasping, there is sickness.

What is grasped? The triple world (*traidhātuka*) is grasped.

And how should one understand (*parijñā*) this grasping (*adhyālambana*)? By clearly understanding that this grasping is a non-perception (*anupalabdhi*). If there is no perception, there is no grasping. And how suppress grasping? By avoiding the two false views (*dṛṣṭidvaya*). What are these two false views? The view of an internal subject (*adhyātmadṛṣṭi*) and the view of an external object (*bahirdhādṛṣṭi*). If these two views are not present, there is no perception (*upalabdhi*). Since there is no more perception, all grasping (*adhyālambana*) is suppressed. And grasping being suppressed, there is no more sickness. If one is oneself without sickness, one can drive away the sickness of (other) beings.

---

[22] Regarding *adhyālambana*, see above, III, § 52, note 103. Here H renders this word by *yüan-lü* 緣慮.

Mañjuśrī, it is thus that a sick Bodhisattva should subdue his mind so as to drive away the sufferings of old age (*jarā*), sickness (*vyādhi*), death (*maraṇa*) and birth (*jāti*). Such is, O Mañjuśrī, the sickness of a Bodhisattva. And if it were not so, his effort (*prayatna*) would be in vain (*anarthaka*). Indeed, just as one calls "hero" (*vīra*) him who slays his enemies (*pratyarthika*), so one calls "Bodhisattva" him who suppresses the sufferings (*duḥkha*) of old age (*jarā*), sickness (*vyādhi*) and death (*maraṇa*).

15. A sick Bodhisattva should make the following considerations (*evam upalakṣitavyam*): Just as my sickness is unreal (*abhūta*) and nonexistent (*asat*), so the sicknesses of beings are also unreal and nonexistent.

Understanding things thus, it is not with a mind invaded by affective views (*anunayadṛṣṭiparyutthitacitta*) that he produces great compassion towards beings (*sattveṣu mahākaruṇām utpādayati*), for it is exclusively to drive away chance passions (*āgantukakleśaprahāṇāya*) that he produces great compassion towards beings. And why?

If his great compassion arose from affective views, a Bodhisattva would feel aversion (*udvega*)[23] for rebirth (*jāti*). But since his great compassion avoids invading by affective views (*anunayadṛṣṭiparyutthānavigata*), a Bodhisattva has no aversion for rebirths. And it is not invaded by the invasion of false views (*dṛṣṭiparyutthānaparyutthita*) that he is born. Being born with an uninvaded mind, he is born (*jāyate*) as one delivered (*mukta*), he comes into existence (*utpadyate*) as one delivered. Being born as one delivered, coming into existence as one delivered, he has the strength (*bala*) and the power (*anubhāva*) to expound the Law which delivers fettered

If a Bodhisattva produced great compassion towards beings with his mind invaded by affective views (*anunayadṛṣṭiparyutthitacitta*), he would feel aversion (*udvega*) for the round of rebirth (*saṃsāra*). But if it is by driving away chance passions (*āgantukakleśaprahāṇa*) that he produces great compassion towards beings, he has no aversion for the round of rebirth. Thus for the sake of beings, a Bodhisattva remains in the round of rebirth without feeling aversion for it and his mind is not invaded (*paryutthita*) by affective views. His mind not being invaded by affective views, he is not bound (*baddha*) to the round of rebirth. Not being bound to the round of rebirth, he possesses deliverance (*vimukti*). Being delivered from the round of rebirth, he has the strength to expound the Good Law (*saddharma*) so that beings may break out of their bondage (*bandhana*) and achieve (*sākṣātkṛ-*) deliverance (*vimukti*).

[23] In Tib.: *phan yon du lta bar ltuṅ nas sñiṅ rje chen pos ni skye ba rnams su byaṅ chub sems dpaḥ skyo bar* [*mi*] *ḥgyur ro.* The negative in brackets should be deleted.

beings (*baddhasattva*) from their
bondage (*bandhana*).

It is with this hidden intention (*etad abhisaṃdhāya*) that the Blessed One declared: "It is impossible, it cannot occur that someone who is himself bound can deliver others of their bondage, but it is possible that someone who is himself delivered can deliver others of their bondage" (*asthānam etad anavakāśo yat kaścid baddhaḥ parān bandhanebhyo mocayet; sthānaṃ ca khalu vidyate yat kaścid muktaḥ parān bandhanebhyo mocayet*)[24]. That is why a Bodhisattva should seek deliverance (*mukti*) and cut through bondage (*bandhana*).

[*Bondage and Deliverance*]

16. For a Bodhisattva, what is bondage (*bandhana*) and what is deliverance (*mukti*)?

For a Bodhisattva, to be free of existence (*bhavamuktiparigraha*) while excluding skillful means (*upāya*), this is bondage. On the contrary, to enter into the world of existence (*bhavajagatpraveśa*) with the aid of skillful means, this is deliverance.

For a Bodhisattva, to taste the flavour (*rasāsvādana*) of the trances (*dhyāna*), the liberations (*vimokṣa*), the concentrations (*samādhi*) and the recollections (*samāpatti*) in the absence of skillful means is bondage. On the contrary, to taste the flavours of the trances (*dhyāna*) and the concentrations (*samādhi*) while having recourse to skillful means is deliverance.

Wisdom not acquired through skillful means (*upāyānupāttaprajñā*) is bondage. On the contrary, wisdom acquired through skillful means (*upāyopāttaprajñā*) is deliverance[25].

Skillful means not acquired through wisdom (*prajñānupāttopāya*) are bondage. On the contrary, skillful means acquired through wisdom (*prajñopāttopāya*) are deliverance.

[*Wisdom and Skillful Means*]

17. What is this wisdom not acquired through skillful means (*upāyānupāttaprajñā*) and which constitutes bondage (*bandhana*)? When

[24] In Pali, *aṭṭhānaṃ etaṃ anavakāso yaṃ*... But the impossibility noted here does not appear in the canonical lists: Majjhima, III, p. 64-67; Aṅguttara, I, p. 26-30; Vibhaṅga, p. 335-338.

[25] Passage quoted in Bhāvanākrama I, p. 194,*8-11*, and Bhāvanākrama III, p. 22, *10-14*: *Yathāryavimalakīrtinirdeśe "prajñārahita* [*upāya*] *upāyarahitā ca prajñā bodhisattvānāṃ bandhanam" ity uktam / upāyasahitā prajñā prajñāsahita upāyo mokṣatvena varṇitaḥ.*

a Bodhisattva subdues himself (*ātmanaṃ niyamati*) by the practice of emptiness (*śūnyatā*), signlessness (*ānimitta*) and wishlessness (*apraṇihita*), but abstains from adorning his body with the primary and secondary physical marks (*lakṣaṇānuvyañjana*), from adorning his Buddha-field (*buddhakṣetrālaṃkāra*) and from helping beings ripen (*sattvaparipācana*), this is wisdom not acquired through skillful means and it is bondage.

What is this wisdom acquired through skillful means (*upāyopātta-prajñā*) and which constitutes deliverance (*mukti*)? When a Bodhisattva subdues his mind (*svacittaṃ niyamati*) by the practice of emptiness (*śūnyatā*), signlessness (*ānimitta*) and wishlessness (*apraṇihita*), when he considers (*parīkṣate*) dharmas with marks (*lakṣana*) and without marks, when he cultivates (*bhāvayati*) realisation (*sākṣātkāra*) and, at the same time, adorns his body with the primary and secondary marks (*lakṣaṇānuvyañjanaiḥ svakāyam alaṃkaroti*), he adorns his Buddha-field (*buddhakṣetram alaṃkaroti*) and helps beings ripen (*sattvān paripacāyati*), this is wisdom acquired through skillful means and it is deliverance.

What are these skillful means not acquired through wisdom (*prajñā-nupāttopāya*) and which constitute bondage (*bandhana*)? When a Bodhisattva settles (*avatiṣṭhati*) into false views (*dṛṣṭi*), the invasion of the passions (*kleśaparyutthāna*), the residual tendencies (*anuśaya*), affection (*anunaya*) and aversion (*pratigha*), but does not transfer to perfect enlightenment the good roots that he has cultivated (*ārabdhāni kuśalamūlāni saṃbodhau na pariṇāmayati*) and implants attachments (*abhini-veśa*), these are skillful means not acquired through wisdom and it is bondage.

What are these skillful means acquired through wisdom (*prajño-pāttopāya*) and which constitute deliverance (*mukti*)? When a Bodhi-sattva rejects (*jahāti*) false views (*dṛṣṭi*), the invasion of the passions (*kleśaparyutthāna*), residual tendencies (*anuśaya*), affection (*anunaya*) and aversion (*pratigha*), and transfers to perfect enlightenment the good roots that he has cultivated (*ārabdhāni kuśalamūlāni saṃbodhau pariṇāmayati*) without producing pride (*garva*), these are skillful means acquired through wisdom and it is deliverance.

18. Mañjuśrī, a sick Bodhisattva should consider dharmas in the following manner:

Understanding that the body (*kāya*), mind (*citta*) and sickness (*vyādhi*) are transitory (*anitya*), painful (*duḥkha*), empty (*śūnya*) and impersonal (*anātman*): this is wisdom (*prajñā*).

Not undertaking rebirth while excluding in advance the sicknesses	Even if the body is sick, always remaining in Saṃsāra and benefitting beings

of the body (*kāyavyādhi*), but without interrupting the round of rebirth (*saṃsāra*), striving to benefit beings (*sattvārtha*): these are skillful means (*upāya*).

without ever flagging: these are skillful means.

Understanding that the body (*kāya*), mind (*citta*) and sicknesses (*vyādhi*) are mutually (*anyo'nyam*) and each in regular succession to the others (*paraṃparayā*) without being new or old: this is wisdom.

Understanding that the body (*kāya*), mind (*citta*) and sickness rest on one another (*ano'nyāśrita*), form a series without beginning or end (*anādikālikasaṃtāna*) and that between their appearance (*utpāda*) and their disappearance (*bhaṅga*) there is neither interval, nor posteriority nor anteriority: this is wisdom.

Not provoking the stilling (*praśamana*) or the extinction (*nirodha*) of the body (*kāya*), mind (*citta*) and sickness (*vyādhi*): these are skillful means.

19. Mañjuśrī, although a Bodhisattva should thus subdue his mind, he cannot adhere (*sthātavyam*) to either the control of the mind (*cittaniyama*) or the license of the mind (*cittāniyama*). And why? Because to adhere to the license of the mind is characteristic of fools (*bāla*), and to adhere to the control of the mind is characteristic of the Listeners (*śrāvaka*). This is why a Bodhisattva cannot adhere to either the control or the license of the mind. Not to adhere to either of these two extremes (*antadvaya*), such is the domain of the Bodhisattva (*bodhisattvagocara*).

[*The Domain of the Bodhisattva*[26]]

20. 1. That which is neither the domain of the worldly (*pṛthagjanagocara*) nor the domain of the holy (*āryagocara*), such is the domain of the Bodhisattva[27].

2. A domain of the round of rebirth (*saṃsāragocara*), but not the domain of the passions (*kleśagocara*), such is the domain of the Bodhisattva.

3. A domain where Nirvāṇa is known (*nirvāṇaprekṣaṇāgocara*), but not the domain of definitive and full Nirvāṇa (*atyantaparinirvāṇagocara*), such is the domain of the Bodhisattva.

[26] The whole of this paragraph is devoted to the contradictory actions or "roundabout ways" (*agati*) of a Bodhisattva. See the Introduction, p. LVII-LX.

[27] K: Not behaving like a *pṛthagjana* and not behaving like an *ārya*, such is the domain of the Bodhisattva. Not committing impure actions and not accomplishing pure actions, such is the domain of the Bodhisattva.

4. A domain where the four Māras are manifested (*caturmāradeśanā*), but which transcends all Māra works (*sarvamāraviṣayasamatikrānta*), such is the domain of the Bodhisattva[28].

5. A domain where omniscience is sought (*sarvajñajñānaparyeṣaṇā*), but without attaining knowledge (*jñāna*) inopportunely (*akālam*), such is the domain of the Bodhisattva[29].

6. A domain where the knowledge of the four truths is sought (*catuḥsatyajñānaparyeṣaṇā*), but without realising these truths (*satyasākṣātkāra*) inopportunely, such is the domain of the Bodhisattva.

7. A domain of introspection (*pratyavekṣā*), but where rebirths in the realm of existence are voluntarily taken on (*saṃcintya bhavajātiparigrahaṇa*), such is the domain of the Bodhisattva.

8. A domain where non-production is fully understood (*anutpādapratyavekṣaṇā*), but without penetrating the absolute certainty of acquiring the supreme Good (*samyaktvaniyāmāvakrānti*), such is the domain of the Bodhisattva[30].

9. A domain where the dependent co-production of phenomena is explored (*pratītyasamutpādavicāraṇa*), but by eliminating all the false views (*dṛṣṭigata*), such is the domain of the Bodhisattva[31].

10. A domain where all beings are frequented (*sarvasattvasaṃsarga*), but sheltered from the residual tendencies of the passions (*kleśānuśaya*), such is the domain of the Bodhisattva[32].

11. A domain where solitude (*viveka*) is cherished, but without seeking the destruction of body and mind (*kāyacittakṣaya*), such is the domain of the Bodhisattva[33].

12. A domain where the triple world (*traidhātuka*) is reflected upon, but without eliminating the element of the Law (*dharmadhātuvyavaccheda*), such is the domain of the Bodhisattva[34].

13. A domain where emptiness (*śūnyatā*) is reflected upon, but where

[28] K: Going beyond Māra's works and nonetheless overcoming the Māras.

[29] K: Seeking the *sarvajñajñāna*, but not seeking it inopportunely.

[30] In H, this paragraph appears under 10. — K: seeing that dharmas are *anutpāda*, but not entering the *samyaktvaniyāma*.

[31] K: Seeing the *dvādaśāṅga pratītyasamutpāda*, but nevertheless entering all the *mithyādṛṣṭi*. — This interpretation is preferable: cf. above, IV, §8, where it is said that a Bodhisattva does not avoid any kind of false view.

[32] K: Welcoming all beings, but without being attached to them.

[33] K: Cherishing *viveka*, but not relying on the *kāyacittakṣaya*.

[34] K: Coursing through the *traidhātuka*, but not harming the *dharmadhātu*. [K always renders *dharmadhātu* by *fa-hsing*].

all kinds of virtues are also sought (*sarvaguṇākāraparyeṣaṇā*), such is the domain of the Bodhisattva [35].

14. A domain where signlessness (*ānimitta*) is reflected upon, but where the liberation of beings (*sattvavimocana*) is kept in view, such is the domain of the Bodhisattva [36].

15. A domain where wishlessness (*apraṇihita*) is reflected upon, but where the course through existences (*bhavasaṃkrānti*) is voluntarily (*saṃcintya*) manifested, such is the domain of the Bodhisattva [37].

16. A domain of inaction (*anabhisaṃskāra*), but where all the good roots are brought into action (*sarvakuśalamūlābhisaṃskāra*) uninterruptedly (*anācchedyam*), such is the domain of the Bodhisattva [38].

17. A domain where the six perfections (*pāramitā*) (are explored), and where the other shore (*pāra*) of the thoughts and practices of all beings (*sarvasattvacittacaryā*) is reached, such is the domain of the Bodhisattva [39].

A domain where the six perfections (*pāramitā*) are explored, but without reaching the other shore (*pāra*) of the wonderful knowledge (*jñāna*) concerning the thoughts and practices of all beings (*sarvasattvacittacaryā*), such is the domain of the Bodhisattva.

18. A domain where the six super-knowledges (*abhijñā*) are explored, but without arriving at the knowledge of the destruction of impurities (*āsravakṣayajñāna*), such is the domain of the Bodhisattva [40].

19. A domain where the Good Law is established (*saddharmasthāpana*), but without taking the wrong paths (*kumārga*) as an object, such is the domain of the Bodhisattva.

20. A domain where the four infinite states (*apramāṇa*) — goodwill (*maitrī*), compassion (*karuṇā*), joy (*muditā*) and equanimity (*upekṣā*) — are reflected upon, but without seeking to be reborn in the Brahmā world (*brahmaloka*), such is the domain of the Bodhisattva [41].

21. A domain where the six contemplations (*anusmṛti*) are reflected upon, but without adapting to the impurities of birth (*jātyāsrava*).

[35] K: Practising the *śūnyatā* [*samādhi*], but planting *kuśalamūla*.

[36] K: Practising the *ānimitta* [*samādhi*], but saving beings.

[37] K: Practising the *apraṇihita* [*samādhi*], but taking on existences.

[38] K: Exercising the *anutpāda*, but producing all the good actions.

[39] K: Practising the six *pāramitā*, but understanding perfectly the *citta* and *caitasikadharma* of beings.

[40] K: Practising the six *abhijñā*, but not destroying the *āsrava*. — In fact, the practice of the sixth *abhijñā*, that is, the knowledge of the destruction of the impurities (*āsravakṣayajñāna*), would transform the Bodhisattva into an Arhat.

[41] K: Practising the four *apramāṇacitta*, but without wishing to be reborn in the *brahmaloka*. — We know that the *apramāṇa* constitute the *brahmavihāra*.

A domain where the destruction of obstacles is reflected upon (*anāvaraṇaprekṣaṇā*), but without desiring defilement (*saṃkleśābhilāṣa*), such is the domain of the Bodhisattva.

22. A domain where the trances (*dhyāna*), the liberations (*vimokṣa*), the concentrations (*samādhi*) and the recollections (*samāpatti*) are reflected upon, but where rebirth (*jāti*) is not regulated by the force (*vaśena*) of these concentrations or these recollections, such is the domain of the Bodhisattva[42].

23. A domain where the four applications of mindfulness (*smṛtyupasthāna*) are explored, but without seeking to be free of the body (*kāya*), sensation (*vedanā*), mind (*citta*) and dharmas, such is the domain of the Bodhisattva[43].

24. A domain where the four right efforts (*samyakpradhāna*) are explored, but without making any distinction between good (*kuśala*) dharmas and bad (*akuśala*) dharmas, such is the domain of the Bodhisattva[44].

25. A domain where the four bases of psychic power (*ṛddhipāda*) are explored, but by effortlessly (*anābhogena*) dominating these bases of psychic power, such is the domain of the Bodhisattva[45].

26. A domain of the five dominant faculties (*pañcendriyagocara*), but also the domain of the knowledge having as its object the degree of the faculties of beings (*sattvendriyavarāvarajñāna*), such is the domain of the Bodhisattva[46].

A domain where the five dominant faculties (*pañcendriya*) are explored, but where the wonderful knowledge (*jñāna*) makes no distinction between the strong faculties and weak faculties (*indriyavarāvara*) of beings, such is the domain of the Bodhisattva.

27. A domain where the five powers are abided in (*pañcabalāvasthāna*),

[42] K: Practising the *dhyāna*, *samāpatti*, *vimokṣa* and the *samādhi*, but without being reborn in their respective spheres.

[43] K: Practising the four *smṛtyupasthāna*, but without absolutely eliminating *kāya*, *vedanā*, *citta* and *dharma*. — Normally the practice of the four *smṛtyupasthāna* leads to the clear vision of the impersonality of all the elements of existence.

[44] K: Practising the four *samyakpradhāna*, but without abandoning physical and mental vigour (*kāyacittavīrya*).

[45] K: Practising the four *ṛddhipāda*, but also obtaining the *ṛddhivaśitā*.

[46] K: Exercising the five *indriya*, but also distinguishing the sharp or blunted faculties (*tīkṣṇamṛdvindriya*) of all beings.

but where the ten powers (*daśabala*) of the Tathāgata are delighted in, such is the domain of the Bodhisattva [47].

28. A domain where the seven limbs of enlightenment are perfected (*saptabodhyaṅgapariniṣpatti*) and where perspicacity and knowledge are excelled in (*matiprabhedajñānakauśala*), such is the domain of the Bodhisattva [48].

A domain where the perfecting of the seven limbs of enlightenment (*saptabodhyaṅgapariniṣpatti*) is abided in, but without seeking after the characteristic attributes of the Buddhas (*buddhadharmaviśeṣa*): the wonderful knowledge and skillful means (*kauśalya*), such is the domain of the Bodhisattva.

29. A domain where the Path is abided in (*mārgāvasthāna*), but without grasping the wrong paths (*kumārga*), such is the domain of the Bodhisattva [49].

A domain where the perfecting of the noble eight-limbed path (*āryāṣṭāṅgamārgapariniṣpatti*) is abided in, but without turning away in disgust (*nirveda*) from the wrong paths (*kumārga*), such is the domain of the Bodhisattva.

30. A domain where the store of tranquillity and insight is sought (*śamathavipaśyanāsaṃbhāraparyeṣṭi*), but without slipping into absolute stillness (*praśamana*), such is the domain of the Bodhisattva [50].

31. A domain where it is reflected that all dharmas have non-arising and non-extinction as their mark (*sarvadharmānutpādānirodhalakṣaṇaparīkṣā*), but where the body is adorned with the primary and secondary physical marks (*lakṣaṇānuvyañjana*) and where all kinds of Buddha works are effected (*nānābuddhakāryapariniṣpatti*), such is the domain of the Bodhisattva [51].

32. A domain where the bodily attitudes of the Listeners and solitary Buddhas are manifested (*śrāvakapratyekabuddheryāpathasaṃdarśana*), but without swerving from the attributes of the Buddhas (*buddhadharmāparityāga*), such is the domain of the Bodhisattva [52].

[47] K: Exercising the five *bala*, but willingly seeking the ten *bala* of the Buddhas. — The five *bala*, identical to the five *indriya*, are *śraddhā*, *vīrya*, *smṛti*, *samādhi* and *prajñā* (cf. Pañcaviṃśati, p. 208,*6*; Mahāvyutpatti, No. 983-987); regarding the ten *bala* of the Buddhas, cf. Mahāvyutpatti, No. 120-129; Kośa, VII, p. 67-71; Pañcaviṃśati, p. 210,*11-23*.

[48] K: Exercising the seven *saṃbodhyaṅga*, but understanding the *buddhajñāna*. — On the seven *saṃbodhyaṅga*, cf. Mahāvyutpatti, No. 989-995; Pañcaviṃśati, p. 208,*8-12*.

[49] K: Even while following the *āryāṣṭāṅgikamārga*, liking to follow the innumerable *buddhamārga*.

[50] K: Even while cultivating the store of *śamatha* and *vipaśyanā*, not slipping into absolute stillness (*praśamana*).

[51] K: Even while exercising the *anutpāda* and *anirodha* of dharmas, adorning the body with the *lakṣaṇa* and *anuvyañjana*.

[52] K: Even while manifesting the *īryāpatha* of the Śrāvakas and Pratyekabuddhas, not abandoning the *buddhadharma*.

33. A domain where naturally pure dharmas are conformed with (*prakṛtiviśuddhadharmānvaya*), but where bodily attitudes are manifested (*īryāpathasaṃdarśana*), depending on the aspirations (*adhimukti*) of beings, such is the domain of the Bodhisattva [53].

A domain where, even while admitting that dharmas are absolutely pure (*atyantaviśuddha*), naturally and eternally calm (*prakṛtiśānta*), bodily attitudes (*īryāpatha*) in conformity with the various aspirations (*nānādhimukti*) of beings are not unadopted.

34. A domain where it is understood that all the Buddha-fields (*buddhakṣetra*) are absolutely imperishable (*avināśin*), immutable (*avikāra*), of spacelike nature (*ākāśasvabhāva*), but where, in diverse and multiple forms, the splendours of the virtues (*guṇavyūha*) of the Buddha-fields are manifested, such is the domain of the Bodhisattva [54].

A domain where all the Buddha-fields (*buddhakṣetra*) are reflected upon as being essentially empty (*svabhāvaśūnya*), calm (*śānta*), unreal (*asiddha*), immutable (*avikāra*) and the same as space (*ākāśasama*), but where Buddha-fields adorned with multiple virtues (*nānāguṇavyūha*) in order to ensure the welfare of beings (*sattvārthakriyā*) are not unadopted, such is the domain of the Bodhisattva.

35. *Saddharmacakrapravartanamahāparinirvāṇasaṃdarśanagocaraś ca bodhisattvacaryāparityāgagocaraś cāyam api bodhisattvasya gocaraḥ* [55].

A domain where the setting in motion of the wheel of the Law and great and full Nirvāṇa are manifested, but where the practices of the Bodhisattvas are never abandoned, such is the domain of the Bodhisattva.

When Vimalakīrti had given this address in which he explained the wonders (*abhutadharma*) of the domain (*gocara*) of the Bodhisattva, eight thousand [H variant: eight hundred thousand] sons of the gods (*devaputra*) among the sons of the gods accompanying Mañjuśrī the crown prince produced the thought of supreme and perfect enlightenment (*anuttarāyāṃ samyaksaṃbodhau cittāny utpāditāni*).

[53] K: Even while conforming to the absolutely pure mark (*atyantaviśuddhalakṣaṇa*) of dharmas, manifesting, according to need, existences [in the world of the round of rebirth].

[54] K: Seeing that the *buddhakṣetra* are eternally calm and like space, but manifesting all kinds of pure *buddhakṣetra*.

[55] An extract from the original text quoted in Śikṣāsamuccaya, p. 273,6-7.

CHAPTER FIVE

THE INCONCEIVABLE LIBERATION

[*The Search for the Law*[1]]

1. Then the Venerable (*āyuṣmant*) Śāriputra had this thought: In this house (*gṛha*), there is not even a chair (*āsana*); on what then are these Bodhisattvas and these Listeners (*śrāvaka*) going to sit?

Then the Licchavi Vimalakīrti, knowing in his mind the thought that had arisen in the mind (*cetasaiva cetaḥparivitarkam ājñāya*) of the Venerable Śāriputra, said to him: Honourable (*bhadanta*) Śāriputra, have you come here to seek the Law (*dharmārthika*) or to seek a chair (*āsanārthika*)?

Śāriputra replied: I have come to seek the Law and not to seek a chair.

2. Vimalakīrti continued: Honourable Śāriputra, he who seeks the Law (*dharmārthika*) does not even care about the life of his own body (*svakāyajīvita*); how then would he seek a chair?

Honourable Śāriputra, he who seeks the Law does not seek form (*rūpa*), sensations (*vedanā*), perception (*saṃjñā*), volition (*saṃskāra*) or consciousness (*vijñāna*). He does not seek the aggregates (*skandha*), the elements (*dhātu*)

Śāriputra, he who seeks the Law does not seek the *skandha* (from *rūpaskandha* to *vijñānaskandha*), does not seek the *dhātu* (from *cakṣurdhātu* to *manovijñānadhātu*), does not seek the *āyatana* (from *cakṣurāyatana* to *dharmāyatana*).

[1] The search for the Law (*dharmaparyeṣaṇā*) was the main preoccupation of early Buddhism. Śākyamuni himself, even when he was already in possession of enlightenment and meditated under the goat-herd's Banyan, sought to find, by way of the world, a monk or brahman whom he could revere and serve. Finding no one superior to himself, he resolved to adhere to the law that he himself had discovered, "so as to honour, respect and serve it": cf. Saṃyutta, I, p. 139-140; Saṃyukta, T 99, ch. 44, p. 321 *c*; Upadeśa, T 1509, ch. 10, p. 131 *c*. Throughout his public ministry, Śākyamuni never stopped advising his disciples: "May the Law be your island, may the Law be your relief, seek no other relief": cf. Dīgha, II, p. 100; III, p. 58, 77; Sanskrit Mahāparinirvāṇa, p. 200; Saṃyutta, III, p. 42; V, p. 154, 163.

Conversely, for Vimalakīrti, the Law is calm and stillness; it is immobile and free of coming and going, for it avoids all affirmation and negation; there is no one to expound it and no one to hear it (see above, III, §6-7). This results in the search for the Law being meaningless. This is the idea that will be developed here.

or the bases of consciousness (*āyatana*).

He who seeks the Law does not seek the world of desire (*kāmadhātu*), the world of form (*rūpadhātu*) or the world of no-form (*ārūpyadhātu*). He who seeks the Law does not seek attachment to the Buddha (*buddhābhiniveśa*), attachment to the Law (*dharmābhiniveśa*) or attachment to the community (*saṃghābhiniveśa*).

3. Honourable Śāriputra, he who seeks the Law does not seek to know suffering (*duḥkha*), does not seek to destroy its origin (*samudaya*), does not seek to achieve its extinction (*nirodha*) and does not seek to practise the Path (*pratipad*). And why? Because the Law is exempt from idle chatter (*niṣprapañca*) and devoid of expression (*akṣarāpagata*). To say and repeat: "Suffering should be known, its origin should be destroyed, its extinction should be achieved, the Path should be practised" (*duḥkhaṃ parijñeyam, samudayaḥ prahātavyaḥ, nirodhaḥ sākṣātkartavyaḥ, pratipad bhāvitavyā*)[2], this is not seeking the Law, but seeking idle chatter (*prapañca*).

Honourable Śāriputra, he who seeks the Law does not seek birth (*utpāda*) and does not seek extinction (*nirodha*). And why? The Law is calm (*upaśānta*) and stilled (*praśānta*). Thus those who are involved in (*samudācaranti*) birth and extinction do not seek the Law, do not seek solitude (*viveka*), but seek birth and extinction.

Besides, Honourable Śāriputra, he who seeks the Law does not seek the stains of craving (*rāgarajas*). And why? The Law is exempt from stain (*araja*) and free of stain (*viraja*). Thus those who are attached to any dharma whatsoever (*dharmasakta*), including Nirvāṇa[3], do not seek the Law, but seek the stains of craving.

[2] Canonical formula in which the four noble truths are condensed. The Sanskrit wording given here is found in Madh. vṛtti, p. 516,*17-18*; Āloka, p. 381,*24*-382,*5*; Kośa, VI, p. 248; Mahāvyutpatti, No. 1316-19. — The Pāli phrasing appears, for example, in Vinaya, I, p. 11; Saṃyutta, V, p. 422: *idaṃ dukkhaṃ ariyasaccaṃ pariññeyyaṃ, idaṃ dukkhasamudayaṃ ariyasaccaṃ pahātabbaṃ, idaṃ dukkhanirodhaṃ ariyasaccaṃ sacchikātabbaṃ, idaṃ dukkhanirodhagāminī paṭipadā ariyasaccaṃ bhāvetabbaṃ.*

[3] This reference to Nirvāṇa appears both in the Tibetan and Chinese versions by K and H. Here Vimalakīrti is intervening in a controversy which is already old: is it permissible to desire Nirvāṇa, the Immortal (*amṛta*), which, by definition, is free of impurities (*anāsrava*)?

The controversy revolves round a passage in the Majjhima, I, p. 4,*23-34*: *Yo pi so bhikkhave bhikkhu arahaṃ khīṇāsavo vusitavā katakaraṇīyo ohitabhāro anuppattasadattho parikkhīṇabhavasaṃyojano samma-d-aññā vimutto so pi nibbānaṃ nibbānato*

He who seeks the Law does not seek objects (*viṣaya*). And why? The Law is not an object. Thus those who pursue objects (*viṣayānusārin*) do not seek the Law, but seek objects.

abhijānāti, nibbānaṃ nibbānato abhiññāya nibbānaṃ na maññati, nibbānasmiṃ na maññati, nibbānato na maññati, nibbānaṃ me ti na maññati, nibbānaṃ nābhinandati. taṃ kissa hetu. pariññātaṃ tassāti vadāmi: "The monk, that holy one who has destroyed the impurities, lived the noble life, done what he had to do, laid down his burden, reached the supreme goal, destroyed the shackles of existence and who is liberated by right views, this monk, say I, in truth knows Nirvāṇa as being Nirvāṇa; he does not consider himself as being Nirvāṇa, as being in Nirvāṇa, as being of Nirvāṇa, as being possessed of Nirvāṇa; he does not delight in Nirvāṇa. And why? Because of his perfect knowledge".

Early exegetes wondered if, in the passage in question, the word *nibbāna* really meant Nirvāṇa, the Immortal, or if it was not more likely describing the five objects of desire (*pañca kāmaguṇa*)?

1. The Pūrvaśailas are of the opinion that it really does concern Nirvāṇa, the Immortal, and they use this passage as an authority to condemn the desire for Nirvāṇa. They therefore assert (Kathāvatthu, I, p. 401,*16*): *amatārammaṇaṃ saññojanaṃ*: "The desire that has the Immortal as object is a fetter". In other words: any desire, even that which has Nirvāṇa as object, is condemned.

2. This is not the opinion of the Theravādins who, in their Kathāvatthu, p. 401-404, dispute this thesis of the Pūrvaśailas. According to the Theravādins, the word *nibbāna* appearing in the Majjhima passage under discussion, does not designate the Immortal, but the enjoyment of the five objects of desire.

In his Commentary of the Majjhima, I, p. 38-39, Buddhaghosa sees in this passage from the Majjhima, the condemnation of an heretical thesis already refuted in the Dīgha, I, p. 36,*23-28*: *idha bhikkhave ekacco samaṇo vā brāhmaṇo vā evaṃvādī hoti evaṃdiṭṭhī: yato kho bho ayaṃ attā pañcahi kāmaguṇehi samappito samaṅgibhūto paricāreti ettāvatā kho bho ayaṃ attā paramadiṭṭhadhammanibbānappatto hotī ti. itth 'eke sato sattassa paramadiṭṭhadhammanibbānaṃ paññāpenti*: "It occurs, monks, that such or such a devotee or brahman upholds this thesis, this view: When this Self, placed in possession of the bundle of the five objects of desire, incorporating them into himself, delights in them, it is indeed so that this Self reaches Nirvāṇa in the present life. Thus some proclaim that a living being possesses Nirvāṇa in the present life".

According to the Theravādins, the Dīgha, I, p. 36, condemns monks who consider the possession of the five objects of desire as Nirvāṇa on earth; and the Majjhima, I, p. 4, condemns the desire for that Nirvāṇa which is considered as being the possession of the five objects of desire, but it does not condemn the desire for true Nirvāṇa, the Immortal.

It is hardly to be doubted that, in the passage from the Majjhima under discussion, the word *nibbāna* shifted from its proper meaning and indicates the five *kāmaguṇa*. As Miss I.B. HORNER puts it so well: "Here *nibbāna* signifies the enjoyment of the five kinds of sensory pleasures. The 'average man' regards these as the highest *nibbāna* in this very life. *Nibbāna* is therefore not being used here in its Buddhist sense" (*Middle Length Sayings*, I, London, 1954, p. 5, note 11).

3. The position of the Sarvāstivādin-Vaibhāṣikas is exactly the same as that of Buddhaghosa and the Theravādins. It is explained in the Vibhāṣā, T 1545, ch. 86,

He who seeks the Law does not seek either grasping (*āyūha*) or rejection (*niryūha*). And why? The Law is without grasping and without rejection (*āyūha-niryūhavigata*). Thus those who grasp or reject dharmas do not seek the Law, but seek grasping or rejection.

4. He who seeks the Law does not seek a resting place (*ālaya*). And why? The Law is not a resting place. Thus those who cherish a resting place (*ālayarata*) do not seek the Law, but seek a resting place[4].

He who seeks the Law does not seek the signs of dharmas (*dharmanimitta*). And why? The Law is signless (*animitta*). Thus those who pursue the signs of consciousness (*vijñānanimittānuparivartin*) do not seek the Law, but seek signs.

He who seeks the Law does not seek a consorting with the Law (*dharmasārdhavihāra*).

p. 445 *a* 1-5: "The Bhadanta Vasumitra said: When there are produced propensities (*anuśaya*) having as their object impure things (*sāsravadharma*) [for example the five objects of desire], the *anuśaya* increase in them progressively [i.e. grow from the fact that these impure things are the object], just as the organ of sight (*cakṣurindriya*) develops in a man who looks at the moon. But when there are produced propensities (*anuśaya*) having as their object pure things (*anāsravadharma*) [namely Nirvāṇa or the Path to Nirvāṇa], the *anuśaya* diminish, like the organ of sight in a man who looks at the sun".

Also see Kośa, V, p. 36: "Craving (*rāgānuśaya*) should be abandoned. But if it has the *anāsrava* [= Nirvāṇa], as its object, it should not be rejected; just as there should not be rejected the aspiration towards good dharmas (*kuśaladharmacchanda*) [which takes the form of desire (*abhilāṣa*), but which is right view (*samyagdṛṣṭi*)]".

All this amounts to saying that the desire for the Good is not a defilement.

4. Here, Vimalakīrti rejects the desire for Nirvāṇa, not for moral reasons, but for metaphysical ones. Saṃsāra and Nirvāṇa are only mere designations (*nāmadheyamātra*) and are both empty and unreal (IV, § 12); there is not a single being who is not already in Parinirvāṇa (III, § 51); if one is truly unbound (*abaddha*), why still seek liberation (*mokṣa*)? Delight in Nirvāṇa (*nirvāṇābhirati*) and repugnance for Saṃsāra (*saṃsāraparikheda*) contravene the principle of non-duality (VIII, § 29).

[4] *Ālaya* "refuge" or "resting place", translated here by *kun-gźi*, *ch'ao-k'u* 巢窟 (Cn), *ch'u-so* 處所 (K) and *shê-tsang* 攝藏 (H), appears in the canonical formula: *ālayarāmā kho panāyaṃ pajā ālayaratā ālayasammuditā* "Beings, most certainly, love the *ālaya*, delight in the *ālaya*, rejoice in the *ālaya*" (Vinaya, I, p. 4,*35*; Dīgha, II, p. 36,*3*; 37,*25*; Majjhima, I, p. 167,*32*; Saṃyutta, I, p. 136,*11*; Aṅguttara, II, p. 131,*30*; Mahāvastu, III, p. 314,*2*). According to its old and canonical meaning, the *ālaya* is the five objects of desire which the worldly consider to be their refuge and their dwelling place: cf. Dīgha Commentary, II, p. 464,*13*: *sattā pañcakāmaguṇesu allīyanti, tasmā te ālayā ti vuccanti*.

Later, the Vijñānavādins were to seek in these canonical texts the justification for the *ālayavijñāna* "store consciousness", keystone of their psychology: cf. Saṃgraha, p. 26-27; Siddhi, p. 180. It goes without saying that, considering its early date, the Vimalakīrti still knows nothing at all of the Vijñānavādin school.

And why? The Law is not a consorting. Thus those who desire to consort with the Law do not seek the Law, but seek a consorting.

He who seeks the Law does not seek that which is seen, heard, thought and known (*dṛṣṭaśrutamatavijñāta*)[5]. And why? The Law cannot be seen, or heard, or thought, or known. Thus those who move (*caranti*) in that which is seen, heard, thought and known seek what is seen, heard, thought and known, but do not seek the Law.

5. Honourable Śāriputra, the Law is neither conditioned (*saṃskṛta*) nor unconditioned (*asaṃskṛta*)[6]. Thus those who hold to a domain of conditioned things (*saṃskṛtagocara*) do not seek the Law, but seek to seize conditioned things.

Śāriputra, he who seeks the Law does not seek conditioned things (*saṃskṛta*). And why? Because the Law is said to be unconditioned (*asaṃskṛta*), devoid of the self-nature of conditioned things (*saṃskṛtasvabhāvavigata*). Thus those who move among conditioned things seek conditioned things and do not seek the Law.

Consequently, O Śāriputra, if you seek the Law, you should not seek any dharma.

When Vimalakīrti had given this homily (*dharmadeśanā*), five hundred sons of the gods acquired the pure eye of the Law regarding dharmas, without dust or stain (*pañcamātrāṇāṃ devaputraśatānāṃ virajo vigatamalaṃ dharmeṣu dharmacakṣur viśuddham*).

[*The Miracle of the Thrones*]

6. Then the Licchavi Vimalakīrti said to Mañjuśrī the crown prince: Mañjuśrī, you have already been in innumerable and incalculable hundreds of thousands of *koṭi* of Buddha-fields (*apramāṇāny asaṃkhyeyāni buddhakṣetrakoṭiśatasahasrāṇi*) spread over the universes of the ten regions (*daśadikṣu lokadhātuṣu*); in which Buddha-field have you seen thrones (*siṃhāsana*) which are the most beautiful (*vara*) and the most endowed with virtues (*guṇasamanvāgata*)?

This having been said, Mañjuśrī the crown prince replied to the Licchavi Vimalakīrti: Son of good family, if, starting from here,

[5] Traditional expression used to designate the whole field of experience (*vyavahāra*). In Pāli, we have *diṭṭhaṃ sutaṃ mutaṃ viññātaṃ* (Dīgha, III, p. 232; Majjhima, I, p. 135,*34*; III, p. 29,*30*; 261,*11*; Aṅguttara, II, p. 246; IV, p. 307). Vaibhāṣikas and Sautrāntikas debate over the exact meaning of these ideas (Kośa, IV, p. 160-162).

[6] In Tib., *chos ni ḥdus byas daṅ ḥdus ma byas med pa ste*. In contrast, in K and H, the Law is called *asaṃskṛta*. The Tibetan reading seems preferable because the theories of *saṃskṛta* and *asaṃskṛta* are interdependent and, in the light of the law of contrasts, the non-existence of the one necessarily implies that of the other.

one traversed, in an Easterly direction, Buddha-fields as innumerable as the sands of the thirty-two [var. thirty-six] Ganges, one would find a universe called Merudhvajā: it is there that the Tathāgata named Merupradīparāja[7] is to be found, lives and exists (*asti pūrvasyāṃ diśi, kulaputra, dvātriṃśadgaṅgānadīvālukopamāni buddhakṣetrāṇy atikramya Merudhvajā nāma lokadhātuḥ. tatra Merupradīparājo nāma tathāgato 'rhan samyaksaṃbuddhas tiṣṭhati dhriyate yāpayati*)[8]. The build (*kāyapramāṇa*) of this Tathāgata is eighty-four hundreds of thousands of leagues (*yojana*)[9], and the height of his throne (*siṃhāsanapramāṇa*) is sixty-eight hundreds of thousands of leagues. The Bodhisattvas who surround him have a build of forty-two hundreds of thousands of leagues, and the height of their thrones is thirty-four hundreds of thousands of leagues. Son of good family, it is in the Merudhvajā universe of this Tathāgata Merupradīparāja that there are to be found thrones which are the most beautiful and the most endowed with virtues.

7. At that precise instant (*tena khalu punar samayena*), the Licchavi Vimalakīrti, having concentrated all his thought (*sarvacetasā samanvāhṛtya*), performed such a supernatural action (*evaṃrūpam ṛddhyabhisaṃskāram abhisaṃskaroti sma*) that the Blessed Tathāgata Merupradīparāja inhabiting the Merudhvajā universe in the Eastern region sent (*preṣayati sma*) thirty-two hundreds of thousands of thrones. These thrones were so high (*prāptāroha*), so large (*viśāla*) and so beautiful (*darśanīya*) that neither the Bodhisattvas, nor the great Listeners (*mahāśrāvaka*), nor the Śakras, nor the Brahmās, nor the Lokapālas, nor the Devaputras had ever seen or heard of anything like them before (*adṛṣṭaśrutapūrva*). Descending from the sky (*upary antarikṣāt*), these thrones came to rest (*pratiṣṭhāpita*) in the house of Vimalakīrti.

These thirty-two hundreds of thrones set themselves down without hindering each other (*avivā-*

The house enlarged and expanded suddenly and was able to contain the thirty-two hundreds of thousands of thrones

[7] The Avataṃsaka, a section of the Gaṇḍavyūha, p. 81,*4-5*, places the Tathāgata Merupradīparāja in the Gandhaprabhāsavatī universe in the Western region. The small Sukhāvatī, p. 204,*8*, also refers to a Tathāgata Merupradīpa whom it places in the Southern region.

[8] Extremely common stock phrase: cf. Aṣṭasāh., p. 879,*5*; 889,*21-22*; Pañcaviṃśati, p. 12,*19*; Sad. puṇḍ., p. 42,*2*; 184,*5*; 409,*3*; 413,*7*; 419,*4*; 423,*6*; 461,*3*.

[9] Here and in the following lines, the measurements proposed by Cn and K are more modest: 84,000 *yojana*, and the rest in proportion.

ryaṃ prajñaptāny abhūvan)[10], and the house seemed to enlarge accordingly. The great town of Vaiśālī experienced no hindrance (*nivāraṇa*) from it; India (*jambudvīpa*) and the four continents (*caturdvīpa*) experienced no hindrance from it. All seemed as before (*yathāpūrvam*).

without them hindering each other. The great town of Vaiśālī, India (*jambudvīpa*), the four continents (*caturdvīpa*) and, in the universes (*lokadhātu*), the towns (*nagara*), villages (*grāma*), boroughs (*nigama*), kingdoms (*rāṣṭra*), capitals (*rājadhānī*), as well as the dwellings (*bhavana*) of the Devas, Nāgas, Yakṣas, Asuras, etc., experienced no hindrance (*nirvāraṇa*) from it. There was no difference from what was seen before.

8. Then the Licchavi Vimalakīrti said to Mañjuśrī the crown prince: Mañjuśrī, after having transformed your body to the size of these thrones (*siṃhāsanānurūpeṇa kāyam adhiṣṭhāya*), take up your place (*niṣīda*) with the Bodhisattvas and the great Listeners (*mahāśrāvaka*).

The great Bodhisattvas, who already possessed the super-knowledges (*abhijñā*), transformed their own bodies (*svakāyān adhiṣṭhāya*) up to forty-two hundreds of thousands of leagues (*dvicatvāriṃśadyojanaśatasahasra*) and, ascending these thrones, sat down comfortably upon them. But the beginner (*ādikarmika*) Bodhisattvas were incapable of seating themselves on these thrones. Then the Licchavi Vimalakīrti expounded the Law to them in such a way that they all obtained the five super-knowledges (*abhijñā*) and, having obtained them, they miraculously transformed their bodies (*ṛddhyā kāyān abhinirmāya*) up to forty-two hundreds of thousands of leagues; after which, they took their places on the thrones.

As for the great Listeners (*mahāśrāvaka*), they were incapable of sitting on the thrones. Then the Licchavi Vimalakīrti said to the Venerable (*āyuṣmant*) Śāriputra: Honourable (*bhadanta*) Śāriputra, sit down on these thrones then. — Śāriputra replied: Worthy man

[10] In Tibetan, the Peking edition has *ma hoṅs par śoṅ ste*; the Narthang one *ma zlogs par śoṅ ste*. I propose the reading *ma zlogs par śoms te*.

Zlog pa "to cause to return, to drive back", in Chinese *fang-ai* 妨礙 "to hinder", normally renders the Sanskrit *nivārayati*, causative of *vṛ*, *vṛṇoti* (cf. J. Nobel, *Wörterbuch zum Suvarṇaprabhāsa*, Leiden, 1950, p. 190). The Mahāvyutpatti, No. 5205, renders *mi zlogs pa* by *avivāryam* which is a *hapax* related to the adjective *avivārin* "which does not set aside, which does not hold back".

As for *śoṅ ba*, confirmed in both Peking and Narthang, its most usual meaning "to empty, remove, carry or take away" is not appropriate here. It should be substituted by *śom pa* "to prepare, make ready", in Sanskrit *prajñāpayati*. This is the verb that is regularly used to indicate the setting out of seats. Thus the traditional expression *prajñapta evāsane nyaṣīdat* (in Pāli, *paññatte āsane nisīdi*) is usually rendered in Tibetan by *gdan bśams pa ñid la bźugs so* "he sat on the seat which had been prepared for him".

(*satpuruṣa*), the thrones are too high (*bṛhat*) and too large (*mahat*): we cannot sit on them. — Vimalakīrti went on: Honourable Śāriputra, then pay homage (*namaskuruta*) to the Blessed Tathāgata Merupradīparāja and ask him to increase your psychic power (*ṛddhibala*); then you will be able to sit down. — The great Listeners paid homage to the Blessed Tathāgata Merupradīparāja and beseeched him to increase their psychic power: immediately, they could sit on the thrones.

9. Then the Venerable Śāriputra said to the Licchavi Vimalakīrti: Son of good family (*kulaputra*), it is a marvel (*āścaryam etat*) that hundreds of thousands of thrones (*siṃhāsana*), so high (*bṛhat*) and so large (*mahat*) can get in such a small (*alpa*) house never hindering each other (*avivāryam*). And yet the great town of Vaiśāli does not experience the least hindrance (*nivāraṇa*); in Jambudvīpa, the villages (*grāma*), towns (*nagara*), kingdoms (*rāṣṭra*) and capitals (*rājadhānī*), as well as the four continents (*caturdvīpaka*) do not experience the slightest hindrance; the dwellings (*bhavana*) of the Devas, Nāgas, Yakṣas, Gandharvas, Asuras, Garuḍas, Kiṃnaras and Mahoragas do not experience the least hindrance either; after as before, all seems the same.

[*The Inconceivable Liberation*[11]]

10. The Licchavi Vimalakīrti replied: Honourable Śāriputra, the Tathāgatas and irreversible (*avaivartika*) Bodhisattvas possess a liberation

[11] This section (V, § 10-18), devoted to the *acintyavimokṣa* of the Bodhisattva is of such importance that it supplied one of the three titles of the Vimalakīrtinirdeśa (see Introduction, p. LIV-LV). It is presented in § 18 as the condensation (*saṃkṣepa*) of an enormous *vaipulyasūtra* the recitation of which would require more than a kalpa.

There exists a vaipulyasūtra entitled *Acintyavimokṣasūtra* "Sūtra of the inconceivable liberation" which is none other than the Avataṃsaka (T 278 and 279). When the Upadeśa quotes the Avataṃsaka, it is always by the title of *Acintyasūtra* (T 1509, ch. 5, p. 94 *b* 13 = NĀGĀRJUNA, *Traité*, p. 311) or *Acintyavimokṣasūtra* (T 1509, ch. 33, p. 303 *b* 24; ch. 73, p. 576 *c* 25; ch. 100, p. 756 *b* 7).

According to Indian and Chinese tradition, the Acintyavimokṣasūtra was compiled by Mañjuśrī, kept for more than six centuries in the Nāgas' palace, discovered in this same palace by Nāgārjuna who learnt the short version in 100,000 *gāthā* by heart. The latter only communicated a very small part of it to his listeners of weak faculties. A version in 36,000 *gāthā*, discovered in Khotan by Fa-ling, between 392 and 408, was translated into Chinese, in Yang-chou, by Buddhabhadra, between 418 and 420: this is the Taishō 278. Another more developed version, in 40,000 *gāthā*, brought from Khotan by Śikṣānanda, was translated in Lo-yang, between 695 and 699: this is the Taishō 279. Finally, when he reached Ch'ang-an in 599-560 after a long journey in

(*vimokṣa*) called "inconceivable" (*acintya*). A Bodhisattva established in this inconceivable liberation (*acintyavimokṣastha*) can, through his psychic power (*ṛddhibala*), insert into a mustard seed (*sarṣapa*) Sumeru,

Central Asia, the Indian Jinagupta told the Chinese of the existence in Khotan, both in the royal palace and on a mountain near the capital, of a rich collection of twelve vaipulyas, each containing 100,000 *gāthā*, among which the Avataṃsaka was to be found. For details and sources see my article on *Mañjuśrī*, in T'oung-Pao, XLVIII, Fasc. 1-3, 1960, p. 40-46; 61-75.

When Vimalakīrti explains here in a condensed form the *acintyavimokṣa* of the Bodhisattvas, he is referring expressly to a greatly developed mahāvaipulya which deals with the same subject. The mahāvaipulya concerned is most probably the Avataṃsaka, also called Acintyasūtra or Acintyavimokṣasūtra.

However, in the two Chinese versions of the Avataṃsaka which have come down to us, it is not a question of the *acintyavimokṣa* of the Bodhisattvas, but of the *acintyadharma* of the Buddhas (T 278, ch. 30-31, p. 590 *b*-601 *a*; T 279, ch. 46-47, p. 242 *a*-251 *b*). The Vimalakīrti may have had access to a more developed version.

We note further that, in this section, Vimalakīrti deals less with the *vimokṣa* in themselves (cf. Kośa, VIII, p. 206-211) than with the psychic and magical powers which are their natural consequence.

Early Buddhism already recognised that the purification of the mind through the *samādhi*, *dhyāna*, *samāpatti* and *vimokṣa* resulted in the acquisition of valuable advantages, especially the six *abhijñā* (cf. Majjhima, III, p. 97-99). When the Śrāvakas mention the concentrations, they are only considering the nine *anupūrvavihāra* or successive grades of mental purification, i.e. the four *dhyāna*, the four *ārūpyāyatana* and the *saṃjñāvedayitanirodha* (Dīgha, II, p. 156; III, p. 265). It is they that produce those enviable psychical powers which are the *abhijñā*.

However, Bodhisattvas are not satisfied with the nine *anupūrvavihāra* of the Śrāvakas and lay claim to possessing a higher thought (*adhicitta*), unknown to the adherents of the Small Vehicle. According to the Saṃgraha (p. 218-231), this higher thought is characterised by six superiorities: 1. superiority in object (*ālambana*), the higher thought pertaining to the teaching of the Great Vehicle; 2. superiority in variety (*nānātva*), Bodhisattvas have at their disposal an infinite number of concentrations (see the lists of the *samādhi* in Pañcaviṃśati, p. 142-144; Śatasāh., p. 825, 1412, 1531; Mahāvyutpatti, No. 506-623); 3. superiority in thwarting (*pratipakṣa*); 4. superiority in aptitude (*karmaṇyatā*); 5. superiority in the results obtained (*abhinirhāra*); 6. superiority in actions (*karman*).

It is this last point which interests Vimalakīrti because, if the *samādhi* of the Śrāvakas produce an ordinary psychic power (*ṛddhi*), those of the Bodhisattvas assure a great psychic power (*maharddhi*).

The prerogatives of the *ṛddhi* of the Śrāvakas or, as they are also called, the *abhijñākarman*, are too well known to stop over here. They are referred to unendingly in both Pāli sources (cf. WOODWARD, *Concordance*, I, p. 164, s.v. *anekavihitaṃ iddhividhaṃ paccanubhoti*) and the corresponding Sanskrit texts (Pañcaviṃśati, p. 83,*8*-84,*2*; Daśabhūmika, p. 34-35; Kośavyākhyā, p. 654,*3-4*; Mahāvyutpatti, No. 215-225): the ascetic, being one, becomes many; being many, he becomes one, etc.

The operation of the *maharddhi* of the Buddhas and Bodhisattvas is infinitely

king of mountains (*parvatarāja*), as high (*evamunnata*), as large (*evaṃmahat*), as noble (*evamārya*) and as vast (*evaṃviśāla*) as it is. However, the Bodhisattva carries out this action (*kriyāṃ saṃdarśayati*) without the mustard seed increasing in size (*na vardhate*) and without Sumeru decreasing in size (*na hīyate*)[12]. The Caturmahārājakāyika devas and the Trāyastriṃśa devas who inhabit Sumeru do not see, do not know where they are going or what they are entering; it is only beings destined to be disciplined by this miracle (*ṛddhivaineya-sattva*) who can know and who can see Sumeru, king of mountains, enter into a mustard seed. Such is, Honourable Śāriputra, among Bodhisattvas, the entry into the realm of inconceivable liberation (*acintyavimokṣaviṣayapraveśa*)[13]. The realm of this inconceivable liberation cannot be fathomed (*anavagāha*) either by Listeners (*śrāvaka*) or by Solitary Buddhas (*pratyekabuddha*).

11. Besides, Honourable Śāriputra, a Bodhisattva established in this inconceivable liberation can, through his psychic power, empty (*chorayati*) into a single pore of his skin (*ekasminn eva romakūpe*) the waters of the four great oceans (*caturmahāsamudrāpkandha*), as deep (*evaṃgambhīra*) and as vast (*evaṃviśāla*) as they are[14].

However, the Bodhisattva carries out this action (*kriyāṃ saṃdarśayati*) without the fish (*matsya*), tortoises (*kūrma*), dolphins

However, the dimensions of the pore do not increase (*na vardhante*) and those of the four great oceans do not decrease (*na hīyante*). Even while carrying out such

richer. The Upadeśa (cf. NĀGĀRJUNA, *Traité*, p. 329-330; 381-386) distinguishes three kinds of psychic powers: 1. displacement (*gamana*) which is of four sorts; 2. creation (*nirmāṇa*) which is of eight or four sorts; 3. *āryarddhi* or noble psychic power. The Bodh. bhūmi, p. 58-63, repeated in part in the Saṃgraha, p. 221-222, distinguishes a *ṛddhi pariṇāmikī*, of transformation, which is manifested in sixteen ways, and a *ṛddhi nairamāṇikī*, of creation, which is of two types.

[12] On this theory, see *Mss. Cecil Bendall* ed. by L. DE LA VALLÉE POUSSIN, JRAS, 1908, p. 49: *ye kecit kulaputrāḥ sattvāḥ sattavadhātusaṃgrahasaṃnihitāḥ dhātvāyatana-saṃniśritās teṣāṃ sattvānāṃ saced ekaikasya sumerupramāṇa ātmabhāvo bhavet parikalpam upādāyaḥ śaktaḥ sa Śākyamunis tathāgatas tān sarvasattvān evaṃrūpātmabhāvān ekasmin sarṣapaphale praveśayitum ekaikaś ca sattvo vistīrṇaviṣayāvakāśāḥ syān na ca parasparaṃ te cakṣuṣā ābhāsam āgaccheran na ca tasyaikasya sarṣapaphalasya sarvasattvamahātma-bhāvapraveśenonnatvaṃ vā pūrṇatvaṃ vā prajñāyeta.*

[13] According to K (p. 546 *b* 29): *Acintyavimokṣadharmaparyāyapraveśa*. It is indeed a reference to a text (*dharmaparyāya*).

[14] Cf. *Mss. Cecil Bendall*, l.c., p. 50: *punar aparaṃ kulaputrā yat kimcid dravatvaṃ prajñāyate tat sarvam abdhātuḥ śaktas sa Śākyamunis tathāgatas taṃ sarvam abdhātum ekabālāgre praveśayituṃ na ca tasyaikasya bālāgrasya sarvābdhātupraveśenonnatvaṃ vā pūrṇatvaṃ vā prajñāyeta.*

(*śiśumāra*), frogs (*maṇḍūka*) and other aquatic animals (*jalajaprāṇin*) suffering from it, and without the Nāgas, Yakṣas, Gandharvas and Asuras knowing what they are entering. And there is for these beings neither torment (*pīḍana*) nor bother (*upāyāsa*).

12. If a Bodhisattva takes in his right hand (*dakṣiṇahasta*), as if it were a potter's wheel (*kumbhakāracakra*), this trichiliomegachiliocosm (*trisāhasramahāsāhasralokadhātu*) and, having turned it (*pravṛtya*), throws it (*ākṣipati*) beyond universes as numerous as the sands of the Ganges (*gaṅgānadīvālukopamā lokadhātuḥ*), beings would not know where they are being thrown or where they came from. Then, when the Bodhisattva recovers the cosmos and puts it back in place, he carries out this action (*kriyāṃ saṃdarśayati*) without beings suspecting either that they had gone or returned.

13. Besides, Honourable Śāriputra, there are beings who are a supernatural action, the Bodhisattva acts so that the Nāgas, Yakṣas, Asuras, etc., do not know and do not see where they are going or what they are entering. Thus the fish (*matsya*), tortoises (*kūrma*), crocodiles (*nakra*) and other aquatic animals, the Nāgas and other divinities, the beings do not suffer either torment (*pīḍana*) or bother (*upāyāsa*). It is only beings destined to be disciplined by this miracle who know and see the waters of the four great oceans emptying into the pore of the skin.

This is how a Bodhisattva is established in this inconceivable liberation which is entered by skillful means (*upāyakauśalya*) and the power of knowledge (*jñānabala*). The realm of this inconceivable liberation cannot be fathomed either by Śrāvakas or by Pratyekabuddhas.

Śāriputra, a Bodhisattva established in this inconceivable liberation can, through his psychic power, take up (*ādadati*) this trichiliomegachiliocosm of such vast dimensions, place it (*sthāpayati*) in his right hand, then, having turned it as fast as a potter's wheel, throw it (*ākṣipati*) beyond universes as numerous as the sands of the Ganges. Finally, he recaptures it (*punar ādadati*) and puts it back in place without this cosmos undergoing either augmentation (*vṛddhi*) or diminution (*hāni*). Even while carrying out such a supernatural action, the Bodhisattva acts so that the inhabitants of the cosmos do not know at all and do not see at all where they have gone or where they have returned from. Thus they do not even produce the notion of going and returning (*gamananirgamanasaṃjñā*) and do not suffer any injury (*vihethana*). It is only beings destined to be disciplined by this miracle (*ṛddhivaineyasattva*) who know and see the cosmos going and returning.

This is how ... (cf. § 11 sub fine).

Śāriputra, a Bodhisattva established in inconceivable liberation examines beings disciplined after an immense period of rebirths (*apramāṇasaṃsāravaineyasattva*) and there are those who are disciplined after a short period of rebirths (*hrasvasaṃsārāvaineya*). A Bodhisattva established in inconceivable liberation, through the power of his discipline (*vinayabalāt*), presents to those who are to be disciplined after an immense period of rebirths a space of seven days (*saptāha*) as lasting for a kalpa. Conversely, to those who are to be disciplined after a short period of rebirths, he presents a kalpa as lasting for seven days. Thus beings due to be disciplined after a long period of rebirths think that the seven days have lasted for a kalpa, while beings due to be disciplined after a short period of rebirths think that the kalpa has lasted for seven days.

who are to be disciplined after a long series of rebirths (*saṃsāradīrghakālaprabandha*) and beings who are to be disciplined after a short series of rebirths (*saṃsārahrasvakālaprabandha*). Through his psychic power (*ṛddhibala*) and going by this two-fold necessity, the Bodhisattva can either prolong seven days into a kalpa so that the former believe themselves to be disciplined at the end of a kalpa, or reduce a kalpa to seven days so that the latter believe themselves to be disciplined at the end of seven days. Thus each being is disciplined according to his perspective. Even while carrying out such a supernatural action, the Bodhisattva acts so that beings already disciplined (*vinīta*) do not even suspect this prolongation or this reduction of time. Thus, it is only those who are to be disciplined by this miracle (*ṛddhivaineyasattva*) who notice this prolongation or this reduction of time.

This is how ... (cf. § 11 sub fine).

14. Besides, a Bodhisattva established in inconceivable liberation can show, in a single Buddha-field (*ekasminn eva buddhakṣetre*), the splendour of the virtues (*guṇavyūha*) of all the Buddha-fields.

And further, a Bodhisattva places all beings in the palm of his right hand (*dakṣiṇakaratala*) and through a feat as rapid as thought (*cittajavanarddhi*) moves around everywhere, but without ever moving from his single Buddha-field.

A Bodhisattva can cause to appear (*saṃdarśayati*) in a single

Besides, Śāriputra, a Bodhisattva established in inconceivable liberation can, through his psychic power, assemble all the pure universes adorned with the attributes of the Buddha and place them in a single Buddha-field so as to show them to beings.

And further, through his psychic power, a Bodhisattva takes hold of all the beings in a single Buddha-field and places them in the palm of his right hand; then with the speed of thought, he goes everywhere in the ten regions while displaying all the Buddha-fields. Even while moving through all the Buddha-fields of the ten regions, he remains in the same Buddha-field, without changing position.

Through his psychic power (*ṛddhibala*), a Bodhisattva can cause to come out of pore of his skin (*romakūpa*) all the offerings (*pūjanā*) destined for the Blessed Lord Buddhas of the ten regions.

a single pore of his skin (*romakūpa*) all the loveliest offerings; then he goes successively through all the universes of the ten regions and offers them to the Buddhas, the Bodhisattvas and Śrāvakas.

Through his psychic power, a Bodhisattva causes to appear (*saṃdarśayati*), in a single pore of his skin (*romakūpa*), all the discs (*bimba*) of the suns (*sūrya*), moons (*candra*) and stars (*tārakā*) existing in all the universes of the ten regions.

Through his psychic power, a Bodhisattva breathes out through his mouth (*mukha*) the tempests (*utthāna*) of the great circles of winds (*vātamaṇḍala*)[15] of all the universes of the ten regions, and yet, his body (*kāya*) does not undergo any harm (*upaghāta*) from it, and the grasses (*tṛṇa*) and woods (*vana*) of these Buddha-fields even while encountering these winds, are not flattened (*na śerante*).

15. At the moment of the kalpa when the Buddha-fields of the ten regions are consumed, the Bodhisattva inserts (*praveśayati*) into his own belly (*svajaṭhara*) the whole mass of burning fires (*ādīptatejaḥskandha*), but he does it with impunity.

Besides, when all the Buddha-fields contained in the universes of the ten regions burn at the end of the kalpa, the Bodhisattva, through his psychic power, inserts (*praveśayati*) into his own belly (*svajaṭhara*) all the fires (*tejas*); and even though the burning flame (*ādīptajvāla*) of these fires is not extinguished, he does not experience in his body the least harm (*upaghāta*).

Having traversed, in the direc-

Besides, and through his psychic power,

[15] The receptacle world (*bhājanaloka*) is founded on three superimposed circles: the circle of wind (*vāyumaṇḍala*), the circle of water (*abmaṇḍala*) and the circle of golden land (*kāñcanamayī bhūmi*): cf. Dīgha, II, p. 107,*23-24*; Kośavyākhyā, p. 15,*27-32*.

The circle of wind which rests in space is sixteen hundred thousand *yojana* thick; it is immeasurable in circumference; it is solid: a *mahānagna* could throw his *vajra* into it, the *vajra* would break without the circle of wind being breached (Kośa, III, p. 139). — Cf. Yogācārabhūmi, p. 37,*12-14*: *trisāhasramahāsāhasralokadhātupramāṇaṃ vāyumaṇḍalam abhinirvartate trisāhasramahāsāhasrasya lokasya pratiṣṭhābhūtam avaimānikānāṃ sattvānāṃ ca.*

At the moment of the kalpa of creation (*vivartakalpa*) there arise in space very light winds which continue to increase and finally constitute the circle of wind (cf. Kośa, III, p. 185).

The kalpa of disappearance (*saṃvartakalpa*) consists of the disappearance of beings (*sattvasaṃvartanī*) and the disappearance of the receptacle world (*bhājanasaṃvartanī*). The latter involves a three-fold disappearance: 1. through fire (*tejas*), due to the seven suns; 2. through water (*ap-*), due to the rains; 3. through wind (*vāyu*), due to disorder in the wind element (cf. Kośa, III. p. 184; 209-210).

According to Vimalakīrti it is these winds and fires that the Bodhisattva can at will inhale through his mouth or put in his belly.

tion of the nadir, Buddha-fields as numerous as the sands of the Ganges (*adhastād gaṅgānadīvālukopamāni buddhakṣetrāṇy atikramya*), the Bodhisattva lifts into the air (*ūrdhvam ārohati*) a Buddha-field; then traversing, in the direction of the zenith, Buddha-fields as numerous as the sands of the Ganges (*upariṣṭād gaṅgānadīvālukopamāni buddhakṣetrāṇy atikramya*), he places on the summit (*ūrdhvam upasthāpayati*) this Buddha-field, in the same way that a strong man lifts a leaf of a jujube tree onto the point of a needle and straightens it (*tadyathā balavān puruṣaḥ sūcyagreṇa badaraparṇaṃ samucchrityonnayati*).

having traversed, in the direction of the nadir region, Buddha-fields as numerous as the sands of innumerable koṭis of Ganges (*punar aparam ṛddhibalenādhastād diśy apramāṇagaṅgānadīkoṭvālukopamāni buddhakṣetrāṇy atikramya*), the Bodhisattva lifts up (*ārohati*) a Buddha-field; then traversing, in the direction of the zenith region, Buddha-fields as numerous as the sands of a koṭi of Ganges (*upariṣṭād diśi gaṅgānadīkoṭivālukopamāni buddhakṣetrāṇy atikramya*), places on the summit (*ūrdhvam upasthāpayati*) this Buddha-field, in the same way that a strong man lifts onto the point of a needle (*sūcyagra*) a small leaf of a jujube tree (*badaraparṇa*) and puts it elsewhere without harming it. While he is carrying out such a supernatural action, beings whom this does not at all concern (*anilambhasattva*) see nothing and know nothing, and there results for them no harm (*upaghāta*). Thus it is that only those beings destined to be disciplined by this miracle (*ṛddhivaineyasattva*) see this wonder.

This is how ... (cf. § 11 sub fine).

16. Equally, a Bodhisattva established in this inconceivable liberation creates for himself the appearances (*pratikṛtyadhiṣṭhānaṃ karoti*) of any being: the appearances of a Cakravartin, a Lokapāla, a Śakra, a Brahmā, a Śrāvaka, a Pratyekabuddha, a Bodhisattva or of a universal Buddha.

Besides, Śāriputra, a Bodhisattva established in this inconceivable liberation can, through his psychic power, create for himself the multiple appearances (*nānāvidhapratikṛti*) of the body of a Buddha, a Pratyekabuddha, a Śrāvaka, a Bodhisattva adorned with the primary and secondary physical marks (*lakṣaṇānuvyañjanasvalaṃkṛta*), a Brahmā, a Śakra devendra, a Cāturmahārājika deva, a Cakravartin king: in short, of any being.

Through his psychic power, he transforms (*pariṇamati*) beings so as to bestow on them the body of a Buddha, or to give them the multiple appearances (*nānāvidhapratikṛti*) of a Bodhisattva, a Śrāvaka, a Pratyekabuddha, a Śakra, a Brahmā, a Lokapāla, a Cakravartin king, etc.

17. The cries (*utkaṇṭha*) and noises (*dhvani*), great (*adhimātra*), medium (*madhya*) or small (*avara*)

Or again, through his psychic power, a Bodhisattva transforms the various sounds of large, medium or small category of all beings of the ten regions, a Bodhisattva changes them supernaturally (*adhitiṣṭhati*) into Buddha voices (*buddhanirghoṣa*), into words of the Buddha, the Law and the Community (*buddhadharmasaṃghaśabda*), and makes them pronounce the words: "Transitory (*anitya*), painful (*duḥkha*), empty (*śūnya*), impersonal (*anātman*)". From these cries and these sounds (*rutasvara*), the Bodhisattva extracts all the instructions of the Law (*dharmadeśanā*) held in whatever form, by the Blessed Lord Buddhas of the ten regions.

uttered by all the beings of the ten regions. He changes them all into Buddha voices (*buddhanirghoṣa*), and these Buddha voices utter various words (*śabdaviśeṣa*) such as: "Transitory (*anitya*), painful (*duḥkha*), empty (*śūnya*), impersonal (*anātman*), definitive Nirvāṇa (*atyantanirvāṇa*), calm (*śānta*), etc." All the instructions (*dharmadeśanā*) of the Buddhas, Bodhisattvas, Śrāvakas and Pratyekabuddhas are uttered in these sounds; the words (*nāman*), phrases (*pada*) and syllables (*vyañjana*) found in the instructions (*dharmadeśanā*) of the Buddhas of the ten regions are all uttered in these Buddha voices (*buddhanirghoṣa*), so well that beings who are able to hear them are disciplined in conformity with the various Vehicles (*yānaviśeṣa*).

Or once again, a Bodhisattva, adopting the various languages (*niruktaviśeṣa*) used by the beings of the ten regions, utters, according to their rules (*yathāyogam*), various words (*nānāvidhaśabda*) so as to expound the Good Law (*saddharma*). Thus each being finds his profit there[16].

18. Honourable Śāriputra, I have only expounded to you a small part (*kiṃcinmātra*) of this Entry into the realm of the Bodhisattvas established in inconceivable liberation (*acintyavimokṣasthabodhisattvaviṣayapraveśa*). With regard to this teaching (*nirdeśa*), I could speak for a kalpa, more than a kalpa or even longer (*bahv api te bhāṣeyaṃ kalpaṃ vā kalpāvaśeṣaṃ vā tato vopari*)[17].

Śāriputra, it is in a condensed form (*saṃkṣepeṇa*) that I have expounded to you this realm of inconceivable liberation (*acintyavimokṣaviṣaya*) which Bodhisattvas penetrate through skillful means (*upāyakauśalya*) and the power of knowledge (*jñānabala*). If I expounded it to you at length (*vistareṇa*), I would spend at it a kalpa, more than a kalpa or even longer, for just as my knowledge (*jñāna*) and my eloquence (*pratibhāna*) are inexhaustible (*akṣaya*), so is the realm of inconceivable liberation inexhaustible because it is immeasurable (*apramāṇa*).

[16] This last paragraph is only found in H.

[17] This paragraph is missing in Cn. — It reproduces a well known stock phrase which can, for example, be found in the Aṣṭasāh., p. 871,*16-20*: *bahv api te Ānandāhaṃ bhāṣeyaṃ prajñāpāramitāyāḥ parīndanām ārabhya kalpaṃ vā kalpāvaśeṣaṃ vā kalpaśataṃ vā kalpasahasraṃ vā kalpaśatasahasraṃ vā kalpakoṭīṃ vā kalpakoṭīśataṃ vā kalpakoṭīsahasraṃ vā kalpakoṭīśatasahasraṃ vā tato vā upari.*

Westerners persist in translating *kalpaṃ vā kalpāvaśeṣaṃ vā* by "for one kalpa

[*Kāśyapa's Wonder*]

19. Then the disciple (*sthavira*) Kāśyapa, having heard this teaching (*nirdeśa*) on the Inconceivable Liberation of the Bodhisattvas, was filled with wonder (*āścaryaprāpta*) and said to the disciple Śāriputra: Venerable (*āyaṣmant*) Śāriputra, if someone were to present to a man blind from birth (*jātyandha*) forms of all kinds (*nānāvidhapratikṛti*), the man blind from birth would not see any of them; equally, O Venerable Śāriputra, when this text (*mukha*) on inconceivable Liberation, a text so difficult to understand (*durvigāhya*), is recited to them, the Śrāvakas and Pratyekabuddhas are deprived of their eyes (*niścakṣus*) like the man blind from birth and understand absolutely nothing of it. Where then is the intelligent son or daughter of good family who, hearing this inconceivable liberation spoken of, would not produce the thought of supreme and perfect enlightenment?

As for ourselves, men with ruined faculties (*praṇaṣṭendriya*) and who, like a burnt and rotten seed (*dagdhapūtikabīja*) [18], have no part in the Great Vehicle (*mahāyāne na bhājanībhūtāḥ*), what should we do? We ourselves, Śrāvakas and Pratyekabuddhas, having heard this teaching of the Law (*dharmanirdeśa*), should give a cry of pain (*ārtasvara*) which would shatter the trichiliomegachiliocosm (*trisāhasramahāsāhasralokadhātu*) [19].

As for the Bodhisattvas, on hearing this inconceivable liberation (*acintyavimokṣa*) spoken of, they must have conceived a great exultation (*prāmodya*), like a young crown prince (*rājaputrakumāra*) when he takes the diadem (*mukuṭa*) at the moment of consecration (*abhiṣeka*) [20]; they must apply to this teaching all the power of their conviction

or for the remainder of a kalpa", "un kalpa ou le reste d'un kalpa", "eine Weltperiode lang oder den noch übrigen Rest einer solchen". I have translated here along with H 或經一劫或一劫餘 "for a kalpa or more than a kalpa".

[18] Classical comparison: cf. Theragāthā, v. 363, 388: *na virūhati saddhamme khette bījaṃ va pūtikaṃ*. Conversely. Aṅguttara, I, p. 153,*3*; III, p. 404,*20*: *seyyathāpi bhikkhave bījāni akkhaṇḍāni apūtīni... sukhette... nikkhittāni*.

[19] In the texts of the Great Vehicle it often happens that Arhats realise that in following the doctrine of the Hīnayāna, they are not as well informed as they should be, but are far from the knowledge of the Tathāgatas: cf. Saddharmapuṇḍ., p. 60,*5-6*; 210,*1-4*; 211,*10*; below, VII, § 4-5.

[20] Another classical comparison: cf. Dīgha, II, p. 227,*1 3*: *seyyathā pi bhante rājā khattiyo muddhāvasitto adhunābhisitto rajjena, uḷāraṃ so labhati devapaṭilābhaṃ, uḷāraṃ so labhati somanassapaṭilābhaṃ*... — H merely says: "All the Bodhisattvas rejoiced greatly and respectfully accepted this Law".

(*adhimuktibala*). In fact, the Māras can do absolutely nothing against those who are convinced of this inconceivable liberation.

When the disciple Mahākāśyapa had given this address, thirty-two thousand sons of the gods (*devaputra*) produced the thought of supreme and perfect enlightenment (*anuttarāyāṃ samyaksaṃbodhau cittāny utpāditāni*).

[*The Tempter-Bodhisattvas*]

20. Then the Licchavi Vimalakīrti said to the Elder (*sthavira*) Mahākāśyapa: Honourable (*bhadanta*) Kāśyapa, the Māras who behave like Māra (that is, the Tempter) in the innumerable universes (*aprameyalokadhātu*) of the ten regions are [mostly] all[21] Bodhisattvas established in inconceivable liberation (*acintyavimokṣa*) and who, through skillful means (*upāyakauśalyena*), behave like Māra in order to ripen beings (*sattvaparipācanārtham*).

Honourable Mahākāśyapa, to the Bodhisattvas inhabiting the innumerable universes of the ten regions, come beggars (*yācaka*) asking for a hand (*hasta*), a foot (*pāda*), an ear (*śrotra*), a nose (*ghrāṇa*), some muscles (*snāyu*), a bone (*asthi*), some marrow (*majjā*), an eye (*cakṣus*), a chest (*pūrvārdhakāya*), a head (*śiras*), a limb (*aṅga*), a minor limb (*pratyaṅga*), a realm (*rājya*), a kingdom (*rāṣṭra*), some country (*janapada*), a wife (*bhāryā*), a son (*dāraka*), a daughter (*dārikā*), a man-servant (*dāsa*), a maid-servant (*dāsī*), a horse (*aśva*), an elephant (*gaja*), a chariot (*ratha*), a vehicle (*yāna*), some gold (*suvarṇa*), silver (*rūpya*), gems (*maṇi*), pearls (*muktikā*), conch shells (*śaṅkha*), crystals (*śilā*), corals (*vidruma*), beryl (*vai-*

Mahākāśyapa, to the Bodhisattvas inhabiting the innumerable and incalculable universes of the ten regions, come certain people asking for a hand (*hasta*), a foot (*pāda*), an ear (*śrotra*), a nose (*ghrāṇa*), a head (*śiras*), an eye (*cakṣus*), some marrow (*majjā*), a clavicle (*jatru*), some blood (*rudhira*), some flesh (*māṃsa*), any limb (*aṅga*) or minor limb (*pratyaṅga*), a wife (*bhāryā*), a son (*dāraka*), a daughter (*dārikā*), a man-servant (*dāsa*), a maid-servant (*dāsī*), a village (*grāma*), a town (*nagara*), a borough (*nigama*), a province (*janapada*), a kingdom (*rāṣṭra*), a capital (*rājadhānī*), an universe of four continents (*caturdvīpaka*) or some other royal fief (*rājya*), some money and seeds (*dhanadhānya*), jewels (*maṇiratna*), gold (*suvarṇa*), silver (*rūpya*), necklaces (*hāra*), corals (*vidruma*), conch shells (*śaṅkha*), shells (*kapardaka*), beryl (*vaiḍūrya*) or some other ornament (*alaṃkāra*), houses (*gṛha*), beds and chairs (*śayanāsana*), clothing (*cīvara*), drink and food (*pānabhojana*), medicaments (*bhaiṣajya*), embellishments (*pariṣkāra*), an elephant (*gaja*), a horse (*aśva*), a chariot

[21] The Tibetan says "all"; K and H say "many", i.e. "mostly".

ḍūrya), and all kinds of jewels (*maṇiratna*), some food (*bhojana*), drink (*pāna*), sweetmeats (*rasa*), and all kinds of clothing (*vastra*).

Beggars (*yācaka*) as demanding as this are ordinarily (*yadbhūyasā*) Bodhisattvas established in inconceivable liberation (*acintyavimokṣa*) and who, through skillful means (*upāyakauśalyena*), desire to highlight (*saṃdarśayitum*) the solidity of high resolve (*adhyāśayasāratā*) in these same Bodhisattvas. And why? Honourable Mahākāśyapa, only Bodhisattvas can display such cruel demands (*evaṃdāruṇa*). The power (*anubhāva*) of creating difficulties (*saṃkaṭa*) for Bodhisattvas does not exist in ordinary people. No, this is not to be found (*anavakāśo 'yam*). They are not capable of tormenting and demanding in this way. No, this is not to be found.

Honourable Kāśyapa, just as a glow-worm (*khadyotaka*) cannot eclipse (*abhibhū-*) the brilliance of the solar disc (*sūryamaṇḍalaprabhāsa*), so it is impossible and it cannot be found (*asthānam etad anavakāśaḥ*) that they should attack Bodhisattvas and make demands on them[22].

Honourable Kāśyapa, if attacked (*tāḍita*) by a dragon-elephant (*kuñjaro nāgaḥ*), an ass (*gardabha*) is unable to resist it

(*ratha*), a vehicle (*yāna*), some vessels (*bhājana*), large or small, or an army (*senā*).

Beggars (*yācaka*) who thus press Bodhisattvas are, mostly, Bodhisattvas established in inconceivable liberation (*acintyavimokṣa*). It is through skillful means (*upāyakauśalyena*) that they do these things so as to test Bodhisattvas and to demonstrate the solidity of their high resolve (*adhyāśayasāratā*). And why? They are great Bodhisattvas who are very cruel (*atiraudra*) and who, for the benefit of beings (*sattvānāṃ hitāya*) manifest such difficult things. The worldly (*pṛthagjana*) and the foolish (*bāla*) do not have such a power (*anubhāva*) and cannot behave like beggars by thus pressing Bodhisattvas.

Mahākāśyapa, just as a glow-worm (*khadyotaka*) cannot eclipse the solar disc (*sūryamaṇḍala*), so the worldly (*pṛthagjana*) and the foolish (*bāla*) are not capable of behaving like beggars by thus pressing Bodhisattvas.

Mahākāśyapa, if a dragon-elephant (*kuñjaro nāgaḥ*) attacks it, an ass (*gardabha*) does not resist. It is only a dragon-elephant that can contest with a dragon-ele-

[22] This paragraph is missing in Cn and K. — Regarding the *khadyotaka*, see above, III, § 22, note 46.

(*na sahate*). Equally, O Honourable Mahākāśyapa, someone who is not a Bodhisattva cannot cause difficulties (*saṃkaṭa*) to a Bodhisattva; it is only a Bodhisattva who can cause difficulties to a Bodhisattva, and only a Bodhisattva can resist the attacks of another Bodhisattva.

phant. Equally, the worldly (*pṛthagjana*) and the foolish (*bāla*) do not have the power to press a Bodhisattva. Only a Bodhisattva can contest with another Bodhisattva.

Such is, O Honourable Mahākāśyapa, the entry into the power of the knowledge of means (*upāyajñānabalapraveśa*) proper to a Bodhisattva established in inconceivable liberation (*acintyavimokṣasthabodhisattva*).

When Vimalakīrti had given this address, eight thousand Bodhisattvas obtained the realm of this inconceivable liberation, this realm which is penetrated by the power of the knowledge of skillful means.

CHAPTER SIX

THE GODDESS

[*The Inexistence of a Living Being*[1]]

1. Then Mañjuśrī the crown prince said to the Licchavi Vimalakīrti: Worthy man (*satpuruṣa*), how should a Bodhisattva see all beings (*kathaṃ bodhisattvena sarvasattvā draṣṭavyāḥ*)?

Vimalakīrti replied: Mañjuśrī, a Bodhisattva should see all beings[2] as

1. an intelligent man (*dakṣapuruṣa*) sees the moon in the water (*udakacandra*),

2. an able illusionist (*dakṣo māyākāraḥ*) sees a man created by an able illusionist (*māyākāranirmitapuruṣa*).

1. a master illusionist (*māyākāra*) sees the object created by his illusion,

2. a clever man sees the moon in the water (*udakacandra*)[3].

3. as a reflection in a mirror (*ādarśamaṇḍale pratibimbam*),

4. the water of a mirage (*marīcyudaka*),

5. the sound of an echo (*pratiśrutkāsvara*),

6. the massing of clouds in space (*ākāśe megharāśiḥ*),

7. the starting point of a ball of foam (*phenapiṇḍe pūrvāntaḥ*),

8. the appearance and disappearance of a bubble of water (*budbudotpattibhaṅga*),

9. the consistence of the trunk of a banana tree (*kadalīgarbhasāratā*),

[1] The *pudgalanairātmya* is common to both Vehicles. For the Small Vehicle the five *skandha*, wrongly taken to be the Self, are not the Self and do not belong to the Self, but they nevertheless possess a self-nature (*svabhāva*) and specific marks (*lakṣaṇa*). The Great Vehicle, which also proclaims the *dharmanairātmya*, goes even further still along the path of negation: dharmas, taken wrongly for the Self, are not only not the Self and do not belong to the Self, but are themselves without a self-nature (*niḥsvabhāva*), without arising or extinction. It is not enough to say that the Self does not exist: the very notion is illogical. Here Vimalakīrti develops, by increasing it considerably, the classic list of the ten comparisons (see above, II, § 9, note 23) which illustrate the absurdity of the notion of a living being.

[2] The Tibetan and Chinese versions introduce each of the 35 comparisons with the phrase; "The Bodhisattva should see all beings..." I have left out these wearisome repetitions.

[3] H here reproduces K's wording.

10. the course of a flash of lightning (*vidyutsaṃkrama*)[4],

11. the fifth great element (*pañcamadhātu*),

12. the sixth aggregate (*ṣaṣṭhaskandha*)[5],

13. the seventh (internal) basis of consciousness (*saptamāyatana*),

14. the thirteenth basis of consciousness (*trayodaśamāyatana*),

15. the nineteenth element (*navadaśamadhātu*),

16. the presence of a formed object in the world of no-form (*ārūpyadhātau rūpyavabhāsaḥ*)[6],

17. the shoot growing out of a rotten seed (*pūtikabījād aṅkura-prādurbhāvaḥ*)[7],

18. the clothing made of tortoise hair (*kūrmaromavastra*)[8],

19. the taste for jesting in him who seeks death (*martukāme krīḍānandanam*)[9],

20. the belief in a personality (*satkāyadṛṣṭi*) in a Srotaāpanna,

21. a third rebirth here below (*tṛtīyabhava*) in a Sakṛdāgāmin,

22. the descent of an Anāgāmin into a womb (*garbhāvakrānti*),

23. the presence of craving (*rāga*), hatred (*dveṣa*) and delusion (*moha*) in an Arhat[10],

24. the thoughts of avarice (*mātsarya*), immorality (*dauḥśīlya*), animosity (*vyāpāda*) and hostility (*vihiṃsā*) in a Bodhisattva in possession of patience (*kṣāntiprāpta*),

25. the pervasions of the passions (*vāsanā*) in a Tathāgata,

26. the sight of colours (*rūpadarśana*) in a man blind from birth (*jātyandha*),

27. the inhalations and exhalations (*āśvāsapraśvāsa*) in an ascetic dwelling in the recollection of extinction (*nirodhasamāpatti*),

28. the tracks of a bird in the air (*ākāśe śakuneḥ padam*)[11],

[4] K: "The length of life of a flash of lightning".

[5] Comparisons No. 12, 14 and 15, which are missing in Tibetan and Cn, are found in K and H. These are comparisons already used by the Vibhāṣā, T 1545, ch. 76, p. 393 *a* 22.

[6] Read, with N: *gzugs med pa dag la gzugs snaṅ ba ltar*.

[7] Regarding *pūtikabīja*, cf. V, § 19, note 18.

[8] The expression *kūrmaroman*, verified by H, is classical: cf. Madh. vṛtti, p. 100,*1*; 180,*7*. In Tibetan we have *sbal paḥi spu* = *maṇḍūkaroman* "frog's hair". Cn and K omit this comparison.

[9] Missing in Cn and K.

[10] K: "The triple poison (*triviṣa*) in an Arhat".

[11] An old comparison already used in the Dhammapada, v. 92, 93, and the Theragāthā, v. 92: *ākāse va sakuntānaṃ padaṃ tassa durannayaṃ*. — Also see Daśabhūmika, p. 10,*17-18*: *yathāntarikṣe śakuneḥ padaṃ budhair vaktuṃ na śakyaṃ na ca darśanopagam*.

29. the erection of a penis (*lāṅgularohaṇa*) in an eunuch (*paṇḍaka*)[12],

30. the confinement of a sterile woman (*bandhyāprasūti*),

31. the passions (*kleśa*) — absolutely unarisen (*anutpanna*) — in the transformations created by the Tathāgata (*tathāgatanirmāṇa*),

32. the visions of a dream (*svapnadarśana*) after awakening,

33. the passions (*kleśa*) in an undiscriminating being (*asaṃkalpa*),

34. a fire breaking out without cause [K var: a fire without smoke],

35. the passage of one who has achieved Nirvāṇa[13] to a new existence (*parinirvṛtasya pratisaṃdhiḥ*).

O Mañjuśrī, it is thus that a Bodhisattva who exactly understands Anātman considers (*pratyavekṣate*) all beings[14].

It is thus that a Bodhisattva should consider all beings. And why? Because all dharmas are originally empty (*ādiśūnya*) and because in reality there is neither *ātman* nor *sattva*.

[*Goodwill*[15]]

2. Mañjuśrī said: Son of good family (*kulaputra*), if a Bodhisattva considers (*pratyavekṣate*) all beings in this way, how does he produce great goodwill (*mahāmaitrī*) towards them?

Vimalakīrti replied:

Mañjuśrī, a Bodhisattva who considers them thus, says to himself: "I am going to expound the Law to beings in the way that I have understood it". Thus he produces towards all beings a goodwill which is truly protective (*bhūtaśaraṇamaitrī*).

A Bodhisattva who considers beings in this way says to himself: "I am going to expound this Law to beings so that they clearly understand it". It is thus that he truly exercises great goodwill (*maitrī*) and he gives to beings a definitive happiness (*atyantasukha*).

So it is that a Bodhisattva exercises:

a calmed (*upaśānta*) goodwill because it is free from attachment (*upādāna*),

a goodwill without warmth (*atāpa*) because it is without passion (*niṣkleśa*),

[12] Missing in Cn and K.

[13] H replaces "one who has achieved Nirvāṇa" by "Arhat".

[14] K concludes in the same way.

[15] Compare this and the following section with the canonical definition of the four *apramāṇa*, also known as *brahmavihāra*: cf. WOODWARD, *Concordance*, II, p. 138 *a* s.v. *mettāsahagatena cetasā*; Kośa, VIII, p. 196 sq.

Here, at the end of § 2, H adds a whole series of qualifications which do not appear in Tibetan, Cn and K.

an exact (*yathābhūta*) goodwill because it is the same (*sama*) in the three phases of time (*tryadhvan*),

a goodwill without obstacle (*aniruddha*) because it avoids the invasion of the passions (*paryutthāṇa*),

a goodwill without duality (*advaya*) for it is not related (*asaṃsṛṣṭa*) to the internal (*adhyātmam*) and the external (*bahirdhā*),

an unshakable (*akṣobhya*) goodwill because it is absolutely fast (*atyantaparyavasita*),

a firm (*dṛḍha*) goodwill because its high resolve (*adhyāśaya*) is as indestructible (*abhedya*) as a diamond (*vajra*),

a completely pure (*pariśuddha*) goodwill because it is naturally pure (*svabhāvapariśuddha*),

an even (*sama*) goodwill because its good intentions (*āśaya*) are the same (*sama*),

an even (*sama*) goodwill[16] because it is the same as space (*ākāśasama*),

a goodwill of an Arhat because it is the slayer of enemies (*arīṇāṃ hatatvāt*)[17],

a goodwill of a Pratyekabuddha because it does not rely on a teacher (*ācārya*),

a goodwill of a Bodhisattva because, ceaselessly (*satatam*), it ripens (*paripācayati*) beings,

a goodwill of a Tathāgata because it penetrates (*anubodhate*) the suchness (*tathatā*) of dharmas,

a goodwill of a Buddha because it awakens beings from their somnolence (*sattvān svapnād vibodhayati*),

an innate (*svarasamaya*) goodwill because it is spontaneously enlightened (*svarasenābhisaṃbuddha*)[18],

a goodwill of awakening (*bodhi*) because it is of even flavour (*samarasa*),

a goodwill without uncalled-for affirmation (*anāropa*) because it is free of affection (*anunaya*) and aversion (*pratigha*),

a goodwill of great compassion (*mahākaruṇā*) because it brings about the shining (*avabhāsayati*) of the Great Vehicle (*mahāyāna*),

a goodwill without repugnance (*aparikheda*) because it takes into

a goodwill without dispute (*araṇa*) because it takes into account (*pratya-*

[16] K: "A goodwill without limit (*aparyanta*)".

[17] Here Vimalakīrti is exploiting one of the many fanciful etymologies of the word Arhat: *arīnaṃ arānañ ca hattatā* (cf. Sumaṅgalavilāsinī, I, p. 146,*10*; NĀGĀRJUNA, *Traité*, p. 127).

[18] K: "A spontancous goodwill for it exists without cause".

account (*pratyavekṣate*) emptiness (*śūnya*) and Non-Self (*anātman*),

vekṣate) Non-Self (*anātman*); a goodwill without repugnance (*parikheda*) because it takes into account intrinsic emptiness (*svabhāvaśūnya*),

a goodwill which practises the giving of the Law (*dharmadāna*) because it is not of those teachers who close their fists (*ācāryamuṣṭi*)[19],

a goodwill which observes pure morality (*śīla*) because it helps ripen immoral beings (*duḥśīlasattvān paripācayati*),

a goodwill which observes patience (*kṣānti*) because it protects (*pālayati*) its own person and that of others so as to avoid all offence (*upaghāta*),

a vigorous (*vīrya*) goodwill because it bears the burden of all beings (*sarvasattvānāṃ bhāram ānayati*),

a goodwill concerned with vigour (*vīrya*) because it undertakes the welfare and happiness (*hitasukha*) of all beings,

a goodwill which devotes itself to transic meditation (*dhyāna*), but only because it abstains from tasting its flavour (*rasāsvādana*)[20],

a goodwill filled with wisdom (*prajñā*) because it obtains it (*prāpnoti*) in due time,

a goodwill which cultivates wisdom (*prajñā*) because, at all times, it understands the Law clearly,

a goodwill linked to skillful means (*upāya*), because everywhere (*sarvatra*) it shows the way (*dvārāṇi deśayati*),

a goodwill which cultivates good vows (*praṇidhāna*) because it is led (*samudānīta*) by innumerable great vows (*apramāṇamahāpraṇidhāna*),

a goodwill which exercises great power (*bala*) because it accomplishes (*sādhayati*) all great things,

a goodwill which cultivates knowledge (*jñāna*) because it discerns (*vijānāti*) the nature (*svabhāva*) and marks (*lakṣaṇa*) of dharmas,

a goodwill which exercises the super-knowledges (*abhijñā*) because it does not disprove the nature (*svabhāva*) and marks (*lakṣaṇa*) of dharmas,

a goodwill which exercises the means of conversion (*saṃgrahavastu*) because it adroitly (*upāyena*) wins over (*saṃgṛhṇāti*) all beings,

a goodwill of detachment (*asaṅga*) because it is free from all obstacles (*āvaraṇa*) and defilements (*saṃkleśa*),

a goodwill without falseness (*dambha*) because of the purity of its good intentions (*āśayaviśuddhi*),

a goodwill without hypocrisy (*mrakṣa*) because of the purity of its efforts (*yogaviśuddhi*),

[19] To make known his unwillingness to teach, the master closes his fist. cf. Dīgha, II, p. 100,*4*; Saṃyutta, V, p. 153,*19*; Sanskrit Mahāparinirvāṇa, p. 196; Lalitavistara, p. 179,*12*; Kāśyapaparivarta, § 1; Bodh. bhūmi, p. 41,*28*; 106,*18*; 363,*14*.

[20] See above, II, § 3, note 10.

a goodwill without guile (*śāṭhya*) because it acts according to its good intentions (*āśaya*),	a goodwill without guile (*śāṭhya*) because it is free from artifice (*akṛtrima*),

a goodwill of high resolve (*adhyāśaya*) because it is undefiled (*niṣkleśa*),

a goodwill without illusion (*māyā*) because it is without artifice (*akṛtrima*),

a goodwill of happiness (*sukha*) because it leads (*niveśayati*) into the happiness of the Buddhas (*buddhasukha*),

Such is, O Mañjuśrī, the great goodwill (*mahāmaitrī*) of the Bodhisattva.

[*Compassion, Joy and Equanimity*]

3. *Mañj.* — What is the great compassion (*mahākaruṇā*) of the Bodhisattva?

Vim. — It is the abandoning (*parityāga*) to beings without retaining any of all good roots (*kuśalamūla*) enacted (*kṛta*) or accumulated (*upacita*)[21].

Mañj. — What is the great joy (*mahāmuditā*) of the Bodhisattva?

Vim. — It is rejoicing in (*saumanasya*) and not regretting (*akaukṛtya*) giving.	It is rejoicing in and not regretting benefiting (*arthakriyā*) all beings,

Mañj. — What is the great equanimity (*mahopekṣā*) of the Bodhisattva?

Vim. — It is benefiting (*arthakriyā*) impartially without hope of reward (*vipāka*).

[*Baselessness*[22]]

4. *Saṃsārabhayabhītena kiṃ pratisartavyam — āha: saṃsārabhayabhītena, Mañjuśrīr, bodhisattvena buddhamāhātmyāṃ pratisartavyam. āha: buddhamāhātmyasthātukāmena kutra sthātavyam. — āha: buddhamāhātmye sthātukāmena sarvasattvasamatāyāṃ sthātavyam. — āha: sarvasattvasamatāyāṃ sthātukāmena kutra sthātavyam. — āha: sarvasattvasamatāyāṃ sthātukāmena sarvasattvapramokṣāya sthātavyam*[23].

Mañj. — A Bodhisattva beset by the fear of rebirth, to where should he withdraw?

[21] On the difference between an action which is done (*kṛta*) and which is accumulated (*upacita*), see Kośa, IV, p. 114; 242-244.

[22] Regarding baselessness in the Madhyamaka system, see Introduction, p. LXIX-LXXII.

[23] Exact from the original text quoted in the Śikṣāsamuccaya, p. 145,*11-15*.

Vim. — A Bodhisattva beset by the fear of rebirth should withdraw into the magnanimity of the Buddhas.

Mañj.—He who desires to abide in the magnanimity of the Buddhas, where should he abide?

Vim. — He who desires to abide in the magnanimity of the Buddhas should abide in the sameness of all beings.

Mañj. — He who desires to abide in the sameness of all beings, where should he abide?

Vim. — He who desires to abide in the sameness of all beings should seek to deliver all beings.

5. *Mañj.* — He who desires to deliver all beings, what should he do?

Vim. — He who desires to deliver all beings should free them from their passions (*kleśa*).

Manj. — He who desires to free them from their passions, what effort should he make (*kiṃ prayoktavyam*)?

Vim. — He who desires to destroy their passions should exercise right effort (*yoniśo prayoktavyam*).	He who desires to destroy the passions of all beings should cultivate investigation (*parīkṣā*) and right mental activity (*yoniśo manasikāra*).
Mañj. — With what kind of effort (*prayoga*) should he exert himself rightly (*yoniśaḥ*)?	He who desires to cultivate investigation and right mental activity, what should he exercise?
Vim. — He should rightly make the effort concerning non-arising (*anutpāda*) and non-extinction (*anirodha*).	He who desires to cultivate investigation and right mental activity should cultivate the non-arising (*anutpāda*) and non-extinction (*anirodha*) of dharmas.
Mañj. — What does not arise and what is not extinguished?	Which are the dharmas that do not arise and which are the dharmas that are not extinguished?

Vim. — Bad (*akuśala*) dharmas do not arise (*notpadyante*) and good ones (*kuśala*) are not extinguished.

Mañj. — What is the root (*mūla*) of good and bad dharmas?

Vim. — They have "aggregation" (*kāya*) as their root[24].

Mañj. — What is the root of aggregation?

Vim. — The root of aggregation is craving (*kāmarāga*).

Mañj. — What is the root of craving?

Vim. — The root of craving is false imagination (*abhūtaparikalpa*).

[24] Here the Tibetan renders *kāya* by *ḥjigs tshogs*, a term which appears in the expression *ḥjigs tshogs la lta ba* = *satkāyadṛṣṭi* "belief in the aggregation of perishable things".

6. *Abhūtaparikalpasya kiṃ mūlam. — āha: viparyastā saṃjñā mūlam. — āha: viparyastāyāḥ saṃjñāyāḥ kiṃ mūlam. — āha: apratiṣṭhānaṃ mūlam. — āha: apratiṣṭhāyāḥ kiṃ mūlam. — āha: yan, Mañjuśrīr, apratiṣṭhānaṃ na tasya kiṃcin mūlam iti hy apratiṣṭhānamūlapratiṣṭhitāḥ sarvadharmāḥ*[25].

Mañj. — What is the root of false imagination?

Vim. — The root of false imagination is distorted perception.

Mañj. — What is the root of distorted perception?

Vim. — The root of distorted perception is the absence of a basis (*apratiṣṭhāna*).

Mañj. — What is the root of the absence of a basis?

Vim. — O, Mañjuśrī, this absence of a basis has no root; that is why all dharmas rest on a baseless root.

[*The Devī and the Miracle of the Flowers*]

7. Then a goddess (*devī*) who lived in the house (*gṛha*) of Vimalakīrti, having heard this teaching of the Law (*dharmanirdeśa*) by the Bodhisattva Mahāsattvas, was filled with astonishment (*āścaryaprāpta*): well-pleased (*tuṣṭa*), delighted (*udagra*), transported (*āttamanāḥ*), she took on a gross material form (*audārikam ātmabhāvam abhisaṃdṛśya*)[26] and scattered heavenly flowers over these great Bodhisattvas and great Listeners (*divyaiḥ puṣpais tān mahābodhisattvāṃs tāṃś ca mahāśrāvakān avakirati sma*). When she had cast them, the flowers that settled (*avatīrṇa*) on the bodies of the Bodhisattvas fell to the ground (*bhūmau prapatanti sma*), while those that settled on the bodies of the great

[25] Extract from the original text quoted in Śikṣāsamuccaya, p. 264,*6-9*. — Śāntideva, in his Śikṣāsamuccaya, p. 264,*3-5*, introduces the quotation with the following thoughts: "If *saṃvṛti* is baseless (*anadhiṣṭhāna*), how can it exist? — Why should it not exist? In the same way that in the absence of a post, one can wrongly imagine that one can see a man. And which is the Śunyavādin who would allow in absolute truth (*paramārthatas*) the existence of a post which could be the support (*āśraya*) of the illusion that one sees a man (*puruṣabhrānti*)? Dharmas are absolutely rootless (*amūla*), for no root exists in reality (*tattvatas*). Thus as the Vimalakīrtinirdeśa teaches...".

Such is not the opinion of the Vijñānavādins. For them, the *saṃvṛti* dharmas exist by reasons of a certain *dharmatā* or *tathatā*, i.e. Mind-only (*vijñaptimātratā*), ineffable, devoid of imagining (*parikalpita*); then again, they are empty (*śūnya*) by reason of a certain emptiness (the non-existence of *parikalpita*).

Regarding the Madhyamaka-Yogācāra conflict, see especially L. DE LA VALLÉE POUSSIN, *Réflexions sur le Madhyamaka*, MCB, II, 1932-33, p. 47-54.

[26] Traditional expression: cf. Dīgha, II, p. 210,*5-6*: *oḷārikaṃ attabhāvaṃ abhinimminitvā pātu bhavati*.

Listeners remained clinging (*sakta*) there and did not fall to the ground. Then the great Listeners resorted to their psychic power (*ṛddhi*) to shake off (*saṃdhotum*) these flowers; but the flowers did not fall away.

8. Then the devī asked the Venerable (*āyuṣmant*) Śāriputra: Honourable (*bhadanta*) Śāriputra, why do you shake off these flowers?

Śāriputra replied: Devī, flowers are not fitting (*ayogya*) to the religious[27]; that is why we reject them (*utsṛjāmaḥ*).

The devī continued: Honourable Śāriputra, say not so. And why? These flowers are perfectly fitting (*yogya*); it is only yourselves, Honourable Sirs, who are not fit. And why is this? These flowers are flowers free of concept (*akalpaka*) and free of discrimination (*nirvikalpaka*); it is only yourselves, the Elders (*sthavira*), who conceive them (*kalpayatha*) and discriminate (*vikalpayatha*) regarding them. Honourable Śāriputra, among those who have renounced the world to take up the religious discipline so well expounded (*svākhyātadharmavinaye pravrajitaḥ*), these concepts (*kalpana*) and discriminations (*vikalpana*) are not fitting (*ayogya*); it is those who conceive of neither concepts nor discriminations who are fit (*yukta*).

Honourable Śāriputra, look well (*paśya*) on these Bodhisattva Mahāsattvas: the flowers do not cling to them because they have dropped concepts and discriminations. Now look at the Listeners: the flowers cling to their bodies because they have not dropped all concepts and discriminations.

Thus non-human spirits (*amanuṣya*) have a hold (*avatāraṃ labhante*)[28] on a fearful man (*bhītajātīya*), but cannot penetrate him who has no fear (*viśārada*). Equally, forms (*rūpa*), sounds (*śabda*), odours (*gandha*), tastes (*rasa*) and tangibles (*spraṣṭavya*) have a hold on those who are fearful of the dangers of rebirth (*saṃsārabhayabhīta*); but what could they do against those who no longer fear the passions of the world of formations (*saṃskārakleśabhayavigata*)?

Flowers cling to those who have not yet dispelled the pervasions of the passions (*aparikṣīṇavāsana*); they do not cling to those who

[27] The seventh *śikṣāpada* forbids monks the use of garlands, perfumes and other adornments: *mālāgandhavilepanadhāraṇamaṇḍanavibhūṣanaṭṭhāna* (*Vinaya*, I, p. 83,*37*; Aṅguttara, I, p. 212,*19*).

[28] Regarding *avatāra* (in Pāli, *otāra*) in the sense of aggression, cf. WOODWARD, *Concordance*, I, p. 445, s.v. *labhati otāraṃ, otārāpekkho*; EDGERTON, *Hybrid Sanskrit Dictionary*, p. 71 *b*, s.v. *avatāra*, No. 4. Add to the references given by the latter, Aṣṭasāh., p. 243,*22*; 885,*26*; Saddharmapuṇḍ., p. 400,*10*; 474,*6*; 476,*8*; below, XII, § 22, note 39.

have dispelled them (*parikṣīṇavāsana*). That is why they do not cling to the bodies (of these Bodhisattvas) who have dispelled all the pervasions of the passions.

[*Deliverance*]

9. Then the Venerable Śāriputra asked the devī: Devī, how long ago (*kiyacciram*) did you come to this house?

Devī. — I have been here since the instant that Śāriputra the Elder (*sthavira*) entered deliverance (*vimukti*).

Śārip. — Devī, have you been in this house for a long time?

Devī. — Has Śāriputra the Elder been in a state of deliverance for a long time?

Upon which, Śāriputra the Elder kept silent (*tūṣṇīṃbhūta*) and did not reply.

The devī continued: Elder (*sthavira*), you, the foremost among the great sages (*mahāprajñāvatām agryaḥ*), you say nothing, you turn away and do not answer the question!

The devī continued: Elder, you are a great Listener (*śrāvaka*), endowed with great wisdom (*prajñā*) and great eloquence (*pratibhāna*). And over this small question, you keep silent and do not answer at all!

Śārip. — Deliverance (*vimukti*) being inexpressible (*anabhilāpya*), I do not know what to say concerning it [29].

Devī. — The syllables pronounced by the Elder are all marks of deliverance (*yāny akṣarāṇi sthavireṇoktāni tāni sarvāṇi vimuktilakṣaṇāni*). And why?

This deliverance is neither inward, nor outward nor apart from either (*na sā vimuktir adhyātmaṃ na bahirdhā nobhayam antareṇa*): it is to be found in the middle (*madhye*) [30]. Equally, syllables (*akṣara*) are neither inward, nor outward nor apart from either: they are to be found in the middle. That is why, O Venerable Śāriputra, you must not speak at all of deliverance as being apart from syllables. And why?

[29] The earliest texts acknowledge that nothing can be said of one who has "gone" (cf. Suttanipāta, v. 1076).

[30] K translates: "This deliverance is neither inward, nor outward nor *between* the two (*nobhayam antareṇa*)"; The Tibetan and H understand: "neither inward nor outward nor *without* the two". In Sanskrit the word *antareṇa* "between, without" allows both interpretations. However H adds further: "it is to be found in the middle". This addition seems to me to be a Vijñānavādin interpolation, for from the Vimalakīrti's point of view, deliverance, which cannot be obtained, does not exist at all.

Because the sameness of all dharmas (*sarvadharmasamatā*) constitutes holy deliverance (*ārya-vimukti*).

Because deliverance and all dharmas are by nature the same (*svabhāvasama*).

Śārip. — But is it not the destruction of craving (*rāga*), hatred (*dveṣa*) and delusion (*moha*) that constitutes deliverance?

Devī. — It is for the distracted (*abhimānika*) that the Buddha said: "The exhaustion of craving, hatred and delusion, this is what is called deliverance" (*rāgakkhayo dosakkhayo mohakkhayo ayaṃ vuccati bhikkhave mutti*)[31]. But for those who are not at all distracted (*anabhimānika*) he has said that craving, hatred and delusion are in themselves (*svabhāvena*) deliverance.

[*Wisdom and Eloquence*]

10. Then the Venerable Śāriputra said to the devī: Excellent, excellent (*sādhu*), O Goddess. What have you obtained (*kiṃ prāpya*), what have you achieved (*kiṃ sākṣātkṛtya*) so as to possess such wisdom (*evaṃrūpā prajñā*) and such eloquence (*evaṃrūpaṃ pratibhānaṃ*)?

Devī. — It is because I have not obtained anything, not achieved anything that my wisdom and my eloquence are such. Those who think they have obtained or achieved something are the distracted ones (*abhimānika*) in the religious discipline so well expounded (*svākhyāta-dharmavinaya*).

[*The Triple Vehicle*]

11. *Śārip.* — Goddess, do you belong to the Vehicle of the Listeners (*śrāvakayānika*), the Vehicle of the Solitary Buddhas (*pratyeka-buddhayānika*) or the Great Vehicle (*mahāyānika*)?

Devī. — Because I expound (*deśayāmi*) the vehicle of the Listeners, I am a Śrāvakayānika; because I have passed through the door of the twelve limbed

Śārip. — In which of the three Vehicles did you set out (*samprasthita*)?

Devī. — I set out in all three Vehicles at once.

Śārip. — With what hidden intention (*kiṃ saṃdhāya*) do you say that?

Devī. — Because I always expound the Great Vehicle so that others may hear it, I am a Śrāvakayānika; because I have understood for myself (*svatas*) the true nature of dharmas (*bhūtadharmatā*), I am

[31] Canonical saying: cf. Saṃyutta, III, p. 26,*6*; 26,*28*; IV, p. 251,*19*; 261,*19*; 359,*11*; 360,*5*; 362,*7*, with slight variations.

dependent co-production (*dvādaśāṅgapratītyasamutpādamukha*), I am a Pratyekabuddhayānika; because I never abandon great compassion (*mahākaruṇā*), I am a Mahāyānika[32].

a Pratyekabuddhayānika; because I never abandon great goodwill (*maitrī*) and great compassion (*karuṇā*), I am a Mahāyānika.

Besides, O Śāriputra, because I convert beings who follow the Vehicle of the Listeners, I am a Śrāvakayānika; because I convert beings who follow the Vehicle of the Solitary Buddhas, I am a Pratyekabuddhayānika; because I convert beings who follow the unsurpassable Vehicle (*anuttarayāna*), I am a Mahāyānika.

[32] In K, § 11 is translated in the following way:

Śāriputra asks the Devī: "Which of the three Vehicles do you pursue?

The Devī replies: Because I convert beings through the law of the Śrāvakas, I am a Śrāvaka; because I convert beings through the law of causation (*nidānadharma*), I am a Pratyekabuddha; because I convert beings through the law of great compassion (*mahākaruṇā*), I am a Mahāyānika. — As can be seen, K is close to the Tibetan; H is much more developed.

The Vimalakīrti does not teach the One Vehicle as clearly as other Mahāyānasūtras. Among these we can quote:

1. Prajñāpāramitāstotra of Rāhulabhadra (reproduced at the beginning of several of the Prajñā manuscripts):

Buddhaiḥ pratyekabuddhaiś ca śrāvakaiś ca nisevitā,
mārgas tvam eko mokṣasya, nāsty anya iti niścayaḥ.

"You are cultivated by the Buddhas, Pratyekabuddhas and Śrāvakas. You are the single path to deliverance; there is no other: this is certain".

2. Saddharmapuṇḍ., p. 40,*13-15*: *ekam evāhaṃ yānam ārabhya sattvānāṃ dharmaṃ deśayāmi yad idaṃ buddhayānam, na kiṃcid dvitīyaṃ va tṛtīyaṃ vā yānaṃ saṃvidyate.*

"It is for a single Vehicle only that I expound the Law to beings. A second or third Vehicle absolutely does not exist".

3. Ibid., p. 46,*11-14*:

Ekaṃ hi yānaṃ dvitiyaṃ na vidyate
tṛtiyaṃ hi naivāsti kadāci loke,
Anyatrupāyā puruṣottamānāṃ
yad yānanānātvupadarśayanti.
Bauddhasya jñānasya prakāśanārthaṃ
loke samutpadyati lokanāthaḥ.
Ekaṃ hi kāryaṃ dvitiyaṃ na vidyate
na hīnayānena nayanti buddhāḥ.

"There is only one Vehicle, a second one does not exist; nor is there a third one either, anywhere whatsoever in the world, except in the case where, making use of the means [at their disposal], the Best of men teach that there are several Vehicles. It is in order to explain the knowledge of the Buddhas that the Leader of the world is born in the world; the Buddhas, in fact, have only a single aim, and do not have a second one; they do not transport [men] in a wretched Vehicle" [Translated after E. Burnouf].

4. Sarvadharmavaipulyasaṃgraha, quoted in Śikṣāsamuccaya, p. 95,*15*: *na mayā*

12. Honourable Śāriputra, just as he who enters a Campaka wood does not smell the (unpleasant) odour of an Eraṇḍa (castor-oil plant), but only smells the fragrance (*gandha*) of the Campaka (magnolia), so those who live in this house perfumed with the virtues of the Buddhadharma (*buddhadharmaguṇagandhopeta*) do not smell the scent of the Listeners (*śrāvaka*) or that of the Pratyekabuddhas.

Honourable Śāriputra, the Śakras, Brahmās, Lokapālas, Devas,

Śāriputra, just as a man entering a Campaka wood smells only the perfume of the Campaka and feels no pleasure in inhaling the scents of other essences, so those who live in this house smell only the perfume of the virtues (*guṇa*) of the Mahāyāna and do not at all appreciate the scents of the virtues of the Śrāvakas or the Pratyekabuddhas. It is because this house is always perfumed (*vāsita*) with the exquisite fragrances of all the Buddhas.

Śāriputra, the Śakras, Brahmās, Cāturmahārājika devas, Nāgas, Yakṣas, Asu-

pṛthak kaścid dharmaḥ śrāvakayānasaṃprayuktaḥ pratyekabuddhayānasaṃprayukto mahāyānasaṃprayukto deśitaḥ. tat te mohapuruṣā imaṃ mama dharmaṃ nānākariṣyanti. idaṃ śrāvakāṇāṃ deśitam idaṃ pratyekabuddhānāṃ idaṃ bodhisattvānām iti. sa nānātvasaṃjñayā saddharmaṃ pratikṣipati.

"Never have I separately expounded a law in relation to the Śrāvaka Vehicle, a law in relation to the Pratyekabuddha Vehicle, a law in relation to the Great Vehicle. But foolish people will bring such distinctions to bear on my words, saying: this has been expounded to the Śrāvakas, that to the Pratyekabuddhas and that again to the Bodhisattvas. It is by conceiving such distinctions that one goes against the Good Law".

5. Laṅkāvatāra, p. 135,2-5 (cf. P. DEMIÉVILLE, *Concile de Lhasa*, p. 53, 132):

yānānāṃ nāsti vai niṣṭhā yāvac cittaṃ pravartate,
citte tu vai parāvṛtte na yānaṃ na ca yāninaḥ.
yānavyavasthānaṃ naivāsti yānam ekaṃ vadāmy aham,
parikarṣaṇārthaṃ bālānāṃ yānabhedaṃ vadāmy aham.

"There is nothing that could be definitive concerning the Vehicles, while the mind is at work. When the mind is converted, there is neither Vehicle nor Vehicle-user. The non-establishment of an old Vehicle, this is what I call the One Vehicle. It is in order to train the foolish that I speak of a multiplicity of Vehicles".

For Vimalakīrti as well, the One Vehicle is the absence of any Vehicle. He indubitably launched, in Ch. III, § 22, a violent attack on the Śrāvakas whom he compares with those who are born blind. But, in Ch. VIII, § 5 and 30, he will deny any distinction between Śrāvaka mind and Bodhisattva mind, between good and bad paths to salvation.

To expound the Law, teach a Vehicle, "it is as if an illusionary man was speaking to other illusionary men". What instruction could there be on anything whatsoever? "The word instructor is an uncalled-for affirmation; the word listener is also an uncalled-for affirmation. Where there exists no uncalled-for affirmation, there is no one to instruct, to hear or to understand" (III, § 7).

As for the rest, "there is no-one who is not already in Parinirvāṇa" (III, § 51); so what is the use of expounding a particular Vehicle of salvation?

Nāgas, Yakṣas, Gandharvas, Asuras, Garuḍas, Kiṃnaras and Mahoragas, who live in this house, hear the Law from the lips of this worthy man (*satpuruṣa*) and, because of the fragrance of the virtues of the Buddha (*buddhaguṇagandha*), hasten to produce the thought of Enlightenment (*bodhicitta*).

Honourable Śariputra, I, who have been in this house for twelve years, have only heard mention (*kathā*) here of great goodwill (*mahāmaitrī*), great compassion (*mahākaruṇā*) and the inconceivable attributes of the Buddhas (*acintyabuddhadharma*); I have not heard anything regarding the Śrāvakas and Pratyekabuddhas.

ras and, in general, all the Manuṣyas and Amanuṣyas who enter this house encounter this worthy man, serve him (*satkurvanti*), venerate him (*gurukurvanti*), pay homage to him (*pūjayanti*) and listen to the great Law: all produce the thought of great Enlightenment (*mahābodhicitta*) and depart once more from this house with the exquisite fragrance of all the virtues of the Buddhas.

Śāriputra, I have lived in this house for twelve years; never have I heard mention here of anything concerning the Śrāvakas and the Pratyekabuddhas; I have only heard mention here of the Great Vehicle, the practices (*caryā*) of the Bodhisattvas, great goodwill, great compassion and the inconceivable attributes of the Buddhas.

[*The Eight Wonders of Vimalakīrti's House*]

13. Honourable Śāriputra, in this house, there are continually (*satatasamitam*) in evidence eight wonderful and extraordinary things (*āścaryādbhutadharma*): What are these eight?

1. Because of the golden-hued brilliance (*suvarṇavarṇaprabhā*) which shines here continually (*satatasamitam*), there is no longer any difference between night (*rātri*) and day (*divasa*); and it could not be said that the moon (*candra*) and the sun (*sūrya*) illumine this house: such is the first wonder (*āścaryādbhutadharma*).

2. *Punar aparaṃ bhadanta Śāriputra ye praviśantīdaṃ gṛhaṃ teṣāṃ samanantarapraviṣṭānāṃ sarvakleśā na bādhante 'yaṃ dvitīya āścaryādbhuto dharmaḥ*[33].

Furthermore, Honourable Śāriputra, all beings — human (*manuṣya*) or non-human (*amanuṣya*) — who come into this house have no sooner entered than no passion torments them any longer: such is the second wonderful and extraordinary thing.

[33] Extract from the original text, quoted in the Śikṣāsamuccaya, p. 269,*11-12*.

3. Furthermore, Honourable Śāriputra, this house is never deserted by Śakra, Brahmā, the Lokapālas nor by the Bodhisattvas who have come from other Buddha-fields (*anyabuddhakṣetrasaṃnipatita*): such is the third wonder.

4. Furthermore, Honourable Śāriputra, this house is never deprived of the sounds of the Law (*dharmaśabda*) nor mention of the six perfections (*ṣaṭpāramitāsaṃprayuktakathā*), nor mention of the irreversible wheel of the Law (*avaivartikadharmacakrasaṃprayuktakathā*): such is the fourth wonder.

5. Furthermore, Honourable Śāriputra, in this house, there can always be heard the drums (*dundubhi*), songs (*saṃgīta*) and music (*vādya*) of gods and men (*devamanuṣya*), and from these drums emanate at all times (*sarvakāle*) the innumerable (hundreds of thousands of) sounds of the Law of the Buddhas (*buddhadharmaśabda*): such is the fifth wonder.

6. Furthermore, Honourable Śāriputra, in this house, there are always to be found the four inexhaustible great treasures (*akṣayamahānidhāna*), filled with all the jewels (*sarvaratnaparipūrṇa*)[34]. Their power

[34] Reference to the four great treasures (*mahānidhi*, *mahānidhāna*) of which Buddhist tradition speaks. They bear the names of their guardians, the *catvāro mahārājāś caturmahānidhiṣṭhāḥ* (Divyāvadāna, p. 61,*1-2*) or *catvāro nidhānādhipatayo nāgarājāno* (Mahāvastu, III, p. 383,*20*). According to most of the sources, they will appear on Maitreya's advent as Buddha. According to others (No. 4 and 5 below), they are already in existence and are made use of by the local inhabitants, every seven years, on the seventh day of the seventh month:

1. A stanza tells where they are located:

Piṅgalaś ca Kaliṅgeṣu, Mithilāyāṃ ca Pāṇḍukaḥ,
Elāpatraś ca Gāndhāre, Śaṅkho Vārāṇasīpure.

Cf. Divyāvadāna, p. 61,*3-4*; Vin. of the Mūlasarv., T 1448, ch. 6, p. 25 *a* 12-15; Maitreyavyākaraṇa, T 455, p. 426 *c* 1-4.

2. As under 1, with the difference that Piṅgala is located in Surāṣṭra: cf. Ekottara, T 125, ch. 44, p. 788 *a* 14-18; ch. 49, p. 818 *c* 6-18; 819 *a* 16-17; Maitreyavyākaraṇa, T 453, p. 421 *b* 19-22; T 454, p. 424 *a* 26-28; T 456, p. 430 *a* 10-13.

3. As under 1, with the difference that Pāṇḍuka is located in Bcom-brlag = Mathurā: cf. the Tibetan version of the Maitreyavyākaraṇa, ed. S. Lévi, *Mélanges Linossier*, II, p. 384, v. 24; ed. N. Dutt, *Gilgit Manuscripts*, IV, p. 194,*13-16*.

4. As under 1, with the difference that Pāṇḍuka is located in Vidiśā: cf. Upāsakaśīlasūtra, T 1488, ch. 5, p. 1063 *a*.

5. As under 1, with the difference that Elāpatra is located in Takṣaśilā: cf. Mahāvastu, III, p. 383,*18-19*: *catvāro mahānidhayo: Saṃkho Vārāṇasyāṃ, Mithilāyāṃ Padumo, Kaliṅgeṣu Piṃgalo, Takṣaśilāyāṃ Elapattro.*

6. Elāpatra in the Northern region, in the town of Takṣaśilā; Pāṇḍuka in Kaliṅga country, in the town of Mithilā; Piṅgala in Vidiśā country, in the town of Surāṣṭra;

is such that all beings, poor (*daridra*), unhappy (*dīna*) and wretched (*kṛpaṇa*), who come to take them are all laden without these treasures ever being exhausted: such is the sixth wonder.

7. Furthermore, Honourable Śāriputra, in this house, the Tathāgatas Śākyamuni, Amitābha, Akṣobhya, Ratnaśrī, Ratnārcis, Ratnacandra, Ratnavyūha, Duṣprasaha, Sarvārthasiddha, Ratnabahula, Siṃhakīrti, Siṃhasvara[35] and the innumerable Tathāgatas of the ten regions (*daśadiktathāgata*) all hasten hither in due time at the first wish of this worthy man (*tasya satpuruṣasya sahacittamātreṇa*) and come to expound the introduction to the Law (*dharmamukhapraveśa*) called the *Tathāgataguhyaka*[36]; after having expounded it, they go back (*nivartante*): such is the seventh wonder.

Śaṅkha in Kaśī country, in the town of Vārāṇasī: cf. the Sūtra of the Conversion of the seven Sons by Anāthapiṇḍada, T 140, p. 862 *b*.

7. Treasure of gold in Gandhāra, guarded by the nāga Elāpatra; treasure of silver guarded by the nāga Pāṇḍuka; treasure of *maṇi* in Surāṣṭra, guarded by the nāga Piṅgala; treasure of *vaiḍūrya* in Vārāṇasī: cf. Maitreyavyākaraṇa, T 457, p. 434 *c*.

8. Simple mention of the four treasures in the *Pūrvāparāntasūtra* of the Madhyama, T 26, ch. 14, p. 513 *a* 15.

9. In the Hsi yü chi, T 2087, ch. 3, p. 884 *c* 8-11, Hsüan-tsang describes, in the region of Takṣaśilā, about thirty li to the south-east of Elāpatra the dragon's pool, one of Aśoka's stūpas, a hundred feet high. This stūpa marked the spot where one of the four great treasures should emerge spontaneously when Maitreya becomes Buddha. Archeologists identify this stūpa with the ruins that overlook present-day Baotī Piṇḍ: cf. Sir John MARSHALL, *Taxila*, I, Cambridge, 1951, p. 348.

Undoubtedly these treasures only existed in the Indians' imagination. In contrast, the Chinese instituted the circulation of the "Inexhaustible Treasure": cf. below, VII, §6, stanza 34.

[35] In enumerating these Tathāgatas, I am here following the order given in the Tibetan version. Śākyamuni, Amitābha and Akṣobhya are well known. Ratnaśrī is mentioned in the Bhadrakalpikasūtra, tr. F. WELLER, *Tausend Buddhanamen des Bhadrakalpa*, Leipzig, 1928, No. 703; Suhkāvatīvyūha, p. 14,*15*; Śikṣāsamuccaya, p. 169,*8*. — Ratnārcis figures in WELLER, No. 362; Lalitavistara, p. 291,*6*; Śatasāh., p. 34,*12*; Śikṣāsamuccaya, p. 169,*7*. — Ratnacandra appears in WELLER, No. 273, 293; Sukhāvatīvyūha, p. 14,*8*; Śikṣāsamuccaya, p. 169,*9*. — Ratnavyūha is mentioned in WELLER, No. 500. — Duṣprasaha appears in Mahāvastu, III, p. 342,*3* and sq.; Sukhāvatīvyūha, p. 142,*1*; Mañjuśrīmūlakalpa, p. 64,*1*; 130,*3*. — Siṃhasvara figures in WELLER, No. 841.

[36] In Tibetan, *de bźin gśegs paḥi gsaṅ ba źes bya baḥi chos kyi sgo*: "The Treatise of the Law (*dharmamukha*) entitled Tathāgataguhyaka". — In Cn (p. 529 *a* 9-10) *Fo hsing wu pu yüeh i* 佛行無不悅懌. — In K (p. 548 *b* 17) *Fo pi yao fa tsang* 佛祕要法藏. — In H (p. 574 *b* 13) *Ju lai pi yao fa mên* 如來祕要法門.

This obviously refers to the Tathāgatācintyaguhyanirdeśa which has already been mentioned above, but without being quoted by name (cf. IV, §1, note 3).

8. Furthermore, Honourable Śāriputra, in this house, there appear all the splendours of the dwellings of the gods (*devabhavanavyūha*) and all the splendours of the Buddha-fields (*buddhakṣetravyūha*): such is the eighth wonder.

Such are, O Honourable Śāriputra, the eight extraordinary wonders which are in evidence in this house. Who, then, after having seen such inconceivable things (*acintyadharma*), could still endorse the doctrines of the Śrāvakas and the Pratyekabuddhas?

[*Equivalence and the Miracle of the Sexes*]

14. *Śārip.* — Devī, why do you not change (*na pariṇamasi*) your womanhood (*strībhava*) [37]?

[37] The physical characteristics of male sexuality (*puruṣendriya*) and of female sexuality (*strīndriya*) appear among the twenty two organs enumerated in the Sūtras (cf. Vibhaṅga, p. 122,*3-4*; Vibhāṣā, T 1545, ch. 142, p. 728 c *7*; Kośa, I, p. 101; Kośavyākhyā, p. 90,*32*). Their reality is not doubted; quite the reverse, feminine sexuality is an object of execration for Buddhist monks, and the old texts are full of attacks against women (cf. Dīgha, II, p. 141; Saṃyutta, IV, p. 238-251; Aṅguttara, I, p. 1; II, p. 82-83; III, p. 68; IV, p. 196-197).

Both Vehicles agree in admitting that no woman can ever become either a Buddha, or Cakravartin king, or Śakra, or Māra, or Brahmā: cf. Aṅguttara, I, p. 28,*9-19*; Majjhima, III, p. 65,*24*-66,*9*; Vibhaṅga, p. 336,*33*-337,*2*; Saddharmapuṇḍ., p. 264,*11*.

However, there is the possibility of a "reversal of the support through the mutation of the female or male organs" (*āśrayaparivṛttiḥ strīpuruṣavyañjanaparivartanāt*: cf. Sūtrālaṃkāra, p. 55,*5*). Buddhist folklore quotes cases of sex changes: Vibhāṣā, T 1545, ch. 114, p. 593 *a* (the eunuch from Kaniṣka and the bulls); Divyāvadāna, p. 473,*14* (story of Rūpavatī who lost both breasts); Dhammapada Commentary, I, p. 325-332 (story of Soreyya, father of two children and mother of two children). Also see E. CHAVANNES, *Cinq cents contes*, I, p. 265, 402. These changes of sex pose disciplinary questions which are taken up in the Kośa, IV, p. 45, 94, 213.

In Mahāyānasūtras, it often happens that women turn into male Bodhisattvas: according to the traditional formula "their female organs disappear and male organs appear" (*strīndriyam antarhitaṃ puruṣendriyaṃ ca prādurbhūtam*). This was notably the case for the daughter of Sāgara, the serpent king, in the Saddharmapuṇḍ., p. 265,*5-6*, the five hundred daughters of Māra in the Mahāsaṃnipāta, p. 43,*1-2* and the thousand wives of King Ajitasena, in the Ajitasenavyākaraṇa, published by N. DUTT, *Gilgit Manuscripts*, I, p. 131,*3*.

So it is quite natural that here Śāriputra should ask the devī to change her womanhood. However, the latter, taking to extremes the theory of the unreality of all dharmas, refuses categorically. By an almost burlesque magical ploy she proves to Śāriputra that sexual characteristics are "neither made nor changed" and that there is no question of modifying them.

We should add that in the Yogācāra system, the expression *āśrayaparāvṛtti* took on a philosophical meaning and signified the reversal of the support [of the mind and

Devī. — For the twelve years that I have lived in this house, I have sought after womanhood, but without ever obtaining it. How then could I change it? Honourable Śāriputra, if a skillful illusionist (*dakṣo māyākāraḥ*) created through transformation (*nirmimīte*) an illusionary woman (*māyāstrī*), could you reasonably ask her why she does not change her womanhood?

Śārip. — Certainly not, O Devī, every illusionary creation being unreal (*aparinispanna*), how could it be changed?

Devī. — Equally, Honourable Śāriputra, all dharmas are unreal (*aparinispanna*) and of a nature created by illusion (*māyānirmitasvabhāva*), and you would think of asking them to change their womanhood?

Equally, the self-nature (*svabhāva*) and marks (*lakṣaṇa*) of dharmas are unreal (*aparinispanna*), like an illusionary creation (*māyānirmāṇa*). How can you ask them if they do not change their womanhood?

15. Then the Devī carried out such a supernatural action (*evaṃrūpam adhiṣṭhānam adhitiṣṭhati sma*) that Śāriputra the Elder (*sthavira*) appeared in every way like the Devī and she herself appeared in every way like Śāriputra the Elder.

Then the Devī changed into Śāriputra asked Śāriputra changed into a goddess: Why then, O Honourable Sir, do you not change your womanhood (*strībhava*)?

Śāriputra changed into a goddess replied: I do not know either how I lost my masculine form (*puruṣarūpa*), or how I acquired a feminine body (*strīkāya*).

The Devī replied:

If, O Sthavira, you were capable of changing a feminine form (*strīrūpa*), then all women could change their womanhood (*strībhava*). Just as, O Sthavira, you appear a woman, so also all women appear in the form of a woman (*strīrūpa*), but it is without being women that they appear in the form of women.

If, O Honourable Sir, you could change your woman's body (*strīkāya*), then all feminine bodies could also be changed. Thus, O Śāriputra, just as, without really being a woman, you manifest a woman's body, so also all women, while manifesting womens' bodies, are not really women.

mental phenomena], namely the six internal *āyatana* which are the primary constituents of a being (*maulasattvadravya*) and, as some might say, a personality. This *āśrayaparāvṛtti* is clearly defined in the Bodh. bhūmi, p. 367-370. Other references in Saṃgraha, p. 79, 261, 16* and 48*.

It is with this hidden intention (*tat saṃdhāya*) that the Blessed One said: Dharmas are neither male or female.

Then the Devī broke off her supernatural action (*adhiṣṭhānaṃ tyaktvā*), and the Venerable Śāriputra regained his previous form.

Then the Devī, having spoken these words, withdrew her psychic power (*ṛddhibalaṃ pratisaṃharate sma*), and both regained their previous forms.

Then the Devī said to Śāriputra: Honourable Śāriputra, where (*kva*) then is your feminine form (*strīrūpa*)?

Śārip. — My feminine form is neither made (*kṛta*) nor changed (*vikṛta*).

Devī. — Excellent (*sādhu sādhu*), O Honourable Sir: in the same way, dharmas, all just as they are, are neither made nor changed. To say that they are neither made nor changed, this is the word of the Buddha (*buddhavacana*).

[*Inaccessible Enlightenment and Impossible Rebirth*]

16. *Śārip.* — Devī, when you leave this world, where will you be reborn (*itaś cyutvā kvotpatsyase*)?

Devī. — I will be reborn wherever the illusionary creations (*nirmāṇa*) of the Tathagata are reborn.

Śārip. — But the illusionary creations of the Tathāgata do not die and are not reborn (*na cyavante notpadyante*). How can you say that you will go wherever they are reborn?

Devī. — It is the same with all dharmas and with all beings (*sattva*): they do not die and are not reborn. How can you ask me where I will be reborn?

Śārip. — Devī, how long will it be before you reach supreme and perfect enlightenment (*kiyacciraṃ tvam anuttarāyāṃ samyaksaṃbodhāv abhisaṃbhotsyase*)?

Devī. — When you yourself, O Sthavira, return to being a worldly one (*pṛthagjana*) with all the attributes of a worldly one, then I myself will reach supreme and perfect enlightenment.

Sārip. — Devī, it is impossible and it cannot occur (*asthānam etad anavakāśo yat...*) that I return to being a worldly one with all the attributes of a worldly one.

Devī. — Equally, Honourable Śāriputra, it is impossible and it cannot occur that I ever attain supreme and perfect enlightenment. And why? Because complete enlightenment (*abhisaṃbodhi*) rests on a non-base (*apratiṣṭhānapratiṣṭhita*). Consequently, in the absence of any base, who could reach supreme and perfect enlightenment?

Śārip. — However, the Tathāgata has said: "Tathāgatas as innumerable as the sands of the Ganges (*gaṅgānadīvālukopama*) reach, have reached and will reach supreme and perfect enlightenment".

Devī. — Honourable Śāriputra, the words "Buddhas past (*atīta*), future (*anāgata*) and present (*pratyutpanna*)" are conventional expressions (*sāṃketikādhivacana*) made up of syllables (*vyañjana*) and numbers (*saṃkhyā*). Buddhas are neither past, nor future nor present, and their Bodhi transcends the three phases of time (*tryadhvasamatikrānta*). Tell me, O Sthavira, have you already obtained the state of holiness (*arhattva*)?

Śārip. — I have obtained it because there is nothing to obtain (*aprāptihetoḥ prāptam arhattvam*).

Devī. — It is the same with Bodhi: it is achieved because there is nothing to achieve (*anabhisaṃbodhanahetor abhisaṃbuddhā bodhiḥ*).

17. Then the Licchavi Vimalakīrti said to the Venerable (*āyuṣmant*) Śāriputra the Elder (*sthavira*): This Devī has already served (*paryupās-*) ninety-two hundreds of thousands of *koṭinayuta* of Buddhas; she is at ease with the super-knowledges and the knowledges (*abhijñājñānavikrīḍita*); she fulfills the vows concerning knowledge and wisdom (*paripūrṇajñānaprajñāpraṇidhāna*); she has acquired the certainty concerning the non-arising of dharmas (*anutpattikadharmakṣānti*); she is assured of never being reversed (*avivartana*) on the way of supreme and perfect enlightenment. Through the strength of her vows (*praṇidhānavaśena*) she is to be found, according to her desires (*yathākāmam*), wherever it is proper for ripening all beings (*sattvaparipācanārtham*).

CHAPTER SEVEN

THE FAMILY OF THE TATHĀGATA

[*The Roundabout Ways of a Bodhisattva*]

1. Then Mañjuśrī the crown prince (*kumārabhūta*) said to the Licchavi Vimalakīrti: Son of good family (*kulaputra*), how does a Bodhisattva follow his way (*gatiṃ gacchati*) in the Buddhadharmas?

Vimalakīrti replied: Mañjuśrī, it is by following a roundabout way (*agatiṃ gacchan*)[1] that a Bodhisattva follows his way in the Buddhadharmas.

Mañjuśrī continued: How does a Bodhisattva follow a roundabout way?

Vimalakīrti replied: A Bodhisattva commits the five acts of immediate fruition (*ānantarya*)[2], but he is free of animosity (*vyāpāda*), hostility (*vihiṃsā*) and hatred (*pradveṣa*).

He enters the destiny of the hell-born (*narakagati*), but he is free of the stains of the passions (*kleśarajas*). — He enters the destiny of the animals (*tiryagyonigati*) but avoids darkness (*tamas*) and ignorance (*avidyā*). — He enters the destiny of the Asuras[3], but he is free from pride (*māna*), presumption (*mada*) and arrogance (*garva*). — He enters the world of the god of death (*yamaloka*), but he accumulates all the stores of merit and knowledge (*puṇyajñānasaṃbhāra*).

He enters the immovable and formless destinies (*acalārūpigati*), but he does not assume (*na samādāpayati*) these destinies[4].

He enters the formless recollections (*ārūpyasamāpatti*), but without liking going there.

[1] According to the genius of the Sanskrit language, *agati* does not mean absence of movement, staying still, but "a movement that is not one", a "false movement". Just as *avidyā* does not mean absence of knowledge, but false knowledge. The Bodhisattva, through expediency, adopts all the grades of life and conforms his conduct to them. However reprehensible this may seem, it is purified by the Bodhisattva's good intentions and altruism. See above, Introduction, p. LVII-LX; II, § 2-6; III, § 3; 16-18; IV, § 20; X, § 19; Bodh. bhūmi, p. 165-166; Saṃgraha, p. 212-217.

[2] Above, III, § 16, note 33.

[3] Like many Mahāyānasūtras, the Vimalakīrti accepts an Asura destiny (cf. NĀGĀRJUNA, *Traité*, p. 613 in the notes).

[4] These five points concern the six destinies (*gati*).

He follows the way of craving (*rāga*), but he is detached (*vītarāga*) from the pleasures of desire (*kāmabhoga*). — He follows the way of hatred (*dveṣa*), but he has neither hatred (*dveṣa*) nor aversion (*pratigha*) for anyone.

He follows the way of delusion (*moha*), but in all things he possesses the clearsightedness of wisdom (*prajñānidhyapti*)[5].

He follows the way of delusion, but he avoids in all things darkness (*tamas*) and ignorance (*avidyā*) because he has disciplined himself (*dānta*) in the light of knowledge (*jñāna*) and wisdom (*prajñā*).

He follows the way of avarice (*mātsarya*), but without a care for his body or his life (*kāyajīvitānapekṣam*), he abandons (*parityajati*) his inward and outward assets (*adhyātmabahirdhāvastu*). — He follows the way of immorality (*dauḥśīlya*) but, seeing the dangers to which the smallest fault leads (*kiṃcitke 'vadye bhayadarśī*), he holds himself to strict observances (*dhutaguṇa*) and complete austerity (*sarvasaṃlekha*) and is content with little (*alpecchatāsaṃtuṣṭa*) — He follows the way of animosity (*vyāpāda*) and aversion (*pratigha*), but he is absolutely without animosity (*vyāpāda*) and firmly established in goodwill (*maitrī*) and compassion (*karuṇā*). — He follows the way of idleness (*kausīdya*), but applies himself ceaselessly to vigour (*satatasamitaṃ vīryābhiyukta*) and strives to seek out all the good roots (*sarvakuśalamūlaparyeṣaṇābhiyukta*). — He follows the way of distraction (*vikṣiptendriya*), but he is always silent, naturally recollected (*samāpanna*) and firm in his trance (*amoghadhyāna*). — He follows the way of false wisdom (*dauṣprajñā*), but he has attained the perfection of wisdom (*prajñāpāramitā*) and he is versed in all worldly and transcendental treatises (*laukikalokottaraśāstrakuśala*)[6].

He follows the way of hypocrisy (*dambha*) and boasting (*lapanā*), but he excels in mental reservations (*abhisaṃdhikuśala*)[7] and in the exercise of skillful means (*upāyakauśalyacaryāniryā-*

He follows the way of guile (*śāṭhya*), but the commands ability in skillful means (*upāyakauśalya*). — He follows the way of mental reservations (*abhisaṃdhi*), of subterfuges (*upāya*) and of pride (*mānastambha*), but it is in order to lay the main girder of the bridge of salvation (*paritrāṇasetu*).

[5] These three points concern the three-fold poison (*triviṣa*): craving, hatred and delusion.

[6] These six points concern the vices, avarice, etc., opposed to the six *pāramitā*. Cf. Pañcaviṃśati, p. 29,*14-18*.

[7] Regarding the four *abhisaṃdhi*, see Sūtrālaṃkāra, p. 82,*13-18*; Saṃgraha, p. 131-132; Abhidharmasamuccaya, p. 85,*1-2*.

ta). — He teaches the way of pride (*māna*), but for the whole world he is a bridge (*setu*) and a palisade (*vedikā*).

He follows the way of all the passions (*kleśa*) of the world, but he is absolutely undefiled (*atyantam asaṃkliṣṭaḥ*) and naturally pure (*svabhāvena pariśuddhaḥ*).

He follows the way of Māra, but with regard to all the Buddhadharmas, he understands them and knows them through personal experience and does not rely on others (*aparapraṇeya*). — He follows the way of the Listeners (*śrāvaka*), but he causes beings to listen (*śrāvayati*) to a Law (*dharma*) that they have never heard before (*aśrutapūrva*). — He follows the way of the Solitary Buddhas (*pratyekabuddha*), but in order to ripen beings (*sattvaparipācanārtham*), he commands great goodwill (*mahāmaitrī*) and great compassion (*mahākaruṇā*). — He follows the way of the poor (*daridra*), but he holds in his jewel-like hand (*ratnapāṇi*) inexhaustible riches (*akṣayabhoga*). — He follows the way of the crippled (*vikalendriya*), but he is beautiful (*abhirūpa*) and adorned with the primary and secondary marks (*lakṣaṇānuvyañjanaiḥ svalaṃkṛtaḥ*). — He follows the way of those of low class (*nīcakulodgata*), but by accumulating stores of merit and knowledge (*puṇyajñānasaṃbhāra*), he augments the noble line of the Tathāgatas (*tathāgatavaṃśa*). — He follows the way of the feeble (*durbala*), the ugly (*durvarṇa*) and the wretched (*dīna*), but he is lovely to behold (*darśanīya*) and possesses a body like that of Nārāyaṇa[8].

Before all beings, he displays the bearing of a sick (*glāna*) and suffering (*asukha*) man[9], but he has gone beyond and overcome the fear of death (*maraṇabhaya*).

He shows himself among the old (*jīrṇa*) and the sick (*glāna*), but he has overcome the root (*mūla*) of old age (*jarā*) and sickness (*vyādhi*) and gone beyond the fear of death (*maraṇabhayasamatikrānta*).

He follows the way of the rich (*bhogin*), but he is without cupidity (*anveṣaṇa*) and he frequently ponders on the notion of impermanence (*anityatāsaṃjñāpratyavekṣābahula*). — He organises numerous harem festivities (*antaḥpuranṛtya*), but he cultivates solitude (*viveka*) and has triumphed over the quagmire of desires (*kāmapaṅka*).

[8] Nārāyaṇa has available in his body, or in each of his articulations, a power which constitutes the seventh term of a series which begins with the elephant and of which each term is worth ten times that of the preceding one; this power is tangible. Cf. Vibhāṣā, T 1545, ch. 30, p. 155 *a* 8; Kośa, VII, p. 72-74.

[9] Cf. II, § 7, note 19; § 6, stanza 18.

He follows the way of the elements (*dhātu*) and the bases of consciousness (*āyatana*), but he retains the formulae (*dhāraṇīpratilabdha*)[10] and is possessed of a multiple eloquence (*nānāpratibhānālaṃkṛta*).

He follows the way of the dumb (*mūka*), but he is possessed of a multiple eloquence (*nānāpratibhānālaṃkṛta*), he retains the formulae (*dhāraṇīpratilabdha*) and there is in him neither loss of mindfulness nor loss of memory (*nāsti smṛtiprajñāyor hāniḥ*).

He follows the way of the sectaries (*tīrthika*) but without being a sectary himself[11].

He follows the way of the sectaries (*tīrthika*) but he saves everyone through the right path.

He follows the destinies of the whole world (*sarvalokagati*), but avoids all destinies (*sarvagatibhyaḥ pratyudāvṛttaḥ*). — He follows the way of Nirvāṇa, but does not abandon (*na parityajati*) the course of Saṃsāra (*saṃsāraprabandha*).

He seems to obtain enlightenment (*saṃbodhi*), to cause the great wheel of the Law (*dharmacakra*) to turn and enter Nirvāṇa, but he practises his function as a Bodhisattva (*bodhisattvacaryā*) continually and uninterruptedly[12].

Mañjuśrī, it is by following these roundabout ways (*agatiṃ gacchan*) that a Bodhisattva follows his way (*gatiṃ gacchati*) in the Buddhadharmas.

[*The Family of the Tathāgata*[13]]

2. Then the Licchavi Vimalakīrti said to Mañjuśrī the crown prince (*kumārabhūta*): Mañjuśrī, what is the family of the Tathāgata (*tathāgatagotra*)? I would like you to tell me about it briefly (*saṃkṣepeṇa*).

[10] In Tibetan, *khams daṅ skye mched kyi ḥgro yaṅ gzuṅs thob ciṅ*... But the connection escapes me between the way of the *dhātu* and the *āyatana* on the one hand, and the *dhāraṇī* on the other. Besides, it is confirmed by K: "He shows himself among the stupid, but he is gifted with eloquence (*pratibhāna*) and his *dhāraṇī* are infallible".

[11] Thus, in the Ratnakāraṇḍavyūha (T 461, ch. 2, p. 461 *c* 8-9; T 462, ch. 2, p. 475 *c* 8-9), Mañjuśrī creates through transformation five hundred Tīrthikas, puts himself at their head and enters a Nirgrantha community directed by Satyaka Nirgranthaputra.

[12] This paragraph is missing in Cn and K. — We read in the Mañjuśrīparinirvāṇasūtra (T 463, p. 480 *c* 18) that, through the power of the Śūraṃgamasamādhi, the Bodhisattva displays at will in the ten regions, the birth (*jāti*), leaving of the world (*naiṣkramya*), Nirvāṇa, Parinirvāṇa and the distribution of the relics: all this for the welfare of beings. See Śūraṃgamasamādhisūtra, tr. É. LAMOTTE, *La Concentration de la Marche Héroïque*, especially p. 122, § 7; p. 140, § 21, No. 97-100; p. 223, § 123; p. 263, § 163.

[13] On this problem, see Appendix, Note VII: *Gotra and Tathāgatagotra*.

Mañjuśrī replied: Son of good family (*kulaputra*), the family of the Tathāgata is the family of the aggregation of all perishable things (*satkāya*), the family of ignorance (*avidyā*) and the thirst for existence (*bhavatṛṣṇā*), the family of craving (*rāga*), of hatred (*dveṣa*) and delusion (*moha*), the family of the four perverted views (*viparyāsa*)[14], the family of the five hindrances (*nīvaraṇa*)[15], the family of the six bases of consciousness (*āyatana*), the family of the seven abodes of the mind (*vijñānasthiti*)[16], the family of the eight depravities (*mithyātva*)[17], the family of the nine causes of irritation (*āghātavastu*)[18] and the family of the ten paths of bad action (*akuśalakarmapatha*)[19]: such is, son of good family, the family of the Tathāgata. Briefly (*saṃkṣepeṇa*), O son of good family, the family of the Tathāgata is the family of the sixty-two kinds of false views (*dṛṣṭigata*), of all the passions (*kleśa*) and of all the bad dharmas (*pāpākuśaladharma*).

3. *Vim.* Mañjuśrī, with what hidden intention (*kiṃ saṃdhāya*) do you say that?

Mañj. — Son of good family, he who, seeing the unconditioned (*asaṃskṛta*), has entered the absolute certainty of acquiring the supreme Good (*avakrāntaniyāma*), is not capable of producing the thought of supreme and perfect enlightenment (*anuttarasaṃyaksaṃbodhicitta*). On the contrary, he who bases himself on conditioned things (*saṃskṛta*) — those mines of the passions (*kleśākara*) — and who has not as yet seen the noble truths (*na dṛṣṭasatya*), he is capable of producing the thought of supreme and perfect enlightenment.

Son of good family, in the jungle (*jāṅgalapradeśa*), flowers (*puṣpa*) like the blue lotus (*utpala*), the red lotus (*padma*), the night lotus (*kumuda*), the white lotus

Elevated and dry ground does not produce the utpala, the padma, the kumuda or the puṇḍarīka; low and damp marshland is needed to produce these four kinds of flowers. Equally, the families (*gotra*) of the Śrāvakas and the Pratyekabuddhas

[14] The four *viparyāsa*: cf. Aṅguttara, II, p. 52; Vibhaṅga, p. 376; Kośa, V, p. 21; Śikṣāsamuccaya, p. 198; NĀGĀRJUNA, *Traité*, p. 925, 1076.

[15] The five *nīvaraṇa*: references in NĀGĀRJUNA, *Traité*, p. 1013, footnote.

[16] The seven *vijñānasthiti*: cf. Dīgha, II, p. 68,*25*; III, p. 253,*9*; 282,*12*; Aṅguttara, IV, p. 39,*15*; V, p. 53,*9*; Vibhāṣā, T 1545, ch. 137, p. 706 *b* 12; Kośa, III, p. 16.

[17] The eight *mithyātva*: cf. above, III, § 13, note 25.

[18] The nine *āghātavastu*: Vinaya, V, p. 137,*25*; 213,*18*; Dīgha, III, p. 262,*25-31*; 289,*11*; Aṅguttara, IV, p. 408,*7-15*; Vibhaṅga, p. 349,*17*; 389,*24-32*; Paṭisambhidā, I, p. 130,*13*; Nettipakaraṇa, p. 23,*21*; Mahāvyutpatti, No. 2104. This concerns irritations brought on by various observations: "He has done, does or will do wrong by me or someone I like; he has done, does or will do right by my enemy".

[19] Above, I, § 13, note 73.

(*puṇḍarīka*) and the waterlily (*saugandhika*) do not germinate (*notpadyante*); it is in the mire (*paṅka*) and on sandbanks (*pulina*) that these flowers germinate. Equally, O son of good family, in beings predestined to the unconditioned (*asaṃskṛte niyāmaprāptāḥ*), the Buddhadharmas do not germinate; it is in beings mingled with the mire and sandbanks of the passions (*kleśa*) that the Buddhadharmas germinate.

who have seen the unconditioned (*asaṃskṛta*) and who have already entered the absolute certainty of acquiring the supreme Good (*avakrāntasamyaktvaniyāma*) absolutely cannot produce the thought of omniscience (*sarvajñānacitta*). It is necessary to be in the low and damp marshlands of the passions (*kleśa*) to be able to produce the thought of omniscience for it is there that the great Buddhadharmas germinate.

In space (*ākāśa*), a seed (*bīja*) does not germinate; put into earth (*pṛthivī*), it germinates (*utpadyate*). Equally, in beings predestined to the unconditioned (*asaṃskṛte prāptaniyāmāḥ*), the Buddhadharmas do not germinate.

Furthermore, son of good family, if one plants (*āropayati*) a seed (*bīja*) in space (*ākāśa*), it does not germinate and does not grow. It should be planted in earth which is low, damp and fertilised for it to germinate and grow. Equally, the families of the Śrāvakas and the Pratyekabuddhas who have seen the unconditioned (*asaṃskṛta*) and have already entered into the absolute certainty of acquiring the supreme Good (*avakrāntasamyaktvaniyāma*) absolutely cannot produce or develop the Buddhadharmas.

Sumerusamāṃ satkāyadṛṣṭim utpādya bodhicittam utpadyate tataś ca buddhadharmā virohanti[20].

It is when there has arisen a belief in a personality as high as Sumeru that there arises the thought of enlightenment and then the Buddhadharmas develop.

Son of good family, it is through these considerations (*etaiḥ paryāyaiḥ*) that it should be understood that all the passions (*sarvakleśa*) are the family of the Tathāgata (*tathāgatagotra*)[21].

[20] Extract from the original text, quoted in Śikṣāsamuccaya, p. 6,*10-11*. — The comparison is possibly taken from the Ratnakūṭa, quoted in Madh. vṛtti, p. 248,*9*: *varaṃ khalu, Kāśyapa, sumerumātrā pudgaladṛṣṭir āśritā* ...

[21] This section comes from K; H has transposed it to the end of the paragraph.

Son of good family, without entering the great sea (*mahāsamudra*) it is impossible to acquire inappreciably precious pearls (*anarghamaṇiratna*). Equally, without entering the sea of the passions (*kleśasamudra*), it is impossible to produce the omniscient thought (*sarvajñacitta*).

Furthermore, son of good family, if one does not enter the great sea, it is absolutely impossible to acquire inappreciably precious pearls, beryl (*vaiḍūrya*) etc. Equally if one does not enter the great sea of the passions of Saṃsāra (*saṃsārakleśa*) it is absolutely impossible to produce that inappreciably precious pearl that is the omniscient thought.

That is why it must be known that the family of all the passions of Saṃsāra (*sarvasaṃsārakleśagotra*) is the family of the Tathāgatas.

[*Mahākāśyapa's Lamentations*]

4. Then the Venerable (*āyuṣmant*) Mahākāśyapa gave his approval (*sādhukāram adāt*) to Mañjuśrī the crown prince: Excellent, excellent (*sādhu sādhu*), O Mañjuśrī, this word is well spoken (*subhāṣita*), is right (*bhūta*): all the passions of Saṃsāra are the family of the Tathāgata.

How could it be possible that people like us produce the thought of enlightenment (*bodhicitta*) and are enlightened (*abhisaṃbudh-*) in the Buddhadharmas? It is necessary to be guilty of the five acts of immediate fruition (*ānantarya*)[22] to be able to produce the thought of enlightenment and be enlightened in the Buddhadharmas.

And why? In us at present, in our thought series (*cittasaṃtāna*) the seed of rebirth (*saṃsārabīja*) is completely rotten (*pūtika*) and we can never produce the thought of perfect enlightenment (*samyaksaṃbodhicitta*). It would be better to become guilty of the five acts of immediate fruition (*ānantarya*) than to be like us holy ones (*arhat*) who are completely delivered (*atyantavimukta*). And why? Because those who become guilty of the five *ānantarya* still have the power to destroy these *ānantarya*, to produce the thought of supreme and perfect enlightenment and gradually (*anupūrveṇa*) attain all the Buddhadharmas. While we, Arhats, who have destroyed our impurities (*kṣīṇāsrava*), will never be capable of it.

5. Over cripples (*vikalendriyapuruṣa*) the five objects of desire (*kāmaguṇa*) are virtueless (*nirguṇa*) and powerless (*asamartha*). Equally, over the Listeners (*śrāvaka*)

Cripples (*vikalendriyapuruṣa*) are powerless (*asamartha*) over the five objects of desire (*kāmaguṇa*). Equally, those who have destroyed their impurities (*kṣīṇāsrava*) and Arhats who have broken the fetters (*parikṣīṇasaṃyojana*) are powerless over

[22] See above, III, § 16, note 33.

who have broken the fetters (*parikṣīṇasaṃyojana*) all the Buddhadharmas are virtueless and powerless and can no longer recapture them.

the Buddhadharmas and no longer consider seeking the lovely Buddhadharmas [23].

That is why, O Mañjuśrī, the worldly (*pṛthagjana*) are grateful (*kṛtajña*) to the Tathāgata, while the Śrāvakas and Pratyekabuddhas are not in the least so. And why? The worldly hear of the virtues (*guṇa*) of the Buddha, of his Law (*dharma*) and of his community (*saṃgha*) and desiring that the family of this triple jewel (*triratnagotra*) may never be interrupted (*samucchinna*), produce the thought of supreme and perfect enlightenment and gradually (*anupūrveṇa*) attain all the Buddhadharmas. Conversely, the Śrāvakas and Pratyekabuddhas, had they heard all their lives (*yāvajjīvam*) of the Buddhadharmas — that is the powers (*bala*) and the convictions (*vaiśāradya*) of the Tathāgata, and so on up to the exclusive attributes of the Buddha (*āveṇikabuddhadharma*), — these Śrāvakas, say I, are incapable of producing the thought of supreme and perfect enlightenment.

[*Vimalakīrti's Stanzas*]

6. Then the Bodhisattva Sarvarūpasaṃdarśana [24], present in the assembly (*tasyāṃ parṣadi saṃnipatitaḥ*), said to the Licchavi Vimalakīrti: Householder (*gṛhapati*), where are your father (*pitṛ*) and mother (*mātṛ*), your sons (*putra*) and your wife (*bhāryā*), your manservants (*dāsa*) and your maidservants (*dāsī*), your labourers (*karmakara*) and your workers (*pauruṣeya*)? Where are your friends (*mitra*), your kinsmen (*jñāti*), your relatives (*sālohita*)? Where are your retinue (*parivāra*), your horses (*aśva*), your elephants (*hastin*), your chariots (*ratha*), your footmen (*pattika*) and your lads (*taruṇa*)?

Thus questioned, the Licchavi Vimalakīrti answered the Bodhisattva Sarvarūpasaṃdarśana with these stanzas (*gāthā*):

1. For pure Bodhisattvas, their mother (*mātṛ*) is the perfection of wisdom (*prajñāpāramitā*), their father (*pitṛ*) is skillfulness in means (*upāyakauśalya*): the Leaders of the world (*nāyaka*) are born of such parents.

2. The joy of the Law (*dharmapramuditā*) is their wife (*bhāryā*);

[23] K and H differ slightly from the Tibetan.

[24] In the Saddharmapuṇḍ., p. 405,*14*; 412,*11*; 435,*9*, *Sarvarūpasaṃdarśana* is the name of a *samādhi*.

goodwill (*maitrī*) and compassion (*karuṇā*) are their daughters (*duhitṛ*); the Law (*dharma*) and truth (*satya*) are their sons (*putra*); the contemplation of emptiness (*śūnyārthacintā*) is their house (*gṛha*).

3. All the passions (*kleśa*) are their disciples (*śiṣya*), who bow to their will. Their friends (*mitra*) are the limbs of enlightenment (*bodhyaṅga*): it is through them that they achieve excellent awakening (*pravarabodhi*).

4. Their companions (*sakhi*), ever present, are the six perfections (*pāramitā*). The means of conversion (*saṃgraha*) are their women (*strī*): their song (*saṃgīta*) is the instruction of the Law (*dharmadeśanā*).

5. The formulae (*dhāraṇī*) constitute a park (*upavana*) for them, with the limbs of enlightenment (*bodhyaṅga*) for blossoms (*kusuma*), the knowledge of deliverance (*vimuktijñāna*) for fruit and the riches of the Law (*dharmamahādhana*) for trees (*vṛkṣa*)[25].

6. The eight liberations (*vimokṣa*) serve them as a pool (*puṣkariṇī*): it is filled with the waters of the concentrations (*samādhi*), covered with the lotuses (*padma*) of the seven purities (*viśuddhi*)[26] and those who bathe there are spotless (*vimala*).

7. The super-knowledges (*abhijñā*) are their lads (*taruṇa*); their vehicle (*yāna*) is great (*mahat*), unsurpassed (*anuttara*); their driver (*sārathi*) is the thought of enlightenment (*bodhicitta*); their path (*mārga*) is the eight-limbed calm (*aṣṭāṅgaśānta*).

The super-knowledges (*abhijñā*) are their elephants (*hastin*) and their horses (*aśva*); the Great Vehicle (*mahāyāna*) is their vehicle (*yāna*); their driver (*sārathi*) is the thought of enlightenment (*bodhicitta*); they take the way of the eight-limbed path (*aṣṭāṅgamārga*).

8. Their ornaments (*ābharaṇa*) are the primary marks (*lakṣaṇa*) and the eighty secondary marks (*anuvyañjana*). Their clothes (*vastra*) are the good dispositions (*ku-*

They are adorned with the primary marks (*lakṣaṇa*) and decorated with the secondary marks (*anuvyañjana*). Modesty and decency (*hrīrapatrāpya*) are their clothes (*vastra*); high resolve (*adhyāśaya*) is their garland (*mālya*).

[25] K: "With the *anāsravadharma* for trees"; H: "With the great dharmas for trees".

[26] In Tib.: "Covered with pure lotuses". But K and H speak of the 'lotuses of the seven purities". Kumārajīva (T 1775, ch. 7, p. 394 *a* 6) and K'uei-chi (T 1782, ch. 5, p. 1089 *c* 27) list these seven purities: 1. purity of the body and speech, or of morality; 2. purity of the mind; 3. purity of the control over the passions, or of vision; 4. purity consisting in overcoming doubt; 5. purity consisting in distinguishing the Paths; 6. purity of the knowledge and vision (*jñānadarśana*) which lead to the destruction of the bonds; 7. purity of Nirvāṇa. — As far as I know, this list is not canonical. I see the purities in question rather more as the seven *saṃbodhyaṅga*.

śalāśaya), modesty (*apatrāpya*)
and decency (*hrī*).

9. They have the Good Law (*saddharma*) for their fortune (*dhana*)[27]; its use (*prayojana*) is the instruction of the doctrine (*dharmadeśanā*); pure conduct (*śuddhapratipatti*) is its great revenue (*mahālābha*); it is inclined (*pariṇata*) towards great Bodhi.

10. Their couch (*śayyā*) is the four trances (*dhyāna*); the pure means of livelihood (*śuddhājīva*) are their covers (*āstaraṇa*). Their awakening (*vibodha*) is knowledge (*jñāna*): they are always awakened (*prabuddha*) and always concentrated (*samāhita*).

11. Their food (*anna*) is ambrosia (*amṛta*); the flavour of deliverance (*vimuktirasa*) is their drink (*pāna*). Pure intention (*viśuddhāśaya*) is their bath (*snāna*). Their perfumes (*gandha*), their unguents (*vilepana*) are morality (*śīla*).

12. Victorious over the passions (*kleśa*) — their enemies (*śatru*) —, they are invincible heroes (*ajitaśūra*). Having subdued the four Māras, they raise the standard on the dais of Bodhi (*bodhimaṇḍe dhvajaṃ samucchrayanti*).

13. Although there is in reality neither arising (*utpāda*) nor extinction (*nirodha*), they voluntarily (*saṃcintya*) take on births (*jāti*). They illumine all the Buddha-fields (*buddhakṣetra*) like a sunrise (*sūryodaya*).

14. All the offerings (*pūjā*) due to the Leaders of the world (*nāyaka*), they offer to millions (*koṭi*) of Buddhas. However, between themselves and the Buddhas they make no distinction (*viśeṣa*).

15. Even though, for the benefit of beings (*sattvahitāya*), they range over all the Buddha-fields, they consider the fields to be like empty space (*ākāśa*) and have no notion of being (*sattvasamjñā*) regarding beings.

Even though they know that Buddha-fields and beings are empty (*śūnya*), they ever cultivate these *kṣetra*, and their good deeds are unending[28].

[27] K: "Their fortune contains the seven riches". — According to Sêng-chao (T 1775, ch. 7, p. 394 *c* 14-15), this would concern the *saptavidha āryadhana*: 1. faith (*śraddhā*), 2. morality (*śīla*), 3. modesty (*hrī*), 4. scruple (*apatrāpya*), 5. learning (*śruta*), 6. generosity (*tyāga*), 7. wisdom (*prajñā*). Cf. Dīgha, III, p. 163,*5-8*; p. 251,*20-22*; Aṅguttara, IV, p. 4,*27-29*; Mahāvyutpatti, No. 1565-1572.

[28] K: "Even though they understand the emptiness of the buddhakṣetras and beings, they always cultivate buddhakṣetras and ripen beings".

16. *sarvasatvāna ye rūpā rutaghoṣāś ca īritāḥ*
ekakṣaṇena darśenti bodhisatvā viśāradāḥ[29].

The forms, articulated sounds and movements of all beings, fearless Bodhisattvas manifest in a single instant[30].

17. They know the feats of Māra (*mārakarman*) and conform (*anuparivartin*) to the Māras. But it is because they have reached the other shore of skillful means (*upāyapāraṃ gataḥ*) that they manifest such feats[31].

18. *te jīrṇavyādhitā bhonti mṛtam ātmāna darśayī,*
satvānāṃ paripākāya māyādharma vikrīḍitāḥ.

They make themselves old and sick and show themselves as if dead, but it is in order to ripen beings that they play with these simulations[32].

19. *kalpoddāhaṃ ca darśenti uddahitvā vasuṃdharām,*
nityasaṃjñina satvānām anityam iti darśayī.

They manifest the final conflagration by burning the earth; thus, to beings who believe in eternity, they demonstrate impermanence[33].

20. *satvaiḥ śatasahasrebhir ekarāṣṭre nimantritāḥ,*
sarveṣāṃ gṛha bhuñjanti sarvān nāmanti bodhaye.

Invited in a single kingdom by hundreds of thousands of beings, they eat in the houses of all of them simultaneously, and incline them all towards enlightenment.

21. *ye kecin mantravidyā vā śilpasthānā bahūvidhāḥ,*
sarvatra pāramiprāptāḥ sarvasatvasukhāvahāḥ.

Whether it concerns magical arts or various techniques, they excel in everything, and bring about the happiness of all beings[34].

22. *yāvanto loka pāṣaṇḍāḥ sarvatra pravrajanti te,*
nānādṛṣṭigataṃ prāptāṃs te satvān paripācati.

In all the heretical orders of the world, everywhere, they become monks; but they ripen beings fallen into all varieties of false views[35].

23. *candrā vā bhonti sūryā vā śakrabrahmaprajeśvarāḥ,*
bhavanti āpas tejaś ca pṛthivī mārutas tathā.

[29] The original text of stanzas 16 and 18 to 41 is quoted in Śikṣāsamuccaya, p. 324,*11* - 327,*4*.

[30] See above, V, § 17.

[31] See above, V, § 20; below, X, § 10 at the end.

[32] See above, II, § 7, note 19.

[33] See above, V, § 14, note 15, and § 15.

[34] See above, II, 2-6.

[35] See above, VII, § 1, note 11.

They become moons, suns, Śakra, Brahmā or Lord of creatures; they become water, fire, earth or the winds[36].

24. *roga antarakalpeṣu bhaiṣajyaṃ bhonti uttamāḥ,*
yena te satva mucyante sukhī bhonti anāmayāḥ.

During the small kalpas of disease[37], these supreme Bodhisattvas are medicament; through this beings are delivered, happy and without ills.

25. *durbhikṣāntarakalpeṣu bhavantī pānabhojanam,*
kṣutpipāsām apanīya dharmaṃ deśenti prāṇinām.

During the small kalpas of famine, they are drink and food; having averted hunger and thirst, they expound the Law to beings.

[36] See above, V, § 16.

[37] Stanzas 24 to 26 refer respectively to the calamities of disease, famine and the knife which will come to the fore at the end of the *antarakalpa*.

Every great kalpa (*mahākalpa*) includes four incalculable kalpas (*asaṃkhyeyakalpa*): 1. a period of disappearance (*saṃvartakalpa*), 2. a period during which the world is in a state of destruction (*saṃvartasthāyikalpa*), 3. a period of creation (*vivartakalpa*), 4. a period during which the world remains created (*vivartasthāyikalpa*). Each of these four incalculable periods lasts for twenty *antarakalpa* "intermediary kalpa" or, as the Chinese often translate it, "small kalpa". A great kalpa thus contains 80 *antarakalpa*.

The sources give us information on the 20 *antarakalpa* of the fourth incalculable period, namely the *vivartasthāyikalpa* during which the world remains created:

1. During the first *antarakalpa* of this period, the life of man, infinite at the beginning, steadily decreases until it is no more than ten years.

2. The *antarakalpa* Nos. 2 to 19 are each subdivided into two phases: *a.* a phase of increase (*utkarṣa*) during which the life of man, ten years at the beginning, increases until it reaches 80,000 years; *b.* a phase of diminution (*apakarṣa*) during which the life of man progressively decreases from 80,000 to ten years.

3. The 20th *antarakalpa* is of increase only: the life of man increases from ten to 80,000 years.

As we can see, the *antarakalpa* Nos. 1 to 19 end when the life of man lasts for ten years. This end is marked by three plagues: the knife (*śastra*), disease (*roga*) and famine (*durbhikṣa*).

a. The knife (*śastra*) lasts for seven days: men, angered and upset, massacre each other.

b. Disease (*roga*) lasts for seven months and seven days: non-human beings, Piśācas, etc., give off nefarious influences; from which come incurable diseases from which men die.

c. Famine (*durbhikṣa*) lasts for seven years, seven months and seven days: the skies stop raining: hence three famines: famine of the casket (*cañcu*), of the white bone (*śvetāsthi*) and of the stick (*śalākā*).

Regarding all this, see Kośa, III, p. 207-209; Yogācārabhūmi, p. 32-33; Bodh. bhūmi, p. 253.

26. *śastra antarakalpeṣu maitrīdhyāyī bhavanti te,*
avyāpāde niyojenti satvakoṭiśatān bahūn.

During the small kalpas of the knife, they meditate on goodwill and compel into kindliness several hundreds of millions of beings.

27. *mahāsaṃgrāmamadhye ca samapakṣā bhavanti te,*
sandhisāmagri rocenti bodhisatvā mahābalāḥ.

In the midst of great battles, they are impartial, for they love peace and concord, these Bodhisattvas with great powers.

28. *ye cāpi nirayāḥ kecid buddhakṣetreṣv acintiṣu,*
saṃcintya tatra gacchanti satvānāṃ hitakāraṇāt.

In all the hells annexed to inconceivable Buddha-fields, they go voluntarily so as to benefit beings [38].

29. *yāvantyā gatayaḥ kāścit tiryagyonau prakāśitāḥ,*
sarvatra dharmaṃ deśenti tena ucyanti nāyakāḥ.

In all the destinies assigned to the animal realm, they expound the Law everywhere; that is why they are called the Leaders of the world.

30. *kāmabhogāṃś ca darśenti dhyānaṃ ca dhyāyināṃ tathā,*
vidhvasta māraṃ kurvanti avatāraṃ na denti te.

They give themselves up to the pleasures of the senses just as to the meditations of the meditators; they cause the fall of Māra and leave him no hold.

31. *agnimadhye yathā padmam abhūtaṃ taṃ vinirdiśet,*
evaṃ kāmāṃś ca dhyānaṃ ca abhūtaṃ te vidarśayi.

Just as it can be affirmed that a lotus in the heart of a fire is an impossibility [39], so they demonstrate that pleasures and meditations are non-existent.

32. *saṃcintya gaṇikāṃ bhonti puṃsām ākarṣaṇāya te,*
rāgāṅku saṃlobhya buddhajñāne sthāpayanti te.

They voluntarily become courtesans to attract men [40], but having won them with the hook of desire, they establish them in the Buddha-knowledge.

33. *grāmikāś ca sadā bhonti sārthavāhāḥ purohitāḥ,*
agrāmātyātha cāmātyāḥ satvānāṃ hitakāraṇāt.

[38] The Kāraṇḍavyūha tells of the descent of Avalokiteśvara into the Avīci hell.

[39] *Abhūta* rendered by *hsi yu* 希有 "extraordinary" in the three Chinese versions. Obviously, the Sanskrit original used by them had *adbhuta* instead of *abhūta*. However, the latter reading is confirmed by the Tibetan *yaṅ dag ma yin*.

[40] See above, II, § 4, note 12.

They continually make themselves village chiefs, caravan masters, priests, prime ministers or ministers, so as to benefit beings[41].

34. *daridrāṇāṃ ca satvānāṃ nidhānā bhonti akṣayāḥ,*
teṣāṃ dānāni datvā ca bodhicittaṃ janenti te.

For the poor, they are inexhaustible treasures; by giving them gifts, they cause them to produce the thought of enlightenment[42].

35. *mānastabdheṣu satveṣu mahānagnā bhavanti te,*
sarvamānasamudghātaṃ bodhiṃ prārthenti uttamām.

Before proud and vain beings, they make themselves great champions and, after having destroyed their pride, they cause them to desire supreme enlightenment.

36. *bhayārditānāṃ satvānāṃ saṃtiṣṭhante 'grataḥ sadā,*
abhayaṃ teṣu datvā ca paripācenti bodhaye.

They always put themselves at the head of beings tormented by fear. Having given them assurance, they ripen them with a view to enlightenment.

37. *pañcābhijñāś ca te bhūtvā ṛṣayo brahmacāriṇaḥ,*
śīle satvān niyojenti kṣāntisauratyasaṃyame.

Representing themselves as recluses endowed with the five superknowledges and practising continence, they compel beings to morality, patience, kindness and discipline.

38. *upasthānagurūn satvān paśyantīha viśāradāḥ,*
ceṭā bhavanti dāsā vā śiṣyatvam upayānti ca.

Here below, fearlessly they see the masters to be served; they make themselves their slaves or servants, and become their disciples.

39. *yena yenaiva cāṅgena satvo dharmarato bhavet,*
darśenti hi kriyāḥ sarvā mahopāyasuśikṣitāḥ.

Of all the means possible to bring a being to delight in the Law, they put them all to use, for they are well practised in skillful means.

40. *yeṣām anantā śikṣā hi anantaś cāpi gocaraḥ,*
anantajñānasaṃpannā anantaprāṇimocakāḥ.

[41] See above, II, § 5.

[42] This humble stanza played an extremely important role in the history of Chinese Buddhism. For it was relying on its authority and that of the Avataṃsaka (T 278, ch. 7, p. 437 *c* 12-13) that, in the seventh century, the school of the Three Stages (or Degrees) (*San chieh chiao*) justified the institution of the circulation of the Inexhaustible Treasure (*wu chin tsang yüan* 無盡藏院). Cf. J. GERNET, *Les aspects économiques du bouddhisme*, Saigon, 1956, p. 210. See also K.K.S. Ch'en, *The Chinese Transformation of Buddhism*, Princeton, 1973, p. 158-63, 177-78.

Regarding the legend of the four treasures, see above, VI, § 13, note 34.

Infinite are their practices, infinite also is their domain. Gifted with infinite knowledge, they deliver an infinite number of living beings.

41. *na teṣāṃ kalpakoṭībhis kalpakoṭiśatair api,*
buddhair api vadadbhis tu guṇāntaḥ suvaco bhavet[43].

Should they wish, throughout millions and hundreds of millions of kalpas, to enumerate the virtues of the Bodhisattvas, the Buddhas themselves would not easily arrive at an end.

42. Except for stupid and base persons (*aprajñahīnasattvān sthāpayitvā*), where then is the astute man (*dakṣa*) who, on hearing this address, would not wish for excellent enlightenment (*agrabodhi*)?

[43] Stanzas 41 and 42 are missing in Cn.

CHAPTER EIGHT

INTRODUCTION TO THE DOCTRINE OF NON-DUALITY

1. Then the Licchavi Vimalakīrti asked the Bodhisattvas present in the assembly: Worthy sirs (*satpuruṣa*), explain to me what, for Bodhisattvas, is the entry into the doctrine of non-duality (*advayadharmamukhapraveśa*)[1]. Have recourse to your own eloquence (*pratibhāna*) and each speak as you so please.

[1] Non-duality (*advaya*), which should not be confused with monism, is accepted by all the theorists of the Great Vehicle, both Mādhyamikas and Vijñānavādins. In his commentaries on the Madhyamakakārikās by Nāgārjuna, Candrakīrti refers continuously to the knowledge of non-duality, the *cittotpāda* adorned with the knowledge of non-duality (*advayajñānālaṃkṛta*), and accompanied by skillful means resulting from great compassion (*mahākaruṇopāyapuraḥsara*): cf. Madh. vṛtti, p. 2,*6-7*; 556,*6*; Madh. avatāra, p. 1,*14*; 6,*8*; 7,*7-8*, etc.

In his Bodh. bhūmi, p. 39-40 (cf. T 1579, ch. 36. p. 486 *c* 24), Asaṅga gives an excellent definition of *advaya* of which I give a free translation here:

"It should be known that the mark of the real (*tattvalakṣaṇa*) is demonstrated (*prabhāvita*) by non-duality (*advaya*). By duality we understand existence and non-existence.

1. Existence (*bhāva*) consists of conventional discourse (*prajñaptivāda*). And since it has always been postulated by man, it is the source of all the conceptions (*vikalpa*) and all the chattering (*prapañca*) that goes on in the world. Thus one talks of form, sensation, perception, volition and consciousness; one talks of eye, ear, nose, tongue, body and mind; one talks of earth, water, fire and wind; one talks of form, sound, odour, taste and touch; one talks of good, bad or undefined action; one talks of arising and extinction; one talks of the dependent co-production of phenomena; one talks of past, future and present; one talks of the conditioned and the unconditioned; one talks of this world and the other world; one talks of sun and moon; one talks of a thing seen, heard, thought, known, acquired, required, analysed or mentally judged; one even talks of Nirvāṇa. Dharmas of this kind, about which the world talks, and which are grafted onto conventional discourse (*prajñaptivādanirūḍha*), are called "existence".

2. As for non-existence (*abhāva*), this is unreality (*nirvastukatā*), the absence of the sign (*nirnimittatā*) of this same conventional discourse concerning form and all the other dharmas up to and including Nirvāṇa. The complete inexistence (*sarveṇa sarvaṃ nāstikatā*) of what supports conventional discourse, the total absence (*asaṃvidyamānatā*) on which conventional discourse relies in order to function, this is what is called "non-existence".

3. Finally, non-duality (*advaya*) is that thing (*vastu*) known as a characteristic of the Law (*dharmalakṣaṇasaṃgṛhīta*), absolutely separated from existence and non-existence (*bhāvābhāvābhyāṃ vinirmuktam*), namely the existence of which we spoke in the first

Then the Bodhisattvas present in the assembly (*tasyāṃ parṣadi saṃnipatitāḥ*) each spoke in turn, as they so pleased (*yathākāmam*).

The Bodhisattva Dharmavikurvaṇa said:

Son of good family (*kulaputra*), arising (*utpāda*) and extinction (*nirodha*) are two. In that which is unarisen (*anutpanna*) and unextinguished (*aniruddha*), there is no disappearance (*vyaya*). The obtainment of the certainty concerning the non-arising of dharmas (*anutpattikadharmakṣāntiprāpti*) is the entry into non-duality (*advayapraveśa*)[2].

Arising (*utpāda*) and extinction (*nirodha*) are two. If Bodhisattvas understand (*avagacchanti*) that dharmas are originally without arising or extinction, they attain (*sākṣātkurvanti*) the certainty concerning the non-arising of dharmas (*anutpattikadharmakṣānti*): this is what is penetrating the doctrine of non-duality.

2. The Bodhisattva Śrīgandha said:

Me (*ātman*) and mine (*ātmīya*) are two. If there is no

2. The Bodhisattva Śrīgupta said:

Ideations (*vikalpa*) concerning me (*ātman*) and mine (*ātmīya*) are two. It is because a me is imagined that a mine is imagined. If Bodhisattvas understand

place and the non-existence we have just spoken of. This non-duality is the Middle Path (*madhyamā pratipad*) and, since it is devoid of both extremes (*antadvayavivarjita*), [namely existence and non-existence], it is "without superior" (*niruttara*).

It is this real with which the pure knowledge of the Blessed Lord Buddhas is concerned, and also the knowledge of the Bodhisattvas, but which is still at the practising level (*śikṣāmārga*)".

Regarding *advaya*, also see Saṃdhinirmocana, I, § 1 and 6; IV, § 9; VII, § 24; X, § 10; Laṅkāvatāra, p. 76,*7-9*; Madh. vṛtti, p. 556,*6*; Ratnāvalī, I, v. 51; IV, v. 96; Paramārthastava, v. 4; Mahāyānaviṃśikā, ed. G. Tucci, p. 202, v. 4; Upadeśa in Nāgārjuna, *Traité*, p. 125, 902, 910, 911; Sūtrālaṃkāra, p. 34,*1*; 36,*9*; 63,*5*; 90,*16*; 94,*18*; Madhyāntavibhaṅga, p. 49,*13*, 50,*1*; 53,*3*; 239,*10*; 253,*16*; 270,*26*; Bodh. bhūmi, p. 54,*20*.

Here, at Vimalakīrti's request, thirty-two Bodhisattvas in turn attempt to define *advaya*. The order of their intervention differs according to the version: I have followed here the order of the Tibetan translation:

Tib.:	1	2	3	4	5	6	7.
Cn:	1	2	6	3	4	5	7.
K and H:	1	2	6	3	4	7	5.

In Cn the definitions given by Dāntamati (§ 13) and Padmavyūha (§ 26) do not yet appear. Also missing is § 33 concerning "Vimalakīrti's silence". These passages were perhaps missing in the original version of the Vimalakīrtinirdeśa.

[2] K: *Utpāda* and *nirodha* are two. Dharmas being originally *anutpāda* are now *anirodha*. To obtain this *anutpādadharmakṣānti* is to enter *advaya*.

uncalled-for ·affirmation of me (*ātmādhyāropa*), the idea of mine is not produced. The absence of uncalled-for affirmation (*anadhyāropa*) is the entry into non-duality [3].

3. The Bodhisattva Śrīkūṭa said:

Defilement (*saṃkleśa*) and purification (*vyavadāna*) are two. If defilement is clearly understood (*parijñāya*), the idea of purification (*vyavadānamanyanā*) is not produced. The destruction of all ideas (*sarvamanyanāpramardana*) and the path which leads to it (*anurodhagaminī pratipad*) are the entry into non-duality [4].

4. The Bodhisattva Bhadrajyotis said:

Distraction (*vikṣepa*) and attention (*manyanā*) are two. If there is no distraction, there is neither attention (*manyanā*) nor reflection (*manasikāra*) nor interest (*adhikāra*). This absence of interest is the entry into non-duality [5].

5. The Bodhisattva Subāhu said:

Bodhisattva mind (*bodhisattvacitta*) and Listener mind (*śrāvakacitta*) are two. If it is seen

that there is neither me nor mine, they penetrate the doctrine of non-duality.

4. The Bodhisattva Śrīkūṭa said:

Ideations (*vikalpa*) concerning defilement (*saṃkleśa*) and purification (*vyavadāna*) are two. If Bodhisattvas understand the identity (*advaya*) of defilement and purification, they no longer have this ideation. To destroy for ever these ideations (*vikalpa*) and follow the path of extinction (*nirodha*), this is penetrating the doctrine of non-duality.

5. The Bodhisattva Bhadrajyotis said:

Ideations (*vikalpa*) concerning distraction (*vikṣepa*) and attention (*manyanā*) are two. If Bodhisattvas understand that there is neither distraction nor attention, then they are free from reflection (*manasikāra*). To be established in the absence of distraction and the absence of attention, not to have reflections, this is penetrating the doctrine of non-duality.

7. The Bodhisattva Subāhu said:

Bodhisattva mind and Śrāvaka mind are two. If Bodhisattvas understand that these two minds are empty of self-nature (*svabhāvaśūnya*) and the same as an illusion (*māyāsama*), they no longer have either

[3] K: *Ātman* and *ātmīya* are two. If there were *ātman*, there would be *ātmīya*, but because there is no *ātman*, there is no *ātmīya*. This absence of *ātman* and *ātmīya* is the entry into *advaya*.

[4] K: *Saṃkleśa* and *vyavadāna* are two. To see the real nature of *saṃkleśa*, is [to understand] that there is no *vyavadānalakṣaṇa* and to penetrate into the *nirodhalakṣaṇa*: this is entering *advaya*.

[5] K: *Vikṣepa* and *manyanā* are two. If there is no *vikṣepa*, there is no *manyanā*; if there is no *manyanā*, there is no *vikṣepa*: to penetrate this is to enter *advaya*.

that these two minds are the same as an illusionary mind (*māyācitta-sama*), there is neither Bodhisattva mind nor Listener mind. This sameness of the mark (*lakṣaṇa-samatā*) of minds is the entry into non-duality [6].

a Bodhisattva mind or a Śrāvaka mind. That these two minds are the same in mark (*lakṣaṇasama*) and the same as an illusion (*māyāsama*), this is penetrating the doctrine of non-duality.

6. The Bodhisattva Animiṣa said:

Grasping (*ādāna*) and rejection (*anādāna*) are two. That which is not grasped (*anātta*) does not exist (*nopalabhyate*). To that which does not exist there cannot be applied either uncalled-for affirmation (*samāropa*) or unjustified negation (*apavāda*). Inaction (*akriyā*), non-functioning (*acaraṇa*) with regard to all dharmas is the entry into non-duality [7].

3. The Bodhisattva Animiṣa said:

Ideations (*vikalpa*) concerning grasping (*ādāna*) and rejection (*anādāna*) are two. If Bodhisattvas understand grasping, they have no more to take hold of. Having no more to take hold of, they abstain from all affirmation (*samāropa*) and all negation (*apavāda*). Not acting, not stopping over dharmas, avoiding all false beliefs (*abhiniveśa*), this is penetrating the doctrine of non-duality.

7. The Bodhisattva Sunetra [8] said:

Singleness of mark (*ekalakṣaṇa*) and absence of mark (*alakṣaṇa*) are two. Not formulating any ideation (*vikalpa*), any imagination (*parikalpa*), this is not postulating either singleness of mark or absence of mark. Understanding a mark and its opposite as being of the same mark (*sama-*

6. The Bodhisattva Sunetra said:

Ideations (*vikalpa*) concerning singleness of mark (*ekalakṣaṇa*) and absence of mark (*alakṣaṇa*) are two. If Bodhisattvas understand that all dharmas are not of a single mark (*ekalakṣaṇa*) or of a different mark (*bhinnalakṣaṇa*) and that neither are they without mark (*alakṣaṇa*), then they know the perfect sameness (*samatā*) of singleness of mark, different mark and markless. This is penetrating the doctrine of non-duality.

[6] K: *Bodhisattvacitta* and *śrāvakacitta* are two. If one considers that the *citta* is empty of mark (*lakṣaṇaśūnya*), like an illusionary creation (*māyānirmāṇa*), there is neither a *bodhisattvacitta* nor a *śrāvakacitta*: this is entering *advaya*.

[7] K: *Ādāna* and *anādāna* are two. If dharmas are *anādāna*, they are inexistent (*anupalabdha*); being *anupalabdha*, they are without seizing (*grāha*), without relinquishing (*tyāga*), without activity (*kriyā*) and without functioning (*caraṇa*): this is entering *advaya*.

[8] Regarding Sunetra, cf. Mahāvastu, II, p. 355,*6*; III, p. 279,*11*; Gaṇḍavyūha, p. 2,25.

lakṣaṇa), this is entering non-duality[9].

8. The Bodhisattva Tiṣya[10] said:

Good (*kuśala*) and Bad (*akuśala*) are two. Not seeking after (*aparimārgana*) either the good or the bad, understanding that the sign (*nimitta*) and the signless (*ānimitta*) are not two, this is penetrating into non-duality[11].

8. The Bodhisattva Puṣya said:

Ideations (*vikalpa*) concerning good (*kuśala*) and bad (*akuśala*) are two. If Bodhisattvas understand the nature (*svabhāva*) of the good and the nature of the bad, they have nothing to undertake (*prasthāna*). The two words, sign (*nimitta*) and signless (*ānimitta*), are the same: they do not consist of either grasping (*grahaṇa*) or discarding (*prahāṇa*): this is entering the doctrine of non-duality.

9. The Bodhisattva Siṃha[12] said:

The blamable (*sāvadya*) and the blameless (*anavadya*) are two. Understanding through the knowledge which cuts like a diamond (*vajracchedikajñāna*) that there is neither bondage (*bandhana*) nor liberation (*mokṣa*), this is penetrating into non-duality[13].

Ideations (*vikalpa*) concerning the blamable (*sāvadya*) and the blameless (*anavadya*) are two. If Bodhisattvas understand that the blamable and the blameless are the same, they penetrate all dharmas through the diamond knowledge (*vajrajñāna*) and know that they consist of neither bondage (*bandhana*) nor liberation (*mokṣa*). This is entering the doctrine of non-duality.

10. The Bodhisattva Siṃhamati said:

To say "this is impure (*sāsrava*) and that is pure (*anāsrava*)" implies duality. If one grasps dharmas from the angle of their sameness (*samatā*), one no longer produces either a notion (*saṃjñā*) of

Ideations (*vikalpa*) concerning impure (*sāsrava*) and pure (*anāsrava*) are two. If Bodhisattvas know the sameness of the nature (*svabhāvasamatā*) of all dharmas, they no longer produce the two notions (*saṃjñā*) of impure and pure. Not being attached (*abhiniviś-*) to a notion of ex-

[9] K: *Ekalakṣaṇa* and *alakṣaṇa* are two. If one knows that the *ekalakṣaṇa* is the *alakṣaṇa*, one no longer clings to the *alakṣaṇa*, but penetrates *samatā*: this is entering *advaya*.

[10] Tiṣya: cf. Gaṇḍavyūha, p. 441,*25*.

[11] K: *Kuśala* and *akuśala* are two. Not to produce either *kuśala* or *akuśala* is to enter the *ānimittānta* and penetrate it in depth: this is entering *advaya*.

[12] Regarding Siṃha, cf. Mahāvastu, II, p. 354,*19*; III, p. 279,*3*; Gaṇḍavyūha, p. 441,*24*.

[13] K: Fault (*āpatti*) and merit (*puṇya*) are two. To understand that the nature of a fault does not differ from merit, to grasp with the diamond-knowledge (*vajrajñāna*) this [single] mark devoid of bondage (*bandhana*) and liberation (*mokṣa*), this is entering *advaya*.

impure or a notion of pure, but one is still not notion-free ... This is penetrating into non-duality[14].

istence (*astitvasaṃjñā*) or to a notion of non-existence (*nāstitvasaṃjñā*), this is entering the doctrine of non-duality.

11. The Bodhisattva Śuddhādhimukti said:

To say "This is happiness (*sukha*) and that is suffering (*duḥkha*)" implies duality. If through the purity of knowledge (*jñānaviśuddhi*) all calculation (*gaṇanā*) is excluded, one's intelligence (*mati*) becomes clear in the same way as space (*ākāśa*). This is penetrating into non-duality[15].

Ideations (*vikalpa*) concerning the conditioned (*saṃskṛta*) and the unconditioned (*asaṃskṛta*) are two. If Bodhisattvas understand the sameness of the nature (*svabhāvasamatā*) of these two dharmas, they avoid all activity (*saṃskāra*), and their intelligence (*mati*) becomes like space. The purity of knowledge (*jñānaviśuddhi*), the absence of grasping (*anupādāna*) and the absence of rejection (*anutkṣepa*), this is penetrating the doctrine of non-duality.

12. The Bodhisattva Nārāyaṇa said:

To say "this is worldly (*laukika*) and that is transcendental (*lokottara*)" implies duality. In this world (*loka*), empty by nature (*svabhāvaśūnya*), there is absolutely no crossing (*taraṇa*), nor entry (*praveśa*), nor moving (*gamana*) nor stopping (*agamana*). Not crossing it, not entering, not moving, not stopping, this is penetrating into non-duality[16].

Ideations (*vikalpa*) concerning the transcendental (*lokottara*) and the worldly (*laukika*) are two. If Bodhisattvas know that the world (*loka*) is originally empty (*śūnya*) and calm (*śānta*), without entry (*praveśa*), without exit (*niḥsaraṇa*), without flow or dispersion, they are not at all attached to it. This is penetrating the doctrine of non-duality.

13. The Bodhisattva Dāntamati said:

Saṃsāra and Nirvāṇa are two. Bodhisattvas who see the self-nature (*svabhāva*) of Nirvāṇa as originally empty (*ādiśūnya*) are not reborn (*na saṃsaranti*) and do not enter Nirvāṇa: knowing this is penetrating into non-duality[17].

[14] K. *Sāsrava* and *anāsrava* are two. If one understands the *dharmāṇāṃ samatā*, one does not produce notions (*saṃjñā*) of *āsrava* or *anāsrava*, one is not attached to the *nimitta* and one does not abide by the *ānimitta*: this is entering *advaya*.

[15] Here the versions differ. — K: *Saṃskṛta* and *asaṃskṛta* are two. If one abandons all calculation (*gaṇanā*), the *citta* becomes like space, and thanks to pure wisdom (*viśuddhaprajñā*), there is no longer any obstacle (*āvaraṇa*): this is entering *advaya*.

[16] K: *Laukika* and *lokottara* are two. But since the *loka* is *svabhāvaśūnya*, it is *lokottara*; it does not consist of either *praveśa*, or *niḥsaraṇa*, or abundance, or dispersion: this is entering *advaya*.

[17] This paragraph is missing in Cn. — K: Saṃsāra and Nirvāṇa are two. If one

14. The Bodhisattva Pratyakṣadarśana said:

Exhaustible (*kṣaya*) and inexhaustible (*akṣaya*) are two. But the exhaustible is absolutely exhausted (*kṣīṇa*), and, since that which is absolutely exhausted has already been exhausted, it becomes "inexhaustible". — The inexhaustible is instantaneous (*kṣaṇika*), but for the instantaneous, there is no exhaustion. Understanding in this way is penetrating the doctrine of non-duality[18].

Ideations (*vikalpa*) concerning the exhaustible (*kṣaya*) and the inexhaustible (*akṣaya*) are two. But Bodhisattvas know that there is nothing exhaustible or inexhaustible. — One calls exhaustible (*kṣaya*) that which is absolutely exhausted (*atyantakṣīṇa*). But since that which is absolutely exhausted can no longer be exhausted again, it should be called inexhaustible. — Furthermore, the exhaustible only lasts for a single instant (*ekakṣaṇika*). But since in a single instant there is no exhaustion, the exhaustible is, in reality, inexhaustible. — The exhaustible not existing at all, the inexhaustible does not exist either. Understanding that the exhaustible and the inexhaustible are empty of self-nature (*svabhāvaśūnya*), this is entering the doctrine of non-duality.

15. The Bodhisattva Parigudha said:

Self (*ātman*) and not-self (*anātman*) are two. The self-nature (*svabhāva*) of the self being non-existent (*anupalabdha*), how could the not-self exist? The non-duality perceived by the vision of these two natures is the entry into non-duality[19].

Ideations (*vikalpa*) concerning self (*ātman*) and not-self (*anātman*) are two. Bodhisattvas understand that the self is non-existent (*anupalabdha*) and thus how much more so (*kiṃ punar vādaḥ*), the not-self. Seeing that the self and the not-self are not two, this is entering the doctrine of non-duality.

16. The Bodhisattva Vidyuddeva said:

Knowledge (*vidyā*) and ignorance (*avidyā*) are two. Knowledge is of the same nature (*svabhāva*)

Ideations (*vikalpa*) concerning knowledge (*vidyā*) and ignorance (*avidyā*) are two. Bodhisattvas understand that the

sees the self-nature of Saṃsāra, [one knows] that there is no Saṃsāra, neither is there *bandhana*, *mokṣa*, *utpāda* or *nirodha*: to understand this is to enter *advaya*.

[18] K: *Kṣaya* and *akṣaya* are two. But whether dharmas are absolutely exhausted (*atyantakṣīṇā*) or inexhausted (*akṣīṇa*), there does not exist in them any mark of exhaustion (*kṣayalakṣaṇa*). Without a mark of exhaustion, they are empty (*śūnya*). Being empty, they have neither a *kṣayalakṣaṇa* nor an *akṣayalakṣaṇa*. To understand this is to enter *advaya*.

[19] K: *Ātman* and *anātman* are two. But if the *ātman* is non-existent (*anupalabdha*), how could the *anātman* exist? To see the real nature of the *ātman* and not to moot duality, this is entering *advaya*.

as ignorance. However, this ignorance is undefined (*avyākṛta*), incalculable (*asaṃkhyeya*) and beyond the path of calculation (*saṃkhyāṃārgātikrānta*). Understanding this is entering non-duality[20].

original nature (*prakṛtisvabhāva*) of ignorance is knowledge, that knowledge and ignorance are both non-existent (*anupalabdha*), incalculable (*asaṃkhyeya*) and beyond the path of calculation (*saṃkhyāmārgātikrānta*). Understanding their sameness (*samatā*), their non-duality (*advaya*), this is penetrating the doctrine of non-duality.

17. The Bodhisattva Priyadarśana[21] said:

Form (*rūpa*) itself is empty (*śūnya*); it is not through the destruction of form (*rūpakṣaya*) that there is emptiness (*śūnya*); the self-nature of form (*rūpasvabhāva*) is emptiness. Equally, to speak of sensation (*vedanā*), perception (*saṃjñā*), volition (*saṃskāra*) and consciousness (*vijñāna*) on the one hand, and of emptiness (*śūnyatā*) on the other, is two. But consciousness (*vijñāna*) is empty; it is not through the destruction of consciousness (*vijñānakṣaya*) that there is emptiness; the self-nature of consciousness (*vijñānasvabhāva*) is emptiness. He who sees in this way the five aggregates of attachment (*upādānaskandha*) and understands them as such through knowledge (*jñāna*) penetrates into non-duality[22].

Form (*rūpa*), sensation (*vedanā*), perception (*saṃjñā*), volition (*saṃskāra*) and consciousness (*vijñāna*) on the one hand, and emptiness (*śūnyatā*) on the other hand, are two. But Bodhisattvas know that the five aggregates of attachment (*upādānaskandha*) are naturally and originally empty (*śūnya*). It is form (*rūpa*) itself which is empty (*śūnya*), and it is not through the destruction of form (*rūpakṣaya*) that there is emptiness. It is the same with the four other aggregates up to and including the consciousness aggregate (*vijñānaskandha*). This is penetrating the doctrine of non-duality.

[20] K: *Vidyā* and *avidyā* are two. But the real nature of *avidyā* is *vidyā*. *Vidyā*, in turn, is ungraspable and evades all calculation. In them there is sameness (*samatā*), non-duality. This is entering *advaya*.

[21] Priyadarśana: cf. Dharmasaṃgītisūtra quoted in Śikṣāsamuccaya, p. 124,*5*.

[22] K: *Rūpa* and *rūpaśūnyatā* are two. But *rūpa* is itself *śūnya*. It is not through the extinction (*nirodha*) of *rūpa* that *rūpa* is *śūnya*; the *svabhāva* of *rūpa* is itself *śūnya*. It is the same for *vedanā*, *saṃjñā*, *saṃskāra* and *vijñāna*. *Vijñāna* and *śūnyatā* are two. But *vijñāna* is itself *śūnya*. It is not through the extinction of *vijñāna* [that *vijñāna* is *śūnya*]; the *svabhāva* of *vijñāna* is itself *śūnya*. To penetrate this is to enter *advaya*.

Here the Vimalakīrti is exploiting a topic that is untiringly repeated in the Prajñāpāramitā: Pañcaviṃśati, p. 38,*2-8*; Śatasāh., p. 118,*18*; 812,*3-5*; 930,*11-16*;

18. The Bodhisattva Prabhāketu[23] said:

To say that the four elements (*dhātu*) are one thing and that the space element (*ākāśadhātu*) is another, is two. But the four elements have space as their nature (*ākāśasvabhāva*); prior time (*pūrvānta*) has space as its nature; posterior time (*aparānta*) has space as its nature, and the present (*pratyutpanna*) also has space as its nature. The knowledge (*jñāna*) that penetrates the elements in this way, is the entry into non-duality[24].

Ideation (*vikalpa*) concerning the four elements (*dhātu*) and ideation concerning space (*ākāśa*) are two. If Bodhisattvas understand that the four elements have space as their nature (*svabhāva*) and that, in their prior, between and posterior times (*pūrvamadhyāparānta*), the four elements have space as their self-nature, then they unerringly (*aviparītam*) penetrate the elements. This is entering the doctrine of non-duality.

19. The Bodhisattva Pramati said:

Eye (*cakṣus*) and form (*rūpa*) are two. But clearly understanding the eye (*cakṣuḥparijñayā*) and not having for form either craving (*rāga*), or hatred (*dveṣa*) or delusion (*moha*), this is calm (*śānta*). Equally, ear (*śrotra*) and sound

Eye (*cakṣus*) and form (*rūpa*), ear (*śrotra*) and sound (*śabda*), nose (*ghrāṇa*) and odour (*gandha*), tongue (*jihvā*) and taste (*rasa*), body (*kāya*) and tangible (*spraṣṭavya*), mind (*manas*) and objects (*dharma*): these ideations (*vikalpa*) are twofold. If Bodhisattvas understand that all these natures (*svabhāva*) are empty (*śūnya*),

T 220, ch. 402, p. 11 *c* 1; T 221, ch. 1, p. 4 *c* 18; T 222, ch. 1, p. 152 *a* 16; T 223, ch. 1, p. 221 *b* 25-221 *c* 10; T 1509, ch. 35, p. 318 *a* 8-22 (followed by a commentary): *na śūnyatayā rūpaṃ śūnyaṃ, nānyatra rūpāc chūnyatā, rūpam eva śūnyatā śūnyataiva rūpam... tathā hi nāmamātram idaṃ yad idaṃ rūpam*: "It is not through emptiness that form is empty; apart from form there is no emptiness; form is emptiness, emptiness is form. In fact form is nothing but a word".

It is stated that the reasoning laid down here concerning *rūpa* applies to the other four *skandha* and all dharmas without exception. — In his turn, Chih Tun 支遁 (314-366), the greatest propagandist of Buddhism amongst the high society of South-Eastern China, based on the present passage of the Vimalakīrtinirdeśa his particular method of exegesis conducive to defining the Mahāyānist concept of emptiness in its relation to the phenomenal world: cf. E. ZÜRCHER, *The Buddhist Conquest of China*, p. 123, and 362, note 215.

Regarding *śūnyatā* and non-existence, see the Introduction, p. LXIX-LXXII.

[23] Prabhāketu: cf. I, § 4, note 13.

[24] K: The four *dhātu* on the one hand and the *ākāśadhātu* on the other hand are two. But the *svabhāva* of the four *dhātu* is the *svabhāva* of the *ākāśadhātu*. *Pūrvānta* and *aparānta* being empty (*śūnya*), *madhyānta* is also empty. To understand in this way the *svabhāva* of the *dhātu* is to enter the *advaya*.

(*śabda*), nose (*ghrāṇa*) and odour (*gandha*), tongue (*jihvā*) and taste (*rasa*), body (*kāya*) and tangible (*spraṣṭavya*), mind (*manas*) and objects (*dharma*) are two-fold. But clearly understanding the mind (*manaḥparijñayā*) and feeling for objects neither craving, hatred nor delusion, this is calm. Being thus established in calm is entering into non-duality[25].

if they clearly see the self-nature of the eye (*cakṣuḥsvabhāva*) and if they do not have for form (*rūpa*) either craving (*rāga*), or hatred (*dveṣa*) or delusion (*moha*); if, little by little, they clearly see the self-nature of the mind (*manaḥsvabhāva*) and if they do not have for objects (*dharma*) either craving, or hatred or delusion, then, say I, Bodhisattvas will hold all this as empty (*śūnya*). Having seen in this way, they are established in calm (*śānta*). This is penetrating the doctrine of non-duality.

20. The Bodhisattva Akṣayamati[26] said:

Giving (*dāna*) and the transference of giving to omniscience (*sarvajñānapariṇāmanā*) are two. But the self-nature (*svabhāva*) of giving is omniscience, and the self-nature of omniscience is transference[27]. Equally, morality (*śīla*), patience (*kṣānti*), vigour (*vīrya*), meditation (*dhyāna*) and wisdom (*prajñā*) on the one hand, and their transference to omniscience on the other hand, are two. But the self-nature of omniscience is transference. The entry into this

Giving (*dāna*) and its transference to omniscience (*sarvajñānapariṇāmanā*) are two. Equally, morality (*śīla*), patience (*kṣānti*), vigour (*vīrya*), meditation (*dhyāna*) and wisdom (*prajñā*) on the one hand, and their transference to omniscience on the other, are two. But if it is understood that giving is the transference to omniscience and that the transference to omniscience is giving, and so on, if it is understood that wisdom is the transference to omniscience, and that the transference to omniscience is wisdom, then the single principle (*ekanaya*) is understood. This is entering the doctrine of non-duality.

[25] K is absolutely identical to the Tibetan.

[26] Akṣayamati is a famous Bodhisattva who gave his name to the Akṣayamatinirdeśasūtra (T 397, ch. 27-30; T 403; OKC 842), one of the great authorities invoked by Mādhyamika authors (cf. Madh. vṛtti, p. 43,*4*; 108,*1*; 276,*9*; Śikṣāsamuccaya, p. 11,*8*; 21,*23*; 33,*13*; 34,*17*; 117,*13*; 119,*3*; 158,*7*; 167,*1*; 183,*4*; 212,*12*; 233,*6*; 236,*1* and *6*; 271,*4*; 278,*4*; 285,*7*; 287,*6*; 291,*8*; 316,*13*; Pañjikā, p. 81,*5*; 86,*5*; 118,*5*; 173,*7*; 522,*12*; 527,*16*). It is a section of the Mahāsaṃnipāta which clearly seems to be one of the sources of the Vimalakīrtinirdeśa (see above, III, § 62, note 121 at the end).

Akṣayamati often figures in Mahāyānasūtras: Rāṣṭrapālaparipṛcchā, p. 2,*1*; Saddharmapuṇḍ., p. 3,*8*; 438,*2*; Mañjuśrīmūlakalpa, p. 311,*14*; 312,*5*; 461,*6*; Mahāvyutpatti, No. 702.

[27] K: Giving (*dāna*) and the transference to omniscience (*sarvajñānapariṇamanā*) are two. But the self-nature of giving is the self-nature of the transference to omniscience, etc.

single principle (*ekanayapraveśa*)[28]
is the entry into non-duality.

21. The Bodhisattva Gambhīramati said:

Emptiness (*śūnyatā*) is one thing, signlessness (*ānimitta*) is another, and wishlessness (*apraṇihita*) is yet another: all this implies duality. But in emptiness (*śūnyatā*), there is no sign (*nimitta*); in signlessness, there is no wish (*praṇidhāna*); in wishlessness, neither thought (*citta*) nor mind (*manas*) nor consciousness (*vijñāna*) function. Seeing that all the three doors to deliverance (*vimokṣamukha*) are contained in a single door to deliverance, this is penetrating into non-duality[29].

22. The Bodhisattva Śāntendriya said:

The three jewels, the Buddha, the Law (*dharma*) and the Community (*saṃgha*) imply duality. But the self-nature (*svabhāva*) of the Buddha is the Law, and the self-nature of the Law is the Community. These three jewels are unconditioned (*asaṃskṛta*); being unconditioned, they are the same as space (*ākāśasama*). The principle of all dharmas (*sarvadharmanaya*) is the same as space. Understanding thus is entering into non-duality[30].

23. The Bodhisattva Apratihatanetra said:

The aggregation of perishable things (*satkāya*) and the extinction of the aggregation of perishable things (*satkāyanirodha*) are two. But aggregation itself is extinction. And why? When the belief in the aggregation of perishable things (*satkāyadṛṣṭi*) does not arise, does not exist, there can be no conception (*kalpa*), no ideation (*vikalpa*), no imagining (*parikalpa*) concerning the aggregation of perishable

The aggregation of perishable things (*satkāya*) and the extinction of the aggregation of perishable things (*satkāyanirodha*) are two. But Bodhisattvas know that the aggregation of perishable things is the extinction of perishable things. Knowing this, they absolutely do not produce the belief in the aggregation of perishable things (*satkāyadṛṣṭi*) Regarding the aggregation of perishable things and the extinction of perishable things, they have no conception (*kalpa*), no ideation (*vikalpa*). They testify (*sākṣātkurvanti*) to the absolute extinction (*atyantanirodhasvabhā-*

[28] Regarding the *ekanaya*, which K always renders by *i-hsiang*, see above, III, § 73, note 144.

[29] K: *Śūnyatā*, *ānimitta* and *apraṇihita* form dualities. But *śūnyatā* is *ānimitta*, and *ānimitta* is *apraṇihita*. If there is *śūnyatā*, *ānimitta* and *apraṇihita*, there is neither *citta*, nor *manas*, nor *vijñāna*. The three *vimokṣamukha* in a single *vimokṣamukha* is the entry into *advaya*.

[30] K: *Buddha*, *dharma* and *saṃgha* form dualities. But the Buddha is the *dharma*; and the *dharma* is the *saṃgha*. These three jewels are *asaṃskṛta* and *ākāśasama*. And all dharmas equally so. To act in conformity with this is to enter *advaya*.

things or the extinction of this aggregation; hence, there is identification with extinction itself (*nirodhasvabhāva*). Non-arising (*anutpāda*) and non-extinction (*anirodha*), this is the entry into non-duality[31].

va) of the two things, without feeling hesitation (*vimati*), or fear (*trāsa*) or dread (*saṃtrāsa*). This is penetrating the doctrine of non-duality.

24. The Bodhisattva Suvinīta said:

The disciplines of the body, speech and mind (*kāyavāgmanaḥsaṃvara*) are not duality. And why? These dharmas are of inactive mark (*anabhisaṃskāralakṣaṇa*). The inactivity of the body is the inactivity of speech, and the inactivity of speech is the inactivity of the mind. The inactivity of all dharmas (*sarvadharmānabhisaṃskāra*) should be known and understood. Knowing it is the entry into non-duality[32].

The three disciplines of the body, speech and mind (*kāyavāgmanaḥsaṃvara*) are, it is said, duality. But Bodhisattvas know that these three disciplines have an inactive mark (*anabhisaṃskāralakṣaṇa*) and that this mark does not consist of duality. And why? The inactivity of the body is the inactivity of speech; the inactivity of speech is the inactivity of the mind; the inactivity of the mind is the inactivity common to all dharmas. Penetrating this mark of inactivity, this is entering the doctrine of non-duality.

25. The Bodhisattva Puṇyakṣetra said:

Actions meritorious, demeritorious and neutral (*puṇyāpuṇyāniñjyābhisaṃskāra*) imply duality. In reality, these meritorious, demeritorious and neutral actions do not constitute a duality. The self-mark (*svalakṣaṇa*) of these actions is empty (*śūnya*). There is neither merit, nor demerit, nor

Ideations concerning meritorious action (*puṇyābhisaṃskāra*), demeritorious action (*apuṇyābhisaṃskāra*) and neutral action (*āniñjyābhisaṃskāra*) imply duality. But Bodhisattvas know that fault, merit and neutral action have an inactive mark and that this mark does not consist of duality. And why? Fault, merit and neutral action are, all three, empty of self-nature and mark. In emptiness these various kinds

[31] K. *Satkāya* and *satkāyanirodha* are two. But the *satkaya* is the *satkāyanirodha*. And why? Because he who sees the *bhūtalakṣaṇa* of the *satkāya*, no longer produces a view concerning the *satkaya* and the *satkayanirodha*. Between *satkāya* and *satkāyanirodha* there is neither duality (*dvaya*) nor mental ideation (*vikalpa*). To stop at that point, without dread or fear is to enter *advaya*.

[32] K: The discipline (*saṃvara*) of *kāya*, *vāc* and *manas* forms dualities. But these three activities all have an *anabhisaṃskāralakṣaṇa*. The inactive mark of the *kāya* is the inactive mark of the *vāc*, and the inactive mark of the *vāc* is the inactive mark of the *manas*. The inactive mark of these three activities is the inactive mark of all dharmas. Those who thus conform to the knowledge of inactivity penetrate *advaya*.

neutral action, nor action. The non-demonstration (*asiddhi*) of this action is the entry into non-duality[33].

(*viśeṣa*) of actions are absent. Understanding thus is penetrating the doctrine of non-duality.

26. The Bodhisattva Padmavyūha[34] said:

That which is born of exaltation of the self (*ātmaparyutthānaja*) is duality. But the real knowledge of self (*ātmaparijñāna*) does not seek out (*na parimārgayati*) duality. In him who bases himself on non-duality (*advayāvasthita*), there is no idea (*vijñapti*), and this absence of idea is the entry into non-duality[35].

All duality is born of the self (*ātmaja*). If Bodhisattvas know the real nature (*bhūtasvabhāva*) of the self, they do not postulate any duality; by not postulating any duality, they no longer have ideas (*vijñapti*) and, no longer having ideas, they no longer have an object of thought. This is penetrating the doctrine of non-duality.

27. The Bodhisattva Śrīgarbha[36] said:

That which arises from an object (*ālambanaprabhāvita*) is duality. The absence of an object (*nirālambana*) is non-duality. That is why not taking anything (*anādāna*) and not rejecting anything (*aprahāṇa*) is entering into non-duality.

All duality is born of an object (*ālambana*). If Bodhisattvas understand that all dharmas are non-existent (*anupalabdha*), they do not take them and do not reject them. Not taking anything and not rejecting anything is penetrating the doctrine of non-duality.

28. The Bodhisattva Candrottara[37] said:

Darkness (*tamas*) and light (*jyotis*) are two. But the absence of darkness and the absence of

Ideations (*vikalpa*) concerning darkness (*tamas*) and light (*jyotis*) are two. But Bodhisattvas know that the real mark

[33] K: The *abhimsaṃskāra puṇya*, *apuṇya* and *āniñjya* imply dualities. But the *bhūtasvabhāva* of these three *abhisaṃskāra* is empty (*śūnya*). Since it is empty, there is neither *puṇya*, nor *apuṇya* nor *āniñjya-abhisaṃskāra*. Not to produce any of these three *abhisaṃskāra* is to enter *advaya*.

[34] Padmavyūha: cf. above, I, § 4, note 32.

[35] This paragraph is missing in Cn. — K: From [the idea] of *ātman* come the two [ideas of *ātman* and *anātman*] which form duality. But he who sees the real mark (*bhūtalakṣaṇa*) of the *ātman* no longer produces these two dharmas. Not abiding in any way in these two dharmas, he has no consciousness (*vijñāna*) nor object of consciousness (*vijñāta*): this is entering *advaya*.

[36] Śrīgarbha: cf. Saddharmapuṇḍ., p. 21,*11*; 26,*5*; Daśabhūmika, p. 2,*6*; Gaṇḍavyūha, p. 442,*9*; Mahāvyutpatti, No. 666.

[37] Candrottarajñānin: cf. Gaṇḍavyūha, p. 2,*15*.

light are a non-duality. And why? For an ascetic entered into the recollection of extinction (*nirodhasamāpatti*), there is neither darkness nor light, and it is thus with all dharmas. Understanding this sameness (*samatā*) is entering into non-duality [38].

(*bhūtalakṣaṇa*) does not consist of either darkness or light and that the nature (*bhāva*) is without duality. Just as for a bhikṣu entered into the recollection of extinction (*nirodhasamāpatti*), there is neither darkness nor light, and so it is with all dharmas. Understanding the sameness (*samatā*) of all dharmas is penetrating the doctrine of non-duality.

29. The Bodhisattva Ratnamudrāhasta [39] said:

Delight in Nirvāṇa (*nirvāṇābhirati*) and repugnance for Saṃsāra (*saṃsāraparikheda*) are two. But the absence of delight in Nirvāṇa and the absence of repugnance for Saṃsāra constitute a non-duality. And why? One must be bound (*baddha*) in order to speak of liberation (*mokṣa*), but if one is absolutely unbound (*atyantābaddha*), why should one seek liberation? The bhikṣu who is neither bound (*baddha*) nor liberated (*mukta*) does not feel either delight (*abhirati*) or repugnance (*parikheda*). This is entering into non-duality [40].

Delight in Nirvāṇa (*nirvāṇābhirati*) and repugnance for Saṃsāra (*saṃsāraparikheda*) are two. But if Bodhisattvas understand Nirvāṇa and Saṃsāra, they have neither delight nor repugnance and there is no longer any duality. And why? One must be bound (*baddha*) by Saṃsāra to seek deliverance (*mokṣa*). But if one knows the bonds of Saṃsāra absolutely do not exist, then why still seek the deliverance of Nirvāṇa (*nirvāṇamokṣa*)? Understanding thus the inexistence of bonds (*bandhana*) and deliverance (*mokṣa*), not delighting in Nirvāṇa and not hating Saṃsāra, is penetrating the doctrine of non-duality.

30. The Bodhisattva Maṇikūṭarāja said:

Right path (*mārga*) and wrong path (*kumārga*) are two. But if Bodhisattvas are established in the right path, they do not follow any of the wrong paths at all. In not following them at all, they have no notions (*saṃjñā*) of right or wrong path. Lacking these two notions, they have no conception of duality. This is penetrating the doctrine of non-duality.

[38] K: *Tamas* and *jyotis* are two. But the absence of *tamas* and the absence of *jyvotis* are not two. And why? If one enters the *saṃjñāvedayitanirodhasamāpatti*, there is neither *tamas* nor *jyotis*. And it is the same for all dharmas. In whatever concerns them, to penetrate *samatā* is to enter *advaya*.

[39] Ratnamudrāhasta: cf. above, I, § 4, note 19.

[40] K is identical with the Tibetan.

31. The Bodhisattva Satyarata said:

Truth (*satya*) and falsehood (*mṛṣā*) are two. But if he who has seen truth (*dṛṣṭasatya*) does not even conceive (*na samanupaśyati*) the nature of truth (*satyatā*), how could he see falsehood? And why? This nature is not seen by the fleshly eye (*māṃsacakṣus*) and is not seen by the wisdom eye (*prajñācakṣus*). It is to the extent that there is neither view (*darśana*) nor vision (*vidarśana*) that it is seen. Wherever there is neither view nor vision is where one enters into non-duality.

Truth (*satya*) and falsehood (*mṛṣā*) are two. But if Bodhisattvas who see the nature of truth (*satyasvabhāva*) do not even see truth, then how could they see falsehood? And why? This nature is not seen by the fleshly eye (*māṃsacakṣus*) or by the other eyes, including the wisdom eye (*prajñācakṣus*). When one sees thus and one has, regarding dharmas, neither vision nor absence of vision, one penetrates the doctrine of non-duality.

32. When the Bodhisattvas present in the assembly had each had their say as they understood it, they together asked Mañjuśrī the crown prince: Mañjuśrī, what really is the entry of the Bodhisattvas into non-duality?

Mañjuśrī replied: Worthy sirs (*satpuruṣa*), you have all spoken well; however, in my opinion, all that you have said still implies duality[41].

Excluding all words and not saying anything, not expressing anything, not pronouncing anything, not teaching anything, not designating anything, this is entering into non-duality[42].

If Bodhisattvas do not say anything, do not speak of anything, do not designate anything and do not teach anything regarding any dharma, they avoid all idle chatter (*prapañca*) and cut off every ideation (*vikalpa*), then they penetrate the doctrine of non-duality.

33. Then Mañjuśrī the crown prince said to the Licchavi Vimalakīrti: Son of good family (*kulaputra*), now that each of us has had his say, it is your turn to expound to us what the doctrine of the entry into non-duality (*advayadharmamukha*) is.

The Licchavi Vimalakīrti remained silent (*tūṣṇībhūto 'bhūt*).

Mañjuśrī the crown prince gave his assent (*sādhukāraṃ adāt*) to the Licchavi Vimalakīrti and said to him: Excellent, excellent, son of good

[41] This sentence is missing in K.

[42] K: In my opinion, not saying anything about any dharma, not speaking of anything, not uttering anything, not knowing anything, omitting all question (*praśna*) and all answer (*vyākaraṇa*), this is entering *advaya*.

family: this is the entry of the Bodhisattvas into non-duality. In this way, syllables (*akṣara*), sounds (*svara*) and concepts (*vijñapti*) are worthless (*asamudācāra*)[43].

These words having been spoken, five thousand Bodhisattvas, having penetrated the doctrine of non-duality, obtained the certainty concerning the non-arising of dharmas (*anutpattikadharmakṣānti*).

[43] In Tibetan: *ḥdi ni byaṅ chub sems dpaḥ rnams kyi gñis su med par ḥjug pa yin te. de la yi ge daṅ sgra daṅ rnam par rig paḥi rgyu med do.*

K translates freely: "By arriving at no longer having either syllables (*akṣara*) or words (*vāc*), this is really entering the *advayadharmamukha*".

In T 1775, ch. 8, p. 399 *b*, Kumārajīva illustrates this philosophical silence with the story of the conversion of Aśvaghoṣa, a story translated in full by S. LÉVI, *La Dṛṣṭāntapaṅkti et son auteur*, JA, July-Sept. 1927, p. 114-115. The bhikṣu Pārśva possessed a great talent for words and excelled in debate. The heretic Aśvaghoṣa introduced himself to him, offering to refute all the theories he supported. Pārśva listened to him debating and remained silent. Aśvaghoṣa considered him with scorn and left him. But, on his way, he reflected: That man has a very profound wisdom; it is I who was defeated. Every word I said can be refuted and I refuted myself. He said nothing and there is nothing to refute. Then Aśvaghoṣa returned to Pārśva, admitted his defeat and offered to have his head cut off. Pārśva suggested that it would be better to be tonsured, for "the tonsure is like death". So Aśvaghoṣa entered the order and became Pārśva's disciple. And Kumārajīva concludes his story with an explanation of the superiority of silence in the matter of the ineffable: "The debate in silence is the supreme debate".

This is indeed the position of the Madhyamaka. When questioned by a logician who asked him if it was really true that the holy ones are free of argument, Candrakīrti, in his Madh. vṛtti, p. 57,7-8, gave the following answer: *kenaitad uktam asti vā nāsti veti. paramārtho hy āryāṇāṃ tūṣṇiṃbhāvaḥ. tataḥ kutas tatra prapañcasaṃbhavo yad upapattir anupapattir vā syāt*: "So who could say whether the holy ones are free or not of argument? In fact the absolute is the silence of the holy ones. How then could a discussion with them on this subject be possible [and how could we know] if they are free or not of argument on this matter?"

On this subject, see G.M. NAGAO, *The Silence of the Buddha and its Madhyamic Interpretation*, Studies in Indology and Buddhology, Kyōto, 1955, p. 137-151.

At the council of Lhasa (792-794), Mahāyāna, the leader of the Chinese faction, used the authority of "Vimalakīrti's silence" to assert that the attribute of the mind is precisely not to have one and, in consequence, to be impredicable (cf. P. DEMIÉVILLE, *Le Concile de Lhasa*, p. 113, 114, 156). Kamalaśīla, Mahāyāna's opponent and leader of the Indian faction at the council, objected that to be legitimate and efficacious, the philosophical silence should be preceded by a long and exact analysis (*bhūtapratyavekṣā*) without which the understanding of emptiness is impossible (Idem, *ibidem*, p. 351).

Let us note in conclusion that this paragraph 33 concerning Vimalakīrti's silence appears in all the versions we have available except in that by Chih Ch'ien which is precisely the oldest. Was this paragraph missing in the original edition of the Vimalakīrti? If so, the interest of this text would be considerably diminished.

CHAPTER NINE

THE OBTAINING OF FOOD BY THE IMAGINARY BODHISATTVA

[*Śāriputra's Anxiety*]

1. Then the Venerable (*āyuṣmant*) Śāriputra had this thought: It is midday (*madhyāhna*) and these great Bodhisattvas occupied in expounding the Law are still not getting up. So when, Listeners (*śrāvaka*) and Bodhisattvas, are we going to eat?

Then the Licchavi Vimalakīrti, knowing in his mind the thought that had arisen in the mind of the Venerable Śāriputra (*tasyāyuṣmataḥ Śāriputrasya cetasaiva cetaḥparivitarkam ājñāya*), said to the Venerable Śāriputra: Honourable (*bhadanta*) Śāriputra, the Tathāgata has expounded to the Listeners (*śrāvaka*) the eight liberations (*vimokṣa*): you should hold to this and not listen to the Law with preoccupations tied up with material things (*āmiṣasaṃbhinnasaṃtāna*). However, if you want to eat, wait a moment (*muhūrtam āgamayasva*), and you will eat such food as has never yet been tasted (*ananubhūtapūrvaṃ bhojanaṃ bhokṣyase*)[1].

[*The Revealing of the Sarvagandhasugandhā Universe*]

2. At that moment (*tena khalu punar samayena*), the Licchavi Vimalakīrti entered into such a concentration (*tathārūpaṃ samādhiṃ samāpede*) and performed such a supernatural action (*tathārūpam ṛddhyabhisaṃskāram abhisaṃskaroti sma*) that he revealed to the Bodhisattvas and Śrāvakas the universe called Sarvagandhasugandhā[2]. This universe can be found if, from here, one traverses, in the direction of the zenith, universes as innumerable as the sands of the forty-two Ganges (*ūrdhvāyāṃ diśi dvācatvāriṃśadgaṅgānadīvālukopamāni buddhakṣetrāṇy atikramya*). It is there that at present the Tathāgata Sugandhakūṭa[3] is to be found (*tiṣṭhati*), lives (*dhriyate*) and exists

[1] On everything that concerns this sacred food that is mentioned in Chapters IX and X, see Appendix, Note VII: *The perfumed Amṛta*.

[2] The reading *Sarvagandhasugandhā* is confirmed by the Śikṣāsamuccaya, p. 270,*2*. The Laṅkāvatāra, p. 105,*9*; and the Madh. vṛtti, p. 333,*6*, simply have *Gandhasugandhā*.

[3] In Tibetan Spos mchog brtsegs pa = Sugandhakūṭa. However, the Laṅkāvatāra

(*yāpayati*). In this universe, the trees (*vṛkṣa*) give off a perfume (*gandha*) far superior (*bahvantaraviśiṣṭa*) to those emitted by the men and gods (*manuṣyadeva*) of all the Buddha-fields (*buddhakṣetra*) situated in the ten regions. In this universe, the very names of Śrāvaka and Pratyekabuddha are not known; there is an assembly (*saṃnipāta*) composed only of great and pure Bodhisattvas, to whom the Tathāgata Sugandhakūṭa expounds the Law. In this universe, the belvederes (*kūṭāgāra*), avenues (*caṅkrama*), parks (*upavana*), palaces (*prāsāda*) and the clothes (*vastra*) are all made of various perfumes (*nānāvidhagandhamaya*), and the perfume of the food eaten by this blessed Lord Buddha and these Bodhisattvas fills (*prasarati*) innumerable universes.

At that moment, the blessed Tathāgata Sugandhakūṭa was sitting with his Bodhisattvas to have his meal (*bhojanam upabhoktum*), and the son of the gods (*devaputra*) Gandhavyūhāhāra, fully pledged to the Great Vehicle (*mahāyānasaṃprasthita*), ensured the service (*upasthana*) and care (*paryupāsana*) of the Blessed One and those Bodhisattvas [4].

and the Madh. vṛtti attribute the Gandhasugandhā universe, not to Sugandhakūṭa, but to Samantabhadra.

Laṅkāvatāra, p. 105,*8-12*: *yathā Mahāmate Animiṣāyāṃ Gandhasugandhāyāṃ ca lokadhātau Samantabhadrasya tathāgatasyārhataḥ samyaksaṃbuddhasya buddhakṣetre 'nimiṣair netraiḥ prekṣamāṇās te bodhisattvā mahāsattvā anutpattikadharmakṣāntiṃ pratilabhante 'nyāṃś ca samādhiviśeṣān*: "And so it is, O Mahāmati, that in the Animiṣā universe and in the Gandhasugandhā universe of the Tathāgata Samantabhadra, the Bodhisattvas acquire the *anutpattikadharmakṣānti* and other kinds of *samādhi* by gazing fixedly, without blinking their eyes".

Madh. vṛtti, p. 333,*6-9*: *tathā āryavimalakīrtinirdeśe*: *tan nirmitabodhisattvena Gandhasugandhāyāṃ lokadhātau Samantabhadratathāgatopabhuktaśeṣaṃ bhojanam ānītaṃ nānāvyañjanakhādyādisaṃprayuktaṃ pṛthak pṛthag vividharasam ekabhojanena sarvam tac chrāvakabodhisattvasaṃgharājarājāmātyapurohitāntaḥpuradauvārikasārthavāhādijanapadaṃ saṃtarpya prītyākāraṃ nāma mahāsamādhiṃ lambhyayāmāseti*: "It is said in the Āryavimalakīrtinirdeśa: Then the imaginary Bodhisattva brought the remains of the food taken in the Gandhasugandhā universe by the Tathāgata Samantabhadra, food blended with all kinds of condiments and victuals and containing, on each occasion, various flavours. When, in a single meal, this food had refreshed the whole population — Śrāvakas, Bodhisattvas, the king, ministers, chaplain, women, door keepers, caravaneers, etc. —, all obtained the great concentration called "Joyful Aspect".

This quotation is certainly not literal; it does not appear in the Tibetan version of the Madh. vṛtti.

[4] According to K: "There were some devaputras there, all named Gandhavyūha and who had produced the *anuttarasamyaksaṃbodhicitta*; they served (*pūjayanti sma*) that Buddha and those Bodhisattvas". But according to the Tibetan version and the Chinese versions by Cn and H, it seems it was a matter of only a single server. The mention of a cup-bearer is surprising, to say the least. It naturally brings to mind

At Vimalakīrti's the whole assembly (*sarvāvatī parṣad*) observed this universe where the Blessed Sugandhakūṭa and his Bodhisattvas were sitting.

[*An Imaginary Bodhisattva's Mission to the Sarvagandhasugandhā*]

3. Then the Licchavi Vimalakīrti, addressing all the Bodhisattvas, said to them: Worthy Sirs (*satpuruṣa*), is there anyone among you who would be capable (*utsāha*) of going to this universe to obtain some food?

But, through the supernatural intervention (*adhiṣṭhāna*) of Mañjuśrī, no-one was capable of it, and all the Bodhisattvas kept silent (*tūṣṇīṃbhūta*).

The Licchavi Vimalakīrti said to Mañjuśrī the crown prince: Mañjuśrī, do you not feel shame (*hrepaṇa*) for such an assembly (*evaṃrūpā parṣad*)?

Mañjuśrī replied: Son of good family, you should not despise (*avaman-*) this assembly of Bodhisattvas. Has not the Tathāgata said that *aśaikṣa* should not be despised [5]?

4. Then the Licchavi Vimalakīrti, without rising from his seat (*anutthāyāsanāt*) and in the presence of the Bodhisattvas, created (*nirmimīte sma*) an imaginary Bodhisattva (*nirmitabodhisattva*): his body was the colour of gold (*suvarṇavarṇa*), he was adorned with the primary and secondary physical marks (*lakṣaṇānuvyañjanasamalaṃkṛta*) and he displayed such colours (*rūpa*) that all the assemblies were eclipsed (*dhyāmīkṛta*) by them.

The Licchavi Vimalakīrti said to this imaginary Bodhisattva: Go then, son of good family, in the direction of the zenith (*gaccha tvaṃ, kulaputra, ūrdhvāyāṃ diśi*); having traversed Buddha-fields as innumerable as the sands of the forty-two Ganges (*dvācatvāriṃśadgaṅ-*

Ganymede, son of Tros and cup-bearer to Zeus (*Iliad*, V, v. 265; XX, v. 232; *Little Iliad* in the Scholia to Euripides, *Orestes*, v. 1392, *Trojans*, v. 821), carried off to Olympus by a whirlwind (*Hymn to Aphrodite*, v. 208), by an eagle (*Aeneid*, V, v. 255), or by Zeus disguised as an eagle (Ovid, *Metamorphoses*, X, v. 155 sq.).

In Gandhāra and Central Asia representations have been found of Garuḍa abducting a Nāgī (cf. A. Foucher, *Art gréco-bouddhique du Gandhāra*, II, fig. 318 to 321; A. von Le Coq, *Bilderatlas zur Kunst und Kulturgeschichte Mittel-Asiens*, Berlin, 1925, fig. 147 to 151). These are crude copies of the Ganymede by Leochares. The Indian sculptors perhaps confused Ganymede's shepherd's crook with a serpent's tail: this led to the substitution of a Nāgī for Ganymede.

[5] Cf. Aṅguttara, I, p. 63,*6-8*: *dve kho gahapati loke dakkhiṇeyyā sekho ca asekho ca. ime kho gahapati dve loke dakkhiṇeyyā ettha ca dānaṃ dātabbaṃ.* Also see Madhyama, T 26, No. 127, ch. 30, p. 616 *a* 10-11; Saṃyukta, T 99, No. 992, ch. 33, p. 258 *c* 14-15.

gānadīvālukopamāni buddhakṣetrāṇy atikramya), you will find the Sarvagandhasugandhā universe; it is there that at present the Tathāgata Sugandhakūṭa is sitting with his Bodhisattvas; having reached him, and after having saluted his feet by touching them with your head (*pādau śirasābhivandya*), you will say to him: "In the nadir region (*adhodiśi*), the Licchavi Vimalakīrti, saluting a hundred thousand times your feet by touching them with his head (*śatasahasrakṛtvo bhagavataḥ pādau śirasābhivandya*), enquires after your health (*glānaṃ pṛcchati*) by asking you if you have little affliction and little suffering, if you are alert and well-disposed, if you are strong, physically well and morally without reproach and if you rejoice in agreeable contacts (*te 'lpābādhatāṃ pṛcchaty alpātaṅkatāṃ laghūtthānatāṃ yātrāṃ balaṃ sukham anavadyatāṃ sukhasparśavihāratām*)[6]. From afar (*dūratas*) and mentally (*cittena*), after having circled round you more than a hundred thousand times (*śatasahasrakṛtvaḥ pradakṣiṇīkṛtya*) and after having saluted your feet by touching them with his head (*pādau śirasābhivandya*), he entreats you to give me the remains of your meal (*upabhuktaśeṣaṃ bhojanam*). With these remains, Vimalakīrti will perform Buddha deeds (*buddhakārya*) in the Sahā universe in the nadir region.

Thus beings with base aspirations (*hīnādhimuktika*) will be animated by noble aspirations (*udārādhimuktika*) and the Tathāgata marks (*tathāgatalakṣaṇa*) will develop"[7].

Thus also beings with base aspirations (*hīnādhimuktika*) will delight in great wisdom, and the innumerable virtues (*apramāṇaguṇa*) of the Tathāgata will be extolled everywhere".

5. Then the imaginary Bodhisattva, having shown his agreement (*sādhv iti kṛtvā*) to the Licchavi Vimalakīrti, obeyed (*pratyaśrauṣīt*). In the presence of the Bodhisattvas, he left, his head held high (*ullokitavadana*), but the

Then the imaginary Bodhisattva, in the presence of the whole assembly, rose into the air (*vaihāyasam abhyudgacchati sma*), and the whole assembly (*sarvāvatī parṣad*) saw him[8]. Miraculously and rapidly, in a single instant (*ekasminn eva kṣaṇalavamuhūrte*), he reached the Sarvagandhasugandhā universe and saluted with

[6] Regarding this formula which will appear again in § 5, see the references above, IV, § 5, note 8.

[7] K: "Vimalakīrti wanted to obtain the remains of the meal (*upabhuktaśeṣa*) of the Bhagavat to perform Buddha deeds (*buddhakārya*) in the Sahā universe in such a way that those who delight in base laws (*hīnadharma*) may obtain great Bodhi all together and so that the Tathāgata's glory may be extolled everywhere".

[8] According to the three Chinese versions, all the Bodhisattvas saw the imaginary Bodhisattva rise into the air; according to the Tibetan version this ascent was so fast that it could not be followed with their eyes.

Bodhisattvas did not see him leave. Then the imaginary Bodhisattva, having reached the Sarvagandhasugandhā universe, saluted with his head the feet of the Blessed Tathāgata Sugandhakūṭa and addressed him with these words:

his head the feet of the Buddha Sugandhakūṭa. He could be heard to say these words:

In the nadir region (*adhodiśi*), the Bodhisattva Vimalakīrti, saluting your feet a hundred thousand times, O Blessed One, enquires after your health (*glānaṃ pṛcchati*) and asks if you have little affliction and little suffering, if you are alert and well-disposed, if you are strong, physically well and morally without reproach and if you rejoice in agreeable contacts (*te 'lpābādhatāṃ pṛcchaty alpātaṅkatāṃ laghūtthānatāṃ yātrāṃ balaṃ sukham anavadyatāṃ sukhasparśavihāratām*). From afar and mentally, Vimalakīrti, after having circled round you more than a hundred thousand times (*śatasahasrakṛtvaḥ pradakṣiṇīkṛtya*) and after having saluted your feet by touching them with his head (*pādau śirasābhivandya*), entreats you to give me the remains of your meal (*upabhuktaśeṣaṃ bhojanam*). With these remains, Vimalakīrti will perform Buddha deeds (*buddhakārya*) in the Sahā universe in the nadir region.

Thus beings with base aspirations (*hīnādhimuktika*) will be animated by noble aspirations (*udārādhimuktika*) with regard to the attributes of the Buddhas, and the Tathāgata marks (*tathāgatalakṣaṇa*) will develop.

Thus beings with base aspirations will delight in great wisdom, and the innumerable virtues of the Tathāgata will be extolled everywhere.

6. Then the Bodhisattvas of the zenith, Bodhisattvas belonging to the Buddhakṣetra of the Blessed Tathāgata Sugandhakūṭa, were filled with astonishment (*āścaryaprāpta*) on seeing this imaginary Bodhisattva, adorned with the primary and secondary marks (*lakṣaṇānuvyañjanasamalaṃkṛta*), of splendid aspect (*viracitaprabhāsa*) and of such amiable qualities (*cāruviśeṣa*). Addressing the Blessed Tathāgata Sugandhakūṭa, they asked him: Blessed One, from where does a personage of this sort (*evaṃrūpo mahāsattvaḥ*) come? Where is the Sahā universe? And who are these beings with base aspirations (*hīnādhimuktika*) of whom he makes mention? We would like the Blessed One to explain all these things to us.

Questioned in this way by his Bodhisattvas, the Blessed Tathāgata Sugandhakūṭa answered them: Sons of good family (*kulaputra*), if, leaving here in the direction of the nadir, one traverses Buddha-fields as innumerable as the sands of the forty-two Ganges (*adhodiśi dvācatvāriṃśadgaṅgānadīvālukopamāni buddhakṣetrāṇy atikramya*), one would find the Sahā universe. It is there that at present the Tathāgata Śākyamuni, holy and perfectly enlightened, is to be found, lives and exists (*tiṣṭhati dhriyate yāpayati*), and in this universe of the five corruptions (*pañcakaṣāya*), he expounds the Law (*dharmaṃ deśayati*) to beings with base aspirations (*hīnādhimuktika*). It is there also that the Bodhisattva Vimalakīrti, established in the doctrine of inconceivable liberation (*acintyavimokṣa*), expounds the Law to the Bodhisattvas of the Sahā universe. This Vimalakīrti has sent (*preṣayati*) to me here this imaginary Bodhisattva (*nirmitabodhisattva*) to extol (*parikīrtana*) my body (*kāya*), my virtues (*guṇa*) and my name (*nāman*), to reveal (*saṃprakāśana*) the advantages (*praśaṃsā*) of our Sarvagandhasugandhā universe and in the hope of developing the good roots (*kuśalamūla*) of the Bodhisattvas of the Sahā universe.

7. All the Bodhisattvas exclaimed: What greatness (*māhātmya*) is that of Vimalakīrti, capable of creating an imaginary being thus gifted with psychic strength (*ṛddhi*), powers (*bala*) and convictions (*vaiśāradya*)!

The Blessed Lord Sugandhakūṭa continued:

The greatness of this Bodhisattva is such that he sends imaginary beings (*nirmāṇa*) to all the Buddhakṣetras of the ten regions and that these imaginary beings perform Buddha deeds (*buddhakāryam upasthāpayanti*) for all the beings of these Buddhakṣetras.

Sons of good family, this great Bodhisattva is gifted with virtues so outstanding (*evaṃviśiṣṭaguṇa*) that in a single instant (*ekasminn eva kṣaṇalavamuhūrte*) he creates by transformation (*nirmimīte*) innumerable (*aprameya*) and infinite (*ananta*) Bodhisattvas and sends (*preṣayati*) them everywhere in the universes of the ten regions (*daśadiglokadhātu*) to perform Buddha deeds (*buddhakārya*) for the benefit and happiness of innumerable beings (*aprameyāṇāṃ sattvānāṃ hitāya sukhāya*).

8. Then the Blessed Tathāgata Sugandhakūṭa poured into a perfumed bowl food which was impregnated with all the perfumes (*sarva gandhasamanvāgate pātre sarvagandhavāsitaṃ bhojanaṃ chorayati sma*) and gave it to the imaginary Bodhisattva sent by Vimalakīrti.

In the Sarvagandhasugandhā universe, ninety hundreds of thousands of Bodhisattvas who wanted to go along (*āgantukāma*) raised their voices together and asked the Buddha Sugandhakūṭa: We want to go with this imaginary Bodhisattva to the Sahā universe in the nadir region to see the Blessed Tathāgata Śākyamuni, to honour him, serve him and hear the Law and also to see the Bodhisattva Vimalakīrti and the other Bodhisattvas (*gamiṣyāmo vayaṃ bhagavaṃs tena nirmitabodhisattvena sārdhaṃ tāṃ Sahāṃ lokadhātuṃ taṃ bhagavantaṃ Śākyamuniṃ tathāgataṃ darśanāya vandanāya paryupāsanāya dharmaśravaṇāya taṃ ca Vimalakīrtiṃ bodhisattvam anyāṃś ca bodhisattvān darśanāya*)[9]. May the Blessed One give us his permission.

The blessed Lord Sugandhakūṭa said: Then go there, sons of good family, if you consider it to be the right time (*gacchata kulaputrā yasyedānīṃ kālaṃ manyadhve*)[10].

But since these beings will certainly be disturbed (*unmatta*) and intoxicated (*pramatta*) by you, go there without your perfumes. Since the beings of this Sahā universe will feel jealousy (*avasāda*) towards you, hide your beauty (*svarūpa*). And finally, do not go and arouse notions of scorn or aversion (*na yuṣmābhis tasyāṃ lokadhātau hīnasaṃjñā pratighasaṃjñotpādayitavyā*). And why? Kulaputras, the (true) Buddhakṣetra is a blank field (*ākāśakṣetra*), but in order to ripen beings (*sattvaparipācanārtham*), the Blessed Ones do not show them completely the (pure) domain of the Buddhas (*buddhagocara*)[11].

However, sons of good family, when you enter the Sahā universe, withhold (*upasaṃharata*) the perfumes of your bodies so that the beings of that universe will not be either disturbed (*unmatta*) or intoxicated (*pramatta*). When you enter the Sahā universe, hide the signs of your beauty (*rūpanimitta*) so that the Bodhisattvas of this universe do not feel before you either shame (*hrī*) or confusion (*apatrāpya*). And finally, do not have for this Sahā universe any notion of scorn (*hīnasaṃjñā*) or aversion (*pratigha*). And why? Because all the Buddhakṣetras, O sons of good family, are the same as space (*ākāśasama*). But the Blessed Lord Buddhas, in order to ripen beings (*sattvaparipācanārtham*), conform to the desires of beings and manifest (*saṃdarśayanti*) Buddhakṣetras of all kinds (*nānāvidha*): some are sullied (*rakta*), others pure (*viśuddha*), others of indeterminate mark (*avyākṛtalakṣaṇa*). But all the Buddhakṣetras are fundamentally pure and indistinguishable (*nirviśiṣṭa*).

[*The Return to the Sahāloka*]

9. Then the imaginary Bodhisattva, having taken the bowl filled with food (*bhojanapūrṇapātra*), departed with the ninety hundreds of

[9] Stock phrase: cf. Saddharmapuṇḍ., p. 367,*6-7*; 425,*1-7*; 427,*7*; 458,*8-11*; 463,*1-3*.

[10] Another very common stock phrase: see WOODWARD, *Concordance*, II, p. 49 *b* 15-25.

[11] K: "The kṣetras of the ten regions are all like space (*ākāśasama*); but the Buddhas, in order to ripen beings animated by base aspirations (*hīnādhimuktika*), do not entirely manifest these pure lands".

thousands of Bodhisattvas, and through the power (*anubhāva*) of the Buddhas and with the supernatural intervention (*adhiṣṭhāna*) of Vimalakīrti, he disappeared (*antarhita*) in an instant (*ekasminn eva kṣaṇalavamuhūrte*) from the Sarvagandhasugandhā universe and entered in the Sahā universe the house of the Licchavi Vimalakīrti.

[*The Sacred Meal*]

10. Then the Licchavi Vimalakīrti supernaturally created (*adhitiṣṭhati sma*) ninety hundreds of thousands of thrones (*siṃhāsana*) in all ways like those which were already there, and the (newly arrived) Bodhisattvas seated themselves on them.

Then the imaginary Bodhisattva gave to Vimalakīrti the bowl filled with food (*bhojanapūrṇapātra*).

The great town of Vaiśālī was permeated with the perfume of that food, and the sweet odour was perceived in all the chiliocosm (*sāhasralokadhātu*).

The perfume of that bowl of food spread throughout the great town of Vaiśālī and the trichiliomegachiliocosm (*trisāhasramahāsāhasralokadhātu*). Because of this immense, boundless and sweet perfume, all the universes gave off a lovely odour.

In the town of Vaiśālī, the brahmans, the householders (*gṛhapati*) and the Licchavi chief (*licchavyadhipati*), the Licchavi Candracchattra, having perceived this odour, were filled with astonishment (*āścaryaprāpta*) and wonder (*adbhutaprāpta*); physically and mentally enchanted (*prasannakāyacitta*), they went, with eighty-four thousand Licchavis, to the house of Vimalakīrti.

In Vaiśālī, the brahmans, the guildsmen (*śreṣṭhin*), the Vaiśyas, beings human (*manuṣya*) and non-human (*amanuṣya*), etc., perceived this odour and were filled with wonder (*adbhutaprāpta*): they experienced great ecstasies, both physical and mental. In Vaiśālī, the chief of the Licchavis named Candracchattra and eighty-four thousand Licchavis went, with all kinds of adornments, to the house of Vimalakīrti.

Seeing, in this house, the Bodhisattvas seated on thrones (*siṃhāsana*) so high (*evam unnata*), so wide (*pṛthu*) and so large (*viśāla*), they were filled with wonder (*adbhutaprāpta*) and experienced a great joy (*pramuditā*). After having saluted all these great Śrāvakas and Bodhisattvas, they stood to one side (*ekānte 'sthuḥ*). The sons of the gods (*devaputra*) who had their spheres on earth (*bhūmyavacara*), in the sphere of desire (*kāmāvacara*) or in the sphere of form (*rūpāvacara*), incited (*codita*) by this perfume, also presented themselves at Vimalakīrti's with innumerable hundreds of thousands of servants.

11. Then the Licchavi Vimalakīrti said to the sthavira Śāriputra and the great Śrāvakas:

Eat, O Honourable Sirs (*bhadanta*), the food of the Tathāgata, ambrosia (*amṛta*) perfumed with great compassion (*mahākaruṇāparivāsita*). But do not conceive any ignoble sentiments (*prādeśikacitta*) for you would not be able to digest (*pariṇam-*) it [12].

Eat, O Honourable Sirs, the food with the flavour of ambrosia (*amṛtarasabhojana*) which is given to you by the Tathāgata. This food is perfumed with great compassion (*mahākaruṇāparivāsita*). But do not eat it with ignoble (*prādeśika*) or base (*hīna*) sentiments (*cittacaritra*), for were you to eat it thus, you would not be able to digest it.

12. Then, in the assembly, a few base Śrāvakas had the following thought: This food is very sparse (*svalpa*); how will it be enough for such a great assembly?

The imaginary Bodhisattva said to these Śrāvakas: Venerable Sirs (*āyuṣmant*), do not identify your small wisdom (*prajñā*) and your small merits (*puṇya*) with the immense wisdom and the immense merits of the Tathāgata. And why? The water of the four great oceans (*mahāsamudra*) would be dried up before this food with its sweet perfume had undergone the slightest diminution (*kiṃcitkakṣaya*). Even if all the beings of innumerable great chiliocosms, for one kalpa or a hundred kalpas, swallowed this food by taking mouthfuls as big as Sumeru (*sumerukalpaiḥ kavaḍīkāraiḥ*), this food would not diminish. And why? Springing from the inexhaustible elements (*akṣayaskandha*) which are morality (*śīla*), concentration (*samādhi*), wisdom (*prajñā*), deliverance (*vimukti*), the knowledge and vision of deliverance (*vimuktijñānadarśana*)[13], the remains of the food (*upabhuktaśeṣam*) of the Tathāgata which are contained in this

[12] Cn: "Bhadantas, eat the food of the Tathāgata which has the flavour of great compassion; but do not have any limited intentions which would bind your mind". — K: "Bhadantas, eat the food of the Tathāgata, food with the flavour of ambrosia (*amṛtarasa*) and perfumed with great compassion (*mahākaruṇāparivāsita*). But do not eat it with limited thoughts (*prādeśikacitta*) for, if you eat it thus, you would not digest it".

In Tibetan we have: *ñi tshe baḥi spyod pa la sems ñe bar ma ḥdogs śig*, literally: "Do not bind your mind with biased (ignoble) intentions". In the Mahāvyutpatti, No. 1610, *ñi tshe ba spyod pa* translates *pradeśakārin*. We find the expressions *prādeśikena jñānena* in Śatasāh., p. 615,*13*; Bodh. bhūmi, p. 236,*13*; *prādeśikacittatā* in Daśabhūmika, p. 25,*22*.

[13] The Tibetan version only mentions *śīla*, *samādhi* and *prajñā*, which make up the three elements (*skandha*) of the Eight-fold Path (cf. Dīgha, I, p. 206,*8-12*; Majjhima, I, p. 301,*1-3*; Aṅguttara, I, p. 125,*25-30*; Itivuttaka, p. 51,*2-7*). The Chinese versions also mention *vimukti* and *vimuktijñānadarśana*: It would then be a matter of the five *dharmaskandha* or Elements of the Law. See above, II, § 12, note 30.

bowl (*pātra*) are inexhaustible, even if all the beings of innumerable trichiliomegachiliocosms (*trisāhasramahāsāhasralokadhātu*) spent hundreds of thousands of kalpas in eating this perfumed food.

13. *Atha tato bhojanāt sarvāvatī sā parṣat tṛptā bhūtā. na ca tad bhojanaṃ kṣīyate. yaiś ca bodhisattvaiḥ śrāvakaiś ca śakrabrahmalokapālais tadanyaiś ca sattvais tad bhojanaṃ bhuktaṃ teṣāṃ tādṛśaṃ sukhaṃ kāye 'vakrāntaṃ yādṛśaṃ sarvasukhamaṇḍitāyāṃ lokadhātau bodhisattvānāṃ sukham. sarvaromakūpebhyaś ca teṣāṃ tādṛśo gandhaḥ pravāti tad yathāpi nāma tasyām eva sarvagandhasugandhāyāṃ lokadhātau vṛkṣāṇāṃ gandhaḥ*[14].

Then the whole assembly was satiated by this food, and the food was in no way exhausted. And the Bodhisattvas, the Śrāvakas, Śakras, Brahmās, the Lokapālas and other beings who had eaten this food, felt descending into their bodies a happiness equal to that of the Bodhisattvas who live in the Sarvasukhamaṇḍitā universe "Adorned with every happiness". And all the pores of their skin gave off a perfume like that of the trees growing in the Sarvagandhasugandhā universe.

[*Sugandhakūṭa's Instruction in his Universe*]

14. Then, addressing the Bodhisattvas come from the Buddhakṣetra of the Blessed Tathāgata Sugandhakūṭa, the Licchavi Vimalakīrti asked them: Sons of good family (*kulaputra*), of what does the instruction (*dharmadeśanā*) of the Tathāgata Sugandhakūṭa consist?

The Bodhisattvas replied: It is not with syllables (*akṣara*) or articulated language (*nirukti*) that the Tathāgata expounds the Law; it is with this very perfume that Bodhisattvas are disciplined (*vinīta*). At the foot (*mūla*) of each perfume tree (*gandhavṛksa*) a Bodhisattva is seated, and from these trees is given off a perfume like this one. Those who perceive it immediately obtain the concentration (*samādhi*) called "Mine of all the Bodhisattva virtues" (*sarvabodhisattvaguṇākara*). As soon as they obtain this concentration, the Bodhisattva virtues arise (*utpadyante*) in all of them.

[*Śakyamuni's Instruction in the Saha Universe*[15]]

15. In their own turn, the Bodhisattvas of the zenith region questioned the Licchavi Vimalakīrti: And here in the Sahā universe, how does the Blessed Lord Śākyamuni expound the Law to beings?

[14] Extract from the original text, quoted in Śikṣāsamuccaya, p. 269.*13*-270.*3*.

[15] This teaching of the Abhidharma, very brief in Cn, is lengthier in the other

Vimalakīrti replied: Worthy Sirs (*satpuruṣa*), these beings are difficult to discipline (*durvaineya*); to those who are unruly (*khaṭuṅka*)[16] and difficult to discipline, Śākyamuni addresses discourses (*kathā*) suitable for disciplining beings who are unruly and difficult to discipline. Which are these discourses? These are they:

This is the hell-destiny (*narakagati*); this is the animal-destiny (*tiryagyoni*); this is the *preta*-destiny; this is the realm of death (*yamaloka*); these are the unfavourable conditions (*akṣaṇa*); these are the crippled (*vikalendriya*).

This is bodily misconduct (*kāyaduścarita*) and that is the fruition (*vipāka*) of bodily misconduct; this is vocal misconduct (*vāgduścarita*) and that is the fruition of vocal misconduct; this is mental misconduct (*manoduścarita*) and that is the fruition of mental misconduct.

This is taking life (*prāṇātipāta*), this is taking the not-given (*adattādāna*), this is sexual misconduct (*kāmamithyācāra*), this is false speech (*mṛṣāvāda*), this is slanderous speech (*paiśunyavāda*), this is harsh speech (*pāruṣyavāda*), this is useless speech (*saṃbhinnapralāpa*), this is covetousness (*abhidhyā*), this is animosity (*vyāpāda*), this is false view (*mithyādṛṣṭi*); and that is the fruition of these paths of bad action (*akuśalakarmapatha*).

This is avarice (*mātsarya*) and that is the fruit (*phala*) of avarice; this is immorality (*dauḥśīlya*) and that is the fruit of immorality; this is anger (*krodha*) and that is the fruit of anger; this is idleness (*kausīdya*) and that is the fruit of idleness; this is distraction (*cittavikṣepa*) and that is the fruit of distraction; this is false wisdom (*dauṣprajñā*) and that is the fruit of false wisdom.

This is the rule of training (*śikṣāpada*) and that is against the rule; this is *prātimokṣa* and that is violation of *prātimokṣa*; this is to be done (*kārya*) and that is to be avoided (*akārya*); this is fitting (*yogya*) and that is not fitting (*ayogya*); this is driving away (*prahāṇa*) and that is not; this is an obstacle (*āvaraṇa*) and that is not an obstacle (*anāvaraṇa*); this is a fault (*āpatti*) and that is release from a fault (*āpattivyutthāna*);

versions. There are many divergencies among the latter which it is impossible to go into here. As usual, I have followed the Tibetan while making some additions from H here and there.

[16] In Pāli, *assakhaḷuṅka* means a "restless, unruly horse", in contrast to *ājāniya* "thoroughbred": cf. Aṅguttara, I, p. 287; IV, p. 397. The Pāli *khaḷuṅka* has the Sanskrit correspondant of *khaṭuṅka, khaṭuka, khaḍuṅka*: cf. WOODWARD, *Concordance*, I, p. 293 *a* s.v. *assakhaluṁke*; EDGERTON, *Dictionary*, p. 202 *b*.

this is the right path (*mārga*) and that is the wrong path (*kumārga*); this is good (*kuśala*) and that is bad (*akuśala*); this is blameworthy (*sāvadya*) and that is irreproachable (*anavadya*); this is impure (*sāsrava*) and that is pure (*anāsrava*); this is worldly (*laukika*) and that is transcendental (*lokottara*); this is conditioned (*saṃskṛta*) and that is unconditioned (*asaṃskṛta*); this is defilement (*saṃkleśa*) and that is purification (*vyavadāna*); this is virtue (*guṇa*) and that is flaw (*doṣa*); this is painful (*duḥkha*) and that is not painful (*aduḥkha*); this is agreeable (*sukha*) and that is disagreeable (*asukha*); this is repugnant and that is pleasant; this should be cut off (*prahātavya*) and that should be cultivated (*bhāvayitavya*); this is Saṃsāra and that is Nirvāṇa. All these dharmas allow of innumerable expositions (*apramāṇa-dharmamukha*).

Thus, then, through multiple interpretations of the Law (*bahuvidha-dharmaparyāya*), does Śākyamuni edify (*pratiṣṭhāpayati*) the minds of those beings who are like unruly horses (*aśvakhaṭuṅka*)[17]. And just as unruly horses (*aśva*) and elephants (*hastin*) are subdued (*vinīta*) by a goad (*aṅkuśa*) that pierces them to the bone (*marmavedha*), so the beings of the Sahā universe, unruly (*khaṭuṅka*) and difficult to discipline (*durvaineya*), are disciplined by discourses (*kathā*) denouncing all suffering (*sarvaduḥkha*). The Tathāgata skillfully resorts to these discourses concerning suffering and these concise teachings in order to discipline them and bring them to the Good Law (*saddharma*).

16. The Bodhisattvas said: The greatness (*mahattva*) of Śākyamuni is established (*sthāpita*). The way in which he converts the lowly (*hīna*), the poor (*daridra*) and the unruly (*khaṭuṅka*) beings is marvellous (*āścarya*). And the Bodhisattvas who are established (*pratiṣṭhita*) in this wretched (*laghu*) Buddhakṣetra have an inconceivable compassion (*acintyamahākaruṇā*).

Having heard these words, the Bodhisattvas come from the zenith region were filled with astonishment (*āścaryaprāpta*) and said these words: He is wondrous (*adbhuta*), this Blessed Lord Śākyamuni who can do these difficult things (*duṣkara*): he hides his innumerable noble virtues (*aprameyān āryaguṇān praticchādayati*) and demonstrates astonishing means of discipline (*evaṃrūpān vinayopāyān saṃdarśayati*); he ripens base and wretched beings (*hīnadaridrasattvān paripācayati*) and resorts to all kinds of means to subdue and captivate them.

As for the Bodhisattvas who inhabit this Sahā universe and who endure all kinds of weariness (*śrama*), they possess

[17] K: "For, among those beings who are difficult to discipline, the mind is like a monkey": Perhaps a canonical recollection: Saṃyutta, II, p. 95: *seyyathāpi bhikkhave makkaṭo araññe pavane caramāno sākhaṃ gaṇhati, taṃ muñcitvā aññaṃ gaṇhati, evaṃ eva kho bhikkhave yad idaṃ vuccati cittaṃ iti.*

a compassion (*mahākaruṇā*) and a vigour (*vīrya*) which are superior (*parama*), wondrous (*adbhuta*), firm (*dṛḍha*) and inconceivable (*acintya*). They uphold (*samavadadhati*) the supreme Good Law (*anuttarasaddharma*) of the Tathāgata and benefit (*arthaṃ kurvanti*) beings who are difficult to discipline (*durvaineyasattva*).

Then the Licchavi Vimalakīrti said: It is indeed so, worthy Sirs, it is indeed as you say (*evam etat, satpuruṣā, evam etad yathā vadatha*). The Bodhisattvas born here have a very firm compassion (*sudṛḍhakaruṇā*). In this universe here, in a single existence (*ekasminn eva janmani*) they benefit beings far more than you do in the Sarvagandhasugandhā universe, even in a hundred thousand kalpas. And why?

Vimalakīrti said: It is indeed so, good Sirs, it is indeed as you say; the Tathāgata Śākyamuni can do difficult things: he hides his innumerable noble virtues and does not fear weariness; through his skillful means he disciplines those beings who are unruly and difficult to discipline. And the Bodhisattvas born in this Buddhakṣetra and who endure all kinds of weariness, possess a compassion and a vigour which are superior, wondrous, firm and inconceivable. They uphold the supreme Good Law of the Tathāgata and benefit innumerable beings.

Know, O worthy Sirs (*satpuruṣa*), that the Bodhisattvas who inhabit this Sahā universe, in a single existence benefit beings far more than do the Bodhisattvas of the Sarvagandhasugandhā universe in a hundred thousand great kalpas and that the virtues (*guṇa*) of the former surpass the virtues of the latter. And why?

[*The Virtues Particular to the Bodhisattvas of the Sahā Universe*]

17. Worthy Sirs (*satpuruṣa*), in this Sahā universe, there exists a collection of ten good dharmas (*daśavidhakuśaladharmasaṃnicaya*) which cannot be found in the other pure Buddhakṣetras in the universes of the ten regions. What are these ten?

1. Converting (*saṃgraha*) the poor (*daridra*) through giving (*dāna*),
2. Converting the immoral (*duḥśīla*) through morality (*śīla*),
3. Converting the irascible (*kruddha*) through patience (*kṣānti*),
4. Converting the idle (*kusīda*) through vigour (*vīrya*),
5. Converting the distracted (*vikṣiptacitta*) through meditation (*dhyāna*),
6. Converting the foolish (*duṣprajña*) through wisdom (*prajñā*),
7. Teaching those who have fallen into the unfavourable conditions

(*akṣaṇapatita*) to overcome (*atikram-*) these eight unfavourable conditions,

8. Teaching the Great Vehicle (*mahāyāna*) to those who follow limited ways (*pradeśakārin*),

9. Converting through good roots (*kuśalamūla*) beings who have not planted good roots (*anavaropitakuśalamūlāḥ sattvāḥ*),

10. Ripening (*paripācana*) beings constantly (*satatasamitam*) through the four means of conversion (*saṃgrahavastu*).

This collection of ten good dharmas which are contained in this Sahā universe cannot be found in the other pure Buddhakṣetras of the universes of the ten regions.

[*Conditions of Access to the Pure Lands*]

18. The Bodhisattvas of the Sarvagandhasugandhā Buddhakṣetra asked further: When the Bodhisattvas have left this Sahā universe (*asyāḥ Sahāyā lokadhātoś cyutvā*), how many conditions (*dharma*) should they fulfil to reach safe and sound (*akṣatānupahata*) a pure (*viśuddha*) Buddhakṣetra?

Vimalakīrti replied: After having left this Sahā universe, the Bodhisattvas who fulfil eight conditions will reach, safe and sound, a pure Buddhakṣetra. What are these eight? The Bodhisattvas should say to themselves:

1. I should be of benefit (*hita*) to all beings, but not expect the slightest benefit from it myself.

2. I should bear the sufferings (*duḥkha*) of all beings and abandon to them all the good roots (*kuśalamūla*) that I may have thus gained.

3. I should have for all beings an even sameness of mind (*cittasamatā*) and not feel any aversion (*pratigha*).

4. Before all Bodhisattvas, I should delight as if they were the Master (*śāstṛ*)[18].	Before all beings, I should eliminate pride and vanity (*mānastambha*) and respect them as joyfully as I do the Buddha.
5. Whether they hear texts (*dharma*) already heard (*śruta*) or not yet heard (*aśruta*), the Bodhisattvas do not reject them[19].	The Bodhisattvas have faith (*śraddhā*) and confidence (*adhimukti*) in the most profound (*gambhīra*) Sūtras which they have not yet heard, and when they do come to hear them, they have neither doubt (*saṃśaya*) nor criticism (*apavāda*).

[18] K confirms the Tibetan.

[19] K: "When they hear Sūtras unheard before, they do not doubt, and do not contradict the Śrāvakas".

6. The Bodhisattvas are without jealousy (*īrṣyā*) of the gain of others (*paralābha*) and without pride (*garva*) in their own gains.

7. The Bodhisattvas discipline their own minds (*svacittaṃ vinayanti*): they examine their own failings (*ātmaskhalita*) and calm the flaws of others (*paradoṣa*).

8. Delighting in heedfulness (*apramādarata*), they collect (*samādadati*) all the good virtues (*guṇa*).	The Bodhisattvas, always without heedlessness, always delight in seeking good dharmas and vigorously cultivate the auxiliary dharmas of enlightenment (*bodhipakṣyadharma*).

If they fulfil these eight conditions, the Bodhisattvas, after having left this Sahā universe, will reach, safe and sound, a pure Buddhakṣetra.

When the Licchavi Vimalakīrti and Mañjuśrī the crown prince had thus expounded the Law to those who were present in that assembly (*tasyāṃ parṣadi saṃniṣaṇṇāḥ*), a hundred thousand living beings produced the thought of supreme and perfect enlightenment (*śatamātrāṇāṃ prāṇisahasrāṇām anuttarāyāṃ samyaksaṃbodhau cittāny utpāditāni*) and ten thousand Bodhisattvas obtained the certainty concerning the non-arising of dharmas (*anutpattikadharmakṣānti*).

CHAPTER TEN

INSTRUCTION REGARDING THE EXHAUSTIBLE AND THE INEXHAUSTIBLE

[*Visit to the Āmrapālīvana*]

1. While the Blessed Śākyamuni was expounding the Law in the Āmrapālīvana, the circular area (*maṇḍalamāḍa*) was enlarged and spread (*vistīrṇo 'bhūd viśālaḥ*), and the assembly (*parṣad*) was tinted as if by a blaze of gold (*suvarṇavarṇeneva bhāsitā*).

Then the Venerable (*āyuṣmant*) Ānanda said to the Blessed One: Blessed One, the Āmrapālīvana is enlarging and spreading, and the whole assembly is tinted by a blaze of gold. Of what is this a presage (*kasya khalv idaṃ pūrvanimittaṃ bhaviṣyati*)[1]?

The Blessed One replied: Ānanda, it is a presage that the Licchavi Vimalakīrti and Mañjuśrī the crown prince (*kumārabhūta*), surrounded and followed by a great assembly (*prabhūtaparivāreṇa parivṛtaḥ puraskṛtaḥ*), are about to come to the Tathāgata.

2. Then the Licchavi Vimalakīrti said to Mañjuśrī the crown prince: Let us go, O Mañjuśrī, with these great beings, to the Tathāgata, to see the Blessed One, to pay homage to him, to serve him and to hear the Law (*gamiṣyāmo vayaṃ tair mahāsattvaiḥ sārdhaṃ tathāgatasya sakāśaṃ taṃ bhagavantaṃ darśanāya vandanāya paryupāsanāya dharmaśravaṇāya*)[2].

Mañjuśrī replied: Let us go, son of good family, if you consider it to be the right time (*gamiṣyāmaḥ kulaputra yasyedānīṃ kālaṃ manyase*).

Then the Licchavi Vimalakīrti performed such a supernatural action (*tathārūpam ṛddhyabhisaṃskāram abhisaṃskaroti sma*) that he placed in his right hand (*dakṣiṇapāṇi*) the whole assembly with its thrones (*siṃhāsana*) and went to where the Blessed One was to be found (*yena bhagavāṃs tenopajagāma*). Having got there, he put the assembly on the ground (*upetya parṣadaṃ bhūmau pratiṣṭhāpayati

[1] Traditional expression: cf. Saddharmapuṇḍ., p. 164,*7*; 427,*1*. *Pūrvanimitta*, in Tib. *sṅa-ltas*, does indeed have the meaning of presage, forerunner: Divyāvadāna, p. 193,*20*; Lalitavistara, p. 76,*9*; 77,*21*; 186,*5*; Saddharmapuṇḍ., p. 17,*2*; 261,*10*; Gaṇḍavyūha, p. 373,*20*; 375,*2*; 531,*4*.

[2] Stock phrase: cf. IX, § 8, note 9.

sma). After having saluted, by touching with his head, the feet of the Blessed One and after having circled round him seven times while keeping him to his right, he stood to one side (*bhagavataḥ pādau śirasābhivandya saptakṛtvaḥ pradakṣiṇīkṛtyaikānte 'sthāt*). Holding his joined hands towards where the Blessed One was (*yena bhagavāṃs tenāñjaliṃ praṇamya*), he remained standing with composure.

Then the Bodhisattvas who had come from the Buddhakṣetra of the Tathāgata Sugandhakūṭa descended from their thrones (*avatīrya siṃhāsanebhyaḥ*) and, after having saluted the feet of the Blessed One and circled round him three times, they stood to one side. Holding their joined hands towards where the Blessed One was, they remained standing with composure.

All the Bodhisattvas and the great Śrāvakas (of the Sahā universe), they too descended from their thrones and, after having saluted the feet of the Blessed One, stood to one side. Equally, the Śakras, Brahmās, the Lokapālas and all the sons of the gods (*devaputra*) also, after having saluted the feet of the Blessed One, stood to one side.

All the great Śrāvakas, Śakras, Brahmās, the four great divine kings, guardians of the world (*lokapālāś cāturmahārājikā devāḥ*), etc., descended from their thrones and, after having saluted the feet of the Blessed One, stood to one side. Holding their joined hands towards where the Blessed One was, they remained standing with composure.

Then the Blessed One, having gladdened these Bodhisattvas and the whole great assembly with a righteous discourse (*dhārmyā kathayā saṃmodanaṃ kṛtvā*), addressed these words to them: Sons of good family (*kulaputra*), take your places on your respective thrones. On this invitation of the Blessed One, they each took their former places and sat down.

[*Duration and Effects of the Sacred Food*]

3. Then the Blessed One said to Śāriputra: Śāriputra, have you seen the miraculous transformations (*vikurvaṇa*) of the Bodhisattvas, the best of beings (*varasattva*)?

Śāriputra replied: Yes, I have seen them, O Blessed One.

The Blessed One continued: What impression (*saṃjñā*) do you derive from them?

Śāriputra replied: The impression that these great beings are inconceivable (*acintya*) and that their actions (*kriyā*), their psychic power (*ṛddhibala*) and their virtues (*guṇa*) are inconceivable to the point of being unthinkable (*acintya*), incomparable (*atulya*), immeasurable (*amāpya*) and incalculable (*gaṇanāṃ samatikrāntaḥ*).

4. Then the Venerable Ānanda asked the Blessed One: Blessed One, this perfume (*gandha*) which has never before been perceived (*apūrvagṛhīta*), to whom does it belong?

The Blessed One replied: It comes from all the pores of the skin (*kāyaromakūpa*) of these Bodhisattvas [3].

Śāriputra in his turn said: Venerable Ānanda, the same perfume is given off equally by all our own pores.

Ānanda. — How is this so?

Śāriputra. — The Licchavi Vimalakīrti obtained food (*bhojana*) originating from the Sarvagandhasugandhā universe, Buddha-field of the Tathāgata Sugandhakūṭa, and this perfume is given off by the bodies of all those who eat it.

Vimalakīrti, through his miraculous power (*vikurvaṇabala*), sent an imaginary Bodhisattva (*nirmitabodhisattva*) in the direction of the zenith, to the Buddhakṣetra of the Tathāgata Sugandhakūṭa. He asked for and obtained the remains of the meal (*upabhuktaśeṣa*) of that Buddha. On his return to Vimalakīrti, he offered it to the great assembly. And all those who have eaten this food give off this perfume through all their pores.

5. Then the Venerable Ānanda asked the Licchavi Vimalakīrti: For how long (*kiyacciram*) will this perfume persist?

Vimalakīrti. — As long as this food is not digested (*pariṇata*).

Ānanda. — And in what length of time will it be digested?

Vimalakīrti. — It will be digested in seven days (*saptāham*) and seven nights (*saptaniśam*). Thus, for seven days, it will persist; but, even though it may not yet be digested, it will cause no harm (*piḍā*).

The strength (*anubhāva*) of this food will remain in the body for seven days and seven nights. After that time, it will gradually be digested. Even though it may be a long time before it is digested, it will not do any harm (*piḍā*).

6. Besides, O Venerable Ānanda:

1. *Yaiś ca bhikṣubhir anavakrāntaniyāmair etad bhojanaṃ bhuktaṃ teṣām evāvakrāntaniyāmānāṃ pariṇaṃsyati* [4].

If monks who have not yet entered the absolute certainty (of

[3] This obviously has to do with a supernatural perfume, quite distinct from the odours that are normally given off by beings, each according to his class. Regarding these odours, cf. Saddharmapuṇḍ., p. 360.

[4] In this paragraph, the underlined passages are extracted from the original text quoted in the Śikṣāsamuccaya, p. 270,4-7. Unfortunately the quotation is incomplete and there are divergencies between the Chinese versions. K adds a sentence which is missing elsewhere: "If those who have not yet produced the thought of the Mahāyāna eat this food, it will only be digested when they have produced it".

acquiring the Supreme Good) eat this food, this food will be digested after they have entered into this absolute certainty.

2. If beings who have not yet renounced all craving (*avītarāga*) eat this food, it will be digested after they have renounced craving.

3. If monks who have entered into the absolute certainty (*avakrāntaniyāma*) eat this food, it will not be digested as long as they are not of perfectly delivered mind (*aparimuktacitta*).

4. If beings who are not yet delivered (*vimukta*) eat this food, it will be digested after they are of perfectly delivered mind (*parimuktacitta*).

5. *Yair anutpāditabodhicittaiḥ sattvaiḥ paribhuktaṃ teṣāṃ utpāditabodhicittānāṃ pariṇaṃsyati.*

If beings who have not yet produced the thought of enlightenment eat this food, it will be digested after they have produced the thought of enlightenment.

6. *Yair utpāditabodhicittair bhuktaṃ teṣāṃ pratilabdhakṣāntikānāṃ pariṇamṣyati.*

If beings who have already produced the thought of enlightenment eat this food, it will be digested after they have obtained the certainty concerning the non-arising of dharmas.

7. If beings who have already obtained the certainty concerning the non-arising of dharmas (*anutpattikadharmakṣāntipratilabdha*) eat this food, it will be digested after they have attained the state of irreversible Bodhisattvahood (*avaivartikasthāna*).

8. If beings who have already obtained the certainty (*pratilabdhakṣāntika*) eat this food, it will be digested when they have become Bodhisattvas separated from the state of Buddhahood by only one existence (*ekajātipratibaddha*).

If beings who have already attained the state of irreversible Bodhisattvahood eat this food, it will be digested when they have become Bodhisattvas separated from the state of Buddhahood by only one existence (*ekajātipratibaddha*).

7. Thus, O Honourable Ānanda, when the medicament (*bhaiṣajya*)

Thus, O Honourable Ānanda, there is in this world a great king of medicaments called "Flavourful" (*sarasa*) enters the stomach, it is not digested (*pariṇata*) as long as all the poisons (*viṣa*) are not eliminated; it is only after that that it is digested. Equally, O Honourable Ānanda, as long as the poisons of all the passions (*sarvakleśaviṣa*) are not eliminated, this food (*bhojana*) is not digested: it is only after that that it is digested[5].

(*mahābhaiṣajyarāja*) called "Most Flavourful" (*surasa*). If someone is afflicted by a poisoning and the poisons (*viṣa*) invade his body, this medicament is administered to him. As long as the poisons are not eliminated, this king of medicaments is not digested. It is only digested when the poisons are destroyed. It is the same with those who eat this food. As long as the poisons of all the passions are not eliminated, this food is not digested; after the passions are destroyed, it is digested.

Then the Venerable Ānanda said to the Blessed One: It is inconceivable (*acintya*), this perfumed food offered by this great being (*mahāsattva*): for beings it actuates a Buddha deed (*buddhakārya*).

The Buddha replied: It is indeed so, O Ānanda, it is indeed as you say (*evam etad yathā vadasi*). It is inconceivable, this perfumed food offered by Vimalakīrti: for beings, it actuates a Buddha deed. It is equally so for the Buddhakṣetras of the ten regions.

[*Skillful Action of the Buddhakṣetras*[6]]

8. There are Buddhakṣetras which actuate Buddha deeds (*buddhakārya*): 1. through Bodhisattvas, 2. through lights (*prabhā*), 3. through

[5] In Tibetan, the name of the medicament is *blo-ldan* = *sarasa*, which K and H seem to have read as *surasa*. However, Cn calls it *a hun t'o* 阿昏陀 i.e. *agada*, the medicament which renders one "disease-free" (*a-gada*). Cf. Apadāna, p. 41,*2*; Milindapañha, p. 121; Sumaṅgalavilāsinī, p. 67,*18*.

Cf. Ratnakūṭa, quoted in Madh. vṛtti, p. 248,*11-13*: *tadyathā, Kāśyapa, glānaḥ puruṣaḥ syāt, tasmai vaidyo bhaiṣajyaṃ dadyāt, tasya tad bhaiṣajyaṃ sarvadoṣān uccārya svayaṃ koṣṭhagataṃ na niḥsaret. tat kiṃ manyase, Kāśyapa, api tu sa puruṣas tato glānyān mukto bhavet. no hīdaṃ. Bhagavan, gāḍhataraṃ tasya puruṣasya glānyaṃ bhavet*: "Let us suppose, Kāśyapa, that a man is sick, that the physician gives him a medicament, that this medicament, after having eliminated all the bad humours of this sick man, remains in his stomach and does not leave it. What do you think, Kaśyapa? Would this man ever be cured of his sickness? — No, certainly not, O Blessed One; on the contrary, this man's sickness would get worse".

However, the perfumed Amṛta to which the Vimalakīrti refers is a medicament that disappears of its own accord once it has eliminated the poison of the passions.

[6] The end of Chapter X contains a series of sections concerning the nature of the Buddha and Bodhisattvas. The explanation is not systematic, but includes all the elements of Mahāyāna buddhology.

1. Paragraphs 8-12 deal with the buddhakṣetras, a matter already gone into in Ch. I, § 11-20 (cf. Appendix, Note I). The Vimalakīrti still knows nothing of the

theory of the three bodies of the Buddha (cf. Saṃgraha, p. 266), but it expatiates at length on the pure buddhakṣetras which spring from the bliss-body (*saṃbhogakāya*).

According to the Saṃgraha, p. 266-267, the bliss-body relies on the Law-body (*dharmakāya*) and is characterised by all kinds of assemblies (*parṣanamaṇḍala*) of Buddhas; it experiences (*anubhavati*) the very pure fields (*pariśuddhakṣetra*) of the Buddhas and the bliss of the Law of the Great Vehicle (*mahāyānadharmasaṃbhoga*).

In § 8 to 11 of the present chapter, the Vimalakīrtinirdeśa lists the different devices to which the Buddhas have recourse in order to perform their Buddha deeds (*buddhakārya*) in the various buddhakṣetras. — Then, in § 12, it proclaims the fundamental identity of all buddhakṣetras. This is the thesis that the Saṃgraha (p. 284-285) was to formulate by saying: "Since their intentions (*abhiprāya*) and activities (*karman*) are identical, the *saṃbhogakāya* [from which the buddhakṣetras spring] are identical. But since their supports (*āśraya*) are different, the *saṃbhogakāya* are different, for they exist in innumerable supports".

2. In § 13, the Vimalakīrti deals with the essential body (*svabhāvikakāya*) of the Buddha. The Saṃgraha (p. 268-274) admits five qualities in the latter. The Vimalakīrti especially emphasizes two points:

a. The sameness of all the Buddhas in that they all possess "the fullness of the Buddha attributes" (*buddhadharmaparipūri*). In the Saṃgraha (p. 269), these attributes are called the "white dharmas" (*śukladharma*): the same Saṃgraha (p. 285-304) lists seventeen of them, and its list is quite similar to that of the Vimalakīrti.

It therefore results, according to the Saṃgraha (p. 271), that one of the qualities of the *dharmakāya* is non-duality with regard to plurality and one-ness (*nānātvaikatvādvayalakṣaṇa*). In other words, there is no plurality of Buddhas because the *dharmakāya*, support (*āśraya*) of all the Buddhas, does not contain any divisions (*abhinna*); but there is no one-ness of Buddhas either because innumerable people, or to be more exact, innumerable mental series (*cittasaṃtāna*) succeed to the *dharmakāya* in turn. In yet other parts, the Saṃgraha (p. 284, 328-29) discusses the question of the plurality and one-ness of the Buddhas.

b. The Vimalakīrti further emphasizes, in § 13, the inconceivability (*acintyalakṣaṇa*) of the Buddhas: "All the beings of the great chiliocosm, had they the learning and mindfulness of Ānanda, would be incapable of grasping the exact meaning of the three words: Samyaksaṃbuddha, Tathāgata, Buddha". On the same subject, the Saṃgraha (p. 274) remarks: "The *dharmakāya* has inconceivability as its mark, for the purity of suchness (*tathatāviśuddhi*) should be known through introspection (*pratyātmavedyā*), has no equal in the world (*loke 'nupamā*) and is not accessible to the speculative (*atārkikagocara*)".

3. Finally, in § 16 to 19, the Vimalakīrti, in the course of a long homily, urges the Bodhisattvas "not to exhaust the conditioned (*saṃskṛta*) and not to abide in the unconditioned (*asaṃskṛta*)". In fact, still according to the Saṃgraha (p. 271), one of the marks of the *dharmakāya* is precisely the non-duality of the conditioned and the unconditioned (*saṃskṛtāsaṃskṛtādvaya*); it explains: "The *dharmakāya* is neither conditioned nor unconditioned for, on the one hand, it is not fashioned (*abhisaṃskṛta*) by action (*karman*) or passion (*kleśa*), and on the other hand, it has the sovereign power (*vibhutva*) of manifesting itself under the aspect of conditioned things".

If, therefore, the Bodhisattva really wants to reach Buddhahood, he cannot either exhaust the conditioned or abide in the unconditioned. Hence his contradictory actions

the tree of enlightenment (*bodhivṛkṣa*)[7], 4. through the vision of the beauty (*rūpa*) and physical marks (*lakṣaṇānuvyañjana*) of the Tathāgata, 5. through imaginary beings (*nirmāṇapuruṣa*), 6. through clothing (*cīvara*), 7. through seats (*āsana*), 8. through food (*āhāra*), 9. through water (*jala*), 10. through groves (*upavana*), 11. through immense palaces (*namātraprāsāda*), 12. through belvederes (*kūṭāgāra*), 13. through empty space (*ākāśa*), or again, 14. through the illumination of space (*ākāśaprasādana*)[8]. And why? Because beings are disciplined (*vinīta*) through such skillful means (*upāya*).

9. Equally, Ānanda, there are Buddhakṣetras which actuate Buddha deeds towards beings by addressing them through syllables (*akṣara*), in articulated language (*nirukti*), or through comparisons (*upamāna*) such as: an illusion (*māyā*), a dream (*svapna*), a reflection (*pratibimba*), the moon in the water (*udakacandra*), an echo (*pratiśrutkā*), a mirage (*marīci*), an image in a mirror (*ādarśapratibhāsa*), a ball of foam (*phenapiṇḍa*), a cloud (*megha*), a town of the Gandharvas (*gandharvanagara*), a phantom (*indrajāla*), etc.[9].

There are Buddhakṣetras which actuate Buddha deeds by making a syllable understood (*akṣara-vijñapti*)[10].

There are Buddhakṣetras which actuate Buddha deeds by teaching through a sound (*ghoṣa*), a word (*vāc*) or a syllable (*akṣara*) the self-natures (*svabhāva*) and marks (*lakṣaṇa*) of all the dharmas.

Ānanda, there are pure (*viśuddha*) and calm (*śānta*) Buddhakṣetras which actuate Buddha deeds through silence (*avacana*), through muteness (*anabhilāpa*), through saying nothing and not speaking[11]. And beings

and roundabout ways to which the Vimalakīrti never stops returning (III, § 3, 16-18; IV, § 20; VII, § 1; X, § 19).

I have here compared the evolving buddhology of the Vimalakīrti with the systematic buddhology of the Saṃgraha, but other Śāstras of the Great Vehicle lend themselves equally well to such contrasting. For further consultation on this subject, see the references concerning the marks of the *dharmakāya* pointed out in my translation of the Saṃgraha, p. 50*.

[7] For example, see the action of the *bodhivṛkṣa* of Amitābha, in Sukhāvatīvyūha, p. 110 sq.

[8] K's list differs slightly.

[9] Regarding these comparisons, see above, II, § 8, note 23.

[10] Cf. Daśabhūmika, p. 79,27-29: *sa dharmāsane niṣaṇṇa ākāṅkṣann ekaghoṣodāhāreṇa sarvaparṣadaṃ nānāghoṣarutavimātratayā saṃjñāpayati.*

This concerns the teaching by a single sound which has been encountered earlier, I, § 10, note 52.

[11] Cf. Laṅkāvatāra, p. 105,3-4: *na ca, Mahāmate, sarvabuddhakṣetreṣu prasiddhābhilāpaḥ; abhilāpo, Mahāmate, kṛtakaḥ.* Hence, "Vimalakīrti's silence" which we met above, VIII, § 33, note 43.

to be disciplined (*vaineyasattva*), because of this calm, spontaneously (*svarasatas*) penetrate the self-nature and the marks of dharmas.

10. Ānanda, among the bodily attitudes (*īryāpatha*), the enjoyments (*bhoga*) and the bliss (*paribhoga*) of the Blessed Lord Buddhas, there is not one that does not actuate Buddha deeds because they are all aimed at disciplining beings.

The Buddhakṣetras spread throughout the universes of the ten regions are infinite in number, and the Buddha deeds accomplished by them are also immense (*apramāṇa*). In truth, the bodily attitudes (*īryāpatha*), the endeavours (*vikrama*), the enjoyments (*bhoga*) and the munificence of the Buddhas are all aimed at disciplining beings. This is why all are called Buddha deeds.

Finally, Ānanda, it is also through the four Māras and the 84,000 kinds of passions (*kleśamukha*) that defile beings that the Blessed Lord Buddhas actuate Buddha deeds [12].

11. Ānanda, this is a *dharmamukha* entitled: Introduction to the doctrine of all the Buddha attributes (*sarvabuddhadharmamukhasaṃpraveśa*).

Bodhisattvas who have entered this introduction to the Law (*tasminn eva dharmamukhe praviṣṭāḥ*) experience neither joy (*muditā*) nor pride (*garva*) before pure (*viśuddha*) Buddhakṣetras, adorned with the splendour of all the noble virtues (*sarvottaraguṇavyūha*); and they experience neither sadness (*viṣāda*), nor repugnance (*āghāta*) before defiled (*kliṣṭa*) Buddhakṣetras, deprived of the splendour of all the noble virtues. But in the presence of all the Buddhas undiscriminatingly, they produce (*utpādayanti*) extreme faith (*adhimātraprasāda*) and great veneration (*manana*).

It is wonderful (*āścarya*) that the Blessed Lord Buddhas who penetrate the sameness of all dharmas (*sarvadharmasamatādhigata*) manifest all kinds of Buddha-fields (*nānāvidhabuddhakṣetra*) in order to ripen beings (*sattvaparipācanārthaṃ*).

It is wonderful that the Blessed Lord Buddhas who fulfil equally all the virtues and penetrate the absolute and real sameness (*atyantabhūtasamatā*) of all dharmas, in order to ripen different beings (*viśiṣṭasattva*), manifest Buddhakṣetras of various kinds.

[*Variety and Similarity of Buddhakṣetras*]

12. Ānanda, just as Buddhakṣetras are varied (*nānāvidha*) in

Understand this well: just as Buddhakṣetras are dissimilar (*asama*) with regard

[12] See above, V, § 20; VII, § 6, stanza 17.

that which concerns such and such a virtue (*guṇa*), but without any spatial difference (*ākāśanirviśeṣa*) as to the sky that covers them (*khasaṃchādita*), so, O Ānanda, among the Tathāgatas, their material bodies (*rūpakāya*) are different (*nānāvidha*), but their knowledge, free from attachment (*asaṅgajñāna*), is identical (*abhinna*).

to the elevations and depressions (*utkūlanikūla*) of the ground that serves as their support (*āśraya*), but unvaried (*nirviśiṣṭa*) with regard to the space (*ākāśa*) which overhangs them, so the Blessed Lord Buddhas, in order to ripen beings (*sattvaparipācanārtham*), manifest all kinds of dissimilar material bodies (*rūpakāya*), but they are all identical in that which concerns the absolute fullness (*atyantaparipūri*) of their unobstructed merits and knowledge (*asaṅgapuṇyajñāna*).

[*The Sameness and Inconceivability of the Buddhas*[13]]

13. Ānanda, all the Tathāgatas are the same (*sama*) in the fullness of all their Buddha attributes (*sarvabuddhadharmaparipūri*), that is, in form (*rūpa*), colour (*varṇa*), brilliance (*tejas*), body (*kāya*), primary and secondary physical marks (*lakṣaṇānuvyañjana*), noble birth (*abhijāta*), morality (*śīla*), concentration (*samādhi*), wisdom (*prajñā*), deliverance (*vimukti*), knowledge and vision of deliverance (*vimuktijñānadarśana*), power (*bala*), convictions (*vaiśāradya*), exclusive Buddha attributes (*āveṇikabuddhadharma*), great goodwill (*mahāmaitrī*), great compassion (*mahākaruṇā*), great joy (*mahāmuditā*), great equanimity (*mahopekṣā*), good intention (*hitābhiprāya*), bodily attitudes (*īryāpatha*), practices (*caryā*), path (*mārga*), life span (*āyuṣpramāṇa*), instruction in the Law (*dharmadeśanā*), ripening of beings (*sattvaparipācana*), liberation of beings (*sattvavimocana*) and purification of the Buddha-fields (*buddhakṣetrapariśodhana*).

And because, among the Tathāgatas, all these Buddha attributes (*buddhadharma*) are the same (*sama*), exceedingly fulfilled (*adhimātraparipūrṇa*) and absolutely inexhaustible (*atyantākṣaya*), the Tathāgatas are called Samyaksaṃbuddhas rightly and perfectly enlightened, Tathāgatas and Buddhas.

Ānanda, were your life span (*āyuṣpramāṇa*) to last for a kalpa, it would not be easy for you to grasp clearly (*adhigam-*) the semantic content (*arthavipulatā*) and the phonetic analysis (*padavigraha*) of these three words (*vākya*). And even if, O Ānanda, the beings belonging to the trichiliomegachiliocosm (*trisāhasramahāsāhasralokadhātu*) were, like you, the foremost of the learned (*bahuśrutānām agryaḥ*) and the foremost of those in possession of mindfulness and formulae (*smṛti-*

[13] See above, X, §8, note 6.

dhāraṇīprāptānām agryaḥ)[14], all these beings like Ānanda, were they to consecrate a whole kalpa to it, would be incapable of grasping the exact meaning (*niyatārtha*) of the three words: Samyaksaṃbuddha, Tathāgata and Buddha. Except for Buddhas, none are capable of an exact understanding (*pravicaya*) of them. Indeed, O Ānanda, the enlightenment (*bodhi*) and virtues (*guṇa*) of the Buddhas are immense (*apramāṇa*); the wisdom (*prajñā*) and eloquence (*pratibhāna*) of the Tathāgatas are inconceivable (*acintya*).

[*Superiority of Bodhisattvas over Śrāvakas*[15]]

14. Then the Venerable Ānanda said to the Blessed One: Blessed One, as from today (*adyāgreṇa*), I shall never again dare to call myself the foremost of those in possession of mindfulness and formulae (*smṛtidhāraṇīprāptānām agryaḥ*) and the foremost of the learned (*bahuśrutānām agryaḥ*).

The Blessed One answered: Reject, O Ānanda, this discouraging thought (*ālīnacitta*). When, formerly, I proclaimed you the foremost of those in possession of mindfulness and formulae and the foremost of the learned, I meant (*abhipretam*) the foremost among Listeners (*śrāvaka*), and not the foremost among Bodhisattvas. Where Bodhisattvas are concerned, stop (*tiṣṭha*), O Ānanda; the latter cannot be fathomed by the wise (*paṇḍita*). It would be possible to fathom the depth of all the oceans (*mahāsamudra*) but, with regard to Bodhisattvas, it is impossible to fathom the depth of their wisdom (*prajñā*), their knowledge (*jñāna*), their mindfulness (*smṛti*), their formulae (*dhāraṇī*) or their eloquence (*pratibhāna*).

You others, Śrāvakas, cannot dream of rivaling things which are of the domain of the Bodhisattvas (*bodhisattvagocaraviṣaya*). And why? Ānanda, the marvels (*vyūhanirdeśa*) performed in a single morning (*pūrvāhṇa*) by this Licchavi Vimalakīrti, Śrāvakas and Pratyekabuddhas gifted with psychic powers (*ṛddhiprāpta*) could never manifest, were they to devote to them, throughout one hundred thousand koṭis of kalpas, all their psychic power (*ṛddhi*) and all feats of transformation (*nirmāṇaprātihārya*).

[*Request of the Bodhisattvas from the Sarvagandhasugandhā Universe*]

15. Then all the Bodhisattvas who had come from the Buddhakṣetra of the Blessed Tathāgata Sugandhakūṭa joined their hands (*pragṛhī-*

[14] See above, III, § 42, note 75.

[15] A purely conventional superiority for, from the point of view of the absolute, there is no difference between Śrāvaka mind and Bodhisattva mind (VIII, § 5).

tāñjali), and saluting the Tathāgata Śākyamuni, addressed him with these words:

Blessed One, when we arrived in this Buddhakṣetra and when we saw its filth, we conceived an unfavourable impression (*hīnasaṃjñā*) of it; now, we are ashamed (*apatrāpya*) and we want to be rid of this conception (*manasikāra*). And why? Blessed One, the realm (*viṣaya*) of the Blessed Lord Buddhas and their skill in means (*upāyakauśalya*) are inconceivable (*acintya*). In order to ripen beings (*sattvaparipācanārtham*) they manifest (*saṃdarśayanti*) such and such a splendour of a field (*kṣetravyūha*) so as to respond to such and such a desire (*kānta*) of beings.

Blessed One, give us, then, a spiritual message (*dharmavisarjana*) which will remind us of the Blessed One when we have returned to the Sarvagandhasugandhā universe.

[*Śākyamuni's Homily on the Exhaustible and the Inexhaustible*[16]]

16. This having been said, the Blessed One spoke: Sons of good family (*kulaputra*), there is a treatise on the liberation of the Bodhisattvas (*bodhisattvavimokṣadharmamukha*) entitled: "Exhaustible and Inexhaustible" (*kṣayākṣaya*): you should instruct yourselves (*śikṣatavyam*) in it. What is it?

Called "Exhaustible" (*kṣaya*) is the conditioned (*saṃskṛta*), that is, the dharmas which arise and are extinguished (*utpannaniruddhadharma*); called "Inexhaustible" (*akṣaya*) is the unconditioned (*asaṃskṛta*), that is, the dharma which is unarisen and unextinguished (*anutpannāniruddhadharma*). A Bodhisattva can neither exhaust the conditioned nor abide in the unconditioned.

17. Not exhausting the conditioned (*saṃskṛtānām akṣayaḥ*), this is not relinquishing great goodwill (*mahāmaitryacyavanam*), not losing great compassion (*mahākaruṇāsraṃsanam*), not forgetting the thought of omniscience originating in high resolve (*adhyāśayasamudānītasya sarvajñacittasyāsaṃpramoṣatā*), never wearying of ripening beings (*sattvaparipācane 'saṃtuṣṭiḥ*), never abandoning the means of conversion (*saṃgrahavastūnām aparityāgaḥ*); so as to maintain the Good Law, sacrificing body and life (*saddharmaparigrāhaṇārthaṃ kāyajīvitotsarjanam*), being insatiable in the search for good roots (*kuśalamūla-*

[16] Regarding *kṣayākṣaya*, taken here in the meaning of *saṃskṛtāsaṃskṛta*, see above, X, § 8, note 6 at the end.

paryeṣaṇe 'tṛptiḥ), delighting in a skillful transference of merits (*pariṇāmanākauśalye saṃlayanam*), excluding all idleness in the search for the Law (*dharmaparyeṣaṇe 'kausīdyam*), not being close-fisted during instruction of the Law (*dharmadeśanāyām anācāryamuṣṭitā*)[17], endeavouring to see and pay homage to the Tathāgatas (*tathāgatadarśanapūjanodyogaḥ*), not being afraid during voluntarily assumed existences (*saṃcintyātmabhāveṣv anuttrāsanam*), not being exultant of successes or discouraged by reverses (*saṃpatsu vipatsv anunnatir anavanatam*), not despising Aśaikṣas (*aśaikṣeṣv anavamānaḥ*) and being kind to Śaikṣas (*śaikṣeṣu priyacittatā*) like the Master (*śāstṛ*) himself; bringing to reason (*yoniśa upasaṃhāraḥ*) those whose passions (*kleśa*) are great; delighting in solitude (*viveka*), but without being attached to it[18]; not being attached to one's own happiness (*svasukha*), but being attached to the happiness of others (*parasukha*); perceiving as hell (*avīcisaṃjñā*) the trances (*dhyāna*), the concentrations (*samādhi*) and the recollections (*samāpatti*) and not tasting their flavour (*rasa*)[19]; considering Saṃsāra like a park (*upavana*) or like Nirvāṇa and not feeling aversion for it; considering beggars (*yācaka*) as good friends (*kalyāṇamitra*); considering the abandoning of all assets (*sarvasvaparityāga*) as the means of achieving omniscience (*sarvajñatā*); considering immoral beings (*duḥśīla*) as saviours (*trātṛ*); considering the perfections (*pāramitā*) as father (*pitṛ*) and mother (*mātṛ*); considering the auxiliary dharmas of enlightenment (*bodhipakṣyadharma*) as servants (*bhṛtya*); not tiring of accumulating good roots (*sarvakuśalamūlasaṃcaye 'tṛptatā*) and setting up one's own field (*svakṣetrasādhana*) with the virtues (*guṇa*) of all Buddhakṣetras; so as to fulfil the primary and secondary physical marks (*lakṣaṇānuvyañjanaparipūraṇārtham*), consenting to pure (*viśuddha*) and infinite (*atyanta*) offerings (*yajña*); while avoiding all wrong doing (*sarvapāpākaraṇāt*), adorning the body (*kāya*), speech (*vāc*) and mind (*citta*);

while purifying the body and the speech and while purifying the mind, taking on rebirths (*saṃsa-*

so as to give substance (*sāra*) and endurance (*kṣānti*) to the body and the mind, avoiding all anger (*krodha*) and all passion

[17] Regarding this expression, see VI, § 2, note 19.

[18] Cf. IV, § 20, clause 11.

[19] Buddhists consider the *dhyāna* associated with enjoyment (*āsvādanasaṃprayukta*) to be impure: see above, II § 3, note 10. The practice of the *samāpatti* is particularly dangerous for the ascetic runs the risk of becoming attached to the recollection and confusing it with the fruits of the Path. On this point, see the mishap of Udraka Rāmaputra in NĀGĀRJUNA, *Traité*, p. 1050-1052.

raṇa) for incalculable periods (*asaṃkhyeyakalpa*);

(*kleśa*); so as to attain rapidly the summit of effort (*bhāvanāniṣṭhāgamanāya*), wandering in the round of rebirth for incalculable kalpas;

so as to give one's own mind a heroic resistance, never tiring (*aviṣāda*) of hearing the innumerable virtues (*apramāṇaguṇa*) of the Buddhas; so as to combat those enemies which are the passions, seizing the sword of wisdom (*kleśaśatrunigrahāya prajñāśastrādharaṇam*); so as to bear the burden of all beings, seeking to understand perfectly the aggregates, the elements and the bases of consciousness (*sarvasattvabhāraharaṇāya skandhadhātvāyatanājñāparyeṣṭiḥ*); so as to destroy the hordes of Māra, stimulating vigour (*māracamūnirghātāya vīryottāpanam*) and fighting idleness (*kausīdya*);

so as to dispel conceit (*māna*), seeking after knowledge (*jñānaparyeṣṭi*); so as to expound the Law, having few desires and being content with little (*dharmavacanārtham alpecchatā saṃtuṣṭiḥ*);

so as to protect the unsurpassed Good Law (*anuttarasaddharmarakṣaṇāya*), dispelling conceit (*māna*) and diligently seeking skillfulness (*kauśalya*) and the knowledge of transformations (*nirmāṇajñāna*);

so as to delight the whole world (*sarvalokasaṃtoṣaṇāya*), not tangling with the worldly states (*lokadharma*)[20];

for the joy and conversion of the world, having few desires (*alpecchatā*), being content (*saṃtuṣṭi*) with little and never tangling with the worldly states (*lokadharma*);

so as to conform to the world (*lokānuvartanārtham*), never abandoning the bodily attitudes (*īryāpatha*); so as to manifest all the practices (*sarvacaryāsaṃprakāśanāya*), producing the super-knowledges (*abhijñā*) and lovely wisdom; causing the benefit and happiness of all beings (*sarvasattvahitasukha*); so as to memorize the good Law already heard (*śrutadhāraṇāya*), possessing the formulae (*dhāraṇī*), mindfulness (*smṛti*) and knowledge (*jñāna*); so as to destroy the doubts of all beings (*sarvasattvasaṃśayacchedanāya*), knowing the degree of their spiritual faculties (*indriyavarāvarajñāna*); so as to teach the Law (*dharmadeśanāya*), having command of invincible supernatural actions (*apratihatādhiṣṭhāna*); possessing the gift of eloquence and thus being in command of an infallible eloquence (*apratihatapratibhāna*); purifying the ten paths of good action (*kuśalakarmapatha*) and thus tasting bliss both divine and human (*devamanuṣyasampadām āsvādanam*); cultivating the four

[20] See I, § 10, note 50.

infinite states (*apramāṇa*) and thus opening up the Brahmā-path (*brahmamārgasthāpana*)[21]; inviting (*adhyeṣaṇa*) the Buddhas to expound the Law, congratulating them (*anumodanā*), praising them (*sādhukāra*), and thus obtaining the sounds of a Buddha's voice (*buddhaghoṣa*)[22]; disciplining the body, speech and mind (*kāyavāgmanaḥsaṃvara*) and thus continuing to progress (*viśeṣagamana*); by not being attached to any dharmas (*sarvadharmāsaktatā*), acquiring the bodily attitudes (*īryāpatha*) of a Buddha; by assembling communities of Bodhisattvas (*bodhisattvasaṃghasaṃgraha*), drawing beings to the Mahāyāna; always and at all times exercising heedfulness (*apramāda*) so as not to lose a single virtue (*guṇa*); so as to ensure the development and growth of good roots (*kuśalamūla*), cultivating joyfully all kinds of great vows (*mahāpraṇidhāna*); so as to adorn all the Buddhakṣetras, cultivating diligently immense good roots; so that the practices (*bhāvanā*) are absolutely inexhaustible (*atyantākṣaya*), always exercising the transference of merits (*pariṇāmanā*) and skill in means (*upāyakauśalya*). Sons of good family, the Bodhisattva who applies himself thus to the Law (*dharmābhiyukta*) is a Bodhisattva who does not exhaust the conditioned.

18. What is not abiding in the unconditioned (*asaṃskṛta*)?

A Bodhisattva practises emptiness, but does not realise emptiness (*śūnyatāṃ parikaroti na tu śūnyatāṃ sākṣātkaroti*). He does the same with signlessness (*ānimitta*), wishlessness (*apraṇihita*) and inaction (*anabhisaṃskāra*)[23].

He is aware that all conditioned things are transitory (*anityāḥ sarvasaṃskārā iti pratyavekṣate*), but never tires of good roots (*kuśalamūla*). He is aware that all conditioned things are painful (*duḥkhāḥ sarvasaṃskārā iti pratyavekṣate*), but voluntarily assumes existences in Saṃsāra (*saṃcintyātmabhāvaṃ parigṛhṇāti*).

He is aware that (all dharmas) are impersonal (*anātmānaḥ sarvadharmā iti pratyavekṣate*), but does not reject the self (*na tv ātmānam utsṛjati*).

He is aware that inwardly (*adhyātmam*) there is no *ātman*, but he does not definitively reject existence (*ātmabhāva*). He is aware that outwardly (*bahirdhā*), there is no *sattva*, but he does not tire of controlling his mind.

He is aware of calm (*śāntaṃ pratyavekṣate*), but does not pro-

He is aware that Nirvāṇa is the absolute calm (*śāntaṃ nirvāṇam iti pratyavekṣate*), but does not definitively slip into calmness.

[21] See I, § 13, note 66; IV, § 20, note 41.

[22] Cf. Hōbōgirin, p. 215, s.v. *Button*.

[23] Paragraph concerning the three *vimokṣamukha*.

voke the definitive calm (*na tu praśamanam utpādayati*)[24].

He is aware of solitude (*viveka*), but he exerts himself in body and mind (*kāyacittena prayatate*)[25].

He is aware of the absolute happiness of solitude (*vivekātyantasukha*), but is not absolutely averse to the body (*kāya*) and mind (*citta*).

He is aware that there is no resting place (*anālayaṃ pratyavekṣate*), but he does not reject the resting place of the white dharmas (*na tu śukladharmāṇām ālayaṃ jahāti*)[26]. He is aware that all dharmas are absolutely unarisen (*anutpādaṃ pratyavekṣate*), but he always bears the burden of beings (*sattvānāṃ tu bhāraṃ harati*). He is aware of the pure elements (*anāsravaṃ pratyavekṣate*), but he follows the course of Saṃsāra (*saṃsāraprabandhaṃ tu parimārgayati*). He is aware of immobility (*apracāraṃ pratyavekṣate*), but he keeps moving so as to ripen beings (*sattvaparipācanārtham tu pracarati*). He is aware of the non-existence of the self (*nairātmyaṃ pratyavekṣate*), but he does not abandon great compassion towards beings (*na tu sattveṣu mahākaruṇām utsṛjati*)[27]. He is aware of non-arising (*anutpādaṃ pratyavekṣate*), but he does not fall into the predestined certainty (*niyāma*) of the Śrāvakas[28].

He is aware that all dharmas are: 1. void (*tucchaka*), 2. vain (*riktaka*), 3. worthless (*asāraka*), 4. dependent (*vaśika*), 5. abodeless (*aniketa*), but he bases himself 1. on merits that are not void (*atucchakāni puṇyāni*), 2. on a knowledge that is not vain (*ariktakaṃ jñānam*), 3. on perfected concepts (*paripūrṇāḥ saṃkalpāḥ*), 4. on the consecration of autonomous knowledge (*svatantrajñānābhiṣeka*) and the effort with regard

He is aware that all dharmas are absolutely void (*tucchaka*), but he does not allow acquired merits (*puṇya*) to become void. He is aware that all dharmas are absolutely vain (*riktaka*), but he does not stray from acquired knowledge (*jñāna*). He is aware that all dharmas are absolutely worthless (*asāraka*), but always bases himself on perfected concepts (*paripūrnasaṃkalpa*). He is aware that all dharmas are dependent (*avaśika*), but he always strives to seek autonomous knowledge (*svatantraṃ jñānam*) He is aware that all dharmas are without a sign of abode (*aniketa*), but he abides in the literal sense (*nītārtha*)

[24] Regarding *anitya, duḥkha, anātman, śānta*, see above, II, §25, note 51; IV, §10, note 15.

[25] Cf. IV, §20, clause 11.

[26] Cf. V, §4, note 4.

[27] See above, VI, §2.

[28] K: "He is aware of the *samyaktvaniyāma*, but does not follow the *hīnayāna*". — H: "He is aware of the *anutpāda*, but does not fall into the *samyaktvaniyāma* of the [first] two Vehicles". — See above, IV, §20, clause 8.

to autonomous knowledge (*svatantrajñānodyoga*), 5. on the family of the Buddhas taken in its literal sense (*nītārthabuddhagotra*)[29].

in the family of the Buddhas (*buddhagotra*).

Sons of good family, the Bodhisattva who adheres to such a Law (*tādṛśadharmādhimukta*) does not abide in the unconditioned and does not exhaust the conditioned.

Sons of good family, the Bodhisattva who applies himself thus to the Law is a Bodhisattva who does not abide in the unconditioned.

19. Besides[30], O sons of good family, a Bodhisattva does not abide in the unconditioned because he collects stores of merit (*puṇyasambhāra*); he does not exhaust the conditioned because he assembles stores of knowledge (*jñānasaṃbhāra*).

He does not abide in the unconditioned because he is endowed with great goodwill (*mahāmaitrīsamanvāgata*) in no way deficient; he does not exhaust the conditioned because he is endowed with great compassion (*mahākaruṇāsamanvāgata*) in no way deficient.

He does not abide in the unconditioned because he ripens all beings (*sarvasattvān paripācayati*); he does not exhaust the conditioned, because he adheres to the Buddhadharmas (*buddhadharmān adhimucyate*).

He does not abide in the unconditioned because he brings about the benefit and happiness (*hitasukha*) of all beings; he does not exhaust the conditioned because he definitively fulfils (*atyantaṃ paripūrayati*) the Buddhadharmas.

He does not abide in the unconditioned because he achieves (*paripūrayati*) a Buddha-body adorned with the primary and secondary physical marks (*lakṣaṇānuvyañjanālaṃkṛtabuddhakāya*); he does not exhaust the conditioned because he acquires the powers (*bala*), the convictions (*vaiśāradya*) and omniscience (*sarvajñajñāna*).

[29] The adjectives *riktaka, tucchaka, asāraka*, etc., are part of a stock of epithets which can be found in the canonical texts of both Vehicles: cf. Dīgha, I, p. 240,*3-4*; Majjhima, I, p. 329,*28-30*; Saṃyutta, III, p. 140-141; Mahāvastu, II, p. 145,*18-19*; Aṣṭasāh., p. 706,*7-9*; Mahāvyutpatti, No. 7316 and sq. — They are explained in Suvikrāntavikrāmin, p. 92, and Āloka, p. 706,*14-18*. — There is some hesitation between *vaśika* (Pāli, *vasika*) and *avaśika* (cf. the note by R. Hikata, in *Suvikrāntavikrāmin*, Index, p. 141, s.v. *vaśika, vaśikasvabhāva*).

K abridges this paragraph considerably: "He is aware that all dharmas are *tucchaka, riktaka, asāraka, niḥpudgala, avaśika, animitta*, but while his original vows (*pūrvapraṇidhāna*) have not been fulfilled, he does not allow *puṇya, samādhi, prajñā* to be in vain".

[30] This paragraph 19 is greatly abridged in K. Once again, he deals with the contradictory actions of the Bodhisattva (see above, II, § 3, note 9).

He does not abide in the unconditioned because he disciplines (*vinayati*) beings through his skillfulness in means (*upāyakauśalya*); he does not exhaust the conditioned because he is resolute in his knowledge (*jñānasuniścita*).

He does not abide in the unconditioned because he purifies (*pariśodhayati*) Buddhakṣetras; he does not exhaust the conditioned owing to the eternal and indestructible supernatural actions of the Buddhas (*buddhādhiṣṭhāna*).

He does not abide in the unconditioned because he perceives (*anubhavati*) the requirements of beings (*sattvārtha*); he does not exhaust the conditioned because he teaches correctly the meaning of the Law (*dharmārthaṃ saṃprakāśayati*).

He does not abide in the unconditioned because he always benefits beings; he does not exhaust the conditioned because he perceives (*pratisaṃvedayati*) the meaning of the Law (*dharmārtha*) without ever stopping.

He does not abide in the unconditioned because he accumulates good roots (*kuśalamūlāni saṃcinoti*); he does not exhaust the conditioned because he has not yet cut off the pervasions of these good roots (*kuśalamūlavāsanā*).

He does not abide in the unconditioned because he fulfils his original vows (*pūrvapraṇidhānāni paripūrayati*); he does not exhaust the conditioned because he does not wish for definitive extinction (*na nirodhaṃ praṇidadhāti*).

He does not abide in the unconditioned because of the purity of his good intentions (*āśayapariśuddhi*); he does not exhaust the conditioned because of the purity of his high resolve (*adhyāśayapariśuddhi*).

He does not abide in the unconditioned because of the play of the five super-knowledges (*pañcābhijñāvikrīḍana*); he does not exhaust the conditioned because of the fullness of the six super-knowledges (*ṣaḍabhijñāparipūri*) constituting Buddha-knowledge (*buddhajñāna*)[31].

He does not abide in the unconditioned because of the fullness of the perfections (*pāramitāparipūraṇa*); he does not exhaust the conditioned because of the fullness of time (*kālaparipūri*)[32].

He does not abide in the unconditioned because of the fullness of his store of perfections (*pāramitāsaṃbhāraparipūraṇa*); he does not exhaust the conditioned because his original mental activities (*pūrvamanasikāra*) are not yet fulfilled.

[31] Regarding the particular value of the sixth *abhijñā*, see above, III, § 30, note 59.

[32] The Bodhisattva cannot exhaust conditioned things and enter Nirvāṇa before the fullness of time, that is, as long as there still remain beings to be converted.

He does not abide in the unconditioned because he accumulates (*saṃgṛhṇāti*) always and tirelessly the riches of the Law (*dharmadhana*); he does not exhaust the conditioned because he does not desire a limited Law (*prādeśikadharma*).

He does not abide in the unconditioned because he gathers (*piṇḍīkaroti*) all the medicaments of the Law (*dharmabhaiṣajya*); he does not exhaust the conditioned because he administers these medicaments of the Law according to need (*yathāyogam*).

He does not abide in the unconditioned because he is firm in his promises (*dṛḍhapratijñā*); he does not exhaust the conditioned so as to overcome the insufficiencies of his promises (*pratijñāhāni*).

He does not abide in the unconditioned because he is firm in his promises and never retreats; he does not exhaust the conditioned so that these promises (*pratijñā*) may be definitively fulfilled (*atyantaparipūrṇa*).

He does not abide in the unconditioned because he accumulates (*saṃcinoti*) all the medicaments of the Law (*dharmabhaiṣajya*); he does not exhaust the conditioned because he distributes these medicaments of the Law according to need.

He does not abide in the unconditioned because he knows perfectly (*parijānāti*) all the diseases of the passions (*kleśavyādhi*); he does not exhaust the conditioned because he appeases (*praśāmayati*) all these diseases.

Sons of good family, it is thus that a Bodhisattva does not exhaust the conditioned and does not abide in the unconditioned. This treatise of the liberation of the Bodhisattvas (*bodhisattvavimokṣadharmamukha*) is called "Exhaustible and Inexhaustible" (*kṣayākṣaya*). Sons of good family, you should instruct yourselves (*śikṣitavyam*) in it.

[*The Return of the Sarvagandhasugandhā Bodhisattvas*]

20. Then the Bodhisattvas who had come from the Sarvagandhasugandhā universe, Buddha-field of the Tathāgata Sugandhakūṭa, after having heard this expounding of the liberation called Kṣayākṣaya, were well-pleased, delighted, transported, joyful, full of contentment and pleasure (*tuṣṭā udagrā āttamanasaḥ pramuditāḥ prītisaumanasyajātāḥ*). In order to pay homage (*pūjanārtham*) to the Buddha Śākyamuni and to pay homage to the Bodhisattvas (of the Sahā universe) as well as to this interpretation of the Law (*dharmaparyāya*), they covered (*ācchādayanti sma*) the ground of the trisāhasramahāsāhasralokadhātu to knee height (*jānumātram*) with powder (*cūrṇa*), perfumes (*gandha*), incense (*dhūpa*) and flowers (*puṣpa*). Having thus covered the entourage (*parṣanmaṇḍala*) of the Tathāgata, after having saluted with their heads the feet of the Blessed One (*bhagavataḥ pādau śirasābhivandya*) and circled round him three times (*triḥkṛtvaḥ pradakṣiṇīkṛtya*), they sang a song of praise (*udānam udānayām āsuḥ*). Then they disappeared (*antarhitāḥ*) from this universe, and, in a single instant (*ekasminn eva kṣaṇalavamuhūrte*), they re-entered the Sarvagandhasugandhā universe.

CHAPTER ELEVEN

THE APPROPRIATION OF THE ABHIRATI UNIVERSE AND VISION OF THE TATHĀGATA AKṢOBHYA

[*The Inexistence of the Tathāgatas*[1]]

1. Then the Blessed One said to the Licchavi Vimalakīrti: Son of good family (*kulaputra*), now that you have come here to see the Tathāgata, how do you see him?

This having been said (*evam ukte*), Vimalakīrti replied to the Blessed One: Blessed One, now that I see the Tathāgata, I see him as if there were nothing to see. And why?

The Tathāgata does not originate in prior time (*pūrvāntād notpadyate*), does not enter posterior time (*aparāntaṃ na saṃkrāmati*) and is not to be found in present time (*pratyutpanne kāle na tiṣṭhati*). And why?

[1] Vimalakīrti once again returns to the problem of the Tathāgata, a subject already dealt with in Chapters II, §12; VII, §2-3; X, §13. Here, he particularly emphasizes the absolute purity of the Tathāgata who can justly be said to be no different from total inexistence.

This is the position of the Prajñāpāramitā (Pañcaviṃśati, p. 146,*9-17*) according to which the Bodhisattva does not perceive (*nopalabhate*) either a being, or dharma, or dependent co-production, or Arhat, or Pratyekabuddha, or Bodhisattva, or Buddha "due to their absolute purity" (*atyantaviśuddhitā*).

This is clearly the opinion of the Madhyamaka (Madh. vṛtti, p. 435) according to which the Tathāgata does not exist in any way at all (*sarvathā na saṃbhavaty eva tathāgataḥ*) and which quotes many of the Vaipulyas in support of its thesis: cf. ibidem, p. 448,*11-15*:

ye māṃ rūpeṇa adrākṣur ye māṃ ghoṣeṇa anvayuḥ,
mithyāprahāṇaprasṛtā na māṃ drakṣyanti te janāḥ.
dharmato buddhā draṣṭavyā dharmakāyā hi nāyakāḥ,
dharmatā cāpy avijñeyā na sā śakyā vijānitum.

"Those who have seen me in a material form and have been guided by my voice, those men, committed to false and ruinous views, will never see me. It is through the Law that the Buddhas should be seen, for the Leaders are Bodies of the Law. The nature of things being itself unknowable cannot be discerned".

Similar declarations can be found in the early canonical Sūtras: cf. Saṃyutta, III, p. 120,*27-31*; Aṅguttara, II, p. 71,*15-16*; Theragāthā, v. 469. — Also see Udānavarga, XXII, v. 12; Divyāvadāna, p. 19,*10-11*; Saptaśatikā, p. 119,*1-10*; Vajracchedikā, p. 56-57; Samādhirāja, XXII, v. 33-39; Pañjikā, p. 421,*10-11*.

The Tathāgata is the self-nature of the suchness of form (*rūpatathatāsvabhāva*), but he is not form (*rūpa*). He is the self-nature of the suchness of sensation (*vedanātathatāsvabhāva*), but he is not sensation (*vedanā*). He is the self-nature of the suchness of perception (*saṃjñātathatāsvabhāva*), but he is not perception (*saṃjñā*). He is the self-nature of the suchness of volition (*saṃskāratathatāsvabhāva*), but he is not volition. He is the self-nature of the suchness of consciousness (*vijñānatathatāsvabhāva*), but he is not consciousness (*vijñāna*)[2].

The Tathāgata is not to be found in the four elements (*dhātu*), but he is the same as the space-element (*ākāśadhātusama*). He is not born of the six bases of consciousness (*āyatana*), but has gone beyond the path of the six faculties (*ṣaḍindriyamārgasamatikrānta*), that is, the path of the eye (*cakṣus*), the ear (*śrotra*), the nose (*ghrāṇa*), the tongue (*jihvā*), the body (*kāya*) and the mind (*manas*).

The Tathāgata is not involved in the triple world (*traidhātukāsaṃbhinna*); he is free of the triple defilement (*malatrayavigata*); he is associated with the triple liberation (*vimokṣatrayānugata*) and endowed with the triple knowledge (*trividyāprāpta*). He is knowledge (*vidyā*) without being knowledge, comprehension (*adhigama*) without being comprehension.

He has reached the summit of detachment in all things (*sarvadharmeṣu asaṅganiṣṭhāgataḥ*), but he is not the limit of reality (*bhūtakoṭi*). He is based on suchness (*tathatāsupratiṣṭhita*), but is deprived of a connection with it[3].

Regarding all dharmas, he has reached the summit of detachment (*asaṅganiṣṭhāgata*). He is at one and the same time the limit of reality (*bhūtakoṭi*) and the non-limit (*akoṭi*), suchness (*tathatā*) and non-suchness (*atathatā*). He does not rely (*apratiṣṭhita*) on the realm of suchness (*tathatāviṣaya*), and he is deprived of light regarding the knowledge of suchness (*tathatājñāna*), but, with that which concerns the realm (*viṣaya*) and the knowledge

[2] As it appears in the Taishō edition, the punctuation in H is at fault: it should be corrected in the light of the Tibetan syntax. Furthermore, H and the Tibetan version seem to have been contaminated by lucubrations of Vijñānavādin origin on the distinction between *skandha* and *tathatā*. There is nothing like them in the two other earlier Chinese versions:

Cn: "The [Tathāgata] is like space: he is not an accumulation of *āyatana* such as *cakṣus*, *śrotra*, *ghrāṇa*, *jihvā*, *kāya* and *manas*".

K: "I do not see the Tathāgata as either *rūpa*, or *rūpatathatā*, or *rūpasvabhāva*; I do not see him as either *vedanā*, *saṃjñā*, *saṃskāra*, *vijñāna*; I do not see him as either *vijñānatathatā* or *vijñānasvabhāva*.

[3] This paragraph is missing in Cn and K.

(*jñāna*) of this suchness (*tathatā*), he is naturally associated and dissociated.

The Tathāgata is not born of causes (*hetusamutpanna*), is not born of conditionality (*pratītyasamutpanna*) and does not depend on conditionality (*pratyayādhīna*). He is neither endowed with a mark (*salakṣaṇa*) nor deprived of a mark (*alakṣaṇa*). He has neither a self-mark (*svalakṣaṇa*) nor other mark (*paralakṣaṇa*), neither a single mark (*ekalakṣaṇa*) nor a multiple mark (*bhinnalakṣaṇa*). He is neither subject (*lakṣya*), nor non-subject nor the same as subject nor different from subject; he is neither predicate (*lakṣaṇa*), nor non-predicate, nor the same as predicate nor different from predicate. He is neither conceived (*kalpita*), nor imagined (*parikalpita*), nor not-conceived (*akalpita*)[4].

The Tathāgata is neither this shore (*apāra*), nor the other shore (*pāra*) nor mid-stream (*madhyaugha*); he is not here (*iha*) or there (*tatra*) or elsewhere (*anyatra*); he is neither on the inside (*adhyātmam*) nor on the outside (*bahirdhā*) nor in the two at the same time (*ubhayatra*).

The Tathāgata has not gone, will not go and does not go; he has not come, will not come and does not come.

The Tathāgata is neither knowledge (*jñāna*) nor realm (*viṣaya*) of knowledge; he is neither consciousness (*vijñāna*) nor the object cognized (*vijñāta*). He is neither hidden (*tirobhūta*) nor overt (*āvirbhūta*), neither darkness (*tamas*) nor light (*prakāśa*). He does not stay still (*na tiṣṭhati*) and he does not move (*na gacchati*).

The Tathāgata has neither name (*nāman*) nor sign (*nimitta*). He is neither powerful (*balin*) nor weak (*durbala*). He is neither localised (*deśastha*) nor unlocalised (*adeśastha*). He is neither good (*kuśala*) nor bad (*akuśala*), neither defilement (*saṃkleśa*) nor purification (*vyavadāna*). He is neither conditioned (*saṃskṛta*) nor unconditioned (*asaṃskṛta*). He is neither extinction (*nirodha*) nor non-extinction (*anirodha*). He is neither something to be taught nor a meaning (*artha*) to be expounded.

The Tathāgata is neither giving (*dāna*) nor greed (*mātsarya*), neither morality (*śīla*) nor immorality (*dauḥśīlya*), neither patience (*kṣānti*) nor animosity (*vyāpāda*), neither vigour (*vīrya*) nor idleness (*kausīdya*), neither meditation (*dhyāna*) nor distraction (*vikṣepa*), neither wisdom (*prajñā*) nor foolishness (*dauṣprajñā*): he is inexpressible (*anabhilāpya*).

The Tathāgata is neither truth (*satya*) nor falsehood (*mṛṣā*), neither exit (*niryāṇa*) nor entrance (*aniryāṇa*), neither going (*gamana*) nor

[4] This sentence is missing in H.

coming (*āgamana*): he is the cutting off of all discussion and of all practice (*sarvavādacaryoccheda*)[5].

The Tathāgata is not a field of merit (*puṇyakṣetra*) nor a non-field of merit; he is neither worthy of offerings (*dakṣiṇīya*) nor unworthy of offerings.

The Tathāgata is neither a grasping subject (*grāhaka*) nor object grasped (*grāhya*), neither a sensing subject (*vedaka*) nor object sensed (*vedayita*); neither sign (*nimitta*) nor signlessness (*animitta*); neither action (*abhisaṃskāra*) nor non-action (*anabhisaṃskāra*).

The Tathāgata is not a number (*saṃkhyā*) and he is free of numbers (*saṃkhyāvigata*); he is not an obstacle (*āvaraṇa*) and he is free of obstacles (*āvaraṇavigata*). He is free of augmentation (*upacaya*) and free of diminution (*apacaya*).

The Tathāgata is the same as sameness (*samatāsama*), the same as the limit of reality (*bhūtakoṭisama*), the same and not the same as the nature of things (*dharmatāsamāsama*).

The Tathāgata is neither weigher (*tulā*) nor weighed (*tulita*), but is beyond all weight (*tulanasamatikrānta*). He is neither measurer nor measured, but is beyond all measure. He is neither ahead (*purastāt*) nor behind (*pṛṣṭhatas*) nor ahead and behind at the same time. He is neither courageous nor timid, but is beyond courage and timidity. He is neither large (*mahat*) nor small (*alpa*), neither broad (*viśāla*) nor narrow (*saṃkṣipta*).

The Tathāgata is neither seen (*dṛṣṭa*), nor heard (*śruta*) nor thought (*mata*) nor known (*vijñāta*)[6]. He eludes all ties (*sarvagranthavigata*). He is cool (*śītībhūta*) and delivered (*vimukta*). He has achieved sameness with omniscient knowledge (*sarvajñajñānasamatāprāpta*). He has obtained the non-duality of all beings[7] (*sarvasattvādvayaprāpta*) and has achieved the indifferentiation of all things (*sarvadharmanirviśeṣaprāpta*).

Everywhere (*sarvatra*), the Tathāgata is without reproach (*avadya*), without excess, without corruption (*kaṣāya*), without flaw (*doṣa*), without obstruction (*vighāta*). He is without conception (*kalpa*) and without imagination (*vikalpa*).

[5] Traditional expression: In Tib., *smra ba dan spyod pa thams cad śin tu chad par*. The Saddharmapuṇḍ., p. 278,*1-2*, mentions *niruktivyavahāravivarjita*, *anabhilāpapravyahṛta* dharmas. Regarding these ideas and expressions, also see Avataṃsaka, T 278, ch. 11, p. 469 *a* 12; Upadeśa, T 1509, ch. 1, p. 61 *b* 7; ch. 5, p. 96 *c* 13; Vijñaptimātratāsiddhi, T 1585, ch. 10, p. 55 *b* 11; Miao fa lien hua ching wên chü, T 1718, ch. 3, p. 42 *a* 13-14; Ta jih ching shu, T 1796, ch. 19, p. 774 *b* 1; P. Demiéville, *Le Concile de Lhasa*, p. 156, note 5.

[6] See above, V, §4, note 5.

[7] The Tibetan mistakenly says: "the non-duality of all dharmas", which duplicates what follows.

He is without activity (*kriyā*), without birth (*jāti*), without arising (*utpāda*), without origination (*samudaya*), without production (*samutpāda*) and without non-production (*asamutpāda*). He is without fear (*bhaya*) and without a resting-place (*ālaya*); without sorrow (*śoka*) and without rejoicing (*nanda*). He is without agitation (*taraṅga*). He cannot express himself (*anirvācya*) in any language (*vyavahāra*).

He is without activity (*kriyā*) and without birth (*jāti*); without falsehood (*mṛṣā*) and without truth (*satya*); without arising (*utpāda*) and without extinction (*nirodha*). He is without past and without future; without fear (*bhaya*) and without defilement (*kleśa*). He is without sorrow (*śoka*) and without rejoicing (*nanda*), without disgust (*nirveda*) and without delight (*nanda*). He cannot be grasped by any idea (*vikalpa*) nor expressed by any language (*vyavahāra*).

Such is the body of the Tathāgata (*tathāgatakāya*). It is thus that he should be seen and not otherwise. He who sees him thus sees him correctly (*samyak paśyati*); he who sees him otherwise sees him wrongly (*mithyā paśyati*).

[*Antecedence of Vimalakīrti*]

2. Then the Venerable (*āyuṣmant*) Śāriputra said to the Blessed One: Blessed One, where then did the son of good family Vimalakīrti die (*kutaś cyutvā*) before coming here to this Sahā universe?

The Blessed One replied: Śāriputra, you ask that worthy man (*satpuruṣa*) where he died before being reborn here.

Then the Venerable Śāriputra questioned the Licchavi Vimalakīrti: Son of good family, where did you die before being reborn here?

Vimalakīrti. — Among all the dharmas ascertained by yourself, O Elder, is there any one that dies and is born (*tvayā sākṣātkṛteṣu dharmeṣu, sthavira, asti kaścid dharmo yo mriyate votpadyate vā*)?

Śāriputra. — No, among them there is not one that dies and is born.

Vimalakīrti. — Honourable (*bhadanta*) Śāriputra, if no dharma dies or is born, why do you ask me where I died before being reborn here? What do you think of this (*tat kiṃ manyase*), O Honourable Śāriputra? If a boy (*dāraka*) or a girl (*dārikā*) created by an illusionist (*māyākāranirmita*) were asked where they died before being reborn here, what would they answer?

Śāriputra. — Son of good family, these illusionary creations (*nirmāṇa*), undergoing neither death (*cyuti*) nor birth (*jāti*), what could they answer?

Vimalakīrti. — Nevertheless, O Honourable Śāriputra, has not the Tathāgata said: "All dharmas are illusionary creations" (*nirmāṇasvabhāvāḥ sarvadharmāḥ*)[8]?

Śāriputra. — It is indeed so (*evam etat*), O son of good family.

Vimalakīrti. — Honourable Śāriputra, if all dharmas are in the nature of illusionary creations (*nirmāṇasvabhāva*), why do you ask me where I died before being reborn here? Honourable Śāriputra, death (*cyuti*) has as its mark (*lakṣaṇa*) the interruption of activities (*abhisaṃskārochheda*), and birth (*jāti*) has as its mark the continuity of activities (*abhisaṃskāraprabandha*). But a Bodhisattva, though he may die, does not "interrupt" the activities of good roots (*kuśalamūla*); and a Bodhisattva, though he may be born, does not "continue" the activities of bad dharmas (*akuśaladharma*).

[*Vimalakīrti comes from the Abhirati Universe*]

3. Then the Blessed One said to Venerable Śāriputra: Śāriputra, this son of good family (*kulaputra*) came from the Abhirati universe and the Tathāgata Akṣobhya[9], and it is in order to save beings that, from there, he was reborn here, in this Sahā universe.

[8] Cf. Pañcaviṃśati, p. 4,*15*; 126,*6*; 226,*21*; 254,*23*; Daśabhūmika, p. 47,*15*.

[9] Akṣobhya is the present Buddha of the East, ruling over the Abhirati universe (Aṣṭasāh., p. 745,*12*; Gaṇḍavyūha, p. 82,*9*). He is therefore one of the four Buddhas of the cardinal points, with Ratnaketu in the South, Amitāyus in the West and Dundubhisvara in the North (Suvarṇabhāsa, p. 7,*11*-8,*3*; 120,*5*-*8*).

We are informed about his *bodhicittotpāda* by the Akṣobhyatathāgatasya vyūhaḥ (T 313, p. 751 *b*-764 *a*; T 310, ch. 19-20, p. 101 *c*-112 *c*; OKC No. 760,*6*). The T 313 is attributed to Chih Lou-chia-ch'an (Lokakṣema of the Yüeh-chih) of the late Han. According to the old catalogue of Chu Shih-hsing drawn up under the Wei (220-264) and quoted in the Li tai san pao chi (T 2034, ch. 4, p. 52 *c* 23) and the K'ai yüan shih chiao mu lu (T 2154, ch. 1, p. 478 *c* 5), the T 313 was composed in the first year of the *chien-ho* period (A.D. 147). But this date is too early for it was only during the second half of the second century that Lokakṣema worked in Lo-yang (cf. P. Demiéville, *Inde Classique*, II, p. 412; E. Zürcher, *The Buddhist Conquest of China*, I, p. 35).

To the East of the Sahāloka, beyond a thousand universes, there is a buddhakṣetra called Abhirati. In bygone days the Tathāgata Mahānetra (*Ta mu* 大目 or *Kuang-mu* 廣目; in Tib., *Spyan chen po*) expounded the Law there to his Bodhisattvas, beginning with the six *pāramitā*. A bhikṣu (whose name is not mentioned) approached the Tathāgata and said to him: Blessed One, I would like to practise the rules (*śikṣāpada*) which you are teaching your Bodhisattvas. The Buddha said to him: These rules are very difficult to practise: these Bodhisattvas do not produce towards beings any thought of anger (*prakopa*) or ill-will (*vyāpāda*).

The bhikṣu declared to the Buddha: Blessed One, as from today, I produce the

Śāriputra said: Blessed One, it is astonishing (*āścaryam etat*) that this worthy man, after having left a Buddhakṣetra as pure (*evaṃviśuddha*) as the Abhirati, should delight (*abhinandate*) in a Buddhakṣetra as full of flaws (*bahudoṣaduṣṭa*) as the Sahā universe.

anuttarasamyaksaṃbodhicitta. Without guile (*śāṭhya*) or deceit (*māyā*), sincerely and without trickery, I seek the knowledge of omniscience (*sarvajñajñāna*). As long as I have not reached *anuttarabodhi*, if I experience towards beings any thought of anger (*krodha*) or ill-will (*vyāpāda*), this would be equivalent to turning my back on the Tathāgata Buddhas who are at present expounding the Law in innumerable universes.

The bhikṣu formulated three further vows (according to T 310, *l.c.*). One of his colleagues acknowledged: This Bodhisattva Mahāsattva, whose *cittotpāda* has arrayed him in the armour of vigour (*vīryasaṃnāha*), is immovable (*akṣobhya*) in his resolve not to feel any anger towards beings.

The text ends by saying: This Bodhisattva, because of that resolve, is today called the Buddha Akṣobhya of the Abhirati universe.

— It is clear that Akṣobhya appears as the Buddha of the present in the Prajñāpāramitā:

The Pañcaviṃśati, p. 91-92 (cf. T 223, ch. 2, p. 229 *b* 2; T 1509, ch. 40, p. 354 *a* 14) contains a prediction concerning three hundred bhikṣuṇīs (or bhikṣus) who, during the *tārakopama kalpa*, will be reborn in Akṣobhya's universe, while 60,000 devaputras will reach Nirvāṇa in the presence of Maitreya.

In the Aṣṭasāh., the Buddha announces that the Gaṅgādevatā will change sex and take on a birth in the Abhirati universe (p. 745,*10-13*); he sings the praises of Bodhisattvas who practise continence under the guidance and example of Akṣobhya (p. 853,*24*; 855,*16*); finally he shows his assembly Akṣobhya's universe (p. 874-875: a passage with several gaps that can be filled with the help of the Śikṣāsamuccaya, p. 351,*9*-352,*6*, and the Chinese versions, T 227, ch. 9, p. 568 *b* 17; etc.).

In the Sukhāvatī, p. 204,*1-6*, the Buddhas of the Eastern region, Akṣobhya at their head, give an account (*nirveṭhana*) of the Sukhāvatīvyūha and extol the wonders of Amitābha's Western Paradise.

Buddhist texts devote some stories to the previous lives of Akṣobhya:

1. Saddharmapuṇḍarīka: In the remotest of times, during the Mahārūpa kalpa, Mahābhijñājñānābhibhū ruled over the Saṃbhavā universe and became a fully and perfectly enlightened Buddha (p. 156,*1-6*). He had sixteen sons, the oldest of whom was named Jñānākara (p. 160,*9*); and, at their request, he turned the wheel of the Law and expounded the *Lotus*. The sixteen princes, who became śramaṇas and reciters of the Law (*dharmabhāṇaka*), are at present the sixteen Buddhas of the ten cardinal points: the first, Jñānākara, is the present Akṣobhya of the Abhirati universe, the ninth is Amitābha, and the sixteenth, Śākyamuni (p. 184-185).

2. Karuṇāpuṇḍarīka, T 157: Formerly, *asaṃkhyeyakalpa* as manifold as the sands of the Ganges having since passed, there lived, in the Saṃtīrana universe, a Cakravartin king named Araṇemin. He had a thousand sons. His minister, Ratnasamudra, fathered a son endowed with the marks of a Mahāpuruṣa, who became Buddha with the name of Ratnagarbha (T 157, p. 174 *c*). Araṇemin and his thousand sons, the ninth of whom was called Mi-su 蜜蘇 (p. 176 *b* 5), gave lodging to the Buddha Ratnagarbha,

The Licchavi Vimalakīrti intervened: Śāriputra, what do you think of this (*tat kiṃ manyase*)? Does sunlight (*sūryaprabhā*) accompany (*sahacarati*) darkness (*andhakāra*)?

Śāriputra. — No, certainly not (*no hīdam*), O son of good family.

Vimalakīrti. — Therefore, they do not go together?

Śāriputra. — No, son of good family, they do not go together and, on the rising of the solar disc (*sūryamaṇḍalodaye*), all darkness (*andhakāra*) disappears.

Vimalakīrti. — Why then, does the sun rise over Jambudvīpa?

Śāriputra. — It is to lighten it (*ālokakaraṇārtham*) and to chase away darkness (*andhakārāpakarṣaṇārtham*).

Vimalakīrti. — Equally, O Śāriputra, a Bodhisattva is reborn voluntarily (*saṃcintya*) in impure Buddhakṣetras so as to purify beings (*sattvapariśodhanārtham*), so as to shed the light of knowledge (*jñānāloka*) and so as to chase away great darkness (*mahāndhakārāpakarṣaṇārtham*). However, he does not consort with the passions (*na kleśaiḥ sārdhaṃ viharati*), but he chases away the darkness of the passions of all beings (*sarvasattvānāṃ kleśāndhakāram apakarṣati*).

[*The Appearance of the Abhirati Universe*]

4. Then all the assemblies felt a yearning (*atha khalu sarvāḥ parṣadas tṛṣitā abhūvan*) to see the Abhirati universe, the Tathāgata Akṣobhya, its Bodhisattvas and its great Śrāvakas.

each for three months, and loaded him with gifts (p. 176 *a* 1). Then, on the advice of the minister, they withdrew from the world and gave themselves over to meditation for seven years. After which, they presented themselves before the Buddha and formulated their vows. The Buddha gave them a prediction by the terms of which they would all reach Buddhahood in the course of time: the king Araṇemin became Amitāyus in the Sukhāvatī universe (p. 185 *a* 20-25); Mi-su, his ninth son, became Akṣobhya in the Abhirati universe (p. 194 *b* 6-13).

3. Survarṇabhāsa, Ch. XIII: At the time of the Buddha Ratnaśikhin, Susambhava, king of Jinendraghoṣā, visited the dharmabhāṇaka bhikṣu Ratnoccaya who recited the Suvarṇabhāsottamasūtra to him. The king, after having expressed his joy, asked for and obtained all kinds of precious objects for beings. In later times, Susaṃbhava was the Buddha Śākyamuni, and the bhikṣu Ratnoccaya was the Tathāgata Akṣobhya (p. 152,*11-18*).

4. In the Pang fo ching, T 831, p. 877 *c* 6, Akṣobhya was the master of the Law, Pratibhānakūṭa.

In esoteric Buddhism, Akṣobhya is one of the five *dhyānibuddha*: cf. Hōbōgirin, p. 40; B. BHATTACHARYYA, *Indian Buddhist Iconography*, 2nd ed., Calcutta, 1958, p. 51-52.

Then the Blessed One, knowing in his mind the thought that had arisen in the minds of the assemblies (*tāsāṃ parṣadāṃ cetasaiva cetaḥ-parivitarkam ājñāya*), said to the Licchavi Vimalakīrti: Son of good family, these assemblies yearn to see the Abhirati universe and the Tathāgata Akṣobhya. So do show them to these assemblies.

Then the Licchavi Vimalakīrti had this thought: I, without rising from my couch (*anutthāya mañcakāt*), through my psychic power (*ṛddhibala*), will myself take hold of the Abhirati universe and all it contains: hundreds of thousands of Bodhisattvas and the dwellings (*bhavana*) of the Devas, Yakṣas, Gandharvas and Asuras bounded by Mount Cakravāḍa. It contains rivers (*nadī*), lakes (*taḍāga*), streams (*udbhida*), water-courses (*saras*), seas (*samudra*) and other depressions (*parikhā*). It contains a Sumeru and chains of mountains (*giri*) all around. It possesses a moon (*candra*), a sun (*sūrya*) and stars (*tārakā*). It incorporates the abodes (*sthāna*) of Devas, Nāgas, Yakṣas and Gandharvas, the abodes and assemblies (*parṣad*) of Brahmās. It contains villages (*grāma*), towns (*nagara*), boroughs (*nigama*), provinces (*janapada*) and kingdoms (*rāṣṭra*), with men (*nara*), women (*narī*) and housing (*gṛha*). It also possesses Bodhisattvas and an assembly of Śrāvakas. The tree of enlightenment (*bodhivṛkṣa*) of the Tathāgata Akṣobhya and the Tathāgata Akṣobhya himself, seated in the midst of an assembly as vast as the sea, expound the Law there. In the ten regions (*daśadikṣu*), lotuses (*padma*) actuate Buddha-deeds (*buddhakārya*) among beings [10]. Three precious ladders (*ratnasopāna*) rise from Jambudvīpa to the heaven of the Trāyastriṃśas; on these ladders, the Trāyastriṃśa gods descend (*avataranti*) to Jambudvīpa to see, honour and serve the Tathāgata Akṣobhya and hear the Law (*tathāgatasya akṣobhyasya darśanāya vandanāya paryupāsanāya dharmaśravaṇāya ca*); on these ladders, the men of Jambudvīpa mount (*ārohanti*) to the heaven of the Trāyastriṃśas to visit the Trāyastriṃśa gods [11].

[10] We have seen above, X, §8, that the *bodhivṛkṣa* can actuate Buddha deeds. The same applies to the precious lotuses, like those of Amitābha (cf. Sukhāvatīvyūha, p. 74,*4-12*).

[11] The Abhirati had precious ladders connecting its earth to the Trāyastriṃśa heavens. In our own Jambudvīpa, these ladders were to be found in Sāṃkāśya and were used in the miracle of the "Descent of the gods" (*devāvatāra*): cf. LAMOTTE, *Histoire*, p. 372 and the notes.

All the Buddhas are expected to accomplish, in the course of their careers, a certain number of obligatory actions (*avaśyakaraṇīya*), particularly that of the descent of the gods to Sāṃkāśya: cf. Divyāvadāna, p. 150,*22-23*; Sumaṅgalavilāsinī, II, p. 424,*11*; Comm. of the Buddhavaṃsa, p. 131,*10*, 298,*3*.

This Abhirati universe, accumulation of innumerable virtues (*apramāṇaguṇasaṃcaya*), I will, like a potter (*kumbhakāra*) with his wheel (*cakra*), reduce to practically nothing, from its circle of waters (*abmaṇḍala*) to the heaven of the Akaniṣṭhas [12]. Then, taking it in my right hand (*dakṣiṇapāṇi*) and carrying it like a garland of flowers (*puṣpamālya*), I will bring it here, to the Sahā universe, and I will show it to all this assembly.

5. Having had this thought, the Licchavi Vimalakīrti without rising from his couch, went into such a [deep] concentration and performed such a supernatural action (*tathārūpaṃ samādhiṃ samāpede tathārūpaṃ carddhyabhisaṃskāram abhisaṃskaroti sma*) that after having reduced the Abhirati universe to practically nothing, he grasped it in his right hand and brought it to the Sahā universe [13].

6. In this universe, the Śrāvakas, the Bodhisattvas and those among the gods and men (*devamanuṣya*) who possessed the super-knowledge of the divine eye (*divyacakṣurabhijñāprāpta*) gave great cries (*ākranda*): "Bhagavat, we are being carried off! Sugata, we are being taken away! May the Tathāgata bring us help (*śaraṇa*)!"

In this Abhirati universe, the Śrāvakas, the Bodhisattvas and the whole of the men and gods (*manuṣyadeva*) who possessed the divine eye (*divyacakṣus*) were gripped with fear (*bhaya*) and all cried together: "Who is carrying us off? Who is taking us away? Help us, Bhagavat! Help us, Sugata!"

With the aim of disciplining them (*vinayanārtham*), the Blessed One said to them: You are being carried off (*ānīta*) by the Bodhisattva Vimalakīrti, and that is not my affair (*madgocara*).

Then the Buddha Akṣobhya, in order to discipline these beings, said to them, with skill in means (*upāya*): You are being carried off (*ānīta*) by the psychic power (*ṛddhibala*) of Vimalakīrti, and I can do nothing about it.

As for the other gods and men, they did not even see that they were being carried off.

As for the mass of beginners (*ādikarmika*), gods and men, of this Abhirati universe, who had in no way as yet obtained the excellent super-knowledge of the divine eye, they remained perfectly calm, without knowing anything and

[12] Regarding the circle of waters, see above, V, § 14, note 15. The Akaniṣṭhas occupy the upper residence of the fourth Dhyāna, the summit of the Rūpadhātu (Kośa, III, p. 2, 168).

[13] Vimalakīrti is making use of his *acintyavimokṣa*, the properties of which have been detailed above (cf. V, § 12).

without seeing anything. It was only after having heard this dialogue that they enquired anxiously and wondered: "Where are we going now?"

Even though the Abhirati universe had been brought into the Sahā universe, there could not be ascertained, in the Sahā universe, either augmentation (*upacaya*) or diminution (*apacaya*): it was neither compressed (*saṃbādhita*) nor impeded (*baddha*). The Abhirati universe itself was also not reduced. Afterwards, both appeared as they were before (*yathāpūrvaṃ tathā paścād dṛśyante sma*).

The Abhirati universe, although brought into the Sahā universe, underwent neither diminution (*apacaya*) nor augmentation (*upacaya*). The Sahā universe itself was also not compressed (*saṃbādhita*). Even though these two universes were mixed one with the other, each saw his dwelling as it was before.

[*Homages paid to Akṣobhya*]

7. Then the Blessed Lord Śākyamuni said to all the assemblies: Friends (*sakhi*), do you see the splendours (*vyūha*) of the Abhirati universe, of the Tathāgata Akṣobhya and of his Buddha-field, and the splendours of these Śrāvakas and these Bodhisattvas?

They replied: We see them, O Blessed One.

Then Vimalakīrti, using psychic power (*ṛddhibala*), created by transformation (*nirmimīte*) all kinds of lovely celestial flowers (*divyapuṣpa*) and delicate perfumes (*gandha*) and, with the assemblies, he scattered them in homage on the Tathāgatas Śākyamuni and Akṣobhya, on the Bodhisattvas, etc.

Then the Blessed Lord Śākyamuni said to the great assemblies: The Bodhisattva who desires to conquer such a Buddhakṣetra should copy (*anuśikṣ-*) all the practices (*caryā*) of the Bodhisattvas of the Tathāgata Akṣobhya.

When Vimalakīrti, through a psychically wondrous feat (*ṛddhiprātihārya*), had thus shown them the Abhirati universe and the Tathāgata Akṣobhya, fourteen [H's var.: eighty-four] *nayuta* of living beings (*prāṇin*) produced the thought of supreme and perfect enlightenment (*anuttarāyāṃ samyaksaṃbodhau cittāny utpāditāni*) and they all formulated the vow (*praṇidhāna*) to be reborn in the Abhirati universe. To them all, the Blessed One predicted (*vyakaroti sma*) that they would be reborn in the Abhirati universe inhabited by the Buddha Akṣobhya.

The Licchavi Vimalakīrti having thus, in the Sahā universe, ripened (*vipacya*) all the beings who were susceptible to ripening, replaced the Abhirati universe exactly in its old position.

Vimalakīrti, through his psychic power (*ṛddhibala*), had taken up the Abhirati universe, the Tathāgata Akṣobhya and his Bodhisattvas, etc., in order to benefit beings of the Sahā universe. When this was finished, he replaced the Abhirati universe in its old position. At the moment the two universes separated, their respective assemblies saw each other.

[*Śāriputra's Wonder*]

8. Then the Blessed One said to Venerable (*āyuṣmant*) Śāriputra: Did you see, Śāriputra, the Abhirati universe, the Tathāgata Akṣobhya and his Bodhisattvas?

Śāriputra replied: I saw them, O Blessed One. I would like all beings to live in a Buddhakṣetra as splendid. I would like all beings to possess merits (*puṇya*), knowledge (*jñāna*) and virtues (*guṇa*) as completed (*paripūrṇa*) as those of the Tathāgata Akṣobhya. I would like all beings to possess psychic powers (*ṛddhi*) like those of that son of good family, the Licchavi Vimalakīrti.

As for ourselves, it is of much advantage to have seen a worthy man like him (*lābhā naḥ sulabdhā yad vayaṃ tādṛśaṃ satpuruṣaṃ paśyāmaḥ*)[14]. Whether the Tathāgata still exists now or whether he has already attained Parinirvāṇa[15], for beings it is of much advantage to have heard this interpretation of the Law (*lābhāḥ sattvānāṃ sulabdhā*

[14] Cf. Dīgha, III, p. 129,*26-28*: *lābhā no āvuso, suladdhaṃ no āvuso, ye mayaṃ āyasmantaṃ tādisaṃ sabrahmacāriṃ passāma.*

We have in Pāli *lābhā ... suladdham* (Dīgha, II, p. 16,*9*; III, p. 129,*26*; Aṅguttara, III, p. 313,*20*; Milindapañha, p. 17,*19*). We find in Sanskrit *lābhā ... sulabdhā* (Mahāvastu, I, p. 226,*14*; Catuṣpariṣad, p. 194,*10-11*; Sanskrit Mahāparinirvāṇa, p. 182,*21*; 378,*25*). Our grammarians have considered *lābhā* in turn to be a dative singular *lābhā* for *lābhāya* (CHILDERS, *Pāli Dict.*, p. 216 *b*; RHYS DAVIDS-STEDE, *Pāli Dict.*, III, p. 41 *a*); a feminine synonym of *lābha* (SENART, *Mahāvastu*, I, p. 550,*19*); or finally, a nominative masculine plural (EDGERTON, *Dict.*, p. 462 *a*). Two passages in the Sanskrit Mahāparinirvāṇa seem to support this last: p. 130,*9*: *ye te lābhā dhārmikā dharmalabdhā antataḥ pātragatāḥ ...*; p. 378,*27* sq.: *asmākam api syur lābhāḥ sulabdhā yad ...*

[15] This section of the sentence appears in K and the Tibetan version; it is missing in H.

yad ime tādṛśaṃ dharmaparyāyaṃ śṛṇvanti). What can be said of those who, after having heard it, will believe it, grasp it, retain it, repeat it, and penetrate it in depth, and who, after having believed it, will teach it, profess it and expound it to others and will apply to it all the effort of meditation (*kaḥ punarvādo ya imam evaṃrūpaṃ dharmaparyāyaṃ śrutvādhimokṣyanty udgrahīṣyanti dhārayiṣyanti vācayiṣyanti paryavāpsyanty adhimucya deśayiṣyanty upadekṣyanti parebhya uddekṣyanti bhāvanākāreṇa prayokṣyante*)[16]?

9. Beings who thoroughly grasp (*udgṛhṇanti*) this excellent interpretation of the Law (*dharmaparyāya*) will obtain the precious treasure of the Law (*dharmaratnanidhāna*).

Those who thoroughly study (*svādhyāyanti*) this interpretation of the Law will become the companions (*sahāyaka*) of the Tathāgata. — Those who pay homage (*satkurvanti*) to and serve (*paryupāsanti*) the adepts of this Law (*taddharmādhimukta*) will be the true protectors of the Law (*dharmabhūtarakṣaka*). — To those who write down (*likhanti*), teach (*deśayanti*) and pay homage (*satkurvanti*) to this interpretation of the Law, the Tathāgata will come into their dwellings. Those who delight (*anumodante*) in this interpretation of the Law will retain all the merits (*sarvapuṇya*). — Those who would teach to others

The beings who believe (*adhimucyante*) this excellent interpretation of the Law will continue the line of the Buddhas (*buddhasaṃtāna*). — The beings who repeat (*vācayanti*) this excellent interpretation of the Law will retain the unsurpassable good Law (*anuttarasaddharma*). — Those who pay homage (*satkurvanti*) to and study this Law will know that there is a Tathāgata in their dwellings. — Those who write down (*likhanti*) and pay homage (*satkurvanti*) to this excellent interpretation of the Law will gain all the merits (*sarvapuṇya*) and omniscience (*sarvajñajñāna*). — Those who delight (*anumodante*) in this excellent interpretation of the Law will make the great offering of the Law (*mahādharmayajña*). — Those who would teach to others be it only a single stanza of four verses of this excellent interpretation of the Law will attain the state of irreversibility (*avaivartikasthāna*). — Those

[16] This stock phrase will be repeated five times in the course of the next chapter (XII, §2, 4, 6, 17, 20); there are some variations, the verbs being in the present, future or optative, and the formula, more or less complete.

We should add that this stock phrase is customary at the end of all Mahāyānasūtras: cf. Aṣṭasāh., p. 205,*13-17*; 212,*16-20*; 868,*1-7*; Vajracchedikā, p. 37,*14-17*; 40,*5-8*; 43,*1-3*; 43,*17-19*; 43,*23*-44,*1*; 44,*19-21*; 45,*15-17*; Samādhirāja, II, p. 273, note 12; Saddharmapuṇḍ., p. 36,*7*; 268,*8-10*; 337,*5-6*; 418,*2-3*; Daśabhūmika, p. 98,*25-27*.

The Mahāyāna introduced into Buddhism the cult of the holy book unknown in the first centuries. On this subject, see É. LAMOTTE, *Sur la formation du Mahāyāna* in Asiatica, Festschrift F. Weller, Leipzig, 1954, p. 381-385.

be it only a single stanza of four verses or a single phrase summarising this interpretation of the Law (*ye kecid ito dharmaparyāyād antaśaś catuṣpādikām api gāthām udgṛhya parebhyo deśayeyuḥ*)[17], would make the great offering of the Law (*mahādharmayajña*)[18]. — Those who consecrate to this interpretation of the Law their conviction (*kṣānti*), their zeal (*chanda*), their intelligence (*mati*), their perspicacity (*vicakṣaṇa*), their vision (*darśana*) and their aspirations (*adhimukti*) are already the subjects of the prediction (*vyākṛta*).

who consecrate to this excellent interpretation of the Law their aspirations (*adhimukti*), their convictions (*kṣānti*), their zeal (*chanda*) and their perspicacity (*vicakṣaṇa*) have already obtained the prediction (*vyākaraṇa*) concerning supreme and perfect enlightenment.

[17] Another very common stock phrase: cf. Vajracchedikā, p. 33,*18*; 37,*8*; 39,*5*; 55,*5*; 61,*10*; Saddharmapuṇḍ., p. 225,*4*; 395,*11*; 415,*7*.

[18] The offering of the Law has been defined above, III, § 69-74.

CHAPTER TWELVE

ANTECEDENTS AND TRANSMISSION OF THE GOOD LAW

[*Śakra's Promises*]

1. Then Śakra, the prince of the gods (*devānām indraḥ*), said to the Blessed One: On other occasions, O Blessed One, I have heard, from the lips of the Tathāgata and Mañjuśrī the crown prince (*kumārabhūta*), several hundreds of thousands of interpretations of the Law (*anekadharmaparyāyaśatasahasra*), but I have never before heard an interpretation of the Law as remarkable (*na mayā jātv evaṃrūpo dharmaparyāyaḥ śrutapūrvaḥ*) as this "Teaching constituting the entry into the method of inconceivable wonder" (*Acintyavikurvaṇanayapraveśanirdeśa*) [1].

2. As I understand the meaning of the words of the Blessed One (*yathāhaṃ bhagavan bhagavato bhāṣitasyārtham ājānāmi*) [2], beings who, having heard this interpretation of the Law, will believe it, grasp it, retain it, teach it, repeat it, penetrate it in depth and expound it widely to others (*ye sattvā imam evaṃrūpaṃ dharmaparyāyaṃ śrutvādhimokṣyanty udgrahiṣyanti dhārayiṣyanti deśayiṣyanti vācayiṣyanti paryavāpsyanti parebhyaś ca vistareṇa saṃprakāśayiṣyanti*), these beings, say I, will be, without the least doubt (*niḥsaṃśayam*), the recipients of the Law (*dharmabhājana*). What can be said of those who will apply to it the effort of meditation

[1] In the Tibetan version, *Rnam par sprul ba bsam gyis mi khyab paḥi tshul la ḥjug pa rab tu bstan pa* = *Acintyavikurvaṇanayapraveśanirdeśa* "Teaching [constituting] the entry into the method (or principle) of inconceivable wonder". Further on, XII, § 23, this title does not reappear.

In K we have *Pu k'o ssŭ i tzŭ tsai shên t'ung chüeh ting shih hsiang ching tien* 不可思議自在神通決定實相經典 = *Acintyavikurvaṇa* [*niyata*]*bhūtanayasūtra* "Sūtra of the true method (or true principle) of inconceivable wonder". Further on, XII, § 23, this title does not reappear.

In H we have *Pu k'o ssŭ i tzŭ tsai shên pien chieh t'o fa mên* 不可思議自在神變解脫法門 = **Acintyavikurvaṇavimokṣadharmaparyāya* "Treatise of the Law concerning the liberation of inconceivable wonder". This title reappears further on, Ch. XII, § 23.

[2] This section of the sentence, missing in Tibetan, is confirmed in K and H. It concerns a well known stock phrase:

Dīgha, I, p. 184,*30*; Majjhima, III, p. 131,*14*; Saṃyutta, IV, p. 299,*15*: *evaṃ kho ahaṃ bhante Bhagavato bhāsitaṃ ājānāmi.* — Vajracchedikā, p. 32,*11*; 47,*14*: *yathāhaṃ Bhagavan Bhagavato bhāṣitasyārtham ājānāmi.*

(*kaḥ punarvādo ye bhāvanākāreṇa prayokṣyante*)? The latter will bar the path to all bad destinies (*durgati*), will open the way to all good destinies (*sugati*), will always see the Buddhas and the Bodhisattvas, will do away with sectaries (*tīrthika*) and adversaries (*parapravādin*), will destroy all the hordes of Māra (*māracamū*), will purify the path of enlightenment (*bodhimārga*), will occupy the seat of enlightenment (*bodhimaṇḍa*) and will penetrate the domain of the Tathāgatas (*tathāgatagocara*).

3. Blessed One, the sons (*kulaputra*) or daughters of good family (*kuladuhitṛ*) who will teach (*deśayiṣyanti*) this expounding of the Law, I and my attendants (*saparivāra*) will pay homage to them and will serve them (*satkāraṃ paryupāsanaṃ kariṣyāmaḥ*).

In the villages (*grāma*), towns (*nagara*), boroughs (*nigama*), provinces (*janapada*), kingdoms (*rāṣṭra*) and capitals (*rājadhānī*)[3] where this interpretation of the Law will be practised (*carita*), taught (*deśita*) and expounded (*prakāśita*), I and my companions (*parivāra*) will go there to hear the Law (*dharmaśravaṇāya*). In unbelievers (*aprasanna*), I will inspire faith (*prasāda*); to believers (*prasanna*), I will assure help and protection against obstacles (*rakṣāvaraṇagupti*)[4].

[In Praise of the Vimalakīrtinirdeśa]

4. This having been said, the Blessed One addressed Śakra, the prince of the gods: Excellent, excellent (*sādhu sādhu*), O Devendra, the Tathāgatas themselves delight (*anumodante*) in your good words (*subhāṣita*).

Devendra, the enlightenment (*bodhi*) of the Blessed Lord Buddhas past (*atīta*), future (*anāgata*) and present (*pratyutpanna*) is expressed (*nirdiṣṭa*) by this actual interpretation of the Law. That is why, O Devendra, the sons or daughters of good family who, having heard this interpretation of the Law, will believe it, will grasp it, retain it, repeat it, penetrate it in depth, write it all down and, enclosing it in one volume, honour it, these sons or daughters of good family will pay homage by this very deed to the Blessed Lord Buddhas past, future and present (*ye hi kecid Devendra kulaputrā vā kuladuhitaro vā ya imaṃ dharmaparyāyaṃ śrutvādhimokṣyanty udgrahīṣyanti dhārayiṣyanti vācayiṣyanti paryavāpsyanty antaśo likhiṣyanti pustakagataṃ vā kṛtvā satkariṣyanti*

[3] Regarding this list, cf. I, § 8, note 43.

[4] The expression *rakṣāvaraṇagupti*, in Pāli *rakkhāvaraṇagutti*, is traditional: cf. Vinaya, II, p. 194,*9*; Dīgha, I, p. 61,*4*; Majjhima, II, p. 101,*20*; Saddharmapuṇḍ., p. 271,*5*; 396,*3*; 397,*6-7*; 399,*1*; 400,*9-10*; 403,*1*; Mahāvastu, I, p. 208,*6*; II, p. 10,*18*.

te kulaputrā vā kuladuhitaro vātītānāgatapratyutpannān buddhān bhagavataḥ pūjayiṣyanti).

5. Let us suppose, O Devendra, that this trichiliomegachiliocosm (*trisāhasramahāsāhasralokadhātu*) were filled (*paripūrṇa*) with Tathāgatas as numerous as the woods (*vana*) of sugar-cane (*ikṣu*), reeds (*naḍa*), bamboos (*veṇu*), mustard bushes (*tila*) or acacias (*khadira*) which cover it, and that a son or daughter of good family, for a kalpa or more than a kalpa, honours them, reveres them, respects them and pays homage to them, by offering them all kinds of offerings and fine embellishments (*kulaputro vā kuladuhitā vā tāṃs tathāgatān, kalpaṃ vā kalpāvaśeṣaṃ vā, satkuryād gurukuryān mānayet pūjayen nānāvidhābhiḥ pūjābhiḥ sukhapariṣkārais ca*).

Let us further suppose that, these Tathāgatas having entered Parinirvāṇa, he desires to honour each of them and raises on their solid and intact bodies a reliquary-stūpa formed of all the jewels, as large as the world of four great continents, reaching in height the Brahmā world, and adorned with parasols, banners, a staff and lamps (*tathāgateṣu ca parinirvṛteṣv ekaikasya tathāgatasya pūjanārtham, ekasminn eva kaṭhore 'kuṇṭhite śarīre śarīrastūpaṃ pratiṣṭhāpayet sarvaratnamayaṃ, caturmahādvīpakalokapramāṇam āyāmena, yāvad brahmalokam uccaistvena cchattrapatākāyaṣṭipradīpopaśobhitam*).

Finally, let us suppose that having raised these Tathāgata stūpas, he consecrates a kalpa or more than a kalpa in honouring them, revering them, respecting them and paying homage to them, by offering them all kinds of flowers, perfumes, flags, banners and lamps and by playing on drums and making music (*teṣāṃ ca sarveṣāṃ tathāgatānāṃ stūpān pratiṣṭhāpya, kalpaṃ vā kalpāvaśeṣaṃ vā, satkuryād gurukuryān mānayet pūjayen nānāvidhaiḥ puṣpagandhadhvajapatākāpradīpair dundubhitūryaghaṭṭanaiś ca*)[5].

This being so, what do you think, O Devendra, would this son or daughter of good family accumulate, as a consequence of this conduct, many merits (*tat kiṃ manyase, devendra, api nu sa kulaputro vā kuladuhitā vā tato nidānaṃ bahu puṇyaṃ prasavet*)[6]?

Śakra, the prince of the gods, replied: Many merits, O Blessed One;

[5] The stūpa as *saptaratnamayo yāvad brahmalokam uccaistvena*, etc., is a stock phrase: cf. Saddharmapuṇḍ., p. 150,*10*; 153,*4*; 239,*2*; 260,*1*; 299,*15*; and especially 338,*8* and sq. where the description is most complete.

[6] Very common stock phrase: Aṣṭasāh., p. 826,*4-6*; Vajracchedikā, p. 33,*3-8*; 51,*22*-52,*4*; Saddharmapuṇḍ., p. 347,*12-13*; 443,*1-2*. — Also see Saddharmapuṇḍ., p. 339,*10*; 395,*7-9*; 414,*13*.

many merits, O Sugata. Were one to consecrate hundreds of thousands of *nayutakoṭi* of kalpas to it, it would be impossible to reach the limit of the mass of merits that this son or daughter of good family would accumulate (*bahu Bhagavan, bahu Sugata. kalpakoṭīnayutaśatasahasrair api na śakyaṃ paryanto 'dhigantuṃ yāvantaṃ puṇyābhisaṃskāraṃ sa kulaputro vā kuladuhitā vā prasaviṣyati*)[7].

6. The Blessed One continued: Have confidence, O Devendra, believe the Tathāgata who will address you with a word of truth. The son or daughter of good family who, having heard this interpretation of the Law entitled "Teaching of the Inconceivable Liberation" will believe it, will grasp it, retain it, repeat it and penetrate it in depth, this one will accumulate much greater merit than the preceding one (*avakalpayasva me, Devendra, abhiśraddadhasva tathāgatasya bhūtāṃ vācaṃ vyāharataḥ*[8]. *yaḥ kulaputro vā kuladuhitā vemam Acintyavimokṣanirdeśaṃ*[9] *dharmaparyāyam adhimucyetodgṛhṇīyād dhārayed vācayet paryavāpnuyāt so 'smād bahutaraṃ puṇyaskandhaṃ prasunuyāt*).

And why? Because, O Devendra, the enlightenment of the Blessed Lord Buddhas comes from the Law (*dharmanirjātā hi, Devendra, buddhānāṃ bhagavatāṃ bodhiḥ*). It is through the homage to the Law (*dharmapūjā*) that they can be honoured, and not through material objects (*āmiṣa*). Devendra, on the basis of this interpreting (*anena paryāyeṇa*), you should know it to be so (*evaṃ veditavyam*).

And why? Because the supreme and perfect enlightenment of the Buddhas comes from the Law (*dharmanirjāta*). It is only through the homage to the Law (*dharmapūjā*) that this interpretation of the Law (*dharmaparyāya*) can be honoured, and not through material objects (*āmiṣa*). Devendra, it must be understood that, the virtues of supreme enlightenment (*anuttarabodhiguṇa*) being numerous, the homage rendered to this Law (*dharmapūjā*) promotes very numerous merits (*puṇya*).

[*Jātaka of Ratnacchattra and his Sons*[10]]

7. Then the Blessed One said to Śakra, prince of the gods: Of old, O Devendra, in times gone by, long before kalpas as innumerable as

[7] Cf. Saddharmapuṇḍ., p. 417,*14*-418,*2*: *eṣāṃ puṇyābhisaṃskārāṇāṃ bauddhena jñānena na śakyaṃ paryanto 'dhigantuṃ yāvantaṃ puṇyābhisaṃskāraṃ sa kulaputro vā kuladuhitā vā prasaviṣyati.*

[8] Another traditional expression: Saddharmapuṇḍ., p. 315,*1-2*. — Variation, *ibid*, p. 44,*3-4*.

[9] K: *Acintyavimokṣasūtra*; H: *Acintyavikurvaṇavimokṣadharmaparyāya*. See above, XII, § 1, note 1.

[10] The presence of this long jātaka (§ 7-15) explains the title of *Pūrvayoga* "Ante-

that which has no number, immense, immeasurable, inconceivable, before this period and well before even that, there appeared in the world the Tathāgata named Bhaiṣajyarāja[11], the holy one, perfectly and fully enlightened, gifted with knowledge and conduct, the Sugata, knower of the world, incomparable driver of men to be tamed, instructor of gods and humans, the Buddha, the Blessed One.

cedents" given to Chapter XII. *Pūrvayoga*, in Pāli *pubbayoga*, means connection (*yoga*) between present events and those of the past (*pūrva*), present actions being explained by old actions performed in the course of previous existences (*jātaka*). So therefore, and whatever F. EDGERTON (*Dict.* p. 352 *a*) may say, the translation "Ancienne application" proposed by Burnouf (*Lotus*, p. 96) is perfectly correct. However, it might be better to explain, for the benefit of foreign readers, that in French "ancienne application" means application to old actions.

Several Buddhist Sūtras contain a chapter of *pūrvayoga*: Ch. I of the Milindapañha, Ch. VII of the Saddharmapuṇḍarīka, Ch. II of the Mahāsaṃnipāta, etc.

For an easier understanding of the text, here is a brief summary of the present jātaka. First of all, we must remember that a great kalpa (*mahākalpa*) contains 80 small kalpas (*antarakalpa*) and that the Buddhas only appear during the 20 small kalpas of the *vivartasthāyikalpa* "period during which the world remains created" (see above, VII, § 6, note 37).

In the remotest of times, at the beginning of the great Vicaraṇa kalpa, there appeared, in the Mahāvyūhā universe, the Buddha *Bhaiṣajyarāja*. There lived, at the same place and the same time, the Cakravartin king *Ratnacchattra* and his thousand sons one of whom was named *Candracchattra*.

a. During the small kalpas 1 to 5, the king Ratnacchattra showered the Buddha Bhaiṣajyarāja with material offerings (*āmiṣadāna*).

b. During the small kalpas 6 to 10, his thousand sons, all together, continued these same material offerings to the Buddha.

c. During the small kalpas 11 to 20, the prince Candracchattra, considering these material offerings to be unworthy of the Buddha, took up the religious life, expounded and protected the Law, thus substituting for material giving (*āmiṣadāna*) the spiritual giving of the Law (*dharmadāna*).

Consequently, during the present great kalpa, called Bhadrakalpa,

a. the old Cakravartin king *Ratnacchattra* is the present Buddha *Ratnārcis*,

b. his *thousand sons* are or will be the *Thousand Buddhas of the Bhadrakalpa*, of whom four (Krakucchanda, Kanakamuni, Kāśyapa and Śākyamuni) have already appeared, the 996 others have yet to appear.

c. the prince *Candracchattra* who practised the giving of the Law is the present Buddha *Śākyamuni*.

[11] This does not concern the famous Bodhisattva Bhaiṣajyarāja who intervenes on several occasions in the Saddharmapuṇḍ., p. 3, 224, 267, 395, 404, 414, 425, 470. Neither does it concern the Buddha Bhaiṣajyaguruvaiḍūryarāja (or prabha) eulogized in the Bhaiṣajyagurusūtra (ed. N. DUTT, *Gilgit Manuscripts*, I, p. 1-32). It could refer to a B. Bhaiṣajyaguru of the past to whom Śākyamuni, during a previous existence, had offered a *chattra* (Lalitavistara, p. 172,8).

He appeared in the Vicaraṇa kalpa, in the universe called Mahāvyūhā (*bhūtapūrvaṃ Devendrātīte 'dhvany asaṃkhyeyaiḥ kalpair asaṃkhyeyatarair vipulair aprameyair acintyais tebhyaḥ pareṇa paratareṇa yadāsīt tena kālena tena samayena Bhaiṣajyarājo nāma tathāgato 'rhan samyaksaṃbuddho loka udapādi vidyācaraṇasaṃpannaḥ sugato lokavid anuttaraḥ puruṣadamyasārathiḥ śāstā devānāṃ ca manuṣyāṇāṃ ca buddho bhagavān Vicaraṇe kalpe Mahāvyūhāyāṃ lokadhātau*)[12].

Of this Bhaiṣajyarāja, Tathāgata, holy one, perfectly and fully enlightened, the life span was of twenty small kalpas (*tasya Bhaiṣajyarājasya tathāgatasyārhataḥ samyaksaṃbuddhasya viṃśaty antarakalpān āyuṣpramāṇam abhūt*)[13].

He also had an assembly of Śrāvakas numbering thirty-six *koṭīnayuta* of individuals, and an assembly of Bodhisattvas numbering twelve *koṭīnayuta* of individuals (*tasya khalu punaḥ ṣaṭtriṃśatkoṭīnayutāḥ śrāvakasaṃnipāto 'bhūd dvādaśakoṭīnayutā bodhisattvasaṃnipāto 'bhūt*)[14].

At the same time and in the same period, O Devendra, there appeared Ratnacchattra, a Cakravartin king, ruling over four continents and endowed with the seven jewels[15]. He had a thousand sons who were heroic, virile, of well-formed bodies and destroyers of enemy armies (*tena khalu punaḥ samayena Ratnacchattro nāma rājodapādi cakravartī cāturdvīpaḥ saptaratnasamanvāgataḥ. pūrṇaṃ cāsyābhūt sahasraṃ putrāṇaṃ śūrāṇāṃ vīrāṇāṃ varāṅgarūpiṇāṃ parasainyapramardakānām*)[16].

[12] Traditional formula to recall the appearance of the Buddhas of the past: Saddharmapuṇḍ., p. 17,*7-11*; 156,*1-5*; 375,*9*-376,*3*; 431,*6-10*; 457,*1-6*. Also see Mahāvastu, I, p. 48,*17*-49,*3*; Vajracchedikā, p. 45,*7-8*; Sukhāvatīvyūha, p. 12,*4-6*; Mahāsaṃnipāta, p. 35,*11-17*.

The ten epithets of the Buddha are explained at length in NĀGĀRJUNA, *Traité*, p. 115-144.

[13] Cf. Saddharmapuṇḍ., p. 144,*7*.

[14] Cf. Saddharmapuṇḍ., p. 404,*13*-405,*1*.

[15] Regarding the seven *ratna* of the Cakravartin, cf. Dīgha, II, p. 172-177; Majjhima, III, p. 172-176; Saṃyutta, V, p. 99; Mahavastu, I, p. 49,*3-4*; 193,*16-17*; Lalitavistara, p. 14-18.

[16] A stock of adjectives which come into the description of the sons of a Cakravartin. In Pāli: *paro sahassaṃ kho pan' assa puttā bhavanti sūrā vīraṅgarūpā parasenappamaddanā* (Dīgha, I, p. 89,*4-5*; II, p. 16,*19-20*). In Sanskrit: *pūrṇāś cāsya bhaviṣyanti sahasraṃ putrāṇāṃ śūrāṇāṃ vīrāṇāṃ varāṅgarūpiṇāṃ parasainyapramardakānām* (Sanskrit Mahāvadāna, p. 95,*15*; Mahāvastu, I, p. 49,*5*; 193,*18*; II, p. 158,*17*; Divyāvadāna, p. 548,*28*; Lalitavistara, p. 18,*6*; 101,*17*).

[*Ratnacchattra's Pūjā*]

8. The king Ratnacchattra for five small kalpas (*antarakalpa*), honoured with all kinds of excellent offerings (*nānāvidhaiḥ sukhapariṣkāraiḥ satkāraṃ cakāra*) the Tathāgata Bhaiṣajyarāja and his retinue (*saparivāra*).

Then the king Ratnacchattra and his retinue (*saparivāra*), for five small kalpas (*antarakalpa*), honoured, revered, respected and paid homage (*satkāraṃ gurukāraṃ mānanāṃ pūjanāṃ cakāra*) to the Tathāgata Bhaiṣajyarāja, and presented to him in homage all kinds of excellent offerings (*sukhapariṣkāra*), divine and human, and all kinds of pleasant dwellings (*sukhavihāra*).

These five small kalpas having passed, the king Ratnacchattra said to his thousand sons: Know that, for myself, I have paid homage to the Tathāgata; now, pay homage to him, in your turn. Then the thousand princes (*rājakumāra*), having given their consent (*sādhukāraṃ dattvā*), obeyed (*pratyaśrauṣuḥ*) the king their father, and, all together, for five small kalpas (*antarakalpa*), they honoured with all kinds of excellent offerings (*sukhapariṣkāra*) the Tathāgata Bhaiṣajyarāja.

[*Candracchattra's Pūjā*]

9. Among them, the prince (*rājaputra*) Candracchattra, having retired into solitude (*ekākī rahogataḥ*), had this thought: It is thus that today we revere, we respect and we pay homage to the Tathāgata Bhaiṣajyarāja. But, is there not a homage (*pūjā*) that is far superior (*bahvantaraviśiṣṭa*) and more noble (*udāratara*) than this one?

Through the supernatural intervention (*adhiṣṭhāna*) of the Buddha, the gods (*deva*), from the height of the heavens (*antarīkṣa*), addressed him: Worthy man (*satpuruṣa*), they said to him, the homage to the Law (*dharmapūjā*) is the best among all homages.

Candracchattra asked them: What is the homage to the Law?

The gods replied: Worthy man, go to the Tathāgata Bhaiṣajyarāja and ask him what the homage to the Law is, and the Blessed One will explain (*vyākariṣyati*) it to you.

Having heard the words of the gods, the prince Candracchattra went to where the Blessed Lord Bhaiṣajyarāja, Tathāgata, holy one, perfectly and fully enlightened, was to be found and, having reached him, after having saluted, by touching with his head, the feet of the Blessed One and after having circled round him three times, he stood to one side; standing to one side, the prince Candracchattra said these words to the Blessed

Tathāgata Bhaiṣajyarāja (*atha khalu Candracchattro rājakumāro yena bhagavān Bhaiṣajyarājas tathāgato 'rhan samyaksaṃbuddhas tenopajagāma; upetya bhagavatpādau śirasā vanditvā triḥkṛtvaḥ pradakṣiṇīkṛtyaikānte 'sthāt; ekāntasthitaś Candracchattro rājaputro Bhagavantaṃ Bhaiṣajyarājaṃ tathāgatam idam avocat*): Blessed One, I have heard speak of the homage to the Law, what is the homage to the Law?

[*Bhaiṣajyarāja's Homily on the Dharmapūjā*]

10. The Blessed Lord Bhaiṣajyarāja replied: Son of good family (*kulaputra*), the homage to the Law (*dharmapūjā*) is that which is rendered to the texts expounded by the Tathāgata (*tathāgatabhāṣitāni sūtrāntāni*).

These texts are lovely (*praṇīta*), profound (*gambhīra*), of profound aspect (*gambhīrāvabhāsa*), difficult to perceive by the world (*sarvalokavipratyanīka*), difficult to believe (*aśraddhadhānīya*), difficult to fathom (*durvigāhya*), difficult to see (*durdṛśa*), obscure (*duravabodha*), subtle (*sūkṣma*) and beneficent (*śiva*), of precise meaning (*nitārtha*), and ungraspable through speculation (*atarkāvacara*)[17].

These texts are contained in the Basket of Bodhisattvas (*bodhisattvapiṭakaparyāpanna*)[18], marked with the seal of the king of formulae and texts (*dhāraṇīsūtrāntarājamudrita*). They reveal the irreversible wheel of the Law (*avaivartikadharmacakrasaṃprakāśaka*). They originate in the six perfections (*ṣaṭpāramitāsaṃbhava*). They completely enclose all that is to be believed and do not contain any false claims (*grāha*).

They are endowed with all the auxiliary dharmas of enlightenment (*bodhipakṣyadharmasamanvāgata*) and realise the seven limbs of perfect enlightenment (*saptasambodhyaṅga*). They bring beings to great compassion (*mahākaruṇā*) and teach great goodwill (*mahāmaitrī*). They

[17] On this stock of adjectives emphasizing the profundity of the *dharma* in general and a *dharmaparyāya* in particular, cf. Vinaya, I, p. 4,*34*; Catuṣpariṣad, p. 108,*12-15*; Mahāvastu, III, p. 314,*1-2*; Lalitavistara, p. 392,*9-10*; 395,*19-22*; Divyāvadāna, p. 492, *18-20*; Aṣṭasāh., p. 616,*5*; Suvarṇabhāsa, p. 81,*7*; Saddharmapuṇḍ., p. 230,*7*; 290,*12*; Mahāvyutpatti, No. 2912-2927.

[18] The expression *bodhisattvapiṭaka* signifies all the Vaipulyasūtras of the Great Vehicle, which have never been reunited in a "basket": cf. Bodh. bhūmi, p. 96,*6*; 160,*16*; 173,*14*; 274,*21*; 297,*10*; 298,*4*; 330,*16*; 336,*11*; Saṃdhinirmocana, IX, § 9, 10, 18; Ratnagotra, p. 70,*9*; Saṃgraha, p. 218; Sūtrālaṃkāra, p. 53,*16-17*. Regarding the Abhidharmasamuccaya, p. 79 (T 1605, ch. 6, p. 686 *a*), cf. LAMOTTE, *Histoire*, p. 162.

The title *bodhisattvapiṭakamātṛkā* (Bodh. bhūmi, p. 157,*4*; 180,*16*; 332,*23*) indicates the Bodhisattvabhūmi, a section of the Yogācārabhūmiśāstra.

avoid all the false views of Māra (*māradṛṣṭigata*). They analyse and manifest the profound dependent co-production (*pratītyasamutpāda*).

11. They are linked (*saṃprayukta*) to the dharmas without self (*nirātmānaḥ*), without sentient being (*niḥsattvāḥ*), without feeding being (*niṣpoṣāḥ*), without personality (*niṣpudgalāḥ*)[19], and also to emptiness (*śūnyatā*), signlessness (*ānimitta*) and wishlessness (*apraṇihita*), inaction (*anabhisaṃskāra*), to non-birth (*ajāta*) and non-arising (*anutpāda*).

They discourse on the dharmas which are inwardly (*adhyātmam*) without self (*nirātmānaḥ*), outwardly (*bahirdhā*) without sentient being (*niḥsattvāḥ*), in both ways (*ubhayatra*) without living being (*nirjīvāḥ*) and without feeding being (*niṣpoṣāḥ*): in brief, absolutely without personality (*atyantaṃ niṣpudgalāḥ*). They are linked (*saṃprayukta*) to emptiness (*śūnyatā*), signlessness (*ānimitta*), wishlessness (*apraṇihita*), inaction (*anabhisaṃskāra*) and non-birth (*ajāta*).

They prepare the seat of enlightenment (*bodhimaṇḍa*) and cause the wheel of the Law to turn (*dharmacakrapravartaka*).

They are applauded (*praśaṃsita*) and praised (*varṇita*) by the rulers (*adhipati*) of the Devas, Nāgas, Yakṣas, Gandharvas, Asuras, Garuḍas, Kiṃnaras and Mahoragas.

They do not interrupt the lineage of the good Law (*saddharmavaṃśa*). They hold the treasure of the Law (*dharmakośa*). They achieve the summit of the homage to the Law (*dharmapūjā*).

They bring beings to the great homage to the Law (*dharmapūjā*). They perfect the great offering to the Law (*dharmayajña*) to be accomplished by beings.

They are adopted (*parigṛhīta*) by all noble beings (*āryajana*). They reveal (*saṃprakāśayanti*) all the practices of the Bodhisattvas (*bodhisattvacaryā*). They attain the infallible penetrations concerning the Law in its true meaning (*bhūtārthadharmapratisaṃvid*)[20]. They proclaim all dharmas as being transitory (*anitya*), suffering (*duḥkha*), impersonal (*anātman*) and calm (*śānta*), thus defining the four summaries of the Law (*dharmoddāna*)[21].

They destroy greed (*mātsarya*), immorality (*dauḥśīlya*), animosity (*vyāpāda*), idleness (*kausīdya*), thoughtlessness (*muṣitasmṛtitā*), foolishness (*dauṣprajñā*) and envy (*avasāda*), as well as the false views (*kudṛṣṭi*) and false beliefs (*abhiniveśa*) of all the sectaries (*tīrthika*) and all adversaries (*parapravādin*).

[19] Regarding the sequence of *ātman, sattva*, etc., see above, III, § 6, note 12.

[20] Regarding the *pratisaṃvid* in general and the *dharmapratisaṃvid* in particular, see the references in Saṃgraha, p. 53*-54*.

[21] The four *dharmoddāna* have been explained earlier, III, § 25, note 51.

They promulgate the high power (*adhibala*) of all good dharmas and destroy the hordes of all the evil Māras (*māracamū*).

They are praised (*stomita*) by all the Buddhas. They counteract the great suffering (*mahāduḥkha*) of Saṃsāra and reveal (*samprakāśayanti*) the great happiness (*mahāsukha*) of Nirvāṇa.

Revealing (*saṃprakāśana*), teaching (*deśanā*), penetrating (*pratisaṃkhyāna*) Sūtrāntas of this kind, and protecting the good Law (*saddharmasaṃgraha*), this is what is called the homage to the Law (*dharmapūjā*).

All the Buddhas of the triple world (*traidhātuka*) and the ten regions (*daśadiś*) together expound these Sūtrāntas. Hearing, believing, retaining, reciting and elaborating these Sūtrāntas; meditating on them and examining their profound meaning so as to clarify it, define it and establish it; analysing, understanding, discerning and clarifying these Sūtrāntas, then expounding them widely to others; finally, protecting the good Law through skillfulness in means, this is what is called the homage to the Law.

12. Besides, son of good family, the homage to the Law consists in understanding the Law according to the Law (*dharmānudharmanidhyapti*), applying the Law according to the Law (*dharmānudharmapratipatti*)[22], conforming to the dependent co-production (*pratītyasamutpādānuvartana*), avoiding false views concerning extremes (*antadṛṣṭivisaṃyoga*), exerting the certainty concerning the non-birth and non-arising of dharmas (*ajātānutpattikadharmakṣāntibhāvanā*), penetrating the dharmas which are without self and without sentient being (*nirātmakaniḥsattvapraveśa*), abstaining from contradicting, criticising and discussing causes and conditions (*hetupratyaya*), avoiding all belief concerning self and of the self (*ātmātmīyagrāhavisaṃyoga*);

1. taking refuge in the spirit and not taking refuge in the letter (*arthapratisaraṇaṃ na vyañjanapratisaraṇam*); 2. taking refuge in direct knowledge and not taking refuge in discursive consciousness (*jñānapratisaraṇaṃ na vijñānapratisaraṇam*); 3. taking refuge in Sūtras of precise meaning and not adhering to conventional Sūtras of indeterminate meaning (*nītārthasūtrapratisaraṇaṃ na neyārthasaṃvṛtisūtrābhiniveśaḥ*); 4. taking refuge in the nature of things and not adhering to the

[22] *Dharmānudharmapratipatti* "to behave in conformity with the doctrine, to apply it in one's actions and in one's life" (cf. W. GEIGER, *Pāli Dhamma*, Munich, 1921, p. 115-116).

opinions of human personalities (*dharmatāpratisaraṇaṃ na pudgala-dṛṣṭyupalabdhitābhiniveśaḥ*)[23];

[23] A textual quotation of a postcanonical topic entitled *Catuṣpratisaraṇasūtra* "Sūtra of the four refuges", of which we possess several versions in Sanskrit, Chinese and Tibetan. The wording differs somewhat depending on the various sources.

The Sanskrit text can be found in the Kośa, IX, p. 246; Kośavyākhyā, p. 704; Madh. vṛtti, p. 43 (taking its quotation from the Akṣayamatinirdeśasūtra, part of the Mahāsaṃnipāta, T 397, ch. 29, p. 205 *a-c*; T 403, ch. 5, p. 603 *c*); Dharmasaṃgraha, § 53; Mahāvyutpatti, No. 1546-1549; Sūtrālaṃkāra, p. 138; Bodh. bhūmi, p. 256 (taking its quotation from the Yogācārabhūmiśāstra, T 1579, ch. 45, p. 539 *a*; T 1582, ch. 6, p. 994 *b*).

Chinese translations: Ta fang pien fo pao ên ching, T 156, ch. 7, p. 163 *c* 29 - 164 *a* 2; Great Parinirvāṇa, T 374, ch. 6, p. 401 *b* - 402 *c*; T 375, ch. 6, p. 642 *a* - 643 *b*; Vikurvaṇarājabodhisattvasūtra, T 420, ch. 1, p. 927 *a-b*; Upadeśa, T 1509, ch. 9, p. 125 *a-b*.

The theory of the *pratisaraṇa* is in preparation in the early canonical Sūtras, debated by the Hīnayāna sects and frequently exploited by Mahāyānasūtras. I have discussed the matter at length in NĀGĀRJUNA, *Traité*, I, p. 536-541, and *La critique d'interprétation dans le bouddhisme*, Annuaire de l'Institut de Philologie et d'Histoire Orientales et Slaves, IX, 1949, p. 341-361.

I will limit myself here to translating the remarkable interpretation of the *pratisaraṇa* given by Kumārajīva in T 1775, ch. 10, p. 417 *a* 10-25:

The Buddha has said: After my Nirvāṇa, you will stand by four rules and you will take them for a great teacher: they consist in relying on the *dharma*. This proves that the four rules can serve as refuges (*pratisaraṇa*), that one can believe them and accept them.

1. *Dharmaḥ pratisaraṇaṃ na pudgalaḥ.* — The *dharma*, that is the teaching of the Sūtras. One should rely on the doctrine of the Sūtras, because one must not depend on a human authority. It is turning one's back on the *dharma* to rely on the *pudgala*.

2. There are two sorts of *dharma*: 1. the *vyañjana* or the letter; 2. the *artha* or the meaning. One should not rely on the *vyañjana*.

3. There are two sorts of *artha*: 1. the *artha* known through discursive consciousnesses (*vijñāna*); 2. the *artha* known through knowledge (*jñāna*). The *vijñāna* only seek after the five objects of desire (*kāmaguṇa*), false and illusory; they do not seek after the real truth. Whereas *jñāna* seeks after the real truth and destroys the five objects of desire. Thus one should rely on the *artha* known through *jñāna* and not rely on the *artha* known through the *vijñāna*. It is in order to seek after the *artha* known through *jñāna* that one relies on *jñāna*.

4. The *artha* known through *jñāna* is also of two sorts: 1. *nītārtha* Sūtra (of explicit meaning); 2. *anītārtha* Sūtra (of indeterminate meaning).

Thus it is an *anītārthasūtra* when the Buddha says (Dhammapada, st. 294; cf. Abhidharmasamuccaya, ed. P. PRADHAN, p. 107,*1-2*): "Having killed his mother and father, the brahman is blameless" (*mātaraṃ pitaraṃ hantvā, anīgho yāti brāhmano*). It is not clear that he is blameless: this is an *anītārtha*.

However, when the Buddha explains: "The father is ignorance (*avidyā*); the mother

understanding dharmas in conformity with the very nature of the Buddhas (*yathābuddhadharmaṃ dharmāṇām avabodhaḥ*); penetrating the absence of a resting place (*anālayapraveśa*) and destroying the resting place (*ālayasamudghāta*)[24]; considering that the outcome of an invincible belief in being (*akṣayasattvadṛṣṭyabhinirhārābhinirhṛta*) is the twelve-fold dependent co-production (*dvādaśāṅgapratītyasamutpāda*) according to which "Through the extinction of ignorance, etc., are extinguished old-age, death, sorrow, lamentation, suffering, grief and despair" (*avidyānirodhād ityādi yāvaj jarāmaraṇaśokaparidevaduḥkhadaurmanasyopāyāsā nirudhyante*).

Son of good family, the non-vision of all views (*sarvadṛṣṭīnām adarśanam*), this is what is called the supreme homage to the Law (*anuttarā dharmapūjā*).

Wishing that all beings abandon all views (*dṛṣṭi*), this is what is called the supreme homage to the Law.

[*Candracchattra, Guardian of the Law*]

13. Continuing his address, the Buddha Śākyamuni said to Śakra, the prince of the gods: Devendra, when the prince Candracchattra had heard from the lips of the Blessed Tathāgata Bhaiṣajyarāja this definition of the homage to the Law, he obtained the preparatory certainty (*anulomikī kṣāntiḥ*). Taking his clothes (*vastra*) and his ornaments (*ābharaṇa*), he offered them to the Blessed Lord Bhaiṣajyarāja and said to him: When the Blessed Tathāgata has entered Parinirvāṇa, I would like to guard this good Law (*saddharma*) so as to protect it (*parigrahāṇa*) and pay homage to it (*pūjana*); may the Tathāgata accord me his supernatural support (*adhiṣṭhāna*) so that I may without difficulty overcome Māra and adversaries (*parapravādin*), protect the good Law of the Blessed One and exercise the practices (*caryā*) of the Bodhisattvas.

is craving (*tṛṣṇā*). They are called father and mother because they are the root (*mūla*) of Saṃsāra. To cut off this root is to put an end to Saṃsāra. This is why I say that he who kills them is blameless": then, it is clear: it is a *nītārthasūtra*.

Or again, when the Buddha says (Itivuttaka, p. 87; Aṅguttara, II, p. 34; III, p. 35; Divyāvadāna, p. 155; Avadānaśataka, I, p. 49-50; 329-330): "Among all beings, the Buddha is the foremost; among all dharmas, Nirvāṇa is the foremost" (*ye kecit sattvā buddhas teṣām agra ākhyātaḥ; ye kecid dharmā nirvāṇaṃ teṣām agram ākhyātam*): then, texts of this type are *nītārtha*. This is why one should rely on the *nītārthasūtra* and not on the *neyārthasūtra*.

[24] See above, V, § 4, note 4.

The Tathāgata Bhaiṣajyarāja, knowing the high resolve (*adhyāśaya*) of Candracchattra, predicted (*vyākaroti sma*) to him that he would be, at the end of the time (*paścime kāle*), in the final period (*paścime samaye*)[25], the protector, the defender and the guardian of the town of the good Law (*saddharmanagara*).

14. Then, O Devendra, the prince Candracchattra, having heard this prediction (*vyākaraṇa*), well-pleased, delighted, transported (*tuṣṭa udagra āttamanāh*), left home in the abundance of his faith so set out on a religious wanderer's life (*śraddhayāgārād anāgārikāṃ pravrajitaḥ*)[26]. Having set

[25] This detail is missing in the Chinese versions, but it concerns a well known formula which can also be found in § 16:

1. *Tathāgatasya parinirvṛtasya paścime kāle paścime samaye* (Saddharmapuṇḍ., p. 234, *3-4*; 268,*3*; 297,*10*): "When the T. has entered complete Nirvāṇa, at the end of the time, in the final period".

2. *Paścime kāle paścime samaye paścimāyāṃ pañcaśatyāṃ vartamānāyām* (Saddharmapuṇḍ., p. 420,*13-14*; 474,*3-4*; 475,*10*; 476,2): "At the end of the time, during the final period, in the last five hundred years".

3. *Tathāgatasya parinirvṛtasya saddharmakṣayāntakāle vartamāne* (Saddharmapuṇḍ., p. 285,*5-6*; 286,*5-6*; *287,11-12*): "When the T. has entered complete Nirvāṇa, when the Good Law has come to an end".

4. *Tathāgatasya parinirvṛtasya paścime kāle paścime samaye paścimāyāṃ pañcaśatyāṃ saddharmavipralope vartamāne* (Saddharmapuṇḍ., p. 282,*9-10*). The same formula, but without *tathāgatasya parinirvṛtasya*, and with *saddharmavipralopakāle* instead of *saddharmavipralope* (Vajracchedikā, p. 30,*17-18*; 40,*4-5*; 45,*13-14*; 53,*16-17*): "When the T. has entered complete Nirvāṇa, at the end of the time, in the final period, in the last five hundred years, when the Good Law is on the decline".

This concerns a belief common to all Mahāyānasūtras, according to which Buddhism will last for five periods of five hundred years and will disappear at the end of the fifth. The Mahāsaṃnipāta, T 397, ch. 55, p. 363 *a-b*, explains: "The Good Law disappears after five periods of five hundred years: in the first, bhikṣus and others are strong in deliberation (in the sense that they will obtain the *satyābhisamaya*); in the second, they will be strong in meditation (*samādhi, dhyāna*); in the third, in Scriptures (*śruta*); in the fourth, the founding of monasteries; in the fifth, disputes and reproaches, and the White Law will become invisible".

Similarly, the Tibetan commentary of the Vajracchedikā (Mdo XVI, fol. 234 *a*) explains: "It is well known that the Bhagavat's teaching lasts for five times five hundred years: that is why the text specifies: *in the last five hundred years*, for then the five corruptions (*kaṣāya*) are on the increase".

The present passage shows that the Vimalakīrti assigns the same date to the disappearance of the Good Law as other Mahāyānasūtras.

Needless to say, yet more dates have been put forward (cf. LAMOTTE, *Histoire*, p. 210-222).

[26] The expression *śraddhayāgārād anāgārikāṃ pravrajitaḥ* is traditional: cf. Saddharmapuṇḍ., p. 180,*7-8*; 465,*3*. Regarding the spelling of *anāgārikā*, or *anagārikā*, cf. EDGERTON, *Dictionary*, p. 19 *a*.

out on this homeless life, he vigorously applied himself to good dharmas (*pravrajitaḥ kuśaleṣu dharmeṣv ārabdhavīryaḥ*). Having applied himself vigorously (*ārabdhavīrya*) and being well established in good dharmas (*kuśaleṣu dharmeṣu supratiṣṭhitaḥ*), he shortly (*naciram*) produced the five super-knowledges (*abhijñā*), understood the formulae (*dhāraṇī*) and obtained invincible eloquence (*anācchedyapratibhāna*). When the Blessed Tathāgata Bhaiṣajyarāja attained Parinirvāṇa, Candracchattra, through the power of the super-knowledges (*abhijñā*) and the formulae (*dhāraṇī*), caused the wheel of the Law to turn (*dharmacakraṃ pravartayati sma*) exactly as the Blessed Tathāgata Bhaiṣajyarāja had caused it to turn, and he caused it to turn for ten small kalpas (*antarakalpa*).

Devendra, while for ten small kalpas (*antarakalpa*), the bhikṣu Candracchattra thus strove (*abhiyukta*) to cause the wheel of the Law to turn and to protect the good Law, a thousand *koṭi* of beings (*sattva*) reached the stage of irreversible (*avaivartika*) Bodhisattva-hood on the path of supreme and perfect enlightenment, fourteen *nayuta* of living beings (*prāṇin*) were converted (*vinīta*) to the Vehicles of the Śrāvakas and the Pratyekabuddhas, and countless beings (*apramāṇasattva*) were reborn in the heavens (*svarga*).

[*Identification of the Personalities in the Jātaka*]

15. Then the Buddha Śākyamuni said to the prince of the gods: Perhaps, O Devendra, you still feel some uncertainty, some perplexity or some doubt and you are wondering if, at that time and in that period, the Cakravartin king Ratnacchattra was not another (than the present Tathāgata Ratnārcis). Well, no, you must not imagine this. And why? Because the present Tathāgata Ratnārcis [27] was, at that time and in that period, the Cakravartin king Ratnacchattra (*syāt khalu punas te Devendraivaṃ kāṅkṣā vā vimatir vā vicikitsā vānyaḥ sa tena kālena tena samayena Ratnacchattro nāmābhūd rājā cakravartī. na khalu punas tvayaivaṃ draṣṭavyam. tat kasya hetoḥ. ayam eva sa Ratnārcis tathāgatas tena kālena tena samayena Ratnacchattro nāma rājā cakravarty abhūt*) [28].

[27] In the Prajñā (Pañcaviṃśati, p. 15,*7-12*; Śatasāh., p. 34 sq), the present Buddha Ratnārcis reigns over the Upaśāntā universe, located on the borders of the Western region. His chief Bodhisattva is a certain Cāritramati.

Ratnārcis is a member of a group of twelve Tathāgatas who regularly frequented Vimalakīrti's house (cf. above, VI, §13, p. 168).

[28] Customary formula used to identify in the present personalities from the past:

As for those who were the thousand sons of the king Ratnacchattra, they are now the thousand Bodhisattvas of the present auspicious period (*bhadrakalpa*). During this auspicious period, a thousand Buddhas come into the world (*utpadyante*). Four among them, Krakucchanda, etc., are already born. The others are yet to be born; they are from Kakutsunda to Roca. The last to be born will be the Tathāgata Roca [29].

The thousand sons of the king Ratnacchattra are the thousand Bodhisattvas of the present auspicious period (*bhadrakalpa*) who will become Buddhas one after the other. The very first to become Buddha was called the Tathāgata Krakucchanda. The very last to become Buddha will be called Roca. Among these thousand Buddhas, four have already appeared in the world; the rest are still in the future.

Divyāvadāna, p. 297,*28*-298,*2*; 328,*1-4*; Rāṣṭrapāla, p. 57,*19-21*; Karmavibhaṅga, p. 56, *14-17* (with one omission doubtless due to the editor); Saddharmapuṇḍ., p. 22,*8-11*; 381,*8-14*; 414,*4-8*; 432,*1-5*; 470; Mahāsaṃnipāta, p. 48-50.

[29] K: "The thousand sons of the king [Candracchattra] are the thousand Buddhas of the present Bhadrakalpa. Krakucchanda was the first to become Buddha; the very last Tathāgata will be called Roca".

With reference to the appearance of the Buddhas, the following points should be remembered:

1. The Buddhas appear during the Period of Stability (*vivartasthāyikalpa*) of the Great Kalpa (*mahākalpa*), which period of stability consists of 20 Small Kalpas (*antarakalpa*). This has already been explained above, VII, § 6, stanza 24, note 37.

2. According to the principle *apakarṣe tu śatād yāvat tadudbhavaḥ* (Kośa, III, p. 192), the Buddhas appear during the phase of diminution (*apakarṣa*) of the *antarakalpa*, phase so named because human longevity is progressively reduced from 80,000 to 10 years. During the first *antarakalpa*, the human lifespan decreases continuously. It also decreases during the second phase of the *antarakalpa* No. 2 to 19. Conversely, it only increases during the 20th *antarakalpa*. It thus results that the Buddhas only appear during the first 19 *antarakalpa* of the 20 that make up the period of stability. Besides, the Buddhas only appear when the average lifespan of man is less than 100 years.

3. Certain Great Kalpas (*mahākalpa*) are called *Bhadrakalpa* "Auspicious Periods": these are the ones when the 1000 Buddhas appear. We belong to one of these *Bhadrakalpa*. It is named *Puṣpika* "Flowered Auspicious Period" (cf. Mahāvastu, III, p. 330,*5*).

4. Amongst the 1000 Buddhas of our Bhadrakalpa, four have already appeared, the 996 others have yet to come: cf. Saddharmapuṇḍ., p. 201,*6-7*; Upadeśa, T 1509, ch. 9, p. 125 *a* (Nāgārjuna, *Traité*, p. 535).

5. The four Buddhas who have already appeared are Krakucchanda, Kanakamuni, Kāśyapa and Śākyamuni. They appeared in turn during the sixth, seventh, eighth and ninth *antarakalpa* of the Bhadrakalpa (Ch'i fo ching, T 2, p. 150 *a* 18-22), or else all during the ninth *antarakalpa* (Fo tsu t'ung chi, T 2035, ch. 30, p. 299 *a* 21),

Perhaps O Devendra, you still wonder if, at that time and in that period, the prince Candracchattra, protector of the good Law of the Blessed Tathāgata Bhaiṣajyarāja, was not another (than myself). Well, no, you must not imagine that. And why? Because I myself was, at that time and in that period, the prince named Candracchattra (*syāt khalu punas te Devendraivaṃ kāṅkṣā vā vimatir vā vicikitsā vānyaḥ sa tena kālena tena samayena Candracchattro nāma rājaputro 'bhūt tasya bhagavato Bhaiṣajyarājasya tathāgatasya saddharmaparigrāhakaḥ. na khalu punas tvayaivaṃ draṣṭavyam. tat kasya hetoḥ. aham eva sa, Devendra, tena kālena tena samayena Candracchattro nāma rājaputro 'bhūvam*).

For this reason (*anena paryāyeṇa*), you should know, O Devendra, that among all the homages (*pūjā*) rendered to the Tathāgatas, the homage to the Law (*dharmapūjā*) is the best. Yes, it is indeed good (*vara*), eminent (*parama*), excellent (*pravara*), perfect (*praṇīta*), superior (*uttara*) and unsurpassed (*anuttara*). That is why, O Devendra, one should pay homage (*pūj-*) to the Tathāgatas, not through material objects (*āmiṣa*), but through the homage to the Law (*dharmapūjā*); one should venerate (*satkṛ-*) them, not through material objects, but through the veneration of the Law (*dharmasatkāra*).

when human longevity was respectively of 40,000, 30,000, 20,000 and 100 years (Dīgha, II, p. 2-7; Sanskrit Mahāvadāna, p. 70; Dīrgha, T 1, ch. 1, p. 2 *b*; Ch'i fo ching, T 2, p. 150 *c*; Ch'i fo fu mu hsing tzŭ ching, T 4, p. 159 *c*; Ekottara, T 125, ch. 45, p. 791 *a*; Ch'u yao ching, T 212, ch. 2, p. 615 *c*). The Upadeśa, which is familiar with these data, disputes them (cf. NĀGĀRJUNA, *Traité*, p. 269 and 299).

For other details on these four Buddhas, see the recapitulative tables by T.W. RHYS DAVIDS, *Dialogues of the Buddha*, II, p. 6-7; E. WALDSCHMIDT, *Sanskrit Mahāvadāna*, p. 169-175; Hōbōgirin, p. 196.

6. Nearly all sources give Maitreya as the immediate successor to Śākyamuni and the fifth Buddha of the Bhadrakalpa. However, here, the Tibetan version of the Vimalakīrti proposes replacing him with Ḥkhor ba ḥjig, or Kakutsunda (cf. Mahāvyutpatti, No. 91). See EDGERTON, *Dictionary*, p. 196 *b*, where he is confused with Krakucchanda.

7. The 996 Buddhas to come are indicated by the expression *ārya-Maitreyapūrvaṃgamāḥ sarvabhadrakalpikā bodhisattvāḥ* (Gaṇḍavyūha, p. 548,5) "The Bodhisattvas of the Auspicious Period headed by Maitreya". The complete list of them can be found in F. WELLER, *Tausend Buddhanamen des Bhadrakalpa nach einer fünfsprachigen Polyglotte*, Leipzig, 1928.

The last of these future Buddhas is Roca. He is also mentioned in the Karuṇāpuṇḍarīka, T 157, ch. 6, p. 203 *b* 16.

[*The Transmission to Maitreya*]

16. Then the Blessed Lord Śākyamuni said to the Bodhisattva Mahāsattva Maitreya: I entrust to you, O Maitreya, this supreme and perfect enlightenment that I only acquired at the end of hundreds of thousands of *koṭīnayuta* of kalpas (*imām ahaṃ Maitreyāsaṃkhyeyakalpakoṭīnayutaśatasahasrasamudānītām anuttarāṃ samyaksaṃbodhiṃ tvayi parindāmi*)[30]. This Sūtrānta has been upheld by the psychic power (*ṛddhibala*) of the Buddha, protected by the psychic power of the Buddha.

I entrust it to you so that, at the end of the time, during the final period, such an interpretation of the Law, protected by your supernatural intervention, spreads throughout Jambudvīpa and does not disappear (*yathā paścime kāle paścime samaye 'yam evaṃrūpo dharmaparyāyas tvadadhiṣṭhānena parigṛhīto Jambudvīpe pracaretana cāntardhīyeta*)[31].

Act in such a way that, after the Parinirvāṇa of the Tathāgata, at the period of the five corruptions (*pañcakaṣāyakāla*), this Sūtrānta, upheld and guarded by your psychic power (*ṛddhibala*), spreads throughout Jambudvīpa and does not disappear.

And why? Maitreya, there will be, in future times (*anāgate 'dhvani*), sons of good family (*kulaputra*), daughters of good family (*kuladuhitṛ*), Devas, Nāgas, Yakṣas, Gandharvas and Asuras who, after having planted good roots (*avaropitakuśalamūla*), will produce the thought of supreme and perfect enlightenment. If they do not hear this interpretation of the Law (*dharmaparyāya*), they will certainly perish[32]. But, if they hear such a Sūtrānta, they will delight, will believe it and will accept it with bowed head. It is in order to protect these sons and daughters of good family that, in that time, O Maitreya, you should disseminate a Sūtrānta such as this one.

[*Beginner Bodhisattvas and Veteran Bodhisattvas*]

17. Maitreya, there are two categories (*mudrā*) of Bodhisattvas. What are these two? 1. The category of those who believe in all kinds of phrases and syllables (*nānāpadavyañjanābhiprasanna*); 2. The

[30] Same formula in Saddharmapuṇḍ., p. 484,*9-10*. — All Mahāyānasūtras are transmitted to Maitreya.

[31] Cf. Aṣṭasāh., p. 869,*14*; 870,*6*; 990,*20*: *yatheyaṃ nāntardhīyeta*.

[32] H: "They will lose immense advantages".

category of those who, without being afraid of the profound tenor of the Law (*gambhīreṇa dharmanayenānuttrāsita*), penetrate it correctly (*yathābhūtaṃ praviśanti*): such are, O Maitreya, the two categories of Bodhisattvas.

Maitreya, you should know that Bodhisattvas who believe and apply themselves to all kinds of phrases and syllables (*nānāpada-vyañjana*) are beginners (*ādikarmika*) and recently come to the religious life (*acirabrahmacārin*). But the Bodhisattvas who read (*paṭhanti*), listen (*śṛṇvanti*), believe (*adhimucyante*) and teach (*deśayanti*) this profound (*gambhīra*) and spotless (*anupalipta*) Sūtrānta, this book (*grantha*) or this section (*paṭala*) entitled "Production of unpaired and inverted (sounds)" (*Yamakavyatyastāhāra*)[33], these Bodhisattvas, say I, are veterans of the religious life (*dīrghakāla-brahmacārin*).

If Bodhisattvas revere (*satkurvanti*) and believe (*adhimucyante*) elegant phrases and syllables (*padavyañjana*), you should know that these are beginner (*ādikarmika*) Bodhisattvas. But if, in the presence of this lovely Sūtrānta, profound (*gambhīra*), spotless (*anupalipta*) and unattached (*asaṅga*), entitled "Interpretation of the Law concerning the Liberation of inconceivable Wonder" (*Acintyavikurvaṇavimokṣadharmaparyāya*), the Bodhisattvas are unafraid (*nirbhaya*); if, after having heard it, they believe it (*adhimucyante*), grasp it, (*udgṛhṇanti*), retain it (*dhārayanti*), repeat it (*vācayanti*), penetrate it in depth (*paryavāpnuvanti*), expound it widely to others (*parebhyo vistareṇa saṃprakāśayanti*), understand it correctly (*yathābhūtam adhigacchanti*) and apply all their efforts to it (*bhāvanāyogena prayuñjanti*); if they then produce a transcendental and pure conviction (*lokottaraviśuddhādhimukti*), then you should know that these Bodhisattvas are long-experienced Bodhisattvas (*ciracaritabodhisattva*).

18. Maitreya, there are four causes[34] through which beginner (*ādikarmika*) Bodhisattvas harm themselves (*ātmano vraṇayanti*) and do not analyse the profound Law (*gambhīraṃ dharmaṃ na nirūpayanti*). What are these four?

1. On hearing this profound (*gambhīra*) Sūtrānta not yet heard before (*aśrutapūrva*), they are afraid (*uttrasta*), hesitant (*saṃśayita*), and do not delight in it (*nānumodante*).

2. By asking themselves: "From where does this Sūtrānta, not yet heard before, come to us?" they put it in question (*adhikurvanti*) and reject it (*pratikṣipanti*).

[33] Note the differences between the versions: Cn and K do not give the title and only talk of *gambhīrasūtra*; H entitles the sūtra *Acintyavikurvaṇavimokṣadharmaparyāya* (as above, XII, § 1, and below, XII, § 23); the Tibetan introduces a new title *Yamakavyatyastāhāra* which it repeats in Ch. XII, § 23. See introduction, p. LVI-LX.

[34] *Four* causes, according to Cn and H; *two*, according to K and the Tibetan.

3. On seeing the sons of good family (*kulaputra*) take up, adopt or expound this profound Sūtrānta, they do not serve them (*na niṣevante*), do not frequent them (*na saṃgacchanti*), do not respect them (*na paryupāsanti*) and do not revere them (*na satkurvanti*).

4. Finally, they even go so far as to address criticisms (*avarṇa*) at them.

Such are the four causes[35] through which beginner Bodhisattvas harm themselves and do not analyse the profound Law.

19. There are four causes[36] through which Bodhisattvas, even while believing in this profound interpretation of the Law (*gambhīradharmaparyāyādhimukta*), harm themselves (*ātmano vraṇayanti*) and do not rapidly obtain the certainty concerning the non-arising of dharmas (*anutpattikadharmakṣānti*). Which are these four?

1. These Bodhisattvas despise (*avamānayanti*) and reprove (*vimānayanti*) the beginner (*ādikarmika*) Bodhisattvas who, even while pledged to the Great Vehicle (*mahāyānasaṃprasthita*), have not exercised the practices for a long time (*aciracarita*).

2. They refuse to receive them and instruct them.

3. Not having great faith in the profound doctrine, they do not have great respect (*bahumāna*) for its very extensive rules (*śikṣāpada*).

4. They help beings (*sattvān upakurvanti*) through material gifts (*āmiṣadāna*) and not through the giving of the Law (*dharmadāna*).

Such are, Maitreya, the four causes[37] through which Bodhisattvas, while believing this profound interpretation of the Law, harm themselves and do not rapidly obtain the certainty concerning the non-arising of dharmas.

[*Maitreya's Promise*]

20. Having heard these words of the Buddha, the Bodhisattva Maitreya, well-pleased (*tuṣṭa*) and delighted (*udagra*), said to the Blessed One:

Blessed One, all the fair words (*subhāṣita*) of the Tathāgata are wonderful (*āścarya*). It is good!

The words of the Tathāgata are marvellous (*adbhuta*); the words of the Tathāgata are wonderful (*āścarya*).

From now on, I shall avoid absolutely the errors (*duṣkṛta*) that you have pointed out to me.

This great Law arising from the supreme and perfect enlightenment

[35] Same remark as in the preceding note.

[36] *Four* causes, according to H; *two* causes, according to Cn, K and the Tibetan.

[37] Same remark as in the preceding note.

(*anuttarasamyaksaṃbodhi*) accumulated by the Tathāgata during immense and countless hundreds of thousands of *koṭīnayuta* of kalpas, I will protect (*ārakṣiṣyāmi*) and guard (*dhārayiṣyāmi*) so that it will not disappear (*yathā nāntardhīyeta*).

As for the sons and daughters of good family who, in the future, will practise the Mahāyāna and will be worthy recipients (*bhājana*) of the true Law, I will place in their hands this profound Sūtrānta. I will give them the power of mindfulness through which, having believed in this very Sūtrānta, they will grasp it, retain it, teach it, repeat it, penetrate it in depth, propagate it, write it all down and expound it widely to others (*teṣāṃ ca smṛtibalam upasaṃhariṣyāmi yenemam evaṃrūpaṃ sūtrāntam adhimucyodgrahīṣyanti dhārayiṣyanti deśayiṣyanti vācayiṣyanti paryavāpsyanti pravartayiṣyanty antaśo likhiṣyanti parebhyaś ca vistareṇa saṃprakāśayiṣyanti*).

Blessed One, I myself will instruct them, and it should be known that at that time those who will believe in this Sūtrānta and propagate it will be upheld by the supernatural action of the Bodhisattva Maitreya (*Maitreyasya bodhisattvasyādhiṣṭhānenādhiṣṭhitāḥ*).

Then the Blessed One gave his approval (*sādhukāram adāt*) to the Bodhisattva Maitreya: Excellent, excellent (*sādhu sādhu*): this is well spoken (*subhāṣita*), and the Tathāgata himself delights in (*anumodate*) and approves (*adhivāsayati*) your fine words.

[*The Bodhisattvas' Promise*]

21. Then all the Bodhisattvas, — those who were part of the assembly and those who had come from remote regions — joined their hands (*añjaliṃ praṇamya*) and all said with one voice (*ekasvaranirghoṣeṇa*): Blessed One, we too, after the Parinirvāṇa of the Buddha, we will come from the various Buddhakṣetras of remote spheres to propagate this great Law arising from the supreme and perfect enlightenment of the Buddha Tathāgata. Thus it will not disappear and will be spread widely.

And the sons of good family will believe it

If the sons and daughters of good family listen to this Sūtra, believe it, grasp it, retain it, repeat it, penetrate it in depth, apply it without error and expound it widely to others, we will protect them and we will give them the power of mindfulness in such a way that they will have no difficulty.

[*The Lokapālas' Promise*]

22. Then the four Mahārājika Devas, present in the assembly, joined their hands, and with one voice, said to the Blessed One:

Blessed One, in all the villages (*grāma*), towns (*nagara*), boroughs (*nigama*), kingdoms (*rāṣṭra*) and capitals (*rājadhānī*)[38] where this interpretation of the Law (*dharmaparyāya*) will be practised (*carita*), taught (*deśita*) and revealed (*saṃprakāśita*), we, the four Great Kings, will go there, with our armies (*bala*), our youths (*taruṇa*) and our attendants (*anucara*) to hear the Law there.

Within a radius of a hundred leagues, we will protect the reciters of this Law, so that any among those who plan or seek to surprise these reciters of the Law will have no hold on them (*vayam api bhagavann ā yojanaśataparisāmantakād evaṃrūpāṇāṃ dharmabhāṇakānāṃ rakṣām kariṣyāmo yathā na kaścit teṣāṃ dharmabhāṇakānām avatārapreksy avatāragaveṣy avatāraṃ lapsyate*)[39].

[*Transmission to Ānanda and Title of the Sūtra*]

23. Then the Blessed One said to the Venerable (*āyuṣmant*) Ānanda: Take then, Ānanda, this interpretation of the Law, retain it and expound it widely to others (*udgṛhṇīṣva tvam Ānandemaṃ dharmaparyāyaṃ dhāraya parebhyaś ca vistareṇa saṃprakāśaya*)[40].

Ānanda replied: I have taken, O Blessed One, this interpretation of the Law (*udgṛhīto me Bhagavann ayaṃ dharmaparyāya iti*). But what is the name of this interpretation of the Law and by what title should I refer to it (*ko nāmāyaṃ Bhagavan dharmaparyāyaḥ, kathaṃ cainaṃ dhārayāmi*)[41]?

The Blessed One replied:

Ānanda, this interpretation of the Law has as its name: "Teaching of Vimalakīrti" (*Vimalakīrtinirdeśa*), or "Production of paired

It has as its name "Teaching of Vimalakīrti" (*Vimalakīrtinirdeśa*), "Interpretation of the Law concerning the liberation of inconceivable wonder" (*Acintyavikurvaṇavimokṣadharmaparyāya*).

[38] Regarding this list, see above, I, § 8, note 43.

[39] Wide-spread stock phrase, but which undergoes variations: cf. Saddharmapuṇḍ., p. 400,*9-11*; 474,*3-7*. — On the meaning of *avatāra*, see above, VI, § 8, note 28.

[40] Stock phrase: cf. Samādhirāja, III, p. 647,*13-15*. — Ānanda is, along with Maitreya, the acknowledged guardian of Mahāyānasūtras. An apocryphal tradition has it that he participated in their compilation (see NĀGĀRJUNA, *Traité*, p. 939-942).

[41] Another stock phrase: cf. Vajracchedikā, p. 37,*21-22*; Bhaiṣajyaguru, p. 31,*11-12*; Tathāgatādhiṣṭhāna, p. 88,*12-13*; Samādhirāja, III, p. 647,*15-16*.

and inverted (sounds) (*Yamakavyatyastābhinirhāra*), or again, "Chapter of the inconceivable liberation" (*Acintyavimokṣaparivarta*): so refer to it thus (*evaṃ cainaṃ dhāraya*)[42]. Thus spoke the Blessed One. Transported with joy, the Licchavi Vimalakīrti, Mañjuśrī the crown prince, the Venerable Ānanda, the great Bodhisattvas, the great Listeners, the whole assembly and the universe with the gods, men, Asuras and Gandharvas, praised what the Blessed One had said (*idam avocad Bhagavān. āttamanā licchavir Vimalakīrtir Mañjuśrīś ca kumārabhūtaḥ sa cāyuṣmān Ānandas te ca mahābodhisattvās te ca mahāśrāvakāḥ sā ca sarvāvatī parṣat sadevamānuṣāsuragandharvaś ca loko Bhagavato bhāṣitam abhyanandann iti*)[43].

---

[42] It is only at the end of a work that Mahāyānasūtras state their titles. I intentionally say titles for it is rare for them to have only one: which does not help in their identification. With regard to the Vimalakīrti, the versions disagree.

Cn gives two titles: 1. *Wei mo chieh so shuo* 維摩詰所說 = Vimalakīrtinirdeśa; 2. *Pu k'o ssŭ i fa mên* 不可思議法門 = Acintyadharmaparyāya.

K also gives two titles: 1. *Wei mo chieh so shuo* 維摩詰所說 = Vimalakīrtinirdeśa; 2. *Pu k'o ssŭ chieh t'o fa mên* 不可思議解脫法門 = Acintyavimokṣadharmaparyāya. [The latter title differs considerably from the title given by K in Ch. XII, § 1, note 1: Acintyavikurvaṇa[niyata]bhūtanayasūtra].

H also gives two titles: 1. *Shuo wu kou ch'êng* 說無垢稱 = Vimalakīrtinirdeśa; 2. As a sub-title, *Pu k'o ssŭ i tzŭ tsai shên pien chieh t'o fa mên* 不可思議自在神變解脫法門 = Acintyavikurvaṇavimokṣadharmaparyāya. [This wording repeats exactly the title already given by H in Ch. XII, §1, note 1; XII, §6, note 9].

The Tibetan gives three titles: 1. *Dri ma med par grags pas bstan pa* = Vimalakīrtinirdeśa; 2. *Phrugs su sbyar ba snrel ži[ṅ] mṅon par bsgrub pa* = Yamakavyatyastābhinirhāra [this repeats the title already given in Ch. XII, § 17, contrasting with that given by H]; 3. *Bsam gyis mi khyab paḥi rnam par thar paḥi leḥu* = Acintyavimokṣaparivarta. [This wording is very close to that already given in Ch. XII, § 6: *Rnam par thar pa bsam gyis mi khyab pa bstan paḥi chos kyi rnam graṅs*: Acintyavimokṣanirdeśo dharmaparyāyaḥ].

Finally we should not forget another title supplied by the Tibetan in Ch. XII, §1: *Rnam par sprul ba bsam gyis mi khyab paḥi tshul la ḥjug pa rab tu bstan pa* = Acintyavikurvaṇanayapraveśanirdeśa. [This wording is somewhat analogous to the title given by H].

[43] This conclusion is customary at the end of Mahāyānasūtras: cf. Vajracchedikā, p. 62,5-8; Sukhāvatīvyūha, p. 156,5-7; Samādhirāja, III, p. 647,19 - 648,2; Bhaiṣajyaguru, p. 32,2-6, etc.

APPENDIX

NOTE I: THE BUDDHAKṢETRAS

(Cf. Ch. I, § 11).

I. *The cosmic system.* — The early writings generally limited their interest to the world of rebirths, the triple world (*traidhātuka*) and its receptacle (*bhājanaloka*) consisting of the universe of four continents (*caturdvīpako lokadhātuḥ*), encircled by a mountain of iron, the Cakravāḍa. A detailed description of this universe can be found in the excellent work by W. KIRFEL, *Die Kosmographie der Inder*, Bonn, 1920, p. 178-207.

However, alongside this limited universe, Buddhists built up a grandiose cosmic system which already appeared in the texts of the Small Vehicle, but which grew in importance in the texts of the Great Vehicle: Dīrgha, T 1, ch. 18, p. 114 *b-c*; T 23, ch. 1, p. 227 *a*; T 24, ch. 1, p. 310 *b*; T 25, ch. 1, p. 365 *c*; Madhyama, T 26, ch. 59, p. 799 *c*; Saṃyukta, T 99, No. 424-426, ch. 16, p. 111 *c*-112 *a*; Aṅguttara, I, p. 227; Cullaniddesa, p. 135; Lalitavistara, p. 150; Kośa, III, p. 170; Mahāvyutpatti, No. 3042-3044; Upadeśa, T 1509, ch. 7, p. 113 *c*-114 *a* (NĀGĀRJUNA, *Traité*, p. 447-449); Pañjikā, p. 52.

This system distinguishes three kinds of complex universes:

1. The small chiliocosm or *sāhasracūḍiko lokadhātuḥ*, containing a thousand universes of four continents.

2. A middling chiliocosm or *dvisāhasro madhyamo lokadhātuḥ*, containing a thousand universes of the preceding type.

3. The great chiliocosm or *trisāhasramahāsāhasro lokadhātuḥ*, containing a thousand universes of the preceding type, i.e. a milliard universes of four continents.

The great chiliocosms "as innumerable as the grains of sand of the Ganges" (*gaṅgānadīvālukopama*) are spread throughout the ten regions (*daśadiś*), that is, the ten points of space: East, South, West, North, North-East, South-East, South-West, North-West, Nadir and Zenith.

II. *The buddhakṣetra.* — Certain great chiliocosms are bereft of a Buddha or, according to the expression in the Mahāvastu, I, p. 122,*3*, deserted by the best of men (*śūnyakāni puruṣapravarehi*). In general, however, the great chiliocosms or multiples of great chiliocosms consist in as many Buddha-fields (*buddhakṣetra*) where "a Tathāgata, a holy one, fully and perfectly enlightened, is to be found, lives, exists and teaches the Law, for the benefit and happiness of many beings, through compassion for the world, for the advantage, benefit and happiness of the great body of beings, men and gods" (*tathāgato 'rhan samyaksaṃbuddhas tiṣṭhati dhriyate yāpayati dharmaṃ ca deśayati bahujanahitāya bahujanasukhāya lokānukampāyai mahato janakāyasyārthāya hitāya sukhāya devānāṃ ca manuṣyāṇāṃ ca*).

Our Sahā universe, situated in the southern region, is or was the buddhakṣetra of the Buddha Śākyamuni. But buddhakṣetras are often multiples of great chiliocosms:

Mahāvastu, I, p. 121,*11*: The *buddhakṣetra* is equal to 61 great chiliocosms, and the *upakṣetra* is worth four times as much.

Upadeśa, T 1509, ch. 92, p. 708 *b* 23: A million (correction: a milliard) moons and suns, a million Sumerus and a million celestial spheres, Cāturmahārājikas, etc., form a *trisāhasramahāsāhasralokadhātu* (= great chiliocosm) and these last, in incalculable and infinite numbers, form a single buddhakṣetra.

Ibid., ch. 50, p. 418 *c*: The *trisāhasramahāsāhasralokadhātu* constitutes a *lokadhātu*. These *lokadhātu* which exist in the ten regions in numbers equal to the sands of the Ganges form a *buddhalokadhātu*. These *buddhalokadhātu* which exist in the ten regions in numbers equal to the sands of the Ganges form a sea (*samudra*) of *buddhalokadhātu*. These *seas* which exist in the ten regions in numbers equal to the sands of the Ganges form a seed (*bīja*) of *buddhalokadhātusamudra*. These *seeds* which exist in the ten regions in numbers equal to the sands of the Ganges form a *buddhakṣetra*.

The buddhakṣetra is the fruit of the great compassion (*mahākaruṇā*) of the Buddha who, in a given field, undertakes to do Buddha deeds (*buddhakārya*), that is, to cause beings to "ripen" (*paripācana*) by developing in them the three "good roots" (*kuśalamūla*), absence of greed (*alobha*), of hatred (*adveṣa*) and of confusion (*amoha*) which are directly opposed to the three basic passions: craving (*rāga*), hatred (*dveṣa*) and delusion (*moha*).

Upadeśa, T 1509, ch. 92, p. 708 *b* 25: In the immense and infinite trisāhasramahāsāhasralokadhātus which constitute a buddhakṣetra, the Buddha performs Buddha deeds. Three times a day and three times a night (*trī rātres trir divasya*), he considers beings with his Buddha-eye (*buddhacakṣuṣā sattvān vyavalokayati*), while saying to himself: In whom could I plant good roots which have not yet been planted (*kasyānavaropitāni kuśalamūlāny avaropayāmi*)? In whom could I develop the good roots which have already been planted (*kasyāvaropitāni vivardhayāmi*)? Whom can I establish in the fruit of deliverance (*kaṃ mokṣaphale pratiṣṭhāpayāmi*)? Having examined them in this way, he makes use of his psychic powers (*ṛddhibala*) and, according to what he has seen, he causes beings to ripen (*sattvān paripācayati*).

In order to do this, the Buddha makes use of the most varied of means, from instruction to absolute silence. The Vimalakīrti lists (X, § 8-9) the various expedients to which the Buddha has recourse.

III. *Diversity of the buddhakṣetras.* — There are as many buddhakṣetras as there are Buddhas, i.e. an infinite quantity. The former can, however, be put in three categories (cf. Upadeśa, T 1509, ch. 32, p. 302 *b* 15; ch. 93, p. 711 *c* 18; Yogācārabhūmi, T 1579, ch. 79, p. 736 *c* 21): the pure (*viśuddha*), impure (*aviśuddha*) and mixed (*miśraka*).

1. Impure is the buddhakṣetra where the sojourn is supposedly disagreeable.

Saṃdhinirmocana, T 676, ch. 5, p. 711 *b*: In impure buddhakṣetras there are eight easy (*sulabha*) and two hard (*durlabha*) things to come by. The eight easy things are: 1. sectaries (*tīrthika*), 2. suffering beings (*duḥkhitasattva*), 3. differences of lineage, etc., 4. people of bad behaviour (*duścaritacārin*), 5. beings devoid of morality (*vipannaśīla*), 6. bad destinies (*durgati*), 7. inferior Vehicles (*hīnayāna*), 8. Bodhisattvas with inferior aspirations and practices (*hīnāśayaprayoga*). — Conversely, hard are: 1. Bodhisattvas with excellent aspirations and practices (*āśayaprayogāvaropeta*), 2. the appearance of Buddhas (*tathāgataprādurbhāva*).

The Sahā universe, of which we are dependents, is a good example of an impure universe. It was here that the Buddha Śākyamuni reached supreme and perfect enlightenment (Pañcaviṃśati, p. 13,*4*; Sad. puṇḍarīka, p. 185,*3*). All the sources present it as a dangerous and wretched universe.

In the Pañcaviṃśati, p. 13,*20*, Ratnākara sends Samantaraśmi to the Sahā universe, but advises him to "take great care, while travelling in that universe".

Sad. puṇḍarīka, p. 425,*9*: That universe has heights and low places, is made of clay, ridged with Kālaparvatas and filled with filth (*sā lokadhātur utkūlanikūlā mṛnmayī kālaparvatākīrṇā gūthoḍillaparipūrṇā*).

Upadeśa, T 1509, ch. 10, p. 130 *a*: In the Sahā universe, the causes of happiness are rare: there are found there the three bad destinies (*durgati*), old age (*jarā*), sickness (*vyādhi*) and death (*maraṇa*), and the exploitation of the soil is difficult. Its inhabitants are filled with disgust (*nirveda*) for that universe. At the sight of old age, sickness and death their thoughts are filled with disgust. On seeing the poor, they know that their deprivation is the result of their former existences (*pūrvajanman*), and their thoughts are full of disgust. It is because of this that their wisdom (*prajñā*) and sharp faculties (*tīkṣṇendriya*) arise... In the Sahā universe, the Bodhisattvas multiply their skill in means (*upāya*); that is why they are difficult to approach.

In the Vimalakīrtinirdeśa, Śāriputra ascertains with horror the impurities of the Sahāloka (I, § 15), and Vimalakīrti himself admires the courage of the Bodhisattvas who consent to establish themselves in this wretched buddhakṣetra (IX, § 16).

2. Pure is the buddhakṣetra of pleasant and agreeable sojourn. Certain recensions of the Saṃdhinirmocana (Tibetan version OKC No. 774; trans. by Hsüan-tsang T 676, ch. 1, p. 688 *b-c*), the Saṃgraha, p. 317-322, and the Buddhabhūmisūtraśāstra, T 1530, ch. 1, p. 292 *b*, enumerate the eighteen excellences (*sampad*) of pure buddhakṣetras: 1. colour (*varṇa*), 2. shape (*saṃsthāna*), 3. dimensions (*pramāṇa*), 4. realm (*deśa*), 5. cause (*hetu*), 6. fruit (*phala*), 7. sovereign (*adhipati*), 8. assistance (*pakṣa*), 9. entourage (*parivāra*), 10. support (*adhiṣṭhāna*), 11. activity (*karman*), 12. beneficence (*upakāra*), 13. fearlessness (*nirbhaya*), 14. beauty (*āspada*), 15. paths (*mārga*), 16. vehicles (*yāna*), 17. doors (*mukha*), and 18. base (*ādhāra*).

In the Sad. puṇḍarīka there is a whole stock of formulae for describing a pure universe: P. 8,7: Lovely, very lovely, presided over and commanded by a Tathāgata (*darśanīyaḥ paramadarśanīyas tathāgatapūrvaṃgamas tathāgatapariṇāyakaḥ*). — P. 202,*2*; 405,*2*: Even, smooth like the palm of a hand, made of the seven jewels (*samaḥ pāṇitalajātaḥ saptaratnamayaḥ*). — P. 65,*9*; 144,*9*; 148,*11*; 151,*8*: It is even, pleasant, charming, most lovely to see, thoroughly pure, flourishing, rich, wholesome and fertile. It rests on a base of beryl or others precious substances. It is devoid of stones, gravel, roughness, torrents, precipices, filth and blemishes. It is adorned with precious trees, covered with enclosures laid out in the form of checkerboards, with golden cords strewn with flowers.

The Auspicious Land, western paradise of the Buddha Amitābha, is the best example of a pure land. The Sukhāvatīvyūha, p. 58-98, describes its vast qualities, its light, assemblies, trees, lotuses, rivers, food, music, palaces, winds, etc.

This Auspicious Land is infinitely superior to the celestial spheres of our universe and even to the Tuṣita heaven, paradise of Maitreya (cf. P. Demiéville, *La Yogācārabhūmi de Saṃgharakṣa*, BEFEO, XLIV, 1954, p. 389, n. 4).

IV. *Identity of the buddhakṣetras.* — Pure or impure, buddhakṣetras are all "Buddha lands" and, as such, perfectly pure. The distinction between pure fields and impure fields is purely subjective.

1. The Buddhas at will transform an impure land into a pure land and vice versa. Thus, in the Prajñāpāramitā (Pañcaviṃśati, p. 5-17; Śatasāh., p. 7-55), Śākyamuni, desiring to expound the Prajñā in Sahāloka, enters into the *samādhirājasamādhi* and projects rays which go out to illuminate the universes of the ten regions and convert beings. He smiles "through all the pores of his skin", and further rays reach the confines of space. He displays his ordinary brilliance, as wide as a span, and all beings are delighted by it. He covers the great chiliocosm with his tongue and thus causes further conversions. He enters into the *siṃhavikrīḍitasamādhi*, and the great chiliocosm is shaken by six earthquakes. The Buddha then brings about the appearance of his light, his splendour, his colours and his eminent forms; then, for the benefit of those who still doubt, he displays his ordinary body, adorned with the primary and secondary physical marks. It goes without saying that a world where such prodigies occur no longer has anything of an impure land about it.

The same phantasmagorias occur in the Sad. puṇḍarīka: P. 244-245: When the Tathāgatas and Bodhisattvas of the ten regions go to the Sahāloka to revere Prabhūtaratna's stūpa, the supposedly impure Sahāloka transforms itself into a pure land. It appears on a foundation of beryl, overlaid with trees of diamonds, trellises of gold and precious jewels, perfumed with the scent of incense, strewn with flowers, adorned with garlands, covered with enclosures in the form of a checkerboard, without villages or town, without mountains or rough surfaces, without oceans or rivers. The hells and the world of death are eliminated. — P. 297: On Śākyamuni's intervention, the Sahā universe splits on all sides and, from the midst of these splits, there surge hundreds of thousands of myriads of Bodhisattvas.

2. It is always permissible for Bodhisattvas to create an oasis of pure land in an impure land. Thus, in the middle of the Sahā universe,

Vimalakīrti's house enjoys all the prerogatives of a pure buddhakṣetra (cf. Ch. VI, § 13).

3. Finally and above all, one and the same buddhakṣetra simultaneously appears pure or impure according to the goodness or badness of those who are looking at it. Thus, in Ch. I, § 15-18, the Sahāloka which appears to Śāriputra to be "full of rises and dips, with thorns, precipices, peaks, chasms, and all filled with filth", seems to Brahmā Śikhin "to be equal in splendour to the paradise of the Paranirmitavaśavartin gods". Śākyamuni only has to touch it with his toe for the Sahāloka to appear completely like the universe called "Precious Splendour of infinite virtues", and for Śākyamuni to explain that "the Sahā universe is always as pure as this".

V. *Emptiness of the buddhakṣetra.* — On several occasions, the Vimalakīrtinirdeśa (see p. 118, 133, 182, 210, 227) proclaims the absolute emptiness of buddhakṣetras. They are devoid of self-nature (*svabhāvaśūnya*), calm (*śānta*), unreal (*asiddha*), immutable (*avikāra*) and the same as space (*ākāśasama*). It is only in order to ripen beings that the Buddhas manifest buddhakṣetras of all kinds, but all the buddhakṣetras are fundamentally pure and indistinguishable. The Bodhisattvas who course through them consider them to be like empty space. According to the formula in the Ratnakūṭa (T 310, ch. 86, p. 493 *b-c*), "all the Buddhas are but one Buddha, and all the buddhakṣetras are but one buddhakṣetra".

The theory concerning the Buddha-fields is conceived within the framework of universal emptiness and absolute non-duality. The Tathāgatas who rule over them are not something, and they should be seen "as if there were nothing to see" (XI, § 1); the living beings who "ripen" in these buddhakṣetras are similarly inexistent (VI, § 1); finally, the materials which could be used to construct them are completely lacking since all dharmas are the same as space (*ākāśasama*) and nothing can be built with empty space (I, § 12).

The buddhakṣetra, then, is nothing but a simple mental construction raised in the minds of beings to be converted.

The Upadeśa, T 1509, ch. 92, p. 708 *c*, strongly emphasizes the close relationship which unites the buddhakṣetra to thought, the external world to the mind: "Thought follows the external object. Confronted with something which conforms to its expectations, it does not produce hatred (*dveṣa*); confronted with things that are impure (*aśuddha*), transitory (*anitya*), etc., it does not produce greed (*lobha*); confronted with inexistent (*anupalabdha*) and empty (*śūnya*) things, it does not produce delusion (*moha*). Thus do Bodhisattvas adorn buddhakṣetras so that beings are easily converted. In the buddhakṣetras this is not difficult, for beings, deprived of the idea of a self, do not experience any passion (*kleśa*), such as avarice (*mātsarya*), craving (*rāga*), animosity (*vyāpāda*), etc. There are buddhakṣetras where all the trees never cease emitting the sounds of the true Law (*dharmaśabda*): "Non-birth (*ajāta*), non-extinction (*anirodha*), non-production (*anutpāda*), non-activity (*anabhisaṃskāra*), etc.". Beings hear only these wonderful sounds, and they do not hear others. Being of sharp faculties (*tīkṣṇendriya*), they grasp the true characteristics of dharmas. These splendours (*vyūha*) of the Buddha-fields are called pure buddhakṣetras, as it is said in the Sūtras of Amitābha (cf. Sukhāvatīvyūha, p. 82,*3*)... Besides, between internal and external dharmas, there is exerted a causality, whether for good or for bad. If bad vocal actions (*akuśalavākkarman*) abound, the land produces thorny bushes; if hypocrisy (*śāṭhya*) and illusion (*māyā*) abound, it produces rises (*utkūla*), dips (*nikūla*) and irregularities; if avarice (*mātsarya*) and greed (*lobha*) abound, the waters evaporate and stagnate, and the land produces sand and gravel. Conversely, if the above-mentioned misdeeds are not committed, the land is even (*sama*) and produces quantities of precious jewels. When the Buddha Maitreya appears, men will observe the ten paths of good action (*kuśalakarmapatha*), and the land will produce many jewels.

VI. *The purification of the Buddha-fields.* — The Bodhisattva who practises the three *vimokṣamukha* of emptiness (*śūnyatā*), signlessness (*ānimitta*) and wishlessness (*apraṇihita*) does not perceive any Buddha-field. However, since his wisdom is completed by great compassion (*mahākaruṇā*) and skill in the means of salvation (*upāyakauśalya*), "he adorns his body with the primary and secondary marks, he adorns his Buddha-field and causes beings to ripen" (Ch. IV, § 17). It is therefore not without reason that, in the present passage (I, § 11), Ratnākara and his companions question the Buddha on the purification (*pariśodhana*) of the buddhakṣetras. The question has already been posed and resolved in the Prajñāpāramitā:

Pañcaviṃśati, T 221, ch. 19, p. 136 *a* 12; T 223, ch. 26, p. 408 *b* 21; T 220, ch. 476, p. 411 *c* 14; Aṣṭādaśa, T 220, ch. 535, p. 749 *c* 20: Subhūti asks the Buddha: How do Bodhisattvas purify the buddhakṣetra? — The Buddha replies: Bodhisattvas who, from the first production of the thought of bodhi (*bodhicittotpāda*), eliminate their own gross actions (*duṣṭhulakarman*) of body (*kāya*), speech (*vāc*) and mind (*citta*) purify through this very deed those of other men. These gross actions are the ten paths of bad action (*akuśalakarmapatha*), from taking life (*prāṇātipāta*) to false views (*mithyādṛṣṭi*).

So therefore purifying the Buddha-fields is no other than purifying one's own mind and, by reaction, those of others. To obtain this result, the Bodhisattva should not only assemble all the Bodhisattva virtues (*guṇa*) but also formulate the great vows (*mahāpraṇidhāna*). It is also said that he secures an immense buddhakṣetra through his vows (*apramāṇabuddhakṣetrapraṇidhānaparigṛhīta*).

The importance of the vow is emphasized by the Upadeśa, T 1509, ch. 7, p. 108 *b*: The adornment of buddhakṣetras is a serious matter. On its own, the practice of the Bodhisattva virtues (*guṇa*) could not achieve it; the power of the vows (*praṇidhānabala*) is also needed. Thus an ox has indeed the strength to pull a cart, but in order to reach its destination, it also needs a driver. It is the same for the vows relating to pure universes: merit (*puṇya*) is comparable to the ox, and the vow (*praṇidhāna*) to the driver.

The purification of the Buddha-field is a long and exacting task, which continues throughout the length of the Bodhisattva's career and consists of at least three steps:

1. From the first stage, the *Pramuditā*, the Bodhisattva formulates ten great vows the seventh of which is concerned precisely with the *buddhakṣetrapariśodhana*: cf. Daśabhūmika, p. 15,*18-23*; Bodh. bhūmi, p. 275,*22*; 328,*19*. — See, for example, the vows formulated at the moment of his *cittotpāda* by Dharmākara, the future Amitābha, in the Sukhāvatīvyūha, p. 24-44.

2. In the third stage, the *Prabhākarī*, the Bodhisattva applies all his good roots to the purification of the buddhakṣetra (*sarvakuśalamūlānāṃ buddhakṣetrapariśodhanāya pariṇāmanā*): cf. Pañcaviṃśati, p. 219,*16*; Śatasāh., p. 1462,*4*; Āloka, p. 100,*10*.

According to the Yogācārabhūmi, T 1579, ch. 79, p. 736 *c* 24, it is from this third stage that the Bodhisattva, through the power of his vow, takes on birth in pure buddhakṣetras.

The Vimalakīrti explains, in Ch. IX, § 18, the conditions to be fulfilled in order to have access to pure lands.

3. Finally, in the eighth stage, the *Acalā*, the Bodhisattva, according to the expression in the Madhyāntavibhāga, p. 105,*21*, enjoys full sovereignty over the purity of the field (*kṣetraviśuddhivaśitā*).

In fact in this stage, knowledge, freed of all the fetters, no longer grasps any characteristic and functions spontaneously without effort:

this is the *anābhoganirnimittavihāra* (Bodh. bhūmi, p. 350,*12*; Siddhi, p. 617). — In the eighth stage, the Bodhisattva is *anutpattikadharmakṣāntiprāpta*, in possession of the certainty of the non-arising of dharmas (Daśabhūmika, p. 64,*5*; Bodh. bhūmi, p. 350,*27*); he receives the definitive prediction (*vyākaraṇa*) concerning his final triumph (Lalitavistara, p. 35,*21*; Sūtrālaṃkāra, p. 20,*15*; 141,*27*; 166,*12*), and he is assured (*niyata, niyatipatita*) of reaching supreme and perfect enlightenment (Bodh. bhūmi, p. 367,*12*); he becomes an *avaivartika*, irreversible Bodhisattva (Bodh. bhūmi, p. 235,*18*), assured of never turning back (*avinivartanīyatā, avinivartanīyadharmatā*: Śikṣāsam., p. 313,*20*). Finally and above all, he abandons his fleshly body (*māṃsakāya*), born of bonds and actions (*bandhanakarmaja*) and subject to birth and death (*cyutyupapatti*), and takes on a body born of the absolute (*dharmadhātujakāya*), released from the existences of the triple world (Upadeśa, T 1509, ch. 12, p. 146 *a* 28; ch. 28, p. 264 *b* 4-7; ch. 30, p. 283 *a* 29-*b* 3; 284 *a* 27; ch. 34, p. 309 *b* 8; ch. 38, p. 340 *a* 2; ch. 74, p. 580 *a* 14-16).

The Pañcaviṃśati, p. 217,*3* and 223,*21*, and the Śatasāh., p. 1458,*1* and 1469,*21*, range among the characteristics of the eighth stage the vision of the Buddha-fields and the adornment of the field in conformity with this vision (*buddhakṣetradarśanaṃ teṣāṃ ca buddhakṣetrāṇāṃ yathādṛṣṭiṃ svakṣetraniṣpādanatā*). The same sources explain: *yad svakṣetra eva sthitvāparimāṇāni buddhakṣetrāṇi paśyati na cāsya buddhakṣetrasaṃjñā bhavati. īśvaracakravartibhūmau sthitas trisāhasramahāsāhasralokadhātūn saṃkrāmati svakṣetraṃ ca niṣpādayati*: "The Bodhisattva, remaining in his own field, sees innumerable Buddha-fields, but no longer has the notion of buddhakṣetras. Holding the rank of a sovereign universal king, he passes through the great chiliocosms and in consequence sets up his own field".

The Upadeśa, T 1509, ch. 50, p. 418 *a* 26, comments on this passage: There are Bodhisattvas who, through the power of their superknowledges (*ṛddhyabhijñā*), pass through the ten regions by flying, contemplate the pure universes and seize their characteristics (*nimittāny udgṛhṇanti*) so as to adorn their own fields with them. There are Bodhisattvas whom a Buddha guides through the ten regions in order to show them the pure universes; they seize the characteristics of these pure worlds, and make the following vow: Just like the Buddha Lokeśvararāja (of the Sukhāvatīvyūha, p. 14,*18*), I shall go to the ten regions, inaugurating the Law and gathering bhikṣus together, and I shall address the pure universes. Finally, there are Bodhisattvas who, even while remaining in their original fields, make use of the Buddha-eye to see the pure universes of ten regions; at first they seize the pure characteristics, but having then obtained detachment of the mind (*asaṅgacittatā*), they revert to indifference.

On the Buddha lands, also see Hōbōgirin, s.v. *Butsudo*, p. 198-203.

NOTE II: CITTOTPĀDA, ADHYĀŚAYA AND ĀŚAYA

(Cf. Ch. I, § 13).

The Bodhisattva career begins with the *bodhicittotpāda* "the production of the thought of *bodhi* or enlightenment" and ends with the *anuttarāyāṃ samyaksaṃbodhāv abhisaṃbodhiḥ* "the arrival at supreme and perfect enlightenment", i.e. omniscience (*sarvajñatā*) which rightfully belongs to the Buddhas.

I. At the time of the *cittotpāda*, the Bodhisattva formulates the vow one day to reach supreme and perfect enlightenment so as to devote himself to the welfare and happiness of all beings.

Bodhisattvaprātimokṣasūtra, IHQ, VII, 1931, p. 274; Bodh. bhūmi, p. 12: *bodhisattvasya prathamaś cittotpādaḥ sarvabodhisattvasamyakpraṇidhānānām ādyaṃ tadanyasamyakpraṇidhānasaṃgrahakam ... sa khalu bodhisattvo bodhāya cittaṃ praṇidadhad evaṃ cittam abhisaṃskaroti vācaṃ ca bhāṣate: aho batāham anuttarāṃ samyaksaṃbodhim abhisaṃbudhyeyaṃ sarvasattvānāṃ cārthakaraḥ syām, atyantaniṣṭhe nirvāṇe pratiṣṭhāpayeyaṃ tathāgatajñāne ca. sa evam ātmanaś ca bodhiṃ sattvārthaṃ ca prārthayamānaś cittam utpādayati... tasmāt sa cittotpādo bodhyālambanaḥ sattvālambanaś ca.*

During the course of the Bodhisattva's career, the *cittotpāda* is continuously evolving, in as much as it is associated with quantities of good dharmas, particularly with high resolve (*adhyāśaya*) and good tendencies (*āśaya, kalyāṇāśaya*).

Akṣayamatisūtra, quoted in Sūtrālaṃkāra, p. 16,*17*: For a Bodhisattva, the first *cittotpāda* is like earth (*pṛthivī*) because it is the soil (*pratiṣṭhā*) in which all the Buddha attributes and the stores (*saṃbhāra*) connected with them should grow. — Associated with good tendencies (*āśaya*), the *cittotpāda* is like pure gold (*kalyāṇasuvarṇa*) because it prevents any modification of the high resolve (*adhyāśaya*) concerned with the welfare and happiness of beings. — Associated with effort (*prayoga*), the *cittotpāda* is like the new moon in a bright fortnight (*śuklapakṣanavacandra*) because it culminates in the increase of good dharmas (*kuśaladharma*). — Associated with high resolve (*adhyāśaya*), the *cittotpāda* is like fire (*vahni*) because it leads to an ever higher superiority (*uttarottaraviśeṣa*), like a fire due to the qualities of a special fuel.

It is possible to single out, with the Sūtrālaṃkārā, p. 14,*7*, four main categories of *cittotpāda* corresponding to four points in the Bodhisattva's career:

1. The *cittotpāda* associated with adherence (*ādhimokṣika*) in the preparatory stage, called Stage of the practice of firm adherence (*adhimukticaryābhūmi*).
2. The *cittotpāda* associated with pure high resolve (*śuddhādhyāśayika*), in the first seven stages.
3. The *cittotpāda* of fruition (*vaipākika*), in stages eight and nine.
4. The obstacle-free (*anāvaraṇika*) *cittotpāda*, in the tenth stage.

II. *Adhyāśaya*, high resolve, is practically synonymous with *cittotpāda*: they are inseparable ideas. In the versions of the Vimalakīrti, *adhyāśaya* is rendered by *lhag paḥi bsam pa*; *shên hsin* 深心 "profound thought" (K); *shang i lo* 上意樂 or *tsêng shang i lo* 增上意樂 "high sentiment" (H).

The Prajñās (Pañcaviṃśati, p. 214,*13*; 217,*20*; Śatasāh., p. 1454,*12*; 1458,*22*) place the *adhyāśaya* at the head of the ten preparations (*parikarman*) of the first stage, the stage later to be called *Pramuditā* or *Śuddhādhyāśayabhūmi* (cf. Bodh. bhūmi, p. 367,*8*), and they define it: *sarvākārajñatāpratisaṃyuktair manasikāraiḥ sarvakuśalamūlasamudānayatā* "the acquisition of all the good roots through reflections concerning knowledge of all the aspects". In other words, the acquisition of the good roots which will culminate in the omniscience proper to the Buddhas.

The Bodh. bhūmi, p. 313,*4* offers a quite similar definition: *tatra śraddhāpūrvo dharmavicayapūrvakaś ca buddhadharmeṣu yo 'dhimokṣaḥ pratyavagamo niścayo bodhisattvasya so 'dhyāśaya ity ucyate*: "High resolve is an adhesion, a comprehension, a determination preceded by faith, preceded by analysis of the Law and directed towards the Buddha attributes".

These definitions directed only towards the Buddha attributes are wanting in that they do not show up enough the altruistic character of *adhyāśaya*. We should not lose sight of the fact that great pity and great compassion are precisely included among these attributes.

Thus the Madhyāntavibhāga, p. 85,*1*, quite rightly speaks of the *sarvasattvahitasukhādhyāśaya*, i.e. the high resolve to bring about the welfare and happiness of all beings.

According to the Bodh. bhūmi, p. 18,*17*, the high resolve "to bring about the welfare (*hita*)" is the desire to put beings in a good position (*kuśale sthāne pratiṣṭhāpanakāmatā*) or establish them in Nirvāṇa; the high resolve "to bring about the happiness (*sukha*)" is the desire to supply the wretched with resources (*vastūpasaṃharaṇakāmatā*).

Just like the *cittotpāda*, the *adhyāśaya* multiplies and diversifies during the course of the Bodhisattva's career. The Avataṃsaka, T 278, ch. 24, p. 551 *a* 26, distinguishes ten kinds of them, and the Bodh. bhūmi, p. 313,*7*, fifteen. These are scholastic distinctions of little value.

According to the Sūtrālaṃkāra, p. 176,*21*, the *adhyāśaya* is impure (*aśuddha*) in Bodhisattvas who have as yet not entered the stages, pure (*viśuddha*) in those who have entered them, very pure (*suviśuddha*) in those who have reached the irreversible stage (*avinivartanīyabhūmi*), i.e. the eighth stage.

III. *Āśaya* or *kalyāṇāśaya*, good tendency, designates a whole collection of good pointers associated with the *cittotpāda* in order to make it progress. In the versions of the Vimalakīrti, *āśaya* is rendered by *bsam pa*; *chih hsin* 直心 "right thought" (K); *shun i lo* 純意樂 "pure sentiment" (H).

The Bodh. bhūmi lists seven *kalyāṇāśaya* (p. 312,*5*) and ten *āśayaśuddhi* (p. 333,*4*).

More generally, the *āśaya*, under different aspects (*ākāra*), favours the practice of the perfections (*pāramitābhāvanā*). These aspects which are six in number — a tendency which is insatiable (*atṛpta*), enduring (*vipula*), joyful (*mudita*), beneficent (*upakāra*), spotless (*nirlepa*) and virtuous (*kalyāṇa*) — are detailed at length in the Sūtrālaṃkāra, p. 102,*13*, and the Saṃgraha, p. 188 sq.

NOTE III: NAIRĀTMYA, ANUTPĀDA AND KṢĀNTI

(Cf. Ch. III, § 19).

I. *Nairātmya*. — 1. The Small Vehicle rejects the belief in the individual (*pudgalagrāha*) and proclaims the inexistence of the individual (*pudgalanairātmya*).

Bodh. bhūmi, p. 280,*21*: *tatredaṃ pudgalanairātmyaṃ yan naiva te vidyamānā dharmāḥ pudgalāḥ, nāpi vidyamānadharmavinirmukto 'nyaḥ pudgalo vidyate*: "The *pudgalanairātmya* signifies that no existing dharma is an individual, and that there is no individual outside existing dharmas".

In contrast, the Small Vehicle accepts that the psycho-physical phenomena of existence (*skandha*), that things (*dharma*), have a self-nature (*svabhāva*) and marks (*lakṣaṇa*). It affirms the existence of the phenomena alone (*skandhamātravāda*).

2. The Great Vehicle rejects both the belief in the individual (*pudgalagrāha*) and the belief in things (*dharmagrāha*) and simultaneously proclaims the inexistence of the individual (*pudgalanairātmya*) and the inexistence of things (*dharmanairātmya*).

a. With regard to the *pudgalanairātmya*, here are a few among the thousands of ceaselessly repeated formulae:

Pañcaviṃśati, p. 39,*3*: *na cātmā upalabhyate na sattvo na jīvo na poṣo na puruṣo na pudgalo na manujo 'py upalabhyante.*

Ibid., p. 99,*17*: *evam ātmasattvajīvapoṣapuruṣapudgalamanujamānavakārakavedakajānakapaśyakāḥ sarva ete prajñaptidharmāḥ sarva ete anutpādā anirodhā yāvad eva nāmamātreṇa vyavahriyante.*

b. Bodh. bhūmi, p. 280,*23*: *tatredaṃ dharmanairātmyaṃ yat sarveṣv abhilāpyeṣu vastuṣu sarvābhilāpasvabhāvo dharmo na vidyate*: "The *dharmanairātmya* signifies that, in all things open to designation, there exists no dharma that is not a mere designation".

Pañcaviṃśati, p. 146,*9*: *bodhisattvo mahāsattva ātmānaṃ nopalabhate yāvat sattvajīvapoṣapuruṣapudgalamanujamānavakārakavedakajānakapaśyakān nopalabhate atyantaviśuddhitām upādāya yāvad vyastasamastān skandhadhātvāyatanapratītyasamutpādān nopalabhate atyantaviśuddhitām upādāya*: "By basing himself on absolute purity the Bodhisattva does not perceive either a self, or a being, or a living being, or a feeding being, or a man, or an individual, or a Manu-born, or a young man, or an active, feeling, knowing or seeing subject. By basing himself on absolute purity, The Bodhisattva does not perceive, isolated or grouped, either aggregates, or elements, or bases of consciousness".

II. *Anutpāda*. — In its interminable Sūtras, the Great Vehicle especially stresses the thesis which is particular to it: the *dharmanairātmya*, i.e. the inexistence, the non-arising (*anutpāda*) of dharmas.

This is demonstrated by Nāgārjuna in a famous *kārikā* (Madh. vṛtti, p. 12,*13*):

na svato nāpi parato na dvābhyāṃ nāpy ahetutaḥ,
utpannā jātu vidyante bhāvāḥ kvacana kecana.

"Not of itself, nor of another, nor of one and the other, nor independently of causes, do entities arise, wherever (*kva cana*), whenever (*jātu*), whatever (*ke cana*)".

1. Things do not arise of themselves: cf. Madh. vṛtti, p. 13,*7*:

tasmād dhi tasya bhavane na guṇo 'sti kaścij
jātasya janma punar eva ca naiva yuktam.

"There is no virtue in this being born of this; it is inadmissible that a thing once born could be born again".

In other words, there is no advantage in something being born of its own substance, in a shoot arising from a shoot, since it already exists. It is inadmissible that something already born should be born again, for if the seed is reproduced as a seed, the shoot, trunk, branches would never arise.

2. Things do not arise of others: cf. Madh. vṛtti, p. 36,*4*:

na hi svabhāvo bhāvānāṃ pratyayādiṣu vidyate,
avidyamāne svabhāve parabhāvo na vidyate.
anyat pratītya yadi nāma paro 'bhaviṣyaj
jāyeta tarhi bahulaḥ śikhino 'ndhakāraḥ,
sarvasya janma ca bhavet khalu sarvataś ca
tulyaṃ paratvam akhile 'janake 'pi yasmāt.

"Things do not arise of others: in fact the self-nature of things does not exist in their [generative] conditions, etc.; the self-nature of things not existing, how could the conditions be of a different nature [from that of the effects]?"

In other words, as long as the effect is not produced, its self-nature does not exist. Hence the conditions which should engender it cannot be of a different nature from that effect, since the latter does not yet exist.

"If another arises by reason of another, then obviously a thick darkness could arise from a flame. All things arise from all things, because the quality of being other [than the effect] is the same [in the cause] and also in all things that are not generative".

In other words, if in order to be a generative cause, it is enough to be other than the effect, anything would arise from anything: a flame could produce darkness, and a barleycorn could yield a rice shoot. In fact the quality of being other than the effect would also apply as much to everything that is not the cause as to the cause itself.

3. Things do not arise of themselves and others at the same time: cf. Madh. vṛtti, p. 38,*1* and 233,*4*: *dvābhyām api nopajāyante bhāvāḥ, ubhayapakṣābhihitadoṣaprasaṅgāt, pratyekam utpādāsāmarthyāc ca. yakṣyati hi:*

syād ubhābhyāṃ kṛtaṃ duḥkhaṃ syād ekaikakṛtam yadi.
yadi hy ekaikena duḥkhasya karaṇaṃ syāt, syāt tadānīm ubhābhyāṃ kṛtaṃ duḥkham. na caikaikakṛtaṃ taduktadoṣāt. na caikaikena prāṇātipāte 'kṛte dvābhyāṃ kṛta iti vyapadeśo dṛṣṭaḥ.

"Things do not arise either of themselves and others at the same time, for this would result in the defects already mentioned in the two preceding theses and because, taken separately, [the self and the other] are incapable of producing [the effect]. It would be said: 'The [world] of suffering could be created by both at the same time, if it could be created by both separately'. If the world of suffering could be brought about by [the self or the other] separately, then it could be created by both at the same time. But it is not created [by the self or the other] separately for the impossibilities mentioned above. If a murder has not been committed by two people taken separately, they cannot be accused of having committed it together".

4. Finally, things do not arise without cause: cf. Madh. vṛtti, p. 38,4: *ahetuto 'pi notpadyante,*
hetāv asati kāryaṃ ca kāraṇaṃ ca na vidyate
iti vakṣyamāṇadoṣaprasaṅgāt.
gṛhyeta naiva ca jagad yadi hetuśūnyaṃ
syād yadvad eva gaganotpalavarṇagandhau
ityādidoṣaprasaṅgāt.

"Things do not arise either without cause, for this would result in the defect we will point out by saying: 'Without causality, there exists neither effect nor cause'; and it would result in this other defect that: 'If the universe were empty of causes, it would not be perceived, just as the colour and scent of a lotus in the sky are not perceived'".

In consequence, since there is no arising either of itself, or of another, or of both, or without cause, things have no self-nature (*svabhāva*). It is for the Ratnameghasūtra (quoted in Madh. vṛtti, p. 225,9) to conclude:

ādiśāntā hy anutpannāḥ prakṛtyaiva ca nirvṛtāḥ
dharmās te vivṛtā nātha dharmacakrapravartane.

"By causing the wheel of the Law to turn, O Master, you have explained that dharmas are originally calmed, unarisen, and are naturally in Nirvāṇa".

III. *Anutpattikadharmakṣānti.* — As it has just been described above, the non-arising of dharmas constitutes the corner-stone of the Mahāyāna, but it is only gradually that the Bodhisattva reaches the certainty of it. This is called *anutpattikadharmakṣānti* "the certainty (or conviction) of the non-arising of dharmas". The analysis of this compound is clear:

Lalitavistara, p. 36,*9*: *anutpattikeṣu dharmeṣu kṣāntiḥ*.

Vajracchedikā, p. 58,*9*: *nirātmakeṣv anutpattikeṣu dharmeṣu kṣāntiḥ*.

Sūtrālaṃkāra, p. 163,*20*: *anutpattikadharmeṣu kṣāntiḥ*.

Normally *kṣānti*, in Pāli *khanti*, means "patience, endurance", but in the expression we are concerned with here, it takes the meaning of *intellectual receptivity* (Edgerton), admission, conviction, certainty.

It is not impossible that *kṣānti*, in the sense of patience, is taken from the root *kṣam* "to endure, bear", while *kṣānti*, in the sense of admission, comes from the root *kam* "to like, be inclined to". In the latter case it would be a wrong Sanskritization of the Pāli *khanti* (cf. G.H. SASAKI, *Khanti, kānti, kṣānti*, Journ. of Indian and Buddhist Studies, VII, No. 1, 1958, p. 359).

In Sanskrit texts, *kṣānti* is the third of the six or ten great perfections (*pāramitā*) of the Bodhisattva. Generally three categories of *kṣānti* are distinguished: 1. the *parāpakāramarṣaṇakṣānti*, patience in enduring the misdeeds of others; 2. the *duḥkādhivāsanakṣānti*, patience in accepting suffering; 3. the *dharmanidhyānādhimuktikṣānti*, patience consisting in contemplating and adhering to the profound Law (Sūtrālaṃkāra, p. 108, *20*; Saṃgraha, p. 191; Bodh. bhūmi, p. 195; cf. NĀGĀRJUNA, *Traité*, p. 865-926). The *anutpattikadharmakṣānti* forms part of this third category.

Like the *cittotpāda* and the *adhyāśaya* (above, Appendix, Note II), it is capable of progression in the course of the Bodhisattva's career: it can be a purely verbal (*ghoṣānugā*) conviction, preparatory (*anulomikī*) or finally definitively acquired (*pratilabdhā*).

This is explained by the Sukhāvatīvyūha, p. 112,*12*: *bodhisattvās tisraḥ kṣāntīḥ pratilabhante yad idaṃ ghoṣānugām anulomikīm anutpattikadharmakṣāntiṃ ca*. — Also see, though with some divergencies, Avataṃsaka, T 279, ch. 44, p. 232 *b* 6-26; Manuṣyendraprajñāpāramitāsūtra, T 245, ch. 1, p. 826 *b* 23-24; Dhyānasamādhisūtra, T 614, ch. 2, p. 285 *a-b*; Samādhirāja, I, p. 76.

1. At the beginning, in the first five stages, the Bodhisattvas accept the idea of the non-arising of things, but this is only through *adhimukti*, adhesion, approbation, verbal professing (*ghoṣānuga*): the Bodhisattvas are not in definitive possession of the certainty. Cf. Aṣṭasāh., p. 856,*25*: *bodhisattvāḥ prajñāpāramitāyāṃ carantaḥ sarvadharmā anutpattikā ity adhimuñcanti na ca tāvad anutpattikadharmakṣāntipratilabdhā bhavanti*.

2. In the sixth stage, the *Abhimukhī*, examining in every way the emptiness of dharmas, they possess an intense preparatory conviction (*anulomikī kṣāntiḥ*), but they still have not gained entry into the true *anutpattikadharmakṣānti*. Cf. Daśabhūmika, p. 47,*17*: *sa evaṃsvabhāvān sarvadharmān pratyavekṣamāṇo 'nusṛjann anulomayann avilomayan śraddadhann abhiyan pratiyann avikalpayann anusaran vyavalokayan pratipadyamānaḥ, ṣaṣṭhīm abhimukhīṃ bodhisattvabhūmim anuprāpnoti tīkṣṇayānulomikyā kṣāntyā. na ca tāvad anutpattikadharmakṣāntimukham anuprāpnoti.*

3. Finally, the Bodhisattvas "obtain" (*pratilabhante*: cf. Sad. puṇḍarīka, p. 136,*9-10*; 419,*6*) the *anutpattikadharmakṣānti*. This is what is called the definitive obtainment (*pratilābha, pratilambha, pratilambhatā*) of the *kṣānti* (Sad. puṇḍarīka, p. 266,*1*; 437,*1*; Lalitavistara, p. 36,*9*; 440,*21*).

According to the unanimous certification of the texts, this obtainment occurs in the eighth stage, the *Acalā*: cf. Daśabhūmika, p. 64,*5*; Sūtrālaṃkāra, p. 122,*2*; 131,*17*; Bodh. bhūmi, p. 350,*27*; Madhyāntavibhāga, p. 105,*11*.

The acquisition of the *kṣānti* is accompanied by a prediction (*vyākaraṇa*) concerning the final triumph of the Bodhisattva: cf. Lalita, p. 35,*21*; Sūtrālaṃkāra, p. 20,*15*; 141,*27*; 166,*12*. This is clearly brought out in a passage of the Sad. puṇḍarīka, p. 266,*1-2*, which attributes to three thousand living beings the joint obtainment of the *anutpattikakṣānti* and the *vyākaraṇa*: *trayāṇāṃ prāṇisahasrāṇām anutpattikadharmakṣāntipratilābho 'bhūt, trayāṇāṃ ca prāṇisahasrāṇāṃ anuttarāyāṃ samyaksaṃbodhau vyākaraṇapratilābho 'bhūt.*

[Naturally here we are dealing with the great *vyākaraṇa*, the definitive prediction, for the texts also distinguish several kinds of *vyākaraṇa*: cf. P. Demiéville, *Le Concile de Lhasa*, Paris, 1952, p. 141 in the notes. See above, III, §50, n. 89.]

Finally, because the Bodhisattvas are in possession of an irreversible conviction (*avaivartikakṣāntipratilabdha*: cf. Sad. puṇḍarīka, p. 259,*13*), the eighth stage where they win it is also called "irreversible stage" (*avivartyabhūmi* in Daśabhūmika, p. 71,*12*, *avaivartikabhūmi* in Bodh. bhūmi, p. 235,*18*).

NOTE IV: MORALITY IN THE TWO VEHICLES

(Cf. Ch. III, § 34).

It is in the realm of morality that the gap between the two Vehicles appears most clearly. The homily addressed by Vimalakīrti to Upāli (III, § 34-35) plainly demonstrates the gulf that separates them. On this subject, see L. DE LA VALLÉE POUSSIN, *Le Vinaya et la pureté d'intention*, in Notes bouddhiques, VII, Brussels, 1929; P. DEMIÉVILLE, *Bosatsukai*, in Hōbōgirin, p. 142-146; NĀGĀRJUNA, *Traité*, p. 770-864.

I. *Morality in the Small Vehicle.* — This is a fine edifice of scholasticism enclosing Buddhists in a whole network of regulations.

1. Morality in general consists in avoiding the offences of body, speech and mind, offences which are essentially actions of thought, voluntary and morally fruitful. The ten offences to be avoided are: 1. taking life (*prāṇātipāta*), 2. taking the not-given (*adattādāna*), 3. sexual misconduct (*kāmamithyācāra*), 4. false speech (*mṛṣāvāda*), 5. slander (*paiśunyavāda*), 6. harsh speech (*pāruṣyavāda*), 7. useless speech (*saṃbhinnapralāpa*), 8. covetousness (*abhidhyā*), 9. animosity (*vyāpāda*), 10. false views (*mithyādṛṣṭi*).

The Karmavibhaṅgas go into long details regarding the pleasant or unpleasant fruit (good or bad destinies) resulting from the observance or the transgression of morality.

Alongside morality in a general sense, simple natural honesty (*prakṛtikauśalya*), there is a morality of commitment (*saṃvaraśīla*) which constitutes the first element of the Buddhist path, the other two being concentration (*samādhi*) and wisdom (*prajñā*). Depending on their state, Buddhists commit themselves by means of vows to observing a certain number of rules of training (*śikṣāpada*).

A lay Buddhist (*upāsaka*) usually pledges himself to undertake the fivefold moral precepts (*pañcaśīla*) and in consequence abstains from:: 1. taking life, 2. taking the not-given, 3. sexual misconduct, 4. false speech, 5. intoxicants (*surāmaireyamadyapāna*). However, four or six days a month, he can also take the eight-fold morality (*aṣṭāṅgaśīla*): he then commits himself to remain for a day and a night in the discipline of fasting (*upavāsa*) consisting in taking only one meal a day, and observing the eight complementary precepts forbidding: 1. taking life, 2. taking the not-given, 3. incontinence (*abrahmacarya*), 4. false speech, 5. intoxicants, 6. meals at the wrong time (*vikālabhojana*), 7. dancing, singing, music and attendance at amusements (*nṛtyagītavādyavisūkadarśana*) as well as the use of perfumes, garlands, unguents and cosmetics (*gandhamālyavilepanavarṇakadhāraṇa*), 8. high seats (*uccaśayanamahāśayana*).

The novice (*śrāmaṇera*) is already committed to ten rules of training (*daśa śikṣāpada*) in the religious life which forbid him, at all times: 1. taking life, 2. taking the not-given, 3. incontinence, 4. false speech, 5. intoxicants, 6. meals at the wrong time, 7. dancing, singing, music and attendance at amusements, 8. the use of perfumes, garlands, unguents and cosmetics, 9. high seats, 10. accepting gold or silver (*jātarūparajatapratigrahaṇa*).

These ten rules of training in the religious life serve as the foundation of the monastic code (*prātimokṣa*) of the monks and nuns who decide how they should be applied. Roughly speaking, the disciplinary code of monks (*bhikṣuprātimokṣa*) consists of 250 articles, and that of nuns (*bhikṣuṇīprātimokṣa*), 500 articles. The prātimokṣa is divided into eight chapters: 1. offences leading to defeat (*pārājika*). 2. offences leading to temporary expulsion from the community (*saṃghāvaśeṣa*), 3. indeterminate (*aniyata*) offences, 4. offences leading to the forfeiture of a wrongfully obtained object (*niḥsargika* or *naiḥsargika pātayantika*), 5. offences leading to expiation (*pātayantika*), 6. offences to be declared (*pratideśanīya*), 7. advice for decent behaviour (*śaikṣa*), 8. procedures for settling disputes (*adhikaraṇaśamatha*).

In Buddhism, the observance of morality is subject to strict control: 1. Once a fortnight, during the celebration of *uposatha*, monks are required publicly to declare their lapses from the prātimokṣa, 2. occasionally, monks and laymen who have been guilty of an infraction (*atyaya*) can admit it before a competent person in such a way as to be absolved from it (cf. above, III, §33, note 63).

II. *Morality in the Great Vehicle* — The Mahāyāna undermined the old Buddhist morality, both for mystical and philosophical reasons:

1. The morality (*śīla*) of the Śrāvaka is replaced by the higher morality (*adhiśīla*) of the Bodhisattva. The Bodhisattva who places his morality at the service of beings partly escapes the regulation: he can commit what the Śrāvakas consider offences of disobedience (*pratikṣepasāvadya*) and carry out any action, whether bodily, vocal or mental, which is favourable to beings, as long as he is irreproachable. Furthermore, because of his skill in means, he can commit any act of nature (*prakṛtisāvadya*), taking life, theft, sexual misconduct, false speech, with the aim of helping others (cf. Saṃgraha, p. 212-217; Bodh. bhūmi, p. 165-166; Hōbōgirin, s.v. *Bosatsukai*, p. 143-146).

2. For philosophical reasons, it is understood that the perfection of morality should be fulfilled by basing oneself on the non-existence of a fault and its opposite (*śīlapāramitā pūrayitavyā āpattyanāpatty-anadhyāpattitām upādāya:* Pañcaviṃśati, p. 18,*10*; Śatasāh., p. 56,*4*). — The Upadeśa (T 1509, ch. 14, p. 163 *c*) remarks: "If morality consists in avoiding wrong and practising good, why speak of the non-existence of a fault and its opposite? To speak of their non-existence is not a false view (*mithyādṛṣṭi*) or an offensive conception (*sthūlacitta*). If the mark of dharmas is penetrated in depth and the concentration on emptiness (*śūnyatāsamādhi*) is practised, then through the wisdom-eye (*prajñācakṣus*) it can be seen that a fault does not exist. If the fault does not exist, its opposite, faultlessness (*anāpatti*) does not exist either. Moreover, a being (*sattva*) not existing, the offence of murder (*atipātāpatti*) does not exist either. The offence not existing at all, the precept (*śīla*) which forbids it does not exist any more. And why? There must be an offence of murder for the forbidding of murder to exist; however, since there is no offence of murder, its forbidding does not exist".

In other words, the *pudgala-* and *dharmanairātnya* remove any basis for morality. Such is Vimalakīrti's opinion (III, § 34-35; VIII, § 8-10, 25).

NOTE V: THE ILLNESSES OF THE BUDDHA

(Cf. Ch. III, § 43).

The question often arises, as much in the canonical texts as the postcanonical, of the illnesses and torments endured by the Buddha: 1. injury to the foot, 2. thorn prick, 3. return with an empty bowl, 4. Sundarī's slander, 5. Ciñcā's slander, 6. chewing of barley, 7. six years of austerities, 8. dysentery, 9. head and back-ache, etc. (See the references in NĀGĀRJUNA, *Traité*, p. 507-509).

How can a being as perfect as the Buddha be subject to suffering? The problem held the attention of adepts of both Vehicles, and scholasticism suggested various answers:

1. *Small Vehicle.* — 1. The first explanation, conforming strictly to the doctrine of the fruition of actions (*karmavipāka*), is that the Buddha, through these torments and illnesses, is expiating certain faults from his earlier existences. The Vinaya of the Mūlasarvāstivādins (T 1448, ch. 18, p. 94-96; *Gilgit Manuscripts* III, Part 1, p. 211-218), the *Pubbakammapiloti* in the Pāli Apadāna, I, p. 299-301, and the Hsing ch'i hsing ching, T 197, p. 164-172 (a work translated into

Chinese in 194 by K'ang Mêng-hsiang) tell of a series of ten misdeeds for which the Buddha was to blame in his previous lives and which incurred the ten torments in question during his last existence. This is because, says the Divya, p. 416,*12*, the Victorious Ones themselves are not freed of their actions (*karmabhis te 'pi jinā na muktāḥ*).

2. It was not long before such a radical application of the Law of Karman appeared shocking in the case of the Buddha. Compromises were found. One of these consists in saying that, whatever may happen to him, the Buddha only experiences pleasant sensations. Cf. the *Devadahasutta* (Majjhima, II, p. 227; Madhyama, T 25, No. 19, ch. 4, p. 444 *c* 16-17): "If beings experience pleasure or suffering because of their past actions, then, O monks, the Tathāgata in bygone days performed good actions since at present he experiences pure and pleasant sensations" (*sace, bhikkhave, sattā pubbekatahetu sukhadukkhaṃ paṭisaṃvedenti, addhā, bhikkhave, tathāgato pubbesu-katakammakārī, yaṃ etarhi evarūpā anāsavā sukhā vedanā vedeti*).

3. By means of another compromise, it is to be noted that besides the torments and illnesses resulting from past actions, there are others which are simply due to present physical conditions. This is what the Buddha himself explains to Sīvaka in Saṃyutta, IV, p. 230-231 (cf. Saṃyukta, T 99, No. 977, ch. 35, p. 252 *c*-253 *a*; T 100, No. 211, ch. 11, p. 452 *b-c*). This sūtra, while not expressly saying it, implies that the Buddha is only subject to discomfort resulting from physical conditions (cf. P. DEMIÉVILLE, in Hōbōgirin, *Byō*, p. 234). This is also the thesis of the Milinda, p. 134-136, which only recalls the Buddha's illnesses — injury to the foot, dysentery (Dīgha, II, p. 127), bodily trouble (Vinaya, I, p. 278-280), wind ailment (Saṃyutta, I, p. 174) — in order to assert forthwith that none of the sensations felt by the Bhagavat result from action (*na -tthi bhagavato kammavipākajā vedanā*).

4. The docetist sects of the Small Vehicle, Mahāsāṃghikas, Uttarāpathakas, quote as their authority a passage of the Scriptures (Aṅguttara, II, p. 38,*30*; Saṃyutta, III, p. 140,*16*): "Just as a lotus, blue, red or white, born in water, grown in water, rises above the surface without being sullied by the water, so the Tathāgata, born in the world, grown in the world, remains vanquisher of the world, unsullied by the world" (*seyyathāpi uppalaṃ vā padumaṃ vā puṇḍarīkaṃ vā udake jātaṃ udake saṃvaddhaṃ udakā accuggamma ṭhāti anupalittaṃ udakena, evaṃ eva kho tathāgato loke jāto loke saṃvaddho lokaṃ abhibhuyya viharati anupalitto lokena*). These sects conclude from this

(Kathāvatthu, p. 271,5) that for the Buddha and the holy one "all dharmas are pure" (*arahato sabbe dhammā anāsavā*) and that the eight worldly states (*lokadharma*), gain, loss, etc., have no grasp on him.

5. The Vaibhāṣikas assert on the contrary that the birth-body (*janmakāya*) of the Buddha is exclusively impure (*sāsrava*), enveloped in ignorance (*avidyānivṛta*), bound by the fetter of desire (*tṛṣṇāsaṃyojana*) and an object of the passion of others. Being led to interpret the scriptural passage invoked above by the Mahāsāṃghikas, they resorted to distinctions: This Sūtra, they say, refers to the Law-body (*dharmakāya*), and is therefore not conclusive. "The Tathāgata, born in the world, grown in the world": this refers to the birth-body (*janmakāya*); "holds himself above the world, is not sullied by worldly dharmas": this concerns the Law-body (Vibhāṣā, T 1545, ch. 76, p. 392 *a*; tr. L. DE LA VALLÉE POUSSIN, MCB, I, 1931, p. 112). The Vibhāṣā goes on to show through concrete examples how it happened that the Buddha encountered the eight worldly dharmas (*lokadharma*): 1. gain (*lābha*), 2. loss (*alābha*), 3. glory (*yaśas*), 4. ignominy (*ayaśas*), 5. blame (*nindā*), 6. praise (*praśaṃsā*), 7. happiness (*sukha*), 8. suffering (*duḥkha*). "Thus the Buddha suffered from ailments of the head, back, stomach; his foot was injured, his blood flowed".

II. *Great Vehicle.* — The general tendency of Mahāyānasūtras, represented here by Vimalakīrti, is to contrast the real body, which goes under the title of *dharmakāya*, with the fictitious bodies (*nirmāṇakāya*) which are manifested in the ten worlds (*daśadhātukāya*). The latter are simple transformations arising from the *upāyakauśalya* of the Buddhas; the former is inexpressible, transcendental: it is neither *skandha*, nor *dhātu*, nor *āyatana*, nor form, nor eye, nor visual understanding...

1. Mahāparinirvāṇasūtra, T 374, ch. 3, p. 382 *c* 27 (cf. Hōbōgirin, p. 178): Then the Blessed One again said to Kāśyapa: The body of the Tathāgata is a permanent body, an indestructible body, a diamond body (*vajrakāya*); it is in no way a body mixed with food; it is the *dharmakāya*. — The Bodhisattva Kāśyapa said to the Buddha: Blessed One, a body such as you speak of is in no way visible to me. I only see a body which is impermanent, destructible, atomic, mixed with food, etc. Why does the Buddha have to enter Nirvāṇa? — The Buddha said: Kāśyapa, do not say that the body of the Tathāgata is fragile and destructible like those of worldlings. Know this, excellent man! The body of the Tathāgata is solid and indestructible for

innumerable millions of kalpas. It is in no way the body of a man or god; it is in no way subject to fear; it is in no way a body mixed with food. It is a body that is in no way a body; it does not entail either arising (*utpāda*) or extinction (*nirodha*), either exercises or practices; it is unlimited, infinite, traceless, consciousnessless, formless, absolutely pure (*atyantaśuddha*), immovable (*acala*), without sensation, without an activator, neither stable nor active, without taste, without mixture, unactivated (*asaṃskṛta*); it is neither action, nor fruit, nor activator, nor extinction, nor mind, nor number; it is forever inconceivable... — The Bodhisattva Kāśyapa said to the Buddha: If the Tathāgata possesses such merits, why does his body have to undergo illness, suffering, impermanence, destruction? Assuredly, henceforth I shall not stop thinking that the body of the Tathāgata is an eternal *dharmakāya*, a bliss body, and this is what I will also teach others; but, O Blessed One, if the *dharmakāya* of the Tathāgata is as indestructible as a diamond, I still do not know the cause. — The Buddha said: O Kāśyapa! It is by retaining possession of the causes and conditions of the Good Law (*saddharmahetupratyaya*) that I have this diamond body.

2. Ratnakūṭa, T 310, ch. 28, p. 154 *c*: How do Bodhisattva Mahāsattvas understand the Tathāgata's cryptic words (*saṃdhāyabhāṣita*)? Bodhisattva Mahāsattvas are skilled in understanding exactly the deep and secret meaning hidden in the Sūtras. O son of good family, when I predict to the Śrāvakas their obtaining of supreme and perfect enlightenment, this is not correct; when I say to Ānanda that I have back-ache, this is not correct; when I say to bhikṣus: "I am old, you should get me an assistant (*upasthāyaka*)", this is not correct. O son of good family, it is not correct that the Tathāgata, in various places, triumphed over over Tīrthikas and their systems one after another; it is not correct that an acacia thorn (*khadirakaṇṭaka*) injured the Tathāgata in the foot. When the Tathāgata again says: "Devadatta was my hereditary enemy, he ceaselessly followed me and sought to flatter me", this is not correct. It is not correct that the Tathāgata, on entering Śrāvastī, went on his alms-seeking round in Śālā, the brahmans' village, and returned with his bowl empty. Neither is it correct that Ciñcāmāṇavikā and Sundarī, attaching a wooden dish to their stomachs [so as to simulate pregnancy], slandered the Tathāgata. It is not correct that the Tathāgata, while dwelling earlier in the land of Verañjā, spent the *varṣa* season in eating only barley.

3. The Upadeśa, T 1509, ch. 9, p. 121 *c* - 122 *b* (Nāgārjuna, *Traité*, p. 507-516) treats this question *ex professo*. It inspects the "nine torments" of the Buddha, then formulates a series of remarks. The Buddha who possesses an immense supernatural power cannot undergo the torments of heat and cold. It is the birth-body (*janmakāya*) which is subject to the retribution of misdeeds; as for the essence-body (*dharmatākāya*), it escapes the laws of *saṃsāra*. The true body of the Buddha, a collection of all the good dharmas, is not subject to the fruition of bad dharmas: it is through skill in means (*upāya*) and so as to convert beings that it feigns suffering. After quoting, in support of its thesis, the present passage of the Vimalakīrtinirdeśa, the Upadeśa concludes: "The illnesses of the Buddha are simulated through skill in means and are not true illnesses; it is the same for the supposed misdeeds that are their cause".

NOTE VI:
PRAJÑĀ AND BODHI IN THE PERSPECTIVE OF THE TWO VEHICLES

(Cf. Ch. III, § 52, n. 96)

Buddhist scholasticism has gone on at length about the *prajñā*, wisdoms, and *bodhi*, enlightenment, in relation to the path of Nirvāṇa. The Small Vehicle distinguishes a whole gamut of wisdoms, from that of the sectaries to the supreme and perfect enlightenment of the Buddhas. The Great Vehicle eliminates all distinctions and posits a *bodhi*, empty of all mental content.

Early scholasticism puts the prajñās in four main classes:

I. Prajñās of the sectaries (*tīrthika*), tainted by the view of the self (*ātmadṛṣṭi*). At first sight, they seem excellent, but in the long run turn out to be baneful. They differ from Buddhist wisdom like ass's milk does from cow's milk. Both are the same colour, but cow's milk, when pressed, yields butter, while ass's milk, when pressed, yields urine (Upadeśa, T 1509, ch. 18, p. 191 *b* - 192 *b*; *Traité* II, p. 1070-1074).

II. *Naivaśaikṣanāśaikṣā* prajñās characterizing worldlings (*pṛthagjana*) who are still neither Śaikṣas (students) nor Aśaikṣas (masters). They are practised in the course of the path of the accumulation of merit (*saṃbhāramārga*) and the preparatory path (*prayogamārga*) of the Buddhist Path proper. These are, for example, the acquisition of good roots (*kuśalamūla*), the acquisition of noble lineages (*āryavaṃśa*), the meditation on the repulsive (*aśubhabhāvanā*) and mindfulness of breathing (*ānāpānasmṛti*), the applications of mindfulness (*smṛtyupasthāna*), and finally the acquisition of the four good roots leading to penetration (*nirvedhabhāgīya*). The latter constitute the superlative preparatory path; they are examined in the Kośa, VI, p. 163 sq.

III. Prajñās of the Śaikṣas or "students" set on the Buddhist path of the vision of the truths (*darśanamārga*) and meditation (*bhāvanāmārga*).

1. The *darśanamārga* consists of sixteen thoughts, eight moments of patience (*kṣānti*) and eight moments of knowledge (*jñāna*), in order to reach the understanding (*abhisamaya*) of the four Buddhist truths (i.e. four moments for each truth). This path eliminates the passions "to be destroyed by vision" (*dṛgheya*), view of the Self, etc. (Cf. Kośa, VI, p. 185-191; É. LAMOTTE, *Histoire*, p. 680-682). The first moment of the *darśanamārga* is a patience relating to the knowledge concerning suffering (*duḥkhe dharmajñānakṣāntiḥ*): this transforms the adept from the worldling (*pṛthagjana*) he was previously into a holy one (*ārya*), firmly established in the certainty of one day acquiring the Absolute Good (*samyaktvaniyāmāvakrānta*), namely, Nirvāṇa.

2. The *bhāvanāmārga* has the effect of eliminating the passions of the triple world "needing to be destroyed through meditation" (*bhāvanāheya*). The triple world comprises nine spheres: the *kāmadhātu*, the four trances (*dhyāna*) of the *rūpadhātu* and the four recollections (*samāpatti*) of the *ārūpyadhātu*. Each of these spheres consists of nine categories of passions, i.e. 81 passions in all. Each of these passions requires elimination through a moment of abandonment (*prahāṇa* or *ānantaryamārga*) and a moment of deliverance (*vimuktimārga*). Therefore 162 moments are required in order to destroy the passions of the triple world.

At the first moment, the ārya wins the first fruit of the religious life (*śrāmaṇyaphala*) and becomes a *srotaāpanna*: he has "entered the stream" and will obtain Nirvāṇa after seven rebirths at the most.

At the 12th moment, the ascetic obtains the second fruit of the religious life and becomes a *sakṛdāgāmin*: he will only be reborn once more in the *kāmadhātu*.

At the 18th moment, the ascetic obtains the third fruit and becomes an *anāgāmin*: he will not be born again in the *kāmadhātu*, but will undergo rebirth among the gods of the *rūpa* or *ārūpyadhātu*.

At the 161st moment, the ascetic abandons the 81st passion, namely the last passion of the realm of non-perception-non-imperception (*naivasaṃjñānāsaṃjñāyatana*) also called the summit of existence (*bhavāgra*). This abandonment (*prahāṇamārga*) bears the name of diamond-like concentration (*vajropamasamādhi*). This abandonment is followed by a 162nd moment — moment of deliverance (*vimuktimārga*) — which inaugurates the stage of master (*aśaikṣa*).

IV. Prajñā of the *aśaikṣa*. This prajñā, final fruit of the religious life, characterizes the *arhat* "holy one, worthy of respect from all" or the *aśaikṣa* "holy one, who has no more to learn (*śikṣ-*) with regard to the destruction of the impurities". The holy one knows that all the vices have been destroyed in him and will never arise again: in scholastic terms, he is in possession of the knowledge of the destruction of the impurities (*āsravakṣayajñāna*) and the knowledge of their non-arising (*anutpādajñāna*): cf. Kośa, VI, p. 240.

This *aśaikṣa* jñāna constitutes *bodhi* (enlightenment) and pertains to the Śrāvaka (listener) who has become an arhat, to the solitary Buddha (*pratyekabuddha*) and to the fully and perfectly enlightened Buddha (*samyaksaṃbuddha*).

It is generally accepted in both Vehicles that deliverance (*vimukti*) — in technical terms, the *pratisaṃkhyānirodha* of the passions — is identical for the Śrāvaka, the Pratyekabuddha and the Buddha. The last declared on several occasions: Regarding this, I deny that there is the slightest difference between one deliverance and another deliverance (Majjhima, II, p. 129; Aṅguttara, III, p. 34; Saṃyutta, V, p. 410: *Ettha kho pan' esāhaṃ na kiñci nānākaraṇaṃ vadāmi yad idaṃ vimuttiyā vimuttiṃ*). See also Vibhāṣā, T 1545, ch. 31, p. 162 *b-c*; Kośa, VI, p. 296; Vasumitra, thesis 37 of the Sarvāstivādins and 22 of the Mahīśāsakas, tr. J. MASUDA, p. 49 and 62; Saṃdhinirmocana, X, § 2; Sūtrālaṃkāra, XI, v. 53; Saṃgraha, p. 327-328; Buddhabhūmiśāstra, T 1530, ch. 5, p. 312 *b* 7-15.

However, there are many differences between the *bodhi* of Śrāvakas (and Pratyekabuddhas) on the one hand and the *anuttarā samyaksaṃbodhiḥ* of the Buddhas on the other. They are pointed out in several texts: Vibhāṣā, T 1545, ch. 143, p. 735 *b*; Upadeśa, T 1509, ch. 53, p. 436 *b*; Upāsakaśīlasūtra, T 1488, ch. 1, p. 1038 *a-c* (analysed in Hōbōgirin, p. 87): Śrāvakas reach *bodhi* by listening, Pratyekabuddhas by reflecting, and they only understand a part of the truth; Buddhas understand everything without a teacher, without listening, without meditating, through the effect of their practices. — Śrāvakas and Pratyekabuddhas only know the general marks (*sāmānyalakṣaṇa*) of things; Buddhas know the particular marks (*bhinnalakṣana*), and they alone are omniscient. — Śrāvakas and Pratyekabuddhas know the four truths (*satya*), but not the causes and conditions (*hetupratyaya*); Buddhas know the causes and conditions. Comparing the waters of the Ganges to the stream of the *pratītyasamutpāda*, the Śrāvaka is like the hare that swims across the river without realising its depth; the Pratyekabuddha is like the horse that realises it at the moment it touches the bottom; the Buddha is like the elephant that comprehends all its depth. — Śrāvakas and Pratyekabuddhas have cut off the passions (*kleśa*), but not their pervasions (*vāsanā*); the Buddhas have pulled up everything right down to the root.

The Bodh. bhūmi, p. 88-94, devotes an admirable chapter to the *bodhi* of the Buddhas, unblemished (*nirmala*) knowledge which drives away all the passions (*kleśāvaraṇaprahāṇa*), unimpeded (*apratihata*) and unobstructed (*anāvaraṇa*) knowledge which drives away the obstacle to the knowable (*jñeyāvaraṇaprahāṇa*). The text points out the seven excellences (*paramatā*) which make this *bodhi* the foremost of all (*sarvabodhīnāṃ paramā*).

Bodhisattvas having not yet definitively driven away the passions do not possess *bodhi*; they do, however, have a great wisdom (*prajñā*) which makes them "close to bodhi".

Seen from the double perspective of the *pudgala* and *dharmanairātmya*, *bodhi* reverts to zero. This is what Vimalakīrti explains in Ch. III, § 52. Once again, he is only returning to considerations already developed in the Mahāyānasūtras:

Pañcaviṃśati, p. 38,*19-21*: *Bodhisattvaḥ prajñāpāramitāyāṃ carann evam upaparīkṣate nāmamātram idaṃ yad idaṃ bodhisattva iti, nāmamātram idaṃ yad uta bodhir iti, nāmamātram idaṃ yad uta buddha iti*: "The Bodhisattva who practises the perfection of wisdom considers that Bodhisattva is only a name, that bodhi is only a name and that Buddha is only a name".

Pañcaviṃśati, p. 46,*10*-47,*7*: *Śūnyatā notpadyate na nirudhyate, na saṃkliśyate na vyavadāyate, na hīyate na vardhate, nātītā nāgatā na pratyutpannā. yā ca idṛśī na tatra rūpaṃ... na mārgo na prāptir nābhisamayo na srotaāpanno na srotaāpattiphalaṃ, na sakṛdāgāmī na sakṛdāgāmiphalaṃ, nānāgāmī nānāgamiphalaṃ, nārhattvaṃ nārhattvaphalaṃ, na pratyekabuddho na pratyekabodhiḥ, na buddho na bodhiḥ*: "Emptiness does not arise and is not extinguished; it is neither defiled nor purified; it neither diminishes nor augments; it is neither past nor future nor present. Wherever there is such an emptiness, there is neither form... nor path, nor acquisition, nor understanding (of the truths); neither srotaāpanna nor srotaāpanna fruit; neither sakṛdāgāmin nor sakṛdāgāmin fruit; neither anāgāmin nor anāgāmin fruit; neither arhat nor arhat fruit; neither solitary Buddha nor solitary bodhi; neither Buddha nor bodhi".

Pañcaviṃśati, p. 261,*8-13*: *asti prāptir asty abhisamayo na punar dvayam. api tu khalu punar lokavyavahāreṇa prāptiś cābhisamayaś ca prajñapyate lokavyavahāreṇa srotaāpanno vā sakṛdāgāmī vā anāgāmī vā arhan vā pratyekabuddho vā bodhisattvo vā buddho vā prajñapyate na punaḥ paramārthena prāptir nābhisamayo na srotaāpanno na sakṛdāgāmī nānāgāmī nārhan na pratyekabuddho na bodhisattvo na buddaḥ*: "There is obtainment and understanding (of the truths), but not duality. Besides, it is in mundane language that there exists the question of obtainment and understanding of the truths; it is in mundane language that there exists the question of srotaāpanna, sakṛdāgāmin, anāgāmin, arhat, pratyekabuddha, bodhisattva or Buddha. In the true sense, there is nothing of all that".

Ratnakūṭa, T 310, ch. 39, p. 227 *a* 14: "Bodhi is not verified by the body (*kāya*) or by the mind (*citta*). And why? The body is naturally without knowledge (*jñāna*) and without activity (*caritra*), like a grass (*tṛṇa*), a piece of wood (*kāṣṭha*), a wall (*bhitti*), a reflection in a polished stone. It is the same with the mind, like an illusion (*māyā*), a mirage (*marīci*), the moon reflected in the water (*udakacandra*). To understand the body and the mind in this way is what is called *bodhi*. It is only in mundane language (*lokavyavahāra*) that there is a question of *bodhi*, but the true nature of bodhi is inexpressible (*anirvācya*). It cannot be obtained (*prāpta*) either by the body or by the mind, either by the *dharma* or the *adharma*, either by the real (*bhūta*) or the false (*abhūta*), either by truth (*satya*) or by falsehood (*mṛṣā*). And why? Because *bodhi* rejects discourse (*vyavahāra*) and rejects every real mark (*dharmalakṣaṇa*). Moreover, *bodhi* is without shape (*saṃsthāna*), without use (*prayojana*) and without discourse (*vyavahāra*). The same as space (*ākāśasama*) and without shape, it is inexpressible (*anirvācya*). To examine all dharmas correctly, is to say nothing of them. And why? Because in dharmas there is no discourse, and in discourse there are no dharmas. Beings do not understand the true principle (*bhūtanaya*) of dharmas. The Tathāgata feels great compassion (*mahākaruṇā*) for them: that is why I am now teaching them the true principle of dharmas so that they can understand it clearly, for this is the truth (*satya*) and the true meaning (*bhūtārtha*)".

Ibid., p. 227 *b* 11: "*Bodhi* is synonymous with emptiness (*śūnyatā*). It is because emptiness is empty that *bodhi* is also empty. Because *bodhi* is empty, all dharmas are empty. The Tathāgata understands all dharmas according to this emptiness. It is not by reason of the emptiness that he understands the emptiness of dharmas; it is through knowledge of the single true principle (*ekabhūtanaya*) that he understands that the nature of dharmas is empty. Emptiness and *bodhi* are not two distinct natures; and since there is no duality, it cannot be said: "This is *bodhi*, that is emptiness (*śūnyatā*)". If there were duality, it could be said: "This is *bodhi*, that is emptiness". But dharmas are without duality and without a mark of duality; without a name, without mark and without activity; absolutely inactive and without purpose (*samudācāra*). Thus the emptiness in question avoids all belief (*grāha*) and attachment (*abhiniveśa*). In absolute truth (*paramārthasatyena*), no dharma exists (*upalabhyate*): It is because they are empty of self-nature (*svabhāvaśūnya*) that they are called empty".

After a similar explanation, the Gayāśīrṣa, T 464, p. 482 *a* 8, concludes: "The mark of *bodhi* transcends the triple world, goes beyond convention (*saṃvṛti*) and the path of language (*vyavahāramārga*). It is by extinguishing all production that the thought of *bodhi* is produced. The production of *bodhi* is non-production".

NOTE VII: GOTRA AND TATHĀGATAGOTRA

(Cf. Ch. VII, § 2).

Gotra "race, family", implies certain mental tendencies, permanent or acquired, which enable someone to obtain Nirvāṇa. *Gotrabhū* (Majjhima, III, p. 256,*7*; Aṅguttara, IV, p. 373,*7*; V, p. 23,*7*) is the name given to the man who will obtain the Ārya state which assures him of Nirvāṇa; *agotraka* is he who does not have this quality.

In the Aṅguttara, V, p. 193-195, the Buddha places among the fourteen restricted points (*avyākṛtavastu*: cf. NĀGĀRJUNA, *Traité*, p. 154-155) the question of knowing whether all beings will reach Nirvāṇa. But all those who will reach it will do so by the Path: the town of existence has only one way out. However Nāgasena answers the same question in the negative: *na kho mahārāja sabbe va labhanti nibbānaṃ* (Milindapañha, p. 69,*17*; P. DEMIÉVILLE, *Les versions chinoises du Milindapañha*, p. 151).

The early sources (Dīgha, III, p. 217) and the Abhidharma (Dhammasaṅgaṇi, p. 186; Kośa, III, p. 137) distinguish three categories (*rāśi*): 1. *samyaktvaniyatarāśi*, those who have entered the Path and will rapidly attain Nirvāṇa; 2. *mithyātvaniyatarāśi*, those who, having committed serious offences, will certainly go to bad destinies, and who, once having left these bad destinies, will pass into the third *rāśi*; 3. *aniyatarāśi*, those who do not come under either the first or second *rāśi*, and can enter either.

In the course of time and the formation of various Vehicles of salvation, the problem of *gotra* became more complicated: cf. Sūtrālaṃkāra, p. 10-11; Bodh. bhūmi, p. 3-11; Siddhi, p. 103, 115, 562.

These sources distinguish: 1. *prakṛtiṣṭha* gotra or "original", innate, without a beginning. possessed through the very nature of things (*paraṃparāgato 'nādikāliko dharmatāpratilabdhaḥ*); 2. *samudānīta* gotra "acquired" through the previous practice of good roots (*pūrvakuśalamūlābhyāsāt pratilabdhaḥ*).

The Siddhi, *l.c.*, posits five categories of people: 1-3. three *niyatagotra* "of determined family": Śrāvakagotra, Pratyekagotra and Tathāgatagotra. They will inevitably attain Nirvāṇa, the first through the Śrāvaka Vehicle, the second through the Pratyekabuddha Vehicle and the third through the Great Vehicle; 4. *aniyatagotra* "of undetermined family": they will certainly attain Nirvāṇa, but they can enter either the Śrāvaka Vehicle or the Pratyekabuddha one and, from there, either before or after having acquired righteousness (*samyaktva*), pass into the Great Vehicle; 5. the *agotraka* "without family", in whom are lacking, from the beginning and forever, the germs of Nirvāṇa. These last are also called *icchantika*, in Tibetan *ḥdod chen po*, "people of great desires". These are either those doomed through predestination, condemned to remain forever below in Saṃsāra for want of the roots of Nirvāṇa, or Bodhisattvas who for the welfare of beings, will never become Buddhas and will always remain in Saṃsāra (Laṅkāvatāra, p. 27,*5*; 65,*17*; Mahāvyutpatti, No. 2210, 2223; Siddhi, Appendice, p. 724).

It is implied (Bodh. bhūmi, p. 4,*10-12*) that the three Vehicles lead respectively to Śrāvakabodhi, Pratyekabodhi and Anuttarā samyaksaṃbodhiḥ, that the first two only purify from the obstacle of the passions (*kleśāvaraṇa*) while the third supresses both the obstacle of the passions and the obstacle to knowledge (*jñeyāvaraṇa*).

However, the question arises of knowing if the three Vehicles really do ensure Nirvāṇa.

1. The great scholars (Nāgārjuna, Asaṅga) accept, it seems, that Nirvāṇa can be reached through the three Vehicles.

Upadeśa, T 1509, ch. 74, p. 581 *c* 24 sq.: Among people of the [first] two Vehicles, when their minds are pure (*anāsrava*), their passions (*kleśa*) are exhausted (*kṣīṇa*): thus, for them, no more fruition, no more merit... Moreover, those of the two Vehicles achieve the *bhūṭakoṭi*: this is why they burn out all the qualities (*guṇa*).

Ibidem, ch. 28, p. 266 *c* 3 sq.: The knowledge (*jñāna*) of a Bodhisattva and the knowledge of a Śrāvaka are but one and the same knowledge. But the latter has no *upāya*, is not adorned with the *mahāpraṇidhāna*, does not possess either *mahāmaitrī* or *mahākaruṇā*, does not seek all the *buddhaguṇa*, does not seek the *sarvākārajñāna* so as to know all dharmas. He is averse only to *jāti*, *jarā*, *maraṇa* and severs the bonds of thirst (*tṛṣṇābandhana*). He goes directly to Nirvāṇa: that is the difference.

Sūtrālaṃkāra, p. 68,*15*: Asaṅga submits the theory of the oneness of the Vehicles, identical on several points, particularly when concerned with the element of the Law (*dharmadhātu*), impersonality (*nairātmya*) and deliverance (*vimukti*), i.e. Nirvāṇa.

Saṃgraha, p. 256, in the notes: "For the Śrāvakas, etc., who dwell in the *nirupadhiśeṣanirvāṇadhātu*, the body (*kāya*) and knowledge (*jñāna*) are extinguished like the flame of a lamp that goes out. Conversely, when Bodhisattvas have become Buddhas, the Law-body (*dharmakāya*) which they achieved (*sākṣātkṛta*) goes right on to the end of the round of rebirth (*āsaṃsārakoṭeḥ*) without undergoing extinction". Here the author is showing the superiority of the *apratiṣṭhitanirvāṇa* of a Buddha over the *nirupadhiśeṣanirvāṇa* of a Śrāvaka. This implicitly admits that the Śrāvaka Vehicle does indeed lead to Nirvāṇa.

Ibidem, p. 326 in the notes: "The three Vehicles, in that they deliver from the obstacle of the passions (*kleśāvaranavimukti*), are identical. Also the Bhagavat has said: Between deliverance and deliverance, there is no difference".

Buddhabhūmiśāstra of Bandhuprabha, T 1530, ch. 5, p. 312 *b* 2-4: "People of determined family (*niyatagotra*) obtain Release (*niḥsaraṇa*) by relying on their own Vehicle. The *aniyatagotra* obtain Release, some by relying on the Great Vehicle, others by relying on the other Vehicles. Here by Release (*niḥsaraṇa*) we mean Nirvāṇa".

The Siddhi, p. 671-672, asserts that the Aśaikṣas of the Small and Great Vehicles possess the *sopadhiśeṣa* and *nirupadhiśeṣa* Nirvāṇa.

2. However several Mahāyānasūtras are diametrically opposed to this. According to them, the Śrāvakas and Pratyekabuddhas are mistaken in thinking they have attained Nirvāṇa: in fact they are far

from it. There is only one efficacious Vehicle: that of the Buddhas and Bodhisattvas, also called Great Vehicle. The Vehicles of the Śrāvakas and Pratyekabuddhas have been taught intentionally (*saṃdhāya*) so as to ripen beings. These, at a certain moment, will abandon their provisional Vehicle to enter the true Vehicle.

So therefore the term *ekayāna* can cover very different conceptions: for the scholars quoted above, there is a single Vehicle because the three Vehicles culminate in the same deliverance (*vimukti*), Nirvāṇa; for the Mahāyānasūtras from which we will quote extracts, there is a single Vehicle because only the third, the Great Vehicle, is efficacious.

Ratnakūṭa, T 310, ch. 119, p. 675 *a* 27: "Arhats and Pratyekabuddhas still have the remains of birth dharmas, they have not practised [to the end] the religious life (*brahmacarya*), they have not done what they had to do (*akṛtaṃ karaṇīyaṃ*), what they had to cut off (*prahātavya*) has not reached completion; they are far from Nirvāṇa. And why? Only Tathāgatas, holy ones, fully and perfectly enlightened, achieve (*sākṣātkurvanti*) Nirvāṇa, are endowed with all the immense and inconceivable virtues (*apramāṇācintyaguṇa*); that which they had to cut off has been completely cut off; they are absolutely pure; they are esteemed by all beings; they have gone beyond the [first] two Vehicles and the realm (*viṣaya*) of the Bodhisattvas. But for Arhats, it is not so. To say that they obtain Nirvāṇa is skill in means (*upāya*) on the part of the Buddha. That is why Arhats are far from Nirvāṇa.

Ibidem, ch. 119, p. 676 *b* 6: Śrāvakas and Pratyekabuddhas all enter the Great Vehicle, and this Great Vehicle is the Vehicle of the Buddhas. That is why the three Vehicles are a single Vehicle (*ekayāna*). To achieve the single Vehicle is to obtain *anuttarā samyaksaṃbodhiḥ*; and *anuttarā samyaksaṃbodhiḥ* is Nirvāṇa. Nirvāṇa is the pure Law-body (*viśuddhadharmakāya*) of the Tathāgatas. That which achieves this Law-body is the single Vehicle. There is no separate Tathāgata, or separate Law-body: it is said that the Tathāgata is the Law-body. That which achieves the definitive Law-body (*atyantadharmakāya*) is the definitive Single Vehicle (*atyantaikayāna*). The definitive single Vehicle is the cutting off of the series (*saṃtānoccheda*).

Saddharmapuṇḍ., references above, VI, § 11, note 32. — In the same text, p. 210,*1-4*, five hundred Arhats themselves admit that they do not possess Nirvāṇa: *atyayaṃ vayaṃ bhagavan deśayāmo yair asmābhir bhagavann evaṃ satatasamitaṃ cittaṃ paribhāvitam idam asmākaṃ parinirvāṇaṃ parinirvṛtā vayam iti yathāpīdaṃ bhagavann avyaktā akuśalā avidhijñāḥ. tat kasya hetoḥ. yair nāmāsmābhir bhagavaṃs tathāgatajñāne 'bhisaṃboddhavya evaṃrūpeṇa parīttena jñānena paritoṣaṃ gatāḥ sma*: "We confess our fault, O Blessed One, we ceaselessly nourished the thought that this was our Nirvāṇa and that we had reached complete Nirvāṇa; it is, O Blessed One, that we are not informed, we are not skilled, we are not instructed as we should be. And why? It is that when we should have reached the enlightenment of the Buddhas in the knowledge of the Tathāgata, we contented ourselves with this limited knowledge of ours".

3. Vimalakīrti takes all these considerations to their furthest extremes:

a. The distinction between the gotra of the Śrāvakas and the Tathāgatagotra does not hold true, for "there is neither Bodhisattva mind nor Śrāvaka mind" (VIII, § 5), and as for *bodhi*, "no-one can draw near or away from it" (III, § 52).

b. There is neither a right or wrong Path to Nirvāṇa (VIII, § 30), nor any Vehicle to traverse it, for "*bodhi* is already acquired by all beings and there is not a single being who is not already in Parinirvāṇa" (III, § 51).

c. Equally empty, Saṃsāra and Nirvāṇa are the same (IV, § 12; VIII, § 13 and 29).

d. In consequence, it is in Saṃsāra that Nirvāṇa should be sought. The holy one (*ārya*), certain of the supreme Good (*avakrāntaniyāma*), and who has seen the truths (*dṛṣṭasatya*) "is not capable of producing *anuttarasamyaksaṃbodhi*" (VII, § 3).

Thus, then, "the *Tathāgatagotra* is the family of the sixty-two kinds of false views (*dṛṣṭigata*), of all the passions (*kleśa*) and of all the bad dharmas [that prevail in Saṃsāra]" (VII, § 2).

NOTE VIII: PERFUMED AMṚTA AND THE SACRED MEAL

(Cf. Ch. IX, § 1, n. 1).

The title of Chapter IX in Tibetan is *Sprul pas zal zas blaṅs pa*, "Obtaining of food by the imaginary (bodhisattva)" (*nirmitena bhojanādānam*). This food, in Ch. IX, § 11, is designated as ambrosia (Sanskrit *amṛta*, Tibetan *bdud-rtsi*, Chinese *kan-lu* 甘露).

In Sanskrit, *amṛta*, taken substantively, has two main meanings: 1. immortality, 2. ambrosia (food or potion of immortality, antidote).

Buddhist texts use it principally in the first meaning and make it a synonym of Nirvāṇa. For the benefit of beings, the Buddha opened the doors to immortality (*apārutā tesaṃ amatassa dvārā*: Vinaya, I, p. 7,*4*; Dīgha, II, p. 39,*21*; 217,*15*; Majjhima, I, p. 169,*24*; Saṃyutta, I, p. 138,*22*) and whosoever is his disciple seeks the Immortal, Nirvāṇa (*amataṃ nibbānaṃ pariyesati*: Aṅguttara, II, p. 247, *33*; Apadāna, I, p. 23,*27*; Mahāniddesa, I, p. 20,*10* etc.).

Texts which use *amṛta* in the sense of ambrosia are much rarer: the Jātakamāla, p. 221,*6*, speaks of a shower of ambrosia (*amṛtavarṣa*), and the Milindapañha, of the ambrosia with which the Blessed One sprinkled the world (*amatena lokaṃ abhisiñci Bhagavā*: Milinda, p. 335,*29*) and the ambrosial remedy (*amatosadha*: p. 247,*22*) which calms the diseases of the passions; it compares (p. 319,*9*) this immortality-remedy (*agado amataṃ*) to immortality-Nirvāṇa (*nibbānaṃ amataṃ*).

It is not only a sacred food, but a feast of immortality that the Vimalakīrtinirdeśa is implying here. It is therefore introducing a new element into Buddhism for which the significance and, if possible, the origin, must be sought.

* * *

In his fine book, *Le Festin d'Immortalité*, Paris, 1924, Mr Georges Dumézil has studied the Hindu cycle of Amṛta in its relationship to other similar cycles. He summarizes (p. 292) the Hindu cycle in the following way:

I. — The Devas fear death. They deliberate over methods of preparing the food of immortality, *amṛta*. On Viṣṇu's advice, they decide to churn the ocean in its "vessel". They make an alliance with the Asuras over this.

Winning of implements: the Devas, among other things, go to ask the Lord of the waters to lend the ocean for the undertaking.

They churn the ocean. The *amṛta* appears, as well as various other divine beings (Lakṣmī ...). A fish, born of the excessive churning, threatens the world; it is swallowed by Śiva.

III. — The Asuras have made off with the *amṛta*, and also claim possession of the goddess Lakṣmī.

Viṣṇu-Nārāyaṇa assumes the form of Lakṣmī and, followed by Nara also disguised as a woman, goes to the Asuras. The latter, maddened by love, give the *amṛta* to the fake goddess who takes it back to the Devas.

II. — The assembled Devas drink the *amṛta*. The Asura Rāhu surreptitiously joins them. He is denounced and decapitated by Viṣṇu. As he falls he shatters the earth.

IV. — All-round conflict. The Asuras, defeated mainly by Viṣṇu, are cast into the waters or under the earth. The Devas keep the *amṛta* for good.

Mr Dumézil compares the Hindu cycle with many other Indo-european legends, expecially that of the Greek cycle of *ambrosia* and the *Oceanides Ambrosia*, and the Bœotian cycle of *Prometheus* and the *Pithos of Immortality*.

* * *

It does not seem that the sacred banquet instigated by Vimilakīrti has much in common with the Hindu cycle of the feast of immortality. Conversely, it lends itself to some comparisons with the accounts of meals and miracles contained in the Buddhist scriptures.

The *amṛta* as conceived in the Vimalakīrtinirdeśa requires certain remarks:

1. *The amṛta comes from above.* — It does not come from the depth of the ocean, but is the ordinary food of the Buddha Sugandhakūṭa and his great Bodhisattvas who inhabit the Sarvagandhasugandhā universe, made only of perfume: the midday meal, taken by both that Buddha and those Bodhisattvas, served by one (or several) cupbearer by the name of Gandhavyūhāhāra, consists of perfumed food (IX, § 2).

The Sarvagandhasugandhā universe is situated on the borders of the zenith (*ūrdhvā diś*), opposite the Sahāloka, our own world, localised in the nadir. When food normally consumed in the Sarvagandhasugandhā universe descends exceptionally to the Sahāloka, it would seem like manna descended from heaven to give life to the world.

2. *The amṛta is humbly pleaded for and generously granted.* — It is not concocted through a great deal of resources, as in the Hindu cycle, or won by force or ruse. Vimalakīrti creates, by transformation, a bodhisattva and sends him to the Buddha Sugandhakūṭa. Putting it in the most refined forms of ancient Indian courtesy, the imaginary bodhisattva pleads, in Vimalakīrti's name, for some remains of the perfumed food consumed in the Sarvagandhasugandhā universe. It will actuate Buddha deeds (*buddhakārya*) in the Sahā universe and convert beings animated by base aspirations (IX, § 4-5).

The food thus requested is granted no less amiably. The Buddha Sugandhakūṭa personally pours some crumbs of his meal into a vessel, or more precisely a begging bowl (*pātra*) and gives it to the imaginary bodhisattva (IX, § 8, at the beginning).

The text reproduces the courtesies exchanged on this occasion in full quite intentionally. Vimalakīrti must know of the divine gift and ask for it in order for it to be granted.

Note should be taken of the role of intermediary played by the bodhisattva who acts as go-between for the Sahāloka and the world above. Created (*nirmita*) and protected (*adhiṣṭhita*) by Vimalakīrti, he speaks and acts at the will of the latter and is a real substitute for him. Regarding this, see Kośa, VII, p. 118-120.

3. *The unworthy guests.* — The *amṛta* is pleaded for and granted "so that beings with base aspirations (*hīnādhimuktika*) would be animated by noble aspirations" (IX, § 4). In all the accounts of sacred meals, unworthy guests appear, even thieves and traitors. In the Hindu cycle, the Asuras make off with the *amṛta*, and the asura Rāhu surreptitiously joins the devas so as to partake of it. Certain versions of the Mahāparinirvāṇasūtra have it that during the meal at the home of the blacksmith Cunda a bad monk stole a cup made of precious metal by hiding it in his armpit (*lohakaroṭakaṃ kakṣeṇāpahṛtavān*) but that, through the all-powerful will of the Buddha, the Master and Cunda were alone in seeing the theft. See Sanskrit Mahāparinirvāṇa, p. 258; Dīrgha, T 1, ch. 3, p. 18 *b* 7-8; T 5, ch. 1, p. 167 *c* 17-19; T 6, ch. 1, p. 183 *b* 5-6; Vin. of the Mūlasarv., T 1451, ch. 37, p. 390 *b* 19-20; Suttanipāta Comm., I, p. 159: texts analysed and translated by E. Waldschmidt, *Beiträge zur Textgeschichte des Mahāparinirvāṇasūtra*, Nachrichten v. d. Gesellschaft der Wissenschaften zu Göttingen, 1939, p. 63-94.

No thief intervenes in Vimalakīrti's feast of immortality, but there is the matter on several occasions of guests animated by base or self-interested aspirations.

The great Śāriputra is the first to be caught (IX, § 1). After having endured a whole morningful of interminable worthy discussions, this thought comes to him: "It is midday and these great Bodhisattvas are still not getting up. So when are we going to eat?" A prosaic anxiety but perfectly justifiable. After midday Buddhists are required to fast. The meeting would have had to be brought to an immediate close so that the hungry listeners could reach Vaiśālī as fast as possible and obtain victuals in a town five li from Vimalakīrti's house. To send them back fasting would be to imperil them to falling through weakness on the wayside.

Vimalakīrti, reading Śāriputra's gluttonous thought, said to him: "Śāriputra, you should not listen to the Law with purely material preoccupations. However, wait a moment and you will eat such food as has never yet been tasted". This was to remind him that man does not live by bread alone and to apprise him of a new food which his forefathers had never eaten before.

A little later, Vimalakīrti is preparing to distribute the sacred food contained in a single vessel to the great assembly. It is then that some disciples — Hsüan-tsang details: some base disciples — had the following thought: "This food is very sparse; how will it be enough for such a great assembly?" (IX, § 12). They immediately draw the reply from the imaginary bodhisattva: "Do not identify your small wisdom and your small merits with the immense wisdom and immense merits of the Buddha. The water of the four great oceans would be dried up before this food with its sweet perfume has undergone the slightest diminution. Even if all the beings inhabiting immense universes, for a kalpa or a hundred kalpas, swallowed this food by taking mouthfuls as big as Mount Sumeru, this food would not diminish" (IX, § 12). And in fact, "the whole assembly is satiated by this food, and the food is in no way exhausted" (IX, § 13).

The theme of the horn of plenty is universal and Buddhist legend is familiar with at least one case of multiplication of the loaves. It is narrated, in identical terms, by the Commentaries on the Dhammapada, I, p. 373, and the Jātakas, I, p. 348: The wife of the śreṣṭhin Maccharikosiya placed a cake (*pūva*) in the Tathāgata's bowl. The Master took as much of it as he needed to sustain himself, and the five hundred monks also took as much as they needed to sustain themselves. The śreṣṭhin then proceeded to distribute milk, ghee, honey, sugar, etc. The Master and the five hundred monks finished their meal; the śreṣṭhin and his wife ate as much as they wanted. Nonetheless, the cakes did no undergo any diminution (*pūvānaṃ pariyosānaṃ eva na paññāyati*). And even when they had been distributed to the monks of the whole monastery and to the beggars, the cakes that remained did not lessen (*pariyanto na paññāyat' eva*). "Master, they said to the Buddha, the cakes are not diminishing (*parikkhayaṃ na gacchanti*)" The Master replied: "Cast them into the store-room, near the Jetavana gate".

4. *The amṛta is not the result of a transformation.* A new food,

susceptible to being multiplied for eternity without ever being exhausted, could well be a magical creation. Whoever possesses the great psychic powers (*maharddhi*: cf. Bodh. bhūmi, p. 58-63; Saṃgraha, p. 221-222) can perform transformations (*anyathībhāvakaraṇa*). Through *adhimukti*, that is, an intense mental application, a superior act of will, he changes the great elements (earth, water, fire, wind) from one into the other, colour-figure (*rūpa-saṃsthāna*) into sound (*śabda*), etc.

Buddhist folklore contains accounts of the altering of food. According to the Atthasālinī, p. 419, and the Visuddhimagga, ed. WARREN, p. 363, a lodging house located in the Vindhya mountains, the Vattaniya senāsana, was the setting for a daily miracle. Seeing the monks eating their food dry, the venerable Assagutta formed the wish that henceforth they should have curds at their disposal. His wish was granted: every day, the waters of the pool which supplied the monastery were transformed at meal-time into curds, then, once the meal was over, went back to being water.

The *amṛta* granted by the Buddha Sugandhakūṭa and distributed by Vimalakīrti is obviously not food of this kind.

5. *The amṛta is a sacred essence, both food and a remedy for the passions, which simultaneously exerts material and spiritual effects.* — It is indeed a sacred essence, given by the Buddha, "perfumed" (*parivāsita*) or "instituted" (*prabhāvita*) by Great Compassion (IX, § 11) and springing from the five Supernatural Elements (*lokottara-skandha*) which ensure deliverance (*vimukti*), salvation (IX, § 12).

It is also a "great king of medicaments" (*mahābhaiṣajyarāja*: cf. X, § 7), a *pharmakon* of immortality. However it is not used in the war against the Giants, as the Greeks would have it (cf. G. DUMÉZIL, *op. cit.*, p. 89, 110, 112, 229): it is an antidote for the passions. "As long as the poisons of all the passions are not eliminated, this food is not digested: it is only after that it is digested" (X, § 7). Hence Vimalakīrti's advice: "Do not eat it with ignoble or base sentiments, for were you to eat it thus, you would not be able to digest it" (IX, § 11). Each must put himself to the test for to partake of it without discernment is to partake of one's own condemnation.

The *amṛta* we are concerned with is a true food (*bhojana*) which produces both material and spiritual effects.

a. "The strength of this food remains in the body for seven days and seven nights. After that time, it will gradually be digested. Even though it may be a long time before it is digested, it will not do any harm" (X, § 5).

b. All those who have eaten it give off a perfume through all their pores, and this perfume persists as long as this food is not digested, i.e. seven days and seven nights (IX, § 13; X, § 4-5).

c. "Those who had eaten this food, felt descending into their bodies a happiness (*sukha*) equal to that of the Bodhisattvas who live in the Sarvasukhamaṇḍitā universe "Adorned with every happiness" (IX, § 13).

d. Finally and most importantly, at the end of seven days and seven nights, when the food is digested, each has advanced a degree on his own particular path. This is explained at length in Ch. X, § 6, although there is some disagreement in the versions. Going by the Sanskrit original quoted in the Śikṣāsamuccaya, p. 270, the Śrāvakas who have not yet entered the absolute certainty concerning the obtainment of Nirvāṇa become *avakrāntaniyāma*, that is, Āryas (holy ones). As for the Bodhisattvas who have not yet produced the thought of enlightenment, they produce it and thus enter the first *bhūmi*; those who have already produced it acquire the certainty concerning the non-arising of dharmas (*anutpattikadharmakṣānti*) and thus come to the eighth *bhūmi*.

* * *

Apart from the spiritual effects, the *amṛta* as it is presented in the Vimalakīrti is not unrelated to the nutritive essence (Sanskrit, *ojas*; Hybrid Sanskrit, *oja* or *ojā*; Pali, *ojā*) which is mentioned in the old Buddhist texts. The gods can insert it directly into the pores of the skin of their favourites or add it to their food. Its high nutritional value makes it particularly indigestible; that is why only the holy ones can tolerate it, and the remains of food thus fortified have to be carefully buried.

While he was practising the austerities on the banks of the Nairañjanā, Śākyamuni one day contemplated abstaining completely from food. The gods approached him and said to him: Sir, beware of abstaining from all food; however if you must, we will introduce the divine nutritive essence into the pores of your skin, and you will be sustained by it (cf. Majjhima, I, p. 245, *8-12*: *mā kho tvaṃ mārisa sabbaso āhārupacchedāya paṭipajji, sace kho tvaṃ mārisa sabbaso āhārupacchedāya paṭipajjissasi tassa te mayaṃ dibbaṃ ojaṃ lomakūpehi ajjhoharissāma, tayā tvaṃ yāpessasīti.* — Mahāvastu, II, p. 131,*2-3*: *vayan te romakūpavivarāntareṣu divyām ojām adhyohariṣyāmaḥ*). However the future Buddha indignantly refused to submit to such a hoax.

Nonetheless, according to the Pāli tradition, but not the Sanskrit, the gods twice introduced the nutritive essence into the Buddha's food: during the last meal, with Sujātā, before Bodhi, and during the last meal, at the home of the blacksmith Cunda, before Nirvāṇa. This is asserted by the Nidānakathā, Jātaka, I, p. 68,*30-32*: *aññesu hi kālesu devatā kabaḷe kabaḷe ojaṃ pakkhipanti, sambodhidivase ca pana parinibbānadivase ca ukkhaliyaṃ yeva pakkhipanti.*

We know that Cunda served the Buddha with *sūkaramaddava* (Dīgha, II, p. 127,*5*). The early exegetists hesitate over the nature of this dish: fresh meat, both tender and fat, of a piglet or ass, neither too young nor too old (*nātitaruṇassa nātijiṇṇassa ekajeṭṭhakasūkarassa mudusiniddhaṃ pavattamaṃsaṃ)*), or soft boiled rice, cooked with a sauce extracted from the five products of the cow (*muduodanaṃ pañcagorasayūsapācanavidhānam*), or bamboo shoots crushed by pigs (*sūkarehi madditavaṃsakaḷīro*), or again mushrooms growing in a spot trampled by pigs (*sūkarehi madditapadese jātaṃ ahicchattakaṃ*), or finally an elixir of life (*rasāyana*). Cf. Buddhaghosa in the Dīgha Comm., II, p. 568 and the note; Dhammapāla, Udāna Comm., p. 399-400.

After having eaten this food, the Buddha fell seriously ill, but he formally forbade the least reproach to be addressed to Cunda. If this food was so indigestible, it was because, according to certain sources (Dīgha Comm., II, p. 568,*16-17*), "the deities had added to it the nutritive essence which is found in the four great continents surrounded by two thousands islands" (*tattha pana dvisahassadīpaparivāresu catūsu mahādīpesu devatā ojaṃ pakkhipiṃsu*). This is doubtless why, according to the Dīgha, II, p. 127, the Buddha asks Cunda not to serve this food to his monks and to bury the remains in a hole, no-one but the Tathāgata being capable of digesting it.

The sacred food served by Vimalakīrti is not so redoubtable: as long as it is taken with good intentions, it is digested at the end of seven days. This is a refined conception of the sacred meal that Buddhism was not alone in imagining.

INDEX

Abbreviations: B. = Buddha(s); Bs. = Bodhisattva(s); Vim. = Vimalakīrti; Vkn = Vimalakīrtinirdeśa.

abhijñā the five or six super-knowledges LV 2 28 40 66 67 & n. 97 114 130 140 157 172 181 231 235 265; *abhijñānābhijñāta* universally known 2

Abhirati, Akṣobhya's universe CV 243-9; introduced into the Sahāloka 246-8

abhisaṃbodhi supreme or complete enlightenment: devoid of base and inaccessible 171-2

abhisaṃdhi mental reservation 174

abhiṣeka royal unction 3; (comparison) 149

abhūtaparikalpa false imagination 159-60

ācāryamuṣṭi "Master's fist", refusal to teach 157 230

Acintyavimokṣa sub-title of the Vkn LIV-LV; and of the *Avataṃsaka* LVLXXXVI

acintyavimokṣa inconceivable liberation of the Bs. 141-50

action(s), contradictory, of the Bs. 29-32 44-5 55-8 128-33 173-6 234-6

ādāna and *anādāna* grasping and rejection 191

ādarśajñāna mirror-like knowledge, XXXVI 98 n.

ādarśamaṇḍale pratibimbam reflection in a mirror 73 153

adhimukti aspiration, confidence 38 41 103 104 251; *hīnādhimuktika* and *udārādhimuktika* animated by base and noble aspirations 207 208

adhiṣṭhāna supernatural supportive power 2 116 170 206 211 231 235 258 263 271

adhyālambana (p'an-yüan; yüan-lü) object of perception 92 124

adhyāropa, see *āropa*

adhyāśaya high resolve CIV 3 16 21 68 96 109 156 170 235 264 284-6

adhyeṣaṇā, *anumodanā* and *sādhukāra* invitation, congratulation and praise to the B. 232

ādikarmika beginner Bs. 140 269-70

advaya non-duality LXVIII-LXIX 91 188-203

agada panacea 223

agati roundabout ways of the Bs. 173-6; see actions, contradictory

āghātavastu nine causes of irritation 177 & n.

Ajita Keśakambala, sectarian master 57

akalpanā avikalpanā absence of imagining and mental construction: same as pure nature 73

Akaniṣṭha(s), gods located at the summit of the *rūpadhātu* world of form 247 & n.

ākāśabīja seed(s) (not germinating) in space (comparison) 178

ākāśe māpayitum to build in empty space (comparison) 15-16

akṣaṇa and *kṣaṇa* unfavourable and favourable conditions for birth 20 & n. 57 79

akṣara, *svara* and *vijñapti* syllables, sounds and conceptions: are worthless 203

Akṣayamati, Bs. 197 & n.

Akṣayapradīpa text LXXXVI 105 & n.

akṣayapradīpa inexhaustible lamp (comparison) 105

Akṣobhya, B. CV 168 & n. 243-9 & n.

Akṣobhyatathāgatasya vyūhaḥ text LXXV 243

ālambana and *nirālambana* object and absence of object: do not constitute duality 200

ālaya illusionary resting place consisting of the five objects of desire XXXV-XXXVI 48 137 & n. 233 242 263

ālayavijñāna store consciousness XXXVI 137

alms round, how to perform it 51-3

āmalakaphala myrobalan (comparison) 67 & n.

āmiṣa and *dharma* contrast between material

goods and Buddhist doctrine: *āmiṣadāna* and *dharmadāna* material gift and gift of the Law 270; *āmiṣapūjā* and *dharmapūjā* homage through material objects and homage to the Law 255 256 n. 258-63 267; *āmiṣayajña* and *dharmayajña* material offering and offering of the Law 107 & n.
Amitābha, B. 168
Āmrapālīvana, vihāra in Vaiśālī C-CI 1 & n.; enlarged and illuminated 219
amṛta immortality (= Nirvāṇa) 10 307-8; *amṛta* ambrosia 3 24 182 212-3 295 307; perfumed *amṛta* and sacred meal 211-3 307-14
anabhisaṃskāra inaction 130 199 232 & n. 260
anācchedyapratibhāna invincible eloquence 2 & n. 114 265
anādāna, see *ādāna*
anāgama and *anirgama* without arrival or departure 116 n.
Ānanda, assistant of the B. 79-81 & n.; in search of milk 80-2; challenged by Vim. 81-4; questions the B. on the enlarging and illumination of the Āmrapālīvana 219; on the origin, duration and nature of the perfumed food 221-3; renounces his superiority over others 228; is entrusted with Vkn and establishes its title 272-3; Ānanda and Vim. in other texts LXXXIII CVII CVIII CIX
Anantaguṇaratnavyūha, universe 24
ānantarya the five acts of immediate fruition: same as deliverance 55 & n. 292; preferable to the complete deliverance of the Arhats 179
anāsrava, see *samatā*
anātman, see *anitya*; *ātman*
Anikṣiptadhura, Bs. 5 & n.
Animiṣa, Bs. 191
ānimitta, see *śūnyatā* and *vimokṣamukha*
anirgama, see *anāgama*
Aniruddha, disciple: brief biography 65-6 & n.; visited by Mahābrahmā 66-7; questioned by Vim. on his divine eye 67-8
anitya, duḥkha, [*śūnya*], *anātman, śānta,* impermanent, painful, [empty], impersonal, calm 63 & n. 64-5 120 127 148 232 260; *anityaṃ darśayati* demonstrating impermanence 183
anta extreme: *antagrāhadṛṣṭi* belief in the extremes consisting of the views on existence and non-existence 57 & n.; *-anta* period of time: *pūrva-* and *aparānta* prior and posterior time 238
antarikṣanirghoṣa voice from the sky 84 & n. 102 258
anulomikī kṣānti, see *kṣānti*
anumodanā, see *adhyeṣaṇā*
anunaya and *pratigha* affection and aversion 97 127 156
anupūrvī kathā gradual oral teachings for the use of the laity 46 n.
anuśaya (*kleśānuśaya*) residual tendencies of the passions 127 129
anusmṛti the six contemplations 109 & n. 130
anutpāda non-arising (of dharmas) LXIV-LXV 130 n. 132 & n. 287-9
anutpattikadharmakṣānti, see *kṣānti*
anyatīrthika, see sects, non-Buddhist
āpatti fault 71-3 192 n. 215; *āpattyanāpattyanadhyāpattitām upādāya* being based on the non-existence of a fault and its opposite 294
apavāda, see *āropa*
Apramāṇa, universe CV
apramāṇa (*apramāṇacitta*) or *brahmavihāra* four infinite states (*maitrī, karuṇā, muditā, upekṣā*) 13 & n. 40 96-7 107-8 130 & n. 155-8 232
apraṇihita, see *śūnyatā* and *vimokṣamukha*
aprāptaphala he who has not obtained the fruit of the religious life 56
Apratihatanetra, Bs. 198
apratiṣṭhāna absence of basis or of first principle LXXII 158-60 171
apratiṣṭhitanirvāṇa, see *nirvāṇa*
araṇā: method of soothing teaching 54 n.; power to prevent others from producing passion 54 n. 57; *araṇādharma*, unconflicting dharmas 109; *araṇāsamādhi* of Subhūti 54 n.
āropa (*adhyāropa, samāropa*) uncalled-for

affirmation 48 & n. 73 90 & n. 190 191; *samāropa* and *apavāda* uncalled-for affirmation and unjustified negation 48 191

ārya, see *pṛthagjana*

Āryadeva, Mādhyamika scholar LXII XCII-XCVI

āryadhana the seven noble riches 182 n.

āryāṇāṃ tūṣṇīṃbhāvaḥ silence of the holy ones 203 n.

Asamadarśana, Bs. 4 5

asaṃskṛta, see *saṃskṛta*

Asaṅga, Yogācāra scholar LXXVIII

asāre sāropādānam taking for substantial that which is not 101 & n. 108

āśaya (*kalyāṇāśaya*) good intentions or resolve 3 16 17 21 60 61 95 96 n. 235 286

āśīviṣa the (four) poisonous snakes (comparison) 37 103

Āśīviṣopamasūtra text LXXXII 38 111 n.

Aśoka, universe 6

āsravakṣayajñāna knowledge of the destruction of the impurities (knowledge particular to the arhat) 103 & n.

āśrayaparāvṛtti reversal of the support 169 n.

āśrayaparivṛtti change of sex 169 n.

Assagutta, Thera 312

Aṣṭamahāsthānacaityastotra: the ratnastūpa of Vim. mentioned in certain versions CIX-CX

aśva and *hastin* horse(s) and elephant(s): tamed by the goad (comparison) 215

aśvakhaṭuṅka unruly horse (comparison) 214 & n. 215 & n.

Aśvaghoṣa, poet: date of XCIV-XCVI: conversion of 203 n.

ātman and *anātman* self and non-self: do not constitute duality 65 194 200 n.

ātman and *ātmīya* I and mine 189; *ātmagrāha* and *ātmīyagrāha* belief in me and mine 47 122 261

ātmasaṃjñā and *dharmasaṃjñā* notion of self and notion of things 122

avaivartika irreversible: Bs. 60 n. 61 141 222 265; bhūmi 85 265; dharmacakra 3 167 259

Avalokiteśvara, Bs. 5

Avataṃsaka, possible source of Vkn LXXXVI-LXXXVII

avatāra aggression: *avatāraṃ dadāti* giving a hold 185; *avatāraṃ labhate* having a hold 161 & n.; *avatāraprekṣin avatāragaveṣin* 272 & n.

āveṇikadharma exclusive attributes: of the B. 4 13 40 & n. 98 180; of the Bs. LVI-LIX

avetyaprasāda (utter) faith of understanding 3 58 n. 103

avidyā ignorance 173 174 177 194 273

avikalpanā, see *akalpanā*

āyatana six internal and six external bases of consciousness 91 177; see also *cakṣus*, *śrotra* etc.

ayuhaniryuhavigata beyond grasping and rejection 92 109 137

bahuśruta erudition 97 109 228

bala: the five powers of the Bs. 20 131 132 n.; the ten powers of the B. 4 13 40 & n. 98 132 180

bandhana and *mukti* bondage and deliverance 126-7; *bandhana* and *mokṣa* bondage and liberation 192 & n.; *baddha* and *mukta* bound and liberated 2

Bhadracinta or Sucinta, Vim.'s son CVII CVIII

Bhadrajyotis, Bs. 190

bhadrakalpa auspicious period 266 & n.

bhaiṣajya medicine: *bhaiṣajyarāja* healing king 4; *dharmabhaiṣajya* medicine of the Law 4 236; the *bhaiṣajya* called Sarasa (var. Surasa) and Agada 222-3 & n.; Bs. who turn themselves into medicaments 184

Bhaiṣajyarāja, B. 256-7 & n.

Bhāvanākrama I and III quote Vkn CXIV 126 n.

bhojana food: spirit in which it should be eaten 55-8; sacred food, see *amṛta*

bhūmi Bs. stages. The *bhūmi* system is largely passed over in silence by Vkn and the oldest versions of the Prajñāpāramitā XCVIII

bhūtakoṭi limit of reality LXXII 47 91 239 241
bhūtapratyavekṣā correct motive 97
bodhi enlightenment: *bodhi* of the Śrāvakas, Pratyekabuddhas and Buddhas 300-1; purely negative concept 90-3 301-3; *anuttarā samyaksaṃbodhiḥ* already acquired by all beings 89
bodhicitta thought of enlightenment: and the young monks 60-1; *bodhicittotpāda* production of the thought of enlightenment CIV 16 & n. 17 25 26 41 53 68 74 79 99 102 111 112 133 150 166 177 179 218 222 244 n. 248 268 284-5 343; constitutes the true leaving of the world (*pravrajyā*) and ordination (*upasampadā*) 79
bodhimaṇḍa seat of enlightenment 94-9 & n. 253 260
bodhipakṣya or *bodhipākṣikadharma* the thirty-seven auxiliiaries of enlightenment 20 & n. 40 44 97 104 111 259
bodhisattva(s): qualities of 2-4; the fifty-six Bs. present in the Vkn assembly 4-5; how they console the sick and comfort themselves 120-6; of what their bondage (*bandhana*) and deliverance (*mukti*) consist 126; how they blend wisdom (*prajñā*) with skillful means (*upāya*) 126-8; thirty-five aspects of their domain (*gocara*) 128-33; capable of transforming their bodies at will 140; inconceivable liberation (*acintyavimokṣa*) of 141-8; "tempter" Bs. 150-2; how they reconcile *nairātmya* and the *apramāṇa* 155-8; "roundabout ways" of 173-6; prosopopoeia of the Bs. 180-2; various conditions assumed by Bs. in order to benefit beings 183-7; the opinion of thirty-three Bs. on non-duality (*advaya*) 188-203; superiority of Bs. over Śrāvakas 228; but identity of the *bodhisattvacitta* and *śrāvakacitta* 190-1; qualities particular to the Bs. of the Sahāloka 216-7; the Bs. of the Sarvagandhasugandhā universe 205 208-10 217 228-9 236-7; they are inferior to the Bs. of the Sahāloka 216; irreversible (*avaivartika*) Bs. 60 n. 61 141 222 265; beginner (*ādikarmika*) Bs. and veteran (*ciracarita*) Bs. 268-70
bodhisattvapiṭaka basket of the Bs. 259 & n.
bodhivṛkṣa tree of enlightenment 225 & n.; of Akṣobhya 246
Brahmā, see Mahābrahmā
Brahmajāla, Bs. 5
brahmavihāra, see *apramāṇa*
buddha (*tathāgata*): body (*kāya*) of 38-41 81 83 224 227 228 242; various epithets 227-8 256; sameness and inconceivablity of the B. 227-8; praise of the B. by Ratnākara 9-14; *buddha-* or *tathāgatagotra* 52 176-9 234 303-7; great compassion 166 212; inexistence of the B. 238-42; fictitious illnesses 81-4; various deeds in the buddhakṣetras 209 223-6; instruction by a single sound 11-13 & n. 225; the B.'s instruction in the Sarvagandhasugandhā universe 213; in the Sahāloka 213-6; rarity of the B.s' appearance 78-9 & n.; the twelve B. present in Vim.'s house 168; the thousand B. of the *bhadrakalpa* 266-7 n.
buddha-dharma-saṃgha, the Triple Jewel: empty as space 198; to be discarded 57 58 n.; also see *triratna*
buddhakṣetra Buddha-field(s) 14; of what they consist 14-22; how to purify them 14-15 21-2; empty and nonexistent 133 182 210; how they actuate B. deeds 223-6; one and diverse 226-7; conditions of access to them 217-8; indifference of the B. regarding them 226; general description 275-84

Cakravāḍa, mountain 7-8 n. 246
cakṣus the five eyes 67 n. 78; *divyacakṣus* divine eye 66-8 & n. 247; *dharmacakṣus* wisdom eye 26 58 67 n. 138; *prajñācakṣus* eye of the Law 49 67 n. 202
cakṣus, *śrotra*, *ghrāṇa*, *jihvā*, *kāya* and *manas*, the six organs (*indriya*) or internal *āyatana* 196-7 239
campaka and *eraṇḍa* champac tree and castor oil plant (comparison) 165
Campakavarṇa, B. CVI
Candracchattra, king of the Licchavis 211

Candracchattra, son of King Ratnacchattra 258-9 263-7
Candrottara, Bs. 200
Candrottaradārikā, Vim.'s daughter CIX
***Candrottaradārikāpariprcchā*, text CVIII-CIX**
***caraka-pāṣaṇḍika* wandering sectaries 30 & n. 82 n.**
caraṇanikṣepaṇe caraṇotkṣepaṇe whether the Bs. lower or raise their feet 98-9
Catalogues, Chinese, and their comments on the tr. of Vkn XXVI-XXXV
catuṣpariṣad the fourfold assembly 6
Catuṣpratisaraṇasūtra, Sūtra of the Four Refuges LXXXIII 262-3 n.
Chih Ch'ien, translator of Vkn XXVI-XXIX LXXXIX XCI CXVI 80
Chih-i, master of the Tien T'ai school: commentary by, on the Vkn (T 1777) XXXIII; theory of, on Expediency and Truth, and the sickness of expediency LVIII-LIX 32-3 n.
Chih Min-tu, catalogue of, entitled *Ching lun tu lu* XXXI; synthetic editions by, of the Vkn and the *Śūraṃgamasamādhisūtra* XXX-XXXI
Chih Tun, treatise of, on the identity of form and emptiness 196
Chinese catalogues, see Catalogues, Chinese
Chinese commentaries, see Commentaries, Chinese
Ching lun tu lu by Chih Min-tu, lost catalogue XXXI
ch'ing-t'an pure conversation in China 113
ch'üan-shih Expediency and Truth LVIII-LIX
ch'üan-shih shuang hsing tao path of the two-fold practice of Expediency and Truth LVIII
Chu Fa-hu, see Dharmarakṣa
Chung ching lu by Nieh Tao-chên, lost catalogue XXX & n.
Chu Shu-lan, translator of Vkn XXIX
Chu Wei-mo-chieh ching "The annotated Sūtra of Vimalakīrti" (T 1775) XXXIII
ciracarita veteran Bs. 269
citta mind, thought: in the two Vehicles LXXII-LXXXI; *cittena nīyate lokaḥ* the world is led by the mind LXXIV, *cittaṃ prabhāsvaraṃ prakṛtiviśuddham* originally luminous and naturally delivered mind or thought LXXIV-LXXVI 73; *cittasaṃkleśāt sattvāḥ saṃkliśyante cittavyavadānād viśudhyante* through defilement of the mind are beings defiled, through purification of the mind are they purified LXXIV LXXXII 72 & n.; *cittam acittam*, non-thought thought or non-mind mind of the Prajñāpāramitās LXXVIII-LXXXI; *cittam arūpy anidarśanam aniśrayam avijñaptikam*, mind that is immaterial, invisible, without support and without intellect 93
citta, manas and *vijñāna* thought, mind and consciousness LXXIII 47 198
cittadama control of the mind 109
cittaniyama and *aniyama* control and licence of the mind 128
cittotpāda*, see *bodhicitta
Commentaries, Chinese, written or oral, on Vkn XXXIII
comparisons, see *upamāna*
confession, private 70-1 n.
contradictory actions of the Bs., see actions, contradictory
Council of Lhasa, invokes Vkn as an authority CXIV
Cunda, the blacksmith 314
cyuti and *jāti* death and birth 88 242 243

dāna giving: *trimaṇḍalapariśuddha* triply pure 51 n.; impartial 112; see *pāramitā*
Dāntamati, Bs. 193
Daśabhūmikavibhāṣā, work by Nāgārjuna translated by Dharmarakṣa XCVII
deśanā, *deśaka* and *śrāvaka* instruction, instructor and listener: non-existence of 48-9
Devakanyās, daughters of the gods: offered to Jagatīṃdhara 101; given to Vimalakīrti 102; converted by him 102-4; sent back to Māra 104-5; counselled by Vim. 105
Devaputras, sons of the gods: of three kinds 611
Devarāja, Bs. 4 5

Devī, goddess living in Vim.'s house 160-72; miracle of the flowers of 160-2; miracle of the sexes of 169-71

Dharma, Buddhist Law: cannot exist or be taught 46-9; or sought 134-8

dharma things or phenomena: *niḥsvabhāva* and *svabhāvaśūnya*, without self-nature and empty of self-nature LXIII; *anutpanna* and *aniruddha* unarisen and unextinguished LXIV-LXV; *ādiśānta* and *prakṛtiparinirvṛta* originally calm and naturally Nirvāṇa-ized LXV-LXVI; *alakṣaṇa*, *anabhilāpya* and *acintya* without marks, inexpressible and unthinkable LXVII-LXVIII; *sama* and *advaya* the same and without duality LXVIII-LXIX; *tucchaka*, *riktaka*, *asāraka*, *vaśika* (or *avaśika*), *aniketa* void, vain, worthless, dependent (independent), abodeless 233; *śūnya* empty 63 65; *nirmāṇasvabhāva* like illusionary creations 243; *niḥsattva*, *nirjīva*, *niṣpoṣa*, *niṣpudgala* without sentient being, living being, feeding being, personality 47 n. 260; see also *āmiṣa*

dharmabhaiṣajya medicine of the Law 4 236

dharmacakra wheel of the Law: of three-fold revolution and twelve aspects 10; three-fold turning 10 n.; *avaivartika*, irreversible 3 167 259

dharmadhana riches of the Law 181 236

dharmadhātu element of the Law LXXII 47 91 115 129

dharmakāya body of the Law LXXVII 39 83 224-5 n. 296-7 305 306

Dharmaketu, Bs. 4 5

dharmanaya principle of the Law or things 28 113 n. 198 269

dharmānudharmanidhyapti understanding the Law according to the Law 261

dharmānudharmapratipatti applying the Law according to the Law 261

dharmaparyeṣṭi search for the Law: consists in not seeking anything 134-8

dharmapūjā homage to the Law 255 259-63 267

Dharmarakṣa or Chu Fa-hu, translator and author of a condensed Vkn XXIX-XXX; translator of *Daśabhūmikavibhāṣā* of Nāgārjuna XCVII

dharmārāmarati pleasure in the garden of the Law 97 103-4

Dharmarātridvayasūtra, source of Vkn LXXXIII 12

dharmasārdhavihāra consorting with the Law 137-8

dharmaskandha the five pure elements of the Law (*śīla*, *samādhi*, *prajñā*, *vimukti*, *vimuktijñānadarśana*) 39 & n. 212 & n. 227

Dharmatāśīla, translator of Vkn and compiler of *Mahāvyutpatti* XXXVII

Dharmavikurvaṇa, Bs. 189

dharmayajña ritual of the giving of the Law 107-11 251 260

Dharmeśvara, Bs. 4 5

dharmoddāna (or *dharmamudrā*, *dharmapūrvāparānta*) summaries of the Law, e.g.: *anityāḥ sarvasaṃskārāḥ*, impermanent are all formations..., etc. 63-5 & n. 120 & n. 127 148 232 260

Dharmottara, śreṣṭhiputra converted by Mañjuśrī 30

dhātu the four great elements 120 121; and the *ākāśadhātu* space element 196 239. – *dhātu* worlds see *traidhātuka*

dhutāṅga the twelve or thirteen ascetic rules 50 n.

dhyāna trance, meditation 96 182; see *pāramitā*

dhyāna, *vimokṣa*, *samādhi* and *samāpatti*, ecstatic states, liberation, concentrations, and recollections 40 131 & n. 230

dhyānarasāsvādana tasting the flavours of the trances 29 & n. 126 157 & n. 230

discipline (*vinaya*) beings are disciplined by means of: various wonders used by Bs. 143-7; Śākyamuni's special discourses 214-6; skillful actions of the Buddhakṣetras 223-6; Akṣobhya's refusal to intervene with Vim. 247

disease (*vyādhi*): 404 bodily diseases 36 & n.; 84,000 diseases caused by the passions 41 & n.; see also illness; sickness

dṛṣṭa, *śruta*, *mata*, *vijñāta*, seen, heard, thought, known: expression describing

the entire field of experience 138 & n. 241 & n.
dṛṣṭi false view(s): *dṛṣṭigata* the 62 kinds of false views (identical to deliverance and forming the *tathāgatagotra*) 44 & n. 57 & n. 119 & n. 127 129 & n. 177 183; rejection of the *dṛṣṭi* constituting *bodhi* 90 125; *dṛṣṭiparyutthāna* being possessed by false views 125 127; *anunayadṛṣṭi* affective views 125 127; *bhavābhavadṛṣṭi* views on existence and non-existence 57 n.; *śāśvatocchedadṛṣṭi* views on eternity and annihilation 57 n.; *satkāyadṛṣṭi* belief in a personality 178
dukha, see *sukha*; *duḥkaṃ parijñeyam* suffering must be known... 135 & n.
Duṣprasaha, B. 111 & n. 168 & n.
dveṣa, see *rāga*

ekajātipratibaddha separated from Buddhahood by only one existence 50 222
ekalakṣaṇa and *alakṣaṇa* single mark and absence of mark: do not constitute duality 191
ekalakṣaṇa and *bhinnalakṣaṇa* single mark and multiple marks 191 240
ekanaya (i hsiang, i li) single principle 109-11 n. 198 & n.; *ekanayajñāna* knowledge of the single principle 109; *ekanaya* and *ekayāna* single principle and the one Vehicle 109 n.
ekaputra only son (comparison) 118
ekasvareṇodāharaṇa teaching in a single sound 11-14 & n. 225 n.
ekayāna, see Vehicles; also *ekanaya*
êrh chiao the two teachings LIX
Êrh chiao lun, text by Tao-an XCIV
êrh chih the two knowledges LIX-LX
Êrh Ch'in lu by Seng-jui, lost catalogue XXXII & n.

Fa-hsien chuan, comment of, on Vaiśālī CI-CII
fault (*āpatti*), non-existent 71-2 294
Fêng fa Yao by Hsi Ch'ao: quotes Vkn (Chih Ch'ien version) 73 n.
field, see *buddhakṣetra*; *puṇyakṣetra*
food, sacred 204 & n. 307-14

Gaganagañja, Bs. 4 & n. 5
gambhīra, gambhīrāvabhāsa... profound, of profound aspect, etc.: series of adjectives descriptive of Buddhist texts 259 & n.
Gambhīramati, Bs. 198
gandha, see *rūpa*
Gandhahastin, Bs. 5 & n.
Gandhakuñjaranāga, Bs. 5
Gandhamādana, mountain 7 & n.
Gandhavyūhāhāra, devaputra 205
gaṇikā courtesan: the Bs. turn into courtesans 185 & n.; see *veśyāgṛha*
Ganymede 205-6 n.
gati destiny 214; various *gatis* assumed by the Bs. 173 & n.
gift of languages, see languages, gift of
Giryagrapramardirāja, Bs. 5
Gītamitra or Ch'i-to-mi, translator of Vkn XXI
glānya, see disease; illness; sickness
gotra and *tathāgatagotra*, various families and the family of the B. 176-9 303-7
guhyasthāna secret reserves of the B. and Bs. 114 & n.
gūthoḍigallaparipūrṇa full of filth 23

Han lu by Chu Shih-hsing, lost catalogue XXVI & n.
Himadri, mountain 7 & n.
house of Vim.: the *fang-chang* of the Chinese CIII-CIV; emptied by Vim 116; furnished with immense thrones 139-40; eight wonders of 166-9
hrī and *apatrāpya* shame and confusion 182; decency and modesty 210
Hsi Ch'ao, on the creative mind 73 n.
Hsieh Ling-yün, poet and philosopher, eulogy by, of the ten comparisons 34 n.
Hsüan-tsang, translator of Vkn XXXIV-XXXVII CXVI; remarks of, on Vaiśālī CII-CIII
Hui-yüan, author of T 1776, commentary on Vkn XXXIII

illness (*glanya*, *vyādhi*): simulated illness of Vim. 32-3; causes and duration of 117-20; illnesses of the B. 80-4 294-8; see also disease; sickness
Indrajāla, Bs. 5 & n.

indriya the five spiritual faculties, faith, etc. 3 20 28 & n.; should be known in order to convert beings 28 49 60 61 131 231; — *indriya* the six sense organs or internal *āyatana*, see *cakṣus*, *śrotra*...
iñjita movement 90
instruction: to the new monks 59-61; to two guilty monks 70-4; through a single sound or through silence 12-13 & n. 148 225
īrṣyā jealousy 218
īryāpatha (bodily) attitudes CVI 28 44 132 133 226 227 231 232

Jagatīṃdhara, Bs.: tempted by Māra 99-102 & n.
Jālinīprabha, Bs. 5 & n.
jāṅgalapuṣpa, flowers growing only in the jungle (comparison) 177-8
jarodāpana old well (comparison) 36 & n.
jātyandha blind from birth (comparison) 22 & n. 52 61 149 154
Jetavana, grove in Śrāvastī 106 & n. 311
ju-i "back-scratcher": attribute of Mañjuśrī 113 n.
jyotis, see *tamas*

Kakuda Kātyāyana, sectarian master 57
Kālaparvata, mountain 7 8 n.
kalpa cosmic period: *mahākalpa* great period 184 n. 266 n.; *asaṃkhyeyakalpa* incalculable kalpa (*saṃvartakalpa*, etc.) 184 n.; *antarakalpa* intermediary or small kalpa 184 & n. 266 n.; *antarakalpa* periods of disease (*roga*), of famine (*durbhikṣā*) and of the knife (*śastra*) 184-5 & n.; *bhadrakalpa* or auspicious period when a thousand Buddhas appear 266 & n.
kalpaṃ vā kalpāvaśeṣaṃ vā: meaning of the expression 148 & n. 254
kalpa, *vikalpa*, *parikalpa*, etc. imagination 73 90 118 159-60 161 198 241
kalpoddāha final conflagration 183 & n.
karmapatha the ten good or bad paths of action 20 & n. 40 177 214 231
kaṣāya the five corruptions 83 n. 84 & n. 264 n.
kathāvatthu the ten good subjects of conversation 59 n.
Kauśika, epithet of Śakra 101 & n.
kāya body (human): deficiencies of 33-8 121-2; see also *buddha*; *dharmakāya*
kāyavāgmanaḥsaṃvara discipline of body, speech and mind 199 & n.
khadyotaka glow-worm (comparison) 60 & n. 151
kleśa passion 159 166 181 182 231; *kleśanirghātana*, *kleśapraśamana* destruction of the passions 98 103; *kleśānuśaya* residual tendencies of the passions 127 129; *kleśaparyutthāna* intrusion, invasion of the passions 92 127 156; *kleśavyādhi* diseases caused by the passions 4 41 & n. 236; *āgantukakleśa* chance passions LXXIV LXXV 125; *saṃskārakleśa*, *saṃsārāvacarakleśa* false passions and imaginations, causes of sickness 121; one should link oneself with all Māras, consort with all the *kleśa* and identify oneself with the self-nature of the passions (*kleśasvabhāva*) 57; the Bs. subjects himself to false views (*dṛṣṭi*) and the invasion of the passions (*kleśaparyutthāna*) 127; the Bs. follows the way of all the *kleśa* of the world, but he is absolutely undefiled (*asaṃkliṣṭa*) and naturally pure (*svabhāvena pariśuddhaḥ*) 175; he who bases himself on conditioned things, those mines of the passions, and who has not yet seen the noble truths (*na dṛṣṭasatya*) is capable of producing the thought of supreme and perfect enlightenment 177; all the passions are the family of the Tathāgata 178; without entering the sea of the passions (*kleśasamudra*), it is impossible to obtain omniscience (*sarvajñāna*) 179; the Bs. does not abide in the unconditioned (*asaṃskṛta*) because he knows perfectly all the diseases caused by the passions (*kleśavyādhi*); he does not exhaust the conditioned (*saṃskṛta*) because he appeases all these diseases 236; the Bs. does not consort with the passions, but chases away the darkness of the passions of all beings 245

klība and *antaḥpura* eunuch and harem 31
Krakucchanda, first B. of the *bhadrakalpa* 266-7 & n.
krīḍādyūtasthāna gaming houses, frequented by Vim. 29
kṛtajña, kṛtajñatā gratitude to the B. 49 105 180
kṛtakṛtya duty 1
kṣaṇa*, see *akṣaṇa
kṣānti conviction, certainty, certain knowledge: *anulomikī kṣāntiḥ* preparatory certainty 25 & n. 58; *anutpattikadharmakṣānti* certainty concerning the non-arising of dharmas 25 & n. 93 172 189 203 218 222 270 289-91; of three kinds: *ghoṣānugā, anulomikī, **pratilabdhā***, verbal, preparatory, definitively acquired 290-2; *pratilabdhakṣantika* 222
kṣānti patience, see *pāramitā*
kṣāntisauratya patience and kindness 40 & n. 96 & n.
kṣaya and *akṣaya* exhaustible and inexhaustible: do not constitute duality 194 & n.
Kṣayākṣayadharmamukha, Treatise of the Law on the Exhaustible and the Inexhaustible 229-36
kṣetra, see *buddhakṣetra*; *puṇyakṣetra*
Kṣetrasamalaṃkāra, Bs. 5
Kṣīraprabhabuddhasūtra (T 809), recension of the *Vatsasūtra* enlarged under the influence of Vkn LXXXIII-LXXXIV CVIII 80-1 n.
***Ku lu*, lost catalogue XXVI & n. XCI**
Kumārajīva, translator of Vkn XXXI-XXXIV CXVI 83 n.; opinion of, on the date of the Nirvāṇa, Aśvaghoṣa, Nāgārjuna and Harivarman XCII-XCVII
kumbhakāracakra potter's wheel (comparison) 144 247
kuñjaranāga and *gardabha* (contest) between dragon-elephant and ass (comparison) 151
kuśala and *akuśala* good and bad: do not constitute duality 192 & n.
Kūtanimittasamatikrānta, Bs. 5

lābhā naḥ sulabdhāḥ (in Pāli, *lābhā... suladdhaṃ*): meaning of 249 & n.
lakṣaṇānuvyañjana primary and secondary marks 7 & n. 109 127 132 175 181 225 230 234
languages, the B.'s and Bs.'s gift of 12 & n. 148
laukika and *lokottara*, worldly and transcendental: do not constitute duality 193 & n.
lekhanāśālā writing-rooms: frequented by Vim. 30
lokadharma the eight worldly states, gain, loss, etc. 11 n. 231 & n. 296
Lokapāla(s), the four great divine kings, world guardians, 6 32 & n; will protect Vkn 272; see also Śakras...
lokottara, see *laukika*
Lung-shu p'u-sa chuan (T 2047), Life of Nāgārjuna XCII XCVII

Maccharikosiya, śreṣṭhin 311
Madhyamaka or Mādhyamika, school of the Great Vehicle: principal scholars of LXII; great tenets of LXII-LXXII; Madhyamaka in the Vkn LXII-LXXII LXXVIII-LXXXI
Madhyamakavṛtti of Candrakīrti, quotes Vkn XXV CXIII
Mahābhijñājñanābhibhū, B. 244 n.
mahābhūta the four great elements (*pṛthivī, ap, tejas, vāyu*) 35 120 & n
Mahābrahmā, king of the Rūpadhātu and leader of the Brahmakāyika gods 6 & n.; does not possess superior knowledge 32 & n ; Mahābrahmā Śikhin: meaning of the epithet 6 & n.; does not see the impurities of the Sahāloka 22-3; Mahābrahmā Śubhavyūha: visits Aniruddha with ten thousand Brahmās, and effects the *cittotpāda* 66-8
Mahācakravāḍa, mountain 7 8 n.
Mahākāśyapa, disciple: brief biography 49-50 n.; seeks alms among the poor 49-51; converted to the Mahāyāna 53; admires the *acintyavimokṣa* of the Bs. and deplores the ignorance of the Śrāvakas 149-50; criticizes the Śrāvakas 179-80
Mahākātyāyana, disciple : brief biography

62-3 n.; explains the *dharmoddāna* to bhikṣus 63; discomfited by Vim. 64-5
Mahāmucilinda, mountain 7 8 n.
Mahānetra, B. 243 n.
Mahāparinirvāṇasūtra (T 374 and 375): concerning the *tathāgatagarbha* LXXVII
Mahāprajñāpāramitopadeśa (T 1509): quotes Vkn extensively XCII CXI; seems to refer to an enlarged version of Vkn XXXIV 83 n.
mahāpuruṣavitarka the eight reflections fit for a Great Man 66 n.
Mahāsāṃghika(s), sect of the Small Vehicle: theory on the luminous mind LXXV; on the silence of the B. 12-13 n.; on the illnesses of the B. 295-6
Mahāsaṃnipāta (T 397): probable source of Vkn LXXXVI-LXXXVII & n.; introduces Vim. into its stories and jātakas CV-CVI
mahāsamudra great sea: intelligence of 28 & n.; emptied into a pore of the skin 143; unfathomable 228
mahāsamudra and *gokhura* the great sea and the footprints of an ox (comparison) 60
mahāsamudre maṇiratnāni precious pearls in the great sea (comparison) 179
Mahāsthāmaprāpta, Bs. 5 & n.
mahāvaidyarāja great king-physician 121
Mahāvana, forest near Vaiśālī 43 & n. 59 66
Mahāvyūha, Bs. 4 & n. 5
Mahāvyutpatti: date of XXXVIII & n.
Mahāyānasūtra(s): Vkn may have been inspired by earliest LXXXIV-LXXXVII; Indian tradition on origin of LXXXVIII-LXXXIX; difficulty of dating XCVI-XCVII
mahāyānavarṇana praise of the Great Vehicle 49
Mahāyānāvatāraśāstra (T 1634) of Sāramati: quotes Vkn CXII-CXIII & n.
Maitreya, Bs.: present in the assembly 5; prerogative as future B. contested by Vim. 85-93; and the great treasure LXXXIV 168 n.; receives transmission of Vkn 268; swears to protect it 270-1
Maitreyaparipṛcchopadeśa (T 1525): quotes Vkn CXI
Maitreyavyākaraṇa, source of Vkn LXXXIV 167-8 n.
manas, see *citta*
mānastabdha proud and vain 186
mānastambha pride 174
Maṇicūḍa, Bs. 5
Maṇikūṭarāja, Bs. 201
Maṇiratnacchattra, Bs. 5
Mañjuśrī, Bs.: present in assembly 5; converts two lovers 30 n.; Mañjuśrī and Vim. represented on carvings 113 n.; agrees to visit Vim. 113-5; exchanges greetings with him 116-7; discusses universal emptiness 118-9; the nature of sickness 119-20; and consolations to be given to the sick 120-6; informs Vim. of the thrones of the Merudhvajā universe 138-9; questions Vim, on *pudgalanairātmya* 153; and the four *apramāṇa* 155; discusses with him the baselessness of all things 158-60; questions Vim. on the roundabout ways of the Bs. 173-6; on the *tathāgatagotra* 176-9; approves Vim.'s silence on nonduality 202-3; immobilizes the Bs. 206; accompanies Vim. to the Āmrapālīvana 219; praises the B. 273
Mañjuśrīmūlakalpa (T 1191): quotes Vkn CX
mantravidyā magical arts 183
manyanā, see *vikṣepa*
Māra, the evil one: role of, in Buddhism 99-101 n.; disguises himself as Śakra in order to mislead the Bs. Jagatīṃdhara 99-102; discomfited by Vim. 102 104-5; the four Māras 100 n. 129 182 336; *Mārakarman*, Māra works 183; *Māragati*, path of Māra 175; *Māracamū*, hordes of Māra 10 231 253; necessity of associating with Māra and imitating him without participating in his works 57 129 185 226; Māra forms the retinue of Vim. 119; Bs. disguised as Māra 150-5
Mārakarmavijetā, Bs. 5
Mārapramardaka, Bs. 5
mārga path: *darśana-* and *bhāvanāmārga* paths of vision and meditation 10 n. 229;

mārga and *kumārga* good and bad paths: do not constitute duality 132 201
Marīci, universe 111-2 & n.
Maskarin Gośālīputra, sectarian master 57
Maudgalyāyana, disciple: brief biography 45-6 n.; instructs the laity 46; discomfited by Vim. 46-9
māyākāranirmita created by an illusionist 153 242
māyāpuruṣa illusionary man 49 52
meditation without content 43-4 n.
Merudhvajā, universe 139
Merupradīparāja, B.: sends thrones to Vim. 139; increases the height of the Śrāvakas 141
miracles, see wonders
mithyātva the eight depravities 53 & n. 177 & n.
mitra friend: *kalyāṇa-* and *pāpamitra* good and bad friends 2 104
moha, see *rāga*
mokṣa, see *bandhana*
morality (*śīla*): according to Vim. 71 3; in the perspective of the two Vehicles 292-4
mountains: various names of 7 8 n.
mrakṣa hypocrisy 21 157
mṛṣā, see *satya*.
Mucilinda, mountain 7 8 n.
muktāhāra pearl necklace: transformed into a belvedere 111-2
mukti, see *bandhana*
Mūrdhābhiṣiktarājasūtra (T 477, 478, 479): devoted to Bhadracinta or Sucinta, son of Vim. CVII-CVIII

Nāgārjuna, Mādhyamika scholar: discovers and memorizes the Mahāyānasūtras LXXXVIII; works of XCI-XCII; Kumārajīva, translator of XCII & n.; date of, according to modern opinion XCIII; according to Kumārajīva and his disciples and contemporaries XCIII-XCVII
nairātmya impersonality: *pudgala-* and *dharmanairātmya* non-existence of individual and things 47 n. 58 73 153 n. 233; non-existence of a being illustrated by thirty-five comparisons 153-5; how it can be reconciled with the virtue of goodwill 155-8
Nandimitrāvadāna (T 2030): mentions Vkn CXIII
Naradatta (Nārada, Nālada, Nālaka), identified with Mahākātyāyana 62 n.
Nārāyaṇa, Bs. 193
nārāyaṇabala power equal to that of Nārāyaṇa 175 n.
Nāstika(s), nihilists: different from Mādhyamikas LXXI & n.
navabhikṣu new monk 59 & n.
nidhāna or *nidhi* treasure: *akṣayanidhāna* inexhaustible treasure (of the Bs.) 186; the four inexhaustible treasures at Vim.'s 29 n. 167-8 & n.; the circulation of the Inexhaustible Treasure in China 186 n.
nirālambana, see *alambana*
Nirālambanadhyāna, Bs. 5
niraya hell: visited by the Bs. 185
Nirgrantha Jñātiputra, sectarian master 57
nirmāṇa, *nirmitapuruṣa* imaginary creature 58 153 209 225
nirmitabodhisattva imaginary Bs., created by Vim. 206; goes to the Sarvagandhasugandhā 207-8; returns to the Sahāloka with the perfumed *amṛta* 210-1; discourses on the inexhaustible food 212-3
nirodhasamāpatti recollection of extinction 44 & n. 154 201 & n.
nirvaṇa: *nirvāṇābhirati* and *saṃsāraparikheda* delight in *nirvāṇa* and repugnance for *saṃsāra*: do not constitute duality 201; whether the desire for *nirvāṇa* is permissible 135-7 n.; *apratiṣṭhitanirvāṇa* not fixed in *nirvāṇa* 45 n.; *nirvāṇa* defined as *apiṇḍa* 52 n.; see *saṃsāra* and *nirvāṇa*
Nirvāṇa of Śākyamuni: date of, according to Kumārajīva XCIV
Niṣparidāha, universe CVI
Nityamuditendriya, Bs. 4 5
Nityapralambahasta, Bs. 4 5
nityasnāpanaparimardanabhedanavidhvaṃsanadharma: meaning of the expression 35 n.
Nityatapta, Bs. 4
Nityodyukta, Bs. 5 & n.

Nityotkṣiptahasta, Bs. 4 & n. 5
nīvaraṇa the five hindrances 177 & n.
niyāma, *samyaktavaniyāma* certainty or predestination to acquire the absolute good or Nirvāṇa 18 n. 177 233 & n.; *niyāmāvakrānti* entry into this certainty 92 129; *avakrānta* and *anavakrāntaniyāma* 221-2; *samyaktvaniyatarāśi*, *mithyātvaniyatarāśi* and *aniyatarāśi* 303-4
noises, various, transformed into teachings 147-8

ojas nutritive essence 313-4
Ovid 105 n.

pādāṅguṣṭhenotkṣipati touching with the toe 23-4 & n.
padmam ivodake jātam like the lotus born in water (comparison) 14 & n.
padmaṃ yathāgnimadhye like the lotus in the heart of a fire (comparison) 185
Padmaśrīgarbha, Bs. 5 & n.
Padmavyūha, Bs. 5 & n. 200
Pañcaguṇa, B. CV-CVI
parable: of the poor wretch and the rich man 31 n.; of the man in the well and the enraged elephant 37 & n.; of the five killers, four poisonous snakes and the empty village 37-8 & n.
pāramitā perfection(s): the six (*dāna*, *śīla*, *kṣānti*, *vīrya*, *dhyāna* and *prajñā*) 17-18 29 96-7 108 130 157 167 216 240 259; and the vices opposed to them (*mātsarya*, *dauḥśīlya*, *vyāpāda*, *kausīdya*, *vikṣepa*, *dauḥprajñā*) 29 174 214 240; the ten perfections (as the six, plus *upāyakauśalya*, *praṇidhāna*, *bala*, *jñāna*) 2 & n.; the *pāramitā* and their transference to omniscience (*sarvajñānapariṇāmaṇā*) do not constitute duality 197
Paranirmitavaśavatin(s), gods of the *kāmadhātu* (world of desire) 23 & n.
Parigūḍha, Bs. 194
parikalpa, see *kalpa*
pariṇāma digestion: of the sacred food 221-3 312-4
pariṇāmanā transference of merit 20 & n. 21 127 230 232
parinirvāṇasaṃdarśana (imaginary) manifestation of full Nirvāṇa 133
Pārśva, Hīnayānist scholar: converts Aśvaghoṣa 203 n.
paścime kāle paścime samaye: meaning of the expression 264 & n. 268
passions, see *kleśa*
perfume-trees 205
piṇḍa, *piṇḍapāta*, *piṇḍāya carati* food and alms-round 49-53; *apiṇḍa* "not eating" = Nirvāṇa 52 & n.; *piṇḍagrāha* belief in a material object 52
Prabhāketu, Bs. 4 & n. 5 196
Prabhāvyūha, Bs.: present in the assembly 4 & n. 5; questions Vim. on the *bodhimaṇḍa* 94
prādeśikacitta ignoble sentiment 212 & n.
pradīpa, *akṣayapradīpa* inexhaustible lamp (comparison) 105 & n.
prajñā wisdom: *upāyopāttā* and *upāyānupāttā* acquired and not acquired through skillful means 126-7; see *pāramitā*
prajñā and *bodhi* in the two Vehicles 298-303
Prajñākūṭa, Bs. 5 & n.
Prajñāpāramitāstotra of Rāhulabhadra XCVII
Prajñāpāramitāsūtra: source of Vkn LXIX LXXXIV-LXXXV XCVIII 195-6 n.
prākṛtapuṇya ordinary merit: value of 31-3 & n.
Pramati, Bs. 5 196
Prāmodyarāja, Bs. 4
praṇidhāna or *mahāpraṇidhāna* the Bs. vows 28 & n. 96 121 157 172 232 235 282
Praṇidhānapraveśaprāpta, Bs. 4
prapañca idle chatter (according to the Chinese translations) 48 135 203 n.
Prasiddhapratisaṃvitprāpta, Bs. 4
Pratibhānakūṭa, Bs. 4 & n. 5
pratigha, see *anunaya*
prātihārya, see wonders
pratipatti religious practice 97 & n. 109;

dharmānudharmapratipatti, apply the Law according to the Law 261 & n.
pratisaṃlayana solitary meditation 43-5 & n. 109
pratisaṃvid the four infallible penetrations 260 & n.
pratisaraṇa the four refuges or exegetical rules 261-3 & n.
pratītyasamutpāda dependent co-production: in reality a non-production LXIV-LXV & n. 3 & n. 4 97 & n. 129 260 263
Pratyakṣadarśana, Bs. 194
pravrajyā leaving the world 75-8 & n. 109; advisability of *cittotpāda* in its stead 79
prayoga effort 17 & & n. 21 159
pre-eminence, Vim.'s, among all classes of beings 31-2
Priyadarsana, Bs. 195 & n.
pṛthagjana and *ārya* the worldly and the holy: identity of 44 & n. 56 & n. 128 & n.
pudgalanairātmya, see *nairātmya*
pūjā homage: *tathāgatapūjā* 254; *dharmapūjā* 255 258-63; *āmiṣapūjā* and *dharmapūjā* 255
puṇya- jñāna- and *prajñāsaṃbhāra* store of merit, knowledge and wisdom 3 103 109 173 175
Puṇyakṣetra, Bs. 199
puṇyakṣetra field of merit: quality not to be aspired to 57 & n.
puṇyāpuṇyāniñjyābhisaṃskāra meritorious, demeritorious and neutral actions: identity of 199-200
Pūraṇa Kāśyapa, sectarian master 57 62 n.
Pūrṇamaitrāyaṇīputra, disciple: brief biography 59 n.; instructions of, to the new monks 59-60; ends by pitying the Śravakas 61
pūrvanimitta presage 219 & n.
pūrvayoga antecedents or retrospective 101 n. 255 & n.
Puṣya, Bs. 192
Puṣyavīrya, jātaka of Vim. CVI
Puṣyayajña, brahman CVI; six sons of CVI
pūtikabījā rotten seed (comparison) 149 & n. 154
rāga, dveṣa and *moha* craving, hatred and delusion: the three basic passions, not to be destroyed as they are themselves deliverance 55 154 163 & n. 174 177 196-7
Rāhula, disciple and son of the B.: brief biography 74-5 n.; teaches the advantages of leaving the world 75
Rāhulabhadra, Mādhyamika scholar XCVII
rakṣāvaraṇagupti help and protection against obstacles 253 & n.
rasa, see *rūpa*
rasāsvādana, dhyānarasāsvādana tasting the flavour of the trances 29 & n. 126 157 230
Ratnabahula, B. 168
Ratnacandra, B. 168 & n.
Ratnacchattra, cakravartin king of the past: heaps offerings on the B. Bhaiṣajyarāja for five *antarakalpas* 258; is the present B. Ratnārcis 265; thousand sons of, continue his offerings for five *antarakalpas* 258; they are or will be the thousand B. of the *bhadrakalpa* 266 & n.
Ratnadaṇḍin, Bs. 5
Ratnadatta, Bs. 5
Ratnākara, śreṣṭhiputra and Bs.: house of, in Vaiśālī CII; offering of parasols by CIII 6-7; stanzas of, to the B. 9-14; enquiry of, regarding *buddhakṣetra* 14-15
Ratnaketudhāraṇīsūtra, section of *Mahāsaṃnipāta*, probable source of Vkn LXXXVII 100-1 n.
Ratnakūṭa, Bs. 4 & n. 5
Ratnakūṭa (T 310), source of Vkn LXXXV LXXXVII
Ratnakūṭacaturdharmopadeśa (T 1526) of Vasubandhu: quotes Vkn CXII
Ratnamudrahasta, Bs. 4 & n. 5 201
Ratnapāṇi, Bs. 4 & n. 5
Ratnaparvata, mountain 7-8 & n.
ratnapātre pūtikabhojanam rotten food in a precious bowl (comparison) 60
Ratnapriya, Bs. 5
Ratnārcis, B.: present in Vim's dwelling 168 & n.; was formerly the king Ratnacchattra 265

Ratnaśrī, B. 168 & n.
Ratnaśrī, Bs. 5 & n.
Ratnaśūra, Bs. 5 & n.
Ratnavyūha, B. 24 & n. 168 & n.
Ratnavyūha, Bs. 4 & n.
Ratnolkāparigṛhīta, Bs. 4-5
ṛddhi psychic power; *ṛddhibala* psychic power of the Bs. 142; *ṛddhi* of the Śrāvakas and *maharddhi* of the Bs. 142-3 n.; *ṛddhipāda* the four bases of psychic power 20 25 131
ṛddhyabhisaṃskāraṃ pratisaṃharati to withdraw psychic power 25 & n.
Roca, last B. of the *bhadrakalpa* 206 & n.
roundabout ways (*agati*) or contradictory actions of the Bs. LVII-LX 20-30 44-5 & n. 55-8 128-33 173-6 234-6
rūpa and *rūpaśūnyatā*: relationship between form and the emptiness of form LXIX 195 & n.
rūpa, śabda, gandha, rasa, spraṣṭavya and *dharma* the six sense objects or external *āyatana* 52 134 161
rūpa, vedanā, saṃjñā, saṃskāra, vijñāna the five aggregates (*skandha*) and their respective *tathatā* 239; also see *skandha*

śabda, see *rūpa*
Saddharmapuṇḍarīka: on the *ekayāna* 164 n.; on Akṣobhya 244 n.; on *paścimakāla*... 264 n.; on pure universes 277-9; on the limited knowledge of the Arhats 306-7
sādhukāra, see *adhyeṣanā*
Sahāloka, Śākyamuni's universe and *buddhakṣetra*: type of impure universe 277-8; seen as impure by Śāriputra 22-3 244; seen as pure by Mahābrahmā 22-3; miraculously transformed by the B. 23-4; visited by the Bs. of the Sarvagandhasugandhā 209-11; superiority of the Bs. of 216-7; absorbs the Abhirati universe 247-8
Śakra, divinity and king of the gods of the *kāmadhātu* (world of desire): twelve thousand Śakras present in the assembly 6; Vim. among the Śakras 32 & n.; Śakra disguised as a brahman 80 n.; Māra disguised as Śakra 99-102 & n.; Śakra promises to protect Vkn 252-3
Śakra, Brahmā and Prajeśvara: the Bs. assume role of 147 184
Śakras, Brahmās, Lokapālas and Devaputras 6 29 115-6 139 147 165 167 213 220
Samadarśana, Bs. 4 5
Samādhivikurvitarāja, Bs. 4 5
Samantabhadra, B. 205 n.
samapakṣa, impartial: epithet of Bs. 185
samāropa, see *āropa*
samatā integral sameness: *dharmasamatā* sameness of all things in relation to one another 11 51 55 92-3 163; in particular, sameness of depravity (*mithyātva*) and righteousness (*samyaktva*) 53; of worldly dharmas and B. dharmas 55; of the *ānantarya* misdeeds and deliverance (*vimukti*) 55; of the Self and Nirvāṇa 123; of sickness (*vyādhi*) and emptiness (*śūnyatā*) 123; of Bs. mind and Śrāvaka mind 190-1; of the single mark (*ekalakṣaṇa*) and the absence of mark 191-2; of the impure (*sāsrava*) and the pure (*anāsrava*) 192-3; of light (*jyotis*) and darkness (*tamas*) 200-1; *sarvasattvasamatā* sameness of all beings 159; *cittasamatā* sameness of mind 23 217
śamatha and *vipaśyanā* tranquillity and insight 17 40 & n. 78 96 132 & n.
saṃbodhyaṅga the seven limbs of enlightenment 20 132 & n. 259
saṃgrahavastu the four means of converting beings 19 & n. 97 108 157 217
Saṃjayin Vairaṭīputra, sectarian master 57
saṃjñā, see *rūpa*
Sāṃkāśya, town 246 n.
saṃkleśa and *vyavadāna* defilement and purification: the same and not constituting duality 57 190 & n. 215 240
saṃlekha austerity 174
saṃsāra round of rebirth : for Bs. the realm of *saṃsāra* is beings 118; *saṃsāra* constitutes the retinue of the Bs. 119
saṃsāra and *nirvāṇa*: whilst remaining in *saṃsāra*, entering *nirvāṇa* 44-5 & n.; not being involved in the round of

rebirth (*saṃsārasthita*) and not being involved in *nirvāṇa* (*nirvāṇasthita*) 53; *saṃsāra* and *nirvāṇa* equally empty 123; *saṃsāra-* and *nirvāṇaprekṣaṇāgocara* constitute the domain of the Bs. 128; following the path of *nirvāṇa* without abandoning the course of *saṃsāra* 176; *saṃsāra* and *nirvāṇa* do not constitute duality 193 & n.; avoiding repugnance for *saṃsāra* (*saṃsāraparikheda*) and delight in *nirvāṇa* (*nirvāṇābhirati*) which are the same 201; sūtra counteracting the great suffering of *saṃsāra* and revealing the great happiness of *nirvāṇa* 261; *apratiṣṭhitanirvāṇa*, see *nirvāṇa*

saṃskāra, see ***rūpa***

saṃskṛta and *asaṃskṛta* conditioned and unconditioned 67-8 & n. 77 138 & n. 193 & n. 215 240; not to exhaust the *saṃskṛta* and not to abide in the *asaṃskṛta* 229-236

saṃskṛtalakṣaṇa the three or four marks of the conditioned 91 & n.

Saṃtuṣita, king of the Tuṣita gods 85 & n.

samyakpradhāna (*samyakprahāṇa*) the four right efforts 20 131 & n.

samyaksaṃbodhi, see *bodhi*

samyaksaṃbuddha, *tathāgata* and *buddha*: depth of meaning of these three words 227-8

samyaktva, see *samatā*

San chieh chiao, sect of the Three Degrees or Stages 186 n.

Sandhakaccānasutta 44 n.

Śāntendriya, Bs. 198

Sāramati (Chien-i or Chien-hui), pre-Yogācāra scholar LXXVII; the question of two Sāramatis CXII-CXIII n.

Śāriputra, disciple: brief biography 42-3 n.; sees the Sahāloka as impure and the B. disabuses him of this with a miracle 15-25; devotee of *pratisaṃlayana* and criticized for this by Vim. 42-5; calls for seats for the assembly 134; cannot increase his height by himself 140-1; cannot shake off the flowers with which the devī has covered him 161; converses with the devī who changes him into a woman 162-72; calls for the midday meal 204 311; participates in the sacred meal 212; gives off a sweet odour and explains its origin 221; questions Vim. on the latter's origin 242-3; again refers to the impurity of the Sahāloka 244-5; expresses his admiration of the Abhirati universe and Vim. 249

Śāriputrābhidharma (T 1548), on the luminous mind LXXV & n.

Sarvabodhisattvaguṇākara, name of a *samādhi* 213

Sarvagandhasugandhā, universe 204 ff.

sarvajñajñāna omniscience 98 108 111 129 241

Sarvārthasiddha, B. 168

Sarvāstivādin-Vaibhāṣika, sect of the Small Vehicle: theory of, on the luminous mind LXXV-LXXVI

Sarvasukhamaṇḍitā, universe 213

sarvavādacaryoccheda cutting off of all discussion and practice 241 & n.

sāsrava, see *samatā*

śāṭhya guile 16 & n. 158 174

satkāya "aggregation of perishable things", personality: has craving as its base 159 & n.; constitutes the *tathāgatagotra* 177; *satkāya* and *satkāyanirodha* do not constitute duality 198-9; *satkāyadṛṣṭi* belief in a personality, indispensable for producing *bodhi* 55 178

Satpuruṣa(s): the sixteen "Worthy Men" 7 n.

satya truth, the four noble truths LX-LXI 10 n. 97 129 135 & n.; he who has not seen them (*na dṛṣṭasatya*) can attain supreme *bodhi* 56 177; truth (*satya*) and falsehood (*mṛṣā*) do not constitute duality 202

Satyarata, Bs. 202

Satyasiddhiśāstra (T 1646) of Harivarman: date of XCIV-XCV XCVI

śauṇḍikagṛha, drinking house(s): frequented by Vim. 30

sāvadānam (Pāli, *sapadānam*) begging in a systematic order 50 n. 55

sāvadya and *anavadya* the blamable and blameless: do not constitute duality 192

sects, non-Buddhist: *caraka-pāṣaṇḍika* 30; *anyatīrthika-caraka-parivrajaka-nirgrantha-jīvika* 82 & n.
Seng-chao, disciple of Kumārajīva: role of, in the trans. of Vkn to which he wrote a preface XXXII-XXXVIII; role of, in the compilation of the *Chu Wei-mo-chieh ching* (T 1775) XXXIII XCVI; testimony of, concerning the date of Nāgārjuna and Āryadeva XCV-XCVI; theory of, regarding the worldly and the holy 44 n.
Sha-mi shih hui chang-chü. work by Yen Fo-t'iao LXXXIX-XC
Shi pu êrh mên the ten non-dual gates LX
Shōtoku, Japanese prince, author of a commentary on Vkn XXXIII
Shui ching chu by Li Tao-yüan mentions Vim.'s house for the first time CII
sickness (*glānya, vyādhi*), causes and duration of Vim.'s sickness 117-20; Chi-i's theory on the sickness of expediency 32-3 n.; the ceremonial of visiting the sick 33 n.; sickness, normal state of the body 34 n.; considerations and consolations to be proposed to the sick Bs. 120-6; simulated sickness of the Bs. 183 & n.; see also disease; illness
śikṣāpada the five or ten rules of training for laity and monks 20 & n. 292
Śikṣāsamuccaya of Śāntideva : quotes Vkn XXV CXIII-CXIV
śīla, see morality
silence, philosophical, constituting the entry into non-duality 202-3; Aśvaghoṣa's silence 203; Vim's silence XXVIII XXXIII 189 n. 202-3 & n.; *paramārtha āryāṇāṃ tuṣṇīṃbhāvaḥ* 203 n.; silence can perform B.-deeds 225; *dharmā niruktivyavahāravarjitā anabhilāpapravyāhṛtāḥ* 241 n.
śilpasthāna technique 183
Siṃha, Bs. 192 & n.
Siṃhakīrti, B. 168
Siṃhamati, Bs. 192
siṃhanāda lion's roar 2 & n. 3 98
siṃhanāda and *sṛgālanāda* lion's roar and jackal's yelp (comparison) 60 & n.
Siṃhanādanādin, Bs. 5
Siṃhasvara, B. 168 & n.
skandha, āyatana and *dhātu* the five aggregates, twelve bases of consciousness and eighteen elements 37 103 134-5; the five *upādānaskandha* 195
spraṣṭavya, see *rūpa*
śrāvaka Listener, see Vehicles
śrāvakaguṇa attributes of the Listeners: list 1-2 & n.
Śrīgandha, Bs. 189
Śrīgarbha, Bs. 200 & n.
Śrīgupta, Bs. 189
Śrīkūṭa, Bs. 190
Śrīmālādevī (T 310): on the *tathāgatagarbha* LXXVII & n.
śṛṅgāṭaka crossroads: frequented by Vim. 30
Sthiramati (An-hui), founder of the Vijñānavāda school in Valabhī CXIII n.
stūpa 254 & n.
Subāhu, Bs. 190
Subhūti, disciple: brief biography 54-5 n.; seeks alms at Vim.'s 55; discomfited by the latter, he withdraws 58
sūcyagreṇa badaraparṇaṃ samucchritam jujube leaf lifted on a needle point (comparison) 147
Sudatta (Anāthapiṇḍaka), upāsaka: brief biography 106 n.; great material offering of 107; offers necklace to Vim. 111
Śuddhādhimukti, Bs. 193
Sujāta, Bs. 5
sūkaramaddava tender pork 314
sukha and *duḥkha* happiness and suffering: do not constitute duality 193
Sumeru, king of mountains: inserted into a mustard seed (*sarṣapa*) 60 142-3; Sumeru in comparisons 6 11 178 212 311
Sunetra, Bs. 191 & n.
śūnyagrāma empty village (comparison) 37-8 & n. 52 103
śūnyatā emptiness: seen as *abhāvamātra*, mere non-existence LXIX-LXXIV; compared to a raft, a drug, an *alagarda* serpent and a magical formula LXX; many synonyms of LXXII 48 n.; same

as the *bodhimaṇḍa* 98; does not imagine itself 118; found in the sixty-two false views 119
śūnyatā, ānimitta and *apraṇihita* emptiness, signlessness and wishlessness (the three *vimokṣamukha*, doors to deliverance): 48 & n. 104 108 127 129-30 232; do not constitute duality 198 & n.
śūnyatāsamādhi concentration on emptiness: practised by Subhūti 54 n.
Śūraṃgamasamādhisūtra: edition compiled by Chih Min-tu XXXI; on the four kinds of predictions 86-7 n.
sūrya and *andhakāra* sun (dispelling) darkness (comparison) 245
Sūryaguhya, Bs., identified with Vim. CV-CVI
Sūryakośagarbha, Bs., identified with Vim. CVI
sūryaprabhā and *khadyotaka* brightness of sun and glimmer of glow-worm (comparison) 60 & n. 151
sūtra(s): as source of Vkn (canonical LXXXII-LXXXIII; paracanonical LXXXIII-LXXXIV; Mahāyānasūtras LXXXIV-LXXXVII); homage to the Law (*dharmapūjā*) rendered to profound *sūtras* 259-61; *sūtras* with precise meaning (*nītārtha*) and the meaning to be determined (*neyārtha*) 261-3 & n.; confidence and respect due to *sūtras* 269-70
Sūtrasamuccaya (T 1635) of Dharmakīrti (alias Śāntideva), quotes Vkn CXIV
Suvarṇacūḍa, Bs. 5
svara, see *akṣara*

Ta ch'êng pên shêng hsin ti kuan ching (T 159), mentions Vim. CIX-CX
tamas and *jyotis* darkness and light: do not constitute duality 200-1
t'an-ping "conversation sceptre", attribute of Mañjuśrī 113 n.
Tao-an, author of the *Êrh chiao lun* XCIV
taraṅga waves (of mental agitation) 47 & n. 92 & n. 242
tathāgata, see *buddha*
Tathāgatācintyaviṣayasūtra (T 300 and 301), mentions Vim. CX
Tathāgatagarbhasūtra (T 666 and 667): on the *tathāgatagarbha* LXXVI
tathāgatagotra, family of the B. 176-9 306-7; also see *gotra*
Tathāgataguhyaka or *Tathāgatācintyaguhyanirdeśa* (T 310), source of Vkn LXXXV 114 n. 168 & n.
tathatā suchness 47 89 91 239; in the perspective of the two Vehicles LX-LXI LXXII
tejaḥskandha mass of cosmic fires swallowed by the Bs. 146
Theravādin(s), sect of the Small Vehicle: theory on the luminous mind and the *bhavaṅga* LXXV
thought, see *citta*
time, the three phases of, merged 172
T'i-p'o p'u-sa chuan (T 2048), Life of Āryadeva XCV
tīrthikaśāstṛ the six sectarian masters 57 & n.
tiryagyoni animals: instructed by the Bs. 185
tisro vidyāḥ triple knowledge 40 & n. 98 239
Tiṣya, Bs. 192 & n.
traidhātuka the triple world (*kāma-*, *rūpa-* and *ārūpyadhātu*) 29 44 98 129 & n. 135 239
translations of the Vkn: Chinese tr. XXVI-XXXVII; Tibetan tr. XXXVII-XLIII; Sogdian and Khotanese tr. XLIII-XLIV
Trāyastriṃśa(s), gods of the *kāmadhātu* 24 & n. 32 n. 143 246 & n.
treasures see *nidhāna*
triratna the triple jewel (*buddha*, *dharma* and *saṃgha*) 11 49; disparaged by Vim. in front of Subhūti 58 & n.; does not constitute duality 198
tṛṇa, vṛkṣa (or *kāṣṭha*), *bhitti, mārga* (or *loṣṭa*), *pratibhāsa*: stock of comparisons applied to the body 35 53
Tsa p'i yü ching (T 205), quotes Vkn CXI
Tun-huang: manuscripts of Tibetan versions of Vkn XXXVII-XLIII; carvings of Vim. and Mañjuśrī in caves of 113 n.
Tuṣita(s), gods of the *kāmadhātu* 85 & n.

uddeśa or *dharmoddeśa* instruction in the Law 63
Ugradattaparipṛcchā (T 332), text translated by An Hsüan and Yen Fo-t'iao XC
upādānaskandha, see *skandha*
Upāli, disciple: brief biography 68-9 n.; receives confession from two monks 70
upamāna, comparisons: stock of ten comparisons illustrating *dharmanairātmya* (ball of foam, bubble of water, mirage, trunk of banana tree, mechanism, illusion, dream, reflection, echo, cloud) quoted more or less completely 34-5 & n. 58 73 93 105 225; stock of thirty-five comparisons illustrating *pudgalanairātmya* 153-5; Eulogy of the ten comparisons by Hsieh Ling-yün 34 n.
upāya and *upāyakauśalya* skill in means and means of salvation 19 & n. 21 29 32 97 109 114 115 150 151 152 174-5 180 183 232; *upāyopāttā prajñā* and *upāyānupāttā prajñā* wisdom acquired and not acquired through the means 126-8
Uttarāpathaka(s), sect of the Small Vehicle: theory of, concerning the illnesses of the B. 295

vadhaka the five killers (comparison) 37 & n.
vaiḍūrya and *kācakamaṇi* beryl and glass gem (comparison) 60 & n.
vaineyasattva, see discipline
Vaiśālī, capital of the Licchavis CI-CIII 1 & n. 29 33 46 50 55 80 81 n. 94 116 140 211
vaiśāradya the four convictions 4 28 & n. 40 & n. 98 180 234
Vākula, arhat: was always in good health 82 n.
vāsanā pervasions of the passions 92 154 161-2
vāta, see *vāyu*
Vatsasūtra (T 808), source of Vkn LXXXIII 80-1 n.
Vattaniya senāsana, monastery 312
vāyu or *vāta* winds: cosmic winds inhaled by the Bs. 146; *vāyumaṇḍala* circle of winds 146 & n.
vedanā, see *rūpa*
Vehicles (*yāna*): the three Vehicles of the Śrāvakas, Pratyekabuddhas and Buddhas 163-4 & n.; various criticisms of the Śrāvakas 53 60-1 149 166 179-80 228; identity of *śrāvakacitta* and *bodhisattvacitta* 190-1; and impossibility of reconciling the attitudes of the Śrāvakas with the B. attributes 132; question of the Single Vehicle (*ekayāna*): viewpoint of various Mahāyānasūtras 164-5 n.; viewpoint of Vkn for which the Single Vehicle is the absence of all Vehicles 48-9 89 165 n. 201 (where the identity of good and bad paths is proclaimed). Whether all Vehicles lead to Nirvāṇa 304-7
veśyāgṛha houses of prostitution: frequented by the Bs. 30 & n.
Vetullaka(s), sect: theory of, on the silence of the B. 13 n.
Vibhajyāvādin(s), sect of the Small Vehicle: theory of, on the luminous mind LXXV-LXXVI
Vidyuddeva, Bs. 5 194
vijñāna, see *citta*; *rūpa*
vijñānasthiti the seven abodes of the mind 177 & n.
Vijñānavādin-Yogācāra(s), school of the Great Vehicle: influence of, on the tr. of Vkn by Hsüan-tsang XXXV-XXXVI; theory of, on *bhūtatathatā* LXXI 160 n.
vijñapti, see *akṣara*
Vijñaptimātratāsiddhi (T 1585), implicitly quotes Vkn CXIII
vikalendriya cripple (comparison) 179
vikalpa, see *kalpa*
vikṣepa and *manyanā* distraction and attention: do not constitute duality 190 & n.
Vikurvaṇarāja, Bs. 5 & n.
vimokṣa the eight liberations 53 97 126 181
vimokṣamukha the three doors to deliverance 48 & n. 104 108 127 129-30 232; do not constitute duality 198 & n.
vimukti deliverance: does not exist apart

from words, not different from the sameness of all dharmas and from the three basic passions 162-3
Vinaya: source of Vkn LXXXIII
***vinaya*, see discipline**
viparyāsa the four perversions 34 73 121 122 177 & n.
vipaśyanā*, see *śamatha
***vīra* hero (comparison) 125**
vīrya*, see *pāramitā
***viśuddhi*, the seven purities 181 & n.**
Viśvabhū, B. CVI
viṭhapanapratyupasthānalakṣaṇa having as its mark being created by mental illusion 26 & n.
viveka or *praviveka* solitude, isolation 29 108 129 & n. 135 175 230 233
vyādhi or *glānya*, see disease; illness; sickness
vyākaraṇa prediction: mechanism of 86-8 n. 291; for Vim. *vyākaraṇa* has neither subject nor object 86-9
vyatyasta inverted: *vyatyastalokadhātu* inverted universe LVI; *vyatyastā samāpatti* inverted recollection LVI; *vyatyastapada* inverted sounds LVII 113 & n.
vyavadāna, see *saṃkleśa*

Wang Hsüan-ts'ê, Chinese envoy who measured Vim.'s house CIII
Wei Wu lu by Chu Tao-tsu, lost catalogue XXVII & n. XXIX
wonders (*prātihārya*): of the parasol 7-8; of the Sahāloka transformed into a pure universe 23-4; of the restoration of memory to the bhikṣus 61; of the voice from the sky 84 102 258; of Māra's immobilisation 102; of the necklace 111-2; of the empty house 116; of the thrones 138-41; of the increase in size of the bodies 140; of the flowers 160-2; of Vim.'s house 166-9; of the change of sex 170-1; of the discovery of the Sarvagandhasugandhā universe 204; of the magically created Bs. 206-8; of the perfumed town 211; of the inexhaustible food 212-3; of the illumination of the Āmrapālīvana 219; of the magical transportation of the assembly 219-20; of the perfumed bodies 221; of the bringing of the Abhirati universe into the Sahāloka 246-8; wonders normally performed by means of the *acintyavimokṣa* of the Bs. 141-8

yamaka "paired": *yamakasamādhi* concentration on conjunction LVIII LIX; *yamakavyatyastāhārakuśala* skilled in producing paired and inverted sounds (exclusive attribute of the Bs). LVI-LIX;
Yamakavyatyastāhāra or *Yamakavyatyastābhinirhāra*, secondary title of Vkn LVI-LX 269 & n. 273 & n.
yāna, see Vehicles
Yen Fo-t'iao: supposedly translated Vkn XXVI-XXVII; tr. is however apocryphal LXXIX-XCI
yogācārabhūmi sphere of the practice of yoga 109

SYNOPSIS OF FORMULAE AND STOCK PHRASES

anityā bata saṃskārāḥ 25
anityāḥ sarvasaṃskārāḥ, duḥkhāḥ sarvasaṃskārāḥ, anātmānaḥ sarvadharmāḥ śāntaṃ nirvāṇam 63-5 120 127 148 232-3 260
animiṣābhyāṃ netrabhyaṃ saṃprekṣamāṇaḥ 9
anyatīrthikacarakaparivrajakanirgranthajīvikāḥ 82
api nu sa kulaputro vā kuladuhitā vā tato nidānaṃ bahu puṇyaṃ prasavet 254
abhikrānte pratikrānte caraṇanikṣepaṇe caraṇotkṣepaṇe 98-9
avakalpayasva me... abhiśraddadhasva tathāgatasya bhūtāṃ vācaṃ vyāharataḥ 255
avidyānirodhād ityādi yāvaj jarāmaraṇaśokaparidevaduḥkhadaurmanasyopāyāsā nirudhyante 263

avaivartikaḥ kṛto 'nuttarāyāṃ samyaksaṃbodhau 61

asthānam etad anavakāśo yat... 82 126 171

āścaryaprāpto 'dbhutaprāptaḥ 8-9 24 53

idam avocad bhagavān. āttamanāḥ... sadevamānuṣāsuragandharvaś ca loko bhagavato bhāṣitam abhyanandann iti 273

imām ahaṃ Maitreyāsaṃkhyeyakalpakoṭīnayutaśatasahasrasamudānītām anuttarāṃ samyaksaṃbodhiṃ tvayi parindāmi 268

udgṛhṇīsva tvam Ānandemaṃ dharmaparyāyaṃ dhāraya parebhyaś ca vistareṇa saṃprakāśaya 272

evam etad... evam etad yathā vadasi 116 223

evaṃrūpam adhiṣṭhānam adhitiṣṭhati sma 170

evaṃrūpam ṛddhyabhisaṃskāram abhisaṃskaroti sma 139 204 219 247

kaccit te satpuruṣa kṣamaṇīyaṃ kaccid yāpanīyaṃ kaccit te dhātavo na kṣubhyante kaccid duḥkhā vedanāḥ pratikrāmanti nābhikrāmanti pratikrama āsāṃ prajñāyate nābhikramaḥ 117

kalpaṃ vā kalpāvaśeṣaṃ vā 148 254 — ***kalpaṃ vā kalpāvaśeṣaṃ vā satkuryād*** *gurukuryān mānayet pūjayet* 254

kasya khalv idaṃ pūrvanimittaṃ bhaviṣyati 219

ko nāmāyaṃ bhagavan dharmaparyāyaḥ kathaṃ cainaṃ dhārayāmi 272

gaṅgānadīvālukopamāni buddhakṣetrāṇy atikramya 139 147 204 206-7 209

gamiṣyāmo vayaṃ... taṃ bhagavantaṃ... tathāgataṃ darśanāya vandanāya paryupāsanāya dharmaśravaṇāya 210 219 246

grāmanagaranigamajanapadarāṣṭra*rājadhanyaḥ* 8 140 141 150 246 253 272

cittasaṃkleśāt sattvāḥ saṃkliśyante cittavyavadānād viśudhyante 72

tat kiṃ manyase 22 58 242 245 254

tatra "..." nāma tathāgato 'rhan samyaksaṃbuddhas tiṣṭhati dhriyate yāpayati 139 204 209

tathāgatasya parinirvṛtasya ***paścime kāle*** *paścime samaye paścimāyāṃ* ***pañcaśat****yāṃ vartamānāyām* 264 n.

tathārūpaṃ samādhiṃ samāpede (samāpadyate sma) 61 204 247

tasya... cetasaiva cetaḥparivitarkam ājñāya 22 42 134 204 246

tasya... pādau śirasābhivandya 43 etc.

tīrṇaḥ pāraṃgataḥ sthale tiṣṭhati 14

tuṣṭa udagra āttamanāḥ pramuditaḥ prītisaumanasyajātaḥ 8-9 160 234 264 270

tena **khalu** *punaḥ samayena "..." nāma rājodapādi cakravarti cāturdvīpaḥ saptaratnasamanvāgataḥ.* ***pūrṇaṃ*** *cāsyābhūt sahasraṃ putrāṇāṃ śūrāṇāṃ virāṇāṃ varāṅgarūpiṇāṃ parasainyapramardakānām* 257

tena hi śṛṇu (tac chṛṇu) sādhu ca suṣṭhu ca manasikuru. bhāṣiṣye 'haṃ te 15

teṣām... anuttarāyāṃ samyaksaṃbodhau cittāny utpāditāni 25 27 41 49 68 74 79 99 111 133 150 218 248

teṣām... anutpattikadharmakṣāntipratilābho 'bhūt 25 93

teṣām... anupādāyāsravebhyaś cittāni vi*muktānn* 26 65

teṣām no bhadanta... atyayam atyayataḥ pratigṛhṇātv āyatyāṃ saṃvarāya 70 70-1 n.

teṣām... virajo vigatamalaṃ dharmeṣu dharmacakṣur viśuddham 26 58 138,

dakṣiṇaṃ jānumaṇḍalaṃ pṛthivyāṃ pratiṣṭhāpya yena bhagavāṃs tenāñjaliṃ praṇamya 9

duḥkhaṃ parijñeyam, samudayaḥ prahātavyaḥ, ***nirodhaḥ*** *sākṣātkartavyaḥ, pratipad bhāvitavyā* 135

devanāgayakṣagandharvāsuragaruḍakiṃnaramahoragāḥ 6 8 141 144 165-6 246 260

dharmacakraṃ triparivartaṃ dvādaśākāram 10

dhārmyā kathayā saṃdarśayāmi samādāpayāmi samuttejayāmi saṃpraharṣayāmi 71

na praṇaśyanti karmāṇi kalpakoṭiśatair api 10 n.

na śakyaṃ paryanto 'dhigantuṃ yāvantaṃ *puṇyābhisaṃskāraṃ sa kulaputro vā kuladuhitā vā prasaviṣyati* 255

nityasnāpanaparimardanabhedanavidhvaṃsanadharma 35
nirmāṇasvabhāvāḥ sarvadharmāḥ 243
padmam ivodake jātam udakena na lipyate 14
pūrvāhṇe nivasya pātracīvaram ādāya 80
bhagavāṃs tasya... sādhukāram adāt: sādhu sādhu yas tvam... 15 202 271
bhagavāṃs tvām alpābādhatāṃ pṛcchaty alpātaṅkatāṃ yātrāṃ laghūtthānatāṃ balaṃ sukham anavadyatāṃ sukhasparśavihāratām 117 207 208
bhūtapūrvam atīte 'dhvany asaṃkhyeyaiḥ kalpair asaṃkhyeyatarair vipulair aprameyair acintyais tebhyaḥ pareṇa paratareṇa yadāsīt tena kālena tena samayena "..." nāma tathāgato 'rhan samyaksaṃbuddho loka udapādi vidyācaraṇasampannaḥ sugato lokavid anuttaraḥ puruṣadamyasārathiḥ śāstā devānāṃ ca manuṣyāṇāṃ ca buddho bhagavān 257
mahāsamudrasarastaḍāgapuṣkariṇīnadīkunadyutsāḥ 7-8 246
ya imam evaṃrūpaṃ dharmaparyāyaṃ śrutvādhimokṣyanty udgrahiṣyanti dhārayiṣyanti vācayiṣyanti paryavāpsyanty adhimucya deśayiṣyanty upadekṣyanti parebhya udekṣyanti bhāvanākāreṇa prayokṣyante (and similar formulae in the optative or indicative) 250 252 253 254 269 271
yathāhaṃ bhagavan bhagavato bhāṣitasyārtham ājānāmi 252
yasyedānīṃ kālaṃ manyase 210 219
ye kecid ito dharmaparyāyād antaśaś catuṣpādikām api gāthām udgṛhya parebhyo deśayeyuḥ 251
ye kecit sattvā buddhas teṣām agra ākhyātaḥ; ye kecid dharmā nirvāṇāṃ teṣām agram ākhyātam 263 n.
rāgakṣayo dveśakṣayo mohakṣaya iyam ucyate muktiḥ 163
lābhā naḥ sulabdhā yad vayaṃ tādṛśaṃ satpuruṣaṃ paśyāmaḥ 349
vayam api bhagavann evaṃrupāṇāṃ dharmabhāṇakānāṃ rakṣāṃ kariṣyāmo yathā na kaścit teṣāṃ dharmabhāṇakānām avatāraprekṣy avatāragaveṣy avatāraṃ lapsyate 272
śarīrastūpaṃ pratiṣṭhāpayati sarvaratnamayaṃ caturmahādvīpakalokapramāṇam āyāmena yāvad brahmalokam uccaistvena 254
śraddhayāgārād anāgārikāṃ pravrajitaḥ 264
sa ca muktāhāras tasya... mūrdhni muktāhāraḥ kūṭāgāraḥ saṃsthito 'bhūc caturasraś catuḥsthūnaḥ samabhāgaḥ suvibhakto darśanīyaḥ 112
sarvadharmān viṭhapanapratyupasthānalakṣaṇān viditvā 26
sādhu bhagavann iti... bhagavataḥ pratyaśrauṣīt 15
sumerur iva parvatarājo bhagavān... bhāsate tapati virocate 6
sūryacandratārakāḥ 8
syāt khalu punas te... evaṃ kāṅkṣā vā vimatir vā vicikitsā vānyaḥ sa tena kālena tena samayena "..." nāmābhūt. na khalu punas tvayaivaṃ draṣṭavyam. tat kasya hetoḥ. ayam (or *aham*) *eva sa tena kālena tena samayena "..." nāma rājā cakravarty abhūt* (or *kulaputro 'bhūvam*) 265 267
svākhyātadharmavinaye pravrajitaḥ 161
himadrimucilindamahāmucilindagandhamādanaratnaparvatakālaparvatacakravāḍamahācakravāḍāḥ 7